# Cultural Backlash

Authoritarian-Populist parties and leaders have advanced in many countries, and gained power in states as diverse as the US, Austria, Italy, the Netherlands, Poland, and Switzerland. Even small parties can still shift the policy agenda, as demonstrated by UKIP's role in catalyzing Brexit. Drawing on new evidence, the book advances a general theory why the silent revolution in values triggered a backlash fuelling support for Authoritarian-Populist forces in the US and Europe. The conclusion highlights the dangers of this development and what could be done to mitigate the risks to liberal democracy.

**Pippa Norris** is the McGuire Lecturer in Comparative Politics at the John F. Kennedy School of Government, Harvard University, Laureate Fellow and Professor of Government and International Relations at Sydney University, and Director of the Electoral Integrity Project. An award-winning author and researcher, her books include *Why Electoral Integrity Matters* (Cambridge University Press, 2014), *Why Elections Fail* (Cambridge University Press, 2015) and *Strengthening Electoral Integrity* (Cambridge University Press, 2017).

**Ronald Inglehart** is Professor of Political Science and Program Director at the Institute for Social Research at the University of Michigan. He has previously collaborated with Pippa Norris on *Rising Tide: Gender Equality and Cultural Change around the World* (Cambridge University Press, 2003) and is the author of many publications including *Modernization and Postmodernization* (1997), *Modernization, Cultural Change and Democracy* (Cambridge University Press, 2005, with Christian Welzel) and *Cultural Evolution* (Cambridge University Press, 2018).

# Cultural Backlash

## *Trump, Brexit, and Authoritarian Populism*

PIPPA NORRIS
*Harvard University*
*Sydney University*

RONALD INGLEHART
*University of Michigan*

CAMBRIDGE
UNIVERSITY PRESS

**CAMBRIDGE**
**UNIVERSITY PRESS**

University Printing House, Cambridge CB2 8BS, United Kingdom

One Liberty Plaza, 20th Floor, New York, NY 10006, USA

477 Williamstown Road, Port Melbourne, VIC 3207, Australia

314–321, 3rd Floor, Plot 3, Splendor Forum, Jasola District Centre, New Delhi – 110025, India

79 Anson Road, #06-04/06, Singapore 079906

Cambridge University Press is part of the University of Cambridge.

It furthers the University's mission by disseminating knowledge in the pursuit of education, learning, and research at the highest international levels of excellence.

www.cambridge.org
Information on this title: www.cambridge.org/9781108426077
DOI: 10.1017/9781108595841



First published 2019

*A catalogue record for this publication is available from the British Library.*

*Library of Congress Cataloging-in-Publication Data*
NAMES: Norris, Pippa, author. | Inglehart, Ronald, author.
TITLE: Cultural backlash : Trump, Brexit, and the rise of authoritarian-populism / Pippa Norris and Ronald Inglehart.
DESCRIPTION: New York, NY : Cambridge University Press, 2018. | Includes bibliographical references.
IDENTIFIERS: LCCN 2018037934 | ISBN: 9781108426077 (hardback) | ISBN: 9781108444422 (pbk.)
SUBJECTS: LCSH: Populism. | Authoritarianism. | Populism—United States. | Authoritarianism—United States. | Populism—Great Britain. | Authoritarianism—Great Britain. | United States—Politics and government—21st century. | Great Britain—Politics and government—21st century.
CLASSIFICATION: LCC JC423 .N6599 2018 | DDC 320.56/62--DC23
LC record available at https://lccn.loc.gov/2018037934

ISBN 978-1-108-42607-7 Hardback
ISBN 978-1-108-44442-2 Paperback

# Contents

*List of Figures* — *page* vii
*List of Tables* — xi
*Preface and Acknowledgments* — xiii

PART I INTRODUCTION

1 Understanding Populism — 3
2 The Cultural Backlash Theory — 32
3 Varieties of Populism — 65

PART II AUTHORITARIAN AND POPULIST VALUES

4 The Backlash Against the Silent Revolution — 87
5 Economic Grievances — 132
6 Immigration — 175

PART III FROM VALUES TO VOTES

7 Classifying Parties — 215
8 Who Votes for Authoritarian-Populist Parties? — 257
9 Party Fortunes and Electoral Rules — 294
10 Trump's America — 331
11 Brexit — 368

PART IV CONCLUSIONS

12 Eroding the Civic Culture 409
13 The Authoritarian-Populist Challenge 443

TECHNICAL APPENDICES

Cultural Backlash: Technical Appendix A: Classification of Parties 473
Technical Appendix B: The Variables and Coding Used in the Multivariate Analysis 487

*Bibliography* 493
*Index* 535

# Figures


| | | |
|---|---|---|
| 1.1 | Vote share for populist parties in Western societies, 1946–2017 | *page* 9 |
| 1.2 | Vote share for Populist parties in Europe, 2000–2017 | 10 |
| 2.1 | The theoretical framework | 33 |
| 2.2 | The size of generational cohorts in Europe 2002–2014 | 37 |
| 2.3 | The educational revolution, US 1948–2012 | 38 |
| 2.4 | Higher education by sex in high-income societies, 1970–2015 | 39 |
| 2.5 | Urbanization in high-income societies, 1960–2015 | 40 |
| 2.6 | Net migration into European regions, 1990–2017 | 41 |
| 2.7 | Model of cleavages in party competition | 51 |
| 4.1 | The proportion of materialist and post-materialists in Europe, 1970–2002 | 94 |
| 4.2 | Socially liberal values correlate with post-materialist values | 95 |
| 4.3 | The silent revolution in socially liberal values in Europe by generation | 96 |
| 4.4 | The silent revolution in socially liberal values by education | 97 |
| 4.5 | Trends in conservative minus liberal self-identification, US by generation, 1994–2014 | 100 |

4.6 Ideological left–right self-identification by generation, Europe, 1970–2007 102
4.7 Socially liberal values are negatively correlated with authoritarian values 103
4.8 The tipping point in authoritarian and libertarian values by generation, Europe 106
4.9 The tipping point in authoritarian and libertarian values by generation and European country 107
4.10 Support for authoritarian values and political mistrust by generational cohort, Europe 120
5.1 Cohort analysis of value change, Europe 1970–2009 147
5.2 Annual economic growth during the financial crisis, Europe and the US 150
5.3 Authoritarian values and populist attitudes by feelings of financial security, Europe 158
5.4 Populist attitudes and personal income insecurity, national level 159
5.5 Authoritarian values and personal income insecurity, national level 159
5.6 Authoritarian values and proportion of persons at risk of poverty or social exclusion, EU 2014 160
5.7 Populist attitudes by per capita GDP, European regions (NUTS2) 163
5.8 Authoritarian values by per capita GDP, European regions (NUTS2) 165
6.1 Net migration into European countries, 1990–2017 178
6.2 Foreign born population as percent of total population, 2005–2015 180
6.3 Perceptions and estimates of proportion of foreign-born living in each European society 181
6.4 Public concern about unemployment and immigration, EU 2005–2017 184
6.5 Anti-immigration attitudes and authoritarian values, Europe 194
6.6 Attitudes toward immigration by authoritarian and populist values 199
6.7 Attitudes toward immigration by authoritarian and populist values 201

7.1 Model of cleavages in party competition in Western societies 222

7.2 Classification of European political parties 238

7.3 Classification of European political parties 243

8.1 Turnout by generation 274

8.2 Authoritarian values and voting for parties with policy positions that are more authoritarian, by country 281

8.3 Authoritarian values and support for parties that are more authoritarian 282

8.4 Populist values and support for parties that are more populist 287

9.1 Mean vote and seats for Authoritarian-Populist parties in Europe, 1946–2015 297

9.2 Voting for Authoritarian-Populist parties by country, 1990–2016 298

9.3 Vote and seat share for Authoritarian-Populist parties by type of electoral system, 1990–2015 319

9.4 The proportionality of votes–seats for Authoritarian-Populist parties, 2010 320

9.5 Rising salience of non-economic issues in the party manifestos of 13 Western Democracies, 1950–2010 323

9.6 Salience of economic and cultural issues, 1920–2016 324

10.1 Party polarization in Congress 335

10.2 The rising salience of cultural issues on the Democrat and Republican Party platforms 336

10.3 Perceptions of the degree of group discrimination by Trump and Clinton voters, US 2016 341

10.4 Vote and materialist/post-materialist values, 1972–2016 343

10.5 The 2012 US presidential vote by materialist/post-materialist values 344

10.6 The 2016 US presidential vote by materialist/post-materialist values 345

10.7 Generational shifts in voting, US presidential elections 1948–2016 346

10.8 Moral conservatism predicts support for Trump and Clinton 361

11.1 UKIP's share of votes and seats in UK European and general elections, 1997–2017 371

11.2 Party voting intentions in UK polls, 2012-2017 372
11.3 The dynamics of the Leave–Remain voting intentions, January–June 2016 374
11.4 Vote Leave by birth cohort 386
11.5 Generation gaps in UKIP voting, 2015–2017 386
11.6 Vote Leave and UKIP by authoritarian–libertarian values 388
11.7 Vote Leave and UKIP by populist values 389
11.8 Vote Leave and UKIP by social class 390
11.9 Populist and authoritarian values of voters in the UK 2017 general election 392
11.10 Populist and authoritarian values of voters in the UK 2015 and 2017 general election 393
12.1 Trends in liberal democracy worldwide, V-Dem, 1900–2016 412
12.2 Trends in democratization worldwide, FH 1972–2017 413
12.3 Approval of democratic governance, US 1995–2017 423
12.4 Approval of governance by experts, US 1995–2017 424
12.5 Approval of governance by strongman rule without elections, US 1995–2017 425
12.6 Approval of army rule, US 1995–2017 426
12.7 Citizen dissatisfaction with the performance of democracy in their own country, EU 1976–2016 427
12.8 Importance of democracy by birth cohort across post-industrial democracies 430
12.9 Institutional trust, EU 2001–2017 432
12.10 European tolerance of immigration 434
13.1 The sequence of steps in the cultural backlash theory 446

# Tables

| | | |
|---|---|---|
| 2.1 | Socially liberal values | *page* 34 |
| 4.1 | The silent revolution in social values in America, 2001–2017 | 99 |
| 4.2 | The balance of conservatives and liberals in America by generation, 2015 | 101 |
| 4.3 | Measuring citizen's authoritarian and libertarian values (Schwartz scales) | 104 |
| 4.4 | Predicting authoritarian values | 109 |
| 4.5 | Predicting socially liberal attitudes | 115 |
| 4.6 | Predicting populist orientations | 118 |
| 4.7 | Correlations between values and generational cohorts | 121 |
| 5.1 | Economic indicators predicting support for authoritarian and populist values | 141 |
| 5.2 | Authoritarian and populist values correlated with income insecurity, 32 countries | 157 |
| 5.3 | Regional predictors of authoritarian values and populist attitudes | 162 |
| 6.1 | Predicting the impact of immigration attitudes on authoritarian values and populist attitudes | 196 |
| 6.2 | Authoritarian and populist values correlated with immigration attitudes, 32 countries | 204 |
| 7.1 | Dimensions of party competition in Europe | 233 |
| 7.2. | Authoritarian-Populist parties in Western Europe, 2000–2015 | 235 |

7.3 Authoritarian-Populist parties in Central and Eastern Europe, 2000–2015 236
7.4 Libertarian-Populist parties in Europe, 2000–2015 237
8.1 Predicting who votes, Europe 272
8.2 Predicting voting support for parties that are more authoritarian 275
8.3 Generational cohorts and voting, by country 283
8.4 Predicting voting support for parties that are more populist 284
9.1 Rules for parliamentary elections for the lower house in the selected case studies 301
10.1 Predicting the Trump vote, US 2016 348
10.2 Cultural scales, US 2016 356
10.3 Predicting the Trump presidential vote, US 2016 357
11.1 Predicting Leave Vote in Brexit 383

# Preface and Acknowledgments

The intellectual foundations for this study build upon a collaborative partnership developed over many years, producing a series of earlier books jointly written by the authors for Cambridge University Press which have compared gender equality in politics, political communications, and religion around the world.

Pippa Norris' research for this book has been generously supported by the research award of the Kathleen Fitzpatrick Australian Laureate from the Australian Research Council. The Electoral Integrity Project is based at Harvard University's John F. Kennedy School of Government and the Department of Government and International Relations at the University of Sydney. She is greatly indebted to Michael Spence, Duncan Ivison, Simon Tormey, and Colin Wight for facilitating the project at the University of Sydney, as well as to all colleagues in the Department of Government and International Relations, and the EIP research team at Sydney including Sarah Cameron, Thomas Wynter, and Megan Capriccio. She is also most appreciative of support from Harvard University, including the John F. Kennedy School of Government, the Roy and Lila Ash Center for Democratic Governance and Innovation, the Minda de Gunzburg Center for European Studies, the Weatherhead Center for International Affairs, and all comments and feedback from colleagues at many seminars and talks as the book developed. We would also like to thank the National Science Foundation for the award for Ronald Inglehart and Jon Miller at the University of Michigan supporting the 2017 US World Values Survey. We build upon the shoulders of giants and it would also not have been possible without many invaluable datasets notably the European Social Survey, developed by the late-Roger Jowell, the European/World Values Survey, and the Chapel Hill Expert Surveys by Liesbet Hooghe and Gary Marks.

As always, this book also owes immense debts to many friends and colleagues who provided comments and feedback about this book during its gestation, including Nancy Bermeo, Bart Bonikowski, John Curtice, Ivor Crewe, E.J. Dionne, Doug Elmendorf, David Farrell, Mark Franklin, Archon Fung, Matthew Goodwin, Peter Hall, Liesbet Hooghe, Jeffrey Isaac, Eric Kaufman, Herbert Kitschelt, Charles Maier, Gary Marks, Jane Mansbridge, Yasha Mounk, Shirin Rai, John Sides, Claes de Vreese, and Daniel Ziblatt. The book has also been influenced by many students who have attended my Harvard classes over the years, where we discuss challenges of democracy and democratization. The idea for the book was originally generated well before the election of President Trump by a short op-ed 'Its not just Trump: Authoritarian populism is rising in the West. Here's why' published by the *Monkey Cage/The Washington Post* on March 11, 2016.[1] The original vision in that piece continues to prove a central thread in this book. Invaluable feedback has been received from panels at many international meetings since then, including the International Political Science Association World Congress in Poznan in 2016 and Brisbane in 2018, the American Political Science Association annual meetings in Philadelphia in 2016, San Francisco in 2017, and Boston in 2018, the Political Science Association of the UK annual conference in Glasgow in 2017, the International Studies Association in Baltimore in 2017, the Canadian Political Science Association in Calgary in 2016, the World Association of Public Opinion Research in Lisbon in 2017, and meetings, panels, and talks at the University of Toronto, University of Bergen, the American Academy of Arts and Sciences, the University of Stockholm, New York University, Duke University, Carleton University, Colorado State University, Warwick University, the London School of Economics and Political Science, the Carnegie Corporation of New York, Harvard's Center for European Studies, and faculty seminars at Harvard's Kennedy School of Government.

Finally, as always, the support of Cambridge University Press has proved invaluable, particularly the patience, efficient assistance, and enthusiasm of our editor, Robert Dreesen, the assistance of Meera Seth, as well as the helpful comments of the reviewers.

[1] www.washingtonpost.com/news/monkey-cage/wp/2016/03/11/its-not-just-trump-authoritarian-populism-is-rising-across-the-west-heres-why/

# PART I

# INTRODUCTION

# 1

# Understanding Populism

Populists have disrupted long-established patterns of party competition in many contemporary Western societies. The most dramatic case is the election of Donald Trump to the White House. How could such a polarizing and politically inexperienced figure win a major party's nomination – and then be elected President? Many observers find it difficult to understand his victory. He has been sharply attacked by conservatives such as George Will, establishment Republicans such as John McCain, Democrats such as Elizabeth Warren, and socialists such as Bernie Sanders. He has been described by some commentators as a strongman menacing democracy, by others as a xenophobic and racist demagogue skilled at whipping up crowds, and by yet others as an opportunistic salesman lacking any core principles.[1] Each of these approaches contains some truth.

We view Trump as a leader who uses populist rhetoric to legitimize his style of governance, while promoting authoritarian values that threaten the liberal norms underpinning American democracy.

Trump is far from unique. Previous demagogues in America include Huey Long's Share the Wealth movement, Joe McCarthy's witch-hunting communists, and George Wallace's white backlash.[2] Trump's angry nativist speeches, anti-establishment appeals, and racially heated language resembles that of many other leaders whose support has been swelling across Europe. Beyond leaders, these sentiments find expression in political parties, social movements, and the tabloid press. Populism is not new; von Beyme suggests that it has experienced at least three successive waves.[3] Its historical roots can be traced back to the Chartists in early Victorian Britain, the People's Party in the US, Narodnik revolutionaries in late nineteenth-century Tsarist Russia, Fascist movements in the interwar decades, Peronism in Argentina, and Poujadism in post-war France. Authoritarianism also has a long history that peaked during the era of Bolshevism and Fascism, and has seen resurgence since the late-twentieth century.

*What is populism?*

Populism is understood in this book minimally as a style of rhetoric reflecting first-order principles about who should rule, claiming that legitimate power rests with 'the people' not the elites. It remains silent about second-order principles, concerning what should be done, what policies should be followed, what decisions should be made.[4] The discourse has a chameleon-like quality which can adapt flexibly to a variety of substantive ideological values and principles, such as socialist or conservative populism, authoritarian or progressive populism, and so on.

As unpacked fully in chapter 3, populist rhetoric makes two core claims about how societies should be governed.[5]

First, populism challenges the legitimate authority of the 'establishment.' It questions pluralist beliefs about the rightful location of power and authority in any state, including the role of elected representatives in democratic regimes. Favorite targets include the mainstream media ('fake news'), elections ('fraudulent'), politicians ('drain the swamp'), political parties ('dysfunctional'), public-sector bureaucrats ('the deep state'), judges ('enemies of the people'), protests ('paid rent-a-mob'), the intelligence services ('liars and leakers'), lobbyists ('corrupt'), intellectuals ('arrogant liberals') and scientists ('who needs experts?'), interest groups ('get-rich-quick lobbyists'), the constitution ('a rigged system'), international organizations like the European Union ('Brussels bureaucrats') and the UN ('a talking club'). In Trump's words, 'The only antidote to decades of ruinous rule by a small handful of elites is a bold infusion of the popular will. On every major issue affecting this country, the people are right and the governing elite are wrong.'[6] The claim is not just that members of the establishment are arrogant in their judgments, mistaken in their decisions, and blundering in their actions, but rather that they are morally wrong in their core values. This claim resonates among critical citizens – those committed to democracy in principle but disillusioned with the performance of elected officeholders and representative institutions, including parties, elections, and parliaments.[7]

In this regard, populist leaders depict themselves as insurgents willing to ride roughshod over long-standing conventions, disrupting mainstream 'politics-as-usual.' Donald Trump's campaign rhetoric has been strongly counter-elitist, emphasizing the need to 'drain the swamp' of corrupt politicians and lobbyists, touching a chord among his supporters.[8] The 'fake media' are labelled 'enemies of the people' and public-sector officials are seen as part of the 'deep state' resisting change.[9] For Marine Le Pen, faceless European Commissioners are the enemy: 'No one knows their name or their face. And above all no one has voted for them.'[10] For pro-Brexit tabloids, 'out of touch' judges seeking to delay Article 50 are vilified as 'Enemies of the People.'[11] In Venezuela, Hugo Chavez's bellicose speeches berated former presidents charged with embezzlement, lambasted the Caracas elite, and attacked American imperialism ('domination, exploitation, and pillage').[12]

Secondly, populist leaders claim that the only legitimate source of political and moral authority in a democracy rests with the 'people.' The voice of ordinary citizens (the 'silent majority,' 'the forgotten American') is regarded as the only 'genuine' form of democratic governance even when at odds with expert judgments – including those of elected representatives and judges, scientists, scholars, journalists and commentators. Lived experience is regarded as a far superior guide to action rather than book-learning. The collective will of 'the people' ('Most people say...') is regarded as unified, authentic, and unquestionably morally right. In cases of conflict, for example, if Westminster disagrees with the outcome of the Brexit referendum, the public's decision is thought to take automatic precedent.

On the night of the Brexit referendum to leave the European Union, for example, the leader of UK Independence Party (UKIP), Nigel Farage, crowed that 'This will be a victory for real people, a victory for ordinary people, a victory for decent people.'[13] For the German protest movement Pegida, 'We are the people' ('Wir sind das Volk').[14] Similarly, Trump's inaugural address proclaimed: 'We are transferring power from Washington, DC and giving it back to you, the American People ... The forgotten men and women of our country will be forgotten no longer.'[15] In the 2017 French presidential elections, the National Front candidate, Marine Le Pen, campaigned to 'free the French people from an arrogant elite.'[16] A few months after Brexit, at the 2016 Conservative Party conference, Prime Minister Theresa May expressed similar views: 'Just listen to the way a lot of politicians and commentators talk about the public. They find their patriotism distasteful, their concerns about immigration parochial, their views about crime illiberal, their attachment to their job-security inconvenient.'[17] And Norbert Hofer, presidential candidate of the Freedom Party of Austria, criticized his opponent: 'You have the haute volée [high society] behind you; I have the people with me.' Elites questioning the wisdom of the people, or resisting its sovereignty, are accused of being corrupt, self-serving, arrogant know-it-alls who are 'traitors declaring war on democracy.'[18] There can be no turning back from the people's decision: Brexit means Brexit.

Therefore, populist rhetoric seeks to corrode faith in the legitimate authority of elected representatives in liberal democracies. But the revolution finds it easier to destroy the old than rebuild the new. The danger is that this leaves the door ajar for soft authoritarians attacking democratic norms and practices. Strongman leaders rise to power by claiming to govern on behalf of the 'real' people, sanctioned by flawed elections and enabled by partisan loyalists. The concept of 'legitimacy' can be best understood, in Seymour Martin Lipset's words, as 'the capacity of a political system to engender and maintain the belief that existing political institutions are the most appropriate and proper ones for the society.'[19] It is the vital quality which ensures that citizens comply with the decisions of their government, not because of the law or threat of force, but because they choose to do so voluntarily. Populist leaders knock-down safeguards on executive power by claiming that they, and they alone, reflect the authentic voice of ordinary people and have the capacity to restore collective security against threats. In Recep Tayyip Erdoğan's words: 'We are the people. Who are you?'[20] Leaders draw fuzzy lines between the interests of the state and their personal interests – along with that of their family and cronies. Democracy is thereby attacked, but not directly, which would raise too many red flags. No coup d'état is hatched. The military stay in the barracks. Elections are not cancelled. Opponents are not jailed. But democratic norms are gradually degraded by populists claiming to be democracy's best friend ('Trust me').[21]

*What is authoritarianism?*

What is important for fully understanding this phenomenon, however, is not just the rhetorical veneer of 'people power,' but also what second-order principles leaders advocate – and thus what cultural values they endorse, what programmatic policies they advocate, and what governing practices they follow. In this regard, know them by what they do – not just by what they say. The populist words of parties such as the French National Front, the Swedish Democrats, or Poland's Law and Justice – and leaders such as Orbán, Berlusconi, and Trump – are the external patina disguising authoritarian practices. It is the combination of authoritarian values disguised by populist rhetoric which we regard as potentially the most dangerous threat to liberal democracy.

The notion of 'authoritarian' is commonly used in comparative politics to denote a particular type of regime and in social psychology to refer to a particular set of personality predispositions or learnt cultural values. Following the latter tradition, in this study, authoritarianism is defined as a cluster of values prioritizing collective security for the group at the expense of liberal autonomy for the individual. Authoritarian values prioritize three core components: (1) the importance of *security* against risks of instability and disorder (foreigners stealing our jobs, immigrants attacking our women, terrorists threatening our safety); (2) the value of group *conformity* to preserve conventional traditions and guard our way of life (defending 'Us' against threats to 'European values'); and (3) the need for loyal *obedience* toward strong leaders who protect the group and its customs ('I alone can fix it,' 'Believe me,' 'Are you in my team?').

The politics of fear drives the search for collective security for the tribe – even if this means sacrificing personal freedoms. In this regard, the 'tribe' refers to an imaginary community demarcated by signifiers of us versus them – our people versus the others. This is often broadly defined by bonds of nationality and citizenship ('We all share the same home, the same heart, the same destiny, and the same great American flag').[22] Or it can be demarcated more narrowly by signifiers of social identity that provide symbolic attachments of belonging and loyalty for the in-group and barriers for the out-groups, signified by, for example, race, religion, ethnicity, location, generation, party, gender, or sex. The notion of a 'tribe' is therefore distinct from simply joining any loose grouping or becoming a formal member of an organization. Tribes are social identity groups, often communities linked by economic, religious, or blood ties, with a common culture and dialect, typically having a recognized leader. Tribes involve loyalty, stickiness, boundaries, and shared cultural meanings and feelings of belonging.

Authoritarian values blended with populist rhetoric can be regarded as a dangerous combination fueling a cult of fear.[23] Populist rhetoric directs tribal grievances 'upwards' toward elites, feeding mistrust of 'corrupt' politicians, the 'fake' media, 'biased' judges, and 'out-of-touch' mainstream parties, assaulting the truth and corroding faith in liberal democracy. Politicians won't/can't defend you. And authoritarians channel tribal grievances 'outwards' toward scapegoat groups perceived as threatening the values and norms of the in-group, dividing 'Us' (the 'real people') and 'Them' ('Not Us'); stoking anxiety, corroding mutual tolerance, and poisoning the reservoir of social trust. If the world is seen as full of gangs, criminals, and fanatics, if our borders are vulnerable to drug cartels, Muslim terrorists, and illegal aliens, if liberal democracy is broken, then logically we need high walls – and strong leaders – to protect us and our nation.

Authoritarian leaders and followers seek collective strength and security because of the triumph of fear over hope, of anxiety over confidence, of darkness over light. The theme of Trump's inaugural address perfectly encapsulates this bleak vision: 'For too many of our citizens, a different reality exists: Mothers and children trapped in poverty in our inner cities; rusted-out factories scattered like tombstones across the landscape of our nation; an education system, flush with cash, but which leaves our young and beautiful students deprived of knowledge; and the crime and gangs and drugs that have stolen too many lives and robbed our country of so much unrealized potential. This American carnage stops right here and stops right now.'[24] This discourse strikes a discordant note because it is so much at odds with the tradition of American 'can do' optimism. Not 'the only thing we have to fear is fear itself' (Roosevelt). Not 'Ask what you can do for your country' (Kennedy). Not 'Its Morning Again in America' (Reagan). Not 'The Audacity of Hope' (Obama).

When authoritarian values and populist rhetoric are translated into public policies, the key issue concerns the need to defend 'Us' ('our tribe') through restrictions on 'Them' ('the other') – justifying restrictions on the entry of immigrants, refugees, asylum seekers, and foreigners, and the use of policies such as official language requirements or bans on certain religious practices. It justifies Guantanamo Bay. It justifies 'zero tolerance' forcibly separating immigrant children from parents at the US border. This orientation underpins and vindicates the intolerance, racism, homophobia, misogyny, and xenophobia characteristic of Authoritarian-Populist parties. In foreign affairs, this viewpoint favors the protection of national sovereignty, secure borders, a strong military, and trade protectionism ('America First'), rather than membership of the European Union, diplomatic alliances, human rights, international engagement, and multilateral cooperation within the G7, NATO, and United Nations. Moreover, Authoritarian Populism favors policies where the state actively intervenes to restrict non-traditional lifestyles, typically by limiting same sex marriage, LGBTQ rights and gender equality, access to contraception and abortion, and affirmative action or quotas – unless, in some cases, these types of liberal policies are framed as a defense of national cultures against attacks by 'others.' Finally, in the public sphere, since liberal democracy has been delegitimized, authoritarian populists favor strong governance preserving order and security against perceived threat ('They are sending rapists' 'radical Islamic terrorists'), even at the expense of democratic norms protecting judicial independence, freedom of the media, human rights and civil liberties, the oversight role of representative assemblies, and standards of electoral integrity. It is the triumph of fear over hope.

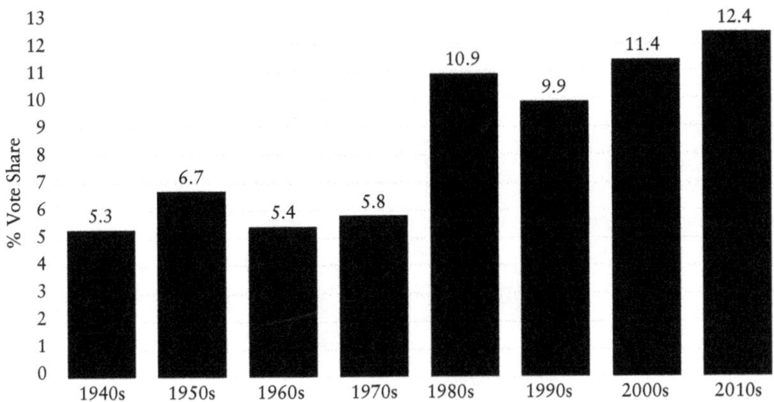


FIGURE 1.1. *Vote share for populist parties in Western societies, 1946–2017*
*Notes:* The mean vote share for populist parties in national elections for the lower (or single) house of parliament from 1945 to 2017 in 32 Western societies containing at least one such party. For the classification of parties, see Chapter 7.
*Sources:* Holger Döring and Philip Manow. 2016. *Parliaments and Governments Database* (ParlGov). www.parlgov.org/; IFES Elections Guide. www.electionguide.org/.

## THE RISE OF AUTHORITARIAN POPULISM

Subsequent chapters classify and measure political parties using systematic evidence and demonstrate that authoritarian populism has taken root in many European countries.

Figure 1.1 illustrates the rising tide in the electorate. Across Europe, the average share of the vote won by these parties for the lower house in national parliamentary elections in Europe has more than doubled since the 1960s, from around 5.4 percent to 12.4 percent today.[25] During the same era, their share of seats has tripled, from 4.0 percent to 12.2 percent. These forces have advanced in some of the world's richest and most egalitarian European societies with comprehensive welfare states and long-established democracies, such as Austria, Norway, and Demark, as well as in countries plagued by mass unemployment, sluggish growth, and shaky finances, such as Greece and Bulgaria.[26] They have won government office in Eastern and Central Europe, such as in Hungary, the Czech Republic, Slovenia, and Poland, and have taken root in the Netherlands and Germany. They have gained in consensus democracies with Proportional Representation elections and federal systems (Belgium and Switzerland), and in countries with majoritarian rules (France) and presidential executives (the United States). By contrast, they are also notably absent, the dog which didn't bark, in several other Western

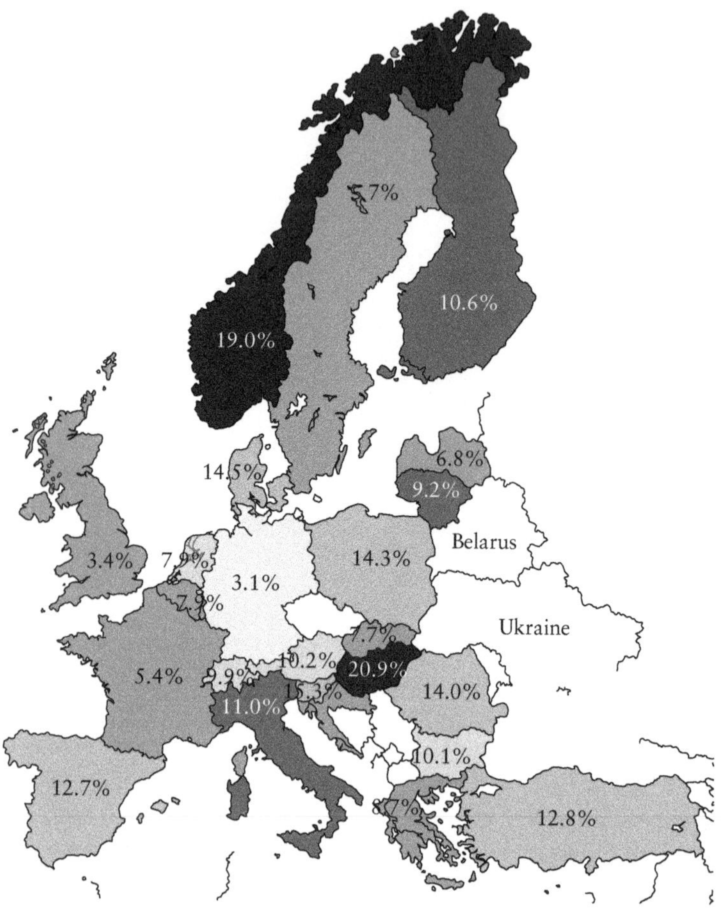


FIGURE 1.2. *Vote share for Populist parties in Europe, 2000–2017*
*Notes:* The mean share of the vote won by Populist parties in national elections for the lower (or single) house of parliament from 1945 to 2017 in European societies containing at least one such party. For the classification of parties, see Chapter 7.
*Sources:* Holger Döring and Philip Manow. 2017. *Parliaments and Governments Database* (ParlGov). www.parlgov.org/; IFES Election Guide www.electionguide.org/.

democracies which were some of the worst affected by the financial crisis, such as Ireland and Iceland.[27]

In later chapters, using reasonable cut-off points, we identify over fifty European political parties that can be classified as 'Authoritarian-Populist.' These have gained a growing presence in parliaments in many countries and entered government coalitions in more than a dozen Western democracies, including in Austria, Italy, New Zealand, Norway, and Switzerland.[28] In long-established democracies, some of the most electorally successful parties during recent decades include the Swiss People's Party, the Norwegian Progress Party, the Freedom Party of Austria, the Danish People's Party, the Party for Freedom and the Forum for Democracy in the Netherlands, and the Finns Party (True Finns). In Central and Eastern Europe, the largest Authoritarian-Populist parties include Viktor Orban's Fidesz in Hungary, Poland's Law and Justice (PiS), the Slovenian Democratic Party, the Bulgarian National Movement II, and the Jobbik Movement for a Better Hungary.[29] Minor parties, capable of influencing the policy agenda, even if less effective in winning seats, include the Flemish Vlaams Belang, the French National Front, the Lega Nord in Italy, Greece's Golden Dawn, Flemish Interest in Belgium, the Alternative for Germany (AfD), and the UK Independence Party. Others in this category include Australia's One Nation Party, New Zealand First, and the Canadian Reform Party (which merged with the Conservatives in 2000). At the extreme fringe, there are also several White Supremacist party organizations, such as the British National Party in the UK, the Party of the Swedes, and the neo-Nazi German National Democratic Party.

Many world leaders have also endorsed authoritarian and populist values, to greater or lesser degree, including Silvio Berlusconi in Italy, Rodrigo Duterte in the Philippines, Prime Minister Andrej Babiš and President Milos Zeman in the Czech Republic, Viktor Mihály Orbán in Hungary, Thaksin Shinawatra in Thailand, Hugo Chávez and Nicolás Maduro in Venezuela, Jair Bolsonaro in Brazil, as well as Narendra Modi in India[30] – and, Donald Trump in America.[31]

By contrast, Libertarian-Populist parties and social movements with a more progressive philosophy are less common but their support has also grown in recent years in several European states. These typically use populist discourse railing against corruption, mainstream parties, and multinational corporations but this is blended with the endorsement of socially liberal attitudes, progressive social policies, and participatory styles of political engagement. This category includes Spain's Podemos Party and the Indignados Movement, Greece's Syriza, the Left Party in Germany, the Socialist Party in the Netherlands, and Italy's Five Star Movement (M5S). In the Americas, Libertarian-Populist leaders are exemplified by Bernie Sanders, as well as the Peronist tradition followed by Cristina Fernández de Kirchner in Argentina, Evo Morales in Bolivia, and Rafael Correa in Ecuador.[32] Arguably, there are also centrist-populist leaders, such as President Emmanuel Macron in France who campaigned as an outsider, criticizing the established parties although governing more like a moderate.

Even in nations where Authoritarian-Populist parties hold few parliamentary seats, they can still exert 'blackmail' pressure on governments and shape the policy agenda.[33] In Britain, for example, the UK Independence Party won only one seat in the May 2015 general election, but its rhetoric fueled rabid anti-European and anti-immigration sentiment, pressuring the Conservatives to call the Brexit referendum, with massive consequences.[34] Similarly, in the September 2017 elections to the Bundestag, the nationalistic, anti-Islamic, and pro-family values Alternative for Germany (AfD) won only 12.6 percent of the vote, but they gained 94 seats in the aftermath of the refugee crisis, entering parliament for the first time and thereby hindering Angela Merkel's negotiations to form a Grand Coalition government, leaving the government in limbo for four months.[35] Mainstream parties can seek to co-opt minor parties in formal or informal governing alliances, and they can adopt their language and policies in the attempt to steal their votes. Popul*ism* and authoritarian*ism* remain potent forces in the contemporary world, even where Authoritarian-Populist parties and leaders don't make substantial or sustained electoral gains.

## WHAT EXPLAINS THESE DEVELOPMENTS?

Many observers seeking to explain developments offer narratives focused on particular high-profile cases and leaders – such as the role of Jean-Marie Le Pen in founding the French National Front (FN),[36] the rightwards shift and revival of the Austrian Freedom Party (FPÖ) during the 1980s under Jörg Haider,[37] and the role of Hugo Chávez in the United Socialist Party of Venezuela.[38]

Similarly, the 2016 US presidential elections can be seen to reflect a contingent series of idiosyncratic events catalyzing the unexpected rise of Donald Trump. Accounts emphasize the role of personalities and leadership styles: the dramatic appeal of Donald Trump, an out-spoken and unpredictable television celebrity, with the public rejecting both 'No drama' Obama's reserved control and cool grace and also Hillary Clinton's policy wonk professionalism.[39] A lot of ink has blamed James Comey's controversial intervention during the final days of the campaign and false journalistic equivalence in negative media coverage of Hillary Clinton's handling of emails and Trump scandals.[40] Others regard the outcome in terms of the evolution of political parties, with the Tea Party and Freedom Caucus pushing House Republicans to the right and deep partisan gridlock emerging in a broken Congress, with Trump inheriting the mantle of Sarah Palin.[41] The FBI has pointed to Putin's meddling through cyberhacking, Facebook bots, and Twitter trolls.[42] Theories of communications emphasize the growth of partisan polarization in the legacy news media and especially social media bubbles, which facilitate the spread of misinformation and conspiratorial thinking.[43] The outcome of the 2016 election can also be attributed to a visceral white backlash against the election of Obama, the first African-American President, toughening the deep scar of racism in the US.[44] Studies emphasize that Trump capitalized upon threats to the declining social status of white working class Americans.[45] Economic accounts seek explanations focused on the after effects of globalization, as trade shocks from cheap Chinese imports shut factories and squeezed paychecks for low-skilled white American workers.[46]

Contingent events clearly do help to account for the outcome of the 2016 American presidential election – for example, it has been estimated that a switch of just 77,744 votes would have tipped Wisconsin, Michigan, and Pennsylvania into the Clinton column, making her President.[47] During the fall campaign, the standard political economy model, combining presidential approval with GNP growth, predicted a tight outcome where the popular vote could have flipped either way.[48] Given the close race, and the decisive role of the Electoral College, mechanical over-determinism should be avoided.

But accounts that focus only on Trump's rise cannot understand the deeper roots of this phenomenon within the Republican Party and the American electorate. And those focused only on America cannot explain why support for populist parties has roughly doubled across Europe in recent decades, with leaders strikingly similar to Trump rising to power in many places around the world. The phenomenon is much broader than any individual and thus requires a more general theory. Any plausible account should be consistent with what is already known from previous research about this phenomenon in the fields of public opinion, elections, political parties, and voting behavior. Claims should also ideally generate propositions testable against a wide range of cross-national and time-series empirical data. And, finally, scientific theories should also be policy relevant, where possible furnishing insights into what can be done by those seeking to mitigate harm to democratic institutions. The plan for this book follows.

## PLAN OF THE BOOK

### I Introduction

Chapter 2 sets out the general theory that lies at the heart of this book. The story of the cultural backlash can be broken down logically into a series of sequential steps involving: (1) long-term social structural changes in the living conditions and security which successive generations experienced during their formative years; (2) the way these developments led to the silent revolution in cultural values; (3) the conservative backlash and authoritarian reflex that this stimulated; (4) medium-term economic conditions and rapid growth in social diversity accelerating the reaction; (5) how the conservative backlash drives voting support for Authoritarian-Populist parties and leaders; (6) how votes translate into seats (and thus government offices) through electoral systems; and finally (7) the broader consequences of this phenomenon, including for the stability of established democracies and hybrid regimes, for party competition and the issue agenda, and for the civic culture.

Building on this narrative, Chapter 3 establishes the book's core concepts. We expand upon the argument that populism is a form of rhetoric, claiming that legitimate authority flows from the vox populi (Us), not the establishment elite (Them). Part of the appeal for the 'deplorables' attending Trump rallies, or media outrage over Tweet transgressions, is reflected in the Punch and Judy theatrical entertainment of cheering attacks on the politically correct liberal consensus, entrenched interests, and hoity-toity elites. But for many European parties, and world leaders, such as Donald Trump, Hungary's Viktor Orban, Venezuela's Nicolás Maduras, and the Philippines' Rodrigo Duterte, behind the populist façade, a darker and more disturbing set of authoritarian values can be identified. Leaders feed upon and foster the politics of fear, anger and resentment. We discuss the core components of our updated concept of authoritarianism and why we believe that drawing upon this notion, rather than conventional labels such as the 'radical right' or 'right-wing populists,' provides a more powerful analytical lens, which accounts for both the attitudes of supporters and the values of political parties and leaders.

These concepts are operationalized and measured separately at both the party and citizen level in subsequent chapters. Citizens' positions are determined using the European Social Survey (ESS) scaled measures of authoritarian–libertarian, populist–pluralist, and left–right attitudes and values in the electorate (Chapter 4). Authoritarianism in the European electorate is gauged not by attitudes toward immigration (which could provide a circular explanation) but by the values of security, conformity, and obedience. Populism is measured by political trust. Left-right economic attitudes are measured through positions toward the role of state vs. markets. The policy positions of 270 European political parties are gauged independently on these dimensions through expert assessments (the Chapel Hill Expert Survey, or CHES) (Chapter 7). The position of

European voters and parties are compared using continuous standardized (0-100-point) scales, avoiding arbitrary boundary errors, allowing shifts over time, and recognizing many shades of grey, not simply black-and-white categories. Thus instead of analyzing support for a specific category of Authoritarian-Populist parties which are classified as belonging to the same family, our models treat adherence to these value scales as matters of degree, where all political parties and voters can be more or less authoritarian–libertarian, populist–pluralist, and left-wing or right-wing.

## II Authoritarian and Populist Values

Our backlash thesis builds upon the extensive body of research demonstrating that long-term social structural developments in post-industrial societies – growing prosperity, rising access to college education, more egalitarian gender roles, and processes of urbanization – led to the silent revolution in socially liberal and post-materialist values, which first became evident at the societal level in the late 1960s and early 1970s. To update the trends, and see whether they are continuing, Chapter 4 presents longitudinal evidence demonstrating the evolving trajectory of value changes during recent decades – the silent revolution shifting the balance between the rising proportion of social liberals and the shrinking proportion of social conservatives in Western societies. We also document the rise of 'critical citizens,' who endorse democracy as the ideal form of government while distrusting politicians as a class.[49] We describe the long-term structural drivers underlying these developments in Western societies, including the role of intergenerational value change, college education, gender roles, ethnicity, and urbanization.

The evidence confirms the importance of generational birth cohorts in Europe and America for authoritarian values and socially conservative attitudes. Authoritarian values may also be shaped by specific periods effects (such as those from 2008 to 2013, the years of the financial crisis) and by life-cycle effects (as people enter middle-age and settle down with marriage and families). Overall, however, such factors are observed to play a secondary role in predicting values compared with birth cohort effects. Longitudinal survey evidence demonstrates that the publics of Western societies have generally become more socially liberal on many issues – but that, as expected, socially conservative values remain strongest among the Interwar generation, non-college graduates, the working class, white Europeans, the more religious, men, and residents of rural communities. These groups are therefore most likely to feel that they have become estranged from the silent revolution in social and moral values, left behind by cultural tides that they deeply reject. The Interwar generation of non-college educated white men – until recently the politically and socially dominant group in Western cultures – has reached a tipping point at which their hegemonic status, power, and privilege is fading. Their values make them potential supporters for parties and leaders promising to restore national sovereignty (Make America Great Again), restrict immigration and multicultural diversity (Build a Wall), and defend traditional religious and conventional moral values ('We stand united behind the customs, beliefs, and traditions that define who we are as a nation and as a people. This is America's heritage: A country that never forgets that we are all, all, every one of us, made by the same God in heaven.')[50]

Theoretically, there are several ways groups could react to the profound cultural changes in society which threaten their core values. One strategy could be self-censorship, the tendency for people to remain silent when they feel that their views are in opposition to the majority, for fear of social isolation or reprisal.[51] Another could be adaptation, as groups gradually come to accept the profound cultural shifts which have become mainstream during their lifetimes, such as growing acceptance of women's equality in the paid workforce and public spheres.[52] A third could be a retreat to social bubbles of like-minded people, the great sorting, now easier than ever in the echo chamber of social media and the partisan press, thereby avoiding potential social conflict and disagreements. We theorize that an alternative strategy, however, is the authoritarian reflex, a defensive reaction strongest among socially conservative groups feeling threatened by the rapid processes of economic, social, and cultural change, rejecting unconventional social mores and moral norms, and finding reassurance from a collective community of like-minded people, where transgressive strongman leaders express socially incorrect views while defending traditional values and beliefs. The tipping point – as formerly predominant majorities become a steadily shrinking but still sizeable share of the population and the electorate – is predicted to trigger the latent authoritarian reflex. Resentment against the inflection point in the silent revolution has spawned a counter-revolutionary conservative backlash. In turn, as the advance of liberal values has stalled, this development has triggered widespread protests and mobilized resistance, especially among the younger generation, women, and minorities.[53] In the long-term, the culture cleavage in the electorate is likely to fade over time through demographic trends and processes of urbanization, as Interwar cohorts without college education, often living in relatively isolated white rural communities, are gradually replaced in the population by college educated Millennials living and working in the ethnically diverse metropolitan cities, who tend to be more open to the values of multiculturalism, cosmopolitanism, and social liberalism. During the tipping point era, however, heated culture wars disrupt politics and society.

Chapter 5 considers the role of economic conditions and material insecurity in accelerating the authoritarian reflex. Many changes are transforming the workforce and society in post-industrial economies through the globalization of economic markets, compounded by the period-effect linked with the deep financial crash and Eurozone sovereign debt crisis.[54] There is overwhelming evidence of powerful trends toward growing wealth inequality and declining real income for most of the population in the West, based on the rise of the knowledge economy, technological automation, and the collapse of the manufacturing industry; the global flows of labor, goods, capital, and people (especially the inflow of migrants and refugees); the erosion of organized labor; shrinking welfare safety-nets; and neo-liberal austerity policies.[55]

The idea that economic conditions have deepened the cultural backlash is supported by studies of electoral geography reporting that Trump supporters were concentrated disproportionately in the Appalachian coal country, rural Mississippi, and rural counties in the Midwestern Rust Belt.[56] In the 2016 US election, the Trump vote was correlated with areas dependent upon manufacturing sectors hit by the penetration of Chinese imports, particularly in Michigan, Wisconsin, Pennsylvania, and North Carolina.[57] Similarly, in Brexit, support for the UK to Leave the EU was concentrated in northern England and the Midlands.[58] Leave votes were disproportionately in 'left-behind' areas characterized by low income, high unemployment, and historic dependence on manufacturing industry.[59] In the second round of French presidential elections in 2017, Marine Le Pen's National Front support was strongest in traditional areas of low-skill employment with double digit unemployment in Northern France, as well as the traditional Mediterranean bastion, while Emmanuelle Macron won by a landslide in Paris and its affluent suburbs.[60] And in the September 2017 Bundestag contests, Alternative for Germany attracted its highest share of the vote in former-East Germany, which lags behind the more prosperous West.[61] Similar regional findings are reported elsewhere in Western Europe.[62] For all these reasons, we expect that economic conditions experienced in some local communities and at individual levels are likely to reinforce authoritarian and populist values.[63]

Building on these observations, we theorize that the authoritarian reflex arising from long-term processes of cultural change is likely to be accelerated and deepened by fears of economic insecurity, including the individual experience of the loss of secure, well-paid blue-collar jobs, and the collective experience of living in declining communities of the left-behinds.[64] Material hardship is likely to make groups more susceptible to the anti-establishment appeals of authoritarian-populist actors, offering simple slogans blaming 'Them' for stripping prosperity, job opportunities, and public services from 'Us.'[65] This chapter considers evidence testing these arguments, at both the individual and community levels.

Chapter 6 turns to the role of migration flows, the refugee crisis, and the growing ethnic diversity of Western societies as other potential accelerants of the authoritarian reflex.[66] Racial resentment in America is often thought to be the driving force behind Trump support, with fears about immigration driving white defection from the Democratic Party to the Republicans. Thus racial divisions in partisanship and voting have been found to outweigh the impact of class, age, gender, and other demographic measures.[67] Similarly, European studies consistently report that anti-immigrant attitudes, and the perceived cultural threat of foreigners, are strong predictors of voting support for radical right parties.[68] We believe that this is indeed an important *part* of the explanation for support for authoritarian populism – but, by itself is over-simplified, because xenophobic, racist, and Islamophobic attitudes are linked with a broader range of socially conservative values. The authoritarian reflex is not confined solely to attitudes toward race, immigration, and ethnicity, but also to the rejection of the diverse lifestyles, political views, and morals of 'out-groups' that are perceived as violating conventional norms and traditional customs, including those of homophobia, misogyny, and xenophobia. Moreover, these sentiments are strongest among those groups, such as homogeneous rural communities and older citizens, who feel the most threatened by the spread of multicultural diversity, and not among the younger generations and university-educated professionals who commonly study, live, and work in metropolitan areas that are typically more socially and ethnically diverse. To explore the survey evidence, we examine attitudes toward immigration across the European Union, testing the links between these orientations and the authoritarian reflex.

## III From Values to Votes

Processes of cultural, economic, and social change are therefore expected to be associated with the endorsement of authoritarian or libertarian values.

Yet comprehensive explanations for the rise of authoritarian populism involve not just 'demand-side' developments in the electorate but also the 'supply-side' conditions under which support for these values can be translated into votes, seats – and power. To examine these factors, we first need to look at voters' values and also at the positions of political parties across the ideological spectrum. Chapter 7 uses the Chapel Hill expert survey (CHES) to identify the policy location of 268 political parties in 31 European countries. Continuous 100-point scales are constructed that identify the location of European political parties on three dimensions. Factor analysis confirms the multidimensional nature of contemporary European party competition, as theorized. The location of European political parties are mapped on these scales. In the four-fold classification illustrated in Figure 7.2, the authoritarian–libertarian cleavage is depicted on the vertical axis. We also demonstrate that this cleavage has become increasingly important since the 1980s, dividing parties over social and cultural issues such as abortion, immigration, Europe, and gay rights. In addition, parties are also classified on the populist–pluralist horizontal axis, based on their position toward the location of legitimate authority in governance. The traditional post-war left–right cleavage also persists, where parties compete over the role of the state versus markets in the economy and welfare services. We identify and map European political parties across these dimensions and use selected case studies to illustrate some of the main contrasts.

Building upon this framework, Chapter 8 examines individual-level cross-national European Social survey data to determine the impact of generational cohorts, period, and life-cycle effects, as well as economic and demographic characteristics, and cultural values on voting for political parties across more than 30 European societies.

This analysis raises a series of methodological challenges. In particular, voting support for minor Authoritarian-Populist parties, that attract only a sliver of the electorate, cannot be analyzed reliably using the standard sample size used in national election surveys. The profile of supporters for Authoritarian-Populist parties attracting a larger share of the vote, such as UKIP, have been analyzed at individual level using standard election surveys in each country.[69] The diversity of these parties, however, along with the instability of voting support over time, make it difficult to generalize from specific cases. Comparative research faces the challenge of measuring voting choices consistently across countries.[70] Electoral studies conventionally use a simple binary variable coded as whether respondents voted for a specific party (1) or whether they voted for any other party (0). This process can be unreliable, however, as it is heavily dependent upon the prior classification of political party families.

The alternative research design employed in this book uses continuous scales (instead of categorical variables for party choice) measuring where all European political parties are positioned across the continuous scales of populist–pluralism, libertarian–authoritarianism, and left–right values, using the CHES expert data. This allows us to compare all European parties based on their positions on these indicators. For the position of citizens, this chapter draws upon the pooled European Social Survey 1–7 (2002–2014) covering 32 countries. It is worth emphasizing that the authoritarian scale used to identify the values of voters avoids asking directly about support for policies, such as attitudes toward immigration or the favorability of leaders, as this would raise risks of endogeneity. Instead, the authoritarian–libertarian scale is measured using the Schwartz scale of personal values.[71] We also examine the effects of authoritarianism and populism separately, since these emerged as distinct dimensions and the drivers of each may be expected to differ.

The evidence confirms our thesis that socially liberal or conservative attitudes, and authoritarian values, in the electorate, predict support for European parties that are more authoritarian and more populist. Moreover, voting support for parties with more authoritarian positions is concentrated among the older birth cohorts and less educated population, as well as among men, the more religious, and ethnic majority populations. By contrast, several economic indicators, such as occupational class and subjective financial insecurity, turn out to be statistically significant but relatively weak predictors of support for parties that are more authoritarian. Overall, cultural values (authoritarian values, political mistrust, and left–right self-placement) are more closely related to voting support for more authoritarian parties than economic indicators. In similar models predicting voting support for the parties that are more populist, the generational effects were reversed, and both economic and cultural factors proved significant.

Chapter 9 examines the fortunes of Authoritarian-Populist parties in Europe, clarifying how the electoral system translates their share of votes into seats. The chapter compares the results of elections for the lower house of parliament held during the post-World War II era under three main types of electoral systems – Majoritarian-Plurality, Mixed, and Proportional Representation Party List – to assess how far the institutional rules of the game can explain the varied results of Authoritarian-Populist parties in gaining seats and ministerial office, even among relatively similar societies. We examine recent elections in six selected case studies, comparing Britain and France using Majoritarian-Plurality electoral systems, Germany and Hungary using Mixed systems, and the Netherlands and Switzerland using Proportional Representation systems.

For a more in-depth case study, Chapter 10 analyzes the reasons behind Donald Trump's victory in the 2016 American presidential election. Many situation-specific factors have been advanced to explain the outcome, the proximate cause of which was the Electoral College rules (Clinton actually won almost three million more votes than Trump). Contributing factors include a Democratic campaign that failed to invest sufficient resources in the 'Blue Wall' of Rust Belt states, the personal strengths and weaknesses of each candidate, the use of a personal email server by Hillary Clinton and the intervention of the FBI, the Russian hacking of the Democratic National Committee computers, Russian trolling via social media, and other situation-specific factors.[72] But the Trump phenomenon was not an isolated event; it was rooted in enduring changes in the Republican Party and in the American electorate, as well as growing party polarization, particularly ideological shifts in cultural politics and social issues that began many years earlier. The Tea Party wing of the Republican Party advocated many of the populist themes that Trump subsequently echoed, including anti-establishment and anti-government appeals, birtherism, and climate change denial.[73] Using the World Values Survey and the American National Election Study, the chapter documents the attitudinal and social basis of the Trump and Clinton supporters, in both the primaries and general election, and long-term changes in the partisan cleavages dividing generations in the American electorate. The evidence confirms, as expected, that Trump's support was concentrated among socially conservative older white men, non-college graduates, and residents in small-town America, especially Republicans endorsing authoritarian values. This was the base particularly susceptible to Trump's promise to 'Make America Great Again,' energized by social pessimism and a nostalgic vision of restoring the traditional social order, jobs, and lifestyles that prevailed decades ago.

Chapter 11 analyzes the populist revolution that shook the foundations of UK party politics just a few months before Trump's victory – the June 2016 Brexit referendum in the UK, as well as the sudden rise and fall in the fortunes of the UK Independence Party (UKIP) in the 2015 and 2017 general elections. The Brexit outcome was also largely unexpected; the opinion polls had predicted a close result, but most commentators assumed that the 'remain' camp would eventually win.[74] Conservative Prime Minister David Cameron decided to hold a referendum on Britain's European Union membership both to appease Eurosceptics within his party and to try to steal votes from UKIP.[75] The results of the analysis confirms the impact of the generation gap, with Millennials supporting 'Remain' – but failing to vote in strong numbers, while the Interwar generation voted for 'Leave' and were much likelier to cast ballots.[76] The subsequent UK general election in June 2017 saw the biggest generational gap in British general elections since the early 1970s, with swings to Labour among the under-40s, and swings to the conservatives among the over 55s.[77] Moreover, in predicting Leave votes, libertarian–authoritarian values and populist attitudes were far stronger factors than social class and experience of unemployment. The series of British contests also illustrates the vulnerability of small populist parties like UKIP when a mainstream party absorbs their language and signature policy issues, as Theresa May's Conservative Party endorsed EU withdrawal, so that authoritarian populism entered the bloodstream of British politics but UKIP failed to win seats. The aftermath of Brexit continued to reverberate in UK politics, dividing parliamentary parties and society.

## IV Conclusions

This book's final part examines the consequences of authoritarian populism and whether liberal democracies are sufficiently robust to resist its damage. This question has aroused intense concern. Debate continues about the potential impact. To understand these issues, Chapter 12 considers several consequences from the rise of authoritarian populism, including for democratic regimes, for party competition over the policy agenda, and for the civic culture.

On the plus side, it is claimed that populism by itself can be a useful corrective for liberal democracy, if it encourages innovative forms of direct participation, highlights genuine public concerns neglected or quarantined by cosmopolitan liberal elites, and brings the cynical back into politics. Liberal democracies have many flaws and reform movements can help to reduce corruption, strengthen participation, and deepen accountability. Populist parties claim to speak for forgotten segments of society and they may potentially mobilize disaffected non-voters and underrepresented groups, thereby boosting campaign activism and turnout.[78]

On the negative side, however, once coupled with authoritarian values, many sound the alarm about the potential threat that the rise of authoritarian populism poses to long-standing norms and institutions of liberal democracy. Populist discourse denigrating 'fake' media, dishonest politicians, and judicial authority, has the capacity to corrode respect for free speech, social tolerance, and confidence in government.[79]

Moreover, when the forces of authoritarian populism rise to power, it is widely feared that they are likely to close borders to refugee families fleeing conflict zones, to erode alliances and multilateral cooperation among Western countries, to embolden bigots and extremist hate groups in society, to corrode social trust and ethnic tolerance, and to replace pluralistic give-and-take in politics with the divisive and polarized politics of animosity, hatred, and fear. The majoritarian principles at the heart of populism put pressures on individual rights, pluralistic diversity, and tolerance of minority dissent.[80] The United States is a resilient democracy but under the Trump administration, the country has been torn apart in the bitter clash between the dystopian vision and divisive rhetoric of the president and his fervent supporters at campaign rallies, on the one side, and the forces of the resistance on numerous issues, on the other side. Divisions are clearest over the investigation into Russian meddling in American elections, reforms to immigration policy and the fate of the Dreamers, the decimation of the Environmental Protection Agency, and culture wars over racial, religious, and sexual politics. It has been estimated that over 8,700 protests occurred in the United States during 2017, involving up to nine million people, with 89 percent protesting against Trump or his policies.[81] In the UK, as well, Brexit has polarized the electorate and deepened splits within the major parties, with Theresa May's government deeply divided in negotiating an exit from the EU. The US and UK, however, are long-establisged democracies which can be expected to prove relatively resilient. Elsewhere, weak institutions of liberal democracy have been pushed to breaking point by populist leaders in hybrid regimes, such as in Hungary, Turkey, and Venezuela, ushering in a reversion to authoritarianism. We examine evidence of trends in democratization and selected cases to see whether anxieties over the rise of authoritarian populism are justified.[82]

In addition, this chapter also considers the 'contagion of the right' thesis, which holds that the advance of Authoritarian-Populist parties has caused mainstream parties and governments to adopt more restrictive policies toward asylum seekers, migrants, and political refugees, for example in Britain and the Netherlands. We conclude that the rise of authoritarian-populist forces is likely to have important impacts on domestic politics – heightening awareness of divisive wedge issues, polarizing party competition, and shaping how mainstream parties like the center-right respond strategically to insurgent challengers, including by adopting at least some of their policy positions. Whether this is positive or negative for the health of liberal democracy remains an open question.

Finally, we also examine debates about the impact of authoritarian populism on confidence in liberal democracy. There is widespread concern that many Western democracies have experienced a long-term erosion of trust in political institutions, along with growing dissatisfaction with democratic performance. Populist support has been fermented in these juices, and their rhetoric criticizing establishment institutions can also be expected to exacerbate mistrust. Yet the evidence is not clear-cut. Thus, many American polls suggest that public confidence in government either remains at an historic low or it is still sinking.[83] Yet recent European studies seeking to detect evidence of any legitimacy crisis present more cautious assessments.[84] Moreover populist parties may be the consequence, as much as the cause, of political discontent.[85] This chapter analyzes trends in institutional confidence and support for democracy and considers the consequences for the legitimacy of liberal democracies.

The concluding chapter 13 reviews the core argument, summarizes the main findings in the evidence, and suggests several alternative strategies which could be employed to mitigate the potential dangers that authoritarian populism poses for plural societies and liberal democracies.

## Notes

1. See E.J. Dionne, Norman Ornstein, and Thomas Mann. 2017. *One Nation under Trump*. New York: St Martin's Press; Brian Klass. 2017. *The Despot's Apprentice: Donald Trump's Attack on Democracy*. New York: Hot Books; Michael Wolff. 2017. *Fire and Fury*. New York: Henry Hold & Co.
2. Michael Kazin. 1995. *The Populist Persuasion*. Ithaca, NY: Cornell University Press; Chip Berlet and Matthew N. Lyons. 2010. *Right-Wing Populism in America: Too Close for Comfort*. New York: Guilford Press.
3. Klaus Von Beyme. 1985. *Political Parties in Western Democracies*. New York: St Martin's Press.
4. As discussed further in Chapter 3, we reject alternative conceptualizations which suggest that populism in politics reflects: (1) a distinct set of policy preferences, specifically, shortsighted economic policies of state-controlled industrialization or protectionist policies that appeal to the poor, (2) a type of party organization with a mass base dominated by charismatic leaders, (3) a type of party defined by its social base, or (4) an ideology. In particular, the minimalist concept of populist rhetoric which we adopt also sets aside notions which introduce unnecessary elements into the notion, notably Cas Mudde's definition of populism as an ideology that considers society to be ultimately separated into two homogeneous and antagonistic groups, 'the pure people' versus 'the corrupt elite,' and which argues that politics should be an expression of the volonté générale (general will) of the people. Cas Mudde. 2004. 'The populist Zeitgeist.' *Government and Opposition* 39(4): 542–563. For a fuller discussion of the concept, see

Chapter 3 and Jan-Werner Muller. 2016. *What is Populism?* Pennsylvania: University of Pennsylvania Press.

5. The rhetoric can be used by a variety of actors, whether presidents, prime ministers, politicians, political parties, journalists or media outlets, social movements, or organizations. In terms of a style of discourse, see Ernesto Laclau. 2005. *On Populist Reason*. London: Verso; Benjamin Moffitt. 2016. *The Global Rise of Populism: Performance, Political Style and Representation*. Palo Alto, CA: Stanford University Press; Toril Aalberg, Frank Esser, Carsten Reinemann, Jesper Stromback, and Claes H. de Vreese. Eds. 2017. *Populist Political Communication in Europe*. London: Routledge; Paris Aslanidis. 2015. 'Is populism an ideology? A refutation and a new perspective.' *Political Studies* 64 (1): 88–104; Elena Block and Ralph Negrine. 2017. 'The populist communication style: Toward a critical framework.' *International Journal of Communication* 11: 178–197.
6. Donald J. Trump. Quoted in *The Wall Street Journal*. April 14, 2016.
7. Pippa Norris. Ed. 1999. *Critical Citizens: Global Support for Democratic Governance*. New York: Oxford University Press.
8. J. Eric Oliver and Wendy M. Rahn. 2016. 'Rise of the Trumpenvolk: Populism in the 2016 Election.' *Annals of the American Academy of Political and Social Science* 667 (1): 189–206.
9. Donald Trump. *Press Conference*. February 16, 2016.
10. Marine Le Pen quoted in *The Daily Express*. www.express.co.uk/news/world/799949/Marine-Le-Pen-Brussels-Frexit-European-Union-Emmanuel-Macron.
11. After the UK High Court ruled that parliament would need to trigger Article 50, the headline below images of the judges in the *Daily Mail* on November 2, 2016 was 'Enemies of the People.' www.dailymail.co.uk/news/article-3903436/Enemies-people-Fury-touch-judges-defied-17-4m-Brexit-voters-trigger-constitutional-crisis.html.
12. Victoria L. Rodner. 2016. 'Populism in Venezuela: When discourse derails institutionalized practice.' *Society* 53 (6): 629–633.
13. Nigel Farage, June 24, 2016. www.express.co.uk/news/politics/686024/Ukip-leader-Nigel-Farage-speeches-resignation-European-Parliament-Brexit-victory.
14. Pegida stands for the 'Patriotische Europäer Gegen die Islamisierung des Abendlandes' ('Patriotic Europeans against the Islamization of the West'), a German protest movement. See www.dw.com/en/german-issues-in-a-nutshell-pegida/a-39124630.
15. Donald Trump. January 20, 2017. *The Inaugural Address*. www.whitehouse.gov/briefings-statements/the-inaugural-address/.
16. www.cnbc.com/2017/04/23/le-pen-time-to-free-french-arrogant-elite.html.
17. Theresa May quoted in *The Independent*. www.independent.co.uk/news/uk/politics/theresa-may-speech-tory-conference-2016-in-full-transcript-a7346171.html.
18. www.dailymail.co.uk/news/article-3903436/Enemies-people-Fury-touch-judges-defied-17-4m-Brexit-voters-trigger-constitutional-crisis.html.

19. Seymour Martin Lipset. 1983. *Political Man: The Social Bases of Politics*. 2nd edn. London: Heinemann, p. 64. The concept of legitimacy is also discussed in Stephen M. Weatherford. 1992. 'Measuring political legitimacy.' *American Political Science Review* 86: 149–166; Bruce Gilley. 2006. 'The meaning and measure of state legitimacy: Results for 72 countries.' *European Journal of Political Research* 45: 499–525.
20. Christopher de Bellaigue. 2016. 'Welcome to demokrasi.' www.theguardian.com/world/2016/aug/30/welcome-to-demokrasi-how-erdogan-got-more-popular-than-ever.
21. Steven Levitsky and Daniel Ziblatt. 2018. *How Democracies Die*. New York: Crown.
22. President Trump. *State of the Union Address to Congress*. January 30, 2018. www.nytimes.com/interactive/2018/01/30/us/politics/state-of-the-union-2018-transcript.html.
23. Ruth Wodak. 2015. *The Politics of Fear: What Right-Wing Populist Discourses Mean*. London: Sage.
24. President Trump. January 20, 2017. *The Inaugural Address*. www.whitehouse.gov/briefings-statements/the-inaugural-address/.
25. See Figure 1.1. Calculated from Holger Döring and Philip Manow. 2016. *Parliaments and Governments Database* (ParlGov) 'Elections' dataset: www.parlgov.org/.
26. See Figure 1.2.
27. Rory Costello. 2017. 'The ideological space in Irish politics: Comparing voters and parties.' *Irish Political Studies* 32 (3): 404–431.
28. Sarah De Lange. 2012. 'New alliances: Why mainstream parties govern with radical right-wing populist parties.' *Political Studies* 60: 899–918; Tjitske Akkerman and Matthijs Rooduijn. 2014. 'Pariahs or partners? Inclusion and exclusion of radical right parties and the effects on their policy positions.' *Political Studies* 62: 1–18.
29. See, for example, an overview by Cas Mudde. 2007. *Populist Radical Right Parties in Europe*. New York: Cambridge University Press.
30. Carlos de la Torre. Ed. 2015. *The Promise and Perils of Populism: Global Perspectives*. Kentucky: University Press of Kentucky; Pasuk Phongpaichit and Chris Bake. 2008. 'Thaksin's populism.' *Journal of Contemporary Asia* 38 (1); Kirk Hawkins. 2009. 'Is Chavez populist? Measuring populist discourse in comparative perspective.' *Comparative Political Studies* 42 (8): 1040–1067; Kirk Hawkins. 2010. *Venezuela's Chavismo and Populism in Comparative Perspective*. Cambridge: Cambridge University Press.
31. Cas Mudde and Rovira Kaltwasse. 2014. 'Populism and Political Leadership.' In R.A.W. Rhodes and Paul't Hart. Eds. *The Oxford Handbook of Political Leadership*. New York: Oxford University Press.
32. Michael L. Conniff. Ed. 1982. *Latin American Populism in Comparative Perspective*. Albuquerque, NM: University of New Mexico Press; Sebastian Edwards. 2010. *Left Behind: Latin America and the False Promise of Populism*. Chicago: University of Chicago Press.
33. Robert Harmel and Lars Svasand. 1997. 'The influence of new parties on old parties platforms: The cases of the Progress Parties and Conservative Parties of Denmark and Norway.' *Party Politics* 3 (3): 315–340.

34. Harold D. Clark, Matthew Goodwin, and Paul Whiteley. 2017. *Brexit: Why Britain Voted to Leave the European Union*. Cambridge: Cambridge University Press.
35. Nicole Berbuir, Marcel Lewandowsky, and Jasmin Siri. 2015. 'The AfD and its sympathisers: Finally a right-wing populist movement in Germany?' *German Politics* 24 (2): 154–178; Rüdiger Schmitt-Beck. 2016. 'The alternative für Deutschland in the electorate: Between single-issue and right-wing populist party.' *German Politics* 26 (1): 124–148.
36. Daniel Stockemer. 2017. *The National Front in France: Continuity and Change under Jean-Marie Le Pen and Marine Le Pen*. Germany: Springer.
37. Göran Adamson. 2016. *Populist Parties and the Failure of the Political Elites: The Rise of the Austrian Freedom Party (FPÖ)*. Germany: Peter Lang.
38. Kirk Hawkins. 2010. *Venezuela's Chavismo and Populism in Comparative Perspective*. Cambridge: Cambridge University Press.
39. www.wsj.com/articles/president-obama-created-donald-trump-1457048679.
40. Deckle Edge. 2017. *Shattered: Inside Hillary Clinton's Doomed Campaign*. New York: Crown; Susan Bardo. 2017. *The Destruction of Hillary Clinton*. New York: Melville House; Thomas E. Patterson. 2017. 'News coverage of the 2016 General Election: How the press failed the voters.' Shorenstein Center, Harvard University, Cambridge, MA. shorensteincenter.org/news-coverage-2016-general-election/; Hillary Clinton. 2017. *What Happened*. New York: Simon & Schuster.
41. http://nymag.com/daily/intelligencer/2016/05/donald-trump-is-the-tea-party.html; Theda Skocpol and Vanessa Williamson. 2012.*The Tea Party and the Remaking of Republican Conservatism*. Oxford: Oxford University Press; J. Eric Oliver and Wendy M. Rahn. 2016. 'Rise of the Trumpenvolk: Populism in the 2016 Election.' *Annals of the American Academy of Political and Social Science* 667 (1): 189–206.
42. Office of the Director of National Intelligence. January 6, 2017. *Assessing Russian Activities and Intentions in Recent US Elections*. Unclassified version. www.scribd.com/document/335885580/Unclassified-version-of-intelligence-report-on-Russian-hacking-during-the-2016-election.
43. P. J. Boczkowski and Z. Papacharissi. Eds. *Trump and the Media*. Cambridge: MIT Press; Elena Block and Ralph Negrine. 2017. 'The populist communication style: Toward a critical framework.' *International Journal of Communication* 11: 178–197.
44. Alan I. Abramowitz. 2017. 'It wasn't the economy, stupid: Racial polarization, white racial resentment, and the rise of Trump.' In Larry Sabato, Kyle Kondik, and Geoffrey Skelley. Eds. *Trumped: The 2016 Elections that Broke all the Rules*. New York: Rowman & Littlefield; Mark Tesler. August 22, 2016. 'Economic anxiety isn't driving racial resentment. Racial resentment is driving economic anxiety.' *The Washington Post/Monkey Cage*; Cornell Belcher. 2016. *A Black Man in the White House: Barack Obama and the Triggering of America's Racial-Aversion Crisis*. www.washingtonpost.com/opinions/trumps-many-bigoted-supporters/2016/04/01/1df763d6-f803-11e5-8b23-538270a1ca31_story.html.

45. Diane Mutz. 2018. 'Status threat, not economic hardship, explains the 2016 presidential vote.'*Proceedings of the National Academy of Sciences.* 115 (19): E4330–E4339.
46. David Autor, David Dorn, Gordon Hanson, and Kaveh Majlesi. 2017. 'A note on the effect of rising trade exposure on the 2016 presidential election.' MIT Working Paper. https://economics.mit.edu/files/12418; Dani Rodrik. 2017. 'Populism and the economics of globalization.' https://drodrik.scholar.harvard.edu/files/dani-rodrik/files/populism_and_the_economics_of_globalization.pdf; Luigi Guiso, Helios Herrera, Massimo Morelli, and Tommaso Sonne. November 21, 2017. 'Populism: Demand and supply.' www.heliosherrera.com/populism.pdf.
47. Larry J. Sabato, Kyle Kondik, and Geoffrey Skelley. Eds. 2017. *Trumped: The 2016 Election that Broke All the Rules.* New York: Rowman & Littlefield, Chapter 1, p. 5.
48. Michael Lewis-Beck and Charles Tien. 2016. 'The political economy model: 2016 election forecasts.' *PS: Political Science and Politics* 49 (4): 661–663.
49. Pippa Norris. Ed. 1999. *Critical Citizens: Global Support for Democratic Governance.* Oxford: Oxford University Press.
50. President Trump speaking at the October 12, 2017 'Values Voters' forum in Washington DC. www.realclearpolitics.com/video/2017/10/13/trump_how_times_have_changed_but_now_theyre_changing_back_again.html.
51. Elizabeth Noelle-Neuman. 1984. *The Spiral of Silence: Public Opinion – Our Social Skin.* Chicago: University of Chicago Press; J.C. Glynn, F.A. Hayes, and J. Shanahan. 1997. 'Perceived support for one's opinions and willingness to speak out: A meta-analysis of survey studies on the "spiral of silence".' *Public Opinion Quarterly* 61 (3): 452–463.
52. Ronald Inglehart and Pippa Norris. 2003.*Rising Tide: Gender Equality and Cultural Change around the World.* New York: Cambridge University Press.
53. Michael Heaney. 2018. 'Making protest great again.' *Contexts* 17(1): 42–47.
54. John B. Judis. 2016. *The Populist Explosion: How the Great Recession Transformed American and European Politics.* New York: Columbia Global Reports; Dani Rodrik. 2017. 'Populism and the economics of globalization.' https://drodrik.scholar.harvard.edu/files/dani-rodrik/files/populism_and_the_economics_of_globalization.pdf.
55. See, for example, Thomas Piketty. 2014. *Capital.* Cambridge, MA: Bellnap Press; Jacob Hacker. 2006. *The Great Risk Shift: The New Economic Insecurity and the Decline of the American Dream.* New York: Oxford University Press.
56. www.nytimes.com/2016/03/13/upshot/the-geography-of-trumpism.html.
57. David Autur, David Dorn, Gordon Hanson, and Kaveh Majlesi. 2016. 'A note on the effect of rising trade exposure on the 2016 presidential election.' NBER Working Paper No. 22637.
58. www.bbc.co.uk/news/uk-politics-36616028.
59. Italo Colantone and Piero Stanig. 2016. 'Global competition and Brexit.' Science Research Network Electronic Paper Collection.

http://ssrn.com/abstract=2870313; Sasha Becker, Thiemo Fetzer, and Dennis Novy. 2017. 'Who voted for Brexit? A comprehensive district-level analysis.' Munich: CESifo Working Papers 6438-2017. Paper presented at the 65th Panel Meeting of Economic Policy. http://cep.lse.ac.uk/pubs/download/dp1480 pdf.

60. Adriana Stephan. 2015. *The Rise of the Far Right: A Sub-Regional Analysis of National Front Support in France*. www.politics.as.nyu.edu/docs/IO/5628/Stephan_Thesis.pdf; www.nytimes.com/interactive/2017/05/07/world/europe/france-election-results-maps.html.
61. http://wahl.tagesschau.de/wahlen/2017-09-24-BT-DE/index.shtml.
62. See Italo Colantone and Piero Stanig. 2017. 'The trade origins of economic nationalism: Import competition and voting behavior in Western Europe.' Carefen Working Papers 2017–49. http://ssrn.com/abstract=2904105.
63. Elizabeth Ivarsflaten. 2008. 'What unites right-wing populists in Western Europe? Re-examining grievance mobilization models in seven successful cases.' *Comparative Political Studies* 41 (1): 3–23.
64. Dani Rodrik. 2017. 'Populism and the economics of globalization.' https://drodrik.scholar.harvard.edu/files/dani-rodrik/files/populism_and_the_economics_of_globalization.pdf.
65. See, for example, Justin Gest. 2016. *The New Minority: White Working Class Politics, Immigration and Inequality*. New York: Oxford University Press; Arlie Russell Hochschild. 2016. *Strangers in Their Own Land: Anger and Mourning on the American Right*. New York: The New Press; J.D. Vance. 2016. *Hillbilly Elegy: A Memoir of Family and Culture in Crisis*. New York: Harper; Katherine J. Cramer. 2016. *The Politics of Resentment: Rural Consciousness in Wisconsin and the Rise of Scott Walker*. Chicago: University of Chicago Press.
66. Christopher Cochrane and Neil Nevitte. 2014. 'Scapegoating: Unemployment, far-right parties and anti-immigrant sentiment.' *Comparative European Politics* 12 (1): 1–32; Anthony Mughan, Clive Bean, and Ian McAllister. 2003. 'Economic globalization, job insecurity and the populist reaction.' *Electoral Studies* 22 (4): 617–633; Richard Wike and Brian J. Grim. 2010. 'Western views toward Muslims: Evidence from a 2006 cross-national survey.' *International Journal of Public Opinion Research* 22 (1): 4–25.
67. Marisa Abrajano and Zoltan L. Hajnal. 2016. *White Backlash: Immigration, Race, and American Politics*. Princeton, NJ: Princeton University Press.
68. Thomas F. Pettigrew. 1998. 'Reactions toward the new minorities of Western Europe.' *Annual Review of Sociology* 24: 77–103; Jens Rydgren. 2008. 'Immigration sceptics, xenophobes or racists? Radical right-wing voting in six West European countries.' *European Journal of Political Research* 47: 737–765; Pippa Norris. 2005. *Radical Right: Voters and Parties in the Electoral Market*. New York: Cambridge University Press, Chapter 8; L.M. McLaren. 2002. 'Public support for the European Union: Cost/benefit analysis or perceived cultural threat?' *Journal of Politics* 64 (2): 551–566.

69. See, for example, Matthew J. Goodwin, Paul Whiteley, and Harold Clarke. 2017. 'Why Britain voted for Brexit: An individual-level analysis of the 2016 referendum vote.' *Parliamentary Affairs* 70 (3): 439–464; David Cutts, Matthew Goodwin, and Caitlin Milazzo. 2017. 'Defeat of the People's Army? The 2015 British general election and the UK Independence Party (UKIP).' *Electoral Studies* 48 (3): 70683; Harold D. Clarke, Matthew Goodwin, and Paul Whiteley. 2017. *Brexit: Why Britain Voted to Leave the European Union*. Cambridge: Cambridge University Press, Chapter 6.
70. Pippa Norris. 2005. *Radical Right: Voters and Parties in the Electoral Market*. New York: Cambridge University Press; Bram Spruyt, Gil Keppens, and Filip Van Droogenbroeck. 2016. 'Who supports populism and what attracts people to it?' *Political Research Quarterly* 69 (2): 335–346; Steven M. van Hauwaert and Stijn van Kessel. 2017. 'Beyond protest and discontent: A crossnational analysis of the effect of populist attitudes and issue positions on populist party support.' *European Journal of Political Research* 57(1): 68–92.
71. Shalom Schwartz. 1992. 'Universals in the content and structure of values: Theoretical advances and empirical tests in 20 countries.' *Advances in Experimental Social Psychology* 25: 1–65.
72. J. Eric Oliver and Wendy M. Rahn. 2016. 'Rise of the Trumpenvolk: Populism in the 2016 election.' *Annals of the American Academy of Political and Social Science* 667 (1): 189–206.
73. Theda Skocpol and Vanessa Williamson. 2012. *The Tea Party and the Remaking of Republican Conservatism*. New York: Oxford University Press.
74. Matthew J. Goodwin, Paul Whiteley, and Harold Clarke. 2017. 'Why Britain voted for Brexit: An individual-level analysis of the 2016 referendum vote.' *Parliamentary Affairs* 70 (3): 439–464; Matthew J. Goodwin and Oliver Heath. 2016. 'The 2016 referendum, Brexit and the left behind? An aggregate-level analysis of the result.' *Political Quarterly*, 87 (3): 323–332.
75. Tim Shipman. 2016. *All Out War: The Full Story of How Brexit Sank Britain's Political Class*. London: William Collins; Sara Hobolt. 2016. 'The Brexit vote: A divided nation, a divided continent.' *Journal of European Public Policy* 23 (9): 1259–1277; Harold D. Clarke, Matthew Goodwin, and Paul Whiteley. 2017. *Brexit: Why Britain Voted to Leave the European Union*. Cambridge: Cambridge University Press.
76. Pippa Norris. 2017. 'Why the younger generation of Corbynistas?' In Einar Thorsen, Daniel Jackson, and Darren Lilleker. Eds. *UK Election Analysis 2017*. Center for the Study of Journalism, Culture & Community, Bournmouth University. http://ElectionAnalysis.UK.
77. www.ipsos.com/en/how-britain-voted-2017-election.
78. Cas Mudde and C.R. Kaltwasser. Eds. 2012. *Populism in Europe and the Americas: Threat or Corrective for Democracy?* New York: Cambridge University Press.
79. Yasha Mounk. 2018. *The People vs. Democracy: Why Democracy Is in Danger and How to Save It*. Cambridge, MA: Harvard University Press;

Steven Levitsky and Daniel Ziblatt. 2018.*How Democracies Die*. New York: Crown.

80. William A. Galston. 2018. *Anti Pluralism: The Populist Threat to Liberal Democracy*. New Haven, CT: Yale University Press.
81. Crowd Counting Consortium. https://sites.google.com/view/crowdcountingconsortium/home.
82. Robert A. Huber and Christian H. Schimpf. 2016. 'Friend or foe? Testing the influence of populism on democratic quality in Latin America.' *Political Studies* 64 (4): 872–889.
83. For example, today only one-fifth of Americans say that they trust the government in Washington to do what is right 'just about always' or 'most of the time' – among the lowest levels in the past half-century. Pew Research Center. 'Public trust in Government: 1958–2017.' www.people-press.org/2017/05/03/public-trust-in-government-1958-2017/.
84. See Pippa Norris. 2011. *Democratic Deficit*. Cambridge: Cambridge University Press; Monica Ferrin and Hanspeter Kriesi. 2016. Eds. *How Europeans View and Evaluate Democracy*. Oxford: Oxford University Press; Carolien van Ham, Jacques Thomassen, Kees Aarts, and Rudy Andeweg. Eds. 2017. *Myth and Reality of the Legitimacy Crisis: Explaining Trends and Cross-National Differences in Established Democracies*. Oxford: Oxford University Press.
85. Matthijs Rooduijn, Wouter van der Brug, and Sarah de Lange. 2016. 'Expressing or fueling discontent? The relationship between populist voting and political discontent.' *Electoral Studies* 43: 32–40.

# 2

# The Cultural Backlash Theory

The cultural backlash theory weaves together old and new claims, as Figure 2.1 illustrates. The electoral marketplace combines three interactive components.[1] Demand-side factors involve societal forces shaping the public's values, attitudes, and beliefs, creating reservoirs of potential support in the electorate that parties attempt to attract. Supply-side factors involve the appeals that parties and leaders use when seeking to mobilize support and the institutional context, especially electoral systems regulating party competition, shaping how popular votes translate into seats and ministerial office. Finally, governance concerns the consequences where parties and leaders gain votes and elected office.

## DEMAND-SIDE: THE SILENT REVOLUTION CATALYZES THE CULTURAL BACKLASH

The first premise in our argument concerns the silent revolution in cultural values that occurred during the second half of the twentieth century, transforming the cultures of post-industrial societies. More than 40 years ago, *The Silent Revolution* argued that the postwar era's unprecedentedly high levels of existential security led to an intergenerational value shift among Western publics.[2] This shift eroded materialist values emphasizing economic and physical security above all, bringing a gradual rise of post-materialist values prioritizing individual free choice and self-expression.

The rise of post-materialist values is the earliest-studied and most thoroughly documented example of changing human values and motivations. Survey data from 1970 to the present demonstrate an

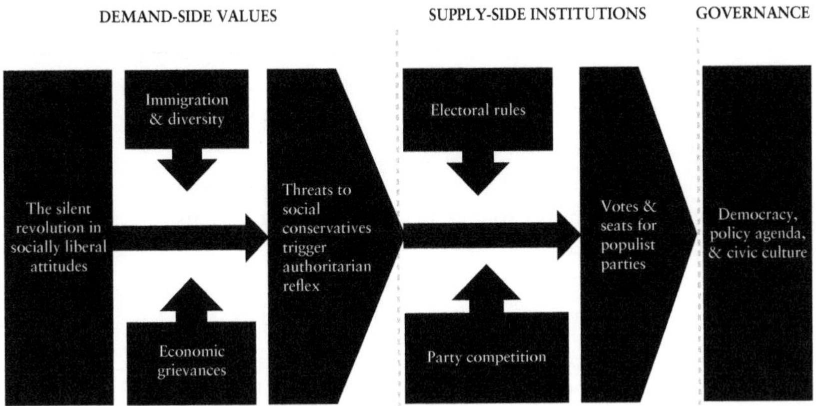


FIGURE 2.1. *The theoretical framework*

intergenerational shift from materialist to post-materialist values in relatively secure high-income societies, but not in less developed ones.[3] The rise of post-materialist values is part of a much broader cultural shift that has brought greater emphasis on environmental protection, peace movements, sexual liberalization, democracy and human rights, gender equality, cosmopolitanism, and respect for the rights of homosexuals, immigrants, handicapped people, and ethnic/racial minorities. These shifts are also associated with the erosion of conventional political participation, such as voting, membership of political parties, trade unions, and voluntary associations, which have given way to protests, demonstrations, and digital activism among the younger generation. Materialist/post-materialist values are only one indicator of this broad cultural shift – but a very good indicator, as Table 2.1 demonstrates. In the 1970s and 1980s, these values and norms were often referred to as 'counter-cultural' – a term that grew outmoded as they gradually became predominant in high-income societies. These values are so closely linked that Inglehart developed an index of survival versus self-expression values based on them.[4] In this book, building on these theories, we refer to this cluster as socially liberal or socially conservative values.

Today, this long-term evolution has transformed the balance of public opinion in post-industrial societies. Traditional moral beliefs, social norms, and behaviors that were conventional and mainstream during the

TABLE 2.1. *Socially liberal values*

| | |
|---|---|
| Abortion, homosexuality, and divorce are justifiable | 62 |
| *Post-materialist rather than materialist values* (12-item index) | 61 |
| Trust people of another nationality | 52 |
| Willing to sign a petition | 51 |
| *Reject* being governed by a strong leader who does not have to bother with parliament | 51 |
| Protecting environment has higher priority than economic growth | 51 |
| When jobs are scarce, men do *not* have more right to a job than women | 49 |

*Note:* First principal component in factor analysis. Based on data from the 2005–2007 wave of the WVS and EVS surveys in the following high-income democracies: Australia, Austria, Belgium, Canada, France, Germany, Italy, Netherlands, Norway, Spain, Sweden, Switzerland, United Kingdom, and United States. This factor explained 29.5 percent of the variance; complete data were available for 14,268 cases.
*Source:* World Values Survey/European Values Survey 2005–2007.

mid-twentieth century, reflecting fixed social identities founded on faith, family, and nation-state, are currently endorsed by a still substantial but shrinking minority of the population. The balance of public opinion has tipped, however, as growing numbers of citizens in Western nations have moved toward post-materialist and socially liberal values.

Economic and physical security have led to pervasive intergenerational cultural changes, bringing a shift from materialist to post-materialist values. People changed from giving top priority to economic and physical safety and conformity to group norms toward increasing emphasis on individual freedom. Growing up under much more secure conditions than their elders, the younger birth cohorts had considerably more tolerant social norms and as they replaced the older cohorts in the adult population, the prevailing culture of their societies were gradually transformed. It took decades for this to happen but it eventually gave rise to a positive feedback loop. People take for granted the world into which they are born. It seems normal and legitimate. The cultural norms of high-income societies were changing, which meant that the gap between contemporary conditions and the world into which one was born was much smaller for Millennials then for the Interwar generation. Conversely, as time went by, the older cohorts experienced a growing gap between the norms of the world into which they had been born, and the world in which they lived. The younger birth cohorts had experienced greater gender equality, tolerant sexual norms, and cultural diversity since birth and they seemed familiar and unthreatening. For many older people, same-sex marriage, women in leadership roles, multicultural diversity in cities, and, in the US, an African-American President were disorienting departures from the norms they had known since childhood; they felt they had become strangers in their own land. The process of cultural change was reinforced by large-scale immigration, rising access to college education, and urbanization. The pace of long-term cultural change can be accelerated or weakened by period-effects associated with shifts in economic conditions and population migration.

The notion of '*values*' refers to deep-rooted and enduring priorities and goals for individuals, organizations, and society. Should society seek to maximize freedom, autonomy, and individual choice or respect for order, tradition, and stability? Should we give top priority to diversity or conformity? Higher wages or more leisure time? Individualism or communitarianism? Open or closed societies? The spiritual or the secular? Nationalism or cosmopolitanism? Minority rights or majority rule? Pluralistic bargaining or strong, decisive leadership? Materialism or post-materialism?

Milton Rokeach defines values as: 'an enduring belief that a specific mode of conduct or end state of existence is personally or socially preferable to an opposite or converse mode of conduct or end state of existence.'[5] Attitudes and opinions are less deep-rooted and enduring than values, shifting more easily in the light of new information or experiences, such as views approving or disapproving of government performance or public policies, and opinions about the risks of climate change or terrorism. But, like the base of an iceberg, values are understood here as bedrock orientations acquired from formative experiences during childhood and adolescence, often persisting for a lifetime, anchoring attitudes and opinions.

## Structural Social Changes Drive Cultural Evolution

If common developments have occurred across diverse post-industrial societies, what underlies the trajectory of cultural evolution? We hypothesize that enduring processes of value change arise from secular processes transforming the deep tectonic plates of Western societies, including generational replacement, the expansion of access to higher education, urbanization, growing gender equality, and greater ethnic diversity. These processes have gradually shrunk the size of the social segments adhering to the core tenants of social conservatism, while expanding the segments of the population endorsing socially liberal attitudes and post-materialist values.

The effects of *generational* change on social values have been extensively documented. This book identifies four main generational cohorts:

- The *Interwar* cohort that lived through two World Wars and the Great Depression (born 1900–1945);
- *Baby Boomers* who came of age during the growing affluence and expansion of the welfare state during the post-World War II era (1946–1964);
- *Generation X* socialized during the counter-culture era of sexual liberalization and student protest (1965–1979); and
- *Millennials* who came of age under the era of neo-liberalism economics and globalization associated with Reagan and Thatcher (1980–1996).

Rapid social change, which transformed the formative experiences of the Interwar and Millennial cohorts growing up in the US and other secure high-income societies, has had profound impacts on cultural values. As Chapter 4 demonstrates, in the US, younger generations hold attitudes that are far more liberal than their elders on a wide range of contemporary social issues – from opinions about the role of women and men to the scope of government, religiosity, homosexuality, race, drugs, guns, and pornography.[6] Similar generation gaps on moral and social issues are evident in Britain.[7] In the 2016 Brexit referendum, for example, age and education divided the UK public more than social class.[8] The Brexit result in 2016 reflects the views of older voters who feared the cultural threat of open borders and migration from Europe.[9]

Inter-generational differences arise from the historical experiences of given birth cohorts which anchor their attitudes and values. The composition of society is gradually transformed through long-term processes of population replacement; each day marks the exit of some older citizens and the entry of new ones. As Figure 2.2 shows, in 2002 the Interwar and Baby Boomer generations constituted almost two-thirds of the European electorate. By 2014, however, these cohorts had shrunken to less than half of the electorate – although they were still a majority of those who actually voted.[10] In America, as well, Millennials alone now comprise almost one-third of the eligible electorate.[11] The evolution of values through demographic processes of generational turnover generates powerful historical tides. As later chapters demonstrate,

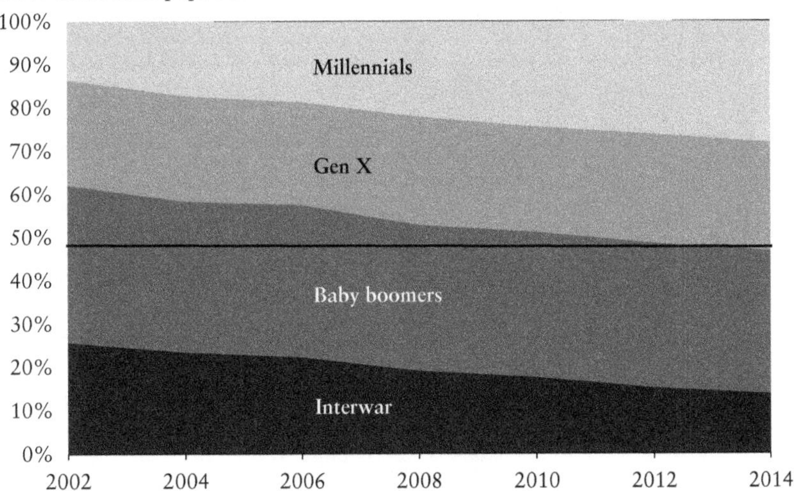


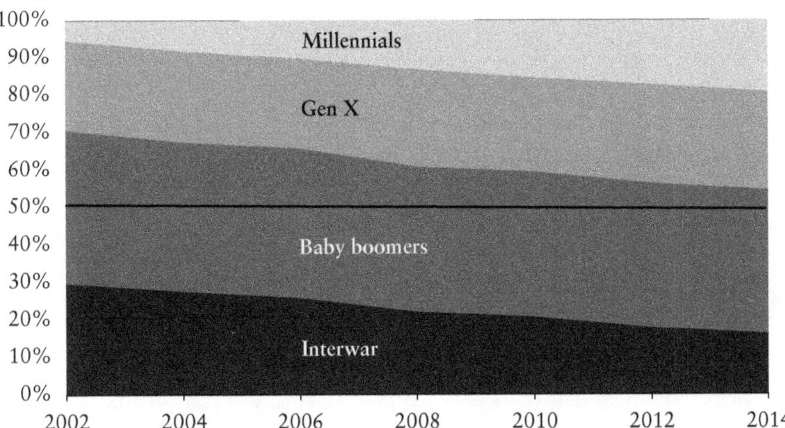


FIGURE 2.2. *The size of generational cohorts in Europe 2002–2014*
*Source:* The European Social Survey, Cumulative File Rounds 1–7.

generational differences are more important for long-term cultural change than period-effects, although we also find fluctuations around major decisive events, as well as life-cycle effects, which alter attitudes as individuals enter the paid workforce, settle down and start a family, and eventually retire.[12]

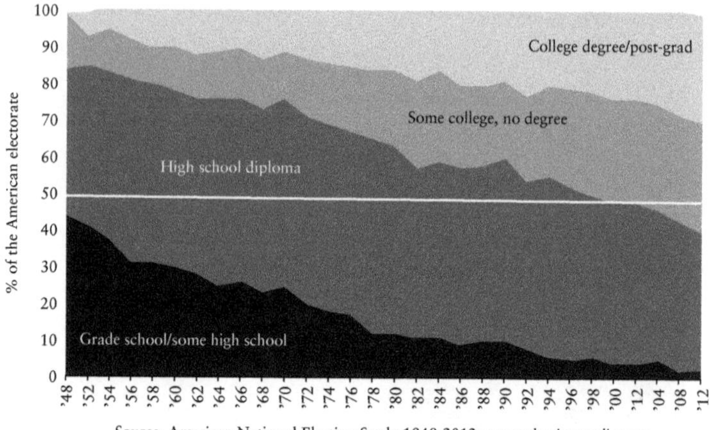


FIGURE 2.3. *The educational revolution, US 1948–2012*

The revolution in *education*, with rapidly growing access to college-level education, has also had a profound impact on Western cultures, helping shift attitudes in a more socially liberal direction. As Figure 2.3 illustrates, the proportion of Americans with only school grade education, or some high school, which was around 45 percent of the electorate immediately after World War II, has shrunk steadily to become a tiny share of the population today. By contrast, a majority of the American electorate now has at least some college education. Similarly, Figure 2.4 shows that across all high-income societies worldwide those enrolling in tertiary education tripled from one-quarter of the student-age population in 1970 to three-quarters today.[13] The transformation was even more marked by sex, where the proportion of women in tertiary education as a share of the student-age population quadrupled during these decades, overtaking men. The experience of attending university has also changed significantly during recent decades, with globalization and the demand for tertiary qualifications expanding student mobility to study abroad, diversifying the college population. Overall, in OECD countries, today around 6 percent of students in higher education are international, with this proportion rising to 20 percent in the UK.[14] In addition to being strongly linked with having post-material values and socially liberal attitudes, education expands

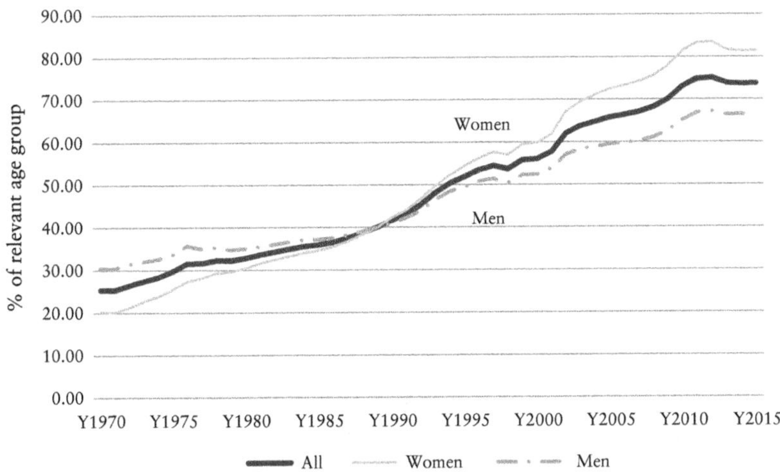


FIGURE 2.4. *Higher education by sex in high-income societies, 1970–2015*
*Notes:* Percentage gross enrollment in tertiary education by sex, as a proportion of the student-age population, high-income societies.
*Source:* World Development Indicators, World Bank, Washington DC, September 2017.

people's cognitive skills, knowledge, and capacities.[15] Millennials have grown up in the information age, where the technological environment has profoundly altered media usage, digital communications, networked connectivity, and geographic barriers to the world beyond local and national communities.[16]

*Urbanization,* combined with growing ethnic diversity in major cities, has reinforced a long-standing center–periphery cultural cleavage. During the twentieth century, the world became predominantly urban, with a majority of the planet's people now living and working in cities. World Bank data indicate that in the 1960s, in high-income societies, about 36 percent of the population lived in rural areas; by 2015, this proportion had shrunk to 19 percent (see Figure 2.5). Urban regions with opportunities for employment have also become the home for rapidly expanding ethnic minority populations. The population growth and cultural diversity of major urban conurbations like New York, London, and Paris contrast with the dwindling predominantly white populations remaining in the rural hinterlands.[17] The lifestyles and values of younger populations in multiethnic conurbations differ sharply from those of older, less-educated, and more homogeneous populations in declining small towns.[18] This has generated deep cultural

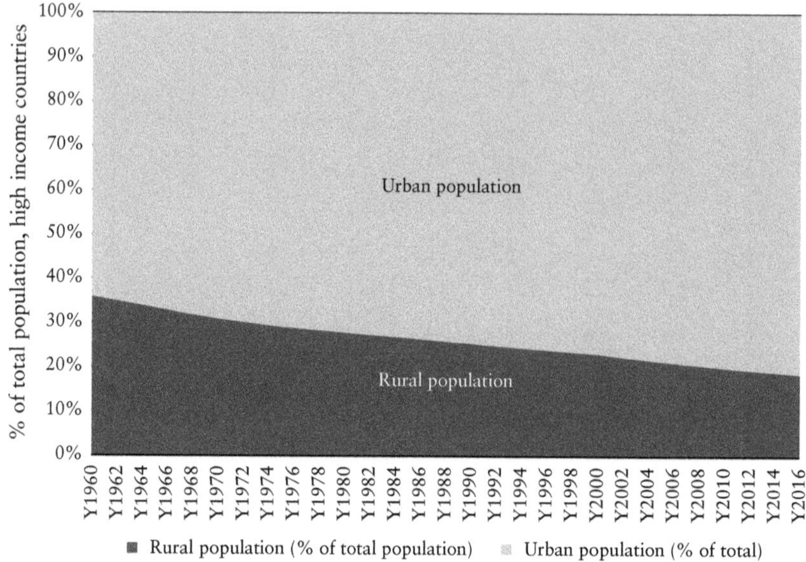


FIGURE 2.5. *Urbanization in high-income societies, 1960–2015*
*Note:* Rural and urban populations (percent of total population).
*Source:* World Development Indicators, World Bank, Washington DC, September 2017.

divisions between America's East coast and the Rust Belt heartland – with similar contrasts between populist support in Greater London versus Northern England, or Paris versus provincial towns.[19]

The growing *ethnic diversity* of post-industrial societies has been transformed by an inflow of immigrants, and the falling fertility rates of white populations, together with the higher fertility rates of non-whites. Younger cohorts also tend to be more accustomed to living in multicultural societies. In America, the youngest (Millennial) generation is the most racially and ethnically diverse; strikingly, almost one-third (30%) are 'new minorities,' born of Hispanic, Asian, and inter-racial couples. In states such as California and Texas, whites have become the minority among the post-Millennial generation that is about to enter adulthood.[20] The ethnic composition of the European Union member states varies greatly and the challenges of integration linked with race, language, and religion differ across the Atlantic.[21] Nevertheless, diversity in EU urban areas has rapidly increased in recent decades due to an influx of immigrants from outside the EU, as well as from the free movement of workers within the EU.[22]

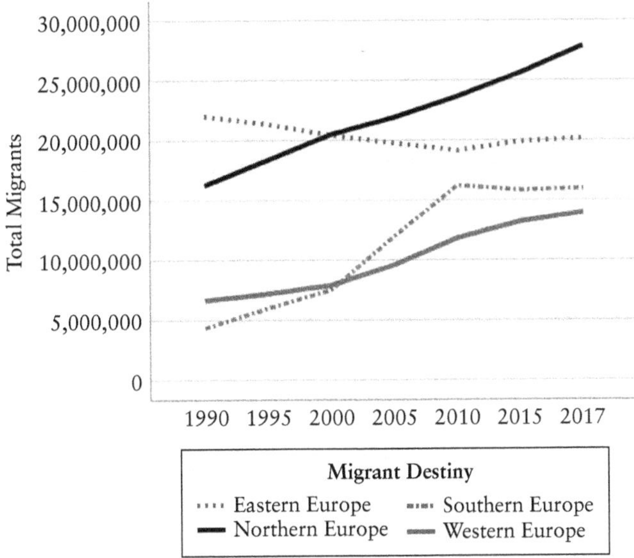


FIGURE 2.6. *Net migration into European regions, 1990–2017*
*Note:* Net migration is defined as the total number of people moving into a country (immigrants) minus the total number of people leaving a country (emigrants), including citizens and non-citizens, for the five-year period.
*Source:* UN Population Division. December 2017. *Migrants Stock by Origin and Destination, 2017*. New York: UNDESA.

Figure 2.6 illustrates some of these developments, as discussed in greater detail in Chapter 6. We can estimate trends in net international migration (the number of immigrants who are not native citizens minus the number of emigrants) in European countries broken down by major regions for five-year periods since the early 1990s. This substantial net migration has transformed Western Europe and Scandinavian societies. The influx of immigrants from the Global South is likely to have profound consequences not just for contemporary European societies but also for the future, because the aging white populations have much lower fertility rates than the immigrant families from developing societies.[23] By contrast, immigration was slower in Mediterranean Europe, while Eastern Europe saw a steady loss of migrants for two decades after the fall of the Berlin Wall, until the numbers stabilized at a lower level. Migration can be driven by many factors, including (1) opportunities to work, study, and live in other countries, and (2) to flee civil wars, economic crises, and the breakdown of political order in countries like Somalia, Libya, Sudan,

Eritrea, or Nigeria. The overall total of migrants includes a number who are at greatest risk – the refugees, asylum seekers, and stateless persons, 6.2 million of whom live in Europe.[24]

### Period Effects Interact with Structural Change

Generational replacement, rising educational levels, growing ethnic diversity, gender equality, and urban growth all contribute to value change. But cultures are also influenced by period-effects, especially those associated with economic insecurity, such as job losses due to the decline of manufacturing industries, as well as rapid changes associated with migrant flows and the perceived risks of terrorism. Social conservatives endorsing social conformity, order, and stability are especially likely to feel threatened by the growing diversity of Western societies. In 2015, in 17 advanced industrial societies of North America and Western Europe, the percent of the population that was foreign born was twice as high as it had been in 1970.[25]

The recession, the refugee crisis in Europe, and major acts of terrorism gave rise to period-effects, which conditioned the impact of social structural change.[26] Public perceptions of these events were stimulated by direct experience, such as the impact of austerity cutbacks on the pocketbook economy among Greek and Spanish households dependent upon unemployment and welfare benefits. Such perceptions are expected to be influenced indirectly by communications through the legacy and digital media, by party campaign rallies, and by leadership discourse, especially messages exploiting popular fears and reinforcing anxieties. Period-effects can accelerate or retard the long-term processes of generational value change, with threats inhibiting the rise of socially liberal attitudes. Moreover, the historical heritage of past cultural values leaves an enduring imprint upon contemporary societies, as has the legacy of Protestantism or Catholicism, or living for decades under democratic governments or under communist rule, even when these experiences gradually fade in importance. Consequently, although the silent revolution has swept over many high-income societies, the pace of change varies considerably.

## SUPPLY-SIDE INSTITUTIONS: FROM VALUES TO VOTES

But under what conditions do secular changes in societies and the evolution of cultural values translate into votes – and then seats in parliament and government offices? In particular, how can structural theories of cultural change explain rising support for authoritarian-populist forces? This is a complex process, where the impact of value change is hypothesized to be mediated by several factors. On the demand-side, one major factor is an authoritarian reaction among social conservatives who perceive that some of their most cherished core values are being eroded. Moreover, a tipping point can occur in the balance between those holding socially liberal and socially conservative values, producing a backlash among the once-dominant group. On the supply-side of the market, leadership appeals and media cues can activate latent authoritarian attitudes among social conservatives in the electorate. Finally, the way that value cleavages in the electorate are translated into votes is conditioned by different rates of electoral turnout – such as the fact that the younger cohorts, whose attitudes are more socially liberal, are less likely to participate than older socially conservative generations. The electoral rules that translate popular votes into elected offices, and the patterns of party competition also matter.[27] Let us unpack these claims.

## The Silent Revolution Reinforces Support for Progressive Forces

Massive but glacially moving shifts in Western cultures have been extensively documented in previous research. But their consequences for voting behavior and party politics have not been fully explained. These value changes motivate the rise of libertarian populists, when the rising tide of social liberalism among the younger, college-educated population is combined with deep disillusionment with the performance of mainstream political parties and leaders. Libertarian populists combine support for socially liberal policies with a sweeping critique of the failure of mainstream parties to address corporate greed, economic inequalities, global capitalism, and social injustice. Campaigning as outsiders, this appeal is likely to mobilize Labour Party members favoring Jeremy Corbyn, Bernie Sanders supporters in Democratic primaries, voters for Jean-Luc Mélenchon's La France Insoumise, the Five Star Movement in Rome, and community activists engaged in Pablo Iglesias' Podemos in Spain.[28] Political parties usually attract older voters, but by adopting digital tools, some like the Five Star Movement (M5S) in Italy, have succeeded in attracting a relatively young membership.[29]

At the same time, levels of youthful enthusiasm are rarely translated into equivalent levels of voting turnout at the ballot box.[30] The Millennial generation in the US and Europe are more likely than their elders to participate in direct protest politics, community volunteering, new social movements, and online activism, but they are usually far less engaged through conventional electoral channels such as voting.[31] Libertarian-Populist parties seeking the support of younger, college-educated voters therefore face stiff competition from social movements championing the progressive agenda on issues such as environmental protection and climate change, LGBTQ rights, gender equality, Black Lives Matter, the 'Me-too' movement against sexual harassment, gun control, immigration rights, human rights and democracy, international development, and social justice. Populists advocating a socially liberal agenda also face competition at the ballot box from mainstream center-left parties and from Green parties, which have became established throughout Western Europe, such as Groen! and Ecolo in Belgium, Les Verts in France, The Greens in Germany, and D66 and GroenLinks in the Netherlands.

## The Counter-Reaction Generates Support for Authoritarian Populism

If socially liberal values have gradually become predominant, shouldn't the silent revolution benefit the electoral fortunes of the standard-bearers for liberal social values, such as the Greens and mainstream social democratic parties advocating progressive policies, as well as social movements among feminists, environmentalists, minority rights, and democratic activists? How do we explain growing voting support for Authoritarian-Populist parties and leaders?

Newton's third law of motion holds that 'For every action, there is an equal and opposite reaction.' And from the start, the spread of post-materialist and other socially progressive policies stimulated a reaction on the part of social conservatives. These changes eventually reached a tipping point in the balance between social conservatives and social liberals in the electorate. This tipping point reflects a threshold effect in public opinion where cultural evolution is not linear. Changes in the relative size of majority and minority groups can spark a decisive shift in collective attitudes and behaviors, catalyzing a reaction when a previously dominant group perceives that their core norms and beliefs are being overwhelmed by social tides and they are losing their hegemonic status. This provides an opportunity for political elites to respond to their cultural grievances.

The 'tipping point' notion suggests that cultural interactions are influenced by the relative proportions of groups within a society. This concept has been explored by previous authors, providing insights into the dynamics of race and gender. In 1969 and 1971, Thomas Schelling published widely cited articles describing a general theory of tipping points to account for racial dynamics.[32] Similarly, Mark Granovetter discussed the idea of racial thresholds, where the size of minority groups living within a local community was seen as triggering 'white flight.'[33] And Malcolm Gladwell popularized notions of tipping points drawn from epidemiology, reflecting the moment when a virus reaches a critical mass and sharply accelerates diffusion in the general population.[34] Thresholds also exist in formal constitutional rules, such as the minimum percentage of votes required before popular support is translated into parliamentary seats.[35]

In the field of gender studies and women's political representation, the concept of a 'critical mass' argues that the effects of women's presence in organizations partly depends on the relative size of the group. Rosebeth Moss Kanter advanced the notion that when only a few token women were included in corporate boardrooms, men, and women behaved similarly. Even if minorities have different interests or behaviors, they are under pressure to conform with established organizational cultures. But once women reached a certain threshold in an organization – constituting perhaps one-third of the board's members – then women could be empowered to express themselves more freely, challenging conventional behavioral norms and cultural attitudes.[36] The notion of a critical mass in organizations also influenced arguments about the design of gender quotas seeking to strengthen women's representation in public affairs. In particular, Drude Dahlerup hypothesized that women's interests are unlikely to have a major impact on political decision-making and the established policy agenda unless women constitute a 'large minority' of elected representatives.[37] This work inspired a substantial debate about the effects of a critical mass on women's access and power in parliaments, a process conditioned by the rules for decision-making within elected bodies.[38]

These diverse accounts share the notion that social change is not necessarily linear; instead, the relative size of groups is important for generating potential threshold shifts.

We argue that the slow process of value change arising from generational, educational, gender, and urban transformations have deepened cultural cleavages in many Western societies and changed the relative balance between liberalism and conservatism. Older social conservatives have gradually lost their hegemonic status, although remaining a large minority of society – and a bare majority of the voting public. In addition, traditional social conservatives are clustered disproportionately in declining rural communities based on manufacturing and agriculture, whereas the younger generations have moved away to cities in pursuit of college degrees and job opportunities, leaving behind aging, overwhelmingly white, and less-educated populations. Thus, in hundreds of counties in America, more people are dying than being born.[39] Conversely, younger social liberals have expanded as a proportion of the overall population – and they are active through community volunteering, protests, and online activism – although they are substantially less likely to vote.[40]

How do people react to the profound cultural changes in Western social values? Several alternative scenarios are possible.

On the one hand, as the proportion of social conservatives erodes in society, their beliefs and behaviors could gradually fade away. In 1974, Elisabeth Noelle-Neumann developed the influential theory that people are more likely to remain silent when they feel that their views are in the minority.[41] The 'spiral of silence' theory posits that people fear social penalties, such as isolation, disapproval, or the loss of status and position, if they are seen to be holding controversial minority views that are not socially desirable, for example by expressing transgressive racial slurs, xenophobia, or misogynistic views in liberal societies. When they feel that their own views are at odds with the majority, people are more likely to self-censor themselves.[42] They tend to feel more comfortable in communicating socially acceptable views that reflect mainstream norms. Hence, social psychologists have found that the public expression of prejudice is strongly related to perceptions of prevailing social norms.[43] People may continue to be prejudiced – such attitudes do not change readily – but they may hesitate to express their views. Such self-censorship seems to underlie resentment against 'political correctness.' If this argument is correct, a snowball or band-wagon effect should be observable in the public square as socially liberal values are seen to gain acceptance in society, such as support for non-traditional families, gay marriage, affirmative action for women and minorities, legalizing recreational drugs, animal rights movements, environmental protection, and transgender rights.

This reaction depends on whether people are aware of changing social norms – which may not happen – for example where distinctive subcultures persist within isolated communities, or if the cues about what is socially acceptable come from media bubbles or dominant opinion leaders, or during periods of rapid transition and intense polarized debate where it may be unclear what social norms should guide acceptable ideas and behavior.[44] Moreover, conservatives who perceive that orthodox moral beliefs are slipping to marginal status within their societies are likely to feel threatened by the loss of respect for their values. If so, even if overt dissent is suppressed, this could trigger anger and resentment on the losing side. The more rapid the shifts in the balance of public opinion, the greater the threat. As later chapters demonstrate, there are strong links between social conservatism (in expressing moral approval on issues such as divorce and abortion) and authoritarian values (as measured by the personal importance of security, conformity, and tradition).[45]

One obvious cultural threat to social conservatives comes from foreigners with different cultural values. But conservatives may view any challenge to conventional norms as threatening, whether linked to race, ethnicity, religion, sexuality, gender identity, lifestyles, or beliefs. Latent feelings of resentment and intolerance may be galvanized into political expression by non-conformity with group morals and values. Conservative reactions can manifest themselves as a violent, nativist force directed against the other, fueled by resentment against globalization, migrants, the closure of factories and plants, the blurring of genders, and the intrusion of different languages. Traditionalists may also reject 'politically correct' views on the benefits of global markets, feminism, diverse lifestyles, and multiculturalism favored by the urban, cosmopolitan liberal elite dominating the media, intellectual life, and parliamentary representatives.

Substantial cultural change has been occurring throughout advanced industrial society. These developments can seem immoral and decadent to those endorsing traditional values, social conformity, tradition, and order. Moreover, large immigration flows, especially from low-income countries, have changed the ethnic makeup of advanced industrial societies. The newcomers speak different languages and have different religions and lifestyles from the existing population – reinforcing the impression that one no longer lives in the society in which one was born. Studies have documented the substantial rise of hate crimes among militant White supremacist and neo-Nazi groups emboldened by the election of Trump in the United States, exemplified by the fatal clashes over the Confederate legacy in Charlottesville, VA.[46] The broader phenomena of Islamophobia has also been rising in Continental Europe, triggering attacks against recently arrived migrants, discrimination in employment and housing, and new laws passed since 2011 in Belgium, France, Austria, and the Netherlands banning the niqab or burqa in public.[47] White nationalist groups typically scapegoat ethnic minorities but they can also be seen to represent a broader reaction against rapid cultural changes that seems to be eroding the basic values and customs of Western societies.

Traditional identities concerning faith, family, ethnicity, and nation, common in the mid-twentieth century, are no longer predominant in Western societies, especially among cultural elites. A tipping point has emerged where social conservatives have become increasingly resentful at finding themselves becoming minorities stranded on the losing side of history. They may also feel that they reflect the 'real' majority in America – especially if they live in isolated communities where friends, family, and neighbors share similar values, if they get much of their political information from conservative media bubbles like Fox TV and like-minded Facebook groups, and if opinion-leaders willing to champion and articulate socially transgressive opinions.[48] Politicians thereby have opportunities to mobilize social conservatives by blaming the erosion of traditional moral values on liberal elites, corrupt politicians, and the mainstream media, as well as denigrating rising out-groups who benefit from socially liberal attitudes and policies, such as women, racial minorities, and immigrants.[49]

Our study is not the first to link the rise of Authoritarian-Populist parties and leaders with the politics of resentment and alienation. In the US, for example, anthropological studies have depicted social trends as the end of white Christian America.[50] Declining rural communities in the American Mid-West and South have been described as inhabited by people who feel that they have become 'strangers in their own land.'[51] The shutting of factories and coal plants has produced declining numbers of secure, unionized jobs, triggering major social problems in which drugs, alcohol, and suicide have led to declining longevity. These social and economic developments may have fueled the politics of resentment, with older whites in rural America blaming global trade, racial minorities, and immigrants for eroding their economic security.[52] In Europe, as well, studies have depicted the white working class as the new minority in politics.[53] Several survey-based studies in particular European countries have demonstrated that populist attitudes, such as mistrust of elites and belief in popular sovereignty, are associated with voting for populist parties.[54] Numerous studies have also linked anti-immigrant and racist attitudes with support for radical right parties in Europe.[55]

But showing that cultural attitudes and values predict support for Authoritarian-Populist parties, by itself, does not account for why these parties have seen rising electoral fortunes in recent years. The impact of long-term cultural shifts, generating a tipping point among social conservatives, has been under-estimated.

Subsequent chapters provide new evidence demonstrating how long-term inter-generational, educational, and urbanization change have gradually shifted the balance between social liberals and social conservatives in Western societies, and how this, in turn, has triggered a cultural backlash among social conservatives with intolerant attitudes.

But much remains to be understood about tipping points in the balance of majority and minority views in public opinion, including the timing, nature, and consequences of these changes in given societies and communities, the way that these developments may serve to mobilize or demobilize citizens to participate at the ballot box, the role of electoral rules for translating voting thresholds into seats, and the broader consequences for party competition, the policy agenda, and liberal democracy.

## Mobilizing Voting Turnout

We hypothesize that the tipping point in public opinion can catalyze social conservatives into voting for authoritarian-populist leaders.[56] But turnout depends on the context. Majorities among the population do not translate directly into representation in liberal democracies for many reasons, including the relative propensity of young and old to vote. In certain contexts, social conservatives may not bother to vote, especially if they are already disenchanted with politics and if the policy programs of mainstream parties fail to reflect the issues they care most about. In this context, those disillusioned with the political classes and disaffected electoral choices, might logically decide to stay home on polling day. On the other hand, where populist parties and leaders who champion their values are on the ballot, this provides a channel for political expression, mobilizing discontented sectors. The Interwar generation (with more traditional values) is also usually far more likely to vote than the millennial generation.[57] As a result, older groups can be disproportionately influential, constituting a majority of those who actually vote, even when they have become a smaller segment of the population.

### *Cleavages in Party Competition*

The success of parties and leaders in using authoritarian-populist appeals to gain votes, seats, and public office is conditioned by electoral systems and institutional rules, patterns of party competition over the key issues, and the role of campaigns. In elections, political demagoguery and media frames can reinforce latent authoritarian values, whipping up fear of 'others,' especially when established authorities have failed to respond to public anxieties. Indeed, mainstream elites, who usually share broadly socially liberal and cosmopolitan values, are regarded by populists as part of the problem of moral corruption – not part of the solution.

From the start, the growing prominence of post-materialist values in the late 1960s and the 1970s stimulated a shift in party competition. As Inglehart pointed out decades ago:

> Environmentalist parties have begun to emerge in many societies in which the electoral system doesn't tend to strangle new parties. Why? The environmentalist cause is only one of many post-modern issues favored by post-materialists. This electorate is distinctive in its entire worldview: they are relatively favorable to women's rights, handicapped groups, gay/lesbian emancipation, ethnic minorities and a number of other causes. But the environmental cause has emerged as the symbolic center of this broad cultural emancipation movement ... Nevertheless, the rise of post-materialist causes has given rise to negative reactions from the very start.[58]

Deepening cultural divisions in the electorate disrupted established party systems. The major political parties in advanced industrial societies were established by the mid-twentieth century when economic issues were dominant, and divisions over social class and religion provided the main cleavages of party competition in the electorate. The classic economic left–right dimension was based primarily on polarization over welfare redistribution and the state role in the economy. On the left, working-class-oriented parties linked to labor unions favored Keynesian economic management and comprehensive welfare states. Parties of the right endorsed free-market policies with a smaller role for the state, as the horizontal dimension of Figure 2.5 indicates. Since the early 1970s, however, the traditional left–right cleavage, dividing political parties over the economic role of markets versus the state, rooted in the classic social identities of class and religion, has gradually faded in importance in many Western countries.[59]

Economic issues such as unemployment, healthcare, welfare, taxation, and social justice remain important problems, especially during periods of recession and financial crisis. But today the most heated political issues in Western societies are cultural, dealing with the integration of ethnic minorities, immigration, and border control, Islamic-related terrorism, same-sex marriage and LGBTQ rights, divisions over the importance of national sovereignty versus international cooperation, the provision of development aid, the deployment of nuclear weapons, and issues of environmental protection and climate change. The changing issue agenda encouraged the emergence of environmentalist parties during the 1980s in West Germany, France, the Netherlands, Belgium, Austria, and Switzerland. In these countries, pure post-materialists were five to 12 times as likely to vote for environmentalist parties as were pure materialists.[60]

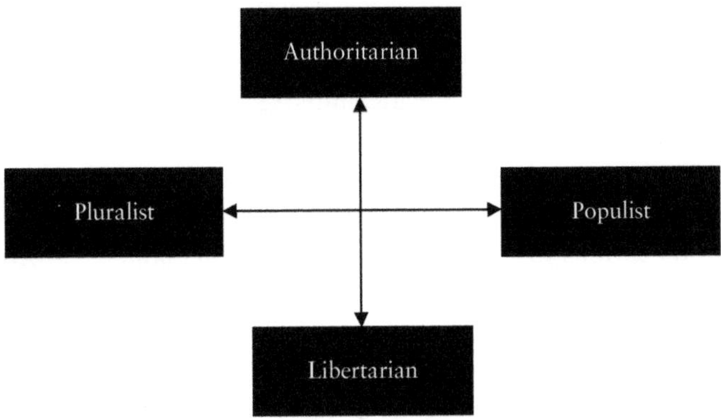


FIGURE 2.7. *Model of cleavages in party competition*

The growing salience of social issues gave rise to a cultural cleavage in party competition that cuts across the left–right economic cleavage.[61] The vertical dimension of Figure 2.7 reflects this cultural dimension, with parties like the Greens at one pole, and those such as France's National Front or the Alternative for Germany at the opposite pole. Other scholars, such as Pierro Ignazi, also argue that the value shift of the 1960s and 1970s stimulated the emergence of left-libertarian parties like the Greens, while simultaneously producing a reactionary backlash among those holding traditional moral values – a 'silent counter-revolution' in favor of the populist right.[62] Similarly, Bornschier suggests that a new cultural cleavage in the electorate identifies extreme right parties in several West European societies.[63]

The changing policy agenda stimulated a cultural backlash in which Authoritarian-Populist parties, leaders and movements channel active cultural resistance against the changes linked with these new issues. The grievances and resentment exploited by Authoritarian-Populists has helped legitimize xenophobic and misogynistic forces, making bigotry respectable in some circles, providing an avenue for its expression at the ballot box. The perceptions of threat among traditionalists have been activated by the message of Authoritarian-Populists, emphasizing fears of threats from 'outsiders' and criticizing the establishment for not responding to genuine public concerns.[64]

Trump's slogan 'Make America Great Again' – and his rejection of 'political correctness' – appeals to a 'golden past' when American society was more homogeneous, US leadership of the Western alliance was unrivalled, threats of terrorism pre-9/11 existed only in distant lands, and sex roles for women and men reflected traditional power relationships. The Us-versus-Them frame is used to stir up fears that provide a support base almost impervious to criticisms of Trump's actual policy performance.[65]

Similarly, the Brexit Leave campaign and UKIP Eurosceptic rhetoric also harks back nostalgically to a time before Britain joined the EU, decades ago, when Westminster was sovereign, society was predominately white Anglo-Saxon, manufacturing and extracting industries – producing steel, coal, cars – still provided well-paid and secure jobs for unionized workers, and, despite the end of empire, Britain remained a major economic and military world power leading the Commonwealth. UKIP rhetoric blends criticism of the European Union with concern about mass immigrations and hostility toward political elites in Westminster and Brussels.[66]

Similar nostalgic messages echo in the rhetoric of other Authoritarian-Populist leaders. This appeal resonates among traditionalists for whom rapid social change and long-term demographic shifts have eroded the world they once knew.[67]

How these value appeals translate into votes – and thus seats and ministerial offices – is conditioned by the institutional rules of the game, especially the electoral system, the strategic response to rivals from mainstream parties, and the campaign communication process through leadership appeals and the media.

## INSTITUTIONAL RULES OF THE GAME

On the supply-side of the political marketplace, conditions that help explain the electoral success of Authoritarian-Populist parties, leaders and candidates include the *institutional rules of the game* regulating party competition during nominations, campaigns, and elections. The opportunities facing parties and candidates are constrained by laws and regulations governing ballot access and the nomination process, the use of Majoritarian, Mixed, or Proportional electoral systems, vote thresholds, as well as the rules governing coverage in the media and political advertising, laws concerning use of referenda and plebiscites, and regulations concerning campaign funding.[68] The legal institutional framework can expand or restrict opportunities for political parties and candidates to compete for votes and seats.

From Duverger on, the classic literature suggests that electoral systems have important impacts on the number of parties that win seats.[69] Minor parties with spatially dispersed support, including authoritarian populists, have more opportunities to gain seats under Proportional Representation, with higher district magnitude and lower thresholds than under Majoritarian systems.[70] Many cross-national studies confirm this point, as do single nation case studies comparing the impact of changes in electoral systems over time.[71] Rules matter. In the 2016 US presidential elections, for example, the use of primary contests in the nomination stage allowed Donald Trump to mount a hostile takeover of the Republican Party. He then won the White House because of the design of the electoral college, despite losing the nation-wide popular vote. Similarly, in the UK, the Leave camp won Brexit with 52 percent of the vote because the rules required only a simple majority, not a super-majority, for passage of constitutional referenda. But rules can change – usually slowly, through piecemeal reforms, so they don't fully explain the timing of fluctuations in support for Authoritarian-Populist parties. Two case studies are selected to provide a fuller account in subsequent chapters that examines in depth the changing electoral fortunes for populist authoritarians in the US and the UK.

## The Strategic Response by Mainstream Parties

The willingness of citizens to desert mainstream parties and support new challengers has been reinforced by social and partisan dealignment, widely documented in previous studies in both the United States and Western Europe.[72] This process has weakened traditional class anchors linking supporters with center-left and center-right political parties, increased potential electoral volatility, and provided opportunities for new populist leaders and parties to mobilize support.[73] The erosion of party loyalties and class identities seems most damaging for the electoral fortunes of center-left Social Democratic parties, but it has also weakened support for mainstream center-right parties. During the 'third-way' era of Clinton and Blair, many left-wing and right-wing parties converged toward the center in their economic policies. Socialists, social democratic, and labour parties on the left sought to broaden their appeal to public-sector professionals, as they could no longer win office if they depended on the shrinking blue-collar trade union base, leading to a decline of social class voting.[74] The public policy agenda also gradually shifted as post-materialists became a larger share of the population, bringing less emphasis on economic redistribution. Economic issues are characteristically incremental, allowing left- and right-wing parties to bargain and compromise over the appropriate levels of taxation, unemployment, and welfare spending. By contrast, cultural issues, and the politicization of social identities, tend to divide into 'Us-versus-Them' tribes, bringing uncompromising and extreme party polarization, as exemplified in American debates about such issues as immigration, abortion, affirmative action, religious freedom, guns, and gay rights.[75]

How have mainstream parties responded to populist rivals? In the supply-side approach, political parties are viewed as rational actors deciding where to position themselves on any given issue dimension, and thus whether to emphasize libertarian-populist or authoritarian-populist appeals.[76] Which social sectors do parties target? Which issues are highlighted in their manifestoes and campaign speeches?

In this regard, established parties may react toward cultural shifts in public opinion and the rise of new challengers through three main strategies.

One approach attempts to delegitimize populist challengers, by drawing attention to their leaders' lack of experience, or the incompatibility of their rhetoric with liberal democratic values.[77]

Alternatively, mainstream parties may seek to isolate populists and exclude them from governing coalitions and party alliances. In the Netherlands, for example, following the March 2017 elections, after lengthy negotiations, in October 2017 Mark Rutte finally assembled a four-party governing coalition designed to keep Geert Wilder's PVV Party out of office, by an agreement involving the People's Party for Freedom and Democracy (VVD), Democrats '66, Christian Democratic Appeal, and Christian Union.[78] Similar grand coalition strategies were used by Angela Merkel to exclude the Alternative for Germany from ministerial office following the September 2017 federal elections. How well governing parties can maintain such a cordon sanitaire, however, depends upon the size of populist parliamentary parties and processes of negotiation over the formation of coalitions with other potential partners.

Finally, mainstream parties may co-opt populist language and adopt a hardline policy stance, promising to restrict immigration or protect trade, or use the anti-elite rhetoric, attempting to squeeze out populist rivals. Single-issue niche parties without a substantial parliamentary or organizational base are particularly vulnerable to hostile issue takeovers of this type. In this way, populist parties may be defeated but populism may still flourish, as exemplified by the British Conservative Party's adoption of UKIP's Euroscepticism and anti-immigration stance.[79]

Finally, political communications through the mainstream broadcast and print media, and opportunities for party leaders to connect directly with their supporters via online social media, can also impact the electoral fortunes of any smaller party, including populists. Many populist leaders gained experience in television, and low-cost platforms such as Twitter and Facebook, and websites such as Breitbart news, have been invaluable for networking extremist social movements, distributing messages to sympathizers, and organizing rallies therefore.[80] The Trump presidency has been characterized by a constant stream of divisive and unsettling Twitter rants, bashing legacy media. There has been growing public concern about the impact of fake news, including the role of Russian bots and ads.[81] Social media have enabled smaller rivals, with limited organizational and financial resources and restricted access to mainstream media, to expand the reach of their communications among their followers, amplifying the impact of rallies therefore. The translation of the electorate's values into support at the ballot box is far from automatic, with the electoral rules, the parties' strategic issue positions, and political communication all helping shape electoral success.

## NEW CHALLENGES FOR REPRESENTATIVE DEMOCRACY

These developments are generating new challenges for party competition, for confidence in democracy, and for democratic representation. If all citizens voted at equal rates, then cultural changes would be directly reflected in the policy agenda and the party composition of democratic assemblies, which would tend to evolve over the long-term in a more progressive direction. As Figure 2.3 shows, the number of Millennials in the electorate now equals the number of Baby Boomers among the population of European societies. But important generation gaps in civic engagement and voting turnout exist.[82] As Chapter 8 points out, citizens born in the Interwar years tend to have traditional values and are almost twice as likely to vote as the Millennials, so they remain a majority of voters. They are also far more likely to be party members. By contrast, Millennials (with progressive values) are more likely than older generations to engage in protest demonstration, but they are consistently underrepresented in voting. This generates a growing misalignment between citizens' preferences and the policy agenda, which lags behind the spread of socially liberal values. The activism gap between young and old reinforces and exacerbates the values gap.

The generational contrasts in cultural attitudes are well established in the literature. In terms of their absolute size, as a proportion of the population, the Interwar generation is a steadily shrinking pool. The Baby Boom cohort has reached a tipping point in contemporary Western societies, as Millennials have become equally numerous. But older cohorts are considerably more likely to vote,[83] and they provide a strong base of electoral support for Authoritarian-Populist parties. The participation–generation gap, in which younger citizens vote at lower levels than their parents and grandparents, has existed for decades. But this generational turnout gap has grown over time: better-educated, more high-income and healthier senior Americans have become *more* likely to vote today than in earlier decades.[84] By contrast, Millennials have become even less likely to vote than young people during earlier decades.[85]

The result of these developments is a growing representational crisis in Western societies. Cultural changes have gradually shifted social values in a steadily more progressive direction in society. But election results over-represent the preferences of the older generations. This disparity means that parties reflecting socially liberal values, like the Greens, tend to be systematically under-represented in elected office relative to the level of public support for environmental policies. Conversely, Authoritarian-Populist parties and leaders are over-represented in elected office, compared with their share of support in society. These tensions are exacerbated most dramatically in contests determined by institutional rules generating winner-take-all majoritarian outcomes, exemplified by the 48:52 victory for the Leave camp in Brexit and by President Trump's victory in the Electoral College despite his loss in the popular vote. This disconnect raises serious concerns about the future of liberal democracy.

## Notes

1. Pippa Norris. 2005. *Radical Right: Voters and Parties in the Electoral Market*. New York: Cambridge University Press.
2. Ronald Inglehart. 1977. *The Silent Revolution: Changing Values and Political Styles among Western Publics*. Princeton, NJ: Princeton University Press.
3. Ronald Inglehart. 2018. *Cultural Evolution: People's Motivations are Changing, and Transforming the World*. New York: Cambridge University Press.

4. Ronald Inglehart and Wayne Baker. 2000. 'Modernization, cultural change and the persistence of traditional values.' *American Sociological Review* 65 (1): 19–51; Ronald Inglehart and Christian Welzel. 2005. *Modernization, Cultural Change and Democracy*. New York: Cambridge University Press. Welzel developed a somewhat similar index of Survival vs. Emancipative values, see Christian Welzel. 2013. *Freedom Rising: Human Empowerment and the Quest for Emancipation*. New York: Cambridge University Press.
5. Milton Rokeach. 1973. *The Nature of Human Values*. New York: The Free Press.
6. Cliff Zukin, Scott Keeter, Molly Andolina, Krista Jenkins, and Michael X. Delli Carpini. 2006. *A New Engagement? Political Participation, Civic Life and the Changing American Citizen*. Oxford: Oxford University Press; James Davies. 2013. 'A generation of attitude trends among US householders as measured in the NORC General Social Survey 1972–2010.' *Social Science Research* 42 (3): 571–583; Achim Goeres. 2009. *The Political Participation of Older People in Europe*. New York: Palgrave-Macmillan.
7. Alison Park and Paula Surridge. 2003. 'Charting change in British values.' In Alison Park, John Curtice, K. Thomson, L. Jarvis, and Catherine Bromley. Eds. *British Social Attitudes: The 20th Report: Continuity and Change over Two Decades*. London: Sage; Alison Park. 2013. 'Changing attitudes towards sex, marriage and parenthood.' In Allison Park, C. Bryson, E. Clery, John Curtice, and Melanie Phillips. Eds. *British Social Attitudes 30*. London: NatCen Social Research.
8. John Curtice. 2017. 'The vote to leave the EU.' *British Social Attitudes* 34. www.bsa.natcen.ac.uk/media/39149/bsa34_brexit_final.pdf.
9. John Curtice. 2017. 'The vote to leave the EU.' *British Social Attitudes* 34. www.bsa.natcen.ac.uk/media/39149/bsa34_brexit_final.pdf.
10. http://ec.europa.eu/eurostat/data/database.
11. See US Census 2015. https://factfinder.census.gov/faces/tableservices/jsf/pages/productview.xhtml?pid=ACS_15_5YR_DP02&src=pt.
12. James Davies. 2004. 'Did growing up in the 1960s leave a permanent mark on attitudes and values? Evidence from the General Social Survey.' *Public Opinion Quarterly* 68 (2): 161–183.
13. 'Tertiary' education is defined by UNESCO as the post-secondary school stage of education involving enrollment in training college or universities. http://uis.unesco.org/indicator/edu-part-er-ger.
14. Oxford University. 2017. *International Trends in Higher Education 2016–17*. www.ox.ac.uk/sites/files/oxford/trends%20in%20globalisation_WEB.pdf.
15. M. Coenders and P. Scheepers. 2003. 'The effect of education on nationalism and ethnic exclusionism: An international comparison.' *Political Psychology* 24 (2): 313–343; Robert Ford. 2008. 'Is racial prejudice declining in Britain?' *The British Journal of Sociology* 59 (4): 609–636; Z. Strabac and Ola Listhaug. 2008. 'Anti-Muslim prejudice in Europe: A multilevel analysis of Survey-data from 30 Countries.' *Social Science Research* 37: 268–286; Ingrid Storm, Maria Sobolewska, and Robert Ford. 2017. 'Is ethnic prejudice declining in Britain? Change in social distance

attitudes among ethnic majority and minority Britons.' *The British Journal of Sociology* 68: 410–434.

16. Pippa Norris. 2000. *Digital Divide*. New York: Cambridge University Press.
17. James H. Spencer. 2014. *Globalization and Urbanization: The Global Urban Ecosystem*. New York: Rowman & Littlefield.
18. See, for example, Cliff Zukin, Scott Keeter, Molly Andolina, Krista Jenkins, and Michael X. Delli Carpini. 2006. *A New Engagement? Political Participation, Civic Life and the Changing American Citizen*. Oxford: Oxford University Press, Chapter 6; James R. Tilley. 2005. 'Research note: Libertarian–authoritarian value change in Britain, 1974–2001,' *Political Studies* 53 (2): 442–453.
19. On the geography of support, see, for example, on France www.nytimes.com/interactive/2017/05/07/world/europe/france-election-results-maps.html?_r=0. On Germany, see www.ft.com/content/1e3facea-9d48-11e7-8cd4-932067fbf946.
20. For a discussion, see www.brookings.edu/blog/the-avenue/2016/06/28/diversity-defines-the-millennial-generation/.
21. Richard Alba and Nancy Foner. 2017. *Strangers No More: Immigration and the Challenges of Integration in North America and Western Europe*. Princeton, NJ: Princeton University Press.
22. Andrew Geddes and Peter Scholten. 2016. *The Politics of Migration and Immigration in Europe*. 2nd edn. London: Sage; Ruud Koopmans, Bram Lancee, and Merlin Schaeffer. Eds. 2015. *Social Cohesion and Immigration in Europe and North America: Mechanisms, Conditions, and Causality*. Abingdon: Routledge, Taylor & Francis Group.
23. http://ec.europa.eu/eurostat/statistics-explained/index.php/Being_young_in_Europe_today_-_demographic_trends.
24. UNHCR. *Global Trends, 2016*. New York: UNHCR. Appendix Table 2. www.unhcr.org/5943e8a34.pdf.
25. This comparison compares the mean percentages of unemployment and foreign-born during the years from 2000 to 2015, with the mean levels in 1970. During this period, the percent foreign born rose from 6 percent to 12 percent and the mean unemployment level rose from 2.7 percent to 7.3 percent in Australia, Belgium, Canada, Denmark, Finland, France, Germany, Italy, Japan, South Korea, Netherlands, Norway, Spain, Sweden, Switzerland, United Kingdom, and the United States. OECD. *Migration – Foreign population – OECD Data*. The OECD. Retrieved 2017-06-01; UNDESA. *Trends in International Migrant Stock: The 2015 Revision*. United Nations Department of Economic and Social Affairs, Population Division. 2015.
26. For the argument that authoritarianism is activated by risk perceptions, see Karen Stenner. 2005. *The Authoritarian Dynamic*. New York: Cambridge University Press.
27. Roger Eatwell. 2003. 'Ten theories of the extreme right.' In Peter Merkl and Leonard Weinberg. Eds. *Right-Wing Extremism in the Twenty-first Century*. London: Frank Cass; Pippa Norris. 2005. *Radical Right: Voters and Parties in the Electoral Market*. New York: Cambridge University Press.

28. The Center for Information and Research on Civic Learning and Engagement. http://civicyouth.org/total-youth-votes-in-2016-primaries-and-caucuses/.
29. Emilie van Haute and Anika Gauja. Eds. 2015. *Party Members and Activists*. New York: Routledge, Chapter 1.
30. Martin P. Wattenberg. 2015. *Is Voting for Young People?* 4th edn. New York: Routledge.
31. Cliff Zukin, Scott Keeter, Molly Andolina, Krista Jenkins, and Michael X. Delli Carpini. 2006. *A New Engagement? Political Participation, Civic Life and the Changing American Citizen*. Oxford: Oxford University Press; Gema M. Garcia-Albacete. 2014. *Young People's Political Participation in Western Europe*. New York: Palgrave Macmillan.
32. Thomas C. Schelling. 1969. 'Models of segregation.' *American Economic Review* 59 (2): 488–493; Thomas C. Schelling. 1971. 'Dynamic Models of Segregation.' *Journal of Mathematical Sociology* 1 (2): 143–186.
33. Mark Granovetter. 1978. 'Threshold models of collective behavior.' *American Journal of Sociology* 83 (6): 1420–1443.
34. Malcolm Gladwell. 2000. *The Tipping Point*. Boston, MA: Little Brown.
35. Rein Tagepeera. 2007. *Predicting Party Sizes: The Logic of Simple Electoral Systems*. Oxford: Oxford University Press.
36. Rosabeth Moss Kanter. 1977. *Men and Women of the Corporation*. New York: Basic Books; Rosabeth Moss Kanter. 1977. 'Some effects of proportions on group life: Skewed sex ratios and responses to token women.' *American Journal of Sociology* 82 (5): 965–980.
37. Drude Dahlerup. 1988. 'From a small to a large minority: Women in Scandinavian politics.' *Scandinavian Political Studies* 11 (4): 275–298.
38. Karen Beckwith and Kimberly Cowell-Meyers. 2007. 'Sheer numbers: Critical representation thresholds and women's political representation.' *Perspectives on Politics* 5 (3): 553–565; Kathleen A. Bratton. 2005. 'Critical mass theory revisited: The behavior and success of token women in state legislatures.' *Politics and Gender* 1 (1): 97–125; Kristin Kanthak and George A. Krause. 2012. *The Diversity Paradox: Political Parties, Legislatures, and the Organizational Foundations of Representation in America*. New York: Oxford University Press; Christopher F. Karpowitz, Tali Mendelberg, and Lauren Mattioli. 2015. 'Why women's numbers elevate women's influence, and when they do not: Rules, norms, and authority in political discussion.' *Politics, Groups, and Identities* 3 (1): 149–177.
39. See, for example, US Department of Agriculture. 2016. *Rural America at a Glance*. 2016 edn. Washington DC: US Department of Agriculture.
40. Russell J. Dalton. 2015. *The Good Citizen: How a Younger Generation Is Reshaping American Politics*. 2nd revised edn. Washington DC: CQ Press; Cliff Zukin, Scott Keeter, Molly Andolina, Krista Jenkins, and Michael X. Delli Carpini. 2006. *A New Engagement? Political Participation, Civic Life and the Changing American Citizen*. Oxford: Oxford University Press.
41. Elizabeth Noelle-Neumann. 1984. *The Spiral of Silence: Public Opinion – Our Social Skin*. Chicago: University of Chicago.

42. J.N. Bassili. 2003. 'The minority slowness effect: Subtle inhibitions in the expression of views not shared by others.' *Journal of Personality and Social Psychology* 84: 261–276; K. Rios and Z. Chen. 2014. 'Experimental evidence for minorities' hesitancy in reporting their opinions: The roles of optimal distinctiveness needs and normative influence.' *Personality and Social Psychology Bulletin* 40: 872–883.
43. C.S. Crandall, A. Eshleman, and L. O'Brien. 2002. 'Social norms and the expression and suppression of prejudice: The struggle for internalization.' *Journal of Personality and Social Psychology* 82 (3): 359–378.
44. E.L. Paluck. 2009. 'What's in a norm? Sources and processes of norm change.' *Journal of Personality and Social Psychology* 96: 594–600.
45. See Karen Stenner. 2005. *The Authoritarian Dynamic*. New York: Cambridge University Press; Marc J. Hetherington and Jonathan Weiler. 2009. *Authoritarianism and Polarization in American Politics*. New York: Cambridge University Press.
46. See Southern Poverty Law Center (SPLC). www.splcenter.org/hate-map.
47. See European Islamophobia Report, 2016. www.islamophobiaeurope.com/executive-summary/2016-2/.
48. Isabelle Portelinha and Guy Elcheroth. 2016. 'From marginal to mainstream: The role of perceived social norms in the rise of a far-right movement.' *European Journal of Social Psychology* 46 (6): 661–671.
49. See also similar arguments in Pierre Ignazi. 1992. 'The silent counter-revolution: Hypotheses on the emergence of extreme right-wing parties in Europe.' *European Journal of Political Research* 22: 3–34; Pierre Ignazi. 2003. *Extreme Right Parties in Western Europe*. Oxford: Oxford University Press; Simon Bornschier. 2010. *Cleavage Politics and the Populist Right: The New Cultural Conflict in Western Europe*. Philadelphia: Temple University Press.
50. Robert P. Jones. 2016. *The End of White Christian America*. New York: Simon & Schuster.
51. Arlie Russell Hochschild. 2016. *Strangers in Their Own Land: Anger and Mourning on the American Right*. New York: The New Press; J.D. Vance. 2016. *Hillbilly Elegy: A Memoir of Family and Culture in Crisis*. New York: Harper.
52. Katherine J. Cramer. 2016. *The Politics of Resentment: Rural Consciousness in Wisconsin and the Rise of Scott Walker*. Chicago: University of Chicago Press.
53. Justin Gest. 2016. *The New Minority: White Working Class Politics, Immigration and Inequality*. New York: Oxford University Press.
54. Agnes Akkerman, Cas Mudde, and Andrej Zaslove. 2014. 'How populist are the people? Measuring populist attitudes in voters.' *Comparative Political Studies* 47 (9): 8–30; K.A. Hawkins, S. Riding, and Cas Mudde. 2012. 'Measuring populist attitudes.' Political Concepts Committee on Concepts and Methods Working Paper Series 55: 1–35.
55. Wouter Van der Brug, Meidert Fennema, and Jean Tillie. 2000. 'Anti-immigrant parties in Europe: Ideological or protest vote?' *European*

*Journal of Political Research* 37 (1): 77–102; Rachel Gibson. 2002. *The Growth of Anti-Immigrant Parties in Western Europe*. Lewiston, NY: The Edwin Mellen Press; Christopher Cochrane and Neil Nevitte. 2014. 'Scapegoating: Unemployment, far-right parties and anti-immigrant sentiment.' *Comparative European Politics* 12 (1): 1–32.

56. Ronald Inglehart. 1997. *Modernization and Post-modernization: Cultural, Economic and Political Change in 43 Societies*. Princeton, NJ: Princeton University Press.
57. Gema Garcia Albacete. 2014. *Young People's Political Participation in Western Europe Continuity or Generational Change?* London: Palgrave Macmillan.
58. Ronald Inglehart. 1997. *Modernization and Postmodernization: Cultural, Economic and Political Change in 43 Societies*. Princeton, NJ: Princeton University Press, pp. 243–246.
59. Paul Nieuwbeerta and Nicholas D. DeGraaf. 1999. 'Traditional class voting in twenty postwar societies.' In Geoffrey Evans. Ed. *The End of Class Politics*. Oxford: Oxford University Press, pp. 23–56; Ola Knutsen. 2004. *Social Structure and Party Choice in Western Europe*. New York: Palgrave Macmillan; Robin E. Best. 2011. 'The declining electoral relevance of traditional cleavage groups.' *European Political Science Review* 3 (2): 279–300; Geoffrey Evans and James Tilley. 2011. 'How parties shape class politics: Explaining the decline of the class basis of party support.' *British Journal of Political Science* 42 (1): 137–161.
60. Ronald Inglehart. 1997. *Modernization and Postmodernization: Cultural, Economic and Political Change in 43 Societies*. Princeton, NJ: Princeton University Press, Chapter 8.
61. Ronald Inglehart. 1984. 'The changing structure of political cleavages in Western society.' In Russell J. Dalton, Scott Flanagan, and Paul A. Beck. Eds. *Electoral Change in Advanced Industrial Democracies: Realignment or Dealignment?* Princeton, NJ: Princeton University Press; Russell J. Dalton. 2013. *Citizen Politics: Public Opinion and Political Parties in Advanced Industrial Democracies*. Washington DC: CQ Press.
62. Pierre Ignazi. 1992. 'The silent counter-revolution: Hypotheses on the emergence of extreme right-wing parties in Europe.' *European Journal of Political Research* 22: 3–34; Pierre Ignazi. 2003. *Extreme Right Parties in Western Europe*. Oxford: Oxford University Press.
63. Simon Bornschier. 2010. *Cleavage Politics and the Populist Right: The New Cultural Conflict in Western Europe*. Philadelphia: Temple University Press; Scott C. Flanagan and Aie-Rie Lee. 2003. 'The new politics, culture wars, and the authoritarian–libertarian value change in advanced industrial democracies.' *Comparative Political Studies* 36 (3): 235–270.
64. Marc Hetherington and Elizabeth Suhay. 2011. 'Authoritarianism, threat, and American support for the war on terror.' *American Journal of Political Science* 55 (3): 546–560; Stijn van Kessel. 2015. *Populist Parties in Europe: Agents of Discontent*. New York: Palgrave Macmillan.

65. Matthew C. MacWilliams 2017. 'Intolerant and afraid: Authoritarians rise to Trump's call.' In Mari Fitzduff. Ed. *Why Irrational Politics Appeals*. Santa Barbara, CA: Praeger.
66. Rob Ford and Matthew Goodwin. 2014. *Revolt on the Right: Explaining Support for the Radical Right in Britain*. London: Routledge; Matthew Goodwin and C. Milazzo. 2015. *UKIP – Inside the Campaign to Redraw the Map of British Politics*. Oxford: Oxford University Press.
67. Eefje Steenvoorden and Eelco Harteveld. 2018. 'The appeal of nostalgia: The influence of societal pessimism on support for populist radical right parties.' *West European Politics* 41(1): 28–52.
68. Arend Lijphart. 1994. *Electoral Systems and Party Systems: A Study of Twenty-Seven Democracies, 1945–1990*. Oxford: Oxford University Press; Elisabeth Carter. 2002. 'Proportional representation and the fortunes of right-wing extremist parties.' *West European Politics* 25 (3): 125–146; Elisabeth Carter. 2004. 'Does PR promote political extremism? Evidence from the West European parties of the extreme right.' *Representation* 40 (2): 82–100; Pippa Norris. 2005. *Electoral Engineering*. Cambridge: Cambridge University Press; K. Arzheimer and Elizabeth Carter. 2006. 'Political opportunity structures and right-wing extremist party success.' *European Journal of Political Research* 45: 419–443.
69. Maurice Duverger. 1954. *Political Parties: Their Organization and Activity in the Modern State*. London: Methuen.
70. See, for example, Giovanni Sartori. 1976. *Parties and Party Systems: A Framework for Analysis*. New York: Cambridge University Press; Arend Lijphart. 1994. *Electoral Systems and Party Systems: A Study of Twenty-Seven Democracies, 1945–1990*. Oxford: Oxford University Press; Gary Cox. 1997. *Making Votes Count*. New York: Cambridge University Press; Elizabeth L. Carter. 2002. 'Proportional representation and the fortunes of right-wing extremist parties.' *West European Politics* 25: 125–146; Matt Golder. 2003. 'Explaining variations in the electoral success of extreme right parties in Western Europe.' *Comparative Political Studies* 36: 432–466; Pippa Norris. 2004. *Electoral Engineering*. New York: Cambridge University Press.
71. Pippa Norris. 2005. *Radical Right: Voters and Parties in the Electoral Market*. New York: Cambridge University Press, Chapter 4.
72. Russell J. Dalton, Scott C. Flanagan, and Paul Allen Beck. Eds. 1984. *Electoral Change in Advanced Industrial Democracies: Realignment or Dealignment?* Princeton, NJ: Princeton University Press; Russell J. Dalton and Martin P. Wattenberg. Eds. 2002. *Parties without Partisans: Political Change in Advanced Industrial Democracies*. Oxford: Oxford University Press; Russell J. Dalton. 2013. *The Apartisan Americans: Dealignment and Changing Electoral Politics*. Los Angeles, CA: Sage/CQ Press.
73. Russell J. Dalton, Scott C. Flanagan, and Paul Allen Beck. Eds. 1984. *Electoral Change in Advanced Industrial Democracies: Realignment or Dealignment?* Princeton, NJ: Princeton University Press; Russell J. Dalton and Martin P. Wattenberg. Eds. 2002. *Parties without Partisans: Political

Change in Advanced Industrial Democracies*. Oxford: Oxford University Press; Russell J. Dalton. 2013. *The Apartisan Americans: Dealignment and Changing Electoral Politics*. Los Angeles, CA: Sage/CQ Press.

74. Geoffrey Evans and James Tilley. 2017. *The New Politics of Class*. Oxford: Oxford University Press.
75. Richard Bond and Jon R. Fleisher. 2001. 'Evidence of increasing polarization among ordinary citizens.' In Jeffrey E. Cohen, Jon R. Fleisher, and Richard Kantor Paul. Eds. *American Political Parties: Decline or Resurgence?* Washington DC: CQ Press, pp. 55–77; Alan I. Abramowitz and Kyle L. Saunders. 2008. 'Is polarization a myth?' *Journal of Politics* 70: 542–555.
76. Anthony Downs. 1957. *An Economic Theory of Democracy*. New York: Harper & Row. See, in particular, Herbert Kitschelt, with Anthony J. McGann. 1995. *The Radical Right in Western Europe: A Comparative Analysis*. Ann Arbor, MI: University of Michigan Press; Bonnie M. Meguid. 2007. *Party Competition between Unequals*. New York: Cambridge University Press.
77. See, for example, Charlotte van Heerden and Wouter van der Brug. 2017. 'Democratization and electoral support for populist radical right parties: A temporary effect.' *Electoral Studies* 47: 36–45.
78. Daniele Albertazzi and Sean Mueller. 2013. 'Populism and liberal democracy: Populists in government in Austria, Italy, Poland and Switzerland.' *Government and Opposition* 48 (3): 343–371; Joost Van Spanje and van der Brug Wouter. 2009. 'Being intolerant of the intolerant: The exclusion of Western European anti-immigration parties and its consequences for party choice.' *Acta Politica* 44: 353–384.
79. David Cutts, Matthew Goodwin, and Caitlin Milazzo. 2017. 'Defeat of the People's Army? The 2015 British general election and the UK Independence Party (UKIP).' *Electoral Studies* 48 (3): 70–83; Joost Van Spanje. 2010. 'Contagious parties: Anti-immigration parties and their impact on other parties immigration stances in contemporary Western Europe.' *Party Politics* 16 (5): 563–586.
80. Gunn Enli. 2017. 'Twitter as arena for the authentic outsider: Exploring the social media campaigns of Trump and Clinton in the 2016 US presidential election.' *European Journal of Communication* 32 (1): 50–61.
81. Diane Owen. 2017. 'Twitter rants, press bashing and fake news: The shameful legacy of media in the 2016 election.' In Larry J. Sabato, Kyle Kondik, and Geoffrey Skelley. 2017. *Trumped: The 2016 Election that Broke All the Rules*. New York: Rowman & Littlefield.
82. Gema Garcia Albacete. 2014. *Young People's Political Participation in Western Europe Continuity or Generational Change?* London: Palgrave Macmillan; Russell J. Dalton. 2015. *The Good Citizen: How a Younger Generation Is Reshaping American Politics*. 2nd revised edn. Washington DC: CQ Press.
83. Achim Goerres. 2009. *The Political Representation of Older People in Europe*. London: Palgrave Macmillan.

84. Russell J. Dalton. 2015. *The Good Citizen: How a Younger Generation Is Reshaping American Politics.* 2nd revised edn. Washington DC: CQ Press; Russell Dalton. 2016. 'Why don't millennials vote?' *Washington Post/Monkey Cage.* www.washingtonpost.com/news/monkey-cage/wp/2016/03/22/why-dont-millennials-vote/.
85. Gema Garcia Albacete. 2014. *Young People's Political Participation in Western Europe Continuity or Generational Change?* London: Palgrave Macmillan.

# 3

# Varieties of Populism

This chapter explains the book's core concepts. Part I unpacks the notion of populism, a concept notoriously difficult to pin down precisely. It is defined here minimally as a form of discourse about the first-order principles of governance, delegitimizing established power structures and the role of elected representatives in liberal democracy while claiming that the people should rule.[1] The antithesis is pluralism, where legitimate authority is understood to rest with elected representatives and liberal democratic institutions providing checks and balances on executive power. Populism reflects a powerful appeal in an era of cynicism but it is silent about second-order ideological values about what governments should do. The discourse is therefore chameleonic in adapting to many colorings. What matters for public policy is the rock not the lizard. Party competition is understood as multidimensional. The main cleavages concern populist–pluralist divisions in orientations toward the legitimate source of governance, left–right divisions over economic values, and authoritarian–libertarian on cultural values. Part II identities the key features of these cleavages in party competition. Part III focuses on one combination, authoritarian populism. We argue that this combination poses the most serious risks for liberal democracy by corroding trust in the established mechanisms safeguarding democratic checks and balances, including the protection of minority rights, the role of the free press, judicial independence, and plural debate in civil society, allowing strongman leaders claiming to speak for the people to step into the vacuum, while simultaneously endorsing social intolerance toward out-groups. Part IV discusses how this conceptual framework help us understand the appeals of diverse populist social movements, parties, and leaders.

## I THE CONCEPT OF POPULISM

We define populism minimally as a rhetorical style of communications claiming that (i) the only legitimate democratic authority flows directly from the people, and (ii) established power-holders are deeply corrupt, and self-interested, betraying public trust. We argue that populist narratives can be reduced to these – and only these – twin components.

### Voice of the People

First, the appeal of populism lies in its claim that legitimate democratic authority is thought to be derived from unconstrained majority rule. The voice of the people should outweigh all countervailing institutions and safeguards designed to protect minorities. Populists assert that 'true' or 'genuine' democracy is *by* ordinary people ('the silent majority'), throwing out corrupt, self-serving elites. Populists claim legitimacy from direct popular expression reflecting the voice of the people, where majority preferences override minority interests. The authority of the voice of the people is valued even when at odds with professional specialists ('Britain has had enough of experts'), legal authorities ('so-called judges'), mainstream media commentators ('fake news'), scientists ('climate change is a hoax'), and elected politicians ('just out for themselves'). Thus in a black-and-white moral vision, the majority of hardworking people are portrayed as homogeneous and inherently 'decent,' betrayed by dishonest pols and corrupt elites ('Crooked' Hillary/'Lyin' Ted).[2] Populist leaders emphasize their authentic grassroot credentials among ordinary people as demonstrated through plebiscites, referenda, demonstrations, mass rallies, and opinion polls. Television talk shows and modern social media such as Twitter are powerful communication tools for mobilizing support by providing a direct and unfiltered link between leaders and followers, by-passing scrutiny by journalists. Old-fashioned mass campaign rallies provide a similar direct link for leaders preaching to the faithful.

### Legitimacy Challenges to the Established Power Structure

Populist rhetoric seeks to undermine the legitimacy of established structures of power in liberal democracies – the elites holding political, cultural, and economic power.[3] The discourse is often transgressive, seeking to outrage and grab headlines. Populists depict themselves as outsiders and radicals, disillusioned with the existing political order and seeking a radical revolution to restore 'real' democracy, sweeping out the money-changers from the temple. Since only the 'real people' are regarded as legitimate, the angry pitchfork brigade denigrates the authority of government officials, the mainstream press, intellectuals and scientific experts, and elected politicians in mainstream political parties.[4]

Populist discourse claims that legitimate authority flows from the people (Us), not the establishment elite (Them).[5] It pits the people against the powerful. Like any powerful drama, it identifies symbolic villains ('the elite') and heroes ('the ordinary people').[6] It suggests both a course of action to solve the problem and a way for leaders to do this ('I alone can fix it'). In his campaign speeches, Trump ran as an authentic outsider to beltway politics, a self-made billionaire leading an insurgency movement on behalf of forgotten Americans disgusted with incompetent politicians, dishonest lobbyists, reckless Wall Street speculators, fake media, incompetent bureaucrats, arrogant intellectuals, foreign powers exploiting America, and politically correct liberals.[7] Populist rhetoric tells a simple story about the silent majority of ordinary, hard-working people rallying behind champions fighting against morally degenerate vested interests.[8] Legitimate authority flows from the popular will. In this regard, despite being located on opposite sides of the political spectrum, Trump's campaign speeches reflect some of the same anti-establishment passion and righteous anger which Bernie Sanders expressed when attacking big corporations, big donors, and big banks.[9] Populism rejects the legitimacy of authority derived from scientific evidence, book learning, and reasoned deliberation. Instead, the discourse celebrates the authenticity of direct experience ('Believe me'), mass opinions ('Many people say...'), and quick applause lines ('Build the Wall'). This form of expression reflects the style of talk-shows and tabloid headlines, websites such as Breitbart news, social media networks, and the everyday language of people. Populists therefore share a common conviction about what they are *against*, depicting themselves as outsiders rooted in the wisdom of 'ordinary folks,' and as insurgents fighting the powerful establishment.[10] This narrative presents a potent story about legitimate decision-making processes in any democratic society.[11] In Barr's words: 'Populism reflects ... a mass movement led by an outsider or maverick seeking to gain power by using anti-establishment appeals and plebiscitarian linkages.'[12] It gains force by using democratic energies against liberal democracy.

Western democracies which have evolved over more than a century are expected to prove relatively resilient from the worst excesses of soft authoritarianism. Layers of safeguards are expected to deter flagrant abuses of executive power – deep-rooted civic cultures, free and fair elections, constitutional limits, independent courts and rule of law, bureaucratic regulations, legislative oversight, opposition scrutiny, public protests, and a vigilant free press.[13] Yet, by their very nature, open societies are far from immune from damage. And protections are even more vulnerable in states governed by hybrid regimes which are not fully democratic. In these settings, strongmen leaders using the façade of populist rhetoric can deal lethal blows to human rights, curtailing freedoms, silencing the press, ramming through constitutional changes, manipulating elections, pocketing state resources, and facilitating backsliding into electoral autocracy. In Hungary, Recep Tayyip Erdoğan has purged thousands of perceived opponents. In Venezuela, Nicolás Maduro has abused electoral malpractices. In Hungary, constitutional amendments weakened checks and balances on Viktor Organ's executive powers.[14] Flawed and failed elections, in particular, facilitate backsliding toward autocracy.[15]

Populist discourse therefore calls for root-and-branch political reforms – but it does not suggest a coherent blueprint for what policies the people's revolution should advance, such as the appropriate way to steer the economy or to conduct foreign affairs.[16] Like related concepts – such as liberal-democracy, deliberative-democracy, plebiscitary-democracy, and so on – many varieties of populism-with-adjectives exist.[17] In this regard, populism has been depicted as a 'thin' ideology.[18] But it would be more accurate to depict it as a political ideology of governance, which is about legitimate authority not substantive policy programs. Not surprisingly, therefore, beyond the common rhetorical style and vision of governance, populist leaders, such as Marine Le Pen and Bernie Sanders, or Silvio Berlusconi and Hugo Chavez, diverge sharply in terms of their worldviews, the policies they advocate, and the types of programs they promise to implement.

## II VARIETIES OF POPULISM

How can types of populist parties and leader be categorized and classified?

For many populist leaders, ranging from Donald Trump and France's Marine Le Pen, Hungary's Viktor Orban, Venezuela's Nicolás Maduras, and the Philippines' Rodrigo Duterte, behind the populist façade, a more disturbing set of *authoritarian values* and policies can be identified. Not all populists endorse authoritarianism, and authoritarian rulers do not necessarily adopt populist appeals, but the combination often occurs. Logical connections tie the two together: populism tends to undermine the legitimacy of democratic checks on executive powers, opening the door for soft authoritarian leaders. And the steady erosion of democratic norms and political freedoms over a sustained period of time leads toward the consolidation of authoritarian regimes, such as Venezuela, which outlast particular leaders.

## Authoritarian Values

Libertarian and authoritarian populists differ in their cultural values rather than in their rhetorical style. The concept of *values* was pioneered by Milton Rokeach who argued that they reflect cultural beliefs about desirable goals.[19] Values are broad objectives that serve to guide attitudes and opinions, behavior and moral judgments. Values reflect broad goals where trade-offs can be identified and ranked, when rival choices conflict. For example, should schools seek to encourage fulfillment, inventiveness, and creativity in children? Or should they emphasize the acquisition of skills in reading, writing, and arithmetic? Should people's lifestyles and careers mainly emphasize material comforts and monetary rewards? Or should they seek self-realization? Should public policies seek to protect society against climate change, or should they aim to protect coal-mining jobs? And should societies promote social cooperation and collaboration – or facilitate individual freedom and initiative? Personal values guide individual goals and behavior, while social values serve a similar function for the family and relationships within communities. Organizational values reflect the goals of companies or administrative units. Similarly, political values shape the salience of public policy issues and perceptions of the most important problems facing the country. Values are first acquired by individuals through formative experiences during early socialization, in the family, schools, and community. Although values can evolve subsequently, they tend to persist as relatively durable orientations throughout adulthood.

But what is the meaning of the values that characterize authoritarian populism? The concept of '*authoritarianism*' builds on a long tradition in social psychology that arose among scholars seeking to explain the rise of European Fascism and Bolshevism.[20] The simplest psychological concept of '*authoritarian*' originally referred to a person favoring obedience over liberty.[21] The notion came into prominence in the interwar years as social psychologists struggled to understand why ordinary citizens willingly supported Bolshevism and Fascism not just through the threat or use of force but also through conviction. Early work by Erich Fromm hypothesized that freedom was a double-edged sword, bringing independence and rationality but also feelings of isolation and anxiety that people sought to escape by following strong leaders who promised to deliver collective security even at the expense of personal liberties.[22] The classical work of Fromm (1941),[23] and Adorno *et al.* (1950),[24] saw authoritarianism as a basic personality trait that served as a defense mechanism against anxieties and insecurities. Adorno and his colleagues hypothesized that these traits stemmed from repressed anger and fear in response to punitive parenting practices and economic hardship.[25] Since the mid-twentieth century, the concept of authoritarianism has typically been treated by social psychologists as an individual personality trait used to explain seemingly irrational feelings such as generalized prejudice, where an individual who dislikes immigrants is also thought likely to prove homophobic, Islamophobic, misogynistic, and so on.[26] Yet others view it – as we do – as the values embedded within a group culture.

The concept was subsequently revised by Altemeyer (1996).[27] In the extensive research literature that has developed, the concept, measurement, and origins of authoritarianism have been widely debated. Several scholars have refined the concept and examined evidence of the impact of authoritarianism on American politics, including Feldman, Stenner, and Hetherington and Weiler.[28] Over the decades, an extensive body of literature has applied this notion in efforts to understand support for fascism, the alt-right, neo-Nazis, and extremist hate groups, psychological feelings of racial prejudice, xenophobia, homophobia, sexism, and Islamophobia, and attitudes toward issues of immigration, minority rights, religious tolerance, racial and gender equality, and cultural protectionism.[29] But as well as applying to individuals, the concept can also be extended to describe the culture permeating groups and societies, meaning their shared values, norms, and beliefs.

For most of history, survival was insecure, with the population rising in response to the food supply and then being held constant by starvation, disease, and violence. Under these conditions, cultures tend to emphasize strong in-group solidarity, conformity to group norms, rejection of outsiders, and obedience to strong leaders. Under extreme scarcity, xenophobia is realistic: if there is just enough land to support one tribe and another tribe tries to claim it, survival becomes a zero-sum struggle. Under perceptions of threat, people tend to close ranks behind a strong leader, forming a united front against outsiders – a strategy that can be called the authoritarian reflex. Conversely, perceptions of existential security generally open the way for greater individual freedom and more openness to diversity, change, and new ideas.

This book conceptualizes 'authoritarian values' in the mass public as a cluster of three related components, emphasizing the importance of (i) *conformity* (strict adherence to group conventions and traditional customs); (ii) *security* (safety and protection of the group against risks, justifying strict enforcement and aggression toward outsiders who threaten the security or the accepted group norms); and (iii) *loyalty* (supporting the group and its leaders). We view these dimensions as expressions of basic social values that represent a strategy for attaining collective security by the group at the expense of individual autonomy. This orientation underpins authoritarian citizens who seek strong group leaders to protect them from outside risks, and who support measures that preserve the collective security of the group, even at the expense of civil liberties. Authoritarian values lead people to close ranks behind tribal leaders, emphasizing in-group solidarity, rigid conformity to group norms, and a rejection of outsiders. Conversely, when people hold values that are more libertarian and progressive, it makes them more open to new ideas and more tolerant of out-groups.[30]

Support for these clusters of social values is measured in this book as a matter of degree on a continuous scale ranging from the most authoritarian, at one pole, to the most libertarian, at the other. At the elite level, authoritarianism relates to a form of governance that disregards the principles and norms of liberal democracy, including political rights and civil liberties. Political actors can display relatively authoritarian or libertarian cultural values, whether ordinary citizens or political elites, as is true of social movements and organizations, or media outlets. This study focuses on analyzing the roots of mass support for political parties that score high on an authoritarianism index, measured by surveys of public opinion and expert estimates of party policy positions. Given the centrality of the concept of authoritarianism to this study, we will spell out the meaning of the component elements in greater detail.

## Conformity and Social Conservatism

Although they are distinct concepts, empirically there are strong links between authoritarian values and social conservatism, because the value of conformity emphasizes the importance of order, tradition, and stability. Conformity means adhering to established ways of doing things, obeying rules and cultural traditions, and respecting orthodox ways of life, rather than emphasizing individual freedoms, personal autonomy, and tolerance of diverse lifestyles – which are associated with social liberalism and post-materialist values.[31]

Given the importance of conformity, authoritarian values justify strict moral sanctions and harsh penalties for those that violate group norms. Those adhering to authoritarian values are therefore generally socially conservative and ethnocentric, seeking to preserve traditional customs rather than endorsing multiculturalism and diversity, preferring conventional gender roles for women and men, while disapproving of gender equality, fluid gender roles, and sexual identities, as well as racial and ethnic diversity, secular moral beliefs, and laws permitting gay marriage, equal rights for women, and the protection of religious minorities. Conformity endorses tradition over novelty, natives over immigrants, localism over cosmopolitanism. Dogmatic attitudes are reinforced by adhering to established lifestyles and not questioning social conventions, so that conformists are less likely to change their minds when presented with new information challenging deeply held beliefs. The emphasis on group conformity divides the world into 'Us' (a community with shared values) and 'Them' (both out-groups *and* powerful elites being regarded as potential threats to socially conservative values). Moral language, which activates symbolic boundaries between insider and outsider groups, generates powerful emotional appeals – as is illustrated by the heated reaction aroused in recent fights in America over the removal of Confederate statues, and between alt-right neo-Nazis and counter-protestors. Some scholars have suggested that the Us-versus-Them, dichotomy is a defining characteristic of authoritarian populism in Europe.[32] But we believe that 'Us-Them' thinking is a defining feature of an *authoritarian* orientation, not populism per se.

In practice, authoritarian and populist values are often closely associated with socially conservative attitudes and behavioral norms. In the words of Duckitt: 'Authoritarians are generally more socially conservative, nationalistic, intolerant of deviance and out-groups, and politically right-wing, preferring strict laws and rules, and supporting tough, punitive social control and authority. At the other pole, people would be generally tolerant and liberal, favoring individual liberties, high levels of personal freedom, self-expression, and individual self-regulation.'[33] But people can hold socially conservative attitudes, such as endorsing traditional views of marriage and sex roles within the family, without adhering to authoritarian values, such as believing that unconventional behavior (transsexuals in the military, recreational use of marijuana, or same sex marriage) should be restricted by society or prohibited by the state. The linkages connecting authoritarianism and social conservatism are contingent not inherent. Moreover, social liberals can also be authoritarian – holding dogmatic attitudes, intolerant of dissent, and enforcing conformity to their vision of politically correct views and identity politics.[34]

By contrast, the antithesis to authoritarianism is libertarianism, emphasizing the importance of personal freedoms, celebrating pluralist diversity, and valuing individuality more than collective security. These values translate into live-and-let-live policies minimizing the role of the state and society in restricting personal choices, exemplified by laws expanding women's and minority rights, facilitating multicultural diversity, and respecting the principles of social justice, human rights, and international cooperation.

To enforce orthodoxy, authoritarians tend to be intolerant of out-groups, rejecting minorities seen as challenging conventional norms, whether the groups are defined in terms of race, ethnicity, nationality, religion, gender, sexuality, or ideology. Authoritarian values are thus closely associated with racism, Islamophobia, misogyny, homophobia, anti-Semitism, and ethnocentrism. Authoritarian language evokes feelings of disgust and anger against out-group scapegoats, who are blamed for socio-economic problems. When confronting their critics, some contemporary Authoritarian-Populist parties and leaders seek to present themselves as the defenders of traditional Western values and national cultures pitted against the values of Muslim immigrants, where Islam is vilified as a religion of fanaticism and intolerance. Leaders typically stoke fears of Muslim-related terrorism in Western societies, heightening public anxieties following violent incidents and promising tough retaliation. This is the essence of the appeal presented by Geert Wilders' Party for Freedom, the Swiss People's Party and the Danish People's Party, the Austrian Freedom Party, the Norwegian Progress Party, and the Sweden Democrats. In the Netherlands, for example, Geert Wilders repeatedly warned in campaign speeches about the perils of Muslim immigrants, proposing to ban the Koran and shut mosques, arguing that only he could help the Dutch to 'regain their own country.' The Norwegian Progress Party made similar claims, and its electoral success led to one of their politicians becoming the first Immigration Minister in 2015, implementing tough laws that dramatically reduced the number of asylum seekers entering the country.[35] These claims erode social tolerance and strike at the heart of cosmopolitan-libertarianism, by blaming foreigners, immigrants, and refugees for society's problems, depicting the outside world as threatening and dangerous, thereby justifying policies of tough law and order and protectionist trade against others.[36]

## Loyalty

Loyalty to the tribal group and its leaders is linked with feelings of conformity and conventionalism, since it implies respect for authorities. It is antithetical to disturbing the status quo. Accordingly, those endorsing loyalty generally support institutions designed to preserve social stability and enforce law and order, including the military, courts, and the police, while deferring to religious leaders and teaching. This deferential orientation empowers strong leaders who seem able to defend the group against outsiders, terrorists, or criminals, even at the sacrifice of personal freedoms. Deference to authority could potentially contradict the populist emphasis on challenging the established structures of power, but the two can be reconciled by emphasizing subservience to leaders who share the in-group's values rather than toward institutionalized power and elites in general. The populist rejection of institutional checks and balances, combined with authoritarian obedience to leaders, can endanger liberal democracy.

Though the authoritarian emphasis on obedience to strong leaders might seem to clash with the populist stress on 'power to the people,'[37] in practice the 'voice of the people' rhetoric provides a convenient smokescreen that legitimates claims to assert sweeping powers unhampered by constitutional safeguards and constraints on executive powers. This is a common tendency among populist leaders, although not an inevitable one; in some cases, they advocate plebiscites and other mechanisms of direct democracy where 'the people' decide.[38] Peronism sought to mobilize unions and poor people, and left-wing populists in Bolivia, Brazil, and Venezuela have encouraged opportunities for participatory decision-making in the governance of local communities, although debate continues about whether these are genuine opportunities for grassroots input, or attempts at hegemonic control by leaders.[39] Spain's Podemos has built substantial electoral success, becoming the country's third largest party in June 2016, partly by utilizing social network channels for online debate. Its grassroots organization was built around local assemblies where people could meet, debate, and vote in person or online.[40]

Nevertheless, skepticism about representative democracy, combined with the absence of effective mechanisms for direct decision-making, lets populist leaders claim to be speaking for the 'forgotten' people. Populist leaders also build support through personalistic appeals and delivering goods and services to loyal allies, unconstrained by internal party democracy. Citizens have only episodic and limited opportunities to express their preferences about genuine political choices; their role is primarily that of a Greek chorus that demonstrates support for the leader. To bolster his legitimacy, Trump has repeatedly emphasized his Electoral College lead and the size of the crowds at his inauguration, while denying that Putin had tipped the electoral scales on his behalf – and alleging, without any evidence, that he lost the popular vote only because millions of fraudulent ballots had been cast for Clinton.[41] His approach is paternalistic: not the communitarian slogan of 'better together,' nor JFK's vision of shared sacrifice, but that of a dark and dangerous world where 'I alone can fix it.'[42]

Trump is far from unique in adopting this tone; populist parties are usually led by charismatic figures such as Giuseppe 'Beppe' Grillo in Italy, Nigel Farage in Britain, Geert Wilders in the Netherlands, Silvio Berlusconi in Italy, Hugo Chavez in Venezuela, Pablo Iglesias in Spain, and Rodrigo Duerte in the Philippines. Leaders depict themselves as outsiders fighting for the common man against established elites. Some like Grillo (a comedian and actor), Trump (star and producer of 'The Apprentice'), and Berlusconi (media tycoon and owner of A.C. Milan) were entertainment celebrities. Colorful, unpredictable leaders communicate using simple slogans, lofty promises, transgressive statements, and blunt everyday language in their speeches – Berlusconi referred to 'bunga bunga' parties, Duterte scatters curse words and slang in his talk, Chavez used belligerent diatribes against the United States and Europe, while Trump adopted classroom bully nicknames for his opponents ('Little Marco,' 'Crooked Hillary,' 'Lyin' Ted').[43] Farage declared that the Brexit referenda victory was 'a victory for real people, a victory for ordinary people, a victory for decent people.' Populist language is characteristically simple, repetitive, and emotionally powerful. Leaders – Trump, Wilders, Berlusconi, or Chavez – use derogatory insults toward opponents ('Crooked Hillary'), vulgar language, and racial slurs toward minorities, and flourish despite corruption and transgressive scandals. This outrages and confuses enemies ('What Happened?'). It reinforces claims to be the authentic voice of the regular people, billionaires but just 'one of us.'[44] This style allows leaders to appeal to diverse groups with heterogeneous grievances, to communicate messages to unsophisticated publics, and, if elected to office, to minimize being held to account in delivering detailed policy pledges. Political inexperience is regarded as a badge of honor by outsiders, untainted by elected office, rather than as a disqualification. Maverick presidents like Duerte in the Philippines, Peron in Argentina, and Chavez in Venezuela claim to articulate the authentic voice, virtue, and experience of 'ordinary people.' Populist leaders characteristically also seek to communicate directly with their followers via public rallies and mass demonstrations, TV shows, and social media, unfiltered by journalists.[45]

In hybrid democratic/authoritarian regimes such as Thailand, Venezuela, Turkey, the Philippines, Poland, and Hungary, Authoritarian-Populist leaders have actively undermined democracy. The rise of similar forces in long-established democracies threatens social inclusion, toleration, and diversity, as well as diminishing public confidence in representative institutions. But the dangers are more profound in states with hybrid regimes, with fewer safeguards preventing backsliding into electoral authoritarianism.

## Security

The focus on security reflects a deep-rooted cultural response to threatening conditions.

The authoritarian emphasis on security stresses the need for protection against outsiders, especially foreigners. It constructs a sharp line between 'Us' (ordinary citizens, our country) and 'Them' (outsiders, foreigners, elites).[46] Authoritarian discourse emphasizes xenophobic nationalism, constructing the myth that the 'people' are a uniform whole, and that nation-states should forcefully oppose threats from foreign countries and cultures. Xenophobia reflects an exaggerated fear of 'outsiders' – especially foreigners and immigrants – and the perceived threats to national identities from different cultures, religions, and languages. Seeing the world as an unstable and threatening place, those holding authoritarian values tend to favor muscular responses to security threats, preferring military action over diplomacy and multilateral engagement. National self-interest is prioritized over international cooperation. Authoritarians tend to reject cosmopolitanism, globalization, and mobility of people, ideas, labor, and goods across national borders. They also tend to disparage the United Nations, the European Union, NATO, and NAFTA and the broader rule-based framework of international law and human rights conventions, which they claim are threats to national sovereignty.

Accordingly, Trump's rhetoric stimulated racial resentment, intolerance of multiculturalism, nationalistic isolationism and belligerence, nostalgia for past glories, mistrust of outsiders, sexism, the appeal of tough leadership, attack-dog politics, and racial and anti-Muslim animosity.

The Trump campaign rally cry 'Build the Wall' and 'America First' perfectly encapsulates the notions of isolationism and protection against threats from outsiders. Similar sentiments underpin his policies to renegotiate or scrap NAFTA, to pull out from the Paris climate accord, and his demands that NATO member states increase their defense spending. Those favoring Britain leaving the European Union echoed similar sentiments, arguing that Brexit would restore national sovereignty, allow Britain to regain control of its borders and restrict the flow of refugees and migrants, and eliminate the UK's financial contributions to the EU.[47]

Debate continues about what threats to security are most likely to activate authoritarian values in such societies as Sweden, the Netherlands, and the UK that have long-established cradle-to-grave welfare states, comfortable living standards, and relatively high per capita incomes. We will examine the evidence in successive chapters of this book, considering the role of (i) cultural change; (ii) economic inequality, stagnant wages, global trade shocks, and unemployment; (iii) the growing ethnic and religious diversity in Western societies due to migration, asylum seekers, and refugees. Each of these factors provides plausible explanations, but untangling their precise effects is complex.

The role of authoritarian values in encouraging support for authoritarian parties and leaders can be reinforced by other forms of insecurity besides material poverty, as the research literature suggests. We argue that a neglected but important part of the explanation lies in the threats posed by value change, which has generated a cultural backlash. High-income societies have experienced unusually rapid and profound changes in both social diversity and cultural values during recent decades, driven by intergenerational population replacement, the expansion of access to university education, and the influx of migrants. We hypothesize that social conservatives feel most threatened by these developments; traditional values and beliefs about the central importance of faith, family, and country, that were once predominant in these societies, have eroded rapidly. Norms that once were important to many people are no longer respected and seemingly are being swept into the dustbin of history by modernizing forces. The predominant cultural majority in these societies has become a new cultural minority, endorsing views about faith, family, and country that are no longer widely respected or generally accepted moral standards.

Among those holding authoritarian values, cultural change can activate deep feelings of social intolerance and resentment directed toward those blamed for change. Resentment can be directed *downwards*, blaming 'out-groups' of perceived lower social status, including feminists, gay activists, immigrants, foreigners, and racial or ethnic minorities. Or, as with populism, cultural resentment can be directed *upwards*, blaming elites with perceived higher social status and progressive values, including intellectuals, experts, politicians, corporate executives, Hollywood producers, and columnists for elite media.[48]

## Libertarian Populists

We see authoritarian populism as constituting one pole of a cultural cleavage that has libertarian values at the opposite pole.[49] While authoritarian populists prioritize social conservatism, order, customary traditions, deference to strong leaders, and social stability; libertarian populists favor post-materialist values, social liberalism, individual autonomy, and tolerance of multicultural lifestyles.

Liberal thought from John Locke and James Madison to John Stuart Mill has emphasized the importance of freedom of speech, religion, association, and a free press, institutional checks and balances with the legislature and states limiting the powers of the federal executive, respect for rule of law and an independent judiciary, and the role of the news media as watchdogs that ensure government accountability and transparency. Liberalism also emphasizes the values of social tolerance, inclusion, social trust, and respect for pluralistic diversity, including constitutional safeguards protecting the rights of diverse religious, ethnic, racial, and other minorities. Representative democracy depends on participation through the conventional channels of elections, membership in mass political parties as well as civil society groups and social movements. Liberalism values pluralistic bargaining and compromise in the legislative process, reducing the dangers of polarization and violent conflict. Contemporary social liberalism also endorses a broad range of moral and social values, including equal rights for women and minorities, flexible sex roles and gender identities and LGBT rights, environmental protection, and secular rather than religious values.

The nativist component of authoritarian populism is sharply at odds with cosmopolitan values, which favor open borders, international engagement, and global cooperation. The concept of 'cosmopolitanism' suggests that all humans live in a single global community – the antithesis of authoritarian nationalism.[50] The distinction between cosmopolitans and locals was developed by Robert Merton in his study of small town America.[51] Cosmopolitans value the benefits of open national borders, shared multicultural values, and the diversity of peoples and lifestyles in outward-looking and inclusive societies. Since World War II, the connections between the people of different nations have become more cosmopolitan, with multiple networks linking their lives. The boundaries of a homogeneous nation-state have become increasingly permeable through flows of workers, expatriate employees, tourists, students, refugees, and immigrants, supported by the post-war architecture of global and regional governance, international standards of human rights, and agencies of international cooperation and economic aid.

On this basis, subsequent chapters go on to operationalize these concepts both in the electorate, to measure public endorsement of these values, and also at the party level, to see how far these values translate into support for Authoritarian-Populist parties. The next chapter considers the evidence concerning the silent revolution, to see whether trends have stalled in recent years or whether the younger generations and societies as a whole continue to move in a more socially liberal direction.

## Notes

1. See, for example, Jan-Werner Muller. 2016. *What is Populism?* Pennsylvania: University of Pennsylvania Press; Matthijs Rooduijn. 2014. 'The nucleus of populism: In search of the lowest common denominator.' *Government and Opposition* 49 (4): 572–598.
2. Margaret Canovan. 1981. *Populism.* New York: Harcourt, Brace, Jovanovich; Robert Barr. 2009. 'Populists, outsiders and anti-establishment politics.' *Party Politics* 15 (1): 29–48.
3. The *Oxford English Dictionary* notes that the modern usage was popularized by a journalist, Henry Farlie, in 1955. www.npr.org/2016/02/11/466049701/how-establishment-became-the-buzzword-of-the-2016-election.
4. Kirk A. Hawkins. 2009. 'Is Chávez Populist? Measuring populist discourse in comparative perspective.' *Comparative Political Studies* 42 (8): 1040–1067.
5. For discussions of the meaning of populism, see Jan-Werner Muller. 2016. *What Is Populism?* Pennsylvania: University of Pennsylvania Press; Ernesto Laclau. 2005. *On Populist Reason.* London: Verso; Benjamin Moffitt. 2016. *The Global Rise of Populism: Performance, Political Style and Representation.* Palo Alto, CA: Stanford University Press; Toril Aalberg, Frank Esser, Carsten Reinemann, Jesper Stromback, and Claes H. de Vreese. Eds. 2017. *Populist Political Communication in Europe.*

London: Routledge; Paris Aslanidis. 2015. 'Is populism an ideology? A refutation and a new perspective.' *Political Studies* 64 (1): 88–104; Elena Block and Ralph Negrine. 2017. 'The populist communication style: Toward a critical framework.' *International Journal of Communication* 11: 178–197.

6. For a discussion, see Paris Aslanidi. 2015. 'Is populism an ideology? A refutation and a new perspective.' *Political Studies* 64 (1): 88–104.
7. J. Eric Oliver and Wendy Rahn. 2016. 'Rise of the Trumpenvolk: Populism in the 2016 election.' *Annals of the American Academy of Political and Social Science* 667 (1): 189–206.
8. Paul Taggart. 2000.*Populism*. Buckingham: Open University Press.
9. Carola Schoor. 2017. 'In the theater of political style: Touches of populism, pluralism and elitism in speeches of politicians.' *Discourse and Society* 28 (6): 657–676.
10. For a discussion, see Jan-Werner Muller. 2016. *What is Populism?* Pennsylvania: University of Pennsylvania Press; Benjamin Moffitt. 2016. *The Global Rise of Populism: Performance, Political Style and Representation*. Palo Alto, CA: Stanford University Press; Toril Aalberg, Frank Esser, Carsten Reinemann, Jesper Stromback, and Claes H. de Vreese. Eds. 2017. *Populist Political Communication in Europe*. London: Routledge; Elena Block and Ralph Negrine. 2017. 'The populist communication style: Toward a critical framework.' *International Journal of Communication*. 11: 178–197.
11. Toril Aalberg, Frank Esser, Carsten Reinemann, Jesper Stromback, and Claes H. de Vreese. Eds. 2017. *Populist Political Communication in Europe*. London: Routledge; Benjamin Moffitt. 2016. *The Global Rise of Populism: Performance, Political Style, and Representation*. Palo Alto, CA: Stanford University Press.
12. Robert R. Barr. 2009. 'Populists, outsiders and anti–establishment politics.' *Party Politics* 15 (1): 29–48.
13. International IDEA. 2017.*The Global State of Democracy: Exploring Democracy's Resilience*. Stockholm: International IDEA. www.idea.int/publications/catalogue/global-state-democracy-exploring-democracys-resilience-overview.
14. Steven Levitsky and Daniel Ziblatt. 2018. *How Democracies Die*. New York: Crown; Arch Puddington and Tyler Roylance. 2018. 'Populists and autocrats: The dual threat to global democracy.' *Freedom in the World 2017*. Washington DC: Freedom House.
15. Pippa Norris. 2013. *Why Electoral Integrity Matters*. New York: Cambridge University Press; Pippa Norris. 2015. *Why Elections Fail*. New York: Cambridge University Press; Pippa Norris. 2017. *Strengthening Electoral Integrity*. New York: Cambridge University Press.
16. Margaret Canovan. 2002. 'Taking politics to the people: Populism as the ideology of democracy.' In Yves Mény and Y. Surel. Eds. *Democracies and the Populist Challenge*. Basingstoke: Palgrave Macmillan, pp. 25–44; Ben Stanley. 2008. 'The Thin Ideology of Populism.' *Journal of Political Ideologies* 13 (1): 95–110.

17. See David Collier and Steve Levitsky. 1997. 'Democracy with adjectives: Conceptual innovation in comparative research.' *World Politics* 49 (3): 430–451.
18. Cas Mudde. 2004. 'The populist zeitgeist.' *Government and Opposition* 39 (4): 541–563.
19. For early discussions about the concept and measurement of values, see Milton Rokeach. 1968. *Beliefs, Attitudes, and Values: A Theory of Organization and Change*. San Francisco, CA: Jossey-Bass; Milton Rokeach. 1973. *The Nature of Human Values*. New York: The Free Press; Ronald Inglehart. 1977. *The Silent Revolution: Changing Values and Political Styles among Western Publics*. Princeton, NJ: Princeton University Press; Shalom Schwartz. 1992. 'Universals in the content and structure of values: Theoretical advances and empirical tests in 20 countries.' *Advances in Experimental Social Psychology* 25: 1–65.
20. For the social psychological debate about the concept of authoritarian dispositions, and measurement, see Theodore W. Adorno, Else Fraenkel-Brunswick, David J. Levinson, and R. Nevitt Sanford. 1950.*The Authoritarian Personality*. New York: Harper & Row; Bob Altemeyer. 1998. 'The other "authoritarian personality".' In M.P. Zanna. Ed. *Advances in Experimental Social Psychology*. New York: Academic Press, pp. 47–91; Bob Altemeyer. 1996. *The Authoritarian Specter.* Cambridge, MA: Harvard University Press; Stanley Feldman. 2003. 'Values, ideology, and the structure of political attitudes.' In Donald Sears, Leonie Huddy, and R. Jervis. Eds. *Oxford Handbook of Political Psychology*. New York: Oxford University Press; Karen Stenner. 2005. *The Authoritarian Dynamic*. New York: Cambridge University Press; Marc J. Hetherington and Jonathan D. Weiler. 2009. *Authoritarianism and Polarization in American Politics*. New York: Cambridge University Press; Stefano Passini. 2017. 'Different ways of being authoritarian: The distinct effects of authoritarian dimensions on values and prejudice.' *Political Psychology* 38 (1): 73–86.
21. *Oxford English Dictionary*. 3rd edn.
22. Erich Fromm. 1941. *Escape from Freedom*. New York: Holt, Rinehart & Winston; Theodore W. Adorno, Else Fraenkel-Brunswick, David J. Levinson, and R. Nevitt Sanford. 1950. *The Authoritarian Personality*. New York: Harper & Row. Prior to Fromm, Wilhelm Reich used Freudian theories to explain authoritarianism. Wilhelm Reich. 1933 [1980]. *The Mass Psychology of Fascism*. New York: Farrar Straus & Giroux.
23. Eric Fromm. 1941. *Escape from Freedom*. New York: Holt, Rinehart & Winston.
24. Theodore W. Adorno, Else Fraenkel-Brunswick, David J. Levinson, and R. Nevitt Sanford. 1950. *The Authoritarian Personality*. New York: Harper & Row.
25. Theodore W. Adorno, Else Fraenkel-Brunswick, David J. Levinson, and R. Nevitt Sanford. 1950. *The Authoritarian Personality*. New York: Harper & Row. See also Milton Rokeach. 1960. *The Open and Closed Mind*. New York: Basic Books.

26. Nazar Akrami, Bo Ekehammar, and Robin Bergh. 2011. 'Generalized prejudice: Common and specific components.' *Psychological Science* 22 (1): 57–59. There is an enormous literature in social psychology where the primary measures of authoritarianism have relied upon scales concerning child-rearing traits, right-wing authoritarianism, and social dominance orientations and these have been widely deployed to explain ethnocentrism and generalized prejudice. See, for example, J.P. Kirscht and R.C. Dillehay. 1967. *Dimensions of Authoritarianism: A Review of Research and Theory*. Lexington, KY: University of Kentucky Press; Bob Altemeyer. 1998. 'The other "authoritarian personality".' In M.P. Zanna. Ed. *Advances in Experimental Social Psychology*. New York: Academic Press, pp. 47–91; Bob Altemeyer. 1996. *The Authoritarian Specter*. Cambridge, MA: Harvard University Press; Stanley Feldman. 2003. 'Values, ideology, and the structure of political attitudes.' In Donald Sears, Leonie Huddy, and R. Jervis. Eds. *Oxford Handbook of Political Psychology*. New York: Oxford University Press; Karen Stenner. 2005. *The Authoritarian Dynamic*. New York: Cambridge University Press; Marc J. Hetherington and Jonathan D. Weiler. 2009. *Authoritarianism and Polarization in American Politics*. New York: Cambridge University Press; John Duckitt, Boris Bizumic, Stephen W. Krauss, and Edna Heled. 2010. 'A tripartite approach to right-wing authoritarianism: The authoritarianism–conservatism–traditionalism model.' *Political Psychology* 31 (5): 685–715; Stefano Passini. 2017. 'Different ways of being authoritarian: The distinct effects of authoritarian dimensions on values and prejudice.' *Political Psychology* 38 (1): 73–86; John Duckitt and Boris Bizumic. 2013. 'Multidimensionality of right-wing authoritarian attitudes: Authoritarianism–conservatism–traditionalism.' *Political Psychology* 34 (6): 841–862; Donald R. Kinder and Lynn M. Sanders. 1996. *Divided by Color*. Chicago: University of Chicago Press; Donald R. Kinder and Allison Dale-Riddle. 2012. *The End of Race? Obama, 2008, and Racial Politics in America*. New Haven, CT: Yale University Press; Michael Tesler and David O. Sears. 2010. *Obama's Race: The 2008 Election and the Dream of a Post-Racial America*. Chicago: University of Chicago Press.
27. Robert Altemeyer. 1996. *The Authoritarian Specter*. Cambridge, MA: Harvard University Press; Robert Altemeyer. 1998. 'The other "authoritarian personality".' In M.P. Zanna. Ed. *Advances In Experimental Social Psychology*. New York: Academic Press, pp. 47–91.
28. For contemporary discussions, see Stanley Feldman. 2003. 'Values, ideology, and the structure of political attitudes.' In Donald Sears, Leonie Huddy, and R. Jervis. Eds. *Oxford Handbook of Politial Psychology*. New York: Oxford University Press; Karen Stenner. 2005. *The Authoritarian Dynamic*. New York: Cambridge University Press; Marc J. Hetherington, and Jonathan Weiler. 2009. *Authoritarianism and Polarization in American Politics*. New York: Cambridge University Press.
29. For a useful discussion, see Marc J. Hetherington and Jonathan Weiler. 2009. *Authoritarianism and Polarization in American Politics*. New York: Cambridge University Press.

30. Ronald Inglehart. 2018. *Cultural Evolution: People's Motivations are Changing, and Transforming the World.* NY: Cambridge University Press.
31. For a discussion of these linkages, see Karen Stenner. 2005. *The Authoritarian Dynamic.* New York: Cambridge University Press, Chapters 5 and 6.
32. Cas Mudde. 2004. 'The populist zeitgeist.' *Government and Opposition.* 39 (4): 541–563. For Mudde, the conceptualization which has become widely accepted in the literature, 'I define populism as *an ideology that considers society to be ultimately separated into two homogeneous and antagonistic groups, "the pure people" versus "the corrupt elite," and which argues that politics should be an expression of the volanté génerale (general will) of the people* ... Populism presents a Manichean outlook, in which there are only friends and foes. Opponents are not just people with different priorities and values, they are *evil!*,' pp. 543–544 (italics in the original). We regard this tendency toward seeing the world simplistically in black-and-white dichotomies as essentially part of the classic concept of authoritarianism, not populism.
33. John Duckitt. 2009. 'Authoritarianism and dogmatism.' In M. Leary and R. Hoyle. Eds. *Handbook of Individual Differences in Social Behavior.* New York: Guilford Press, pp. 298–317.
34. Mark Lilla. 2017. *The Once and Future Liberal after Identity Politics.* New York: HarperCollins.
35. www.newsinenglish.no/2017/03/21/progress-party-proud-of-sharp-decline-in-asylum-seekers/.
36. Ruth Wodak. 2015. *The Politics of Fear: What Right-Wing Populist Discourses Mean.* London: Sage.
37. Paulina Ochoa Espejo. 2011. *The Time of Popular Sovereignty.* Pennsylvania: University of Pennsylvania Press.
38. David Altman. 2011. *Direct Democracy Worldwide.* New York: Cambridge University Press.
39. Mónica Barczak. 2001. 'Representation by consultation? The rise of direct democracy in Latin America.' *Latin American Politics and Society* 43 (3): 37–59; Matthew Rhodes-Purdy. 2015. 'Participatory populism: Theory and evidence from Bolivarian Venezuela.' *Political Research Quarterly* 68 (3): 415–427; Saskia P. Ruth and Kirk A. Hawkins. 2017. 'Populism and democratic representation in Latin America.' In Christina Holtz-Bacha, Oscar Mazzoleni, and Reinhard Heinisch. Eds. *Handbook on Political Populism,* Baden-Baden: Nomos; Saskia P. Ruth, Yanina Welp, and Laurence Whitehead. Eds. 2017. *Let the People Rule? Direct Democracy in the Twenty-first Century.* Colchester: ECPR Press.
40. Jose Castillo-Manzano, Lourdes Lopez-Valpuesta, and Rafael Pozo-Barajas. 2017. 'Six months and two parliamentary elections in Spain: December 2015 and June 2016. The end of the two-party system?' *Electoral Studies* 45: 157–160.
41. See Peter Bakes and Maggie Haberman. May 13, 2017. 'The election is over, but Trump can't seem to get past it.' *New York Times.*

42. Yoni Appelbaum. July 21, 2016. 'I alone can fix it.' *The Atlantic*. www.theatlantic.com/politics/archive/2016/07/trump-rnc-speech-alone-fix-it/492557/.
43. Benjamin Moffitt. 2016. *The Global Rise of Populism: Performance, Political Style, and Representation*. Palo Alto, CA: Stanford University Press.
44. Juha Herkman. 2017. 'Old patterns on new clothes? Populism and political scandals in the Nordic countries.' *Acta Sociologica*. https://doi.org/10.1177/0001699317737816.
45. Sven Engesser, Nicole Ernst, Frank Esser, and Florin Buechel. 2017. 'Populism and social media: How politicians spread a fragmented ideology.' *Information Communication and Society* 20 (8): 1109–1126.
46. See Toril Aalberg, Frank Esser, Carsten Reinemann, Jesper Stronback, and Claes H. de Vreese. Eds. 2017. *Populist Political Communication in Europe*. London: Routledge.
47. Sara Hobolt. 2016. 'The Brexit vote: A divided nation, a divided continent.' *Journal of European Public Policy* 23 (9): 1259–1277.
48. J. Duckitt. 1989. 'Authoritarianism and group identification: A new view of an old construct.' *Political Psychology* 10 (1): 63–84; Stanley Feldman and Karen Stenner. 1997. 'Perceived threat and authoritarianism.' *Political Psychology* 18: 741–770.
49. Similar distinctions are used in Scott Flanagan and Aie-Rie Lee. 2003. 'The new politics, culture wars, and the authoritarian–libertarian value change in advanced industrial democracies.' *Comparative Political Studies* 36 (3): 235–270; Jan-Werner Muller. 2016. *What is Populism?* Pennsylvania: University of Pennsylvania Press. By contrast, others have conceptualized the cultural cleavage as one between universalistic social values and traditionalist-communitarians, see Simon Bornschier. 2015. 'New cultural conflict, polarization, and representation in the Swiss party system, 1975–2011.' *Swiss Political Science Review* 21 (4): 680–701.
50. For useful discussions of the concept, see Ulf Hannerz. 1990. 'Cosmopolitans and locals in world culture.' In Mike Featherstone. Ed. *Global Culture: Nationalism, Globalization and Modernity*. London: Sage; John Tomlinson. *Globalization and Culture*. Chicago: University of Chicago Press; Steven Vertovec and Robin Cohen. Eds. 2002. *Conceiving Cosmopolitanism: Theory, Context and Practice*. Oxford: Oxford University Press.
51. Robert Merton. 1957. *Social Theory and Social Structure*. Glencoe, IL: Free Press.

# PART II

# AUTHORITARIAN AND POPULIST VALUES

# 4

# The Backlash Against the Silent Revolution

This chapter first describes our theory and the empirically testable propositions it implies. We then present updated empirical data documenting the silent revolution in cultural values. The next part examines the drivers of these values and begins disentangling the impact of birth-cohort effects from life-cycle and period-effects. The conclusion reflects on the implications of the findings and considers the economic and social conditions most likely to stimulate an authoritarian reflex.

## THE SILENT REVOLUTION THEORY

Our theory argues that a cultural silent revolution has heightened polarization over cultural issues in the electorate, provoking an authoritarian backlash among social conservatives. We hypothesize that socially liberal values are spreading through intergenerational population replacement and demographic shifts, causing traditionalists (concentrated among the less-educated and older birth cohorts) to feel threatened, perceiving that respect for their core values and social mores is rapidly eroding. These developments have cumulated over time to reach a tipping point in high-income Western societies. The once-dominant cultural majority has gradually become a minority, endorsing views and norms that were considered normal during earlier eras but are no longer widely respected by the rest of society. Once widely accepted norms such as sexual abstinence before marriage, readiness to fight for one's country, and regular church attendance, now seem quaint to a growing share of society, as do traditional views about the role of women, the subordinate status attributed to racial and ethnic minorities, and intolerance toward outsiders.

A large body of survey research supports this argument, providing widespread evidence of changing attitudes toward sex and gender, increasing tolerance of homosexuality, abortion, and equal rights for women,[1] as well as growing secularization and the decline of religiosity in high-income societies,[2] and the spread of cosmopolitan orientations rejecting rigid national borders limiting the flow of people, ideas, and products.[3] Since about 1970, high-income Western societies have seen growing emphasis on post-materialist and socially liberal values, especially among the younger birth cohorts and the better-educated strata of society.[4] This has brought rising emphasis on environmental protection, increased acceptance of gender and racial equality, and rights for the LGBTQ community. These sweeping changes have fostered growing tolerance of diverse lifestyles, religions, and cultures; international cooperation and aid for human development; views toward criminal justice that are more liberal; support for democratic governance and civil rights and liberties.[5] Social movements motivated by these values have brought environmental protection, same sex marriage, minority rights, and gender equality to the center of the political agenda, drawing attention away from the classic economic redistribution and welfare issues.

We hypothesize that long-term structural changes in high-income post-industrial societies have been at the heart of culture shifts, particularly intergenerational population replacement, the rapid expansion of access to tertiary education, the growth of gender equality, migration flows creating societies that are more socially diverse, and processes of urbanization. In Western democracies, we argue that these structural developments have gradually eroded traditional bedrock identities that prevailed well into the twentieth century.

There is considerable evidence in the research literature identifying the factors driving the silent revolution. Previous research has established that birth cohort is one of the strongest predictors of support for post-materialist values and socially liberal policy attitudes.[6] Age-related differences in basic values and attitudes might theoretically be attributed to life-cycle effects, as people enter schooling and then the paid labor force, settle down with a partner to raise a family, and then eventually retire. They might also be interpreted as period-effects, arising from watershed events stamping an indelible mark on public opinion, like feelings of security that existed on American soil before the perceived risks of terrorism after 9/11. But they also might also reflect enduring intergenerational differences based on birth-cohort effects: socialization theory suggests that growing up under radically different circumstances from those that shaped earlier birth cohorts can leave an enduring mark on core values that subsequently endure throughout one's life. We argue that cultural evolution largely occurs through processes of population replacement, as younger cohorts gradually replace older ones in the adult population. The prevailing values of post-industrial societies evolved through this process, as the post-war birth cohorts, who grew up in prosperous and peaceful societies with comprehensive welfare states during the years after World War II, gradually replaced older cohorts whose formative years had been shaped by mass unemployment and deprivation during the Great Depression, and bloody conflict and destruction during World War I and World War II.

A substantial body of evidence confirms that existential security is conducive to open-mindedness, social tolerance, and trust, secularization, and acceptance of diverse lifestyles, identities, and values.[7] Since the post-war birth cohorts became old enough to be politically relevant, they have altered conventional moral norms and social attitudes in high-income post-industrial societies. The process of intergenerational population replacement in these societies has been gradually transforming Western cultures and challenging ideas that were common among the older generations. As Figure 2.2 demonstrated, the proportion of the European population who spent their pre-adult years during the Interwar era has been steadily shrinking. By 2012, the Interwar and Baby Boom generations had become a minority of the adult population in Europe – yet they remain a bare majority of voters, since they are far more likely to cast a ballot than the young. In the US as well, today Millennials surpass Baby Boomers as the largest sector of the adult *population*, though there are lagged effects in the *electorate*.[8]

Many other factors also seem to play a role in reinforcing the prevailing trajectory of cultural change, particularly the expansion of universities.[9] The college-educated in Western societies are among the strongest proponents of socially liberal and post-materialist values, partly because graduates were likely to have grown up in relatively well-off families. The chasm between the college and non-college educated has been widely observed as one of the clearest and most consistent divisions in the profile of Leave and Remain supporters in the Brexit referendum.[10] Similar patterns have been observed among Trump supporters; for example the CNN exit polls in the 2016 GOP primaries and caucuses reported that, on average, only one-quarter of college graduates voted for Trump, compared with almost half (45%) of those with high school education or less.[11] The educational revolution has transformed the composition of Western societies: one-third of the Interwar generation in Europe had only lower secondary education, compared with around 6 percent of Generation X and Millennials.[12] Younger college educated generations have brought socially liberal mores and lifestyles into the mainstream, moving from the era of Mad Men to the era of Modern Family.

Moreover, the role of sex and gender also seem important. Traditional patriarchal values about fixed sex roles, once the predominant view in Western societies, have gradually been displaced by norms favoring women and men's equality in the home, the economy, and politics, more fluid self-ascribed gender identities, and diverse arrangements of cohabitation, marriage and divorce, child-rearing, and families. A wealth of research in sociology, public opinion, and gender studies has documented birth-cohort-linked change in sex role attitudes, in the US and Europe.[13] These studies report that a gender gap can be observed among the more egalitarian younger generations, with women's views shifting further and faster than men's, due in part to women's experience of rising educational levels (see Figure 2.4), growing labor force participation, the ideological impact of the second-wave women's movement, and declining religiosity and marriage rates.

Finally, racial, national, and ethnic identities also predict values. Authoritarian-populist rhetoric is closely associated with rejection of the 'Other,' directed toward diverse targets – thus heightening racism, Islamophobia, misogyny, homophobia, anti-Semitism, and ethnocentrism. These issues are explored in depth in Chapter 6, where we examine the role of belonging to the ethnic majority or a minority group, and of nationality and type of faith on attitudes.

For all these reasons, we expect to find that support for socially conservative attitudes and authoritarian values is disproportionately concentrated among certain social sectors, notably the older generations, white men, rural communities, and the non-college educated. These are all shrinking segments of the population – although they remain a substantial sector of the active electorate that turns out to vote.

The tipping point hypothesis holds that traditional socially conservative values have gradually fallen out of step with the changing cultures of contemporary Western societies. This might conceivably generate a spiral of silence effect, where social conservatives retreat from the public sphere, suppressing the overt expression of politically incorrect views. But growing threats to traditional norms might also be expected to generate feelings of resentment, anger, and a sense of loss – especially for those with authoritarian predispositions that emphasize social conformity and intolerance of out-groups. These feelings would tend to make these groups susceptible to racist, sexist, or nativist leadership appeals.[14]

We hypothesize that long-term cultural changes have reached a 'tipping point' where members of the former cultural majority, who still adhere to traditional norms, have come to feel like strangers in their own land. People with socially conservative values have lost their cultural hegemony, activating feelings of resentment toward groups blamed for change. They can blame out-groups with lower social status, such as feminists, LGBTQ activists, immigrants, foreigners, and racial or ethnic minorities. Or cultural resentment can be directed upwards toward elites with higher social status and progressive values, such as academics and intellectuals, Hollywood movie producers, elected politicians, Wall Street executives, and journalists or media commentators. Populist leaders exploit and deepen mistrust of elites, channeling popular resentment against liberal proponents of value change ('Lock her up'), mobilizing anxieties ('radical Islamic terrorists'), identifying enemies ('Fake news'), and providing simple solutions ('Build a wall').

## NEW EVIDENCE OF THE SILENT REVOLUTION IN CULTURAL VALUES

We hypothesize that distinctive shared formative experiences shape the attitudes and values of given generations.[15] Consequently, in analyzing new survey evidence for these arguments, we group US and European birth cohorts into generations. Several alternative demarcation points can be identified.[16] The periodization used in this study is based on shared experiences during key turning points in European history that seem likely to have left a mark on each cohort during their formative years of socialization. Thus, World War I, the Great Depression, and World War II are likely to have shaped the formative experiences of older birth cohorts, making their childhood and adolescence much less secure than those of younger cohorts, who spent their formative years in prosperous and peaceful post-war societies with cradle-to-grave welfare systems and expanded educational opportunities.

On this basis, this study identifies four main generational groups:

- The *Interwar* cohort that lived through two World Wars and the Great Depression (born before 1945);
- *Baby Boomers* who came of age during the growing affluence and expansion of the welfare state during the post-World War II era (1946–1964);

- *Generation X* socialized during the counter-culture era of sexual liberalization and student protest (1965–1979); and
- *Millennials* who came of age under the era of neo-liberalism economics and globalization associated with Reagan and Thatcher (1980–1996).

These cohorts reflect major historical watersheds common across many Western societies, making them suitable for pooled analysis. There are also other major events that could be turning points in specific societies, such as the fall of dictators and subsequent periods of democratization during the 1970s in Spain and Portugal, the era of the military junta in Greece, the 1989 fall of the Berlin Wall and reunification in Germany, the Thatcherite years in the UK, and the impact of 9/11 in the United States. The transition from Communist party rule during the 1990s had a decisive impact on the politics of Central and Eastern Europe, with divergent pathways of regime change in countries such as Ukraine, Slovakia, Latvia, and Bulgaria. Not every generation marches in lockstep. But the periods used in this study were chosen to reflect major shared events that impacted on a large number of post-industrial societies.

We can compare several indicators of values across generational cohorts and over time, including (i) adherence to materialist or post-materialist values; (ii) attitudes toward socially liberal and socially conservative policy issues, such as gay rights, gender equality, and immigration; (iii) ideological self-identification as liberals or conservatives; (iv) support for authoritarian or libertarian personal values, such as obedience and security; and finally (v) political trust, as an indicator of the appeal of populist rhetoric. To confirm the robustness of our key findings, we examine trends in each of these variables, drawing on a range of alternative surveys where time-series data are available in America and in Europe.

## Post-Materialism

The first component of our argument, the 'silent revolution' theory of value change, holds that conditions of existential security experienced by Western societies during the post-war decades brought an intergenerational shift toward post-materialist and socially liberal values. A substantial body of survey evidence has documented the cultural transformation that occurred during the last half century.[17] Time-series and cohort analysis has demonstrated growing support for socially liberal attitudes among the younger generations and the college educated in Western societies.[18] The spread of post-materialist values arises primarily through long-term processes of inter-generational replacement, as the Interwar cohort fades away and Baby Boomers and the Millennials replace them in the adult population. Time-series survey data demonstrate the intergenerational value shift in six European countries, from a 4:1 preponderance of materialists over post-materialists in 1970, to a preponderance of post-materialists over materialists by the late twentieth century.[19]

More than 45 years ago, it was argued that 'a transformation may be taking place in the political culture of advanced industrial societies. This transformation seems to be altering the basic value priorities of given generations as a result of changing conditions influencing their basic socialization.'[20] In the 1990s, the Beliefs in Government project analyzed the Eurobarometer data and concluded that an overall rise in post-materialism had occurred across much of Western Europe during the prior two decades – and the shift was consonant with the effects of generational replacement.[21] Subsequent birth cohort analysis in EU member states during the longer period 1970–1999 (when measurement ended in the Eurobarometer surveys) confirmed that post-war birth cohorts continued to bring an intergenerational shift from materialist to post-materialist values, as the younger cohorts gradually replaced the older ones in the adult population.[22] This analysis also reveals clear period-effects, reflecting the current economic conditions: the intergenerational differences persist, but all cohorts shift toward views that are more materialist in times of economic downturn during the late-1970s (with the OPEC oil crisis) and again in the early 1980s (with the surge in unemployment). With subsequent economic recovery, each cohort shifts back again toward their long-term baseline, so that across this 30-year span, given cohorts remain at least as post-materialistic as they were at the start.

The time-series results from the Mannheim Eurobarometer trend file can also be compared across nine diverse European societies. As Figure 4.1 shows, the proportion of post-materialists and materialists varies across countries. Thus, Denmark displays the clearest crossover effect, where the proportion of materialists in the population has steadily dropped and post-materialists have displaced them. In several other countries, including France, Italy, Luxembourg, and the UK, the evidence suggests that materialists were the predominant group in society during the early 1970s, but this proportion dropped sharply, closing the gap between materialists and post-materialists. Some distinctive patterns can also be observed in certain societies, notably in Germany after reunification between West and East.

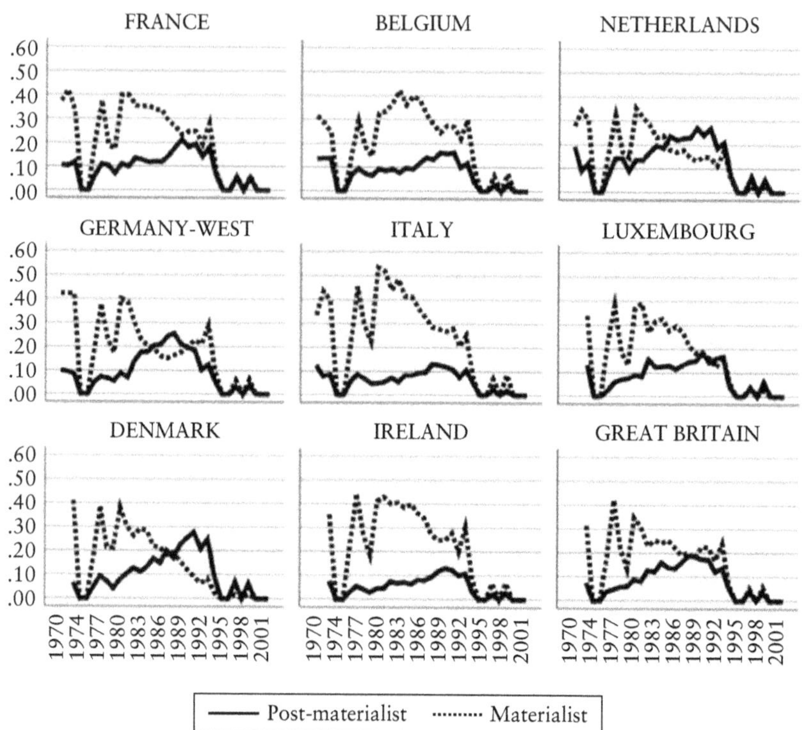


FIGURE 4.1. *The proportion of materialist and post-materialists in Europe, 1970–2002*

*Note:* Calculated as the proportion of materialists and post-materialists in nine EU member states (France, Belgium, Netherlands, Germany, Italy, Luxembourg, Denmark, Ireland, and Britain).

*Source:* The Mannheim Eurobarometer Trends File 1970–2002.

## Socially Liberal and Conservative Attitudes Toward Policy Issues

To broaden the analysis of longitudinal trends in cultural values, we turn to other measures. Evidence from the World Values Survey demonstrates that Western societies have been getting steadily more socially liberal on many issues over several decades, especially among the younger generation and college-educated middle classes. The trajectory of value change first became evident in Western societies during the early 1970s, bringing an era of student protests.[23] This cultural revolution was expressed through shifts toward social liberalism in mainstream left-wing political parties, as well as the rise of Green parties, and the mobilization of new social movements advocating environmental protection and fighting climate change;

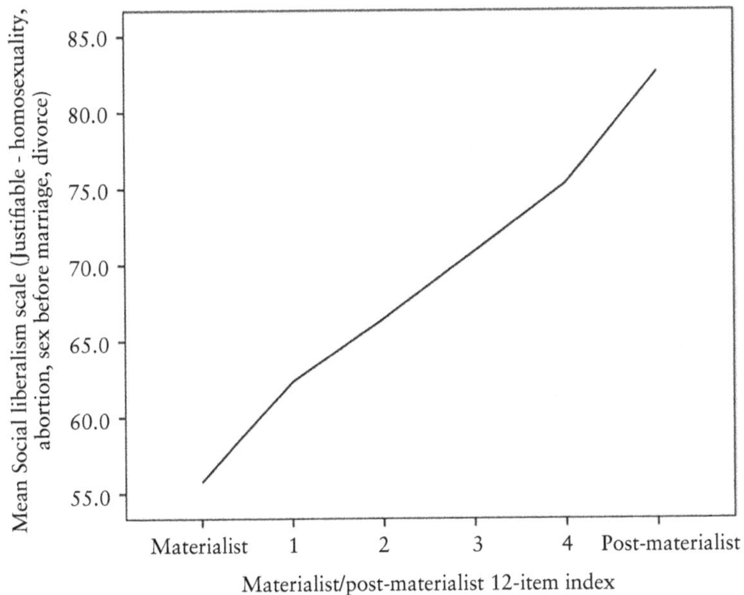


FIGURE 4.2. *Socially liberal values correlate with post-materialist values*
*Note:* The socially liberal value scale (100-point standardized) includes how far the following are seen as justifiable: homosexuality, abortion, sex before marriage, and divorce. The materialist/post-materialist index is based on 12 value items. Data are from the WVS-6 (2010–2014) in the following seven post-industrial societies: Australia, Germany, Netherlands, New Zealand, Spain, Sweden, and United States.
*Source:* World Values Survey 2010–2014, Wave 6. N. 10,576.

LGBTQ rights to employment in the military, adoption, and same sex marriage; civil rights for minorities like the Black Lives Matters movement; feminist networks with global mobilization on behalf of gender quotas in elected office; anti-domestic violence, and anti-sexual harassment, international assistance for humanitarian disasters and economic development, and human rights around the world.[24] Drawing on data from seven post-industrial societies from the World Values Survey (6th wave), Figure 4.2 shows the strong association between socially liberal attitudes, as measured on scales monitoring tolerance of homosexuality, abortion, divorce, and pre-marital sex, with the 12-item scale of post-material values.

This growth of liberal values is confirmed when replicated elsewhere in Western societies using other survey evidence. Hence, after reviewing public opinion trends toward a range of domestic and foreign policy issues, using data from the International Social Survey Program, the NORC General

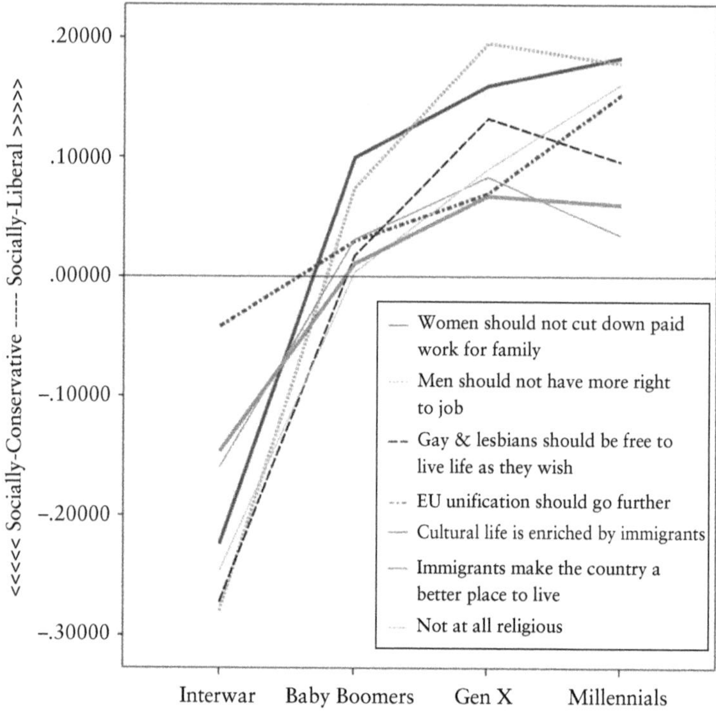


FIGURE 4.3. *The silent revolution in socially liberal values in Europe by generation*
*Note:* All items have been standardized around the mean (using Z-scores).
*Source:* The European Social Survey, Cumulative File Rounds 1–7.

Social Survey, and Gallup, Dalton concluded that one consistent trend has been the growing tolerance of social liberalism: 'Contemporary publics are becoming more tolerant of individual diversity and are more interested in protecting individual freedoms. These trends appear in attitudes toward social equality, moral issues, and the quality of life. Paralleling these changes is a decline in respect for authority.'[25] The European Social Survey illustrates these trends; Figure 4.3 displays some of the substantial shifts in social values by birth cohorts in a wide range of more than 30 European societies, with the younger birth cohorts being substantially more liberal and cosmopolitan than their parents or grandparents, whether monitored by feelings toward European Union unification, the positive impact of immigrants for multiculturalism, tolerance of gay and lesbian lifestyles, more secular identities, and egalitarian attitudes toward the role of women in the paid workforce. The tipping

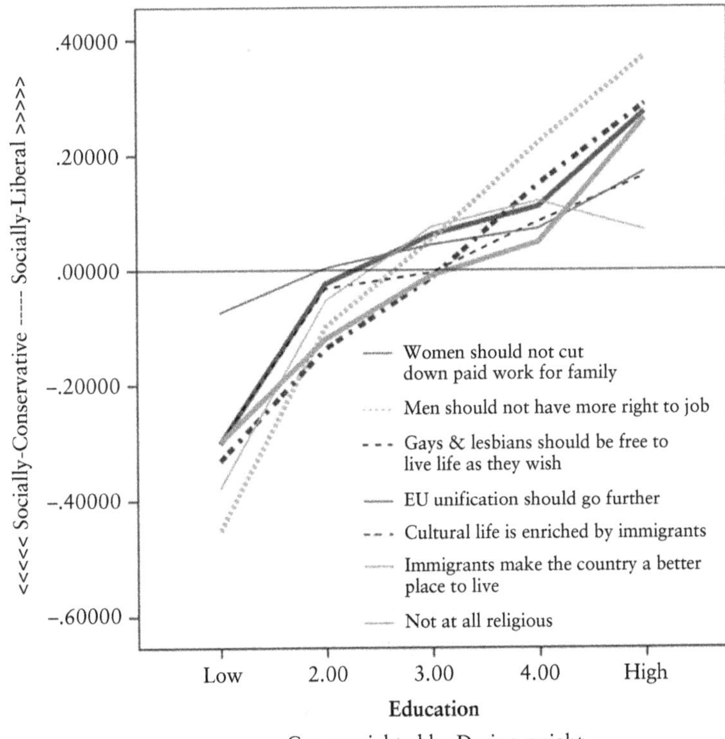


FIGURE 4.4. *The silent revolution in socially liberal values by education*
*Note:* All items have been standardized around the mean (using Z-scores).
*Source:* The European Social Survey, Cumulative File Rounds 1–7.

point in the balance of opinion occurs among the Baby Boomers, with liberalism continuing to rise among the Millennials and Generation X.

When the same issues are compared by level of educational attainment, a similar pattern can be observed (see Figure 4.4): those with college education consistently express attitudes that are more liberal than those with only secondary school education. Needless to say, age and education are closely correlated, because of the expansion of higher educational levels during recent decades.

The United States differs culturally from European societies in many respects, including the strength of religiosity and church-going practices.[26] Accordingly, data from the International Social Survey Program show that the US public is more conservative than comparable West European societies, with Americans favoring a smaller role for government on healthcare, pensions, housing, and less state intervention in providing jobs, reducing income differentials, and controlling prices.[27] Similarly, cross-national differences have been found in attitudes toward the family, marriage, children, and gender roles, when comparing Britain, Ireland, the US, and Germany. But the differences between the young and old were much larger than the Transatlantic differences.[28]

The trajectory of value change on social issues in America closely mirrors European trends by generation and education. Since 2001, for example, Gallup's annual Values and Beliefs polls have monitored moral approval of a wide range of issues, showing that today an overwhelming majority of Americans approve of birth control, divorce, extramarital sex, gay or lesbian relations, birth out of wedlock, and doctor-assisted suicide.[29] American public opinion has moved in a steadily more socially liberal and tolerant direction on 13 out of the 19 issues monitored by Gallup since the beginning of the twenty-first century – and none of these issues shows a significant shift toward values that are more conservative (see Table 4.1). Since 1994, the Pew Research Center has also regularly monitored American attitudes toward fundamental social values, such as the role of government in aiding the poor, views on racial discrimination, attitudes toward immigration, and opinions toward environmental protection. Pew reports that the gap between the Democrats and the Republicans on these types of issues widened during the Obama years, and reached record levels under Trump.[30] Party polarization on social values has become greater than gaps by race, religion, education, and age.

## Ideological Identities

Are these patterns of values and attitudes reflected in how people see themselves ideologically?[31] It is not clear that most people have consistent ideological views in their policy attitudes across a range of dimensions and over time. In a classic article, Philip Converse argued that most Americans cast ballots based on group identities, not ideological considerations.[32] Ordinary Americans continue to display weakly constrained and inconsistent policy attitudes.[33] Nevertheless most people can and do offer a position when asked in surveys where they place themselves on left–right scales, and whether they regard themselves as Liberal or Conservative, suggesting that these labels are meaningful to many respondents. This type of information therefore provides another useful clue about the self-identified location of the electorate.

TABLE 4.1. *The silent revolution in social values in America, 2001–2017*

| | First year asked % | 2017 % | Change % |
|---|---|---|---|
| **MORE LIBERAL VIEWS** | | | |
| Gay/lesbian relations | 40 | 63 | 23 |
| Having a baby outside of marriage (2002) | 45 | 62 | 17 |
| Sex between an unmarried man and woman | 53 | 69 | 16 |
| Divorce | 59 | 73 | 14 |
| Medical testing on animals | 65 | 51 | −14 |
| Polygamy (2003) | 7 | 17 | 10 |
| Human embryo stem cell research (2002) | 52 | 61 | 9 |
| Doctor-assisted suicide | 49 | 57 | 8 |
| Cloning humans | 7 | 14 | 7 |
| Pornography (2011) | 30 | 36 | 6 |
| Suicide | 13 | 18 | 5 |
| Death penalty | 63 | 58 | −5 |
| Sex between teenagers (2013) | 32 | 36 | 4 |
| **NO CHANGE** | | | |
| Extramarital affairs | 7 | 9 | 2 |
| Gambling (2003) | 63 | 65 | 2 |
| Birth control (2012) | 89 | 91 | 2 |
| Abortion | 42 | 43 | 1 |
| Cloning animals | 31 | 32 | 1 |
| Animal fur clothing (buying/wearing) | 60 | 57 | −3 |

*Note:* The items were first asked in the survey in 2001 unless otherwise indicated.
*Source:* Gallup Annual Values and Beliefs poll, 2001–May 2017.[34]

Consequently, it is significant that in 1999 Gallup found that 39 percent of Americans said that their views on social issues were conservative or very conservative, while 21 percent said that they were liberal or very liberal – a conservative preponderance of almost two to one. But by 2015, Gallup found that as many Americans described themselves as socially liberal as said they were socially conservative.[35] This does not mean that public opinion is consistently socially liberal on all policies, and there are significant variations in attitudes toward specific issues such as gun control, abortion, or civil rights. But quite strikingly, while

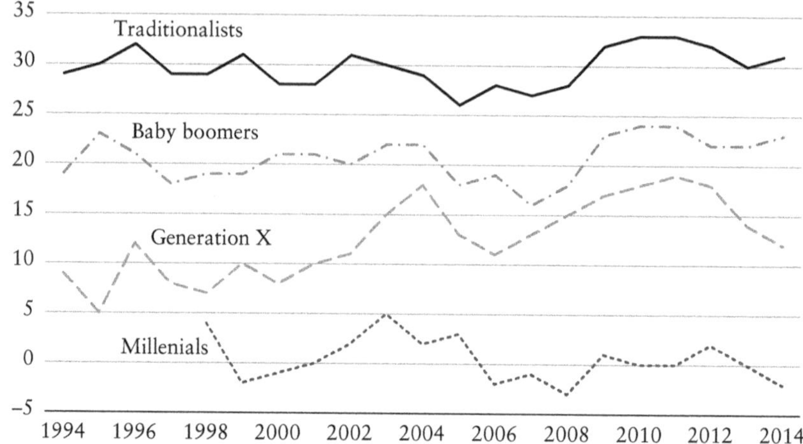


FIGURE 4.5. *Trends in conservative minus liberal self-identification, US by generation, 1994–2014*

*Note:* The figures are the percentage identifying as conservative minus the percentage identifying as liberal in each year. Positive scores indicate a conservative advantage. Millennials born 1980–1996; Generation X born 1965–1979; Baby boomers born 1946–1964; Traditionalists born 1900–1945.

*Source:* Gallup Polls 2015, http://news.gallup.com/poll/181325/baby-boomers-likely-identify-conservative.aspx.

most older Americans see themselves as ideologically conservative, this pattern reverses itself among the young. By 2015, Gallup reports that among the Interwar generation (born before 1945), 17 percent describe their political views as liberal, while almost three times as many (48 percent) see themselves as conservatives. This pattern reverses itself among younger birth cohorts; among the Millennials born after 1980, 30 percent see themselves as liberal and only 28 percent describe their views as conservative. As later chapters demonstrate, this generation gap in ideological identities is also reflected in party preferences and voting choices.

The relative conservatism and liberalism of each American generation has been consistent. The age-related gap in liberal/conservative values does not reflect life-cycle effects, where younger people become more socially conservative as they age. Instead, cultural evolution is driven by generational replacement, as older cohorts are gradually replaced by Millennials and Generation X in the US population. As Figure 4.5 demonstrates, in annual Gallup polls since the mid-1990s, Millennials (born 1980–1996) have consistently been the most liberal generation, while the Interwar

TABLE 4.2. *The balance of conservatives and liberals in America by generation, 2015*

| Generation | Birth years | Conservative | Moderate | Liberal | Conservative–liberal gap |
|---|---|---|---|---|---|
| Millennials | 1980–1996 | 28 | 40 | 30 | −2 |
| Generation X | 1965–1979 | 35 | 39 | 23 | +12 |
| Baby boomers | 1946–1964 | 44 | 33 | 21 | +23 |
| Interwar | 1900–1945 | 48 | 33 | 17 | +31 |
| All | | 38 | 36 | 24 | +14 |

*Note:* Proportion responding to 'How do you usually see yourself?'
*Source:* Gallup Polls 2015, http://news.gallup.com/poll/181325/baby-boomers-likely-identify-conservative.aspx.

generation (born 1900–1945) have consistently been the most conservative. Through the glacial but irresistible process of population replacement, as older Americans die and younger cohorts take their place, this is gradually shifting the overall balance of American public opinion in a more liberal direction. Adherence to traditional views has not disappeared. A large minority of older Americans express conservative views on such issues as the acceptance of legal abortions, global climate change, racial and sexual equality, immigration, gun rights, the legalization of marijuana, and same sex marriage. But the direction of ideological change in American public opinion, especially the social liberalism of the Millennial generation, is consistent with similar developments observed across the Atlantic.[36]

In Europe, we compare where respondents place themselves on left–right scales that are used to monitor ideological identities, with the analysis broken down by generational cohort. The scales sum up party positions across a wide range of issues, although the specific meaning of 'Left' and 'Right,' and the policies associated with them, vary over time and across societies.[37] Previous studies using survey data have analyzed how supporters of radical right parties identify themselves ideologically, reporting that they usually locate themselves on the extreme right on 10-point left–right scales.[38]

The results in Figure 4.6 show a generation gap similar to the one observed in the US; the Pre-War and Interwar generations consistently show the most right-wing identities throughout the 35-year period, with the Baby Boomers and Generation X closely positioned, while Millennials display the least right-wing position. The cohort differences persist over the decades of Eurobarometer surveys.

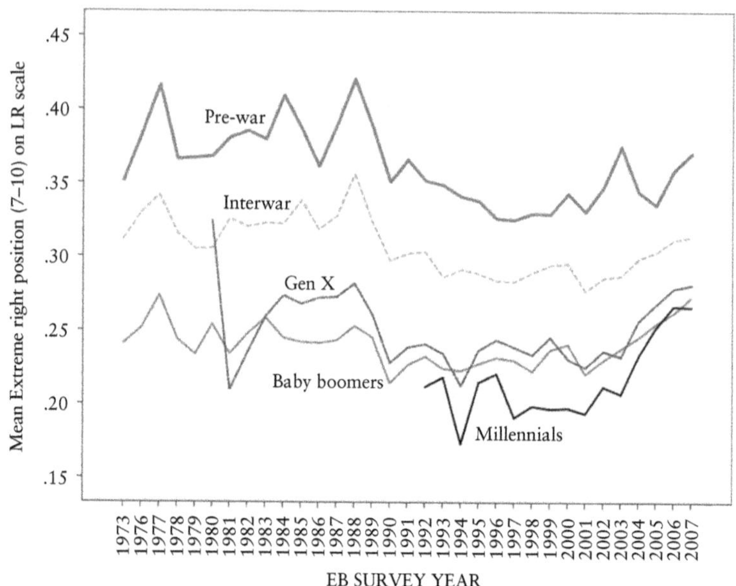


FIGURE 4.6. *Ideological left–right self-identification by generation, Europe, 1970–2007*
*Note:* Ideological position on the extreme right (7–10) are compared by ideological self-placement on a 10 point left–right scale.
*Source:* Eurobarometer 1970–2007.

## Authoritarian Values

Our theory argues that social conservatives are a shrinking share of the overall population, *and* they tend to have authoritarian predispositions, making them intolerant of non-conformity with established social norms. Consequently, social liberals accepting new norms concerning gender identities, secular ethics, sex before marriage, and racial equality are not merely seen as different, but are condemned by conservatives as morally corrupt. Normative threats, such as feelings of moral decay, national decline, and social disorder, dramatically magnify the impact of authoritarianism by exacerbating racial, political, and moral intolerance, strengthening the use of stereotyping and discrimination against minorities.[39]

Analysis of the World Values Survey data covering seven high-income societies, presented in Figure 4.7, demonstrates the strong association between endorsement of authoritarian values (the Schwartz using items measuring the personal importance of security, conformity, and tradition), and a battery of items monitoring socially conservative or liberal attitudes (using 10-point scales concerning the justifiability of homosexuality,

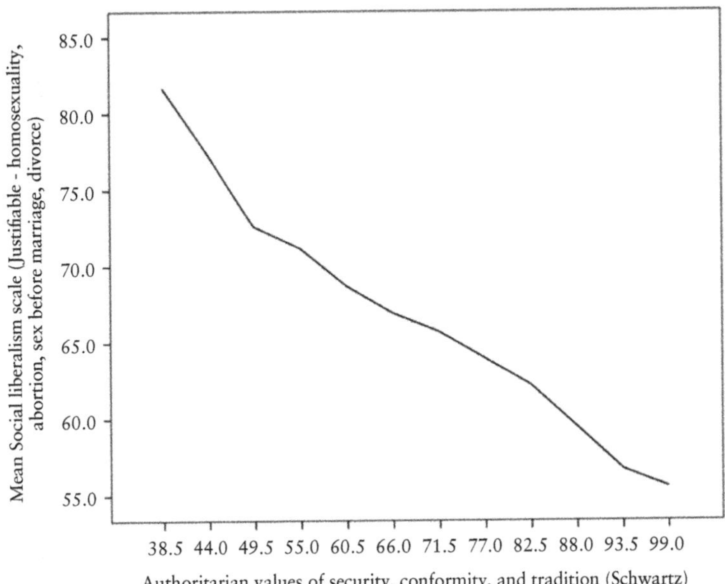


FIGURE 4.7. *Socially liberal values are negatively correlated with authoritarian values*

*Note:* The social liberalism 100-point standardized scale includes how far the following are seen as justifiable: homosexuality, abortion, sex before marriage, and divorce. The authoritarian values index is based on combining five items using the Schwartz scale to measure the personal values of security, conformity, and tradition. Data are from the WVS-6 (2010–2014) in the following seven societies: Australia, Germany, Netherlands, New Zealand, Spain, Sweden, and United States.

*Source:* World Values Survey 2010–2014, Wave 6. N. 10576.

abortion, pre-marital sex, and divorce). As the graph shows, those with authoritarian values are by far the most socially conservative toward these moral issues, with the relationship showing a steady linear pattern.

Many other previous studies have observed the links between generations and social liberalism that we have also documented here. But to what extent have Western societies reached a tipping point in the balance between authoritarians and libertarians in the electorate? To answer this question, we draw on the pooled European Social Survey, waves 1–7. To measure authoritarianism, the study selected five items from a battery originally developed by Schwartz for cross-national comparisons of personal values, as listed in Table 4.3. The preamble asks: '*Now I will briefly describe some people. Please listen to each description and tell me how much each person is or is not like you.*' Respondents are presented with a wide range of statements designed to reflect diverse values. Five of the items listed in Table 4.3 were selected to monitor adherence

TABLE 4.3. *Measuring citizen's authoritarian and libertarian values (Schwartz scales)*

| Variables | Description | Authoritarian values | Libertarian values |
|---|---|---|---|
| ipbhprp | *It is important to her/him always to behave properly. She/he wants to avoid doing anything people would say is wrong.* | .728 | |
| impsafe | *It is important to her/him to live in secure surroundings. She/he avoids anything that might endanger her/his safety.* | .711 | |
| ipstrgv | *It is important to her/him that the government ensures her/his safety against all threats. She/he wants the state to be strong so it can defend its citizens.* | .704 | |
| imptrad | *Tradition is important to her/him. She/he tries to follow the customs handed down by her/ his religion or her/his family.* | .652 | |
| ipfrule | *She/he believes that people should do what they're told. She/he thinks people should follow rules at all times, even when no one is watching.* | .652 | |
| impdiff | *She/he likes surprises and is always looking for new things to do. She/he thinks it is important to do lots of different things in life.* | | .783 |
| ipadvnt | *She/he looks for adventures and likes to take risks. She/he wants to have an exciting life.* | | .710 |
| ipcrtiv | *Thinking up new ideas and being creative is important to her/him. She/he likes to do things in her/his own original way.* | | .700 |
| impfree | *It is important to her/him to make her/his own decisions about what she/he does. She/he likes to be free and not depend on others.* | | .601 |
| ipudrst | *It is important to her/him to listen to people who are different from her/him. Even when she/he disagrees with them, she/he still wants to understand them.* | | |

*Note:* The Schwartz value scales in the European Social Survey (ESS) use the following question: 'Now I will briefly describe some people. Please listen to each description and tell me how much each person is or is not like you. Use this card for your answer.' Response categories to the above questions in 6-point scales range from 1 'Not very much like me' to 6 'Very much like me.' The coefficients in the table are generated by principal component factor analysis with varimax rotation and kaiser normalization. The scales have a high level of reliability.

*Source:* The European Social Survey, Cumulative File Rounds 1–7.

to authoritarian values, including the core concepts of conformity (the importance of behaving properly and following traditions), security (the importance of living in secure surroundings and that of a strong government to protect against threats), and deference (the importance of following rules and doing what one's told). To measure libertarian values, five other items were selected, reflecting the values of non-conformity, independence, and personal autonomy (the importance of being free and not dependent on others). Principal component factor analysis with varimax rotation confirmed the dimensionality of the selected items listed in Table 4.3 and the expected division between Authoritarian and Libertarian values. The scales displayed a high level of reliability when compared with equivalent measures.[40] The value scales were each summed from these items and then standardized around the mean (Z-scores) for ease of comparison.

It should be emphasized that these items refer to individual predispositions and personal value preferences.[41] In this regard, they are similar to the older items used to measure authoritarianism in terms of the importance of teaching children about the values of manners, obedience, and conformity. The selected items are designed to tap personal values across multiple societies. They do not seek to gauge public attitudes toward specific public policy issues, such as the rights of minorities, equal opportunities for women, or strengthening police powers, which might be influenced by support for given candidates or parties, and thus be open to the risk of endogeneity.

Figure 4.8 shows the tipping point in the proportion of the electorate endorsing authoritarian and libertarian values (as measured by the Schwartz scales) across Europe. The overall results show strikingly divergent patterns between birth cohorts, and a tipping point in these values among European publics, as predicted by our theory. Thus, across Europe, the Interwar generation displays the highest levels of authoritarian values, while support for these values steadily declines among the younger generation and Millennials. By contrast, the reverse pattern is evident for the libertarian values scale, which shows growing support as we move from older to younger birth cohorts, with the strongest endorsement among the Millennials. As a result, the trend lines cross, showing the hypothesized tipping point in the balance of rising levels of libertarian versus authoritarian values by cohorts. Thus, among the Interwar generation, in the pooled European data, authoritarian values clearly outweigh libertarian values. The reverse situation can be observed among Millennials.

The patterns also reflect the distinctive experiences of different countries; Figure 4.8 shows how the tipping point varies by birth cohort across countries in different European regions. Thus, the cross-over between

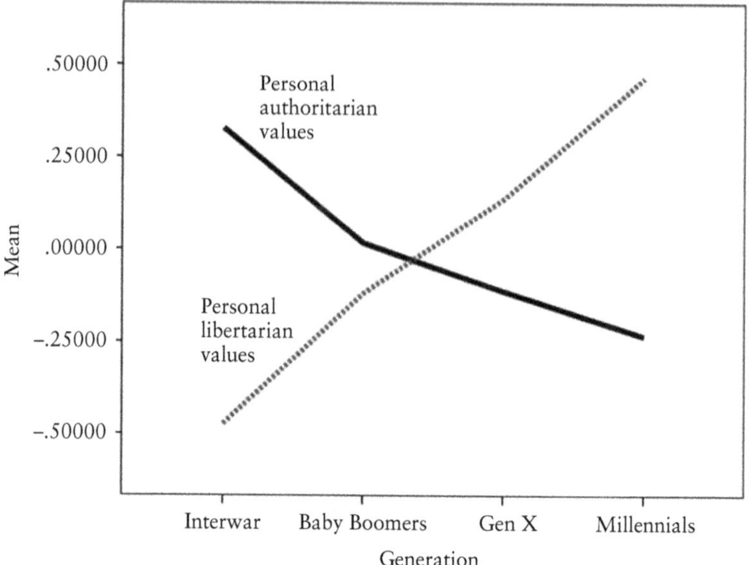


FIGURE 4.8. *The tipping point in authoritarian and libertarian values by generation, Europe*
*Note:* The trend lines illustrate the mean standardized (z-scores) for the Schwartz authoritarian and libertarian value scales. For their construction, see Table 4.3.
*Source:* The European Social Survey, Cumulative File Rounds 1–7.

authoritarian and libertarian values, reverses earliest among the Baby Boom generation in Norway, Denmark, and Finland, all affluent post-industrial societies and long-established liberal democracies, with strong egalitarian cultural traditions and comprehensive cradle-to-grave welfare states. Several Northern European societies show a similar profile, such as France, the Netherlands, and Switzerland – all affluent knowledge economies. By contrast, the tipping point is reached later (among Generation X, born in the mid-1970s), in Mediterranean countries such as Spain, Greece, and Italy. The gap barely reverses itself in post-communist Europe, such as in Ukraine, Slovakia, Bulgaria, and in Turkey (where no reversal occurs), reflecting the sluggish economic growth and the later (and unstable) democratic development of several states in this region.

## ANALYZING AGE–COHORT–PERIOD EFFECTS

What are the underlying drivers of authoritarian values, socially conservative attitudes, and populist orientations? And how can we disentangle

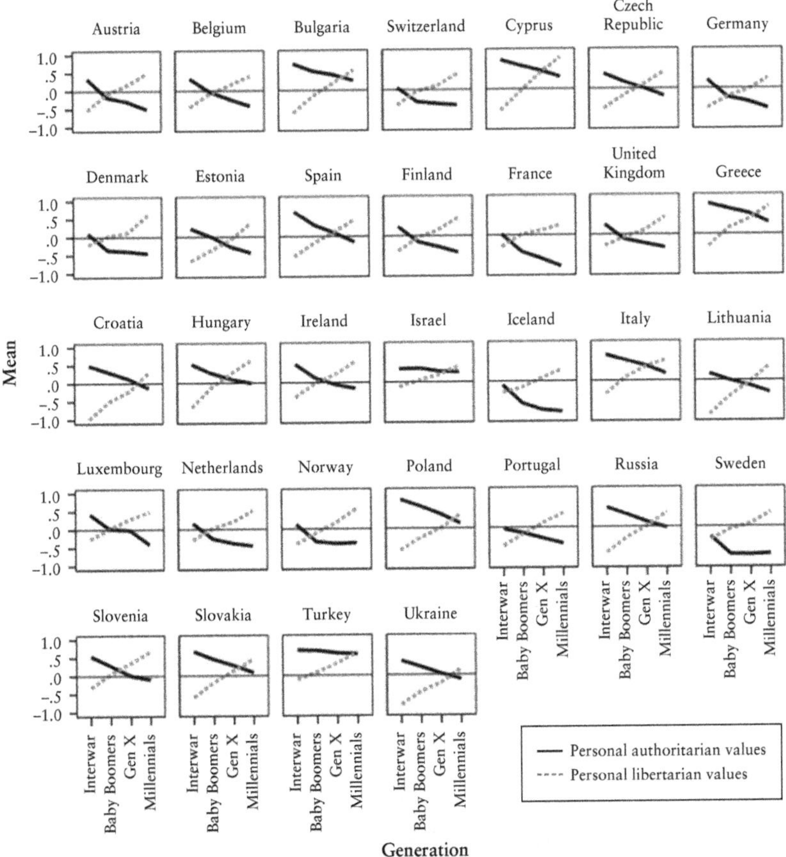


FIGURE 4.9. *The tipping point in authoritarian and libertarian values by generation and European country*
*Note:* The trend lines illustrate the mean standardized (z-scores) for the Schwartz authoritarian and libertarian personal value scales. For their construction, see Table 4.3.
*Source:* The European Social Survey, Cumulative File Rounds 1–7.

birth cohorts (generations) from the effects of life cycles (as people age) and periods (defined as events like the financial crash happening during particular years)? The classic identification problem is that each of these may possibly be influencing cultural values and two of these effects are always confounding. If socially liberal values are increasing this could be attributed to generational differences in attitudes among Interwar and Millennial cohorts, or it could be because people become more conservative as they age, or it could be because events mean that all people have changed their values over time.

To disentangle these effects we use both panel and cross-sectional datasets. Following Tilley, age is measured indirectly using the underlying indicators of social ageing, in particular marriage and children.[42] This allows us to model the significance of the birth cohort (generation), the years of the survey, from 2002 to 2014 (period), and marriage and children as the proxy indicators of the life cycle (age).

A series of models entering these variables in blocks using OLS regression was used for the analysis. In each table, Model 1 tests the effects of generation (birth cohort). Model 2 adds controls for the year of the European Social Survey, to see whether there are any significant period-effects, which can be interpreted as associated with the occurrence of specific events, such as the 2007 financial crash or the migrant crisis. Model 3 adds controls for compositional effects arising from education, sex, social class (using the Goldthorpe scheme), religiosity, and urbanization, since older and younger generations vary systematically in these characteristics. The aim is to establish the effects of generation, independently of the fact that Millennials are better educated, more urbanized, and less religious than the Interwar generation. Finally, Model 4 also controls for life-cycle effects associated with ageing, in particular marriage and children.

Subsequent chapters will expand this framework by analyzing additional economic factors (including socio-tropic indicators such as household income, subjective feelings of financial security, and the experience of long-term unemployment, and ego-tropic indicators, such as satisfaction with the performance of the national economy), as well as the effects of ethnicity (such as race, type of religious faith, citizenship, immigration status, and nationality).

## Authoritarian Values

Table 4.4 predicts support for authoritarian values, as measured by the Schwartz scale. The results in the successive models confirm that birth cohort is an important predictor of support for authoritarian values. As expected, in Model 1, the Interwar generation proved significantly more likely to endorse authoritarian values than successive generational cohorts, with Millennials being the most libertarian. Authoritarianism fades steadily in the pooled European sample as we move from older to younger birth cohorts, supporting the cultural change thesis, which emphasizes the process of generational population replacement.

Model 2 adds the year of the ESS survey to the analysis, serving as a proxy for period-effects from 2002 to 2014. In particular, two events

TABLE 4.4. *Predicting authoritarian values*

| Models | | Model 1 | | | | Model 2 | | | | Model 3 | | | | Model 4 | | | |
|---|---|---|---|---|---|---|---|---|---|---|---|---|---|---|---|---|---|
| | | B | d. Error | Beta | Sig. | B | d. Error | Beta | Sig. | B | d. Error | Beta | Sig. | B | d. Error | Beta | Sig. |
| Generation | Interwar (1900–1945) (Ref) | 0.00 | | | | | | | | | | | | | | | |
| | Boomers (1946–1964) | −4.48 | 0.07 | −0.15 | *** | −4.61 | 0.07 | −0.15 | *** | −3.12 | 0.07 | −0.10 | *** | −3.52 | 0.07 | −0.12 | *** |
| | Generation X (1965–1979) | −6.38 | 0.07 | −0.19 | *** | −6.51 | 0.07 | −0.20 | *** | −4.46 | 0.07 | −0.13 | *** | −4.90 | 0.08 | −0.15 | *** |
| | Millennial (1980–1996) | −8.15 | 0.08 | −0.23 | *** | −8.48 | 0.08 | −0.24 | *** | −6.66 | 0.08 | −0.19 | *** | −6.33 | 0.08 | −0.18 | *** |
| Year | Y2002 (Ref) | | | | | 0.00 | | | | 0.00 | | | | 0.00 | | | |
| | Y2004 | | | | | 0.88 | 0.10 | 0.02 | *** | 0.80 | 0.10 | 0.02 | *** | 0.81 | 0.10 | 0.02 | *** |
| | Y2006 | | | | | −0.02 | 0.10 | 0.00 | N/s | 0.24 | 0.10 | 0.01 | *** | 2.11 | 0.13 | 0.05 | *** |
| | Y2008 | | | | | 2.33 | 0.10 | 0.06 | *** | 2.38 | 0.09 | 0.06 | *** | 4.23 | 0.12 | 0.11 | *** |
| | Y2010 | | | | | 2.52 | 0.10 | 0.07 | *** | 2.74 | 0.09 | 0.07 | *** | 4.59 | 0.12 | 0.12 | *** |
| | Y2012 | | | | | 2.52 | 0.10 | 0.07 | *** | 2.19 | 0.10 | 0.06 | *** | 3.96 | 0.13 | 0.10 | *** |
| | Y2014 | | | | | 1.45 | 0.10 | 0.03 | *** | 1.48 | 0.11 | 0.03 | *** | 3.25 | 0.13 | 0.08 | *** |
| | Manager | | | | | | | | | −1.93 | 0.10 | −0.04 | *** | −2.08 | 0.10 | −0.05 | *** |
| | Routine non-manual | | | | | | | | | −1.15 | 0.08 | −0.03 | *** | −1.27 | 0.08 | −0.04 | *** |
| | Petty bourgeoisie | | | | | | | | | −1.00 | 0.09 | −0.02 | *** | −1.19 | 0.08 | −0.03 | *** |
| | Skilled manual | | | | | | | | | 0.43 | 0.10 | 0.01 | *** | 0.27 | 0.10 | 0.01 | *** |
| | Manual (Ref) | | | | | | | | | 0.00 | | | | 0.00 | | | |
| Education | Education (5-point scale low to high) | | | | | | | | | −0.62 | 0.02 | −0.06 | *** | −0.63 | 0.02 | −0.06 | *** |

(*continued*)

TABLE 4.4 (*continued*)

| Models | | Model 1 | | | | Model 2 | | | | Model 3 | | | | Model 4 | | | |
|---|---|---|---|---|---|---|---|---|---|---|---|---|---|---|---|---|---|
| | | B | d. Error | Beta | Sig. | B | d. Error | Beta | Sig. | B | d. Error | Beta | Sig. | B | d. Error | Beta | Sig. |
| Sex | Men (Ref) | | | | | | | | | 0.00 | | | | 0.00 | | | |
| | Women | | | | | | | | | −0.83 | 0.05 | −0.03 | *** | −0.74 | 0.05 | −0.03 | *** |
| Urbanization | Urbanization (1–5 scale urban to rural) | | | | | | | | | 0.28 | 0.02 | 0.02 | *** | 0.30 | 0.02 | 0.03 | *** |
| Religiosity | How religious are you? (10-pt scale) | | | | | | | | | 1.11 | 0.01 | 0.23 | *** | 1.09 | 0.01 | 0.23 | *** |
| Children | No children under 18 | | | | | | | | | | | | | 0.00 | | | |
| | Children under 18 | | | | | | | | | | | | | 1.23 | 0.06 | 0.04 | *** |
| Marital status | Never married | | | | | | | | | | | | | 0.00 | | | |
| | Married | | | | | | | | | | | | | 3.00 | 0.12 | 0.07 | *** |
| | Separated or divorced | | | | | | | | | | | | | 1.71 | 0.15 | 0.02 | *** |
| | (Constant) | 77.31 | 0.05 | | *** | 75.95 | 0.09 | | *** | 71.32 | 0.13 | | *** | 69.27 | 0.15 | | *** |
| | Adjusted R2 | 0.04 | | | | 0.04 | | | | 0.11 | | | | 0.11 | | | |

*Notes:* OLS regression models predicting citizen's support for authoritarian values measured by the Schwartz scale. P *** .001, ** .01, * .05, N/s = Not significant. The Interwar generation and the unskilled manual class are the excluded reference categories.

*Source:* The European Social Survey Cumulative File Rounds 1–7. N. 330,315 respondents in 31 European countries.

during this period can be expected to have catalyzed latent authoritarian feelings. The first was the 2007–2013 financial crisis in OECD countries, especially the effects on unemployment and austerity cuts in social welfare in Mediterranean Europe, which heightened feelings of economic insecurity. The migrant crisis is another landmark event, which brought refugees and asylum seekers flooding into Europe in leaky boats that had crossed the Mediterranean and arduous overland journeys through Southern Europe. Migrants came from diverse religions and cultures, but the majority were Muslims, often seeking to escape conflict in Syria, Afghanistan, and Iraq, as well as from poorer countries like Eritrea in North Africa and elsewhere in the Middle East. Eurostat estimates show the number of refugees seeking asylum in the European Union rose slowly from 2006 to 2012, increasing in 2012–2014, then accelerating sharply following Angela Merkel's open door policy for Syrian refugees into Germany, announced in the summer of 2015, before stabilizing in 2016 at the higher level, then falling again in 2017.[43]

It is not possible to disentangle the impact of such events cleanly at aggregate levels. But the initial results in Model 2 show a pattern of trendless fluctuations in authoritarian values from 2002 to 2006, but a significant jump observed for 2008–2012. This suggests that the shock of these events may have reinforced these values – an issue explored in depth later in this book.

Model 3 shows that even after controlling for the social background characteristics of younger and older cohorts, the generation gap in authoritarian values remains significant and large. In other words, contrasts in libertarian and authoritarian attitudes among Interwar and Millennial generational cohorts are not attributable only to the different social characteristics of these groups.

In addition, education also proves significant and negative, confirming as expected that support for values that are more authoritarian is concentrated among the less-educated sectors of the population. This finding confirms decades of research, having been repeatedly observed ever since the earliest studies of this topic, including Gordon Allport's work on the nature of prejudice, Samuel Stouffer's study of support for communism, and Seymour Martin Lipset's thesis of working-class authoritarianism, all published in the mid-twentieth century.[44] Education is consistently associated with attitudes that are more tolerant toward out-groups, including ethnic, religious, and racial minorities.[45]

The precise reasons *why* the more educated are more socially liberal and tolerant are difficult to disentangle, however, since the association could be attributed to both cultural and material insecurities.

On the one hand, differences in socio-economic status may be important, since access to higher education is skewed toward those coming from relatively prosperous middle-class families. Moreover, formal educational qualifications help to determine subsequent life-chances, social mobility, and occupational careers (and thus future economic status and material security). Writers, academics, journalists, artists, and scientists may also have liberal views on race, sexuality, and diversity because they are more likely to thrive under conditions of openness, meritocracy, and social change than those with lower knowledge, skills, and abilities.[46]

At the same time, however, studies seeking to determine the origins of socially liberal views have concluded that education is far more important than occupational class.[47] Moreover, the education correlation in Model 3 persists even with controls for social class. Instead of an economic thesis, several scholars suggest that the linkage mechanism connecting education with views that are more libertarian may well arise from socialization effects.[48] Hence, it has been argued that tolerance of diversity and difference is fostered through the cultural values, knowledge, and cognitive skills learned through formal schooling.[49] Multicultural educational programs may also serve to strengthen intergroup relations, with textbooks integrating awareness of diverse experiences and cultures, and citizenship or civics education.[50] Informal processes may also play a role, if the experience of attending schools and colleges promotes intergroup contact and expands interpersonal networks. Contact theory, developed in the 1950s by Gordon Allport, holds that under certain circumstances, connections between majority and minority group members can promote tolerance and acceptance, especially where groups have equal status and share common goals.[51] Similarly, Putnam has argued that personal communications and associational networks among people from diverse backgrounds, with different ideologies, and characteristics, can build 'bridging' social capital, promote social trust, and facilitate social cooperation.[52] And Russell Hardin emphasizes that knowledge builds social trust.[53] From this perspective, ignorance and dogmatic thinking are likely to be closely associated with practices of intolerance, prejudice, and stereotyping. Where people lack understanding about individuals, peoples, or places, then observable group characteristics are more likely to function as heuristic shortcuts to form blanket judgments. Politics may be seen by those with little schooling and few analytical skills in simplistic black-and-white terms, attracting them to demagogic populist leaders, promising easy short-term fixes and offering slogans instead of policy programs to address complex social problems ('Build a Wall').

Among the other controls for compositional effects, occupational class was strong and significant. Compared with the unskilled manual workers, which serve as the default category, middle-class groups are less likely to endorse authoritarian values, with professional and managerial groups displaying the least support. In 1959, Seymour Martin Lipset observed that the working class were usually less progressive than the middle class, where liberalism was defined in non-economic terms such as by respect for individual liberty, equality for ethnic and racial minorities, tolerance for internationalist foreign policies, and support for liberal immigration laws. As Lipset characterized this orientation, the lower strata and less educated are less sophisticated and therefore predisposed to view politics in black-and-white terms, making them more likely to support extremist movements and leaders that promise quick and easy fixes rather than viewing problems of reform in complex gradualist terms.[54] Almost six decades later, the evidence suggests that this pattern can still be observed.

As reported in previous studies, a modest gender gap can be observed, with men being slightly more likely to endorse authoritarian values than women; the exact reasons for the gender gap are difficult to establish.[55] One factor could be that men may generally feel a stronger sense of cultural grievances from the impact of feminism, their loss of predominant bread-winner status, and changing attitudes toward gender equality in the home, workforce, and public sphere. These developments may be perceived by older generations as violating traditional social norms about the roles of women and men which prevailed during earlier decades, threatening patriarchal beliefs about status and power.

Urbanization was also negatively related, with support for authoritarian values strongest in rural and non-metropolitan areas, rather than in urban areas that have multicultural populations – an issue explored in more depth in Chapter 6.

The strength of religiosity, closely linked with conformity toward a wide range of traditional values, is also positively and strongly associated with authoritarian values. Religious attitudes, beliefs, and behaviors are often closely linked with social conservatism, as well as being far more pervasive among the older generations in Europe.[56]

In short, authoritarian values are generally strongest among the working class, men, the less-educated, residents living in rural areas, and among the most religious.[57] Nevertheless, even with these controls, the impact of generation on authoritarian values remains significant and is the second strongest predictor (after religion) in model 3.

Finally, Model 4 adds controls for marriage and children as proxy variables for life-cycle effects. Both factors are significant but their effects are weaker than those observed for birth cohorts.[58] Authoritarian values may be strengthened by life-cycle effects as people age, and seem to have been affected by period-effects linked with the 2007 financial crisis – although further scrutiny is given in the next chapter to examine this interpretation. But the largest differences observed in these values are between older and younger generational cohorts. Controls for all these variables do not weaken the significant generational gaps already observed in Europe and the United States, revealing large differences between the authoritarian cultural beliefs of the Interwar cohorts from subsequent generations, especially the Millennials, who widely reject these values.

## Socially Liberal Attitudes

Are these results found only in the specific items we have used to gauge cultural values? As an additional robustness test, Table 4.5 uses a similar design to predict endorsement of social liberalism or conservatism. This is measured in a composite scale constructed from the items listed in Figure 4.5 concerning approval of women's role in the paid labor force, men's right to a job, homosexual freedoms, EU unification, religiosity, and immigration.

The results of successive models in Table 4.5, predicting socially liberal attitudes, display a similar profile to that already observed, confirming the importance of birth cohorts, as well as the role of education, social class, religiosity, and urbanization. This is hardly surprising given the close correlation between socially conservative attitudes and adherence to personal authoritarian values that was documented earlier (see Figure 4.8). Birth cohort is important, with the Millennial birth cohorts being much more socially liberal than the Interwar generation. The role of education is also strong and significant, as observed previously in Figure 4.5, confirming the link between formal schooling and liberal attitudes, such as tolerance toward gay rights, immigrants, and gender equality. In addition, women, middle-class households, the urban, and the secular were somewhat more socially liberal. And with the proxies for life-cycle effects, those with children and those who were married were slightly more conservative, but the generation gaps persisted even with these controls. The overall factors predicting greater social liberalism or

TABLE 4.5. *Predicting socially liberal attitudes*

| Models | | Model 1 | | | | Model 2 | | | | Model 3 | | | | Model 4 | | | |
|---|---|---|---|---|---|---|---|---|---|---|---|---|---|---|---|---|---|
| | | B | SE | Beta | Sig. | B | SE | Beta | Sig. | B | SE | Beta | Sig. | B | SE | Beta | Sig. |
| Generation | Interwar (1900–1945) (Ref) | | | | | | | | | | | | | | | | |
| | Boomers (1946–1964) | 2.73 | 0.10 | 0.10 | 0.00 | 2.65 | 0.10 | 0.09 | 0.00 | 1.61 | 0.10 | 0.06 | 0.00 | 1.70 | 0.10 | 0.06 | 0.00 |
| | Generation X (1965–1979) | 3.10 | 0.10 | 0.10 | 0.00 | 3.00 | 0.10 | 0.10 | 0.00 | 1.50 | 0.10 | 0.05 | 0.00 | 1.52 | 0.12 | 0.05 | 0.00 |
| | Millennial (1980–1996) | 3.33 | 0.11 | 0.10 | 0.00 | 3.10 | 0.11 | 0.09 | 0.00 | 2.53 | 0.11 | 0.08 | 0.00 | 2.20 | 0.12 | 0.07 | 0.00 |
| Year | Y2002 (Ref) | | | | | | | | | | | | | | | | |
| | Y2004 | | | | | −1.76 | 0.09 | −0.06 | 0.00 | −1.39 | 0.09 | −0.05 | 0.00 | −0.30 | 0.13 | −0.01 | 0.02 |
| | Y2008 | | | | | 1.08 | 0.09 | 0.04 | 0.00 | 1.19 | 0.08 | 0.04 | 0.00 | 1.19 | 0.08 | 0.04 | 0.00 |
| Class. | Manager | | | | | | | | | 2.73 | 0.13 | 0.07 | 0.00 | 2.81 | 0.13 | 0.08 | 0.00 |
| | Routine non-manual | | | | | | | | | 1.67 | 0.09 | 0.06 | 0.00 | 1.74 | 0.09 | 0.06 | 0.00 |
| | Petty bourgeoisie | | | | | | | | | 0.53 | 0.12 | 0.01 | 0.00 | 0.63 | 0.13 | 0.02 | 0.00 |
| | Skilled manual | | | | | | | | | 0.27 | 0.13 | 0.01 | 0.04 | 0.34 | 0.13 | 0.01 | 0.01 |
| | Manual (Ref) | | | | | | | | | 0.00 | | | | 0.00 | | | |
| Education | Education (5-point scale low to high) | | | | | | | | | 1.04 | 0.03 | 0.11 | 0.00 | 1.03 | 0.03 | 0.11 | 0.00 |
| Sex | Men (Ref) | | | | | | | | | 0.00 | | | | 0.00 | | | |
| | Women | | | | | | | | | −1.11 | 0.07 | −0.04 | 0.00 | −1.16 | 0.07 | −0.04 | 0.00 |

*(continued)*

TABLE 4.5 (*continued*)

| Models | | Model 1 B | SE | Beta | Sig. | Model 2 B | SE | Beta | Sig. | Model 3 B | SE | Beta | Sig. | Model 4 B | SE | Beta | Sig. |
|---|---|---|---|---|---|---|---|---|---|---|---|---|---|---|---|---|---|
| Urbanization | Urbanization (1–5 scale rural to urban) | | | | | | | | | −0.24 | 0.03 | −0.02 | 0.00 | −0.25 | 0.03 | −0.02 | 0.00 |
| Religiosity | How religious are you on 10-pt scale | | | | | | | | | −0.24 | 0.01 | −0.05 | 0.00 | −0.23 | 0.01 | −0.05 | 0.00 |
| Children | No children under 18 (Ref) | | | | | | | | | | | | | 0.00 | | | |
| | Children under 18 | | | | | | | | | | | | | −0.37 | 0.08 | −0.01 | 0.00 |
| Marital status | Never married (Ref) | | | | | | | | | | | | | 0.00 | | | |
| | Married | | | | | | | | | | | | | −1.63 | 0.15 | −0.05 | 0.00 |
| | Separated or divorced | | | | | | | | | | | | | −1.63 | 0.20 | −0.03 | 0.00 |
| | (Constant) | 54.84 | 0.07 | | 0.00 | 55.12 | 0.09 | | 0.00 | 53.94 | 0.17 | | 0.00 | 54.09 | 0.17 | | 0.00 |
| | Adjusted R2 | 0.01 | | | | 0.017 | | | | 0.045 | | | | 0.046 | | | |

*Notes:* OLS regression models predicting citizen's support for the socially liberal attitudes scale. P *** .001, ** .01, * .05, N/s = Not significant. The Interwar generation and the unskilled manual class are the excluded reference categories.

*Source:* The European Social Survey Cumulative File Rounds 1–7. N. 330,315 respondents in 31 European countries.

conservatism largely confirm the patterns observed for authoritarian values, strengthening confidence in the results.

## Populist Orientations

Finally, are similar associations found among those endorsing anti-establishment attitudes, as measured by distrust of core democratic institutions? Populist leaders combine condemnation of politicians, parliaments, and mainstream parties, with claims that the only legitimate authority derives from the people. The ESS survey lacks suitable measures of faith in the people (an issue examined further with other survey data in chapter 11) but it does measure confidence in parliaments, political parties, and politicians. Combining these items allows us to construct a 30-point populism scale, where a higher score reflects deeper institutional mistrust.

In contrast to the previous analysis, Table 4.6 demonstrates a mixed pattern of political mistrust by birth cohort: compared with the Interwar generation (as the default category), Baby Boomers and Generation X showed slightly more mistrust in political institutions but the Millennials were fairly similar to the oldest cohort. Model 1 in Figure 4.10 illustrates how authoritarian values clearly and consistently divide generational cohorts, but *populism does not show a similar pattern.* In fact, Baby Boomers and Generation X were slightly more critical of these political institutions than the Interwar and the Millennial cohorts. These results are largely consistent with those found in previous studies.[59]

These generational patterns persisted in successive models applying the standard controls. Model 2 adds the year of the survey. Instead of a steadily linear growth in political mistrust over time, the results suggest that levels were steady from 2002 to 2006, before peaking in 2010–2012, and then falling back to the levels observed at the start of the series. This suggests a potential period-effect and Chapter 5 will explore how far this can be explained by economic conditions during these years.

As Model 3 indicates, men also expressed slightly more confidence in political institutions than women, a long-standing pattern observed elsewhere.[60] Mistrust was also stronger among the working classes and less educated. By contrast, slightly more confidence in political institutions was expressed by those employed in professional and managerial occupations and by the college educated, who also have more political knowledge. Finally, to examine life-cycle effects, those with children and the married were more cynical about political institutions than those without children or the never married.

TABLE 4.6. *Predicting populist orientations*

| Models | | Model 1 | | | | Model 2 | | | | Model 3 | | | | Model 4 | | | |
|---|---|---|---|---|---|---|---|---|---|---|---|---|---|---|---|---|---|
| | | B | SE | Beta | Sig. | B | SE | Beta | Sig- | B | SE | Beta | Sig. | B | SE | Beta | Sig. |
| Generation | Interwar (1900–1945) (Ref) | 0.00 | | | | | | 0.00 | | | | 0.00 | | | | | |
| | Boomers (1946–1964) | 1.66 | 0.12 | 0.04 | *** | 1.54 | 0.12 | 0.03 | *** | 2.35 | 0.12 | 0.05 | *** | 1.85 | 0.12 | 0.04 | *** |
| | Generation X (1965–1979) | 1.32 | 0.13 | 0.03 | *** | 1.19 | 0.13 | 0.02 | *** | 2.38 | 0.13 | 0.05 | *** | 1.53 | 0.14 | 0.03 | *** |
| | Millennial (1980–1996) | 0.26 | 0.13 | 0.01 | *** | −0.08 | 0.13 | 0.00 | N/s | −0.29 | 0.14 | −0.01 | * | −0.29 | 0.14 | −0.01 | * |
| Year | Y2002 (Ref) | | | | | 0.00 | | | | 0.00 | | | | 0.00 | | | |
| | Y2004 | | | | | −5.59 | 0.15 | −0.09 | *** | −5.99 | 0.14 | −0.10 | *** | −6.61 | 0.21 | −0.11 | *** |
| | Y2006 | | | | | −5.05 | 0.15 | −0.08 | *** | −4.99 | 0.15 | −0.08 | *** | −4.99 | 0.15 | −0.08 | *** |
| | Y2008 | | | | | −2.92 | 0.14 | −0.05 | *** | −2.99 | 0.14 | −0.05 | *** | −3.00 | 0.14 | −0.05 | *** |
| | Y2012 | | | | | −1.41 | 0.14 | −0.02 | *** | −2.93 | 0.16 | −0.05 | *** | −2.93 | 0.16 | −0.05 | *** |
| | Y2014 | | | | | −4.95 | 0.15 | −0.08 | *** | −6.53 | 0.17 | −0.10 | *** | −6.51 | 0.17 | −0.10 | *** |
| Class | Manager | | | | | | | | | −5.07 | 0.17 | −0.07 | *** | −5.08 | 0.17 | −0.07 | *** |
| | Routine non-manual | | | | | | | | | −2.97 | 0.13 | −0.06 | *** | −2.99 | 0.13 | −0.06 | *** |
| | Petty bourgeoise | | | | | | | | | −1.00 | 0.15 | −0.01 | *** | −1.09 | 0.15 | −0.02 | *** |
| | Skilled manual | | | | | | | | | 1.36 | 0.18 | 0.02 | *** | 1.29 | 0.18 | 0.02 | *** |
| | Manual (Ref) | | | | | | | | | 0.00 | | | | 0.00 | | | |
| Education | Education (5-point scale low to high) | | | | | | | | | −1.47 | 0.04 | −0.09 | *** | −1.48 | 0.04 | −0.09 | *** |
| Sex | Men (Ref) | | | | | | | | | 0.00 | | | | 0.00 | | | |
| | Women | | | | | | | | | −2.05 | 0.09 | −0.05 | *** | −1.91 | 0.09 | −0.04 | *** |

| | | | | | | | | | | | | | | | | | |
|---|---|---|---|---|---|---|---|---|---|---|---|---|---|---|---|---|---|
| Urbanization | Urbanization (1–5 scale rural to urban) | | | | | | | | | 0.80 | 0.04 | 0.04 | | 0.82 | 0.04 | 0.05 | |
| Religiosity | How religious are you on 10-pt scale | | | | | | | | | −0.60 | 0.02 | −0.08 | *** | −0.61 | 0.02 | −0.08 | *** |
| Children | No children under 18 (Ref) | | | | | | | | | | | | | 0.00 | | | |
| | Children under 18 | | | | | | | | | | | | | 1.73 | 0.10 | 0.04 | *** |
| Marital status | Never married (Ref) | | | | | | | | | | | | | | | | |
| | Married | | | | | | | | | | | | | 0.57 | 0.24 | 0.01 | * |
| | Separated or divorced | | | | | | | | | | | | | 1.75 | 0.32 | 0.01 | *** |
| | (Constant) | 61.45 | 0.09 | | *** | 64.76 | 0.13 | | *** | 71.87 | 0.22 | | *** | 71.60 | 0.22 | | *** |
| | Adjusted R2 | 0.00 | | | | 0.01 | | | | 0.033 | | | | 0.034 | | | |

*Notes:* OLS regression models predicting support for the populist orientations – scale measured by mistrust in politicians, parties, and parliaments. P *** .001, ** .01, * .05, N/s = Not significant. The Interwar generation and the unskilled manual class are the reference categories.
*Source:* The European Social Survey Cumulative File Rounds 1–7. N. 330,315 respondents in 31 European countries.

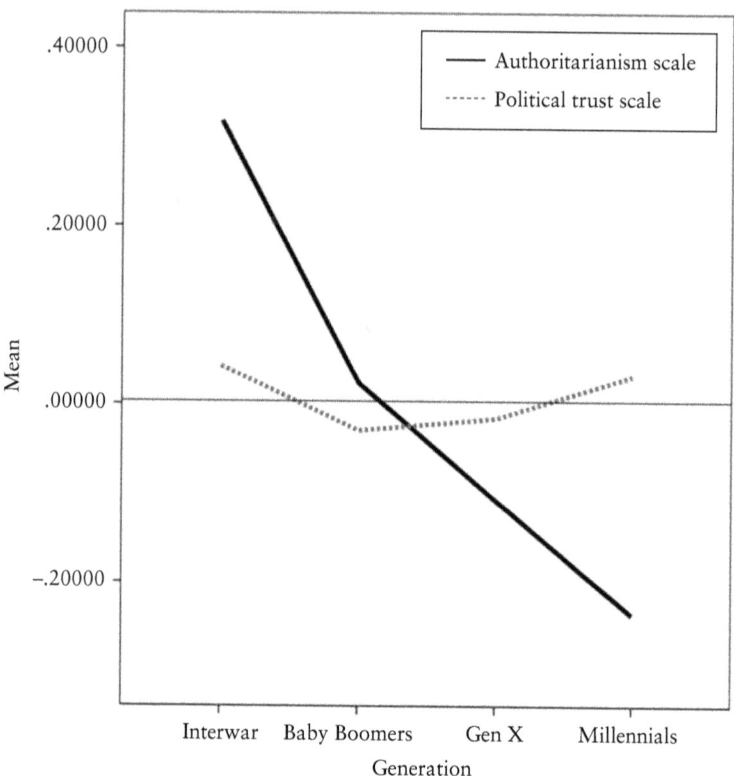


FIGURE 4.10. *Support for authoritarian values and political mistrust by generational cohort, Europe*
*Note:* The trend lines illustrate the mean standardized (z-scores) for the Schwartz authoritarian and the political trust scales.
*Source:* The European Social Survey, Cumulative File Rounds 1–7.

To examine the results by country, we compare the simple correlations between generations and authoritarian, socially liberal and populist values for each of the 32 countries in the ESS. Table 4.7 shows that *generation is significantly linked with authoritarianism in every country under comparison*, in a consistent pattern, with the older cohorts always endorsing authoritarian values more than the Millennials.

The correlations between generation and socially liberal values were observed across two dozen diverse countries, with the younger cohorts being more liberal than the older ones – but this pattern was significant and reversed in four post-communist states (Russia, Ukraine, Lithuania, and Bulgaria) and it was insignificant in three other post-communist

TABLE 4.7. *Correlations between values and generational cohorts*

| | Authoritarian values | | Social Liberalism | | Populism | |
|---|---|---|---|---|---|---|
| Austria | −0.27 | ** | 0.14 | ** | 0.01 | N/s |
| Belgium | −0.29 | ** | 0.17 | ** | −0.09 | ** |
| Bulgaria | −0.17 | ** | −0.04 | ** | 0.05 | ** |
| Switzerland | −0.17 | ** | 0.20 | ** | −0.09 | ** |
| Cyprus | −0.23 | ** | 0.08 | ** | 0.20 | ** |
| Czech Republic | −0.22 | ** | 0.00 | N/s | −0.07 | ** |
| Germany | −0.24 | ** | 0.07 | ** | −0.06 | ** |
| Denmark | −0.18 | ** | 0.11 | ** | −0.04 | ** |
| Estonia | −0.03 | ** | 0.02 | N/s | −0.03 | ** |
| Spain | −0.31 | ** | 0.20 | ** | 0.06 | ** |
| Finland | −0.24 | ** | 0.12 | ** | −0.09 | ** |
| France | −0.25 | ** | 0.20 | ** | 0.00 | N/s |
| UK | −0.21 | ** | 0.24 | ** | −0.04 | ** |
| Greece | −0.22 | ** | 0.05 | ** | 0.14 | ** |
| Croatia | −0.24 | ** | 0.11 | ** | 0.02 | N/s |
| Hungary | −0.22 | ** | 0.04 | * | 0.01 | N/s |
| Ireland | −0.22 | ** | 0.21 | ** | 0.05 | ** |
| Israel | −0.05 | ** | 0.08 | ** | 0.01 | N/s |
| Iceland | −0.22 | ** | 0.09 | * | −0.02 | N/s |
| Italy | −0.21 | ** | 0.11 | * | 0.02 | N/s |
| Lithuania | −0.20 | ** | −0.08 | ** | −0.01 | N/s |
| Luxembourg | −0.23 | ** | 0.20 | ** | 0.01 | N/s |
| Netherlands | −0.21 | ** | 0.17 | ** | −0.08 | ** |
| Norway | −0.16 | ** | 0.02 | N/s | −0.05 | ** |
| Poland | −0.28 | ** | 0.10 | ** | −0.02 | N/s |
| Portugal | −0.16 | ** | 0.04 | ** | −0.03 | ** |
| Russia | −0.22 | ** | −0.15 | ** | 0.02 | * |
| Sweden | −0.16 | ** | 0.16 | ** | −0.08 | ** |
| Slovenia | −0.26 | ** | 0.10 | ** | 0.03 | * |
| Slovakia | −0.22 | ** | 0.00 | N/s | 0.08 | ** |
| Turkey | −0.06 | ** | 0.04 | * | 0.03 | * |
| Ukraine | −0.17 | ** | −0.05 | ** | 0.09 | ** |

*Source:* The European Social Survey Cumulative File Rounds 1–7. N. 330,315 respondents in 32 European countries.

societies (Czech Republic, Slovakia, and Estonia). This suggests that there were important contrasts in the formative experiences shaping birth cohorts in Western and Eastern Europe – above all, the effects of the transition from Soviet rule, an issue examined further in Chapter 5.

Finally, the correlations for populism, as measured by distrust of politicians, parties and parliaments, were far more variable across countries. Thus in around one-third of the countries under comparison, including several in Southern and Eastern Europe, older cohorts were *more* populist than the younger cohorts. In Scandinavia and Northern Europe, however, this situation was reversed, with the Millennials more populist than the Interwar generation. And other cases, including France, Hungary, and Poland, showed no significant generational gaps in political mistrust. Chapter 8 explores whether similar generational patterns can be observed, not just in values but also in votes for Authoritarian-Populist parties.

## CONCLUSIONS

This chapter suggests several major findings.

First, updating previous research, the evidence demonstrates that *the silent revolution continues to transform Western societies on a wide range of social issues,* including those involving sexuality and gender, religion and faith, race and ethnicity, and national versus cosmopolitan identities. Far from a conservative revival, or slow-down in progressive change, the survey data confirm that the long-term trajectory of cultural evolution has continued to move Western cultures in a more socially liberal direction over successive decades. It should be noted that these developments predated the impact of situation-specific effects like the banking crash of 2007, or the influx of migrants flowing into Europe following Angela Merkel's decision to open German borders in 2015, or Donald Trump's victory in the 2016 Electoral College. Subsequent chapters will examine the impact of period-effects, linked to such contingent events, in accelerating the effects of long-term culture shifts.

Secondly, we tracked the primary drivers of these culture shifts. The evidence confirms that *the silent revolution during the second half of the twentieth century was closely associated with processes of intergenerational value change*. This was also reinforced by the expansion of university education in knowledge societies that demand more skilled employees, by growing gender equality as women enter the paid workforce and political leadership, and by urbanization as younger professionals leave rural areas to study, work, and live in multicultural metropolitan cities. These findings are in line with many previous studies, which have also found that libertarian and authoritarian values vary substantially by birth cohort. The more libertarian values of younger citizens can be seen as primarily generational, rather than the result of life-cycle effects linked with getting married and having children, or period-effects linked with specific events like passage of same-sex marriage laws.[61] The factors predicting support for socially conservative and authoritarian values – particularly generational cohort, education, religiosity, and urbanization– are consistent with the sociology of the voting support for radical right parties documented in many previous studies.[62]

Thirdly, we argue that *the silent revolution has catalyzed a major cultural backlash*. Socially conservative and authoritarian values are strongest among the Interwar generation (1900–1945) and Baby Boomers (1946–1964), a steadily shrinking sector of the general population due to demographic turnover. Social conservatives with authoritarian orientations are likely to react to these trends with growing feelings of resentment at the erosion of respect for their core values and beliefs. This is the essence of the backlash against 'political correctness,' in which sexist language, anti-foreigner sentiments, or the expression of racist attitudes are condemned by the liberal consensus and silenced in mainstream political debate. Traditionalists believing in the importance of social conformity are likely to feel that modern social mores taken for granted by the younger generations, such as the acceptance of multicultural lifestyles, tolerance of ethnic diversity, cosmopolitan borders, and fluid gender identities, are not simply mistaken – they are morally wrong.[63] Traditionalists have reacted against cultural changes that have left them feeling like strangers in their own land – and feeling that they have lost status and respect in their own societies. Moreover this is not simply a myth or an irrational belief; traditionalists *have* lost battles in culture wars. The authoritarian reflex is likely to fuel resentment both upwards toward elites and downwards toward out-groups of lower status. This orientation makes people open to the appeals of populist leaders, where the 'fake media' are claimed to be 'enemies of the people,' so-called experts and intellectuals are denigrated as partisan hacks, mainstream parties are seen as out-of-touch with the 'real' people, and elites are regarded as deeply corrupt in their moral values. Bitterness is also likely to be directed 'downwards,' scapegoating immigrants and ethnic minorities that are seen as threatening to Western lifestyles, security, and Christian traditions.

Fourthly, what are the political consequences? *Polarization among those endorsing socially conservative and socially liberal values in Western societies is expected to increase the salience of the cultural cleavage in party competition and the public policy agenda.* Demands for restrictions on immigration and the expression of ethnic and religious identities, such as wearing the hijab, fears of Islamic terrorism, hostility toward LGBTQ rights, and appeals to xenophobic nationalism, are now potent wedge issues. These cut across the traditional left–right axis of post-war party competition over the economy, social and foreign policy. Cultural issues generate opportunities for Authoritarian-Populist leaders to exploit public disaffection and to propose actions addressing public concerns.[64] Cultural divisions also heighten tensions among ideological factions within mainstream parties, such as Trump's hostile takeover within the Republican Party. Similar cultural divisions have split the UK Conservative Party over whether Britain should negotiate a hard or soft exit from the European Union. An extensive body of research demonstrates that public support for extremist social movements, intolerant hate groups, and radical right-wing parties is especially strong among those holding authoritarian values.[65] Values on the 'demand' side of the political marketplace, however, are not automatically translated into votes, legislative seats, ministerial office and inclusion in governing coalitions, and the 'supply-side' of this complex process is analyzed in subsequent chapters.

Finally, *the generational differences shown here are expected to help explain important variations observed in the social profile and strategic appeals of different types of populist parties.* On the one hand, libertarian populists, exemplified by Bernie Sanders, the Five Star Movement, and Podemos, seek to mobilize support among younger cohorts by criticizing corrupt mainstream parties and establishment elites, while simultaneously endorsing gay rights, environmental protection, and social justice for minorities. By contrast, Authoritarian-Populist parties typically target older generations through anti-establishment rhetoric while also defending traditional conservative values linked with family, faith, and patriotism, rejecting tolerance of diverse lifestyles, open borders, and multiculturalism. The cultural backlash is expected to lead toward support for Authoritarian-Populist leaders and parties that promise to resist the winds of change and the liberal consensus, making 'America great again.'

The theory seems to fit many cases, notably the older profile of the Leave supporters in Brexit and Trump voters in America, as documented in later chapters. But populist parties do not march in lock-step and they respond strategically to the cultural legacies of each country.

Thus, xenophobic nativist appeals on certain dimensions coexist in some cases with greater tolerance of sexually liberal values on others. For example, the Alternative for Germany (AfD) has a stridently anti-foreigner platform, regarding Islam as alien to Germany. AfD challenged Angela Merkel's decision to let in around 1.3 million undocumented migrants and refugees, mainly from the Middle East, and demanded strict border controls against EU policy. It has also used populist rhetoric, for example in the neo-Nazi phrase 'Lügenpresse' ('lying press'). Yet, since 2015, Alice Weidel, an openly lesbian woman, has been one of the co-leaders of the party, suggesting that homophobia is not inevitably linked consistently with nationalism. Similarly, in the Netherlands the founding leader of the xenophobic List Pim Fortuyn was openly gay, positioning the party as a defender of traditional Dutch socially tolerant values against the traditional culture of immigrants drawn from Muslim-majority countries. The platform of the Danish People's Party also claims to protect the cultural heritage of the Danish people, and defends freedom of expression, freedom of assembly, and freedom of belief, while simultaneously rejecting multiethnic and multicultural assimilation of migrants.[66] Populist parties are not identical across countries, or over time. Nevertheless, as Chapter 7 will demonstrate, many Authoritarian-Populist parties consistently adopt socially conservative policies across a wide range of issues, campaigning against immigration and adopting anti-European Union rhetoric, as well as taking hardline conservative positions on issues such as reproductive rights, gay rights, and Christianity.

Before examining these issues, however, we need to consider the intervening impact of medium-term conditions that many expect to deepen the authoritarian reflex. Debate continues about the role of economic insecurity on values and votes, including conditions of unemployment, the impact of global trade, and the decline in jobs in factories and mills. Similarly, the growth of multicultural diversity, especially the sudden influx of refugees and immigrants and the resultant European refugee crisis, is also widely blamed for fueling support for nationalism. The next chapters go on to explore the impact of both economic downturns and the growing ethnic diversity of Western societies on authoritarian and populist values.

## Notes

1. Ronald Inglehart and Pippa Norris. 2004. *Rising Tide: Gender Equality in Global Perspective.* Cambridge: Cambridge University Press; C. Lundmark, Jan W. van Deth, and Elinor Scarbrough. 1995. 'Feminist political

orientations.' *The Impact of Values*. New York: Oxford University Press; Johannes Bergh. 2006. 'Gender attitudes and modernization processes.' *International Journal of Public Opinion Research* 19 (1): 5–23; Rosalind Shorrocks. 2016. 'A feminist generation? Cohort change in gender-role attitudes and the second-wave feminist movement.' *International Journal of Public Opinion Research* 42: 237–248.

2. Pippa Norris and Ronald Inglehart. 2011. *Sacred and Secular*. 2nd edn. New York: Cambridge University Press.
3. Pippa Norris and Ronald Inglehart. 2013. *Cosmopolitan Communications*. New York: Cambridge University Press. For details, see www.worldvaluessurvey.org/.
4. Ronald Inglehart. 1977. *The Silent Revolution: Changing Values and Political Styles among Western Publics*. Princeton, NJ: Princeton University Press; the most recent evidence is summarized in Ronald Inglehart. 2018. *Cultural Evolution: People's Motivations Are Changing, and Reshaping the World*. New York: Cambridge University Press.
5. On the US, see, for example, Benjamin Page and Robert Y. Shapiro. 1992. *The Rational Public: Fifty Years of Trends in Americans' Policy Preferences*. Chicago: University of Chicago Press, Chapter 3. On global trends across diverse societies, see Christian Welzel. 2013. *Freedom Rising: Human Empowerment and the Quest for Emancipation*. New York: Cambridge University Press.
6. Christian Welzel. 2013. *Freedom Rising: Human Empowerment and the Quest for Emancipation*. New York: Cambridge University Press.
7. Ronald Inglehart and Christian Welzel. 2005. *Modernization, Cultural Change and Democracy: The Human Development Sequence*. New York: Cambridge University Press.
8. See the Pew Research Center. 2017. *How America Changed during Barack Obama's Presidency*. www.pewresearch.org/2017/01/10/how-america-changed-during-barack-obamas-presidency/.
9. Russell Dalton. 2014. *Citizen Politics*. 6th edn. Thousand Oaks, CA: Sage Publications.
10. Matthew J. Goodwin, Paul Whiteley, and Harold Clarke. 2017. 'Why Britain voted for Brexit: An individual-level analysis of the 2016 referendum vote.' *Parliamentary Affairs* 70 (3): 439–464; Harold D. Clarke, Matthew J. Goodwin, and Paul Whiteley. 2017. *Brexit! Why Britain Voted to Leave the European Union*. Cambridge: Cambridge University Press.
11. Pippa Norris. March 11, 2016. 'Its not just Donald Trump: Authoritarian populism is rising across the West. Here's why.' *Washington Post/Monkey Cage*. Estimates calculated from http://edition.cnn.com/election/primaries/polls.
12. See Figure 2.4.
13. J. Scott, D. Alwin, and M. Braun. 1996. 'Generational changes in gender-role attitudes: Britain in a cross-national perspective.' *Sociology* 30: 471–492; K. Brewster and I. Padavic. 2000. 'Change in gender ideology, 1977–1996: The contributions of intra-cohort change and population turnover.' *Journal of Marriage and Family* 62: 477–487; Ronald Inglehart and Pippa Norris. 2003. *Rising Tide: Gender Equality and Cultural Change*

around the World. New York: Cambridge University Press; Michael Braun and Jacqueline Scott. 2009. 'Changing public views of gender roles in seven countries, 1988–2002.' In Max Haller, Roger Jowell, and Tom Smith. Eds. *Charting the Globe: The International Social Survey Programme, 1984–2009*. London: Routledge; S. Dorius and D.F. Alwin. 2011. 'The global development of egalitarian beliefs: A decomposition of trends in the nature and structure of gender ideology.' Population Studies Center Research Report No. 10-723. Population Studies Center, University of Michigan; D. Cotter, J. Hermsen, and R. Vanneman. 2011. 'The end of the gender revolution? Gender role attitudes from 1977 to 2008.' *American Journal of Sociology* 117 (1): 259–289; F. Pampel. 2011. 'Cohort change, diffusion, and support for gender egalitarianism in cross-national perspective.' *Demographic Research* 25: 667–694.

14. Terri E. Givens. 2004. 'The radical right gender gap.' *Comparative Political Studies* 37 (1): 30–54.
15. Larry Bartels and Simon Jackman. 2014. 'A generational model of political learning.' *Electoral Studies* 33: 7–18; Maria Teresa Grasso. 2014. 'Age–period–cohort analysis in a comparative context: Political generations and political participation repertoires.' *Electoral Studies* 33: 63–76; Maria Teresa Grasso, Stephen Farrall, Emily Gray, Colin Hay, and Will Jennings. 2017. 'Thatcher's children, Blair's babies: Political socialization and trickle down value change.' *British Journal of Political Science* 41 (2): 259–285; Maria Teresa Grasso. 2016. *Generations, Political Participation and Social Change in Western Europe*. London: Routledge.
16. Maria Teresa Grasso. 2014. 'Age–period–cohort analysis in a comparative context: Political generations and political participation repertoires.' *Electoral Studies* 33: 63–76.
17. Ronald Inglehart. 1990. *Cultural Shift in Advanced Industrial Society*. Princeton, NJ: Princeton University; Ronald Inglehart. 1997. *Modernization and Postmodernization: Cultural, Economic and Political Change in 43 Societies*. Princeton, NJ: Princeton University Press; Ronald Inglehart and Pippa Norris. 2003.*Rising Tide: Gender Equality and Cultural Change around the World*. New York: Cambridge University Press; Ronald Inglehart and Christian Welzel. 2005. *Modernization, Cultural Change and Democracy: The Human Development Sequence*. New York: Cambridge University Press; Christian Welzel. 2013. *Freedom Rising: Human Empowerment and the Quest for Emancipation*. New York: Cambridge University Press; Ronald Inglehart and Pippa Norris. 2017. 'Trump and the populist authoritarian parties: The silent revolution in reverse.' *Perspectives on Politics* 15 (2): 443–454.
18. Pippa Norris and Ronald Inglehart. 2009. *Cosmopolitan Communications*. New York: Cambridge University Press.
19. Ronald Inglehart. 2008. 'Changing values among Western publics, 1970–2006: Postmaterialistic values and the shift from survival values to self-expression values.' *West European Politics* 31 (1–2): 130–146.
20. Ronald Inglehart. 1971. 'The silent revolution in Europe: Intergenerational change in post-industrial societies.' *American Political Science Review* 65 (4): 991–1017.

21. Elinor Scarbrough. 1994. 'Materialist–post-materialist value orientations.' In Jan W. van Deth and Elinor Scarbrough. Eds. *The Impact of Values.* Oxford: Oxford University Press, Chapter 5.
22. See Ronald F. Inglehart. 2008. 'Changing values among Western Publics, 1970–2006: Postmaterialist values and the shift from survival values to self-expression values.' *West European Politics* 31 (1–2): 130–146.
23. Ronald Inglehart. 1990. *Cultural Shift in Advanced Industrial Society.* Princeton, NJ: Princeton University; Ronald Inglehart. 1997. *Modernization and Post-Modernization: Cultural, Economic and Political Change in 43 Societies.* Princeton, NJ: Princeton University Press; Ronald Inglehart and Christian Welzel. 2005. *Modernization, Cultural Change and Democracy: The Human Development Sequence.* New York: Cambridge University Press; Christian Welzel. 2013. *Freedom Rising: Human Empowerment and the Quest for Emancipation.* New York: Cambridge University Press.
24. Ronald Inglehart. 1977. *The Silent Revolution: Changing Values and Political Styles among Western Publics.* Princeton, NJ: Princeton University Press.
25. Russell Dalton. 2014.*Citizen Politics.* 6th edn. London: Sage.
26. Pippa Norris and Ronald Inglehart. 2010. *Sacred and Secular: Religion and Politics Worldwide.* 2nd edn. New York: Cambridge University Press.
27. See Peter Taylor-Gooby. 1993. 'What citizens want from the state.' In Roger Jowell, Lindsay Brook, and Lizanne Dowds. Eds. *International Social Attitudes: The 10th BSA Report.* Aldershot: Dartmouth Publishing, Chapter 4. See also Max Haller, Roger Jowell, and Tom Smith. Eds. 2009. *Charting the Globe: The International Social Survey Programme, 1984–2009.* London: Routledge; J.W. Becker, James A. Davis, Peter Ester, and Peter P. Mohler. Eds. 1990. *Attitudes to Inequality and the Role of Government.* Rijswijk, Netherlands: Sociaal en Cultureel Planbureau; Roger Jowell, Sharon Witherspoon, and Lindsay Brook. Eds. 1989. *British Social Attitudes: Special International Report.* Aldershot: Gower.
28. Jacqueline Scott, Michael Braun, and Duane Alwin. 1993. 'The Family Way.' In Roger Jowell, Lindsay Brook, and Lizanne Dowds. Eds. *International Social Attitudes: The 10th BSA Report.* Aldershot: Dartmouth Publishing, Chapter 2.
29. http://news.gallup.com/poll/210542/americans-hold-record-liberal-views-moral-issues.aspx.
30. www.people-press.org/2017/10/05/the-partisan-divide-on-political-values-grows-even-wider/.
31. Pamela Conover and Stanley Feldman. 1981. 'The origins and meaning of liberal/conservative self-identifications.' *American Journal of Political* Science 25 (4): 617–645.
32. Philip Converse. 1964. 'The nature of belief systems in mass publics.' In D.E. Apter. Ed. *Ideology and discontent.* New York: The Free Press, pp. 206–261.
33. Donald R. Kinder and Nathan Kalmoe. 2017. *Neither Liberal nor Conservative.* Chicago: University of Chicago Press.

34. http://news.gallup.com/poll/210542/americans-hold-record-liberal-views-moral-issues.aspx.
35. http://news.gallup.com/poll/183386/social-ideology-left-catches-right.aspx.
36. See Anthony Heath, Geoffrey Evans, and J. Martin. 1994. 'The measurement of core beliefs and values: The development of balanced socialist/laissez faire and libertarian/authoritarian scales.' *British Journal of Political Science* 24 (1): 115–132.
37. Dieter Fuchs and Hans-Dieter Klingemann. 1990. 'The left–right schema.' In M. Kent Jennings & Jan W. van Deth. Eds. *Continuities in Political Action: A Longitudinal Study of Political Orientations in Three Western Democracies*. Berlin: de Gruyter, pp. 203–234; J.D. Huber. 1989. 'Values and partisanship in left–right orientations: Measuring ideology.' *European Journal of Political Research* 17 (5): 599–621; Andre Freire. 2006. 'Bringing social identities back in: The social anchors of left–right orientation in Western Europe.' *International Political Science Review* 27 (4): 359–378; Y. Piurko, Shalom Schwartz, and E. Davidov. 2011. 'Basic personal values and the meaning of left–right political orientations in 20 countries.' *Political Psychology* 32 (4): 537–561; Catherine E. De Vries, A. Hakhverdian, and B. Lancee. 2013. 'The dynamics of voters' left/right identification: The role of economic and cultural attitudes.' *Political Science Research and Methods* 1 (2): 223–238.
38. Hans-George Betz and Stefan Immerfall. Eds. 1998. *The New Politics of the Right: Neo-Populist Parties and Movements in Established Democracies*. New York: St Martin's Press; Siegfried Schumann and Jurgen Falter. 1988. 'Affinity towards right-wing extremism in Western Europe.' *West European Politics* 11 (2): 96–110.
39. Karen Stenner. 2005. *The Authoritarian Dynamic*. New York: Cambridge University Press.
40. The Cronbach Alpha for the five-item authoritarianism scale is 0.720. By contrast, the reliability of the similar Heath–Evans libertarian–authoritarian value 6-item scale from the British Election Study is 0.53, see Anthony Heath, Geoffrey Evans, and J. Martin. 1994. 'The measurement of core beliefs and values: The development of balanced socialist/laissez faire and libertarian/authoritarian scales.' *British Journal of Political Science* 24 (1): 115–132. The equivalent Tilley scale of Authoritarian values from the BES had a Cronbach Alpha of 0.51. See James R. Tilley. 2005. 'Research note: Libertarian–authoritarian value change in Britain, 1974–2001.' *Political Studies* 53: 422–453.
41. Shalom Schwartz. 1992. 'Universals in the content and structure of values: Theoretical advances and empirical tests in 20 countries.' *Advances in Experimental Social Psychology* 25: 1–65.
42. James R. Tilley. 2005. 'Research note: Libertarian–authoritarian value change in Britain, 1974–2001.' *Political Studies* 53: 422–453.
43. http://ec.europa.eu/eurostat/statistics-explained/index.php/File:Asylum_applications_(non-EU)_in_the_EU-28_Member_States,_2006-2016_(thousands)_YB17.png.

44. Gordan Allport. 1954. *The Nature of Prejudice*. Cambridge, MA: Addison-Wesley; Samuel Strouffer. 1955. *Communism, Conformity and Civil Liberties*. New York: Doubleday; Seymour Martin Lipset. 1959. 'Democracy and working class authoritarianism.' *American Sociological Review* 24: 482–502. See also, for example, David L. Weakliem. 2002. 'The effects of education on political opinions: An international study.' *International Journal of Public Opinion Research* 13: 141–157.
45. Cecil Meeusen, Thomas de Vroome, and Mark Hooghe. 2013. 'How does education have an impact on ethnocentrism? A structural equation analysis of cognitive, occupational status and network mechanisms.' *International Journal of Intercultural Relations* 37: 507–522.
46. David Goodhart. 2017. *The Road to Somewhere: The Populist Revolt and the Future of Politics*. London: Hurst & Company.
47. H.G. Van de Werfhorst and N.D. de Graaf. 2004. 'The sources of political orientations in post-industrial society: Social class and education revisited.' *British Journal of Sociology* 55 (2): 211–235; Cecil Meeusen, Thomas de Vroome, and Mark Hooghe. 2013. 'How does education have an impact on ethnocentrism? A structural equation analysis of cognitive, occupational status and network mechanisms.' *International Journal of Intercultural Relations* 37: 507–522.
48. Rune Stubager. 2008. 'Educational effects on authoritarian–libertarian values: A question of socialization.' *British Journal of Sociology* 59 (2): 327–350; Paula Surridge. 'Education and liberalism: Pursuing the link.' *Oxford Review of Education* 42 (2): 146–164.
49. Anders Todal Jenssen and Heidi Engesbak. 1994. 'The many faces of education: Why are people with lower education more hostile toward immigrants than people with higher education?' *Scandinavian Journal of Educational Research* 38: 33–50; Paul W. Vogt. 1997. *Tolerance and Education: Learning to Live with Diversity and Difference*. Thousand Oaks, CA: Sage Publications; Becky L. Choma and Yaniv Hanoch. 2017. 'Cognitive ability and authoritarianism: Understanding support for Trump and Clinton.' *Personality and Individual Differences* 106: 287–291.
50. Werner Wiater and Doris Manschke. Ed. 2011. *Tolerance and Education in Multicultural Societies*. Frankfurt: Peter Lang; Lenka Drazanowa. 2017. *Education and Tolerance: A Comparative Quantitative Analysis of the Educational Effect on Tolerance*. Frankfurt: Peter Lang.
51. Gordon W. Allport. 1954. *The Nature of Prejudice*. Cambridge, MA: Perseus Books.
52. Robert Putnam. 2000. *Bowling Alone: The Collapse and Revival of American Community*. New York: Simon & Schuster.
53. Russell Hardin. 2002. *Trust and Trustworthiness*. New York: Russell Sage Foundation.
54. Seymour Martin Lipset. 1959. 'Democracy and Working-Class Authoritarianism.' *American Sociological Review* 24 (4): 482–501. See also Dick Houtman. 2003. 'Lipset and "Working-Class" Authoritarianism.' *The American Sociologist* 34 (1/2): 85–103.

55. Niels Spierings and Andrej Zaslove. 2017. 'Gender, populist attitudes, and voting: Explaining the gender gap in voting for populist radical right and populist radical left parties.' *West European Politics* 40(4): 821–847.
56. Pippa Norris and Ronald Inglehart. 2011. *Sacred and Secular: Religion and Politics Worldwide*. 2nd edn. New York: Cambridge University Press; Walter G. Stephan and Paul W. Vogt. 2004. Eds. *Educational Programs for Improving Intergroup Relations: Theory, Research and Practice*. London: Teacher's College Press; Jaak Billiet. 1995. 'Church involvement, ethnocentrism, and voting for a radical right-wing party: Diverging behavioral outcomes of equal attitudinal dispositions.' *Sociology of Religion* 56 (3): 303–326.
57. Pippa Norris. 2005. *Radical Right: Voters and Parties in the Electoral Market*. New York: Cambridge University Press.
58. There are also questions about interpreting the direction of causality in the correlation, since authoritarians who emphasize social conformity may be more likely to marry and have children.
59. Pippa Norris. Ed. 1999. *Critical Citizens: Global Support for Democratic Governance*. Oxford: Oxford University Press; Pippa Norris. 2011. *Democratic Deficit*. Cambridge: Cambridge University Press, e.g. see Table 10.5.
60. Ronald Inglehart and Pippa Norris. 2004. *Rising Tide: Gender Equality in Global Perspective*. Cambridge: Cambridge University Press.
61. James R. Tilley. 2005. 'Research note: Libertarian–authoritarian value change in Britain, 1974–2001.' *Political Studies* 53: 422–453.
62. Matthew J. Goodwin and Oliver Heath. 2016. 'The 2016 Referendum, Brexit and the left behind? An aggregate-level analysis of the result.' *Political Quarterly* 87 (3): 323–332; Edwards J. Arnold, Ed. 2000. *The Development of the Radical Right in France: From Boulanger to Le Pen*. Basingstoke: Macmillan Press.
63. Hans-George Betz and C. Johnson. 2004. 'Against the current – stemming the tide: The nostalgic ideology of the contemporary radical populist right.' *Journal of Political Ideologies* 9: 311–327.
64. Göran Adamson. 2016. *Populist Parties and the Failure of the Political Elites: The Rise of the Austrian Freedom Party (FPÖ)*. Germany: Peter Lang.
65. For previous analysis suggesting that radical right voting support is often concentrated more heavily among older citizens, see Pippa Norris. 2005. *Radical Right: Voters and Parties in the Electoral Market*. New York: Cambridge University Press, Tables 6.1 and 6.6; Sara Hobolt. 2016. 'The Brexit vote: A divided nation, a divided continent.' *Journal of European Public Policy* 23 (9): 1259–1277.
66. https://danskfolkeparti.dk/politik/principprogram/.

# 5

# Economic Grievances

Newton's third law of motion holds that 'For every action, there is an equal and opposite reaction.' Societal changes are more complicated than physical ones, but they can reach a tipping point that brings an analogous response. As Chapter 4 demonstrated, long-term processes of intergenerational population replacement have brought a gradual shift toward socially liberal values in Western societies. Like Newton's third law, this triggered a reaction among authoritarian conservatives who felt threatened by these developments. But the gradual process of intergenerational value change cannot explain the relatively rapid fluctuations in public opinion and party fortunes. This chapter explores how economic grievances can bring rising support for Authoritarian-Populist parties. This issue has aroused considerable debate in the research literature and in popular commentary, often pitting economists against sociologists. After setting out the theoretical arguments, we analyze individual-level, longitudinal, and spatial evidence.

Part I outlines the best-known economic grievance theory, which argues that the least prosperous citizens in advanced industrialized economies– the 'losers' from globalization – provide the strongest support for authoritarian and populist values.[1] To consider the evidence, Part II draws on the pooled European Social Survey 2002–2014 (ESS) to test whether authoritarian values and populist attitudes are systematically strengthened at the individual level by various economic factors. To do so, we extend the models presented earlier by adding objective measures of occupational class and household income, direct experience of long-term unemployment, dependency on state benefits, and employment in manufacturing industry, as well as such subjective measures as feelings of personal income insecurity and dissatisfaction with the overall performance of the national economy. We also examine evidence of the timing of attitudinal changes across successive waves of the ESS survey. The period-effects thesis suggests that a sudden economic downturn, such as the financial crash of 2007 or the sovereign debt crisis in the Eurozone member states in 2009, would tend to fuel economic grievances and thereby strengthen authoritarian values and populist attitudes. The impact of various economic characteristics on values and attitudes are compared at the individual level in models containing a comprehensive range of controls for generational, period (year), and life-cycle effects, building on the findings presented in Chapter 4. The results indicate that economic factors do have an impact on cultural values – but that generational effects outweigh economic factors in predicting who holds authoritarian values.

We also consider the possibility that the impact of economic change on enduring social values might only become evident over several decades, and that economic conditions might also interact with the formative experience of the birth cohorts that grew up during the hard times of the interwar years and the Great Depression– versus those who grew up under the growing economic and physical security of post-war Europe. To illuminate long-term trends, Part III analyzes longitudinal survey evidence, examining annual changes in the proportion of those holding materialist and post-materialist values in given birth cohorts during the period from 1970 to 2008 in six West European societies. These data allow us to monitor the impact of changes in economic conditions, such as inflation and unemployment, on post-material values over almost 40 years, well before the impact of the 2007 financial crisis. The trends demonstrate strong birth cohorts effects in adherence to materialist or post-materialist values – but demonstrate that period-effects are also observed. The timing of major economic downturns, such as annual changes in levels of inflation and unemployment during these decades, correlates with upturns or downturns in cultural values across all cohorts.

The impact of economic conditions can also vary substantially both *across* and *within* countries, as is illustrated by the dramatic contrasts between the impact of economic recession and exposure to the Eurozone debt crisis evident in Northern and Mediterranean European countries.[2] Part IV compares 32 Western societies, examining how the financial crash in 2007/2008, and then the Eurozone debt crisis in 2009/2010, strengthened authoritarian and populist values among citizens living in the debtor economies most vulnerable to these shocks, such as Greece and Spain, while having less impact on creditor countries, such as Germany and the Netherlands.

Values may also be shaped by the experience of living in economically depressed regions *within* a society, regardless of personal levels of prosperity.[3] For everyone in a given area, rich or poor, can be affected – at least psychologically – by that area's socio-economic conditions. When Ford closed the automobile plants in Dagenham, or when the coal mines ceased production in the Ruhr Valley, for example, the knock-on effects depressed house prices and the business prospects for local shops, businesses, and the construction industry. Populations shrank as the more mobile employees and younger college educated professionals left for job opportunities elsewhere, reducing tax revenues supporting schools, healthcare and police, and exacerbating social problems – and contributing to a sense of insecurity even among those who still had jobs. Thus, wide regional disparities are observed in voting behavior, such as the National Front's share of the vote in Marseilles versus Paris, Brexit support in Greater London versus the West Midlands, and the AfD vote in former East Germany versus the West. We consider how far cultural values reflect local socio-economic conditions. In particular, we examine the impact of the local economy on authoritarian values and populist attitudes of political mistrust.[4] The results are consistent with the individual-level analysis: economic indicators are a stronger and more consistent predictor of populist attitudes (political mistrust) than authoritarian values (measured by the Schwartz scale).

Part V summarizes the key findings about the impact of economic grievances and considers their implications for understanding the drivers of partisan change and voting behavior.

## I THEORIES OF ECONOMIC GRIEVANCES AS DRIVERS OF CULTURAL VALUES

The argument that support for extremist movements reflects economic anxieties dates back to classic accounts by Seymour Martin Lipset and Daniel Bell in the mid-twentieth century, who sought to explain the appeal of Fascism in Weimar Germany, Poujadism in France, and McCarthyism in the United States.[5] These movements were seen as authoritarian reactions against modernity, with support coming mainly from small entrepreneurs, shopkeepers, self-employed artisans, and farmers – squeezed between the power of big businesses, on the one hand, and organized labor on the other.

Fascist parties and extremist movements tapped into the fear of downward mobility and falling social status among those who lost out to industrialization. As Lipset argued: 'Extremist movements have much in common. They appeal to the disgruntled and psychologically homeless, to the personal failures, the socially isolated, the economically insecure, the uneducated, unsophisticated, and the authoritarian persons.'[6]

Contemporary concern about working-class authoritarianism has revived today, stimulated by the emergence of a poorly educated, underclass in Western societies (the 'precariat'), with increasingly stark disparities of income and wealth dividing rich and poor during the late-twentieth century.[7] The growing electoral success of Authoritarian-Populist parties and leaders has often been attributed to several related economic developments occurring during the late twentieth century. They include the advanced globalization of labor, finance, investment, trade and goods flowing across national borders, coupled with economic liberalization and deregulation, deteriorating job security for unskilled workers, the loss of manufacturing industries, and growing economic inequality.[8] Millions of people in low and middle-income countries, particularly China and India, have benefitted from international trade and finance – and by the remarkable growth in GDP, which has halved the proportion of the world's population living in extreme poverty since 1990, and reduced income inequality and raised living standards in these countries.[9]

The less-educated population in advanced industrialized economies have been losers from global markets. The 'left-behinds' in developed societies, suffering from sluggish job growth, stagnant wages, and deteriorating public services, seem most vulnerable to the call of authoritarian populism. National governments have increasingly lost their capacity to control the role of international markets and multinational corporations. In particular, center-left social democratic parties have been unable to implement social policies that provide a sense of security for the unemployed and under-privileged who have lost from globalization. As a result, it is argued that many of their core blue-collar supporters have turned to populists like Donald Trump and Bernie Sanders, both of whom campaigned for trade barriers designed to protect workers from foreign competition. In Britain, as well, support for withdrawal from the European Union, particularly among less-educated, poorer, and older Leave voters, is thought to reflect a reaction against Conservative austerity cutbacks in the NHS and welfare benefits, as well as the internationalization of labor and trade markets, particularly the influx into the UK of workers from EU member states like Poland.[10]

As one study argues: 'The "losers" of globalization are people whose life chances were traditionally protected by national boundaries. They perceive the weakening of these boundaries as a threat for their social status and their social security. Their life chances and action spaces are being reduced. The "winners," on the other hand, include people who benefit from the new opportunities resulting from globalization, and whose life chances are enhanced.'[11] Entrepreneurs and salaried professionals – international financiers in London, company executives in Milan, bankers in Paris, and professors in Oxford – can most easily take advantage of the opportunities to live, work, study, and travel in a borderless Europe. The cosmopolitan, secular, and mobile middle classes, with college education and professional or executive careers, may be equally at home in London, Sydney, or New York. By contrast, the 'left behinds' are more rooted in loyalty to particular groups and local communities, unlikely to move even when opportunities call elsewhere. This sector – especially older white men and non-graduates – feels marginalized economically. And urban elites look down on them for holding retrograde views about the flag, faith, and community that are no longer politically correct.[12] Resentment of the establishment, and adherence to the older values of traditional Christian morality, fitting in, and deference toward authority ('Queen and country'), are said to flourish among the 'left-behinds.'[13]

Thomas Piketty's influential work has called attention to rising levels of income and wealth inequality.[14] In recent decades, the US and UK and other high-income countries have experienced sharply rising income inequality; despite substantial economic growth, the gains have gone almost entirely to the top 10 percent of the population.[15] Yet advanced economies differ, with income inequality rising much faster and further in the United States than in the European Union. Inequality has been exacerbated by growing automation and outsourcing, globalization, the erosion of labor unions, government austerity policies, the growth of the knowledge economy, and the limited capacity of governments to regulate investment decisions by multinational corporations or to stem migration flows. The financial crisis also reduced tax revenues and squeezed public sector borrowing, restricting the capacity of states to respond through welfare provisions. Piketty argues that inequality has been rising steeply in many advanced economies since about 1970.[16] All but one of the OECD countries for which data are available saw growing income inequality before taxes and transfers from 1980 to 2009. OECD nations closely integrated into the global economy have seen large-scale layoffs, stagnant wages, and job losses in the manufacturing sector in recent years, as local industries have been unable to compete with lower labor costs abroad and the influx of cheaper imported goods. Deregulation and liberalization of the economy is also blamed for inequality.[17] In the light of these trends, it is not surprising that growing electoral support for populism has been attributed to public resentment of rising income inequality, the shrinkage of well-paid manufacturing jobs, reductions in welfare benefits, and stagnant wages following decades of automation, consolidation, and relocation.[18]

What matters is not just economic conditions, however, but also the political response to them. Where mainstream social democratic parties have been unable to address economic grievances, many scholars argue that this has expanded opportunities for populist demagogues who blame foreigners and immigrants for 'jumping the queue' in welfare services like housing and benefits, preferring to reserve social entitlements for legal residents, a phenomenon known as 'welfare chauvinism' or 'exclusionary nationalism.'[19] For example, UKIP campaigned by promising to limit free access to the National Health Service to legal residents. Some populist parties are pro-market in their economic philosophy, but, following the financial crisis, others like the French National Front became far more protectionist in their policies toward trade and labor markets.

There is widespread agreement that globalization has generated new 'winners' and 'losers' in advanced industrialized societies – providing opportunities for political parties to mobilize the latter. The question this chapter tackles, on which there is far less agreement, concerns the political consequences of these economic developments, and whether Authoritarian-Populist and Progressive-Populist parties have actually managed to mobilize the 'left-behinds.' If the answer is yes, then supporters of Authoritarian-Populist parties in Europe should be concentrated among the losers from globalization – in particular, unskilled workers in manufacturing industry, low-income households with minimal savings, and those dependent on unemployment benefits. At the local level, voting support for populist parties should also be disproportionately concentrated in those communities that have lost most from economic globalization.

There is some systematic evidence that radical right parties generally gain electorally after banking crashes; a comparison of historical financial crises in 20 advanced economies since the 1870s reported that far-right parties increased their average vote share by 30 percent after such events, although similar effects were not observed for non-financial economic shocks or normal recessions.[20] Econometric research supporting the economic grievance thesis has also been conducted at the regional level in Europe, finding that the share of votes cast for populist parties/leaders in local areas is correlated with the loss of jobs in the types of manufacturing industries that are most vulnerable to competition from cheaper Chinese imports.[21] In the US as well, the exposure of local labor markets to increased trade from China has been found to have affected voting in the 2016 US presidential election, with rising import competition strengthening Republican vote share gains.[22] But there is little consensus about these claims; in the case of the 2016 Brexit referendum, for example, ward-level analysis suggests that very little variation in the vote to leave the EU is explained by a local authority area's exposure to immigration and trade, or by the quality of public services and fiscal consolidation. Rather, a significant amount of the variation is linked to characteristics such as educational attainment, demography, and industry structure.[23]

The macro-level approach is often inconclusive because it is unable to disentangle economic features, such as the loss of blue-collar employment, from other characteristics of a given area. In particular, American counties switching from Blue to Red in the 2016 presidential election are distinctive culturally and in their social make-up, containing a higher proportion of older and less educated residents, as well as in their economic characteristics.[24] Thus, macro-level analysis is a blunt instrument for interpreting the meaning of factors correlated with the vote swings observed in local precincts. One difficulty facing analysts is that globalization is expanding networks of interdependence that follow the increasingly swift movement of ideas, money, goods, services, ecology, and people across territorial borders.[25] In practice, multiple dimensions of this phenomenon are often closely correlated, including open borders for the flow of refugees and media communications, and trade alliances, and membership of multilateral organizations.[26] In the Netherlands, for example, does resentment of resident Turks, Moroccans, and Indonesians reflect their willingness to take low-paid manual jobs, or does it reflect a broader intolerance against Muslim religious practices, or resentment of the fact that low-income immigrant families have access to welfare services?[27]

The macro-level evidence underpinning such claims remains inconclusive and debate continues about the relative importance of economic factors compared with cultural grievances, such as the role of authoritarianism, xenophobia, and racial prejudice.[28] Individual-level survey data allow far more fine-grained analysis, and do not provide consistent and clear-cut support for the economic insecurity thesis; for example, Americans working in manufacturing jobs – the sector most vulnerable to declining wages and security from global trade – were *not* more likely to have voted for Trump.[29] Similarly, the 2016 US election exit poll showed that the least well-off households (with annual household incomes below $50,000) voted disproportionately for Hillary Clinton, not Donald Trump, and household income levels were a poor predictor of candidate support.[30] Even if people feel economically insecure, or feel that the national economy is heading in the wrong direction, this does not necessarily mean that they blame the government for this problem – or that they want government to take a more active stance to redress the situation. Concern about rising inequality is strongest among liberals, stimulating the progressive populism linked with Bernie Sanders, but it is not an issue of great concern to Trump supporters and conservatives.[31]

## II TESTING INDIVIDUAL-LEVEL EVIDENCE FOR THE ECONOMIC GRIEVANCE THESIS

It is not clear that rising electoral support for populism is due to worsening economic conditions, such as growing income inequality, the loss of blue-collar jobs, exposure to trade shocks, or the impact of the financial crisis. The evidence needs to be carefully reexamined. What survey data allow us to test the economic grievance thesis?

If the thesis is correct, authoritarian and populist values should be most strongly endorsed by those living in low-income households, those with inadequate savings, people who have experienced long-term unemployment, blue-collar workers in manufacturing industries, and those living in households dependent on welfare benefits. Overall satisfaction with the performance of the national economy may also be important, if attitudes and values are shaped more by how people think the country is doing (reflecting 'socio-tropic' concerns), as standard theories of political economy suggest, rather than by their personal pocket-book finances (or ego-tropic concerns).[32] Negative valuations of economic conditions in each country would be expected to predict dissatisfaction with political elites and governing parties.

The individual-level survey evidence from the ESS allows us to test these propositions and see whether authoritarian and populist values are indeed strengthened, as these arguments predict, by 'objective' indices measuring occupational class (using the 5-category Goldthorpe schema)[33] and household income, employment in the manufacturing sector, direct experience of long-term unemployment (12 months or more), and dependency on state benefits (excluding pensions, to minimize age-effects). Our models also include 'subjective' feelings of financial insecurity (measured by the reported difficulty of living on the household's income) and satisfaction with the overall performance of the national economy.[34] The objective measures probably provide evidence that is more reliable to test the economic grievance thesis, because they are less likely to be contaminated by prior beliefs, such as partisanship or candidate preferences. By contrast, subjective attitudes are more vulnerable to problems of endogeneity. Nevertheless, similar findings with both types of indicators would increase confidence in the robustness of the results. In this chapter, OLS regression models for both authoritarian values and populist values are run separately. All models were tested to be free of multicollinearity. Evidence from the pooled European Social Survey 2002–2014 build upon the core models (distinguishing generational, period, and life-cycle effects) and the controls like education, religiosity, and sex, which were discussed in the previous chapter.

Table 5.1 presents the results of the OLS regression analysis models predicting support for authoritarian and populist values, generating several important findings.

Firstly, *both authoritarianism and populism are usually generally significantly stronger among less prosperous respondents*, confirming that these cultural values are indeed found among those people most likely to feel a sense of economic insecurity and grievances. In particular, five of the seven selected indices are indeed significant predictors of these cultural orientations, in the expected direction. Thus authoritarian values and populist attitudes are strongest among the working class, low-income households, those employed in the manufacturing sectors, people reporting subjective income insecurity (finding it difficult to live on their current household income), and those dissatisfied with the present state of the national economy. The primary exceptions – and these are important ones – concern indicators of direct experience of long-term unemployment and dependency upon state benefits, which were in the reverse direction to that expected theoretically.

At the same time, however, when the strength of the standardized betas are compared, important differences can be observed across both cultural dimensions.

TABLE 5.1. *Economic indicators predicting support for authoritarian and populist values*

| | | Model 1 Authoritarian values | | | | Model 2 Populist values | | | |
|---|---|---|---|---|---|---|---|---|---|
| | | B | SE | Beta | Sig. | B | SE | Beta | Sig. |
| Generation | Interwar (1900–1945) (Ref) | 0.00 | | | | 0.00 | | | |
| | Boomers (1946–1964) | −3.30 | 0.09 | −0.11 | *** | 0.74 | 0.13 | 0.02 | *** |
| | Generation X (1965–1979) | −4.44 | 0.10 | −0.14 | *** | 0.84 | 0.15 | 0.02 | *** |
| | Millennials (1980–1996) | −5.77 | 0.10 | −0.16 | *** | 0.85 | 0.14 | 0.02 | *** |
| Year | 2002 (Ref) | 0.00 | | | | 0.00 | | | |
| | 2004 | 1.09 | 0.12 | 0.03 | *** | −1.81 | 0.23 | −0.03 | *** |
| | 2006 | 2.20 | 0.16 | 0.05 | *** | 0.23 | 0.15 | 0.00 | N/s |
| | 2008 | 3.17 | 0.15 | 0.08 | *** | −3.43 | 0.14 | −0.06 | *** |
| | 2010 | 4.16 | 0.15 | 0.11 | *** | −3.43 | 0.14 | −0.06 | *** |
| | 2012 | 3.58 | 0.16 | 0.10 | *** | −0.66 | 0.16 | −0.01 | *** |
| | 2014 | 3.16 | 0.16 | 0.08 | *** | −0.86 | 0.16 | −0.01 | *** |
| Social | Education | −0.53 | 0.03 | −0.05 | *** | −0.46 | 0.04 | −0.03 | *** |
| | Sex (male) | −0.42 | 0.06 | −0.01 | *** | −0.01 | 0.09 | 0.00 | N/s |
| | Urbanization (1–5 scale Most rural to most urban) | 0.23 | 0.02 | 0.02 | *** | 0.09 | 0.03 | 0.01 | *** |
| | How religious are you on 10-pt scale | 1.09 | 0.01 | 0.23 | *** | −0.47 | 0.01 | −0.06 | *** |
| | Children | 1.17 | 0.07 | 0.04 | *** | 0.80 | 0.10 | 0.02 | *** |
| | Married | 2.66 | 0.15 | 0.07 | *** | 0.46 | 0.26 | 0.01 | N/s |
| | Separated or divorced | 0.92 | 0.20 | 0.01 | *** | 0.36 | 0.36 | 0.00 | N/s |

*(continued)*

TABLE 5.1 (*continued*)

| | | Model 1 Authoritarian values | | | | Model 2 Populist values | | | |
|---|---|---|---|---|---|---|---|---|---|
| | | B | SE | Beta | Sig. | B | SE | Beta | Sig. |
| Class | Manager | −1.79 | 0.12 | −0.04 | *** | −1.12 | 0.17 | −0.02 | *** |
| | Routine non-manual | −1.08 | 0.09 | −0.03 | *** | −0.43 | 0.13 | −0.01 | *** |
| | Petty bourgeoisie | −1.07 | 0.10 | −0.02 | *** | 0.59 | 0.15 | 0.01 | *** |
| | Skilled manual | 0.00 | 0.12 | 0.00 | N/s | 0.54 | 0.19 | 0.01 | *** |
| | Manual (Ref) | 0.00 | | | | 0.00 | | | |
| Economic | Work in manufacturing industry | 0.79 | 0.08 | 0.02 | *** | 1.58 | 0.12 | 0.03 | *** |
| | Household net income | −0.34 | 0.01 | −0.06 | *** | −0.22 | 0.02 | −0.03 | *** |
| | Subjective income insecurity | 1.18 | 0.04 | 0.07 | *** | 2.34 | 0.06 | 0.09 | *** |
| | Ever been unemployed for a period of 12 months or more | −1.37 | 0.07 | −0.04 | *** | 0.99 | 0.10 | 0.02 | *** |
| | Main source of income is unemployment or other social benefit | −2.69 | 0.15 | −0.04 | *** | −3.24 | 0.20 | −0.03 | *** |
| | How satisfied with present state of economy in country | −0.30 | 0.01 | −0.05 | *** | −4.36 | 0.02 | −0.50 | *** |
| | (Constant) | 69.99 | 0.23 | | *** | 80.31 | 0.29 | | *** |
| | $R^2$ | 0.14 | | | | 0.32 | | | |
| | N | 218,587 | | | 197,543 | | | | |

*Notes:* OLS regression models predicting citizen's support for authoritarian and populist values. P *** .001, ** .01, * .05, N/s Not significant. Note that the Interwar generation and the unskilled manual class are the excluded reference categories. For the construction of all measures, see Appendix B. The '*Authoritarian values*' standardized scale is based on combining five items using the Schwartz scale to measure the personal values of security, conformity, and tradition. The '*Populist attitudes*' standardized scale is based on combining mistrust in parliament, parties, and politicians.

*Source:* The European Social Survey, Cumulative File Rounds 1–7. N. 330,315 respondents in 31 European countries.

In particular, *authoritarian values are predicted more strongly by generational cohorts than by any of the economic indicators*. This implies that endorsement of values such as the importance of security against external threats, social conformity with traditional norms, racial prejudice and intolerance of ethnic minorities, and deferential loyalty toward authorities may be influenced most deeply by enduring experiences shared by each generational cohort during their formative years, such as the Interwar generation growing up during the era of the Great Depression and the outbreak of World War II, compared with Baby Boomers coming of age in a resurgent Europe with the establishment of welfare capitalism, then the era of sexual liberalization and the celebration of youth culture during the 1960s and 1970s. Generational experiences are stronger predictors of authoritarianism than any of the economic characteristics, such as occupational class and household income. This interpretation also implies that these orientations are likely to endure, providing a potential pool of older supporters for parties endorsing these values, even after any economic crisis passes and prosperity returns.

By contrast, however, although both economic and cultural factors are significant, *populist attitudes (mistrust of politicians, parliaments, and parties) are predicted slightly more strongly by subjective economic characteristics (feelings of economic insecurity and especially approval of the state of the national economy) than by birth cohort*. Even after controlling for many other factors, such as education, sex, and religiosity, households struggling to live on their income are more mistrustful of politics than those living more comfortable lives.[35] By far the strongest predictor of political mistrust, however, is how people felt about the state of the national economy. Those most dissatisfied with the performance of the economy expressed far less confidence in political institutions. These findings are consistent with previous findings that trust in political institutions and satisfaction with the performance of democracy are driven by macroeconomic performance (as measured by rates of inflation rates, unemployment, changes in real GDP and the size of the budget deficit).[36]

A note of caution is needed when interpreting these relationships. Although subjective economic attitudes are closely correlated with mistrust, the direction of causality in this association is not easily established from cross-sectional survey data. The way that governments mishandled the financial and debt crises would be expected to deepen mistrust. But the linkages may be reversed; citizens may judge the performance of the economy, and assign government responsibility for economic conditions, through the prism of their prior political preferences – avoiding cognitive dissonance and leading people to confirm what they already believe. For example, in the US there was a substantial jump in the proportion of Republicans expressing positive evaluations of the economic situation after Trump entered the White House, with the proportion saying that these conditions were 'very good' or 'somewhat good' doubling from 31 percent in February 2016 to 61 percent a year later. Yet the underlying economic indicators suggest only slow and steady improvements occurred during the same 12 month period, and Democratic views improved by only four percentage points.[37] Experimental research points to similar conclusions about how partisanship frames evaluations of government performance.[38] Moreover, according to the standardized betas, the impact on mistrust of the *objective* economic indices, such as occupational class, experience of long-term unemployment or household income, were similar in strength to those for the generational cohort effects.

Are authoritarian and populist values also shaped by period-effects, with these values and attitudes becoming less favorable during the years when the European financial and debt crisis worsened economic conditions? In the pooled survey, the association between the survey year and authoritarian values strengthened over successive surveys from 2002 to 2010, before subsequently weakening somewhat. These effects increased as the crisis progressively deepened, before falling again slightly, after the recovery started in many European countries. On the other hand, the impact of period-effects on populist values was inconsistent. European countries varied substantially in how they fared following the 2007 financial crash; hence unemployment soared for many years following the Eurozone debt crisis in Spain, Portugal, and Greece, while the stronger economies in Northern Europe and Scandinavia recovered relatively well.[39] To explore this issue further, we need to consider the different performances of the economy among debtor and creditor European countries, as examined in Part IV, rather than assuming that the effects of the crisis were common across all societies.

## III LONGITUDINAL EFFECTS

To throw additional light on long-term trends, we can consider longitudinal survey evidence examining annual changes in the proportion of materialist and post-materialist values by birth cohort for the period from 1970 to 2008 for six West European societies. The data allow us to examine the impact of rising and falling economic conditions, such as the levels of inflation and unemployment, on post-material values over more than a quarter century, well before the onset of the 2007 financial crisis. Longitudinal data over this extended period allow us to examine whether normal fluctuations in economic conditions function as period-effects, reinforcing or modifying the effects of cohort change.

The previous chapter showed how support for socially conservative and authoritarian values reflects a long-term process of cultural evolution, triggering a backlash among traditionalists seeking to hold back the rising tide of social liberalism. Millennials endorse socially liberal attitudes and post-materialist values, while the oldest (Interwar) cohort holds values that are more socially conservative and authoritarian, in an enduring intergenerational clash.[40] But during recent decades rising economic inequality and declining job security, together with the 2007–2013 financial crisis in Europe triggered by the US housing crash, may have generated a period-effect. The literature suggests that insecurity is conducive to in-group solidarity, rigid conformity to group norms, and rejection of outsiders, leading people to seek strong, authoritarian leaders to protect them from dangerous outsiders seen as threatening peoples' jobs and personal safety.[41]

The fact that birth-cohort effects can coexist with period-effects is not intuitively obvious and tends to be overlooked. But birth-cohort effects can help explain why given *individuals* endorse authoritarian and populist values – while at the *societal* level, support for authoritarian and populist values may become stronger or weaker across all birth cohorts in response to current conditions.

More than 40 years ago, *The Silent Revolution* argued that when people grow up taking survival for granted, they become more open to new ideas and more tolerant of out-groups. Accordingly, the growing affluence experienced in the European recovery after World War II, rebuilding the economy and welfare states, gave rise to an intergenerational shift toward post-materialist values. Baby Boomers, born between 1946 and 1964, grew up under conditions of peace and unprecedented prosperity. These conditions were present from their earliest memories and they took them for granted – bringing an intergenerational shift toward post-materialist and socially liberal values. Economic reconstruction and welfare states emerged soon after 1945 but their impact on prevailing values involved a long time-lag – it did not become evident until the Baby Boomers first became old enough to be politically relevant, launching the student protest of the late-1960s and 1970s. While materialists give top priority to economic and physical security, Post-Materialists are less conformist, more open to new ideas, less authoritarian, and more tolerant of out-groups. Rising security brought growing emphasis on freedom of expression, democratization, environmental protection, gender equality, and tolerance of gays, handicapped people, and foreigners.[42] Conversely, our theory holds, economic downturns have the opposite effect. In keeping with our theory, post-materialist values are most widespread among the younger, more secure strata of developed societies, and are almost absent in low-income countries. Growth in GDP has continued, but in recent decades, almost all of the gains have gone to the top 10 percent; the losers from economic globalization have experienced declining real income and status that has stimulated the authoritarian-populist backlash.

What data support the period-effects thesis? Materialist/post-materialist values have been measured in Eurobarometer and World Values Surveys carried out in several West European countries for almost every year from 1970 to 2009, providing a detailed time series covering four decades – making it possible to carry out the cohort analysis needed to determine whether the hypothesized period-effects exist. These surveys asked people which goals they considered most important, choosing between such aspects as economic growth, rising prices, maintaining order, and the fight against crime (which tap materialist priorities); and freedom of speech, giving people more say in important government decisions, and more say on the job (which tap post-materialist priorities).[43] Representative national surveys in 1970 asked these questions in Great Britain, France, Italy, West Germany, Belgium, and the Netherlands.

The responses revealed large differences between the values of younger and older generations in all six countries. Among those aged 65 and older, people with materialist values outnumbered those with post-materialist values by more than 14:1 But as one moves from older to younger cohorts, the balance gradually shifts toward a growing proportion of post-materialists. Among the youngest cohort (those 18 to 25 years old in 1970), post-materialists outnumber materialists.

But do these age differences reflect enduring birth cohort effects or transient life-cycle effects? A life-cycle interpretation implies that the post-war Baby Boom cohort became increasingly materialist as they aged, so that by the time they were 65 years old they were just as materialist as the 65 year olds were in 1970 – and society as a whole will not change at all. The generational-effects interpretation implies that the younger birth cohorts will remain relatively post-materialist over time – so that as they replace the older, more materialist cohorts, society's prevailing values *will* change.

Figure 5.1 shows the results of a cohort analysis based on over 300,000 interviews that follows given birth cohorts over four decades.[44]

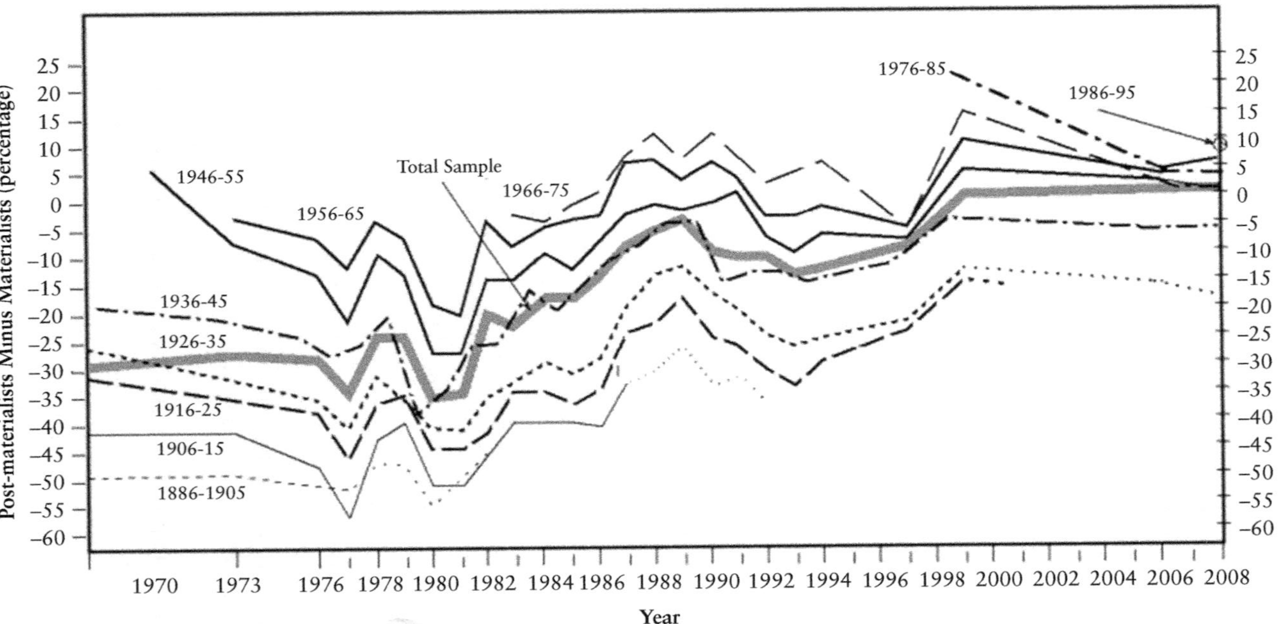


FIGURE 5.1. *Cohort analysis of value change, Europe 1970–2009*
*Note:* Percentage of post-materialists minus percentage of materialists by birth cohort in six West European countries, 1971 to 2009 (countries are Britain, France, West Germany, Italy, Belgium, and the Netherlands).
*Source:* Data from 1970 through 1997 are from Euro-Barometer surveys; data for 1999, 2006, and 2008–2009 are from European Values Study/World Values Survey.

This figure pools the data from all six countries in order to provide sufficiently large samples to estimate each cohort's position at a given time – which is calculated by subtracting the percentage of materialists from the percentage of post-materialists. Thus, at the zero point on the vertical axis, the two groups are equally numerous. The proportion of post-materialists increases as one moves up, while the proportion of materialists increases as one moves down.

If the age differences in Figure 5.1 reflected life-cycle effects, then each of the lines on this figure would shift downward as they moved to the right, with each cohort becoming more materialist as it aged. If the age differences reflected stable birth cohort effects, the lines would be horizontal, with each cohort remaining about as post-materialist at the end of the time series as it was at the start.

But we also need to take period-effects into account. Our theory implies that events that undermine existential security, such as major recessions, terrorist attacks, or a banking crash, will push all cohorts downward in response to current conditions. The detailed data from the long time series in Figure 5.1 show that period-effects clearly *are* present. These fluctuations reflect contemporary economic conditions, particularly inflation.[45] During periods of economic downturn, each birth cohort becomes more materialist; with recovery, each birth cohort moves back up – but the *differences* between given generations remain stable. The younger cohorts remain relatively post-materialist despite short-term fluctuations. Over four decades, we find no overall tendency for the members of given birth cohorts to become more materialist as they age.

During this four-decade span, the three oldest birth cohorts left the sample. They were replaced by three younger cohorts, born in 1956–1965, 1966–1975, and 1976–1985. This brought a substantial shift toward post-materialist values. The heavy shaded line on Figure 5.1 shows the net shift toward post-materialist values among the adult population as a whole at various time points. In the early 1970s, materialists heavily outnumbered post-materialists in all six countries. During the ensuing years, major shifts occurred. By 1999, post-materialists were slightly more numerous than materialists in Western Europe (and twice as numerous as materialists in the US). The predicted shift toward post-materialist values took place. From 1970 to 1999, the shaded line rose from −30 to the zero point where post-materialists are as numerous as materialists.

But the upward trend shown by the heavy shaded line on Figure 5.1 subsequently leveled off; from 1999 to 2008, the trend was flat. Although intergenerational population replacement is still taking place, in recent years it seems to have been offset by powerful period-effects linked with declining economic security. Millennials face greater risk of unemployment, stagnant wages, welfare cuts, and growing levels of student debt, so they are no longer growing up under dramatically more secure conditions than their elders. The declining strength of organized labor, economic liberalization, and the opening of borders to the free flow of labor, goods, trade, and services, has brought falling real income and the loss of job security to unskilled workers and the less educated populations in Western societies.

## IV COMPARING COUNTRIES AND REGIONS

Another way to understand these issues is through comparing geographic variations across EU member states as well as across local regions within each society. The cultural and political impact of long-term trends in economic globalization, opening markets to the flow of goods and labor across national borders, is expected to be deepened and accelerated by the shock of the financial and Eurozone debt crisis. The banking crash first struck in late 2007 and developed into a full-blown crisis with the collapse of the investment bank Lehman Brothers on September 15, 2008. Many Americans lost their homes to foreclosure and house prices plummeted (in December 2008 the Case–Shiller home price index reported its largest price drop in its history), in scope and scale representing the worst downturn since the Great Recession of the 1930s.[46] As a result, the US economy contracted from 2007 to 2009, as Figure 5.2 shows; millions were thrown out of work, countless companies went bankrupt, and consumer confidence nosedived.

Like dominoes, the aftershocks spread across the Atlantic, catalyzing the Eurozone debt crisis in late 2009.[47] Some members of Europe's 19-country euro-currency union saw a sharp decline in GDP growth, which then recovered relatively fast, as shown by trends in annual GDP growth in Figure 5.2. Thus, Germany, which suffered a sharp downturn in 2009, snapped back quickly, thanks to strict banking and credit regulations and Chinese hunger for German products, which compensated for lost sales in the slumping Eurozone. Growth in several other EU member states, like Austria, Belgium, and France, fell temporarily then pulled back to former levels. Among the post-communist economies, as Figure 5.2 shows, after a period of growth, several states saw a deep plunge – notably in Estonia, Latvia, Lithuania, and Ukraine, before subsequently recovering.

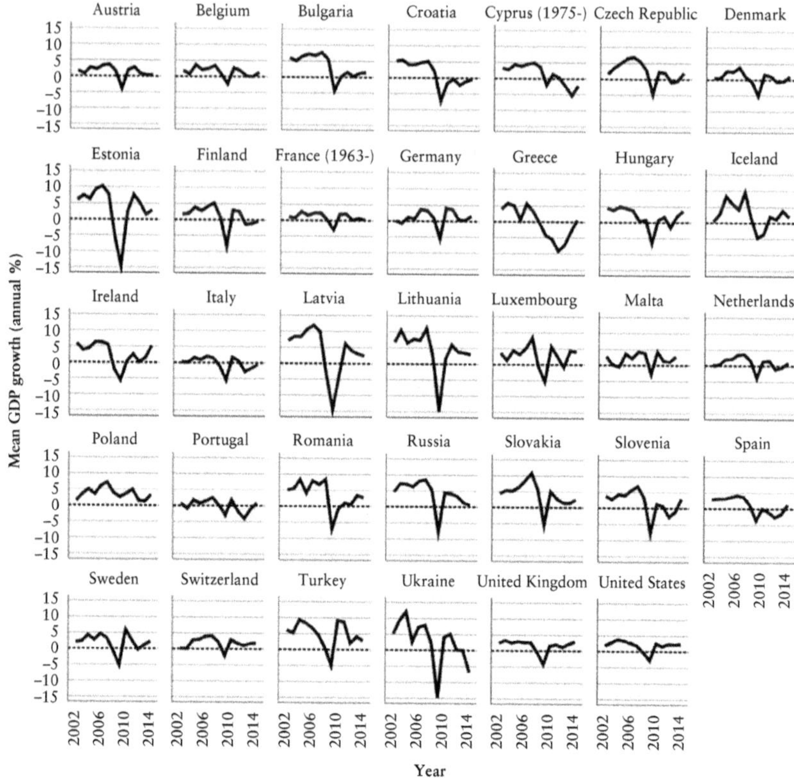


FIGURE 5.2. *Annual economic growth during the financial crisis, Europe and the US*

*Note:* Annual percent change in GDP, Europe, and the US.

*Source:* World Development Indicators, World Bank, Washington DC. https://data.worldbank.org/indicator/NY.GDP.PCAP.CD?end=2016&start=1978.

The effects were deeper and more protracted in Southern Europe, which experienced major destabilization. To be part of the Eurozone, member states had to meet the terms of the treaty in their budget deficits, inflation, interest rates, and other monetary requirements. When they failed to do so, governments in Greece, Spain, Portugal, and Cyprus (as well as Ireland) were unable to repay their debt or bail out banks, forcing them to adopt austerity packages and structural reforms as part of the IMF and EU rescue. The most extreme case is Greece; economic output has fallen by more than one-fourth since 2010, about a quarter of the work force is unemployed, and about half of all bank loans are in default.[48] The Greek economy still had not recovered by late 2017: per capita GDP was under $18,000, about half the level of its pre-crisis peak in 2008. The dramatic shock to the Greek economy might explain the political backlash, including the rise of the ultranationalist Golden Dawn, which gained seats for the first time in 2012.[49] Major financial crises (characterized by bank runs, sharp increases in default rates, bankruptcies, and large losses of capital) also seem to fuel support for political extremism; one longitudinal study examined parliamentary election results in 20 post-industrial societies from 1870 to 2014, finding that far right parties experienced an average rise of about 30 percent in their vote share in the five years after a systemic financial crisis.[50] By contrast, no equivalent gains were recorded for far left parties (and no similar effects were observed for recessions or economic downturns without a financial crash).

As Figure 5.2 shows, the 2008 financial crisis had very different impacts across Europe.[51] The rise of the ultranationalist and racist Golden Dawn in Greece, led by Nikolaos Michaloliakos, and the conservative populist Independent Greek (ANEL) party seem to reflect the consequences of the financial crash in a relatively straightforward fashion.[52] Even as the world was recovering from the 2008 meltdown, Greece provoked a Eurozone crisis in 2009–2010, when it revealed that it was far deeper in debt than official figures showed. Greek leaders have been in nearly continuous conflict with other Eurozone states over the terms of aid needed to prevent the economy from collapsing. Greece suffered more than any other Eurozone country from the consequences of the crash. Golden Dawn had been a fringe factor in Greek elections before the crash, but it entered parliament for the first time in 2012 with 21 seats and 7 percent of the popular vote, maintaining this level in subsequent contests. The party has been accused of carrying out acts of violence against immigrants, political opponents, homosexuals, and ethnic minorities.[53] The 2007–2013 financial crisis had destabilizing effects on Greece: a large share of the professional middle class employed in the public sector experienced declining real wages and loss of job security. This country has also been at the forefront of a massive influx of sea-borne immigrants and refugees seeking to escape conflict and extreme poverty in Syria, Afghanistan, and Ethiopia, through the route across the Mediterranean.

Similarly, in Spain, the rise of Podemos, founded in March 2014 by Pablo Iglesias as a progressive populist party, has been widely interpreted as a response to economic conditions, including the Eurozone debt crisis and the subsequent recession, problems of corruption and inequality, and record levels of youth unemployment.[54] In the December 20, 2015 parliamentary elections, Podemos surged to receive 21 percent of the vote, becoming Spain's third largest party in parliament, with 69 out of 350 seats. Nevertheless, the role of the economy in explaining the new party's success in the polls has been challenged, with some arguing that it was more closely tied to declining support for Spain's two party system.[55] Moreover, Podemos supporters are not the primary losers from globalization and the economic crisis; instead, they are characterized by a combination of protest, anti-mainstream sentiment, and unfulfilled expectations.[56]

The cases of Greece and Spain therefore seem to fit the economic narrative. Previous research finds that the financial crisis weakened citizen's trust in political institutions most in Southern Europe, where the crisis had the most severe impact on the economy.[57] More broadly, economic dissatisfaction may also engender criticism of the regime and distrust of politicians; other studies find that perceptions of the state of the economy also influence both satisfaction with, and support for, democracy in Europe.[58] Instrumental theories suggest that populist feelings in the electorate are likely to rise and fall with economic ups and downs.

But other previous cross-national evidence examining the national-level correlations between economic factors and votes for radical right parties has shown mixed results. Hence, some researchers have found a positive association between party votes and unemployment rates,[59] while others have found negative effects.[60] Another study also found a poor fit between a country's exposure to the financial crisis and the electoral fortunes of far-right parties, concluding: 'When looking at the overall picture, indicators such as unemployment, inequality, immigration and perceptions of immigration do not seem to have a clear-cut effect on the rise of far right-wing parties.'[61]

Several national cases also seem to undermine the economic grievance thesis: some European countries badly affected by the financial crash, including Ireland and Portugal, have not seen populist contenders enter their party systems. Conversely, authoritarian-populist forces have gained ground in Sweden, Germany, Norway, and Denmark, some of the most egalitarian and affluent European societies, with cradle-to-grave welfare systems, containing some of the world's best educated and most secure populations.

In Sweden, for example, the socially conservative and nationalist Swedish Democrats led by Jimmie Åkesson entered the Riksdag for the first time in 2010, winning 5.7 percent of the vote and 20 seats, more than doubling their support in 2014 to become the third largest party with 12.9 percent of the vote and 49 seats. In the September 2018 elections, they advanced further, gaining 62 seats with 17.5 percent of the vote. The Swedish economy contracted deeply in 2008–2009, but then recovered. Sweden currently enjoys a per capita GDP of $53,000, the 11th highest in the world.[62] Likewise in Germany, the powerhouse of the European economy with export-led growth and low unemployment, the radical anti-immigrant AFD broke through to enter the Bundestag for the first time in 2017.

Similarly, Norway, ranks 4th globally in per capita gross domestic product, education, and life expectancy.[63] It comes near the top among all nations in happiness, which is attributed to high levels of caring, freedom, generosity, honesty, health, income, and good governance.[64] Norway has a generous and comprehensive welfare state, with lengthy paid parental leave, free university education, and long-term unemployment benefits. The rate of unemployment in recent years has been below 4.5 percent. Norway's total poverty rates and levels of income inequality are both ranked 7th lowest among all OECD countries.[65] In 2014, the Norwegian economy was hurt by falling energy prices but since then jobs and consumer confidence have recovered; in 2016, the World Bank estimated that Norway ranked as the world's 4th most prosperous country, with its per capita GDP of US$70,812 (in purchasing power parity).[66]

Nevertheless, in the September 11, 2017 Norwegian parliamentary elections, the Progress Party (FrP) led by Siv Jensen came third with 15.2 percent of the vote and 27/169 seats, beating more than 20 rivals including the Green Party, the Liberal Party, and the Center Party.[67] The Social Democrats were again defeated by the right despite their historical predominance. Jensen campaigned as a hard-liner on immigration, pushing through tighter controls on migrants entering from Sweden and via the border with Russia. In its party conference before the election, the Progress Party (FrP) voted to ban hijabs in public schools, as well as forbidding the Jewish rite of circumcision. The ruling minority coalition of the Conservatives and the populist Progress Party, together with two small center-right allies, was returned to government with a slim governing majority of 89 seats in the 169-seat parliament under Prime Minister Erna Solberg. The fact that Authoritarian-Populist parties have become powerful, even in societies with widespread prosperity and comprehensive welfare services such as Norway, Denmark, Switzerland, the Netherlands, and Sweden, implies that the economic grievance thesis alone cannot explain their electoral success.

In Central and Eastern Europe, Hungary, Poland, the Czech Republic, and Slovakia have enjoyed rising living standards and rapid economic growth, compared with other post-communist societies, yet they have also experienced a series of populist gains. A comparative study of the region concluded that the emergence of this party family cannot be linked straightforwardly to adverse economic conditions.[68] Nor do populist parties follow a common economic philosophy; thus, some such as SNS in Slovakia are market oriented, while others such as Ataka in Bulgaria and Jobbik in Hungary favor a partial return to state ownership.

In Hungary, the Movement for a Better Hungary (Jobbik) was on the fringe in the 2006 parliamentary elections, with only 2.2 percent of the vote. But their support shot up to 16.7 percent in the elections of 2010 and to 20.7 percent in April 2014. It is defined as a 'conservative and radically patriotic' party based on Christian moral values, anti-immigrant, and anti-Roma, with protectionist left-wing economic policies. The party has also influenced the agenda of Fidetz, whose leader, Victor Orban became Prime Minister for his second term in 2010. As well as building tighter border walls restricting the flow of immigrants, and refusing to take even a small quota of refugees, he has implemented illiberal constitutional changes that have centralized executive power, curbed civil liberties, restricted freedom of speech, and weakened the Constitutional Court and judiciary. In Poland, the socially conservative and anti-immigrant populist Law and Justice (PiS) party almost tripled its support in 2005 to win 27 percent of the vote, before advancing to form a government with an outright parliamentary majority in 2015. The government has subsequently cracked down on the private news media for covering opposition protests, as well as passing laws giving PiS the power to appoint judges and dismiss members of the supreme court.[69] In the Czech Republic, Andrej Babis, an oligarch and wealthy businessman, controlling several media outlets, founded a movement in 2012. He then rode a wave of anger toward the corruption and complacency of conventional politics, winning a resounding election to become Prime Minister in October 2017. Babis has advocated strengthening the powers of the executive and like other East European leaders, he takes a hardline against accepting migrants, especially Muslims. The rise of populism in all of these countries has occurred despite experiencing a sustained period of economic growth and increased prosperity since they joined the European Union, with growing consumer confidence and investment – and, as Figure 5.1 shows, per capita GDP was fairly steady during the last decade.

Moreover, according to the World Inequality Database (WID), there are striking cross-national variations in contemporary levels of social and economic inequality that reflect each country's history. Sweden stands out: though it had substantially more inequality than the US in the early twentieth century, by the 1920s Sweden had attained more egalitarian distribution of wealth and income than America – and it has maintained these conditions to the present. In the US, the top decile got almost half of the total income in 2014, while in Sweden it got only 30 percent (World Inequality Database [WID] WID.world). The advanced welfare state culture introduced by Sweden's long-dominant Social Democrats, had lasting effects. Conversely, in Anglo-American democracies, the neo-conservative regimes led by Ronald Reagan and Margaret Thatcher in the 1980s left a heritage in which conservatives in those countries seek to reduce government expenditures with almost religious zeal – and the US and United Kingdom now show greater income inequality than most other developed capitalist societies. In America, although real income has stagnated or shrunk for a growing share of the population, the inflation-controlled cost of attending college for four years has more than doubled since 1981, making social mobility increasingly difficult.[70] This is shaping how many Americans see their social position: in 2000, 33 percent of the public described themselves as 'working class'; by 2015, that figure had risen to 48 percent.[71] The safety net is unraveling, as politicians and corporations cut back on healthcare, income security, and retirement pensions.[72] Stiglitz argues convincingly that a minority of extremely rich individuals has attained tremendous political influence in the US, which they are using to shape policies that systematically increase the concentration of wealth, undermining economic growth, and diminishing investment in education, research, and infrastructure.[73] Similarly, Hacker and Pierson argue that politics in the US is dominated by an alliance between big business and conservative politicians that has cut maximum taxes for the rich from 75 percent in 1970 to less than 35 percent in 2004 and sharply reduced regulation of the economy and financial markets.[74] The Republicans under Trump have slashed taxes for corporate America, while leaving most middle-class households largely unchanged.[75]

To examine the cross-national evidence, levels of political mistrust in European societies can be compared with several aggregate economic performance indicators in each country, such as rates of unemployment and growth. But any correlations would be conditioned by the accuracy of citizen's awareness and knowledge of such indicators. Public perceptions of socio-tropic economic performance are also potentially colored by cues derived from prior partisanship or information from the media. A more reliable test of the thesis comes from comparing the relationship in each society between populist attitudes (measured by citizen's political distrust of parties, politicians, and parliaments) and feelings of personal economic insecurity (as measured on a four-point scale ranging from whether respondents reported living comfortably to those saying it was very difficult to live on their current household income). Reports of one's personal experiences may be conflated by a social desirability bias but they are less vulnerable to potential problems of endogeneity.

As Table 5.2 indicates, the results show that populism was significantly correlated with feelings of personal income insecurity in 30 out of 32 societies under comparison (the exceptions were Turkey and Luxembourg). The correlations were particularly strong in Belgium, Germany, Estonia, and the Netherlands. In general, Figure 5.4 demonstrates how personal income insecurity consistently deepens feelings of political distrust. These findings make intuitive sense and are consistent with standard instrumental theories of economic voting; on rational grounds, citizens' confidence in representative institutions in democratic societies and trust in politicians should fluctuate according to their evaluations of policy performance.[76] Where governing parties and elected representatives are seen as delivering prosperity for the country – and where citizens are satisfied with the pocket book economy – this should engender greater trust in the political system and satisfaction with the its performance. By contrast, citizens should become more critical of governing elites, and less trusting of established parties and politicians, in countries afflicted with rising levels of unemployment, growing rifts between rich and poor, and austerity cuts to public services. Figure 5.4 illustrates how populist values were strongly correlated with personal income insecurity at national level, showing a linear relationship, with countries such as Bulgaria and Ukraine displaying the greatest political distrust and income insecurity – in stark contrast to Denmark, Switzerland, and Norway, where attitudes toward politics were more trusting and people's lives were more comfortable.

Now let us compare correlations between authoritarian values (as measured by the Schwartz scale) and income insecurity in each country. Here the results are less consistent; the correlations were significant in most countries under comparison (19 out of the 32), but the relationships were relatively weak. As Figure 5.5 illustrates, support for authoritarian values varied far less than populism according to one's level of income insecurity. Authoritarian values seem to be more enduring than political mistrust, with emphasis on social conformity and rejection of outsiders being mainly linked with pre-adult formative experiences, although contemporary socio-economic conditions also have some effect. Figure 5.5 illustrates that at the national level, reported income insecurity was correlated with authoritarian values – but the relationship was relatively weak. It is also noteworthy that despite both Spain and Greece being hard-hit by the Eurozone debt crisis, these countries are not located close together on either scatterplot.

TABLE 5.2. *Authoritarian and populist values correlated with income insecurity, 32 countries*

| | Authoritarian values | | Populist values | |
|---|---|---|---|---|
| Austria | 0.03 | ** | 0.13 | ** |
| Belgium | 0.11 | ** | 0.21 | ** |
| Bulgaria | 0.07 | ** | 0.09 | ** |
| Switzerland | 0.07 | ** | 0.11 | ** |
| Cyprus | −0.01 | N/s | 0.10 | ** |
| Czech Republic | 0.04 | ** | 0.15 | ** |
| Germany | 0.03 | ** | 0.22 | *** |
| Denmark | 0.01 | N/s | 0.14 | ** |
| Estonia | 0.11 | ** | 0.20 | *** |
| Spain | 0.05 | ** | 0.13 | *** |
| Finland | 0.00 | N/s | 0.17 | ** |
| France | 0.08 | ** | 0.17 | *** |
| UK | 0.01 | N/s | 0.17 | ** |
| Greece | 0.01 | N/s | 0.14 | ** |
| Croatia | 0.06 | ** | 0.05 | ** |
| Hungary | 0.02 | N/s | 0.14 | *** |
| Ireland | 0.00 | N/s | 0.23 | ** |
| Israel | 0.09 | ** | 0.13 | ** |
| Iceland | −0.03 | N/s | 0.19 | *** |
| Italy | 0.06 | ** | 0.15 | *** |
| Lithuania | −0.02 | N/s | 0.17 | *** |
| Luxembourg | 0.06 | * | 0.03 | N/s |
| Netherlands | 0.06 | ** | 0.24 | *** |
| Norway | 0.00 | N/s | 0.15 | *** |
| Poland | 0.09 | ** | 0.12 | ** |
| Portugal | 0.01 | N/s | 0.17 | ** |
| Russia | 0.07 | ** | 0.09 | ** |
| Sweden | 0.09 | ** | 0.15 | *** |
| Slovenia | 0.13 | ** | 0.16 | *** |
| Slovakia | 0.01 | N/s | 0.10 | ** |
| Turkey | 0.00 | N/s | 0.00 | N/s |
| Ukraine | 0.06 | ** | 0.05 | ** |

*Note:* The '*Authoritarian values*' standardized scale is based on combining five items using the Schwartz scale to measure the personal values of security, conformity, and tradition. The '*Populist attitudes*' standardized scale is based on combining mistrust in parliament, parties, and politicians. Correlations. P *** .001, ** .01, * .05, N/s Not significant. For the construction of all measures, see Appendix B.

*Source:* The European Social Survey, Cumulative File Rounds 1–7. N. 330,315 respondents in 32 European countries.

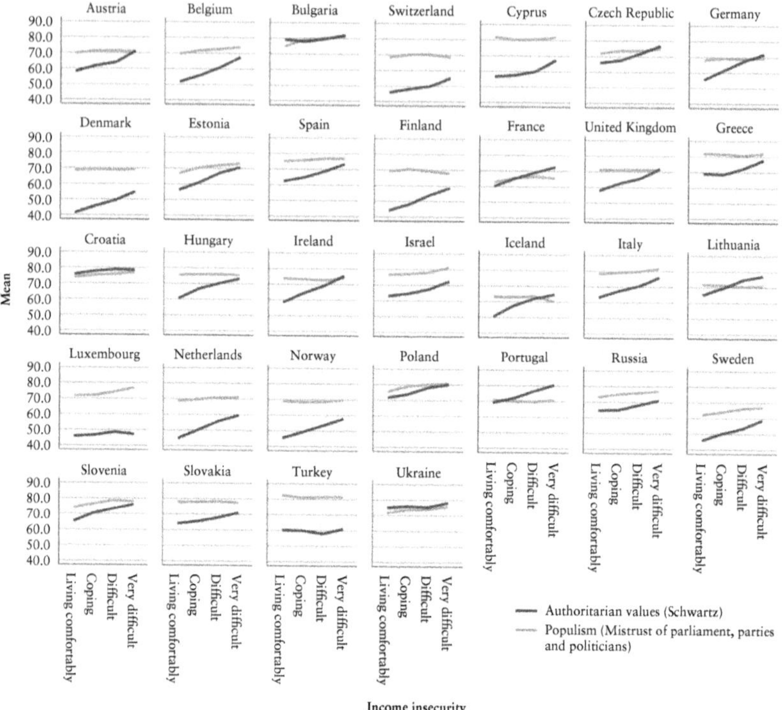


FIGURE 5.3. *Authoritarian values and populist attitudes by feelings of financial security, Europe*

*Note:* The '*Authoritarian values*' standardized scale is based on combining five items using the Schwartz scale to measure the personal values of security, conformity, and tradition. The '*Populist attitudes*' standardized scale is based on combining mistrust in parliament, parties, and politicians. The trend lines illustrate the mean scores for these scales by subjective feelings of income insecurity, measured by the reported difficulty of living on the household's present income. For the construction of all measures, see Appendix B.

*Source:* The European Social Survey, Cumulative File Rounds 1–7. N. 330,315 respondents in 32 European countries.

Reported levels of personal income insecurity may reflect a more general feeling of hard-times colored by cultural grievances, such as the feeling that, regardless of one's take home pay, other groups are moving ahead faster. Do objective official statistics support this idea? Here we can turn to Eurostat estimates of the proportion of people at risk of poverty in each country, based on their income, material deprivation, and social exclusion. This includes persons with a disposable income below 60 percent of the national median disposable income (after social transfers). Material deprivation covers living conditions such as being unable to pay rent or utility bills, keep their home adequately warm, and without access

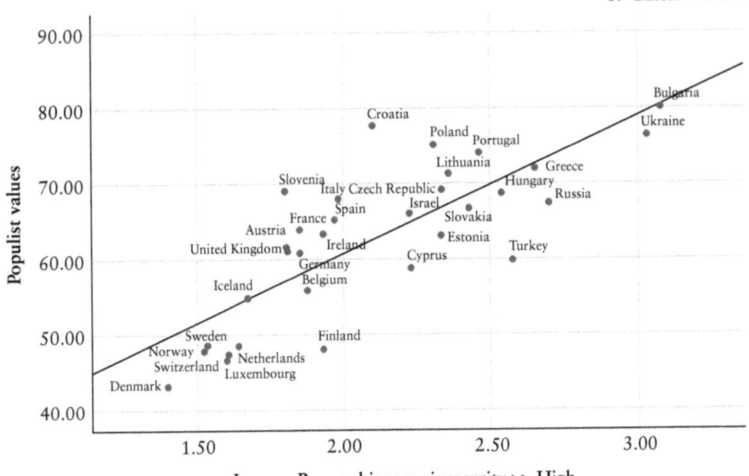


FIGURE 5.4. *Populist attitudes and personal income insecurity, national level*
*Note:* The '*Populist attitudes*' standardized scale is based on combining mistrust in parliament, parties, and politicians. Personal income insecurity 4-point scale ranging from 'living comfortably' to 'very difficult to live on present income,' (ESS). For the construction of all measures, see Appendix B.
*Source:* The European Social Survey, Cumulative File Rounds 1–7.

$R^2$ Quadratic = 0.481

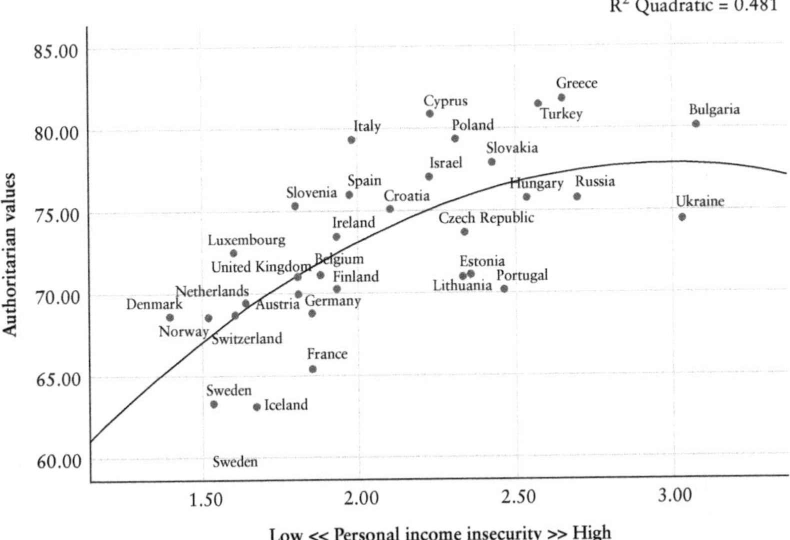


FIGURE 5.5. *Authoritarian values and personal income insecurity, national level*
*Note:* The '*Authoritarian values*' standardized scale is based on combining five items using the Schwartz scale to measure the personal values of security, conformity, and tradition. Personal income insecurity 4-point scale ranging from reporting, 'living comfortably' to reporting 'very difficult to live on present income,' (ESS). For the construction of all measures, see Appendix B.
*Source:* The European Social Survey, Cumulative File Rounds 1–7.

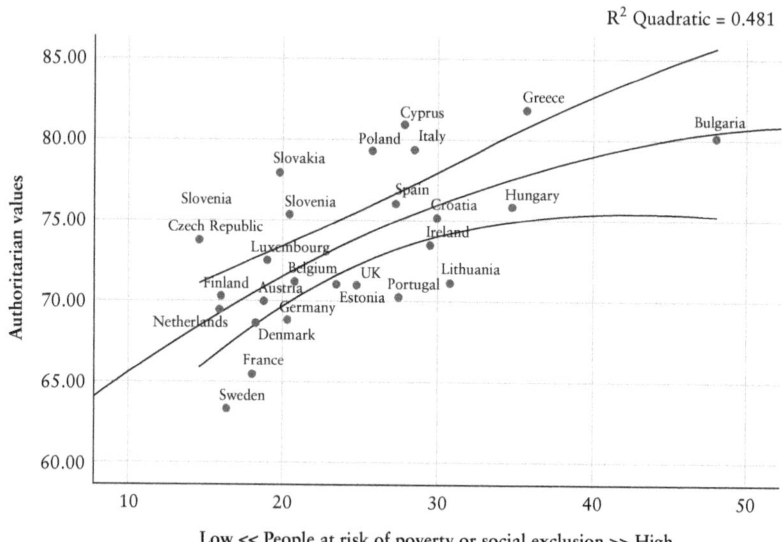


FIGURE 5.6. *Authoritarian values and proportion of persons at risk of poverty or social exclusion, EU 2014*

*Notes:* The '*Authoritarian values*' standardized scale is based on combining five items using the Schwartz scale to measure the personal values of security, conformity, and tradition. The *proportion of persons at risk of poverty or social exclusion* in each country is derived from the Eurostat estimates combining disposable income, material deprivation, and low work intensity. See the text for details.

*Sources:* The European Social Survey, Cumulative File Rounds 1–7. Eurostat http://ec.europa.eu/eurostat/web/products-datasets/-/tsdsc100.

to consumer durables such as a washing machine, a color TV, or a telephone. People living in households with very low work intensity, where the adults had worked a fifth or less of their total work potential during the past year. As shown in Figure 5.6, authoritarian values are strongly predicted by the proportion of people at risk of poverty in EU countries (R = 0.634** N.25). Countries with the highest risks of poverty, such as Bulgaria, Greece, and Hungary, are also with the highest endorsement of authoritarian values. By contrast, European nations with the lowest risks of poverty and deprivation, such as Sweden, France, and Denmark, had relatively low levels of authoritarian values.

But nation-level comparisons are only part of the story. We also need to consider the geographic effects on cultural values of living in certain regions. This argument gains support from American evidence showing widening political–geographic divisions between the Republican heartland and the Democratic coastal cities. Thus, in the 2016 election, the white rural counties in key Mid-West states such as Pennsylvania and Michigan swung disproportionately toward Trump, while the Democrats performed better in large metropolitan areas and surrounding suburbs.[77] Socio-economic indicators – poverty levels, median earnings, labor force participation, longevity, and unemployment rates – are generally worse in American counties dependent upon farming, mining, and manufacturing than in urban areas.[78] Trump also strongly outperformed the Romney vote in counties with severe social and economic problems, including substance abuse, alcoholism, and suicide rates, exemplified by the scourge of soaring white opioid addiction and its devastating effects on local communities.[79] Trump performed best in places where the economy was at its worst, beating Clinton in counties with slower job growth and lower wages, and far outperforming her in counties where jobs were most threatened by automation or offshoring. Similarly, the vote shifted most strongly from Obama (in 2012) to Trump (in 2016) in counties that experienced economic decline.[80]

Yet local economic conditions are not necessarily the main reason underlying the geographic divide in the American electorate, since rural and urban counties also differ sharply in many other respects. This includes the distribution of Democrat-leaning college-educated populations and the proportion of black and Hispanic residents in coastal cities, and the location of Republican-leaning white Evangelicals and older populations in heartland America. Cultural grievances may also be critical, if rural residents living in fly-over states feel resentful that their concerns are neglected by the political elites in Washington.[81] There are strong indications from individual-level survey data that economic factors alone are not a sufficient explanation for the outcome of the 2016 elections. In both exit polls and the ANES, the lowest income households (with less than $50k annually) were sharply divided by race, with Clinton winning a plurality of voters in this category as a whole, but with Trump having an edge among poor *white* households. The economic grievance thesis has also been applied to analyses of the spatial distribution of voting support for populist parties in European countries and sub-regions, where studies find that the populist vote is strongest in areas with high unemployment and poor economic conditions.[82]

To examine the European evidence, Table 5.3 examines the linkage between 14 indicators of socio-economic conditions at the regional level in 112 sub-national areas, and our measures of support for authoritarian values and populist attitudes. Like the national-level patterns already observed, the results of these region-level analyses confirm that populist

TABLE 5.3. *Regional predictors of authoritarian values and populist attitudes*

| | Authoritarian values | | Populist attitudes | |
|---|---|---|---|---|
| | R | P | R | P |
| GDP at current market prices – Euro per inhabitant, 2014 | −0.48 | ** | −0.74 | ** |
| Total population change, 2014 | −0.27 | ** | −0.64 | ** |
| Net migration plus statistical adjustment, 2014 | −0.24 | * | −0.59 | ** |
| Fertility rates, 2014 | −0.60 | ** | −0.41 | ** |
| Crude rate of natural change of population, 2014 | −0.16 | | −0.33 | ** |
| Life expectancy at age less than one year, 2014 | −0.51 | ** | −0.27 | ** |
| Population density, 2014 | 0.14 | | −0.09 | |
| Natural change of population, 2014 | −0.24 | * | −0.07 | |
| Area ($km^2$), 2015 | 0.01 | | 0.19 | * |
| Homicides recorded by the police, 2010 | −0.08 | | 0.29 | ** |
| Population size – Total 2015 | −0.05 | | 0.30 | ** |
| Unemployment by age 15–24 years in 1000s, 2015 | 0.03 | | 0.32 | ** |
| Deaths (total), 2014 | −0.01 | | 0.40 | ** |
| Long-term Unemployment (12 months and more), percent of active population 2015 | 0.29 | ** | 0.44 | ** |

*Notes:* The '*Authoritarian values*' standardized scale is based on combining 5 items using the Schwartz scale to measure the personal values of security, conformity, and tradition. The '*Populist attitudes*' standardized scale is based on combining mistrust in parliament, parties, and politicians. NUTS-2 level (N.112) * Correlation is significant at the 0.05 level (2-tailed). ** Correlation is significant at the 0.01 level (2-tailed). For the construction of all measures, see Appendix B. In Austria, Belgium, Switzerland, Denmark, Spain, France, Netherlands, Norway, Poland, and Portugal.

*Source:* The European Social Survey, Cumulative File Rounds 1–7. N. 48,746 respondents in 10 European countries.

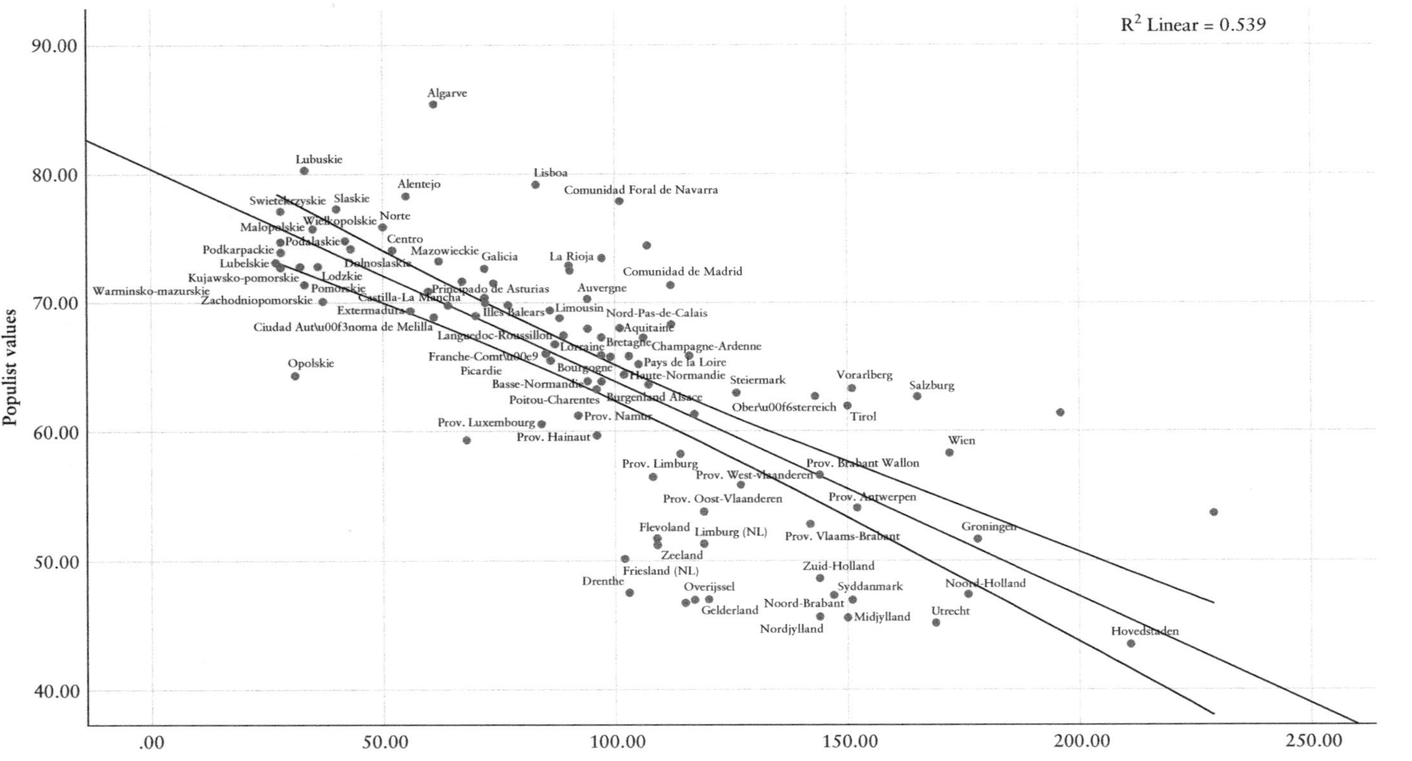


FIGURE 5.7. *Populist attitudes by per capita GDP, European regions (NUTS2)*

*Note:* The '*Populist attitudes*' standardized scale is based on combining mistrust in parliament, parties, and politicians. GDP at current market prices – purchasing power standard per inhabitant (2014). For the construction of all measures, see Appendix B.

*Source:* The European Social Survey, Cumulative File Rounds 1–7. N. 48,746 respondents in 10 European countries and 112 regions.

attitudes of political trust tend to be significantly correlated with socio-economic conditions. The strongest correlation is with per capita GDP (R = –0.74 ***), as illustrated in Figure 5.8. The poorest rural areas in Europe tend to have high levels of political mistrust. By contrast, urban areas that are more affluent show greater political trust. Distrust in politicians and parties was also higher in areas with declining populations, low fertility rates, and low levels of life expectancy – and with high rates of long-term unemployment, youth unemployment, and homicides.

Authoritarian values are also the strongest in poorer regions, as Figure 5.8 demonstrates, but in general there is a 'flatter' profile across the middle and more affluent areas, with the cubic line providing the best fit. While the economic and demographic conditions do help predict attitudes such as xenophobia, racial intolerance, and respect for social conformity, at the individual, regional, and national levels, these factors are less powerful in explaining support for authoritarianism over populism.

## V CONCLUSIONS

Heated debate continues over the role of economic conditions and cultural grievances in fueling support for Authoritarian-Populist parties. Many accounts see authoritarian and libertarian populism as consequences of economic globalization, viewing rising support for these parties as largely the product of stagnant and declining real incomes, growing income inequality, and loss of faith that mainstream parties have the capacity or will to respond to these concerns.[83] Globalization and the free flow of peoples, goods, services, and ideas does generate winners and losers – and authoritarian populism is often assumed to be endorsed most strongly by blue-collar workers who have lost manufacturing jobs, by those living in declining areas, and by households struggling to pay the rent.[84]

This chapter has shifted the available European evidence concerning these claims, analyzing three types of evidence: (1) individual-level survey data concerning the direct effects of economic insecurity and evaluations of the performance of the national economy; (2) longitudinal cohort analysis used to examine period-effects of support for post-material values associated with economic conditions; and (3) spatial analysis of national and local economic conditions. This allows us to test several interrelated claims.

Firstly, at the individual level, is *support for authoritarian values and populist attitudes concentrated among the 'losers,' from processes of*

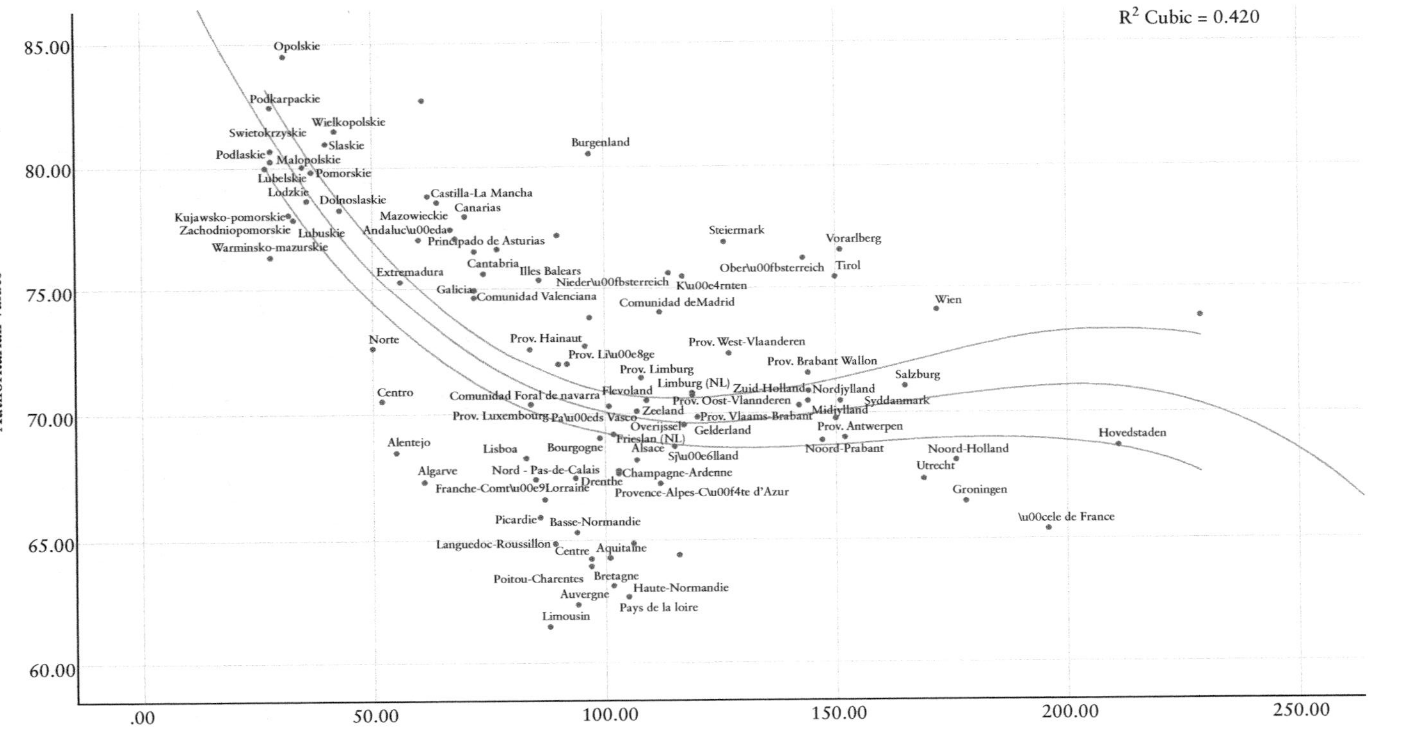


FIGURE 5.8. *Authoritarian values by per capita GDP, European regions (NUTS2)*
*Note:* The '*Authoritarian values*' standardized scale is based on combining five items using the Schwartz scale to measure the personal values of security, conformity, and tradition. GDP at current market prices – purchasing power standard per inhabitant (2014) from Eurostat. For the construction of all measures, see Appendix B.
*Source:* The European Social Survey, Cumulative File Rounds 1–7. N. 48,746 respondents in 10 European countries and 112 regions.

*economic globalization*, the manual workers, and low-income families, as commonly assumed? The results demonstrate that five of the seven economic indices are significant predictors of cultural values in Europe, in the expected direction. That is, both authoritarian and populist values are consistently stronger among less well-off people, who are most likely to feel a sense of economic insecurity. The key exceptions – and they are important theoretically – are those who have experienced long-term unemployment and dependency on state benefits.

But economic grievances do not have the same impact on authoritarian values and populist attitudes. Authoritarian values are more strongly linked with the respondent's birth cohort than with any of the economic indicators. This suggests that the perceived importance of security, conformity, and loyalty are more strongly influenced by each generational cohort's formative experiences than by immediate economic conditions.

By contrast, populist attitudes – that is, trust in parties, politicians, and parliaments – are more strongly influenced by personal experience of economic insecurity and by perceptions of the national economy's performance. Period-effects are also evident, with populist attitudes, increasing around the time when the financial crisis deepened. This is consistent with instrumental theories, which suggest that political trust varies according to how effectively the government maintains prosperity and peace.

Secondly, *do long-term fluctuations in economic conditions affect adherence to post-material values by different birth cohorts?* The longitudinal analysis of support for values in six West European countries from 1970 to 2008 demonstrates the existence of distinct birth cohort effects, like geological layers, with the youngest birth cohort being consistently the most post-materialist, while the oldest cohort is consistently the most materialist. But it is also clear that period-effects exist, with all birth cohorts shifting toward materialist values when there are economic downturns, and moving back toward post-materialist values with economic recovery.

Finally, *are authoritarian and populist values strongest in the localities most vulnerable to economic decline?* The evidence provided strong confirmation that populist attitudes were indeed strongly linked with economic conditions within the regions of European countries. People are most mistrustful of mainstream political parties, parliaments, and politicians in poorer regions that have suffered from declining populations– providing a natural constituency for populist appeals. But the effects of social deprivation were less consistent and weaker as predictors of authoritarian values. Whether these findings reflect economic or cultural grievances among the 'left behinds' is not yet clear. These areas have suffered economically, but they are also disproportionately rural areas with older white residents, where younger people have left for educational, and employment opportunities in metropolitan areas.

Economic grievances seem to help drive support for populist parties – but they may also have indirect effects, exacerbating anxieties about the migrants and refugees flooding into Europe and the perceived job losses, crime, concern about overloaded welfare services, and fears of terrorism – all of which will be explored in the next chapter.[85] Socially disadvantaged groups, Betz argues, are most prone to blame ethnic minorities and migrant populations for deteriorating conditions, loss of manufacturing jobs, and inadequate welfare services.[86] Consequently, we need to explore the impact of global migration flows, growing racial and ethnic diversity, and the perceived risks of terrorist threats, which could also help explain the cultural backlash we are witnessing.

## Notes

1. Lorenza Antonucci, Laszlo Horvath, Yordan Kutiyski, and Andre Krouwel. 2017. 'The malaise of the squeezed middle: Challenging the narrative of the "left behind" Brexiter.' *Competition and Change* 21 (3): 211–229.
2. Veronica Fagerland Kroknes, Tor Georg Jakobsen, and Lisa-Marie Grønning. 2016. 'Economic performance and political trust: The impact of the financial crisis on European citizens.' *European Societies* 17 (5): 700–723.
3. Daniel Stockemer. 2017. 'The success of radical right-wing parties in Western European regions: New challenging findings.' *Journal of Contemporary European Studies* 25 (1): 41–56; Richard Harris and Martin Charlton. 2016. 'Voting out of the European Union: Exploring the geography of Leave.' *Environment and Planning* 48 (11): 2116–2128.
4. The European Union regional classification for NUTS (Nomenclature of territorial units for statistics) are explained here: http://ec.europa.eu/eurostat/web/nuts. This includes categories for NUTS1 (98 major socio-economic regions), NUTS2 (276 basic regions for the application of regional policies), and NUTS3 levels (1,342 small regions for specific diagnoses).
5. Seymour Martin Lipset. 1960. *Political Man: The Social Basis of Politics.* New York: Doubleday, Chapters 4 and 5, p. 175. See also Daniel Bell. Ed. *The Radical Right.* 3rd edn. New Brunswick, NJ: Transaction Publisher (first published in 1955 as *The New America Right*, subsequently expanded in the 2nd edition in 1963); W. Sauer. 1967. 'National socialism: Totalitarianism or fascism?' *American Historical Review* 73 (4): 404–424.
6. Seymour Martin Lipset. 1960. *Political Man: The Social Basis of Politics.* New York: Doubleday, p. 175.

7. See, for example, G. Esping-Anderson. 1990. *The Three Worlds of Welfare Capitalism*. Princeton, NJ: Princeton University Press.
8. D. Swank and H.G. Betz. 2003. 'Globalization, the welfare state and right-wing populism in Western Europe.' *Socio-Economic Review* 1: 215–245; Anthony Mughan, Clive Bean, and Ian McAllister. 2003. 'Economic globalization, job insecurity and the populist reaction.' *Electoral Studies* 22 (4): 617–633; Hanspeter Kriesi, E. Grande, R. Lachat, M. Dolezal, S. Bornschier, and T. Frey. 2006. 'Globalization and the transformation of the national political space: Six European countries compared.' *European Journal of Political Research* 45 (6): 921–925; Dani Rodrik. 2017. 'Populism and the economics of globalization.' https://drodrik.scholar.harvard.edu/files/dani-rodrik/files/populism_and_the_economics_of_globalization.pdf; David Autor, David Dorn, Gordon Hanson, and Kaveh Majlesi. 2017. 'A note on the effect of rising trade exposure on the 2016 presidential election.' MIT Working Paper. https://economics.mit.edu/files/12418.
9. https://unstats.un.org/sdgs/files/report/2017/TheSustainableDevelopmentGoalsReport2017.pdf.
10. Sara Hobolt. 2016. 'The Brexit vote: A divided nation, a divided continent.' *Journal of European Public Policy* 23 (9): 1259–1277. See, however, Lorenza Antonucci, Laszlo Horvath, Yordan Kutiyski, and Andre Krouwel. 2017. 'The malaise of the squeezed middle: Challenging the narrative of the "left behind" Brexiter.' *Competition and Change* 21 (3): 211–229.
11. Hanspeter Kriesi, Edgar Grande, Romain Lachat, Martin Dolezal, Simon Bornschier, and Timotheos Frey. 2006. 'Globalization and the transformation of the national political space: Six European countries compared.' *European Journal of Political Research* 45 (6): 921–925. See also Luigi Guiso, Helios Herrera, Massimo Morelli, and Tommaso Sonne. November 8, 2017. 'Populism: Demand and supply.' www.heliosherrera.com/populism.pdf; Luigi Guiso, Helios Herrera, Massimo Morelli, and Tommaso Sonne. Forthcoming. 'Global crisis and populism: The role of Eurozone Institutions.' *Economic Policy*.
12. David Goodhart. 2017. *The Road to Somewhere: The Populist Revolt and the Future of Politics*. London: Hurst & Company.
13. Hans-Georg Betz. 1994. *Radical Rightwing Populism in Western Europe*. New York: St Martin's Press, Chapters 1 and 5; Piero Ignazi. 2003. *Extreme Right Parties in Western Europe*. New York: Oxford University Press. See also Herbert Kitschelt, with Anthony J. McGann. 1995. *The Radical Right in Western Europe: A Comparative Analysis*. Ann Arbor, MI: University of Michigan, Table 2.11; J.G. Anderson and T. Bjorkland. 1990. 'Structural changes and new cleavages: The Progress Parties in Denmark and Norway.' *Acta Sociologica* 33 (3): 195–217.
14. Thomas Piketty. 2014. *Capital*. Cambridge, MA: Bellnap Press.
15. http://wir2018.wid.world/part-2.html.
16. Thomas Piketty. 2014. *Capital*. Cambridge, MA: Bellnap Press.
17. Robert M. Marsh. 2016. 'What have we learned from cross-national research on the causes of income inequality?' *Comparative Sociology* 15 (1): 7–36; Andreas Bergh and Therese Nilsson. 2010. 'Do liberalization

and globalization increase income inequality?' *European Journal of Political Economy* 26 (4): 488–505; Giray Gozgor and Priya Ranjan. 2017. 'Globalisation, inequality and redistribution: Theory and evidence.' *World Economy* 40 (12): 2704–2751.

18. Simon Bornschier. 2010. *Cleavage Politics and the Populist Right: The New Cultural Conflict in Western Europe*. Philadelphia: Temple University Press; John B. Judis. 2016. *The Populist Explosion: How the Great Recession Transformed American and European Politics*. New York: Columbia Global Reports; Dani Rodrik. 2017. 'Populism and the economics of globalization.' https://drodrik.scholar.harvard.edu/files/dani-rodrik/files/populism_and_the_economics_of_globalization.pdf.
19. J.G. Andersen. 1992. Denmark: The Progress Party – populist neo–liberalism and welfare state chauvinism. In Paul Hainsworth. Ed. *The Extreme Right in Europe and the USA*. London: Pinter; Keith Banting. 2010. 'Is there a progressive's dilemma in Canada? Immigration, multiculturalism and the welfare state.' *Canadian Journal of Political Science* 43 (4): 797–820; A.H. Bay and A. Pedersen. 2006. 'The limits of social solidarity: Basic income, immigration and the legitimacy of the universal welfare state.' *Acta Sociologica* 49 (4): 419–436.
20. Manuel Funke, Moritz Schularick, and Christoph Trebesch. 2016. 'Going to extremes: Politics after financial crises, 1870–2014.' *European Economic Review* 88: 227–260.
21. Italo Colantone and Piero Stanig. 2017. 'The trade origins of economic nationalism: Import competition and voting behavior in Western Europe.' Carefen Working Papers 2017–2049. http://ssrn.com/abstract=2904105.
22. David Autor, David Dorn, Gordon Hanson, and Kaveh Majlesi. 2017. 'A note on the effect of rising trade exposure on the 2016 presidential election.' MIT Working Paper. https://economics.mit.edu/files/12418.
23. Sasha Becker, Thiemo Fetzer, and Dennis Novy. 2017. 'Who voted for Brexit? A comprehensive district-level analysis.' Munich: CESifo Working Papers 6438-2017. Paper presented at the 65th Panel Meeting of Economic Policy. http://cep.lse.ac.uk/pubs/download/dp1480.pdf; Matthew J. Goodwin and Oliver Heath. 2016. 'The 2016 referendum, Brexit and the left behind? An aggregate-level analysis of the result.' *Political Quarterly* 87 (3): 323–332.
24. Dante J. Scala and Kenneth M. Johnson. 2017. 'Political polarization along the rural–urban continuum? The geography of the presidential vote, 2000–2016.' *The Annals of the Academy of Political and Social Science* 672: 162.
25. Pippa Norris and Ronald Inglehart. 2003. *Cosmopolitan Communications*. New York: Cambridge University Press. See also David Held, Anthony McGrew, David Goldblatt, and Jonathan Perraton. 1999. *Global Transformations: Politics, Economics, and Culture*. Stanford, CA: Stanford University Press; Anthony McGrew and David Held. Eds. 2007. *Globalization Theory: Approaches and Controversies*. Cambridge: Polity.
26. Axel Dreher, Noel Gaston, and Pim Martens. 2008. *Measuring Globalisation: Gauging Its Consequences*. New York: Springer; *KOF Globalisation Index*. KOF Swiss Economic Institute. http://globalization.kof.ethz.ch/; Jens

Bartelson. 2000. 'Three concepts of globalization.' *International Sociology* 15 (2): 180–196.

27. Willem de Koster, Peter Achterberg, and Jeroen van der Waal. 2013. 'The new right and the welfare state: The electoral relevance of welfare chauvinism and welfare populism in the Netherlands.' *International Political Science Review* 32 (1).
28. Brian Rathbun, Even Evegennia Iaknis, and Kathleen Powers. October 19, 2017. 'The new poll shows that populism doesn't stem from people's economic distress.' *Washington Post/Monkey Cage.*
29. Jonathan Rothwell. 2017. 'The miniscule importance of manufacturing in far-right parties.' *Washington Post/ The Upshot.* September 15, 2017. www.nytimes.com/2017/09/15/upshot/the-minuscule-importance-of-manufacturing-in-far-right-politics.html.
30. 'Election 2016: US Exit poll.' *New York Times.* November 8, 2016. www.nytimes.com/interactive/2016/11/08/us/politics/election-exit-polls.html.
31. 'Election 2016: US Exit poll.' *New York Times.* November 8, 2016.
32. See Donald R. Kinder and Roderick D. Kiewiet. 1981. *Sociotropic Politics: The American Case.* SSRN: https://ssrn.com/abstract=1156460.
33. For details, see Geoffrey Evans. 1992. 'Testing the validity of the Goldthorpe class schema.' *European Sociological Review* 8 (3): 211–232.
34. Subjective income insecurity is measured as follows:'*Which of the descriptions on this card comes closest to how you feel about your household's income nowadays? Living comfortably on present income, coping on present income, finding it difficult on present income, or finding it very difficult on present income?*'
35. See also Luigi Guiso, Helios Herrera, Massimo Morelli, and Tommaso Sonne. November 8, 2017. 'Populism: Demand and supply.' www.heliosherrera.com/populism.pdf; Luigi Guiso, Helios Herrera, Massimo Morelli, and Tommaso Sonne. Forthcoming. 'Global crisis and populism: The role of Eurozone Institutions.' *Economic Policy.*
36. Pedro Magalhaes. 2017 'Economic outcomes, quality of governance and satisfaction with democracy.' In Carolien van Ham, Jacques Thomassen, Kees Aarts, and Rudy Andeweg. Eds. 2017. *Myth and Reality of the Legitimacy Crisis: Explaining Trends and Cross-National Differences in Established Democracies.* Oxford: Oxford University Press; Klaus Armingeon and R. Stein. 2014. 'Democracy in crisis? The declining support for national democracy in European countries, 2007–11.' *European Journal of Political Research* 53 (3): 423–442.
37. Bruce Stokes. 2017. '"As Republicans" views improve, Americans give the economy its highest marks since financial crisis.' Pew Research Center. www.pewresearch.org/fact-tank/2017/04/03/americans-give-economy-highest-marks-since-financial-crisis/.
38. James Tilley and Sara Hobolt. 2011. 'Is the government to blame? An experimental test of how partisanship shapes perceptions of performance and responsibility.' *Journal of Politics* 73 (2): 316–330.
39. Jean Pisani-Ferry. 2014. *The Euro Crisis and Its Aftermath.* Oxford: Oxford University Press.

40. Ronald Inglehart. 1997, *Modernization and Postmodernization: Cultural, Economic and Political Change in 43 Societies*. Princeton, NJ: Princeton University Press, Chapter 8.
41. See Ronald Inglehart. 2016. 'Modernization, existential security and cultural change: Reshaping human motivations and society.' In M. Gelfand, C.Y. Chiu, and Y.-Y. Hong. Eds. *Advances in Culture and Psychology*. New York: Oxford University Press.
42. Ronald Inglehart. 1977. *The Silent Revolution: Changing Values and Political Styles among Western Publics*. Princeton, NJ: Princeton University Press; Ronald Inglehart. 1990. *Culture Shift in Advanced Industrial Society*. Princeton, NJ: Princeton University Press.
43. For fuller detail on how materialist/post-materialist values are measured, and validation of the measures, see Ronald Inglehart. 1977. *The Silent Revolution: Changing Values and Political Styles among Western Publics*. Princeton, NJ: Princeton University Press, Chapter 1; Ronald Inglehart. 1990. *Culture Shift in Advanced Industrial Society*. Princeton, NJ: Princeton University Press, Chapter 1.
44. The samples are weighted to reflect each country's population. Since the 2006 World Values Survey did not include Belgium, we used data from the 1999 Belgian survey in the pooled analysis. This tends to reduce the amount of change observed from 1999 to 2006, but the distortion is minimal since Belgium contains only 4 percent of the six countries' population.
45. Ronald Inglehart and Christian Welzel. 2005. *Modernization, Cultural Change and Democracy: The Human Development Sequence*. New York: Cambridge University Press.
46. George K. Zestos. 2016. *The Global Financial Crisis: From US Sub-Prime Mortgages to European Sovereign Debt*. New York: Routledge.
47. Jean Pisani-Ferry. 2014. *The Euro Crisis and Its Aftermath*. Oxford: Oxford University Press.
48. Jean Pisani-Ferry. 2014. *The Euro Crisis and Its Aftermath*. Oxford: Oxford University Press.
49. S. Vasilopoulou and Daphne Halikiopoulou. 2015. *The Golden Dawn's Nationalist Solution: Explaining the Rise of the Far Right in Greece*. New York: Palgrave.
50. Manuel Funke, Moritz Schularick, and Christoph Trebesch. 2015. *Politics in the Slump: Polarization and Extremism after Financial Crises, 1870–2014*. http://ec.europa.eu/economy_finance/events/2015/20151001_post_crisis_slump/documents/c._trebesch.pdf.
51. See also Hans-Peter Kriesi and T.S. Pappas. Eds. 2015. *European Populism in the Shadow of the Great Recession*. Colchester: ECPR Press.
52. V. Georgiadou. 2013. 'Right-wing populism and extremism: The rapid rise of Golden Dawn in crisis-ridden Greece.' In R. Melzer and S. Sebastian. Eds. *Right-wing Extremism in Europe*. Berlin: Friedrich Ebert Stiftung, pp. 75–102.
53. S. Vasilopoulou and Daphne Halikiopoulou. 2015. *The Golden Dawn's Nationalist Solution: Explaining the Rise of the Far Right in Greece*. New York: Palgrave.

54. José Fernández-Albertos. 2015. *The Voters of Podemos: From the Party of the Indignant to the Palada of the Excluded.* Madrid: La Catarata Books; Davide Vittori. 2017. 'Podemos and the Five Star Movement: Populist, Nationalist or What?' *Constellations* 24 (3): 324–338; L. Ramiro and R. Gomez. 2017. 'Radical-left populism during the great recession: Podemos and its competition with the established radical left.' *Political Studies* 65 (1): 1–19; Richard Gillespie. 2017. 'Spain: The forward march of Podemos halted?' *Mediterranean Politics* 22 (4): 537–544.
55. Lluis Orriols and Guillermo Cordero. 2016. 'The breakdown of the Spanish two-party system: The upsurge of Podemos and Ciudadanos in the 2015 General Election.' *South European Society and Politics* 21 (4): 469–492; Sonia Alonso and Cristóbal Rovira Kaltwasser. 2016. 'Spain: No country for the Populist Radical Right?' *South European Society and Politics* 20 (1): 21–45.
56. Luis Ramiro and Raul Gomez. 2017. 'Radical-left populism during the great recession: Podemos and its competition with the established radical left.' *Political Studies* 65: 108–126.
57. Veronica Fagerland Kroknes, Tor Georg Jakobsen, and Lisa-Marie Grønning. 2016. 'Economic performance and political trust: The impact of the financial crisis on European citizens.' *European Societies* 17 (5): 700–723.
58. Guillermo Cordero and Pablo Simón. 2015. 'Economic crisis and support for democracy in Europe.' *West European Politics* 39 (2): 305–325.
59. Robert W. Jackman and K. Volpert. 1996. 'Conditions favouring parties of the extreme right in Western Europe.' *British Journal of Political Science* 26 (4): 501–521.
60. P. Knigge. 1998. 'The ecological correlates of right-wing extremism in Western Europe.' *European Journal of Political Research* 34: 249–279.
61. Daphne Halikiopoulou and Tim Vlandas. 2015. 'The rise of the far right in debtor and creditor European Countries: The case of European Parliament elections.' *Political Quarterly* 85 (2): 279–288.
62. *World Development Indicators*. Washington DC: The World Bank.
63. Jeff Sachs *et al.* 2017. *SDG Index and Dashboards Report 2017.* New York: Bertelsmann Stiftung and Sustainable Development Solutions Network. http://sdgindex.org/assets/files/2017/2017-SDG-Index-and-Dashboards-Report–regions.pdf.
64. John Helliwell, Richard Layard, and Jeffrey Sachs. Eds. 2017. *World Happiness Report, 2017.* New York: Sustainable Development Solutions Network. http://worldhappiness.report/ed/2017/.
65. https://data.oecd.org/inequality/income-inequality.htm.
66. https://data.worldbank.org/indicator/NY.GDP.PCAP.CD.
67. See also A. R. Jupskas. 2015, 'Institutionalised right-wing populism in times of economic crisis: a comparative study of the Norwegian progress party and the Danish people's party.' In Hans Kriesi and T.S. Pappas. Eds. *European Populism in the Shadow of the Great Recession*, Colchester: ECPR Press, pp. 23–40.

68. Andrea Pirro. 2017. *The Populist Radical Right in Central and Eastern Europe: Ideology, Impact, and Electoral Performance.* London: Routledge, p. 197.
69. The US estimates that the total number of people living in extreme poverty fell significantly worldwide from 1.7 billion in 1999 to 767 million in 2013, although progress remains uneven. United Nations 2017. *The Sustainable Development Goals Report 2017*. New York: United Nations. https://unstats.un.org/sdgs/files/report/2017/TheSustainableDevelopmentGoalsReport2017.pdf.
70. Joseph Stiglitz. 2015. *Creating a Learning Society: A New Approach to Growth, Development, and Social Progress.* New York: Columbia University Press, p. 166.
71. www.gallup.com/poll/182918/fewer-americans-identify-middle-class-recent-years.aspx.
72. Joseph Hacker. 2006. *The Great Risk Shift: The New Economic Insecurity and the Decline of the American Dream.* Oxford: Oxford University Press.
73. Joseph Stiglitz. 2013. *The Price of Inequality: How Today's Divided Society Endangers Our Future.* New York: W.W. Norton.
74. Joseph Hacker and Paul Pierson 2011. *Winner-Take-All Politics: How Washington Made the Rich Richer – and Turned Its Back on the Middle Class.* New York: Simon & Schuster.
75. Congressional Budget Office. December 21, 2017. *Distributional Effects of Changes in Taxes and Spending Under the Conference Agreement for H.R. 1.* Washington DC. www.cbo.gov/publication/53429.
76. Heinz Eulau and Michael S. Lewis-Beck. Eds. 1985. *Economic Conditions and Electoral Outcomes: The United States and Western Europe.* New York: Agathon Press; Michael S. Lewis-Beck. 1988. *Economics and Elections: The Major Western Democracies.* Ann Arbor, MI: University of Michigan Press.
77. Dante J. Scala and Kenneth M. Johnson. 2017. 'Political polarization along the rural–urban continuum? The geography of the presidential vote, 2000–2016.' *The Annals of the Academy of Political and Social Science* 672: 162–169.
78. US Department of Agriculture. 2017. *Rural America at a Glance.* 2017 edn. Washington DC: US Department of Agriculture. www.ers.usda.gov/webdocs/publications/85740/eib-182.pdf.
79. Shannon Monnat. 2016. 'Deaths of despair and support for Trump in the 2016 presidential election.' Department of Agricultural Economics, Sociology and Education Research Brief 12/04/16. Pennsylvania State University. http://aese.psu.edu/directory/smm67/Election16.pdf.
80. Dante J. Scala and Kenneth M. Johnson. 2017. 'Political polarization along the rural–urban continuum? The geography of the presidential vote, 2000–2016.' *The Annals of the Academy of Political and Social Science* 672: 162; Five Thirty Eight. 2016. 'Trump was stronger where the economy was weaker.' http://fivethirtyeight.com/features/trump-was-stronger-where-the-economy-is-weaker.

81. Katherine J. Cramer. 2016. *The Politics of Resentment: Rural Consciousness in Wisconsin and the Rise of Scott Walker.* Chicago: University of Chicago Press.
82. Yann Algan, Sergei Guriev, Elias Papaionnou, and Egenia Passari. 2017. 'The European trust crisis and the rise of populism.' *Brookings Papers on Economic Activity.*
83. Michael Hirsh. February 28, 2016. 'Why Trump and Sanders were inevitable.' *Politico Magazine.* www.politico.com/magazine/story/2016/02/why-donald-trump-and-bernie-sanders-were-inevitable-213685; *The Economist.* April 2, 2016. 'European social democracy: Rose thou art sick.' www.economist.com/news/briefing/21695887-centre-left-sharp-decline-across-europe-rose-thou-art-sick.
84. Italo Colantone and Piero Stanig. 2017. 'The trade origins of economic nationalism: Import competition and voting behavior in Western Europe.' Carefen Working Papers 2017–49. http://ssrn.com/abstract=2904105; Enrique Hernandez and Hanspeter Kriesi. 2016. 'The electoral consequences of the financial and economic crisis in Europe.' *European Journal of Political Research* 55 (2): 203–224; G. Lucassen and Marcel Lubbers. 2012. 'Who fears what? Explaining far-right-wing preference in Europe by distinguishing perceived cultural and economic ethnic threats.' *Comparative Political Studies* 45: 547–574; David Autor, David Dorn, Gordon Hanson, and Kaveh Majlesi. 2017. 'A note on the effect of rising trade exposure on the 2016 presidential election.' MIT Working Paper. https://economics.mit.edu/files/12418.
85. Christopher Cochrane and Neil Nevitte. 2014. 'Scapegoating: Unemployment, far-right parties and anti-immigrant sentiment.' *Comparative European Politics* 12 (1): 1–32.
86. Hans-Georg Betz. 1994. *Radical Rightwing Populism in Western Europe.* New York: St Martin's Press.

# 6

# Immigration

Long-term intergenerational value change, and the expansion of education, have transformed the basic cultural values of Western societies, generating a backlash that has been strengthened by periods of declining economic security. To what extent have other major changes contributed to this backlash – particularly the influx of people with different nationalities, religions, languages, customs, and ethnic backgrounds? Many socially conservative people feel that their basic values are being eroded by rapid cultural change, a feeling reinforced by growing ethnic diversity and the specter of Islamic terrorism.

Part I discusses Europe's rising levels of ethnic diversity in recent decades and the hardline opposition to immigration it has evoked from Authoritarian-Populist parties and leaders. Part II sets out our theoretical arguments. There is little doubt that xenophobia, racist resentment, and Islamophobia are closely linked with voting for parties with anti-immigrant platforms.[1] Our theory cultural tipping points predicts that threat perceptions and feelings of insecurity among the losers from long-term cultural change will lead to latent authoritarian predispositions.[2] But debate continues about why immigration is perceived as a threat.[3] Are anti-immigrant sentiments mainly driven by fear of competition from low-skilled workers?[4] Or are concerns about the erosion of European cultural norms, the decline of Christianity, and threats to white predominance more important?[5] Or are anti-immigrant sentiments more closely interlinked with the threat of terrorism?[6] And are all immigrants seen to be equally threatening, or are fears most intense concerning those of different racial and ethnic backgrounds?

Part III analyzes our core hypotheses, using individual-level survey evidence from the pooled European Social Survey. This enables us to expand our explanation of support for authoritarian and populist orientations to include the respondents' religion, country of origin, and citizenship. We also test a range of subjective attitudes, including anti-immigrant anxieties linked with economic grievances, cultural threats, and terrorist fears, and attitudes toward immigrants with various racial and ethnic characteristics. We will also compare the European host countries most and least effected by the refugee crisis to determine to what extent authoritarian values and populist attitudes are linked with given levels or rates of immigration.

Part IV summarizes our key findings and considers their implications for understanding changes in voting behavior and party competition. The evidence points to three key findings. First, as expected, *hostility toward immigration is a significant predictor of authoritarian values*, which emphasize the importance of security against threats, conformity with traditional customs, and obedience to group leaders. This finding is not surprising, given the wealth of literature linking these attitudes. Authoritarianism is, by definition, the rejection of out-groups that are seen as threats to the in-groups. But this finding confirms an important component of our tipping point thesis. Moreover, we find that *cultural threats associated with immigration are more strongly linked with authoritarian and populist values than with instrumental concerns* about protecting economic interests, such as jobs and wages. It is racial and ethnic differences, not immigration per se, that is most closely associated with authoritarian values. Finally, even after controlling for attitudes toward immigrants and economic conditions, the *respondent's generation (or birth cohort) persists as the strongest predictor of authoritarian values.*

## I RISING LEVELS OF IMMIGRATION AND THE AUTHORITARIAN-POPULIST RESPONSE

### The Growing Ethnic Diversity of European Societies

What are the effects of immigration on European societies' cultural values – and thus potential support for Authoritarian-Populist parties? Immigrants can bring valuable talent and stimulate the economy. They form a disproportionate share of entrepreneurs; for example, in 2016, 40 percent of Fortune's list of the 500 top US firms were owned by immigrants or their children.[7] Advanced industrialized societies like Germany with an aging population, a shortage of skilled labor, and declining fertility rates, can expand the working-age population, consumption, and productivity through the successful integration of young migrants.[8] In America, many legal immigrants are highly educated scientists, engineers, and entrepreneurs; others are young workers with little education who are employed in highly manual-intensive occupations.[9] The willingness of low-skilled immigrants to do work involving hard physical labor fills important needs in farm-work, building construction, home services, and food preparation.[10]

But the rapid influx of large numbers of immigrants, refugees, and asylum seekers into Europe from poorer societies generates social tensions. The refugee crisis, with the number of people applying for asylum in the EU peaking at 1.26 million in 2015, including many from Muslim-majority societies, raised difficult challenges for European policymakers in managing welfare, maintaining social cohesion, and providing educational training services for the refugees. The transformation of European societies through the migrant population flows and growing multicultural diversity has been dramatic. The United Nations estimates that in 2015, 248 million migrants lived outside their country of birth.[11] This figure has doubled since 1960 and continues to rise. Many migrants move to high-income European societies, which now contain 74 million or around 30 percent of the world's migrants. Europe now hosts more migrants than any other region.[12] In absolute numbers, however, the United States has a larger immigrant population than any other country, with 49.7 million immigrants in 2017.[13]

Figure 6.1 shows the trends in net international migration (the number of immigrants who are not native citizens minus the number of emigrants) in European countries since the early 1990s. This process has transformed European societies. West European nations and Scandinavia had the greatest influx. This movement of people from the global South to Europe will have profound consequences not only for contemporary European societies but also for the future, because the aging white populations have much lower fertility rates than the younger immigrant families from developing societies.[14] Eastern Europe saw a steady loss of migrants for two decades after the fall of the Berlin Wall, until the numbers stabilized at a lower level. Migration is driven by many factors, including opportunities to work and study in other countries, and to flee civil wars, economic crises, and the breakdown of political order. Refugees, asylum seekers, and stateless persons are at greatest risk, and 6.2 million of them live in Europe.[15]

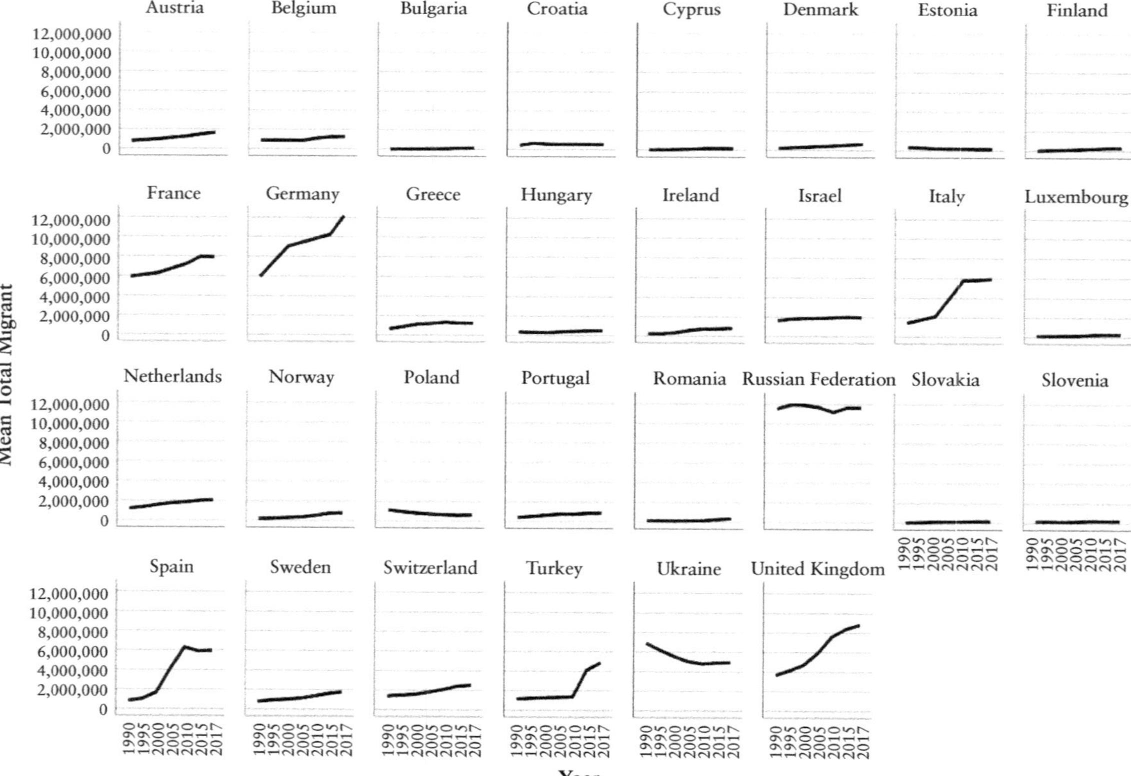


FIGURE 6.1. *Net migration into European countries, 1990–2017*

*Note:* Net migration is defined as the total number of people moving into a country (immigrants) minus the total number of people leaving a country (emigrants), including citizens and non-citizens, for the five-year period.

*Source:* UN Population Division. December 2017. *Migrants Stock by Origin and Destination, 2017*. New York: UNDESA.

Several large European countries such as Germany and the UK stand out with the substantial increase in the number of net migrants they have received during these years. Germany's desirability as a destination for asylum seekers is long standing: over the past 30 years it has received 30 percent of all asylum applications in Europe – a greater share than any other country. In 2015, Angela Merkel adopted an 'open border' policy and the country took in 890,000 refugees and received 476,649 formal applications for political asylum – the highest number in history. In 2016, the government reinstated border controls. An agreement between the EU and Turkey allowed Greece to return 'irregular migrants' to Turkey and made it more difficult for refugees from the Middle East to reach Western Europe overland. As a consequence, the total number of refugees arriving in Germany in 2016 dropped to 280,000. In addition to Germany's image as a safe and prosperous country with liberal asylum laws, the strong diaspora networks that built up over time, particularly with Middle Eastern countries, helped pull in new arrivals. Germany also invests generously in integration policies, providing refugees and asylum seekers with linguistic, cultural, and vocational training.[16] Large surges in immigration help explain why some of the most prosperous and (until recently) most tolerant Western countries, such as Sweden, Denmark, Norway, Germany, and the Netherlands, have seen rising support for Authoritarian-Populist parties. These societies have been the target of immigration flows because they are secure, prosperous countries with strong social welfare safety nets that (until recently) were relatively hospitable to refugees and immigrants.

Though refugees may enter the European Union through South Eastern Europe, relatively few choose to settle there. Conditions are much more attractive in Northern Europe, due to the lack of economic opportunities, and the contraction of welfare benefits in Greece, Italy, and Spain, which were badly hit by the recession. Turkey saw a notable shift, starting in 2010, due to the exodus of refugees from Syria, fleeing the bloody disaster of the civil war. By contrast, several Central and Eastern European societies saw a net outflow of people, as Poles sought educational and economic opportunities in Britain, and Ukrainians fled their country's instability and conflict. Compared with Germany, the number of refugees admitted into the US is relatively small: 85,000 people were admitted into America in 2016, about half of them from Muslim-majority countries.[17] The Trump administration sought to limit the number of refugee admissions far further for 2018.

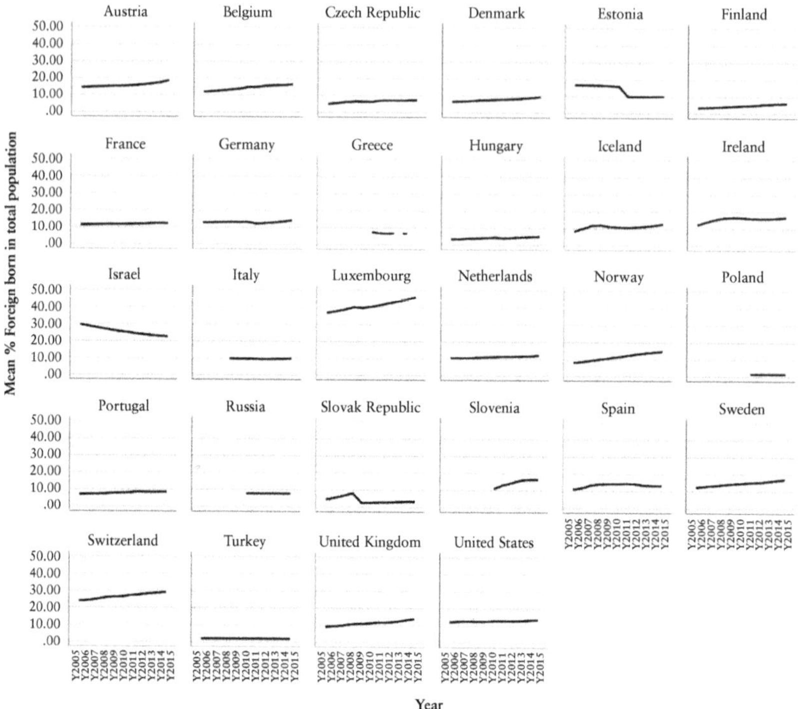


FIGURE 6.2. *Foreign born population as percent of total population, 2005–2015*
*Notes:* The 'foreign born' population is defined by the OECD as all people who have ever migrated from their country of birth to their current country of residence, as a proportion of the total population of the host country. The OECD data include those expatriates born abroad as nationals of their current country of residence.
*Source:* OECD. 2017. *International Migration Outlook, 2017 – Statistical Annex*. Version 2. Last updated June 8, 2017. www.oecd-ilibrary.org/social-issues-migration-health/international-migration-outlook-2017_migr_outlook-2017-en.

The recent waves of refugees and asylum seekers are only one component of a society's ethnic diversity. Figure 6.2 shows the proportion of the total population in European societies and the US that is estimated to be foreign-born. Accurate figures are difficult to compile for those without legal status but substantial differences can be observed across countries, with the greatest levels of diversity being found in small high-income European states with a high demand for skilled labor, such as Luxembourg and Switzerland. The proportion of foreign-born is far smaller in less prosperous countries such as Turkey, the Czech Republic, and Poland. Overall, the proportion of foreign-born population has risen since 2005 in all but four of the 26 societies for which time-series data

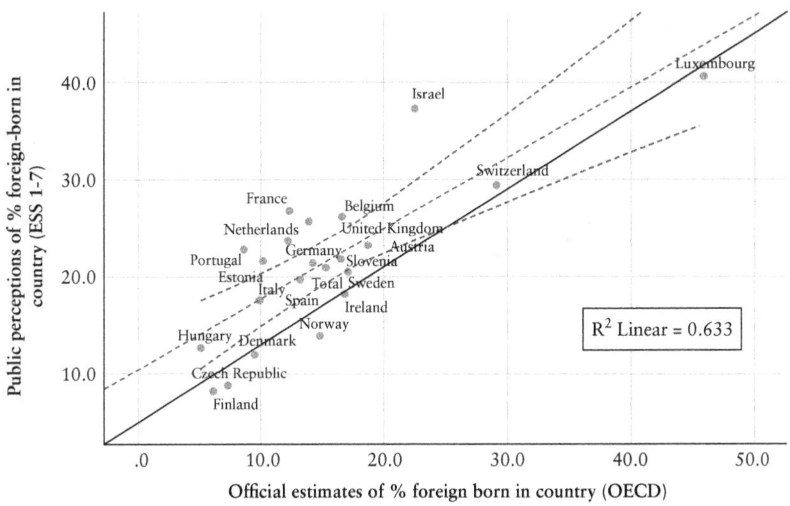


FIGURE 6.3. *Perceptions and estimates of proportion of foreign-born living in each European society*

*Notes:* Public perceptions are measured in the ESS survey by the question: 'Of every 100 people in the country, how many do you think are born outside the country?' The official estimates from the OECD data on the 'foreign born' population are defined by the OECD as all people who have ever migrated from their country of birth to their current country of residence, as a proportion of the total population of the host country.

*Sources:* OECD. *International Migration Outlook, 2017.* http://dx.doi.org/10.1787/migr_outlook-2017-en; The European Social Survey, Cumulative File Rounds (1–7). N. 330,315 respondents in 32 European countries. www.europeansocialsurvey.org/.

are available.[18] In 1970, Sweden was inhabited almost entirely by ethnic Swedes, but by 2015 it had a foreign-born population of 17 percent. Similarly in 2015 the proportion of foreign born had risen to 12 percent in both the Netherlands and France, 14 percent in both Germany and the UK, 19 percent in Austria, and 29 percent in Switzerland.[19] Despite having a large absolute number of immigrants, in 2014 the proportion of foreign born in the United States was 13 percent – close to the European average of 12.6 percent.[20] Moreover, the US proportion of foreign-born residents rose only 1.4 percent since 2005, a slower rate than in Europe.

What matters for cultural attitudes and electoral behavior is not just the number of migrants that arrive, but public perceptions of them, which are affected by personal experiences and media accounts. The public may misperceive the extent of ethnic diversity, and of crime rates and unemployment. Figure 6.3 compares the estimated proportion of foreign-born residents living in each European society, from OECD data, with public perceptions of the proportion of foreign born. The public tends to exaggerate the number of foreigners, with this disparity being particularly strong in Israel, France, the Netherlands, and Portugal – although in Luxembourg, Sweden, and Denmark public perceptions are relatively accurate.

## The Response of Authoritarian-Populist Parties

The transformation of Western societies through growing ethnic diversity has been highly controversial. Authoritarian-Populist parties vary from country to country but they are uniform in their hostility toward immigration – along with nationalism, nativism, xenophobia, and cultural protectionism. Reflecting these values, these parties seek to restrict the movement of peoples within the European Union, to limit the inflow of migrants, refugees, and asylum seekers from outside Europe, to integrate immigrants into national cultures, through opposition to oppose multiculturalism in languages, religions, and lifestyles, and to propose stricter measures to prevent terrorism. These sentiments are coupled with blaming the loss of national sovereignty to the European Union, with several parties proposing that EU membership should be subjected to a referendum. Nationalistic appeals tap into fears, resentment, and intolerance of native Europeans against the 'other.' The extreme right in Europe traditionally used anti-Semitic and racist rhetoric, and these themes have not faded away, but since the events of 9/11, and the influx of Muslims fleeing conflict, Islamophobia has strengthened its grip, with countless cases of discrimination, hate speech, physical attacks, and anti-Muslim campaigns.[21]

Hostility toward multiculturalism, racial equality and minority rights, ethnic diversity, and immigration is widely regarded as the defining feature of the Authoritarian-Populist (and radical right) parties, although progressive populists are more tolerant on these issues.[22] Some populist right parties succeed in attracting electoral support without campaigning on economic grievances or elite corruption, but Ivarsflaten finds that all successful populist parties mobilized support on the immigration issue.[23] Similarly, in the mid-1990s, Betz argued that support for parties such as the National Front was driven by resentment against immigrants: 'The emergence and rise of radical right-wing populist parties in Western Europe coincided with the growing tide of immigrants and particularly the dramatic increase in the number of refugees seeking peace, security, and a better life in the high-income societies of Western Europe. The reaction to the new arrivals was an outburst of xenophobia and open racism in a majority of West European countries ... This has made it relatively easy for the radical populist Right to evoke, focus, and reinforce preexisting xenophobic sentiments for political gain.'[24]

Debate about migration in the EU became more salient following EU enlargement in 2004 to include Estonia, Latvia, Lithuania, Poland, Czech Republic, Slovakia, Slovenia, Hungary, Malta, and Cyprus, and, in 2007, Romania and Bulgaria. But it became a top priority with the influx of refugees, asylum seekers, and economic migrants from war-torn Syria, Afghanistan, Iraq, Somalia, and South Sudan.[25] Concern peaked after Angela Merkel decided to open Germany's borders to one million refugees and asylum seekers between autumn 2015 and spring 2016.[26] This decision sent shockwaves across the EU, with Greece and Italy receiving boatloads of refugees fleeing across the Mediterranean and Austria, Bulgaria, Croatia, and Hungary suddenly dealing with border chaos at their frontiers along the Balkan route for entry.

These developments exacerbated social tensions; the Eurobarometer tracks public opinion about the two most important problems facing each country. As Figure 6.5 shows, the effects of the US housing and banking crisis in 2007 triggered economic recession across the Atlantic, with European concern about unemployment rising sharply from mid-2008 until mid-2010, before eventually falling again in 2013. Within the EU, public concern about immigration had been lower than worries about unemployment, but the importance of the immigration issue rose steadily in Europe from mid-2013 until peaking in late 2015, matching levels of concern about unemployment, before declining slightly. Member states differed however on the importance of these issues, as shown by the contrasts between Greece and Germany.

The heated controversy over the entry of refugees and asylum seekers from outside the region, and the free flow of peoples within the European Union has enabled authoritarian populists to campaign on these issues, using provocative posters depicting immigrants as criminals, sometimes conflating the image of the immigrant with that of the Islamist terrorist.[27] EU states vary in the strength of anti-immigrant and anti-Muslim rhetoric, and the response of European governments.

The most hardline policies in the European Union have been enacted by Hungary's Prime Minister Viktor Orbán, who has consolidated power since 2010, revising the constitution to reduce judicial independence, electoral integrity, and press freedom. An Authoritarian-Populist party with

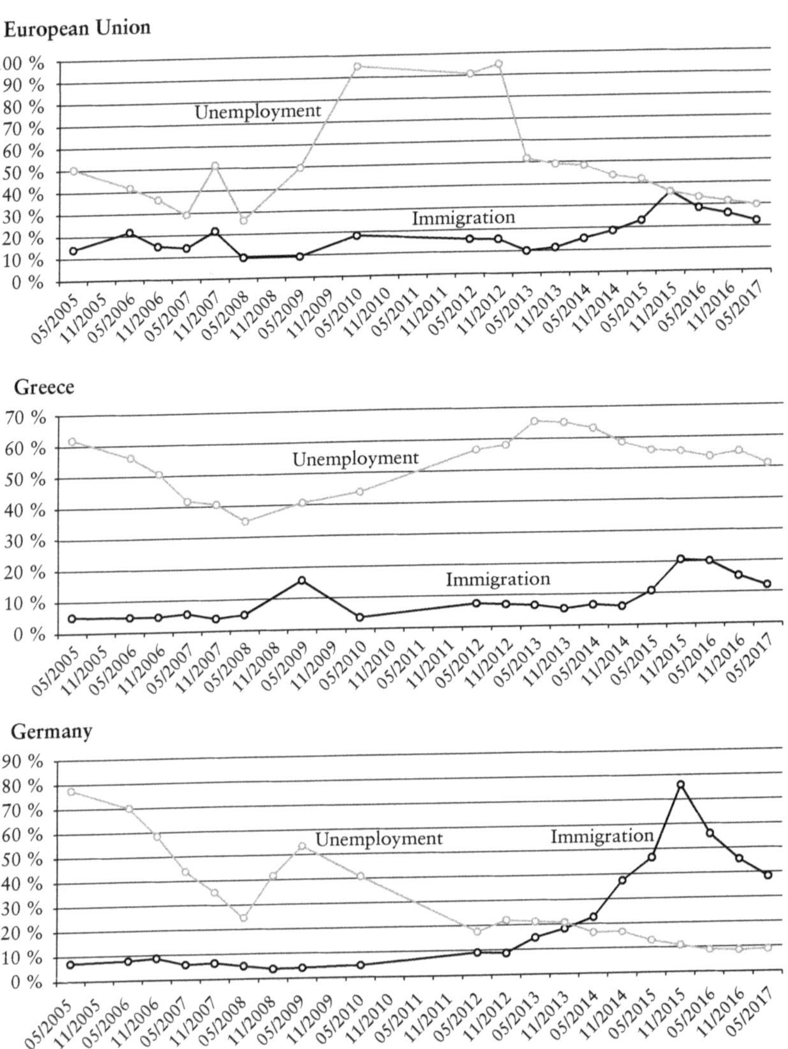


FIGURE 6.4. *Public concern about unemployment and immigration, EU 2005–2017*

*Notes:* What do you think are the two most important problems facing our country at the moment? The proportion of Europeans responding 'unemployment' (light grey) or 'immigration' (dark grey).

*Source:* European Commission. Euro-barometers. http://ec.europa.eu/commfrontoffice/publicopinion/index.cfm/Chart/getChart/themeKy/42/groupKy/208.

an absolute majority in parliament, Fidesz is outflanked on these issues by Jobbik, the third largest party in the National Assembly, describing itself as a radical patriotic Christian party. Orbán uses harsh and inflammatory anti-immigrant rhetoric, arguing that migrants have no rights to enter the EU.[28] In 2015, at the height of the refugee crisis, Hungary built a fence on the southern borders with Serbia and Croatia to keep out refugees. Orbán strongly opposed the EU's refugee reallocation quota program, designed to ease the burden on Germany, Greece, and Italy. His government refuses to accept Hungary's designated quota of just over 1,000 refugees, despite losing legal battles over the issue in the European Court of Justice. He proposed that financial assistance and migration reception centers should be established by the European Commission in African countries that agree to take back refugees.

In the Netherlands, Geert Wilders' Party for Freedom (PVV) expresses similarly radical anti-immigration sentiments; their program in the 2017 elections called for an end to immigration from Islamic countries, closing all mosques, banning Muslim headscarves, as well as strengthening policing and holding a referendum on Dutch membership in the EU.[29] Wilders' transgressive language has been extreme, such as, when launching his 2017 election, calling Moroccan migrants 'scum who make the streets unsafe' and telling his supporters to 'make the Netherlands ours again.'[30]

Another example comes from the Danish People's Party (DF), which has run on a platform hostile to uncontrolled immigration since its founding in the late-1990s, attracting support from social conservatives opposed to multiculturalism and rejecting the transfer of sovereignty to Brussels.[31] The party's current policies call for tighter border controls, voluntary repatriation, and for immigrants to follow Danish values and laws, as well as supporting traditional Danish institutions such as the monarchy, Christianity, and cultural heritage.[32] The party's leader, Kristian Thulesen Dahl, seeks to withdraw from the EU's Schengen free-movement area and reinstate border controls with Germany and Sweden, opposing further EU integration.

Britain's traditional anti-immigrant parties, the National Front and the British National Party, have faded in strength in recent years. But the UKIP's manifesto in the June 2017 election campaign, advocating a 'hard' Brexit from the EU, sought to ban the burqa, outlaw sharia law, impose a temporary moratorium on new Islamic schools, and require annual checks against female genital mutilation for high-risk girls, as well as introducing a net migration target of zero in five years.[33]

In France, Marine Le Pen has sought to temper the extreme racism of her father, who denied the Holocaust and once called the Nazi gas chambers a 'detail of history.'[34] She also depicts herself as more open toward certain socially liberal issues, such as women's rights and gender equality, with party campaign images giving female French National Front (FN) candidates greater prominence. In the 2017 French presidential elections, however, she called for massive reductions in legal immigration and proposed ending free schooling for the children of undocumented immigrants, holding a referendum on EU membership, giving preference in welfare services to French nationals, and stripping dual-nationality Muslims with extremist views of their French citizenship.

In the European Parliament, the Europe of Nations and Freedom (ENL) coordinates Authoritarian-Populist parties in an alliance of the FN, the Austrian Freedom Party (FPÖ), the Flemish Vlaams Belang (VB), the Alternative for Germany (AfD), the Italian Northern League, the Dutch PVV, and the British UKIP, among others. These parties share a deeply Eurosceptic philosophy, seeking to restore national sovereignty, to roll back Brussels bureaucracy, and to control immigration. As the ENL website proclaims: 'Our European cultures, our values and our freedom are under attack. They are threatened by the crushing and dictatorial powers of the European Union. They are threatened by mass immigration, by open borders and by a single European currency: one size does not fit all.'[35]

Across the Atlantic, Trump has repeatedly advocated tightening America's borders against illegal aliens and limiting legal immigration. In addition to his campaign pledge to build a wall on the US–Mexican border, his administration's actions include employing more immigration officials to round up illegal aliens, barring Muslims from entering the country, limiting the number of refugees and asylum seekers, rescinding the rights of undocumented 'Dreamers,' brought into the country illegally as children – which had been recognized by the Obama administration – strengthening vetting of asylum seekers, and cracking down on 'sanctuary' cities.[36] As the official White House website summarizes these policies: 'The United States must adopt an immigration system that serves the national interest. To restore the rule of law and secure our border, President Trump is committed to constructing a border wall and ensuring the swift removal of unlawful entrants. To protect American workers, the President supports ending chain migration, eliminating the Visa Lottery, and moving the country to a merit-based entry system. These reforms will advance the safety and prosperity of all Americans while helping new citizens assimilate and flourish.'[37]

Beyond immigration policies, Wodak argues that the hallmark of right-wing populism is to amplify the politics of fear, using simple transgressive language, identifying scapegoats as the culprits blamed for 'our' problems, and legitimating Us/Them exclusion.[38] Trump's derogatory language against diverse minorities has been widely noted, such as when attacking Gold Star Muslim parents, African-American NFL football players, suggesting that Haitian immigrants 'all have AIDS' and Nigerians in the United States 'would never go back to their huts,' and that Mexicans are rapists and criminals.[39] His campaign speeches about the need for tough actions to protect America's borders against 'the flood' of illegal immigrants linked those seeking entry with threats to security: 'We have people that are criminals, we have people that are crooks. You can certainly have terrorists. You can certainly have Islamic terrorists.'[40] It has been suggested that Trump's nativist and nationalistic policies reflect his personal fear of foreign peoples, predating his entry into politics.[41] These views are certainly longstanding, as evidenced by his reviving the 'Birther' conspiracy against President Obama in March 2011, years before announcing his candidacy.[42] But his derogatory comments and racist language may also be a strategy to mobilize his white base.[43] In any case, Trump's executive actions seeking to implement his goals to limit immigration have been deeply divisive, marking a clear break from the Republican Party's long-standing claims about the economic value of migrant workers, and the Democratic Party's commitment to respect the rights of refugees and lawful migrants seeking a path to American citizenship. They also go against a long historical tradition defining America as a nation built on waves of immigrants.

## II THEORIES OF INSTRUMENTAL INTEREST, CULTURAL IDENTITIES, AND TERRORIST FEARS

Anti-immigrant, nativist, Islamophobic, and nationalist appeals are defining characteristics in the rhetoric and policy platforms of Authoritarian-Populist parties and leaders. Concern about these issues has risen among the electorates. There is overwhelming evidence that these views are closely linked with a broad range of authoritarian values and socially conservative views in the electorate. A large body of survey data indicate that attitudes hostile toward 'outsiders' – including foreigners, immigrants, and ethnic minorities – triggers an authoritarian reflex linked with in-group conformity and xenophobia.[44] Authoritarians characteristically emphasize the importance of maintaining in-group social conformity with traditional social mores and conventional practices, respecting customs, and defending the established way of life against the threat of change by group outsiders.

Nevertheless, debate continues about the factors driving these expressions of authoritarian sentiments, particularly the relative importance of (1) concerns about the impact of immigration on jobs, wages, and benefits, versus (2) the impact of anxieties about the impact of multiculturalism on traditional European identities, lifestyles, and symbols, and (3) the influence of fears of Muslim terrorist violence.[45] Understanding the reasons behind anti-immigrant attitudes is important both theoretically and for understanding how policymakers can best respond to these fears.

## Instrumental Concerns

Interest-based theories of immigration hold that competition over scarce resources, and threats to material well-being trigger opposition to immigration.[46] The political debate about immigration policies is framed in terms of their threats to jobs and wages when counterbalanced against the economic gains from admitting skilled professionals, software engineers, scientists, and entrepreneurs, as well as unskilled laborers to do the hard manual jobs that many native-born workers avoid, like harvesting crops, providing home services for the elderly, and food preparation and packing.[47] The debate about material costs and benefits also concerns the perceived impact of immigration on crime, schools, and welfare programs, where it is argued that the native population who have contributed toward insurance schemes should have priority in access to public services, a phenomenon known as 'welfare chauvinism' or 'exclusionary nationalism.'[48] Foreigners and immigrants are accused of 'jumping the queue' in services like public housing and unemployment benefits, and anti-immigrant parties advocate reserving social entitlements for legal residents who have contributed toward programs like national healthcare. 'Nativism' promotes the interests of native-born citizens over those of immigrants. From this perspective, opposition to immigration would be expected to be greatest among low-income workers, and those living on benefits, the sector most directly threatened by the loss of employment or public services. Instrumental accounts also suggest that attitudes toward immigrants will reflect macro-level economic conditions, like rates of unemployment, with hostility growing during hard times.

Prior research provides some empirical support for interest-based theories. Opposition to immigration and support for anti-immigrant political parties have been found to increase with rates of unemployment, especially where radical right parties blame immigrants for these conditions.[49] Similarly, feelings toward the European Union have been attributed to rational calculations about the instrumental benefits, such as access to regional development aid and trade markets, or the costs, such as the loss of national sovereignty and the need to comply with EU regulations.[50] Studies of welfare chauvinism find that immigrants, refugees, and foreigners are blamed for lack of access to welfare services, such as healthcare and schools.[51] In the Brexit campaign, for example, the Leave side notoriously claimed (falsely) that an extra £350m would be available to be spent on the NHS every week from diverted EU spending, an argument subsequently widely discredited once EU rebates, and public investments were taken into account. The Leave camp also claimed – again falsely – that the trade benefits of Britain remaining part of the European market would continue after negotiations, while regaining control over the free movement of people and immigration. If the instrumental thesis is correct, attitudes should be related to the perceived consequences of immigration for matters like jobs and wages. Moreover, rational attitudes should be for or against the free flow of peoples across national borders, regardless of racial, religious, linguistic, or national characteristics.

## Cultural Anxieties

By contrast, the cultural anxieties explanation holds that anti-immigrant feelings are generated by nativism, white resentment, racial prejudice, Islamophobia, and xenophobia. Blumer theorized that these feelings arise among the dominant groups of a society as a response to concerns about losing privileges to subordinate groups.[52] Similarly, as the tipping point thesis argues, cultural grievances may be strongest when previously dominant groups are threatened by major value shifts in public opinion, as when the older generations of less-educated Europeans and Americans continue to endorse socially conservative views although the balance of public opinion has gradually tipped toward socially liberal values. Symbolic politics emphasizes values and identities, and affective feelings override the importance of material concerns. Authoritarians seek to exclude 'outsiders' who threaten traditional social values, whether based on tribal identities of national, faith, race, and ethnicity.

Large numbers of immigrants, who are often visibly different in appearance, tend to trigger feelings of threat. This reaction is strengthened by the open flow of peoples across national borders in the European

Union, by the numbers of immigrants drawn from developing societies, by terrorist-linked Islamophobia, and by the perceived failure of mainstream governing parties to manage population flows effectively.[53] The classic literature on tolerance and prejudice suggests that threat perceptions are central to in-group rejection of out-groups – but several distinct risks may be at work.[54] Studies of Islamophobia in Western societies find that perceived cultural threats stimulate physical and existential security, leading to negative attitudes toward Muslims.[55] The context also matters. Contact theories suggest that growing up in ethnically diverse metropolitan areas is conducive to more social trust and tolerance of multiculturalism than growing up in isolated and homogeneous rural settings, with little direct experience of living with people with different lifestyles and customs.[56]

Cultural distances also seem to be important. And attitudes vary according to the immigrants' economic background (such as skilled professionals versus unskilled laborers), humanitarian considerations (such as refugee families with children fleeing war), and their religious faith (such as Assyrian Christians, and Sunni Muslims from Iraq).[57] Some people see Muslims in France, the UK, and the Netherlands as seeking to create a society entirely separate from the mainstream.[58] White Europeans also often disapprove of traditional Muslim forced marriages, polygamy, domestic violence, and honor killings, which are at odds with their social norms. Populists like Geert Wilders argue that patriarchal beliefs about the traditional roles of women in the family, and the wearing of the hijab, or burqa, undermine the more egalitarian gender roles, liberal social values, and secular legal framework of the Netherlands.[59] Moreover, although anti-immigrant attitudes tend to be strong predictors of authoritarian values, those holding these views are not necessarily distrustful of their country's political institutions, but they may be if they feel that their concerns about stricter limits on the number of asylum seekers or restrictions on multiculturalism are denigrated as racist or Islamophobic and thereby dismissed and excluded from serious parliamentary debate due to the liberal consensus shared across parties on the center-right and center-left.[60]

People tend to take the world into which they are born for granted: it seems familiar and normal. And in recent decades, each successive birth cohort in high-income societies has been born into a world with more immigrants than were present during their formative years. Consequently, older cohorts feel most threatened and disoriented by racial and ethnic diversity.

This principle also applies to geographic differences. For those born in New York or London in 1960, ethnic diversity was familiar. If born in 1960 in rural Montana or Sweden, it was not. A sudden influx of immigrants from diverse cultures into relatively homogeneous societies can lead to a situation in which some people (especially the older ones) feel that they have become strangers in their own land: the world they live in is no longer the one in which they grew up. This can produce genuine anxiety and intense disorientation. Dismissing people as bigots, racists, or deplorables does not solve the problem. In the long run, it can bring surging support for the French National Front or the Alternative for Germany or Donald Trump.

The literature provides considerable support for the cultural grievance thesis. Several recent studies have found that support for the Leave outcome in the Brexit referendum was strongly associated with prejudice against foreigners, measured by right-wing authoritarianism.[61] Similarly, in the run up to the Brexit referendum, Curtice found that many British people saw EU membership as economically beneficial, but expressed concern about its cultural consequences.[62] Survey results also suggested that respondents expressing concerns about immigration into Britain were more likely to vote Leave.[63] Other research on European attitudes based on analysis of the 2002 ESS survey showed that, even after controlling for standard socio-economic and demographic variables, voting for the radical right was significantly linked with negative attitudes toward immigrants, refugees, and multiculturalism in seven West European countries, including Denmark, France, and the Netherlands.[64] A parallel process may have emerged in Eastern Europe, where authoritarian-populist success has been attributed to resentment against ethnic minorities.[65]

In the US 2016 presidential election, feelings of racial resentment and whether or not voters supported a path for citizenship for undocumented immigrants, was strongly associated with vote switching from Obama in 2012 to Trump in 2016. Clinton maintained many of Obama's white voters with positive views toward immigration, but she lost about a third of those with negative views.[66] MacWilliams argues that Trump's rise during the 2016 primaries was fueled by his appeal to authoritarian voters who responded to his unvarnished, us-versus-them rhetoric against Mexicans and Muslims.[67] President Trump's signature issue of immigration ('Build a Wall'), and his dog-whistle appeals to racism, in contrast to Hillary Clinton's support of ethnic diversity, may have reinforced the white flight from the Democratic Party which already was under way during Obama's presidency. In the 2016 United States election, white working-class fears of cultural replacement and immigration were more powerful factors in predicting support for Trump than economic concerns.[68] White working-class voters in the study who said that they felt like strangers in their own land, and who believed that the US needs protection against foreign influence, were 3.5 times as likely to favor Trump as those who did not share these concerns. These findings support the cultural anxiety thesis.

## Fears of Terrorism

Contemporary events have intensified public concerns about the integration of Muslim immigrants and the risks of mass violence by ISIS sympathizers. Examples include ethnic tensions rising in the Netherlands after the murder of film-maker Theo van Gogh in November 2004; heated protests in many countries following the September 2005 publication of the 'Muhammad' cartoons in Denmark – the cartoons were seen as blasphemous by Muslims, whose demands for their suppression raised Western concerns about freedom of expression; and violent riots occurred a few months later in suburban Paris housing projects involving disaffected Franco-Maghrebi immigrants.[69]

Even deeper concerns about social instability and deadly violence were evoked by terrorist events, particularly the 2001 terrorist attacks in the United States, as well as the bombings in Madrid (2004), London (2005), and Paris (2008).[70] Citizens of the UK found it shocking that British-born second-generation Muslim youths of Pakistani and Bangladeshi descent, with good education and job prospects, carried out the 2005 London bombings. These events raised fears that second-generation Muslims were becoming alienated from democratic norms and radicalized by developing closer sympathies with extremist Islamic movements. Terrorist acts seem to have reinforced authoritarian feelings in America where, even before the election of Trump, authoritarian-driven partisan polarization was linked with increasing fear of real and imagined threats, fueled by terrorist incidents abroad and at home.[71] For all these reasons, fears of terrorism seem likely to have a direct impact on Islamophobia, and an indirect effect in strengthening authoritarian values.

## The Liberal Elite Consensus and Populist Mistrust

Do anti-immigrant feelings also predict populist attitudes? A distinction can be drawn between 'exclusionary' forms of populism, such as that of

Le Pen and Trump, and more 'inclusive' forms that seek to expand participation among historically excluded social groups, such as as that of Bolivian President Evo Morales and Venezuelan President Hugo Chavez.[72] But if this is a valid distinction, it is unclear whether all European parties fall into the 'exclusionary' category today, given the rise of progressive populists like Podemos and the Five Star Movement, which seem closer to their Latin American counterparts. It is an empirical question to what extent anti-immigrant feelings predict support for all types of populist parties.

Moreover, there are reasons why anti-immigrant attitudes may be linked not just with authoritarian orientations but also with populist support. The educated elites dominating most mainstream political parties, mass media commentators, civil servants, and intellectuals have generally been hesitant to respond to public concern about the growing multiculturalism of modern European societies by advocating tougher immigration policies.[73] During the post-World War II era, European politicians and civil servants have been drawn mainly from middle-class, meritocratic backgrounds.[74] Elite education provides one of the most consistent predictors of liberal values, tolerant attitudes toward multiculturalism, and approval of racial/ethnic equality. European elites governing prosperous democracies with generous welfare states, egalitarian values, and deep-rooted civic cultures differed on many important issues, but they share a broadly similar worldview. Core components of this liberal world view emphasize the value of the UN, NATO, the EU, and other agencies of global governance, of respect for human rights and democratic governance, of providing development aid to overcome world poverty, and of responding to humanitarian disasters, as well as the importance of close cooperation with allies with shared values. In managing the economy, a broad liberal consensus emphasized the benefits of a borderless European community with free flow of goods, ideas, and peoples, maintaining the welfare safety-net and regulating capitalism, as the conditions most conducive to prosperity. And this worldview among educated elites has been underpinned by broadly shared socially liberal values, respecting diversity, social tolerance and trust, equality of opportunity for women and ethnic minorities, and the protection of minority rights. Consequently, there may be a link between anti-immigrant feelings and populist mistrust of elites, if the elite liberal consensus on these issues makes mainstream parties reluctant to respond to genuine public concerns about growing diversity and globalism, thereby deepening the lack of confidence in political elites.

## III EUROPEAN INDIVIDUAL-LEVEL EVIDENCE

Let us examine the empirical evidence concerning how far attitudes toward immigration shape support for authoritarian values and populist attitudes in the European electorate. The pooled ESS contains several items measuring public perceptions of immigration, including whether immigrants are good or bad for the country's economy (the instrumental thesis), whether they are good or bad for cultural life (the cultural grievance thesis), and whether they make the host country a better or worse place in which to live (which could relate to either perspective). These items can be summed into a single consistent standardized scale measuring positive or negative attitudes toward immigration, with high reliability.[75] We find that across European societies, each nation's mean immigration attitudes scale is strongly and significantly correlated with authoritarian values (R = .46, P.008, N.32). As shown in Figure 6.5, Greece

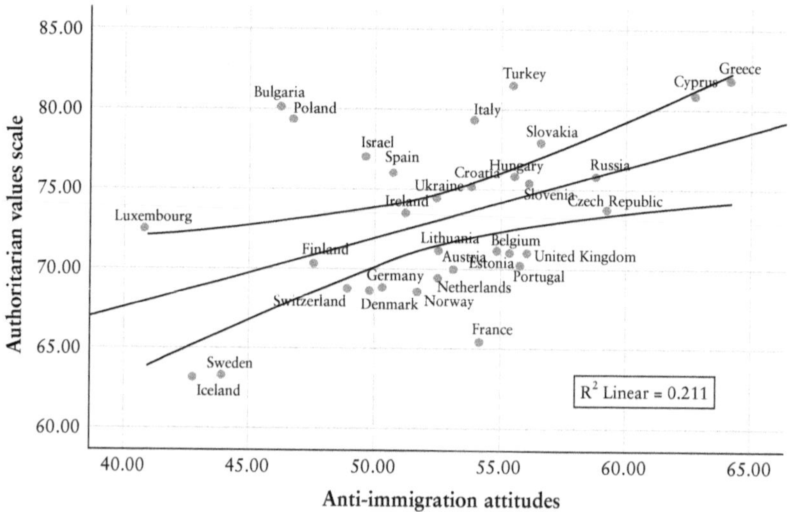


FIGURE 6.5. *Anti-immigration attitudes and authoritarian values, Europe*
*Notes: 'Authoritarian values'* are measured in a standardized 100-point scale by combining five items in the Schwartz value scales concerning the personal importance of security, conformity, and obedience. See Table 4.3. *Anti-Immigration attitudes* are measured in a standardized 100-point scale by combining whether respondents thoughts that immigration was good or bad for the economy, for the country's cultural life, and for making the country a better or worse place to live.
*Source:* The European Social Survey, Cumulative File Rounds 1–7. N. 330,315 respondents in 32 European countries.

and Cyprus have both the strongest authoritarian values and the greatest hostility to immigrants. Greece has been at the forefront of the Eurozone debt crisis, and at the forefront of the refugee transit zone across the Mediterranean. Several Central and Eastern European countries such as Russia, Slovenia, and Slovakia were also high on both dimensions, although Poland and Bulgaria had more positive attitudes toward immigration. Many other countries were far more open toward immigration and far less authoritarian, including the Scandinavian countries and several Western European states such as Germany. But the national-level correlation between immigration attitudes and the populism scale is considerably weaker and not statistically significant (R =.34, P.081, N.27).

To probe further, we also analyze these relationships at the individual level in order to understand the reasons underlying positive or negative feelings, in particular whether cultural grievances or economic interests are stronger predictors of authoritarian populism. Attitudes toward immigration can be influenced by many factors, such as generation (or birth cohort), class, and education, so we will use multivariate analysis. Table 6.1 expands the models used in previous chapters to include indicators of national citizenship and whether one was born in the country of residence, the ethnic diversity of the place where respondents lived, minority group membership, adherence to Muslim faith, and the indicators of attitudes toward immigration described above.

The results of this analysis confirm that even after controlling for all of the social, demographic, and economic factors, negative attitudes both toward the impact of immigration on the country's cultural life, and on making the country a worse place to live, are significant predictors of authoritarian values, but the economic consequences are not significant. Fears about the loss of one's cultural identity is more closely associated with authoritarianism than fears about the impact of immigrant competition on jobs, wages, or benefits.

Figure 6.6 illustrates how attitudes toward immigration are consistently associated with both authoritarian and populist values. Of the three indicators, the impact on undermining or enriching cultures is most distinctive, with respondents making little distinction between the economic consequences and whether immigrants make their country a better or worse place to live.

How important is one's cultural distance from other groups? If the cultural grievances thesis is correct, the public distinguishes between immigrants having similar or different characteristics. Consequently, the survey asked how people feel about the entry of peoples from similar or

TABLE 6.1. *Predicting the impact of immigration attitudes on authoritarian values and populist attitudes*

| | | Authoritarian values | | | | Populist attitudes | | | |
|---|---|---|---|---|---|---|---|---|---|
| | | B | SE | Beta | Sig. | B | SE | Beta | Sig. |
| Generation | Interwar (1900–1945)(Ref) | 0.00 | | | | 0.00 | | | |
| | Boomers (1946–1964) | −3.10 | 0.10 | −0.10 | *** | 1.34 | 0.14 | 0.03 | *** |
| | Gen X (1965–1979) | −4.17 | 0.11 | −0.13 | *** | 1.62 | 0.16 | 0.03 | *** |
| | Millennials (1980–1996) | −5.43 | 0.11 | −0.15 | *** | 1.67 | 0.15 | 0.03 | *** |
| Year | 2004 | 1.58 | 0.15 | 0.04 | *** | 0.20 | 0.29 | 0.00 | N/s |
| | 2006 | 2.46 | 0.18 | 0.06 | *** | 1.78 | 0.23 | 0.03 | *** |
| | 2008 | 3.07 | 0.18 | 0.08 | *** | −1.66 | 0.22 | −0.03 | *** |
| | 2010 | 4.32 | 0.18 | 0.11 | *** | 1.18 | 0.22 | 0.02 | *** |
| | 2012 | 4.14 | 0.18 | 0.11 | *** | 0.86 | 0.20 | 0.02 | *** |
| | 2014 | 3.30 | 0.17 | 0.08 | *** | | | | |
| Social | Education | −0.32 | 0.03 | −0.03 | *** | −0.22 | 0.04 | −0.01 | *** |
| | Sex (male) | −0.47 | 0.07 | −0.02 | *** | 0.12 | 0.09 | 0.00 | *** |
| | Urbanization (1–5 scale Most rural to most urban) | 0.13 | 0.03 | 0.01 | *** | 0.12 | 0.04 | 0.01 | *** |
| | How religious are you on 10-pt scale | 1.06 | 0.01 | 0.22 | *** | −0.38 | 0.02 | −0.05 | *** |
| | Children | 0.94 | 0.07 | 0.03 | *** | 0.74 | 0.10 | 0.02 | *** |
| | Married | 2.31 | 0.15 | 0.06 | *** | 0.19 | 0.27 | 0.00 | N/s |
| | Separated or divorced | 0.76 | 0.22 | 0.01 | *** | −0.15 | 0.38 | 0.00 | N/s |
| Class | Manager | −1.19 | 0.13 | −0.03 | *** | −0.62 | 0.18 | −0.01 | *** |
| | Routine non–manual | −0.73 | 0.10 | −0.02 | *** | −0.44 | 0.14 | −0.01 | *** |

| | | | | | | | | | |
|---|---|---|---|---|---|---|---|---|---|
| | Petty bourgeoisie | −1.01 | 0.11 | −0.02 | *** | 0.75 | 0.15 | 0.01 | *** |
| | Skilled manual | 0.04 | 0.14 | 0.00 | N/s | 0.30 | 0.20 | 0.00 | N/s |
| | Unskilled manual (Ref) | 0.00 | | | | 0.00 | | | |
| Economic | Work in manufacturing industry | 0.70 | 0.09 | 0.02 | *** | 1.48 | 0.12 | 0.03 | *** |
| | Household Net Income (10-pt scale) | −0.29 | 0.01 | −0.05 | *** | −0.24 | 0.02 | −0.03 | *** |
| | Subjective income insecurity | 0.78 | 0.05 | 0.05 | *** | 2.00 | 0.06 | 0.08 | *** |
| | Ever been unemployed for a period of 12 months or more | −1.10 | 0.07 | −0.03 | *** | 1.20 | 0.10 | 0.03 | *** |
| | Main source of income is unemployment or other social benefit | −2.33 | 0.16 | −0.03 | *** | −3.06 | 0.22 | −0.03 | *** |
| | How satisfied with present state of economy in country | −0.17 | 0.01 | −0.03 | *** | −4.08 | 0.02 | −0.46 | *** |
| Citizen | Citizen of country | −0.69 | 0.19 | −0.01 | *** | 1.65 | 0.28 | 0.02 | *** |
| | Born in country | −0.96 | 0.13 | −0.02 | *** | 0.77 | 0.19 | 0.01 | *** |
| Diversity | Almost no minority race or ethnic members in locality | 0.83 | 0.13 | 0.02 | *** | 0.89 | 0.24 | 0.01 | *** |
| | Some minority race or ethnic members in locality (Ref) | 0.00 | | | | 0.00 | | | |
| | Many minority race or ethnic members in locality | −0.23 | 0.21 | 0.00 | N/s | 0.21 | 0.36 | 0.00 | N/s |
| Ethnicity | Member of an ethnic minority | 1.68 | 0.15 | 0.03 | *** | 0.87 | 0.22 | 0.01 | *** |
| | Muslim | 4.58 | 0.19 | 0.06 | *** | −2.98 | 0.27 | −0.02 | *** |

*(continued)*

TABLE 6.1. (*continued*)

| | | Authoritarian values | | | | Populist attitudes | | | |
|---|---|---|---|---|---|---|---|---|---|
| | | B | SE | Beta | Sig. | B | SE | Beta | Sig. |
| Immigration | Immigration bad for country's cultural life | 0.46 | 0.02 | 0.07 | *** | 0.57 | 0.03 | 0.06 | *** |
| | Immigration makes country a worse place to live | 0.17 | 0.02 | 0.02 | *** | 0.72 | 0.03 | 0.07 | *** |
| | Immigration bad for the economy | 0.02 | 0.02 | 0.00 | N/s | 0.22 | 0.03 | 0.02 | *** |
| | Allow few immigrants of same race/ethnic group as majority | –0.36 | 0.05 | –0.02 | *** | –0.11 | 0.08 | 0.00 | N/s |
| | Allow few immigrants of different race/ethnic group from majority | 1.18 | 0.07 | 0.07 | *** | –0.20 | 0.09 | –0.01 | * |
| | Allow few immigrants from poorer countries outside Europe | 0.67 | 0.06 | 0.04 | *** | –0.29 | 0.08 | –0.01 | *** |
| | (Constant) | 62.86 | 0.34 | | *** | 66.10 | 0.46 | | *** |
| | $R^2$ | 0.16 | | | | 0.32 | | | |
| | N. | 183,492 | | | | 166,467 | | | |

*Notes:* OLS regression models predicting citizen's support for authoritarian and populist values. P *** .001, ** .01, * .05, N/s Not significant. Note that the Interwar generation and the unskilled manual class are the excluded reference categories. For the construction of all measures, see Appendix B. The '*Authoritarian values*' standardized scale is based on combining five items using the Schwartz scale to measure the personal values of security, conformity, and tradition. The '*Populist attitudes*' standardized scale is based on combining mistrust in parliament, parties, and politicians.

*Source:* The European Social Survey, Cumulative File Rounds 1–7. N. 199,389-191,062 respondents in 32 European countries.

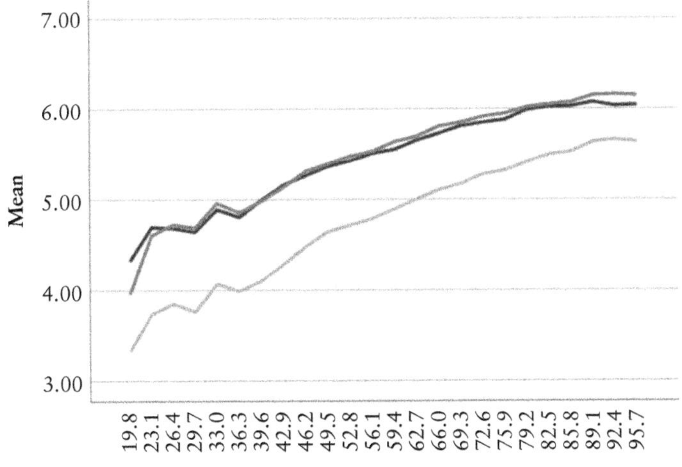


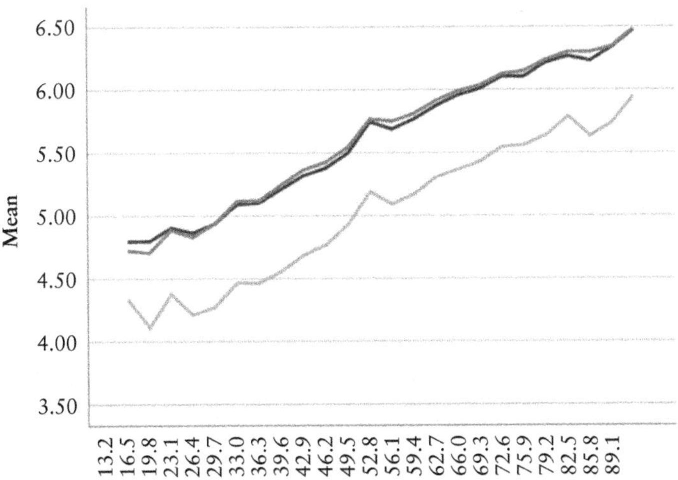


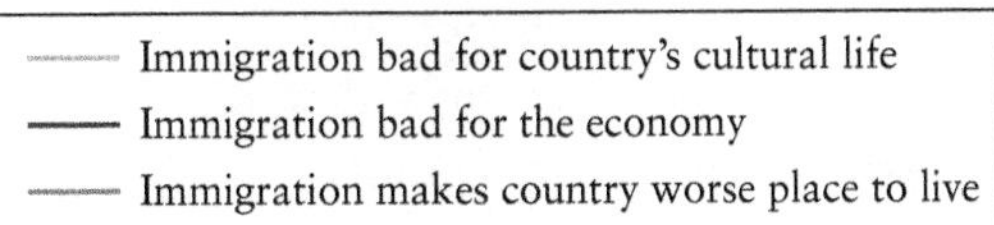


FIGURE 6.6. *Attitudes toward immigration by authoritarian and populist values*
*Notes:* The Authoritarian values standardized scale is based on combining 5 items using the Schwartz scale to measure the personal values of security, conformity, and tradition. The Populism standardized scale is based on combining mistrust in parliament, parties, and politicians. The three items measuring immigration attitudes use 10-point scales ranging from 0 (negative) to 10 (positive). See Appendix B for details.
*Source:* The European Social Survey, Cumulative File Rounds 1–7. N. 330,315 respondents in 32 European countries.

different racial or ethnic groups, and from less developed countries outside Europe. Here, even clearer findings emerge about the reasons underlying public concern about immigration. Allowing immigrants of the *same* race or ethnicity as the country's majority population was not significantly correlated with authoritarianism. But allowing immigrants from a *different* race or ethnic group was strongly associated with authoritarian values. A similar but weaker correlation was observed for immigrants from poorer countries. Apparently, it is attitudes toward immigration by people of a different race or culture – not immigration per se – that is most strongly linked with authoritarianism. Authoritarianism seems to be catalyzed by fear of the ethnically or racially different 'other,' more than by concern about the free flow of peoples across national borders. Figure 6.7 displays how authoritarian and populist values are strongly and consistently related to these attitudes. People distinguished sharply between allowing fewer immigrants of the same race or ethnicity as the majority in the country and admitting people of a different race or ethnicity or from poorer countries.

Some researchers have studied local effects; in Austria, for example, the percentage of immigrants in a community was found to have a significant impact on the community's vote for the Freedom Party (FPÖ), explaining roughly a sixth of its regional variation.[76] And in Belgium, support for the Vlaams Belang was related to the proportion of Muslims living in an area.[77] Other studies report that *changes* in the rate of immigration, but not levels, predict radical right support across Western Europe.[78] On the other hand, in America the Trump vote was strongest in predominately white communities like rural Wisconsin, areas of population decline that attract relatively few immigrants, Hispanic workers, or African-American minorities.[79] The diversity of the neighborhood also mattered, with authoritarianism and populism being strongest among those living in areas with *little* intergroup contact with ethnic minorities in their area, not those who lived in diverse multicultural areas, such as Paris, London, or Berlin. As contact theory suggests, personal interactions and familiarity with neighbors from diverse backgrounds seems to promote tolerance and trust of immigrants and minorities.[80] During the late twentieth century, many metropolitan cities like Stockholm, Berlin, and Paris, that once had a homogeneous religious heritage, and homogeneous linguistic, racial, and national identities, have become transformed into multiethnic communities, attracting many immigrants and refugees from Muslim-majority states.[81] The data examined here suggest that these cities tend to gradually become more socially tolerant due to intergroup

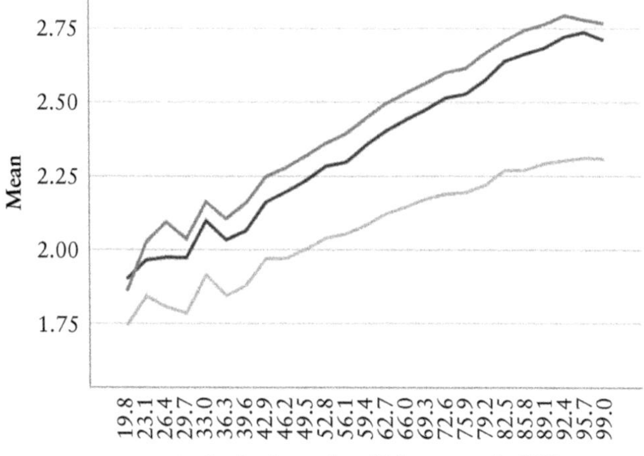


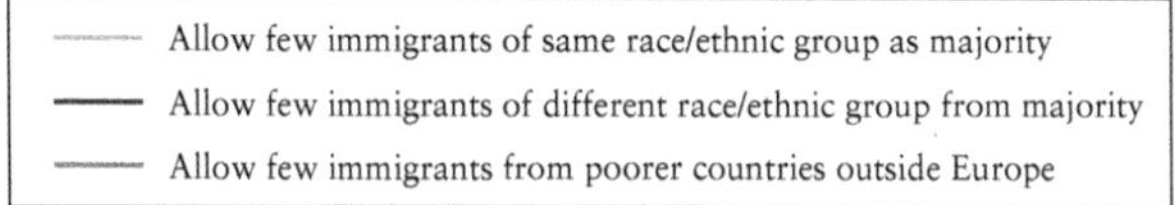


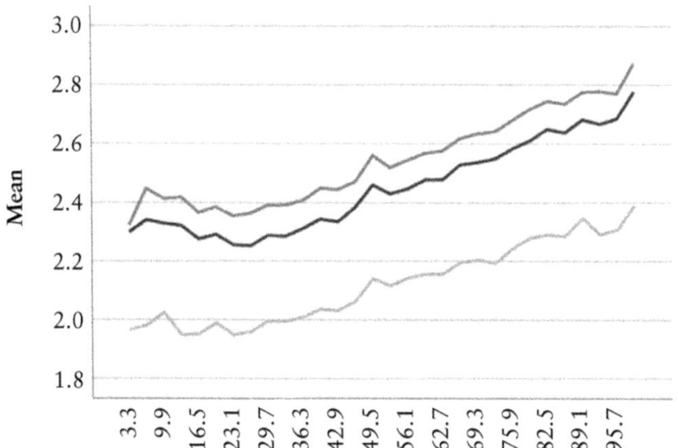


Allow many/few immigrants of same race/ethnic group as majority
Allow many/few immigrants of different race/ethnic group from majority
Allow many/few immigrants from poorer countries outside Europe

FIGURE 6.7. *Attitudes toward immigration by authoritarian and populist values*
*Notes:* The '*Authoritarian values*' standardized scale is based on combining five items using the Schwartz scale to measure the personal values of security, conformity, and tradition. The '*Populist attitudes*' standardized scale is based on combining mistrust in parliament, parties, and politicians. The three items measuring immigration attitudes use 10-point scales ranging from 0 (negative) to 10 (positive). See Appendix B for details.
*Source:* The European Social Survey, Cumulative File Rounds 1–7. N. 330,315 respondents in 32 European countries.

contact – but at the same time more isolated peripheral areas of economic decline, which attract far fewer immigrants, are more likely to have intolerant and authoritarian attitudes.

Finally, ethnic minorities, especially Muslims, strongly endorsed authoritarian values concerning social conformity, security, and respect for leaders. Many immigrants are drawn from developing countries in Africa, Asia, and the Middle East, and these societies tend to have strongly traditional attitudes toward family and marriage, religion, and gender roles.[82]

The remaining findings are consistent with those of earlier chapters, with authoritarian values being strongest among the older birth cohorts, the less educated, the most religious, and manual workers and less well-off. The strongest predictor of authoritarianism was the respondent's generation (or birth cohort) – which had more impact than all of the indicators of ethnicity and immigrant attitudes.

## Cross-National Comparisons

Evidence from the Brexit referendum suggests that *levels* of migration, trade, and EU transfers to UK regions were weak predictors of the Leave vote.[83] By contrast, the *growth rate* of immigrants into Britain from the countries that joined the EU in 2004 and 2007 was significantly linked at regional levels to the Leave vote share. Latent authoritarian fears may be triggered by increases in the numbers of visibly different minorities. Concern about long-term cultural change, coupled with the effect of sudden changes in the influx of refugees, may make older Europeans feel that they are no longer living in the society in which they grew up – thereby stimulating support for Authoritarian-Populist parties that promise to slow down immigration, crack down on undocumented aliens, and strengthen cultural integration, with laws restricting Muslim schools and 'Burka bans.'[84]

Variations in ethnic diversity also differ widely across European societies regardless of recent rates of refugees and asylum seekers. The continent contains several long-standing multilingual federal states such as Switzerland and Belgium, as well as multicultural societies that traditionally contain substantial ethno-national, ethno-racial, and ethno-religious minorities in their borders, such as the Roma in Hungary. Other societies, such as Norway and Sweden, were historically relatively homogeneous ethnically. The macro-level evidence that levels of ethnic diversity or rates of immigration influence voting support for the radical right has produced inconclusive findings; several previous European studies have found only mixed evidence linking the proportion of immigrants or foreign born populations in a country with voting support for radical right parties.[85]

Table 6.2 presents the simple correlations between negative attitudes toward immigration, using the composite scale from the three items discussed above, and both authoritarian values and populist attitudes. The results confirm that a significant relationship links anti-immigration attitudes with authoritarian values in around two-thirds of the countries under comparison. Particularly strong links are found in some of the most high-income European societies such as Switzerland, Germany, Denmark, and Austria, which have seen an influx of migrants in recent years and where radical right parties have made considerable electoral gains. By contrast, the correlations were not significant in several lower-income countries, including several post-communist societies such as Ukraine, Russia, and Poland, which have seen a net outflow of migrants to Western Europe. Anti-immigration attitudes were also significantly correlated with greater support for populism (mistrust of parties, parliaments, and politicians) in all but five societies under comparison, being especially strong in Scandinavia and Northern Europe. Governing elites in countries such as Norway and Sweden were reluctant to implement hardline policies limiting refugees and asylum seekers from poorer societies. By failing to respond to genuine public concerns about these issues, they may have undermined confidence in democratic institutions.

## V CONCLUSIONS

Throughout advanced industrial society, social changes have been occurring that seem shocking to those with traditional values. Immigration flows, especially from lower-income countries, have transformed the ethnic makeup of Western Europe. The newcomers speak different languages and have different religions and lifestyles from those of the native population – reinforcing the impression that traditional norms and values are rapidly disappearing. In a joint press conference with Theresa May on July 13, 2018, Trump warned European leaders that they had better watch themselves because immigration is changing the culture and security of European societies, echoing the claims of Authoritarian-Populist leaders from Hungary to France. By contrast, in response, UK prime minister Theresa May provided a strong defence for liberal tolerance: 'The UK has a proud history of welcoming people who are fleeing persecution to our country. We have a proud history of welcoming people who want

TABLE 6.2. *Authoritarian and populist values correlated with immigration attitudes, 32 countries*

| | Authoritarian values | | Populism | |
|---|---|---|---|---|
| Switzerland | 0.19 | ** | 0.13 | ** |
| Iceland | 0.17 | ** | 0.09 | ** |
| Germany | 0.17 | ** | 0.20 | ** |
| Austria | 0.16 | ** | 0.09 | ** |
| Denmark | 0.16 | ** | 0.21 | ** |
| Sweden | 0.16 | ** | 0.28 | ** |
| France | 0.15 | ** | 0.11 | ** |
| Israel | 0.12 | ** | 0.04 | ** |
| Belgium | 0.12 | ** | 0.19 | ** |
| UK | 0.12 | ** | 0.19 | ** |
| Norway | 0.12 | ** | 0.32 | ** |
| Netherlands | 0.12 | ** | 0.25 | ** |
| Finland | 0.11 | ** | 0.25 | ** |
| Spain | 0.10 | ** | 0.11 | ** |
| Italy | 0.10 | ** | 0.03 | N/s |
| Ireland | 0.06 | ** | 0.16 | ** |
| Lithuania | 0.06 | ** | 0.12 | ** |
| Slovenia | 0.06 | ** | 0.09 | ** |
| Slovakia | 0.05 | ** | 0.01 | N/s |
| Czech Republic | 0.04 | ** | 0.08 | ** |
| Estonia | 0.02 | * | 0.08 | ** |
| Hungary | 0.02 | * | 0.06 | ** |
| Luxembourg | 0.01 | N/s | 0.08 | ** |
| Greece | 0.01 | N/s | 0.08 | ** |
| Turkey | 0.00 | N/s | 0.03 | N/s |
| Poland | 0.00 | N/s | 0.06 | ** |
| Portugal | −0.01 | N/s | 0.05 | ** |
| Bulgaria | −0.01 | N/s | 0.02 | N/s |
| Russia | −0.02 | N/s | 0.06 | ** |
| Croatia | −0.02 | N/s | −0.06 | ** |
| Cyprus | −0.03 | N/s | 0.08 | ** |
| Ukraine | −0.07 | ** | 0.03 | * |
| ALL | 0.10 | ** | 0.14 | ** |

*Note:* Correlations. P ** .01, * .05, N/s Not significant. For the construction of all measures, see Appendix B.

*Source:* The European Social Survey, Cumulative File Rounds 1–7. N. 330,315 respondents in 32 European countries.

to come to our country to contribute to our economy and contribute to our society. Over the years, overall, immigration has been good for the UK. It has brought people with different backgrounds, different outlooks here to the UK.'[86] The rise of anti-immigrant Authoritarian-Populist parties seems to reflect, above all, a reaction by social conservatives against rapid social and cultural changes that seem to be eroding the bedrock values and historical customs of Western societies. This chapter has examined one part of this thesis, the impact of immigration on authoritarian and populist values.

Overall three findings stand out.

Firstly, the evidence examined here confirms extensive previous research linking anti-immigration attitudes with authoritarian *values.* Authoritarianism is about protecting 'Us' from 'Them' – those who transgress community norms. Immigrants who differ from the native population in the color of their skin or their religion, lifestyle, or language tend to be perceived as dangerous – especially by those living in isolated rural areas with little direct personal contact with ethnic minorities. These results, while not novel, confirm an important building block in our tipping point thesis.

Secondly, we find that cultural threats from immigration are more strongly correlated with authoritarian and populist values than with instrumental concerns about protecting economic interests. Cultural grievances are particularly strong among the older generation of white social conservatives, the people most likely to feel disconcerted by the rapid transformation of their societies. The evidence suggests that rapidly growing racial and ethnic diversity, not immigration per se, is most closely associated with authoritarian values.

Finally, even after controlling for the impact of a wide range of attitudes toward immigrants and economic conditions, *the respondent's generation remains the most important predictor of authoritarian values.* Long-term intergenerational population replacement is transforming the predominant values of European societies, and it is accelerated by immigration. But the reaction to rapidly growing ethnic diversity by social conservatives who feel threatened by these developments should not be underestimated: this is the group most likely to support Authoritarian-Populist parties.

How values are translated into votes, however, is far from straightforward. The anti-immigrant backlash provides opportunities for Authoritarian-Populist parties to harvest votes by advocating hard-line nationalist policies. They can exploit this issue, particularly where mainstream politicians share a liberal consensus that deters them from following suit. But if mainstream parties react by adopting immigration policies that are more restrictive and nationalistic language, stealing their rival's clothes while simultaneously ostracizing Authoritarian-Populist parties, the latter may find themselves squeezed out.[87] This is a plausible explanation for the outcome of the June 2017 UK general elections, where UKIP support faded following Theresa May's Conservative Party pledge to implement tighter migration restrictions on EU citizens. The policy was defended by May to prevent the wages of unskilled workers being undercut in the UK.[88] Regaining control of free movement of peoples from Europe was justified by the Conservative government as important even at the expense of access to the single market. Similarly, in Scandinavia, mainstream parties have been losing support to radical, anti-immigrant populist movements. But some mainstream parties have counter-attacked by absorbing these issues; in seeking to prevent further gains by the anti-immigrant Sweden Democrats (SD), for example, in 2017 the Moderate Party shifted to support implementing permanent limits on the length of time that those granted asylum can stay in Sweden, with polls suggesting that they subsequently regained some of the support they had lost to SD.[89] Patterns of competition and issue ownership evolve as parties learn in response to new issues, electoral results, and shifts in public opinion. The following chapter classifies Authoritarian-Populist parties and then examines how far values explain electoral support.

## Notes

1. Elizabeth Ivarsflaten. 2008. 'What unites right-wing populists in Western Europe? Re-examining grievance mobilization models in seven successful cases.' *Comparative Political Studies* 41 (1): 3–23; Tjitske Akkerman. 2012. 'Comparing radical right parties in government: Immigration and integration policies in nine countries (1996–2010).' *West European Politics* 35 (3): 511–529.
2. Stanley Feldman and Karen Stenner. 1997. 'Perceived threat and authoritarianism.' *Political Psychology* 18 (4): 741–770; Stanley Feldman. 2003. 'Enforcing social conformity: A theory of authoritarianism.' *Political Psychology* 24 (1): 41–74.
3. Jens Hainmueller and Daniel J. Hopkins. 2014. 'Public attitudes toward immigration.' *Annual Review of Political Science* 17: 225–249; Alin M. Ceobanu and Xavier Escandell. 2010. 'Comparative analyses of public attitudes toward immigrants and immigration using multinational survey data: A review of theories and research.' *Annual Review of Sociology* 36: 309–328; John Sides and Jack Citrin. 2007. 'European opinion about

immigration: The role of identities, interests and information.' *British Journal of Political Science* 37(3): 477–504.

4. D. Swank and H.-G. Betz. 2003. 'Globalization, the welfare state and right-wing populism in Western Europe.' *Socio-Economic Review* 1: 215–245.
5. Robert P. Jones. 2016. *The End of White Christian America.* New York: Simon & Schuster.
6. A. Yunas Samad and Konrad Sen. Eds. 2007. *Islam in the European Union: Transnationalism, Youth and the War on Terror.* Oxford: Oxford University Press.
7. http://research.newamericaneconomy.org/report/nearly-6-million-workers-employed-at-immigrant-owned-businesses-new-report-finds/.
8. www.imf.org/en/News/Articles/2015/09/28/04/52/mcs050916.
9. https://clas.berkeley.edu/research/immigration-economic-benefits-immigration.
10. www.pewresearch.org/fact-tank/2017/03/16/immigrants-dont-make-up-a-majority-of-workers-in-any-u-s-industry/.
11. OECD. 2017.*International Migration Outlook, 2017 – Statistical Annex.* Version 2. Last updated June 8, 2017.
12. OECD. 2017. *Key Statistics on Migration in OECD Countries.* www.oecd.org/els/mig/keystat.htm.
13. United Nations Population Division, Department of Economic and Social Affairs. 2017. *International Migrant Stock, 2015.* New York: United Nations. www.un.org/en/development/desa/population/migration/data/estimates2/estimates15.shtml.
14. http://ec.europa.eu/eurostat/statistics-explained/index.php/Being_young_in_Europe_today_-_demographic_trends.
15. UNHCR. *Global Trends, 2016.* New York: UNHCR. Appendix Table 2. www.unhcr.org/5943e8a34.pdf.
16. https://wenr.wes.org/2017/05/lessons-germanys-refugee-crisis-integration-costs-benefits.
17. www.pewresearch.org/fact-tank/2017/01/30/key-facts-about-refugees-to-the-u.
18. The exceptions are Greece, Slovakia, Estonia, and Israel, but it is likely that the OECD estimates for Greece do not take account of the effects of the 2015 refugee crisis.
19. OECD. 2017. *International Migration Outlook, 2017 – Statistical Annex.* Version 2. Last updated June 8, 2017. www.oecd-ilibrary.org/social-issues-migration-health/international-migration-outlook-2017_migr_outlook-2017-en.
20. The US Census Bureau estimates that in 2014, out of a total US population of 313,401 million, 272,658 were native born, with 40,743 million (13 percent of the total) who were foreign born. Among the foreign-born population, about half subsequently become naturalized citizens. www2.census.gov/programs-surveys/demo/tables/foreign-born/2014/cps2014/2014-nativity-table1.1.xlsx.

21. John L. Esposito and Ibrahim Kalin. Eds. 2011. *Islamophobia: The Challenge of Pluralism in the 21st Century*. New York: Oxford University Press.
22. For a discussion, see Hans-Georg Betz. 1994. *Radical Rightwing Populism in Western Europe*. New York: St Martin's Press, Chapter 3; Roger Karapin. 2002. 'Far right parties and the construction of immigration issues in Germany.' In Martin Schain, Aristide Zolberg, and Patrick Hossay. Eds. *Shadows Over Europe: The Development and Impact of the Extreme Right in Western Europe*. Houndsmill: Palgrave Macmillan; Cas Mudde. 1999. 'The single-issue party thesis: Extreme right parties and the immigration issue.' *West European Politics* 22 (3): 182–197; Rachel Gibson. 2002. *The Growth of Anti-Immigrant Parties in Western Europe*. Lewiston, NY: The Edwin Mellen Press.
23. Elizabeth Ivarsflaten. 2008. 'What unites right-wing populists in Western Europe? Re-examining grievance mobilization models in seven successful cases.' *Comparative Political Studies* 41 (1): 3–23.
24. Hans-Georg Betz. 1994. *Radical Rightwing Populism in Western Europe*. New York: St Martin's Press, p. 81.
25. www.europarl.europa.eu/external/html/welcomingeurope/default_en.htm.
26. Robin Alexander. 2017. *Die Getriebenen*. Berlin: Siedler.
27. Nicole Doerr. 2017. 'How right-wing versus cosmopolitan political actors mobilize and translate images of immigrants in transnational contexts.' *Visual Communication* 16 (3): 315–336.
28. Agnes Bolonyai and Kelsey Campolong. 2017. 'We mustn't fool ourselves "Orbanian" discourse in the political battle over the refugee crisis and European identity.' *Journal of Language Aggression and Conflict* 5 (2): 251–273.
29. Koen Vossen. 2016. *The Power of Populism: Geert Wilders and the Party for Freedom in the Netherlands*. New York: Routledge. See also www.geertwilders.nl/.
30. www.theguardian.com/world/2017/feb/18/geert-wilders-netherlands-describes-immigrants-scum-holland.
31. Priscilla Southwell and Eric Lindgren. 2013. 'The rise of neo-populist parties in Scandinavia: A Danish case study.' *Review of European Studies* 5 (5): 128–135.
32. https://danskfolkeparti.dk/politik/stramninger-paa-udlaendingepolitikken/.
33. James Dennison and Matthew Goodwin. 2015. 'Immigration, issue ownership and the rise of UKIP.' *Parliamentary Affairs* 68 (1): 168–187.
34. Daniel Stockemer and Mauro Barisione. 2017. 'The "new" discourse of the Front National under Marine Le Pen: A slight change with a big impact.' *European Journal of Communication* 32 (2): 100–115; Daniel Stockemer. 2017. *The National Front in France: Continuity and Change under Jean-Marie Le Pen and Marine Le Pen*. Germany: Springer.
35. www.enfgroup-ep.eu/.
36. Michael D. Shear and Julie Hirschfeld David. 2017. 'Stoking fear, Trump defied bureaucracy to advance immigration agenda.' *New York Times*. www.nytimes.com/2017/12/23/us/politics/trump-immigration.html.
37. www.whitehouse.gov/issues/immigration/.

38. Ruth Wodak. 2015. *The Politics of Fear: What Right-Wing Populist Discourses Mean*. London: Sage.
39. Massimiliano Demata. 2017. '"A great and beautiful wall" Donald Trump's populist discourse on immigration.' *Journal of Language Aggression and Conflict* 5 (2): 274–294; Natalia Knoblock. 2017. 'Xenophobic Trumpeters.' *Journal of Language Aggression and Conflict* 5 (2): 295–322.
40. Donald Trump. Speech on January 24, 2016. Des Moines, Iowa. www.c-span.org/video/?403832-1/ presidential-candidate-donald-trump-rally-des-moines-iowa.
41. Michael D. Shear and Julie Hirschfeld David. 2017. 'Stoking fear, Trump defied bureaucracy to advance immigration agenda.' *New York Times*. www.nytimes.com/2017/12/23/us/politics/trump-immigration.html.
42. www.politico.com/story/2016/09/birther-movement-founder-trump-clinton-228304.
43. Joan C. Williams. 2017. *White Working Class*. Cambridge, MA: Harvard Business Review Press, Chapter 8.
44. Ronald Inglehart. 2018. *Cultural Evolution: People's Motivations are Changing, and Reshaping the World*. New York: Cambridge University Press; Ronald Inglehart, Mansoor Moaddel, and Mark Tessler. 2006. 'Xenophobia and in-group solidarity in Iraq: A natural experiment on the impact of insecurity.' *Perspectives on Politics* 4 (3): 495–505.
45. John Sides and Jack Citrin. 2007. 'European opinion about immigration: The role of identities, interests and information.' *British Journal of Political Science* 37 (3): 477–504.
46. Jack Citrin, Donald P. Green, C. Muste, and C. Wong. 1997. 'Public opinion towards immigration reform: The role of economic motivations.' *Journal of Politics* 59: 858–881; V.M. Esses, L.M. Jackson, and T.L. Armstrong. 1998. 'Intergroup competition and attitudes toward immigrants and immigration: An instrumental model of group conflict.' *Journal of Social Issues* 54: 699–724; G. Lahav. 2004. *Immigration and Politics in the New Europe*. Cambridge: Cambridge University Press; Paul M. Sniderman, L. Hougendoorn, and Marcus Prior. 2004. 'Predispositional factors and situational triggers: Exclusionary reactions to immigrant minorities.' *American Political Science Review* 98: 35–50.
47. Julien L. Simon. 1999. *The Economic Consequences of Immigration*. 2nd edn. Ann Arbor, MI: University of Michigan Press; George Borjas. 2003. 'The labor demand curve is downward sloping: Reexamining the impact of immigration on the labor market.' *Quarterly Journal of Economics* 118 (4): 1335–1374.
48. J.G. Andersen. 1992. 'Denmark: The Progress Party – populist neo-liberalism and welfare state chauvinism.' In Paul Hainsworth. Ed. *The Extreme Right in Europe and the USA*. London: Pinter; Keith Banting. 2010. 'Is there a progressive's dilemma in Canada? Immigration, multiculturalism and the welfare state.' *Canadian Journal of Political Science* 43 (4): 797–820; A.H. Bay and A. Pedersen. 2006. 'The limits of social solidarity: Basic income, immigration and the legitimacy of the universal welfare state.' *Acta Sociologica* 49 (4): 419–436.

49. R.W. Jackman and K. Volpert. 1996. 'Conditions favouring parties of the extreme right in Western Europe.' *British Journal of Political Science* 26: 501–521; Christopher Cochrane and Neil Nevitte. 2014. 'Scapegoating: Unemployment, far-right parties and anti-immigrant sentiment.' *Comparative European Politics* 12 (1): 1–32.
50. L.M. McLaren. 2002. 'Public support for the European Union: Cost/benefit analysis or perceived cultural threat?' *Journal of Politics* 64 (2): 551–566.
51. J.G. Andersen. 1992. 'Denmark: The Progress Party – populist neo-liberalism and welfare state chauvinism.' In Paul Hainsworth. Ed. *The Extreme Right in Europe and the USA*. London: Pinter; Keith Banting. 2010. 'Is there a progressive's dilemma in Canada? Immigration, multiculturalism and the welfare state.' *Canadian Journal of Political Science* 43 (4): 797–820; A.H. Bay and A. Pedersen. 2006. 'The limits of social solidarity: Basic income, immigration and the legitimacy of the universal welfare state.' *Acta Sociologica* 49 (4): 419–436.
52. H. Blumer. 1958. 'Race prejudice as a sense of group position.' *The Pacific Sociological Review* 1: 3–7.
53. See, for example, Jeff Crisp. 2003. 'The closing of the European gates? The new populist parties of Europe.' In Sarah Spencer. Ed. *The Politics of Migration*. Oxford: Blackwell; Grete Brochmann and Tomas Hammar. Eds. 1999. *Mechanisms of Immigration Control: A Comparative Analysis of European Regulation Policies*. New York: Berg.
54. J.L. Sullivan, J.E. Piereson, and G.E. Marcus. 1982. *Political Tolerance and American Democracy*. Chicago: The University of Chicago Press; Jocelyn Cesari. 2004. *When Islam and Democracy Meet: Muslims in Europe and the United States*. New York: Palgrave Macmillan; D.W. Davis and B.D. Silver. 2004. 'Civil liberties v. security: Public opinion in the context of terrorist attacks on America.' *American Journal of Political Science* 48: 28–46.
55. Richard Wike and Brian J. Grim. 2010. 'Western views toward Muslims: Evidence from a 2006 Cross-National Survey.' *International Journal of Public Opinion Research* 22 (1): 4–25.
56. Thomas F. Pettigrew and L.R. Tropp. 2006. 'A meta-analytic test of intergroup contact theory.' *Journal of Personality and Social Psychology* 90 (5): 751–783.
57. K. Bansak, J. Hainmueller, and D. Hangartner. 2016. 'How economic, humanitarian, and religious concerns shape European attitudes toward asylum seekers.' *Science* 354: 217–222.
58. Bruce Bawer. 2007. *While Europe Slept: How Radical Islam Is Destroying the West from Within*. New York: Anchor; Douglas Murray. 2017. *The Strange Death of Europe: Immigration, Identity, Islam*. London: Bloomsbury.
59. Conny Roggeband and Mieke Verloo. 2007. 'Dutch women are liberated, migrant women are a problem: The evolution of policy frames on gender and migration in the Netherlands, 1995–2005.' *Social Policy and Administration* 41 (3): 271–288.
60. Wouter Van der Brug, M. Fennema, and James Tillie. 2000. 'Anti-immigrant parties in Europe: Ideological or protest vote?' *European Journal of Political Research* 37 (1): 77–102.

61. Agnieszka Golec de Zavala, Rita Guerra, and Claudia Simao. 2017. 'The relationship between the Brexit Vote and individual predictors of prejudice: Collective narcissism, right-wing authoritarianism, social dominance orientation.' *Frontiers In Psychology* 8. https://doi.org/10.3389/fpsyg.2017.02023.
62. John Curtice. 2015. 'A question of culture or economics? Public attitudes to the European Union in Britain.' *Political Quarterly* 87 (2): 209–218.
63. Sara B. Hobolt. 2016. 'The Brexit vote: A divided nation, a divided continent.' *Journal of European Public Policy* 23 (9): 1259–1277.
64. Pippa Norris. 2005. *Radical Right: Voters and Parties in the Electoral Market.* New York: Cambridge University Press, pp. 182–183. See also Tjitske Akkerman. 2012. 'Comparing radical right parties in government: Immigration and integration policies in nine countries (1996–2010).' *West European Politics* 35 (3): 511–529; E. Davidov, B. Meuleman, J. Billiet, and P. Schmidt. 2008. 'Values and support for immigration: A cross-country comparison.' *European Sociological Review* 24 (5): 583–599.
65. L. Bustikova. 2014. 'Revenge of the radical right.' *Comparative Political Studies* 47: 1738–1765.
66. John Sides, Michael Tesler, and Lynn Vavreck. 2017. 'How Trump lost and won.' *Journal of Democracy* 28 (2): 34–44.
67. Matthew C. MacWilliams. 2016. 'Who decides when the party doesn't? Authoritarian voters and the rise of Donald Trump.' *PS: Political Science and Politics* 49 (4): 716–721.
68. Daniel Cox, Rachel Lienesch, and Robert P. Jones. 2017. *Beyond Economics: Fears of Cultural Displacement Pushed the White Working Class to Trump*. www.prri.org/research/white-working-class-attitudes-economy-trade-immigration-election-donald-trump/.
69. Rafaela M. Dancygier. 2010. *Immigration and Conflict in Europe*. Cambridge: Cambridge University Press.
70. Rik Coolsaet. Ed. 2008. *Jihadi Terrorism and the Radicalisation Challenge in Europe*. Farnham: Ashgate.
71. Marc Hetherington and Jonathan Weiler. 2009. *Authoritarianism and Polarization in American Politics*. New York: Cambridge University Press. See also M. Abrajano and Z.L. Hajnal. 2015. *White Backlash: Immigration, Race, and American Politics*. Princeton, NJ: Princeton University Press.
72. Cas Mudde and Cristóbal Rovira Kaltwasser. 2012. 'Exclusionary vs. Inclusionary Populism in Europe and Latin America.' *Government and Opposition* 48 (2): 147–174; Dani Filc. 2015. 'Latin American inclusive and European exclusionary populism: Colonialism as an explanation.' *Journal of Political Ideologies* 20 (3): 263–283.
73. Andrew Geddes and Peter Scholten. 2016. *The Politics of Migration and Immigration in Europe*. London: Sage.
74. Mark Bovens and Anchrit Wille. 2017. *Diploma Democracy: The Rise of Political Meritocracy.* Oxford: Oxford University Press.
75. Reliability tests for the three items on immigration generated a high Cronbach Alpha (0.826).

76. Martin Halla, Alexander F. Wagner, and Josef Zweimuller. 2014. 'Immigration and voting for the Extreme Right.' www.econ.jku.at/papers/2012/wp1205.pdf.
77. Hilde Coffé, Bruno Heyndels, and Jan Vermeir. 2007. 'Fertile grounds for extreme right-wing parties.' *Electoral Studies.* 26: 142.
78. Daniel Stockemer. 2017. 'The success of radical right-wing parties in Western European regions: New challenging findings.' *Journal of Contemporary European Studies* 25 (1): 41–56.
79. Katherine J. Cramer. 2016. *The Politics of Resentment: Rural Consciousness in Wisconsin and the Rise of Scott Walker.* Chicago: University of Chicago Press.
80. Thomas F. Pettigrew and L.R. Tropp. 2006. 'A meta-analytic test of intergroup contact theory.' *Journal of Personality and Social Psychology* 90 (5): 751–783.
81. Jytte Klausen. 2005. *The Islamic Challenge: Politics and Religion in Western Europe.* Oxford: Oxford University Press; John L. Esposito and Ibrahim Kalin. Eds. 2011. *Islamophobia: The Challenge of Pluralism in the 21st Century.* New York: Oxford University Press.
82. Ronald Inglehart and Christian Welzel. 2005. *Modernization, Cultural Change and Democracy: The Human Development Sequence.* New York: Cambridge University Press.
83. Sascha O. Becker, Thiemo Fetzer, and Dennis Novy. 2017. 'Who voted for Brexit? A comprehensive district-level analysis.' Munich: CESifo Working Papers 6438-2017. Paper presented at the 65th Panel Meeting of Economic Policy. http://cep.lse.ac.uk/pubs/download/dp1480.pdf; Sascha O. Becker and Thiemo Fetzer. 2016. 'Does migration cause extreme Voting?' Coventry: University of Warwick. CAGE working paper 306/2016.
84. www.nytimes.com/2017/10/19/world/europe/quebec-burqa-ban-europe.html.
85. For a discussion, see Thomas F. Pettigrew. 1998. 'Reactions toward the new minorities of Western Europe.' *Annual Review of Sociology* 24: 77–103; Herbert Kitschelt, with Anthony J. McGann. 1995. *The Radical Right in Western Europe: A Comparative Analysis.* Ann Arbor, MI: University of Michigan; Marcel Lubbers, Mérove Gijsberts, and Peer Scheepers. 2002. 'Extreme right-wing voting in Western Europe.' *European Journal of Political Research* 41 (3): 345–378; Pippa Norris. 2005. *Radical Right: Voters and Parties in the Electoral Market.* New York: Cambridge University Press.
86. Donald Trump and Theresa May joint press conference, Chequers. https://www.cnn.com/2018/07/13/politics/trump-europe-immigration/index.html.
87. Rooduijn Matthijs, S.L. De Lange, and Wouter van der Brug. 2014. 'A populist Zeitgeist? Programmatic contagion by populist parties in Western Europe.' *Party Politics* 20 (4): 563–575; Joost van Spanje and Nan Dirk de Graaf. 2018. 'How established parties reduce other parties' electoral support: The strategy of parroting the pariah.' *West European Politics* 41 (1): 1–27.
88. www.theguardian.com/politics/2017/sep/06/theresa-may-backs-new-eu-immigration-controls-after-brexit-leak.
89. www.politico.eu/article/ulf-kristersson-swedish-opposition-latest-approach-to-the-far-right-talk-to-the-hand/.

PART III

# FROM VALUES TO VOTES

# 7

# Classifying Parties

Can parties such as the Swedish Democrats, the Jobbik Movement for a Better Hungary, the French National Front/National Rally, and the Italian Lega Nord all be classified consistently as part of the same family? Are there shared values among leaders as apparently diverse as Donald Trump, Recep Tayyip Erdoğan, Marine Le Pen, Viktor Orban, Miloš Zeman, Hugo Chavez, Bernie Sanders, and Nigel Farage? There is little dispute that certain long-established cases fall into the same boat – a broad consensus regards the French National Front, the Freedom Party of Austria, and the Danish People's Party as sharing many characteristics. But other cases raise arguments about concept-stretching and boundary issues – particularly when mainstream center-right or center-left parties take on populist colorings. Can Corbyn, Macron, and May be categorized as populist? Researchers also use a bewildering plethora of labels to classify party families such as 'radical right,' 'far-right,' 'right-wing populism,' 'alt-right,' 'extreme right' and 'populist right,' and so on. The lack of consistency raises red flags. Accordingly, to clear the decks, this chapter clarifies the underlying concepts and presents the party typology used in this book.

Part I of this chapter summarizes the conceptual framework and the meaning of both populism and authoritarianism, ideas discussed earlier in Chapter 3. Building on this, Part II discusses the pros and cons of alternative methods for gathering evidence useful to categorize party families. Part III describes how party positions are measured in this study and mapped on a multidimensional issue space. The Chapel Hill Expert Survey (CHES) is used to create indices of left–right, authoritarian–libertarianism, and populism–pluralism, each measured as continuous standardized scales. These are used to compare the position of 270 political parties in this CHES dataset. The location of party position on the 100-point scales indicates how far each party endorses each of these dimensions. The indices are therefore treated in this book primarily as matters of degree, rather than as categorical types.[1] Identifying party positions on continuous scales avoids sharp-edged boundary issues and potential risks of misclassifications, as well as facilitating granular analysis. Researchers often treat party choices in the electorate as discrete (yes/no) categories but this is theoretically implausible, especially in multiparty systems, if people have ranked utilities ('I like X, but also Y and Z'). This practice is also statistically problematic with the standard size of national survey samples when analyzing voting for small parties using conditional logit and multinomial logit techniques; quite simply, researchers have too few cases and too many confounding conditions, as well as sharply skewed distributions.[2] At the same time, we recognize that it is also useful to identify specific categories which exemplify types of parties for other purposes, such as when selecting concrete case studies. For this purpose, a stricter categorization is used, focusing on parties which score very highly on the Indexes. Part IV maps European political parties on these scales – including Authoritarian-Populist parties – across a wide range of European countries. We also discuss how best to classify presidential leaders. This enables us, in the next chapter, to identify the key determinants of how values translate into voting support for political parties located across the authoritarian and populism indices.

## I THE CONCEPTUAL FRAMEWORK

The meaning of populism continues to be debated but in recent years a broad consensus has emerged among many scholars. Chapter 3 used a minimalist definition of populism as a form of discourse making two core claims, namely that: (i) the only legitimate democratic authority flows directly from the people, and (ii) establishment elites are corrupt, out of touch, and self-serving, betraying the public trust and thwarting the popular will. In the political sphere, populist arguments challenge the legitimacy of intermediate power structures linking citizens and the state in liberal democracies, including that of elected representatives, mainstream political parties, elected assemblies and parliaments, as well as the courts, judges, and rule of law, and public-sector bureaucrats and mainstream media, along with the broader range of policy technocrats, professional think-tanks, academic opinion-formers, and scientific consultants. The roots of populism can be traced back to concepts of direct democracy and the voice of the people in Jean-Jacques Rousseau's *The Social Contract* (1762). In this regard, populism is treated not as a distinct type of leadership, or even a family of political parties, as is often assumed, but rather as a discourse about governance that can be adopted by actors across the entire ideological spectrum.[3] We reject the notion that populism, in itself, makes other ideological claims about substantive or programmatic claims, about what should be done; instead, it is a rhetoric about the rightful location of governance authority in any society. In Western democracies, the most common antithesis of populism is 'pluralism,' emphasizing the importance of tolerating multiculturalism and social diversity in society, governance through liberal democratic institutions, the role of checks and balances on executive powers, and respect for minority rights to counter-balance the majoritarian voice of the people. In non-democratic countries, however, populism may also be contested by those advocating 'elitism' – claiming that power should rest in the hands of a single leader, a leadership elite, or a predominant party.

Beyond the expressive rhetoric, however, as a philosophy of *who* should govern and *how* legitimate power should be exercised, populism by itself, like pluralist theories of liberal democracy, does not furnish a roadmap prescribing any consistent set of substantive programmatic policies or provide a coherent set of beliefs about what governments should do. What matters for the public policy agenda on issues such as managing the economy, handling international relations, or dealing with social problems is not populism alone, but how this narrative is used in conjunction with alternative ideologies. As discussed earlier, parties and leaders endorsing authoritarian values (i) advocate conformity with conventional moral norms and traditions within a group, expressing intolerance of out-groups perceived to threaten accepted group mores; (ii) expect deference and loyalty to the group and its leaders, being intolerant of dissent; and (iii) seek to strengthen collective security against perceived group threats. They reject the libertarian emphasis on the values of individualism, free-spiritedness, and personal liberation. The conjunction of populism and authoritarianism is common, since populism undermines the legitimacy of institutional checks on executive powers, opening the door for authoritarian rulers. But this is a contingent relationship not a necessary condition. Both populist discourse and authoritarian values can be endorsed by all sorts of actors – leaders, political parties, organizations, social movements, media, and ordinary citizens – located on both the economic right and left.

How can the conceptual framework be applied to classify political parties and leaders?

## Ideological Diversity and the Multidimensional Issue Space

The first challenge is to consider how these concepts relate to the dimension of 'left' and 'right' which traditionally permeate studies of party competition. The dominant research tradition, building upon standard classifications of political parties in Western Europe, reflects conventional approaches by retaining the familiar left–right terminology but tacking on 'populism.' Thus, parties are categorized as 'right-wing populist,' as well as alternative related terms, such as 'radical right,'[4] 'populist radical right,'[5] 'far right,' or 'extreme right' parties, and so on.[6] More recently, the term 'alt-right' has been adopted in America to describe a loose network composed chiefly of white supremacists, neo-Nazis, neo-fascists, and other fringe hate groups. The plethora of terms common in the research literature, and practices of concept stretching where these labels are extended to cover diverse cases, are indicative of problems that are more severe.

Attention in the research literature has also traditionally focused upon studying only one side of the left–right cleavage, namely right-wing forms of populism, the type most commonly observed in Western Europe. Yet populist parties around the world range across the ideological spectrum from market-oriented neo-liberalism (as advocated by Alberto Fujimoro) to state socialism (as advocated by Hugo Chavez). This combination is particularly common in Latin America.[7] Thus, Chavez railed against 'predatory' political elites, economic austerity measures, and the neo-colonial foreign policies of the United States, while inspiring a socialist revolution in Venezuela.[8] Studies comparing the Americas, Central and Eastern Europe, and Asia have identified many populist parties and leaders that favor state economic management, wealth redistribution, and social justice, policies which can be classified as part of the 'populist left.'[9]

Similarly, there are several left-wing populist parties in Western Europe, including Podemos in Spain and the Five-Star Movement in Italy. It has also become fairly common for left-wing parties and politicians like Jeremy Corbyn and Bernie Sanders to use populist rhetoric when criticizing financial elites and the power of multinational corporations and big business. The discourse of radical left parties in Europe, traditionally communist and socialist, have been found to have become more populist in recent years, making broad claims about 'the good people' not just appealing to the working class.[10]

In the United States, as well, populism is associated historically with the left. The Populist Party founded in 1891 was an anti-elite rural movement on the left that was critical of capitalism, especially banks, and associated with organized labor.[11] Following this long historical tradition in America, in his run for the Democratic nomination during the 2016 election, Senator Bernie Sanders campaigned as a left-wing populist. His speeches attacked economic inequality, globalization, and capitalism, and he proposed redistributive taxation and programs of social justice designed to expand access to food, housing, healthcare, and education for the poor, as well as being progressive on issues of environmental protection and climate change, sexual and gender identities, civil rights, and immigration.

## Ideological Inconsistency and Ambiguity

Another practical difficulty in classifying populist parties and leaders along the traditional left–right spectrum lies in the (intentional?) ambiguity of their programmatic appeals. Clearly, it is important to distinguish several varieties of populism where the rhetoric is the façade attached to diverse ideologies. One challenge about this process is that populist rhetoric concerns first-order principles about legitimate government concerning vague anti-establishment appeals, simplistic slogans, and sweeping promises to fight for 'the silent majority,' and end corruption. But the discourse typically eschews detailed policy prescriptions about second-order policy programs about what governments should do. As a result, rather than having a consistent common location on the classic economic left–right continuum, populist parties and leaders differ in their views, for example toward the appropriate level of investment in welfare protection, public-sector spending, taxation, and state regulation.

As a result, many populist leaders and parties also refuse to fit neatly into left–right programmatic policy boxes. This can be illustrated by the first year of President Trump's administration. Trump is often thought to exemplify the 'populist right' yet the President's speeches, tweets, and executive actions mix together advocacy of inconsistent principles across the conventional left–right spectrum. Some economic priorities are right-wing: this includes supporting small-state laissez faire economic policies, which reflect the mainstream Republican Congressional leadership and the role of the GOP Freedom Caucus on issues such as the aggressive deregulation of environmental protection, seeking to repeal Obamacare, and rolling back corporate taxes. His economic policy positions strongly favor the rich, exemplified by the regressive 2017 Tax Cut and Jobs Act cutting the corporate tax rate permanently from 35 percent to 21 percent, with benefits flowing mainly to wealthy executives and shareholders. But Trump has also followed economic protectionism for American industry, imposing tariffs on trade, renegotiating NAFTA, and seeking to restore coal-mining jobs.[12]

Similarly, in international affairs, President Trump may be seen as an isolationist. His 'America First' rhetoric has signaled US withdrawal from multilateral agreements and alliances, such as the TPP, the Paris climate accord, the Iran accord, and America's leadership role of the free world, as well as tearing up the State Department's investment in democracy promotion, human rights, and the United Nations. President Trump has sharply attacked the G7, NATO, and the European Union, breaking diplomatic norms and deeply undermining the pillars of the liberal world order. He has attacked and sought to destabilize some of America's most stalwart allies, including leaders in Canada, Germany, and the UK, while expressing warm admiration for many authoritarians around the world, such as in Russia, China, North Korea, the Philippines, and Saudi Arabia. Yet his administration has also maintained several foreign policies; for example, the Pentagon has signaled the continuing engagement of troops in Afghanistan and Iraq.

On culture issues, while social conservatives like Ted Cruz suspected that Trump's colorful life and 'New York values' were relatively liberal before he was elected to the White House, President Trump has sought to roll back tolerant live-and-let-live social liberalism.[13] Through a series of executive orders, legislative bills, and the selection of judicial and agency appointments, his administration has worked to enforce conformity with traditional social norms and limit personal freedoms. His administration has sought to oppose state laws deregulating recreational drugs, to limit voting rights, to restrict women's access to reproductive rights, to defend gun ownership, to repeal DACA and end the citizenship rights of Dreamers, to advocate stronger libel laws, and to limit the role of transsexuals in the military. The white nativist appeals have been most overt in his attempts to restrict all Hispanics seeking entry into the US, even those with legal appeals to asylum, including dividing families and incarcerating children crossing the border. He also displays authoritarian values in governance, undermining norms of American democracy in numerous ways, including through deepening partisan and factional rancor, dividing the country instead of providing moral leadership on issues of race and diversity, challenging the independence of the judiciary and rule of law, undermining the news media through constantly lambasting 'fake' news, failing to observe standards of transparency and integrity in separating his office from financial dealings and enriching his family, threatening his opponent with imprisonment, displaying sexism in his treatment of women and racism in his remarks toward African-Americans and Hispanics, failing to defend an attack on US elections by a foreign power, appealing only to his base rather than seeking to expand his support, and proving deeply incompetent at the process of legislative bargaining and inept in the art of brokering political deals across both parties.

## Collective Party Ideologies

Finally, a further challenge arises because even where the left–right policy position of individual leaders can be classified, such as through analyzing their speeches, or the collective policy positions of a political party can be determined, through the platform, this does not mean that this signifies the position of leadership factions, activists, and grassroots members. Party platforms and manifestos are taken to reflect common principles as blueprints which guide party campaigns and subsequent government programs.[14] But these documents may be inadequate guides to collective issue preferences in factionalized and poorly institutionalized political parties with low party discipline, which are common outside of Western Europe. The US Republican Party, for example, has become more authoritarian populist under the Trump administration, exemplified by the influence of Steve Bannon as chief strategist in the White House during the first seven months after Trump took office, the resignation of many moderate Republican House lawmakers in the run up to the 2018 mid-term contests, and the role of cabinet members in zealously implementing Trump's vision of America, notably Scott Pruitt's tenure in the Environmental Protection Agency and Ryan Zinke at the Interior. But this does not mean that all agency heads are in 100 percent agreement or that all Republican lawmakers marched in lockstep. Multiple ideological factions within the party, such as the Freedom Caucus, continue to battle in public with its heart and soul on issues such as the budget, immigration, and free trade. Nor would most Republicans in Congress ever regard themselves as populists – even if they collaborate with the Trump administration to implement a shared legislative agenda. Similarly, the British Conservative parliamentary party has long been deeply split between its Eurosceptic and pro-EU wings. And platform documents may prove a poor guide to party positions in leadership-dominated parties, common with Authoritarian-Populist parties, as well as in candidate-centered campaigns and in coalition governments. For all these reasons, classifying political parties based on their policy position on the traditional one-dimensional left–right cleavage, based on programmatic disagreements about the appropriate role of the state versus markets, fails to capture competition over many other party positions.

Figure 7.1 depicts how we expect party policy positions will map onto the core cleavages. We want to establish the position of parties on the pluralism–populism dimension of party competition, reflecting contention about where legitimate power lies in the nation-state. This divides populists, claiming that governance should reflect the preferences of the vox populi, from pluralists, arguing that decisions should be made by the elected officials and divided among governing institutions in liberal democracy.

This can be distinguished from party positions on the second dimension reflecting the authoritarian–libertarian cultural cleavage, reflecting their stand on issues such as environmental protection and climate change, multiculturalism and sexual equality, human rights, international development aid, and cosmopolitan or nationalistic policies.

Finally, we also want to see how these dimensions relate to the classic left–right economic cleavage over the role of markets versus the state, which traditionally dominated party competition in established Western democracies during the mid-twentieth century.[15] Communist, socialist, and social democratic parties are predicted to be located on the economic left, favoring state management of the economy, redistribution through progressive taxation, and generous welfare states, social policies, and

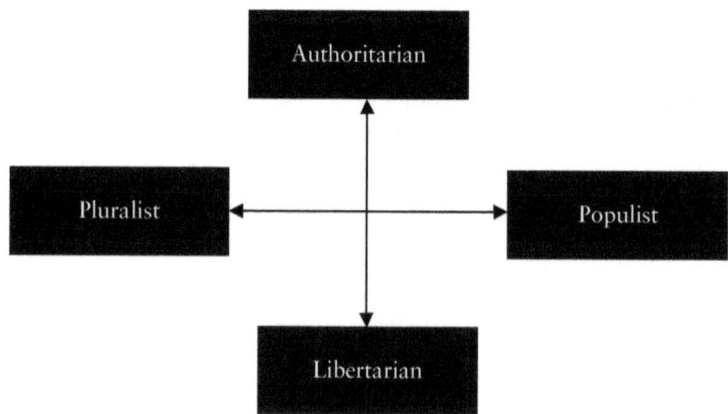


FIGURE 7.1. *Model of cleavages in party competition in Western societies*

public services. By contrast, liberal, conservative, and Christian democratic parties are expected to be located on the economic right, favoring free markets and private enterprise, a minimal role for the state, deregulation, and low taxation.

## II WAYS TO MEASURE PARTY POSITIONS IN THE THREE-DIMENSIONAL ISSUE SPACE

What evidence allows us to operationalize, categorize, and compare where European political parties position themselves in terms of the dimensions of left–right, authoritarian-libertarian, and populism-pluralism? How can these concepts be measured on a reliable, consistent, and valid basis? Attempts to categorize parties into distinct families have used various methods, including classifying them according to party names and organizational affiliations; analyzing the discourse in leadership speeches and press releases; coding the contents of programmatic party platforms or manifestos; using expert surveys to assess party positions across the ideological spectrum; conducting surveys of elected representatives, parliamentary candidates, activists and party members; and using national election surveys to measure the policy preferences of party supporters in the general electorate.[16] Each approach has certain distinct pros and cons.

### Party Affiliations

Scholars of party politics often seek to classify distinct party families through common organizational networks, such as membership in the European People's Party, or institutional affiliations with transnational federations, such as the Liberal International and the Global Greens. This is useful for classifying older party families such as the scores of labour parties, social democratic parties, and socialist parties that are affiliated with the Socialist International.[17] This method is relatively straightforward to apply using publically accessible information. It also reflects the way that political parties seek to build alliances and share resources with sister organizations. But these alliances are far from stable, with members and parties shifting alliances; for example, the Italian Northern League belonged to the Rainbow Coalition in the European Parliament before moving in 1994 to join the Euro-liberals. Political parties can also be members simultaneously of different associations at European, national, and regional levels.

Authoritarian-Populist parties are also divided in their affiliations. Several parties in the European Parliament are currently associated with the Europe of Nations and Freedom (ENF) group. This provides a loose alliance for the Austrian Freedom Party, the Flemish Vlaams Belang (FB), the French National Front (FN), the Alternative for Germany (AfD), the Italian Lega Nord, the Dutch Party for Freedom (PVV), and some individual MEPs from other countries. In the words of Marcel de Graff, the ENF's co-president: 'Our European cultures, our values and our freedom are under attack. They are threatened by the crushing and dictatorial powers of the European Union. They are threatened by mass immigration, by open borders and by a single European currency: one size does not fit all.'[18]

However, the Europe of Freedom and Direct Democracy (EFD) provides another rival group in the European Parliament, linking UKIP, the Alternative for Germany, the Five Star Movement, the Lithuanian Order and Justice Party, the Swedish Democrats, and other members. The EFD is Eurosceptic, with Nigel Farage as the president, claiming to reflect 'the people's voice' by fighting 'big government, big banks, and big business' which are 'strangling national identities.'[19] Favoring the populist principles of direct democracy, the Charter for the EFD advocates referenda: 'Convinced that the legitimate level for democracy lies with the nation-states, their regions and parliaments since there is no such thing as a single European people; the Group opposes further European integration (treaties and policies) that would exacerbate the present democratic deficit and the centralist political structure of the EU. The Group favours that any new treaties or any modification of the existing treaties are to be submitted to the peoples' vote through free and fair national referenda in the Member States. The Group does believe that the legitimacy of any power comes from the will of its Peoples and their right to be free and democratically ruled.'[20] Compared with the EFN, the EFD Charter also presents a more moderate position committed to direct democracy, arguing that it seeks to restore rights to national sovereignty in Europe, but it simultaneously rejects xenophobia, anti-Semitism, and other forms of discrimination.

Finally, not all Authoritarian-Populist parties in the EU belong to these two groupings; for example, the Danish People's Party and the Finns Party are members of the center-right European Conservatives and Reformists. Therefore, it is far from easy to identify the common ideological principles and shared values of Authoritarian-Populist political parties based on shifting allegiances to formal institutional affiliations.

## Party Names

Other party typologies have relied on shared party names, such as 'Social Democrats,' 'Christian Democrats,' 'Liberals,' and 'Greens.' The titles that parties adopt goes to the heart of their brand name in the political marketplace and their historical origins. It seems a straightforward approach. But in practice, party labels can disguise deep ideological divisions, such as those between neo-classical laissez faire liberals and social liberals. Moreover, identical party labels have been adopted by parties with very different platforms and ideologies. The same name can also mask major ideological shifts over time within a party, such as the British Labour Party experienced under the leadership of Tony Blair and Jeremy Corbyn. Similarly, Trump mounted a hostile take-over of the GOP, so that the policies of the party under his leadership diverged sharply from the Republican Party of George W. Bush, such as the contrasts between the international promotion of democracy in the Middle East by the Neo-Cons and the 'American First' withdrawal from this role in Rex Tillerson's State Department. Newer populist parties, wanting to burnish their outsider credentials, also adopt *sui generis* names to avoid being associated with traditional party labels, exemplified by the Italian Five Star Movement, the Greek Golden Dawn, and the Spanish Podemos. Parties that scholars consider populist or authoritarian use a variety of labels that don't refer to these concepts, and, like authoritarian regimes, they may even use Orwellian language that refers to their antonym, such as the Swedish Democrats, the Federal Democratic Union of Switzerland and the Croatian Democratic Union. Party names also change over time; for example, in June 2018 the French National Front (FN) rebranded itself as the National Rally (Rassemblement national, RN).

## Rhetorical and Discourse Analysis

An approach common in communication studies focuses on the speeches, social media, and press releases of political party leaders and the contents of the media messages. Techniques have included human and computerized content analysis of text and visual images. From this perspective, populism is viewed as a style of communication and a language claiming 'power to the people' and a critique of the establishment, rather than a set of ideological beliefs about substantive public policies on issues like the economy.[21]

Moreover, the style of communication is not confined to political parties – populist language can be adopted by any actor, such as individual politicians and leaders, social movements and political organizations, media communication outlets, such as the tabloid press, news channels such as Fox TV, websites, such as Breitbart news, and by ordinary citizens. In political communications, the rise of populist leaders as diverse as Forza Italia's Silvio Berlusconi in Italy and Podemos' Pablo Iglesias in Spain are closely associated with 'soft' news outlets, such as the tabloid press and cable news channels.[22] The tabloid press uses a populist style of language and vernacular aimed to build mass circulation though appealing to the common people. Years before the electoral success of UKIP and Brexit, British papers such as *The Sun, Express*, and *Daily Mail* had a long history of publishing exaggerated or invented cartoonish tall stories reflecting Eurosceptic diatribes and myths about Brussels regulations (the tale of banning 'bendy bananas'), as part of their flag-waving nationalism, as well as using colorful headlines and graphics attacking 'politically correct' liberal views toward feminism and the women's movement, refugees and immigration, and racial tolerance.[23] The Eurosceptic tabloid press shapes reader's views toward the EU, especially when the media cues coincide and reinforce partisan preferences.[24] In the Nordic countries, as well, populist parties have gained from media coverage.[25] Nevertheless, further communications research is needed to examine populism across a wide range of media outlets, and debate continues about how far the tabloid press in different countries consistently reflect an 'anti-elite' or 'anti-establishment' perspective.[26] Studies have started to examine populism in the mass media in particular countries but cross-national data remains limited.[27]

For populist leaders, the content of speeches can be analyzed in terms of ethos (focusing leadership character and credibility), pathos (using emotions, such as patriotism, compassion, or anger), and sources of supporting evidence. Populist campaign communications can also be scrutinized in terms of the focus on anti-elitism and appeals to the people, an informal style and anti-intellectualism, and emotional negative appeals to the politics of fear.[28] For example Bart Bonikowski and Noam Gidron examined the discourse used in over 2000 US presidential speeches from 1952 to 1996 and found that populist language was used by both Democrats and Republicans – but especially by challengers and outsiders.[29] Others have scrutinized Trump's campaign speeches to understand his appeal to his white working-class base.[30] His constant Twitter feed has been deconstructed for its meaning, including the way that it provides an informal, direct, and provoking communication style, boosting his image while denigrating his enemies.[31] The visual cues from Le Pen's National Front campaign materials have been deconstructed for their meaning.[32] Similarly, the rhetoric of speeches by chief executives in Latin America and 17 other countries have been studied to understand the key features, drawing contrasts between populist and pluralist discourse.[33] Discourse analysis provides useful insights documenting the evolution of party leadership appeals and media coverage over time within countries. But the evidence from this approach is often highly context-specific, and systematic cross-national and time-series data derived from leadership speeches and party campaign communications materials, such as posters and election broadcasts, are not yet available to classify parties across the wide range of European societies compared in this book.[34]

## Party Elites, Activists, and Supporters

Another alternative approach is to classify parties according to the ideological values of their elites, mid-level activists, or voting supporters. This includes surveys of parliamentary candidates and Members of Parliament,[35] party members,[36] campaign managers and party officials, and partisan identifiers and party voters in the electorate. These are all potentially useful approaches, which could be utilized more fully. For example, mass election surveys allow researchers to establish how citizens see their own left–right position and where they perceive their own location and that of the major parties across diverse issue scales. However, the results may not prove reliable as ordinary citizens may misperceive the issue position of parties by seeing them as either closer to their own views or further away than they are in reality. Ordinary people may mistake party issue positions because of motivated reasoning, selective perceptions used to reduce cognitive dissonance, confused signals about policy positions arising from internal ideological divisions within political parties, or from simple lack of political information and awareness.[37]

## Programmatic Policy Platforms and Issue Positions

The most common practice in the comparative literature has sought to distinguish the location of political parties, and the similarities across party families, based on content analysis of policy manifestos and programmatic platforms. The Comparative Manifesto Project provides the most extensive resources, widely used in the research literature, covering party manifestos published in more than 50 countries since 1945.[38] These documents have been analyzed to identify issue salience (the amount of coverage or prominence) as well as issue positions (the direction of statements for or against issues) published in party election programs and related proxy documents. Directional theories of party competition assume that parties vary primarily in how much prominence party manifestos devote to certain issues such as unemployment, healthcare, or inflation.[39] Most attempts at party classification based on these data have used the familiar 'left–right' cleavage, including redistributive economic issues reflecting the class cleavage, such as party positions for or against taxation, welfare spending, privatization or nationalization.[40] These were key to patterns of party competition in many European countries during the post-war era. Using the CMP data, the next chapter also demonstrates that the left–right cleavage has faded in importance since the 1980s as party programs have given greater prominence to socially liberal and socially conservative issue positions reflecting contemporary cultural battles.[41]

The CMP data were not used for classifying parties in this study for two reasons. Firstly, questions remain as to whether the dataset has the capacity to capture the two core components of populism, including appeals to vox populi as well as anti-establishment critiques. There is an item on government corruption in general, an issue central to many anti-establishment populist appeals, but the CPM dataset is not designed to capture party populism as a style of discourse making claims about restoring legitimate power to the people and constraining the power of the establishment.

Secondly, the CMP is particularly effective for capturing changes in traditional left–right cleavages during the post-war decade when European parties could be classified with some degree of reliability across the economic spectrum, with Keynesian economic policies, pro-welfare state, and public ownership, on the center-left, and free-market policies favoring a smaller role for the state, deregulation, and low taxes on the center-right. These ideological divisions reflected the classic social cleavages that Lipset and Rokkan saw as dividing party families in Western Europe by social class, religion, and center-periphery.[42]

But the traditional left–right economic policy cleavage provides a poor guide to the contemporary cultural cleavages in party competition and the modern policy agenda revolving around socially liberal versus socially conservative values and policies. For example, the coding scheme is largely gender blind by neglecting the politics of sexuality and gender identities, and the modern agenda of the feminist and LGBTQ rights movements. The codebook instructions make a single reference to classifying manifesto statements making favorable mentions to 'special interest groups,' which are defined to include 'women, university students, and age groups.' A second item also codes favorable references to 'under-privileged minorities' – specified as 'handicapped, homosexuals, immigrants, and indigenous populations.' But there is no explicit reference to coding the range of contemporary policy issues revolving around the politics of sexuality and gender, including sex equality, affirmative action, and equal opportunities policies, women's rights, equal pay laws, feminism, maternity or paternity leave, maternity health and childcare, gender and sexual identities, gay and transsexual rights, affirmative action in the workplace and public sphere, rights to same sex marriage and civil unions, gender quotas in elected bodies, sexual harassment, domestic violence, women serving in the military, and so on. The CMP contains an item coding policy statements for or against traditional morality, such as support for abortion/divorce, traditional families, and the role of religious institutions in the state, but this is unlikely to capture the full dimension of policy debates over cultural issues. The coding schema is also skewed in direction by recording positive statements about social justice and equality but not negative statements critical of these rights, for example where parties seek to assert 'traditional family values' and restrict reproductive rights, to enforce conformity with certain religious or gender-related dress codes, or to roll back LGBTQ equal treatment under the law.

## III MEASURING PARTY POSITIONS IN THE THREE-DIMENSIONAL ISSUE SPACE

How can the three-dimensional model be operationalized to classify European parties? Their policy location is assessed and classified most consistently using systematic evidence derived mainly from expert surveys of party positions across ideological scales, supplemented by the Comparative Manifesto Project.[43]

For empirical evidence of where parties fall on these dimensions, we use the Chapel Hill Expert Survey (CHES) to identify the ideological location of each country's political parties.[44] Expert surveys are a technique that has been used increasingly to gauge complex phenomenon where we lack objective data across and within nation-states – for example, to assess levels of democracy and human rights, problems of corruption and lack of press freedom, and the quality of electoral integrity.[45] CHES asks experts to estimate the ideological and policy positions of political parties in the country with which they are most familiar. The survey has been conducted roughly every four years from 1999 to 2014 and we rely primarily on the 2014 wave, which has the closest fit to the pooled ESS survey data. The wave of the CHES used in this chapter includes data collected between December 2014 and February 2015. The number of parties covered has gradually expanded over time, with the 2014 CHES survey covering 268 political parties in 37 post-industrial societies, including all EU member states plus Norway, Switzerland, and Turkey.[46] This study includes a wide range of societies, including long-standing democracies, such as Switzerland and

France, as well as post-communist states that have had divergent trajectories of democratization, such as Poland, Slovakia, and Hungary. Many of these societies enjoy high standards of living but others are middle-income, with diverse levels of economic growth, unemployment, and human development. Countries also vary in their level of integration into global markets. The CHES expert assessments of party positions have been widely used in the social sciences and validated against independent data based on content analysis of party platforms from the Comparative Manifesto Project.[47] Factor analysis with principal component rotation examined the dimensionality of 13 selected indicators contained in the dataset, listed in Table 3.1, where experts rated the position of European parties using 10-point scales.

*Populism–pluralism* is treated as the first dimension that divides parties. When it comes to measuring populism, the crucial element is the importance of appeals calling for power to the people and critiquing the corrupt power of the establishment. In established liberal democracies, the antithesis is pluralism asserting the legitimacy of elected officials and the established institutions of governance. To measure this dimension, two proxy indicators were selected from the CHES dataset: (1) the importance of anti-establishment and anti-elite rhetoric, and (2) the salience of anti-corruption. One important qualification should be noted: these CHES items helps to capture the typical populist critique of corrupt elites, although unfortunately the dataset does not yet gauge populist claims about the moral legitimacy of the voice of the people or the elected representatives.[48]

The *authoritarian–libertarian* values are the second dimension in our framework. This dimension divides authoritarian parties with policy positions favoring the values of conformity with conventional social norms, collective security, and loyalty toward group leaders from Libertarian parties with policy positions favoring personal freedoms, pluralism, and individualism. The term 'Liberal' is one which can prove confusing on both sides of the Atlantic, and it can refer to both economic (laissez faire) liberalism as well as social (welfare) liberalism. For these reasons, the term 'Libertarianism' is used to refer to parties that value live-and-let-live policies minimizing the role of the state in restricting personal choices, exemplified by laws protecting women and minority rights, tolerance of diversity, and respect for the principles of social justice, human rights, and international cooperation. The authoritarian–libertarian values of parties are measured by experts from their policy positions on seven issue items: (1) the 'Galtan' summary measure in CHES designed to distinguish authoritarian parties valuing order, tradition and stability from libertarian parties favoring expanding personal freedoms and rights; (2) whether parties favored nationalism or cosmopolitanism; (3) law and order or civil liberties; (4) policies of multiculturalism or assimilation of immigrants; (5) liberal positions on homosexuality; (6) restrictions on immigration; and (7) rights for ethnic minorities – all of which are linked with the cultural cleavage dividing authoritarians and libertarians.

Finally, for comparison, the left–right cleavage conventionally divides parties with policy positions located on the economic left (favoring regulated markets, state management of the economy, wealth redistribution, and public spending) from those on the economic right (favoring deregulation and free markets, opposing wealth redistribution, and favoring tax cuts). To gauge where political parties were located on the left–right economic cleavage, four standard issue items were used from the CHES dataset, estimating party positions toward (1) market deregulation, (2) state management of the economy, (3) redistributive taxes, and (4) preferences for either tax cuts or more public services.

In addition, several items were first included in the 2014 CHES survey, but not in earlier waves, preventing systematic comparisons over time. The analysis assumes that the measures of party positions reflect fairly stable characteristics of parties, which evolve relatively slowly in their ideological values and policy positions. Certainly discontinuities, realignments, or decisive breaks can occur, shifting parties in a different direction, particularly under new leadership, after factional splits, or following critical elections.[49] Fringe and minor parties tend to be poorly institutionalized and unstable. There can also be important shifts in party issue positions over time, especially in reaction to new events such as the European financial crisis or the Brexit decision. For example, in an attempt to broaden the appeal of the National Front (FN), Marine le Pen sought to adopt a more populist tone and soften the hardline immigration policies advocated by her father.[50] By contrast, in the October 2017 election, Angela Merkel shifted toward advocating caps that were more restrictive on immigrant numbers flowing into Germany, in response to threats from the rival AfD. The changes in party positions and factional splits are far more common in Central and Eastern Europe. The measures of party positions should therefore be treated as a cross-national snapshot comparing European party competition in 2014. Ideally, party positions should be monitored over time to detect shifts in ideological positions but in practice these sorts of turning points tend to be fairly rare in long-established party systems. Subsequent CHES datasets will facilitate comparisons of the stability of these estimates. The analysis we present comparing party and voter positions assumes that the expert measurement in 2014 provides a proxy guide to party positions throughout the 2002–2014 waves of the European Social Survey.

The results of the principal components factor analysis with varimax rotation, presented in Table 7.1, confirm that the economic left–right, authoritarian–libertarian, and populist items form three dimensions of party competition, as hypothesized. The empirical results confirm our argument that parties adopting populist rhetoric are scattered across the map of ideological values. Populists do not necessarily endorse authoritarian cultural values; this is not surprising, given the vagueness and ubiquity of politicians claiming to stand 'for the people' and against elites. Similarly, populist language is not adopted by all traditional authoritarians on the extreme left or right, such as neo-Nazis, White Supremacist, and hate groups advocating anti-Semitism, racial separation, and ethnic purity. The items measuring each of these dimensions were added to generate separate ideological scales, measuring populism, authoritarianism, and left–right economic policy positions, and then standardized to 100-point scales for ease of comparison. These scales are normally distributed and display a high degree of internal consistency, as measured by Cronbach's Alpha.[51]

The continuous standardized scales provide fine-grained comparisons across all European parties for analysis with the European Social Survey monitoring the values of the electorate. Nevertheless, categories can also be useful, especially for selecting typical cases which aid understanding of concrete examples. To develop categories, 'authoritarian parties' are defined as those with policy position scales that scored more than 80 points on the standardized 100-point authoritarian–libertarian index. Left-wing and right-wing parties are defined as those with policy position scales that fall above or below the mean score (50) on the 100-point left–right index. Similarly, populist parties are categorized as those located at extreme positions (over 80/100) on the populism scale. The more detailed classification and CHES scores of all European Authoritarian-Populist parties included in our study are listed in Appendix A. The ideological scales constructed from the CHES dataset allow the expert-rated locations of European political party policy positions to be compared across these dimensions.

It should be noted that attempts to move from continuous scales to categorize parties as distinct groups or even families requires drawing dividing lines where judgments are inevitably somewhat arbitrary. Moreover, contagion effects can arise if leaders from mainstream center-right or

TABLE 7.1. *Dimensions of party competition in Europe*

| CHES Variable name | Description | Cultural cleavage | Populist rhetoric | Economic cleavage |
|---|---|---|---|---|
| | **AUTHORITARIAN VALUES** | | | |
| Galtan | Party positions toward democratic freedoms and rights; libertarian parties favor expanding personal freedoms; authoritarian parties value order, tradition, and stability. | .935 | | |
| Nationalism | Pro-nationalism | .923 | | |
| Civlib_laworder | Favors tough measures to fight crime rather than the protection of civil liberties | .921 | | |
| Multiculturalism | Against multiculturalism and the integration of immigrants and asylum seekers | .911 | | |
| Sociallifestyle | Opposes liberal social lifestyles (e.g. homosexuality) | .904 | | |
| Immigrate_policy | Favors restrictive policy on immigration | .894 | | |
| Ethnic_minorities | Opposes rights for ethnic minorities | .876 | | |
| | **POPULIST RHETORIC** | | | |
| Anti-corrupt salience | Salience of anti-corruption | | .712 | |
| Anti-elite_salience | Salience of anti-elite and anti-establishment rhetoric | | .932 | |
| | **LEFT–RIGHT ECONOMIC VALUES** | | | |
| Deregulation | Favors market regulation or deregulation | | | .965 |
| Econ_interven | Favors or opposed to state intervention on the economy | | | .954 |
| Redistribution | Favors or opposed to redistribution of wealth from the rich to the poor | | | .928 |
| Spendvtax | Favor or opposes cutting taxes and public services | | | .911 |

*Notes:* CHES 2014 expert survey of political party positions in 31 countries, including all EU member states plus Norway, Switzerland, and Turkey, Dec 2014–Feb 2015. Factor analysis with rotated varimax and Kaiser normalization.

*Source:* Ryan Bakker, Erica Edwards, Liesbet Hooghe, Seth Jolly, Gary Marks, Jonathan Polk, Jan Rovny, Marco Steenbergen, and Milada Vachudova. 2015. '2014 Chapel Hill Expert Survey.' Version 2015.1. Available on chesdata.eu. Chapel Hill, NC: University of North Carolina, Chapel Hill (subsequently referenced as the 2014 Chapel Hill Expert Survey or just abbreviated as CHES 2014).

center-left parties, in attempting to steal supporters, adopt some of the populist language or the xenophobic rhetoric and strict immigration policies espoused by authoritarians. For these reasons, in subsequent chapters the analysis of voting support is measured using the position of all parties on the authoritarian–libertarian and the populism indices, although categories are employed for selecting cases.

For a robustness check on the validity and reliability of the CHES measures, the results were compared with independent evidence. The Immerzeel, Lubbers, and Coffé expert judgment survey of European Political Parties, conducted in 2010, provides one source.[52] This research used a similar expert survey methodology to estimate the scores of political parties in 38 European countries, focusing on populist issues such as nationalism and immigration. The two independent datasets proved to be highly correlated in the perceived position of parties on the ideological scales, lending further confidence to the CHES estimates.[53] In addition, for face-value validity, the list of parties ranked according to the CHES cultural values scale was found to be generally consistent with previous classifications of right-wing populist parties.[54]

Parties are also ranked by their average share of the vote for the lower house in national legislative elections since 2000 and categorized into major parties (10 percent or more), minor parties (4.0–9.9%), and fringe parties, which often fail to win any parliamentary seats (less than 4.0%). Each of these categories are also inevitably somewhat arbitrary but the choice of a 4 percent cut off for fringe parties reflects the common minimum vote threshold used to qualify for parliamentary seats.

## IV COMPARING EUROPEAN PARTY COMPETITION

Table 7.2 and 7.3 list political parties in Western and Eastern Europe which we classify as authoritarian populist from 2000 to 2015 while Table 7.4 lists the libertarian-populist category. To examine the comparisons visually, Figure 7.2 illustrates the patterns of European party competition.

### Authoritarian-Populist Parties

As can be observed from the scatterplot, the Authoritarian-Populist parties are located in the top-right quadrant. This category includes several parties in Scandinavia such as Jimmie Kasson's Swedish Democrats, Jussi Halla-aho's Finns Party, Siv Jensen's Progress Party in Norway, and Kristian Thulesen Dahl's Danish People's Party (DF). Similar parties and leaders

TABLE 7.2. *Authoritarian-Populist parties in Western Europe, 2000–2015*

| | Party Name (English) | Abr. | % Vote | N. elec | SD |
|---|---|---|---|---|---|
| **MAJOR** (7) | | | | | |
| Switzerland | Swiss People's Party | SVP-UDC | 27.9 | 4 | 1.5 |
| Norway | Progress Party | Fr | 19.0 | 4 | 4.1 |
| Austria | Freedom Party of Austria | FPÖ | 14.8 | 4 | 5.1 |
| Denmark | Danish People's Party | DF | 14.5 | 5 | 3.5 |
| Netherlands | Pim Fortuyn List | LPF | 11.4 | 2 | 8.0 |
| Finland | Finnish Party – True Finns | SP-P | 10.6 | 4 | 9.0 |
| Netherlands | Party for Freedom | PVV | 10.5 | 3 | 4.8 |
| **MINOR** (10) | | | | | |
| France | National Front | FN | 9.7 | 3 | 4.9 |
| Belgium | Flemish Block | VB | 8.8 | 4 | 3.9 |
| Luxembourg | Action Comm. Pensions ǀ Alt. Demo Ref | ARǀADR | 7.9 | 3 | 1.2 |
| Greece | People's Association – Golden Dawn | XA | 6.8 | 4 | 0.3 |
| Greece | Independent Greeks | AE | 6.6 | 4 | 3.1 |
| Sweden | Sweden Democrats | SD | 5.7 | 4 | 5.1 |
| Austria | Team Stronach | TS | 5.7 | 1 | |
| Italy | Northern League | LN | 5.6 | 3 | 2.3 |
| UK | United Kingdom Independence Party | UKIP | 4.9 | 4 | 5.2 |
| Germany | Alternative for Germany | AfD | 4.7 | 1 | |
| **FRINGE** (9) | | | | | |
| Greece | Popular Orthodox Rally | LAOS | 2.9 | 6 | 1.7 |
| Belgium | National Front | FN | 2.0 | 2 | 0.0 |
| Italy | Brothers of Italy – National Centre-right | FdI-CN | 2.0 | 1 | . |
| United Kingdom | British National Party | BNP | 1.9 | 1 | . |
| Netherlands | Political Reformed Party | SGP | 1.7 | 5 | 0.2 |
| Germany | National Democratic Party | NPD | 1.5 | 3 | 0.2 |
| Switzerland | Federal Democratic Union of Switzerland | EDU-UDF | 1.3 | 3 | 0.0 |
| France | Movement for France | MF | 1.0 | 2 | 0.3 |
| Switzerland | Ticino League | LdT | 0.6 | 3 | 0.2 |

*Note:* The list includes 27 Authoritarian-Populist parties in Western Europe which contested elections for the lower house of the national parliament. The percentage vote is the mean share of the vote for each party (and the standard deviation) in parliamentary elections from 2000 to 2015. For the party classification, see Chapter 8.

*Source:* Vote share calculated from Holger Döring and Philip Manow. 2016. *Parliaments and governments database* (ParlGov) 'Elections' dataset. www.parlgov.org/.

TABLE 7.3. *Authoritarian-Populist parties in Central and Eastern Europe, 2000–2015*

| | Party | Abr. | % Vote | N. elec | SD |
|---|---|---|---|---|---|
| **MAJOR** (9) | | | | | |
| Hungary | Fidesz – Hungarian Civic Union | Fi-MPSz | 41.1 | 1 | . |
| Croatia | Croatian Democratic Union | HDZ | 29.9 | 5 | 5.6 |
| Poland | Law and Justice | PiS | 27.2 | 5 | 10.6 |
| Slovenia | Slovenian Democratic Party | SDS | 24.2 | 5 | 5.8 |
| Bulgaria | National Movement Simeon II | NDSV | 21.9 | 3 | 19.9 |
| Hungary | Jobbik Movement for a Better Hungary | Jobbik | 18.4 | 2 | 2.5 |
| Romania | People's Party – Dan Diaconescu | PP-DD | 14.0 | 1 | . |
| Turkey | National Action Party | MHP | 12.8 | 5 | 3.0 |
| Lithuania | Order and Justice – Liberal Democratic | TT-LDP | 10.5 | 3 | 2.8 |
| **MINOR** (13) | | | | | |
| Slovakia | Ordinary People and Independent | OLaNO | 8.6 | 1 | . |
| Slovakia | Christian Democratic Movement | KDH | 8.5 | 4 | 0.3 |
| Lithuania | The Way of Courage | DK | 8.0 | 1 | . |
| Croatia | Croatian Peasant Party | HSS | 7.5 | 4 | 6.2 |
| Bulgaria | Attack | Ataka | 7.3 | 4 | 2.1 |
| Latvia | For Latvia from the Heart | NsL | 6.9 | 1 | . |
| Latvia | Latvian Association of Regions | LRa | 6.7 | 1 | . |
| Slovenia | New Slovenia – Christian People's Party | NSI | 6.3 | 5 | 2.5 |
| Slovakia | Slovak National Party | SNS | 6.2 | 4 | 3.8 |
| Bulgaria | Bulgaria Without Censorship | BBZ | 5.7 | 1 | . |
| Bulgaria | National Front for the Salvation of Bulgaria | NFSB | 5.5 | 2 | 2.5 |
| Croatia | Croatian Party of Rights | HSP | 4.6 | 4 | 1.6 |
| Hungary | Hungarian Justice and Life Party | MIEP | 3.3 | 2 | 1.5 |

| | Party | Abr. | % Vote | N. elec | SD |
|---|---|---|---|---|---|
| **FRINGE (5)** | | | | | |
| Croatia | Croatian Democratic Alliance of Slavonia | HDSSB | 2.0 | 3 | 0.9 |
| Poland | Real Politics Union – Congress of the New Right | UPR\|KNP | 1.3 | 2 | 0.4 |
| Croatia | Croatian Party of Rights of 1861 | HSP-1861 | 1.1 | 1 | . |
| Croatia | Croatian Democratic Peasant Party | HDSS | 1.0 | 1 | . |
| Croatia | Croatian Party of Rights – Dr. Ante Star | HSP-AS | 0.6 | 1 | . |

*Note:* The list includes 26 Authoritarian-Populist parties in Central and Eastern Europe which contested elections for the lower house of the national parliament. The percentage vote is the mean share of the vote for each party (and the standard deviation) in parliamentary elections from 2000 to 2015. For the party classification, see Chapter 8.
*Source:* Vote share calculated from Holger Döring and Philip Manow. 2016. *Parliaments and governments database* (ParlGov) 'Elections' dataset. www.parlgov.org/.

TABLE 7.4. *Libertarian-Populist parties in Europe, 2000–2015*

| | Party Name (English) | Abr. | % Vote | N. elec | SD |
|---|---|---|---|---|---|
| Italy | Five Star Movement | M5S | 25.6 | 1 | |
| Greece | Coalition of the Radical Left | SYRIZA | 18.3 | 7 | 14.6 |
| Spain | Podemos – We Can | P | 12.7 | 1 | . |

*Note:* The list includes three Libertarian-Populist parties in Europe which contested elections for the lower house of the national parliament. The percentage vote is the mean share of the vote for each party (and the standard deviation) in parliamentary elections from 2000 to 2015. For the party classification, see Chapter 8.
*Source:* Vote share calculated from Holger Döring and Philip Manow. 2016. *Parliaments and governments database* (ParlGov) 'Elections' dataset.

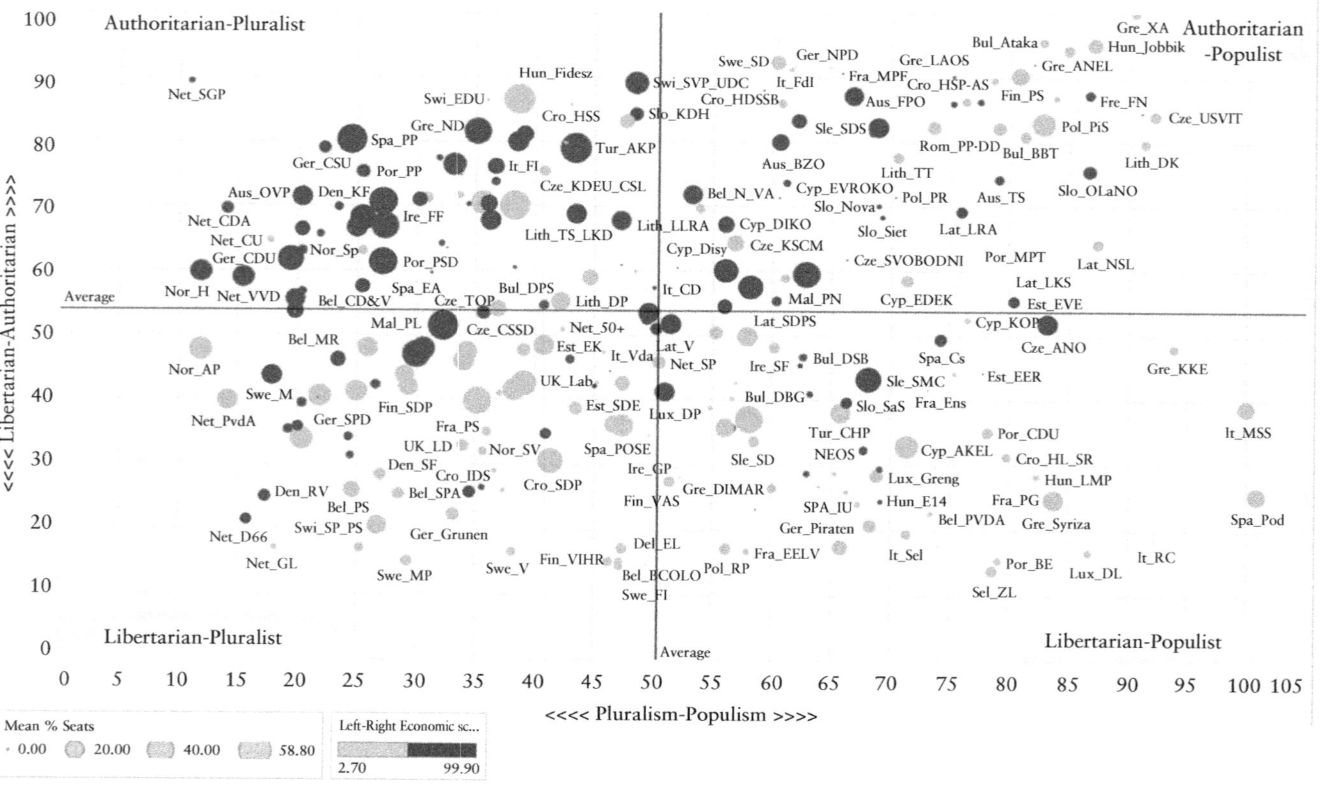


FIGURE 7.2. *Classification of European political parties*
*Notes:* For the scale components, see Table 7.1. Party scores on all dimensions are standardized scales.
*Source:* 2014 Chapel Hill Expert Survey.

in Northern Europe are Albert Rösti's Swiss People's Party (SVP), Geert Wilder's Freedom Party (PVV) in the Netherlands, Heinz-Christian Starches Austrian Freedom Party (FPÖ), Marine Le Pen's National Front (FN), Alexander Garland's Alternative for Germany (AfD), Tom Van Grieken's Flemish Vlaams Belang (VB), and Nigel Farage's UK Independence Party (UKIP).[55] In Central and Eastern Europe, as well, several parties fall into the authoritarian-populist category, including Bulgaria's Ataka, the Polish Law and Justice party (PiS), the Czech Republic's Freedom and Direct Democracy (SPD) Party, the Polish Congress of the New Right (Kongres Nowej Prawicy or KNP), and Slovakia's Christian Democratic Movement (KDH). In order to explain the electoral appeal, this is the core group of parties we focus on in subsequent chapters.

An extreme Authoritarian-Populist party is exemplified by Golden Dawn in Greece with one of the highest scores on the authoritarian index in Europe due to policies which are extremely anti-immigrant, ultra-nationalistic, and hardline Eurosceptic. This has led some to classify Golden Dawn and the Independent Greeks ANEL parties as extreme right, neo-Nazi, or fascist.[56] Yet these categorizations are potentially confusing, since the labels conflate social with economic conservatism, according to the expert assessments in the CHES data. In fact, Golden Dawn is also anti-capitalist in its economic policies, for example its 'National Plan' advocates nationalizing banks and natural resources and strengthening trade agreements with Russia, Iran, and China. The party first entered parliament in May 2012 and just a few years later, in the January 2015 general elections, Golden Dawn had become the third largest party in the national parliament, winning 17 seats.[57]

In post-communist Europe, another example of extreme Authoritarian-Populist parties is Ataka (Attack) in Bulgaria, positioned close to Hungary's Jobbik. The party was created by Volen Siderov in April 2005 and in parliamentary elections since then, Ataka has been in fourth place in Bulgaria. Its program advocates ultra-nationalist and xenophobic policies, especially directed against Muslim, Turkish and Roma minorities. The party seeks to assert traditional Bulgarian values, including by recognizing the Orthodox Church as the official religion of the country. It also endorses classic left-wing economic and social policies, such as restoring state ownership of major industries and increasing spending on education, welfare, and healthcare.[58] The party blames capitalism, neo-liberal markets, globalization, the IMF, the World Bank, and United States-led pro-Western forces for the country's economic problems and seeks to withdraw Bulgaria from NATO.[59] In the March 2017 elections, the party formed a coalition, United Patriots, with other nationalist and populist parties, including the National Front for the Salvation of Bulgaria, the Bulgarian National Movement (IMRO), and the Union of the Patriotic Forces. United Patriots won 9 percent of the parliamentary vote and came third with 27 seats. Based on this result, United Patriots entered a government coalition led by Boyko Borisov, and nominated one-third of the Council of Ministers.

### Libertarian-Populist Parties

Libertarian-Populist parties, combining socially liberal values and progressive policies with populist rhetoric, are located in the bottom-right quadrant in the figure. This includes Spain's Podemos (We Can), Greece's Syriza, Germany's The Left (Die Linke), and Italy's Five-star Movement.[60] These parties blend more socially liberal attitudes with anti-capitalist appeals calling for social justice and the end to austerity cuts, and some newer forms of participation within local communities.[61]

This position is exemplified by the Greek Coalition of the Radical Left (Syriza), a coalition of the radical left formed in 2004. In the January and September 2015 elections, in the midst of the sovereign debt crisis in the Eurozone, Syriza led coalition governments as the largest parliamentary party, in partnership the Independent Greeks (ANEL).[62] The sovereign debt crisis in Greece, discussed in Chapter 5, formed the backdrop for the rise of Syriza, which fought the January 2015 elections on a platform pledged to end austerity, rewrite the bailout, and achieve substantial debt relief, and attacking the international financial institutions of the EU, IMF, and European Central Bank, as well as foreign governments such as Germany, which sought public-sector spending cuts as a condition of debt relief. The party is also socially liberal, implementing same-sex civil unions in 2015, despite opposition from its coalition partner, ANEL, and the Orthodox Church.

### Authoritarian-Pluralist Parties

Authoritarian-Pluralist parties with socially conservative values, but which endorse less populist philosophies toward governance, are shown in the top-left quadrant. This quadrant contains parties such as Hungary's Fidesz, Norway's Freedom Party, and the Danish People's Party scoring more highly on the authoritarian index, which experts rate as reflecting socially conservative values but with weaker emphasis on populist appeals.

This category is exemplified by the Swiss People's Party (SVP), which is socially conservative in its values but relatively moderate in its degree of populist discourse. SVP was established in 1971 as a farmer's agrarian party, but its electoral support remained limited in the 1970s and 1980s, attracting around 11 percent of the vote mainly from cantons in the rural countryside. Party fortunes were transformed in the early 1990s, however, under the leadership of Christoph Blocher, a wealthy industrialist, when the SVP became more Eurosceptic, advocating keeping Switzerland out of the European Economic Area and the EU, and opposed to mass immigration. The party became more hierarchically organized around the leader and a tight circle of party officials, and it adopted more aggressive anti-establishment discourse.[63] The party program promoted a philosophy of national conservatism and identity politics, advocating a limited role for government in the economy and the welfare state, and the preservation of traditional Swiss values against the supranational integration of Europe and the threat of foreigners.[64] Asylum seekers and refugees were blamed for the rise of crime and drugs and insufficient security.

The transformation of the party into the Swiss standard bearer for the socially conservative right led to its growing electoral success.[65] From 1959 to 2003, out of the four parties represented in the seven member Swiss Federal Council, the executive governing body, the SVP had one member. In 2004, after the party had gained in strength and representation in the federal parliament, they were allocated two seats – the Christian Democrats were reduced to one.[66] Currently chaired by Albert Rösti and led by Toni Brunner, the SVP's economic policies oppose deficit spending, government regulation, environmental protection, military engagement abroad, and closer ties with NATO.[67] On cultural issues, the party has emphasized Euroscepticism, strict asylum laws, and opposition to multiculturalism and immigration. For example, its party manifesto says: 'The SVP is fighting the failed asylum policy that leads to skyrocketing costs, more crime, and housing problems.'[68] The electoral success of the SVP at municipal, cantonal, and national levels polarized the Swiss party system, especially on cultural issues.[69] In 2009, in one of its most controversial moves, claiming to 'stop the creeping Islamization of Switzerland,' it pushed successfully to ban the construction of minarets – an initiative that subsequently became an amendment to the Swiss Constitution.[70] As we have seen in Chapter 6, Switzerland is a multiethnic and multilinguistic country with around one-third of its population foreign-born (see Figure 6.3), and one of the highest proportions in Europe. Following the October 2015 federal elections, and spurred by the European migration crisis, the SVP became the largest party in the Federal Assembly, winning a record number of around one-third of the seats (65/200) with 29.4 percent of the votes. The SVP backs a referendum campaign to limit the free movement of EU citizens into the country, a bilateral accord agreed earlier to give Switzerland access to the EU single market. At the same time, the party managed to be in government without giving up its 'anti-system' image and rhetoric and without experiencing internal factionalism.[71] Therefore, the SVP flourishes in a highly educated plural society – as well as a stable consociational democracy and federal state. Switzerland is also one of the affluent societies, which the World Bank estimates has the second highest per capita GDP in the world ($78,813), with low unemployment.[72]

### Libertarian-Pluralist Parties

The lower left-hand quadrant depicts the Libertarian-Pluralist parties, usually long-established and mainstream parties favoring socially liberal policies and traditional forms of liberal democratic governance, including the many social democratic and socialist parliamentary parties in Western Europe. Mainstream parties in this group, include many Christian Democrat, Social Democrat, Conservative, Liberal, and Green Parties, sharing a liberal consensus concerning the value of cooperation and engagement in international affairs, generally supporting multilateral institutions of global governance, cooperation, development assistance, and humanitarian engagement, and the benefits of open borders for the free movement of capital, trade, goods, and labor. On the cultural dimension, Libertarian-Pluralist parties endorse socially liberal policy positions, reflecting the expansion of personal freedoms and individual rights on moral issues, tolerance of pluralistic diversity, supported by liberal democratic institutions and norms of governance. Parties in this quadrant differ from each other primarily on the traditional left–right cleavage over the importance of free markets versus state management of the economy and thus policy positions toward issues of redistribution, taxation, regulation, and social justice, as well as the role and size of the public sector and welfare states.

## V CLASSIFYING LEFT–RIGHT PARTIES

How do parties compete across the left–right dimension? To examine these patterns, we can look at Figure 7.3 which shows the authoritarian–libertarian and the left–right cleavages broken down by country.

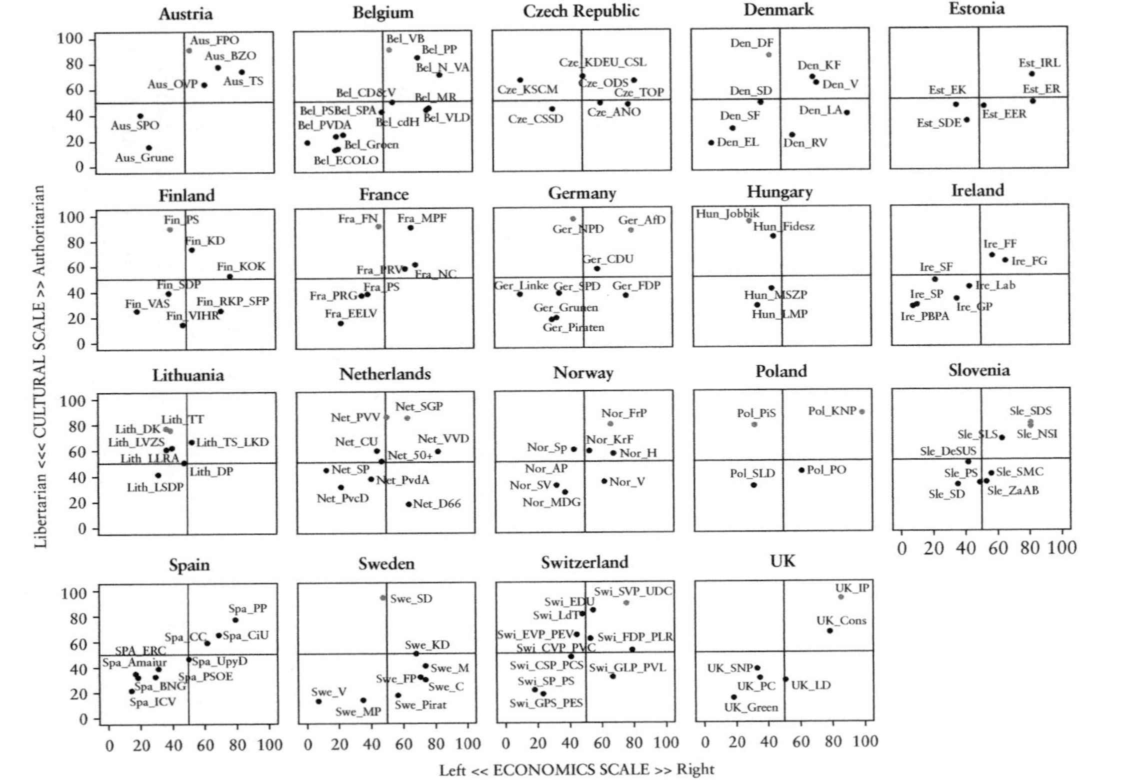


FIGURE 7.3. *Classification of European political parties*
*Notes:* For the scale components, see Table 7.1. Party scores on all dimensions are standardized scales. *Source:* 2014 Chapel Hill Expert Survey.

## Authoritarian Right

The top-right quadrant contains the authoritarian right parties. These parties typically favor pro-market policies with a small role for the state on issues such as public-sector spending and taxation, and are socially conservative on issues such as preserving traditional family values and religious traditions, and deeply Eurosceptic and nationalistic in international affairs. Overall 17 European parties fall into this category. Many of these parties are also populist – denigrating the legitimacy of established elites at home or abroad – but not all. We can observe far more parties located in the authoritarian right quadrant than in the authoritarian left quadrant. When the position of all political parties in the 2014 CHES dataset is compared, we can observe a moderately strong and significant correlation between the authoritarian–libertarian scale and the left–right scale (R = –.074** P.000, N.270).

## Authoritarian Left

The top-left quadrant in Figure 7.2 contains the athoritarian left parties – again many but not all populist in their discourse toward governance authority. Overall, 22 parties fall into this category but in Western Europe and Nordic Europe, although many voters blend socialist views toward redistribution and the welfare state with adherence to traditional cultural values around issues like nationalism, it is notable that relatively few parties offer policy positions endorsing this combination, generating a representation gap.[73] Elsewhere around the world, however, many parties are of this category.[74] In post-communist Europe, this includes the Lithuanian Way of Courage (DK), the governing Polish Law and Justice Party (PiS), the Slovak National Party, the National Front for the Salvation of Bulgaria and the Bulgarian National Movement, the Czech Party of Civic Rights, and Jobbik (Movement for a Better Hungary).[75] In Latin America, as well, the Peronist tradition reflects this combination of socialist state-managed economics with populist authoritarian leaders in many countries, notably Hugo Chávez and Nicolás Maduro in Venezuela (becoming increasingly authoritarian over time), Cristina Fernández de Kirchner in Argentina, Eva Morales in Bolivia, and Rafael Correa in Ecuador.[76] Latin America has a long history of populist leaders on both the economic left and right that dates back to the 1940s, when Argentina's Juan Perón came to power.[77] The resurgence of populism in Latin America during the last decade is exemplified by the success of Cristina Fernández in Argentina and Rafael Correa in Ecuador, commonly seen as a reaction against the economic stagnation and financial crises that hit the region during the late 1990s. Similar arguments about economic inequality have been made to explain the case of the United Socialist Party of Venezuela (Partido Socialista Unido de Venezuela, PSUV).[78] The election of Hugo Chavez as Venezuela's president in 1998, less than seven years after his unsuccessful military coup attempt, marked one of the most dramatic political transformations in the nation's history. This was followed in 2013 by his successor, Nicolás Maduro.[79] Venezuela illustrates the dangers of authoritarian left populist leaders in hybrid regimes, and how democratic institutions like elections can be destroyed by them.

### Libertarian Right and Libertarian Left

Finally, the majority of European parties can be observed to fall into the libertarian left (99) and libertarian right (130) categories in the bottom quadrants in Figure 7.2. This includes many mainstream center-right governing parties close to the middle of the political spectrum, such as the British Conservatives, the Swiss People's Party (SVP), the German CSU, and Ireland Fianna Fail.

## VI CLASSIFYING AUTHORITARIAN-POPULIST LEADERS

Finally, several presidents can also be classified as authoritarian populists. The technique of discourse analysis of leadership speeches has been used to identify these but unfortunately systematic data are lacking across many countries so judgments have to be more impressionistic.[80]

Does President Trump fit the authoritarian-populist classification? We think so.[81] His speeches feature a mélange of xenophobic fear-mongering and Islamophobia, narcissism, misogyny and racism, conspiracy theories ('millions of fraudulent votes'), and isolationist 'America First' policies. It is in his legitimation of authoritarian values that Trump represents the gravest threat to American democracy with his equivocal treatment of neo-Nazi and white supremacist hate groups, his open approval of some of the world's most repressive regimes, attacking the press and using Twitter to slam 'fake news,' seeking border limits on migrants from Muslim-majority countries and promising to build a wall to keep out Mexicans, casting doubts on the integrity of American elections and the independence of the judiciary, prioritizing military security and American jobs over defending democracy and human rights abroad, weakening multilateral cooperation and international conventions, and disparaging the rule of law. Like other authoritarian rulers, he shows a casual disregard for the truth and a willingness to challenge the legal constraints on his powers. Many of the tensions observed in his administration arise from his rejection of democratic constraints. On the other hand, he can also be regarded as a consummate populist without any moral compass, an inconsistent and mercurial decision-maker who blows with the wind in response to crowds, advisors, and TV commentary. His belligerent Tweet attacks against perceived critics and detractors seem to be driven by narcissistic ego and by Fox news than by any coherent set of ideological principles.[82] Given his impulsiveness and inconsistency, more than many leaders, it remains difficult to sort the sound from the signal. But even where the Trump administration lacks detailed coherent policy proposals which could be translated into workable legislative proposals, the mix of xenophobia, anti-immigrant, and racist values are a consistent thread in his rhetoric and policy priorities.

Trump is the first authoritarian populist to reach the White House but he is not unique in American politics. Other demagogues spewing the politics of resentment include Joe McCarthy's witch-hunt for communists and George Wallace's white backlash,[83] and the historical roots of populism can be traced back to the late-nineteenth-century progressive movement, the Prohibitionists, and Huey Long's Share the Wealth movement. Indeed populist discourse has permeated modern American presidential campaigns, with (on the Republican side) the 1952 Eisenhower campaign, the 1996 Dole campaign, and the 1968 Nixon campaign, and (on the Democratic side) the 1988 Dukakis campaign, the 1972 McGovern campaign, and the 1992 Clinton campaign with the slogan 'Putting People First.'[84] Analysis of presidential speeches suggest that many US presidential candidates from across the political spectrum, including Jimmy Carter, Ronald Reagan, and Ross Perot, have depicted themselves as outsider reform crusaders vowing to clean up the corruption in Washington DC, to throw out beltway lobbyists, and to reform government.[85]

Trump's angry anti-establishment tone and his authoritarian-populist tendencies also echo that of many other presidential leaders around the world.[86] Latin America also has a long history of presidents using populist rhetoric to decry the corrupt establishment from the left-wing side of the political spectrum, preaching social justice, pacifism, anti-globalism, and anti-capitalism.[87] In Asia, several political leaders have been seen as populist; including Indian Prime Minister Narendra Modi, Thailand's Thaksin Shinawatra,[88] and the Philippines' President Rodrigo Duterte.[89] In Sub-Saharan Africa, several leaders are seen to have also adopted populist strategies, such as Zambia's Michael Sata and South Africa's Jacob Zuma.[90]

## VII CONCLUSION

Populist rhetoric asserts the legitimacy of popular sovereignty – if necessary, over-riding the pluralist principles of minority rights, elite expertise, conventional power structures in liberal democracy, and decision-making by elected representatives and professional bureaucrats. Populism thereby delegitimizes institutional checks-and-balances on the powers of the executive, undermining faith in the impartiality of the courts and rule of law, elections, the independent news media, intellectuals and scientists, civil society organizations and interest groups, opposition parties, civil servants, and elected legislators. There is broad agreement in the literature that populism emphasizes the value of faith in the wisdom and virtue of ordinary people over the 'corrupt' elite.[91]

This rhetoric reflects first-order principles about the moral foundations of legitimate governance. At the same time, populism provides little if any guidance about what should be done, however, and thus it is silent about second-order principles in any ideology about public policies, so populists are not necessarily defined by the traditional state v. market left–right cleavage over economic and social welfare policies nor are populists necessarily associated with one side or other in the authoritarian–libertarian cleavage.[92] Actors of various political persuasions who adopt populist discourse share a common language about what they are *against*, depicting themselves as radical outsiders rooted in the wisdom and experience of 'ordinary folks,' with their leaders seen as insurgents fighting the establishment on behalf of the people. They attack the liberal conviction of moral superiority and politically correct nostrums.

The evidence in this chapter suggests two main conclusions about where populists are located in patterns of party competition.

Firstly, political parties can be classified on a systematic basis from expert survey data to identify how far they reflect the left–right and authoritarian–libertarian cleavages, as well as whether they adopt populist or pluralist discourse. The results suggests that populism is not best understood as a phenomenon confined to a specific party type, as so much of the literature assumes, but instead it is a pervasive discourse or style. Politicians of many political stripes and persuasions can adopt populist language – especially challengers and outsiders running for office by running against the office – because this is an effective way to tap into a mood of public disenchantment with the performance of mainstream parties and other representative institutions. How else, after all, could Eurosceptic politicians campaign when seeking election to the European Parliament, the very body they attack? Even policies often most closely regarded as the signature issue of 'populists' – such as nativism, nationalism, and anti-immigration – are more a product of the ideologies attached to populism, rather than an intrinsic feature. Populism is about who should govern – not what is to be done.

Secondly, the classification in this chapter seeks to scrap and replace the conventional language of 'radical right,' 'extreme right,' 'populist right,' and all the rest as both conceptually flawed and confusing. Instead, experts identify party positions in a wide range of European parties on three dimensions. The measures capture contemporary patterns of party competition in European societies, distinguishing the old left–right economic cleavage, the authoritarian–libertarian cultural cleavage and the populist–pluralist dimension which overlays both. These data are used to estimate continuous scales for all parties, used in subsequent chapters. Parties are also categorized based on these dimensions. Parties scoring highly in populism are located across the political spectrum. Finally, we identify the sub-category of parties which combine both authoritarianism and populism, the combination we regard as potentially most dangerous for undermining liberal democracy.

What explains mass support for Authoritarian-Populist parties and leaders? The next chapter examines cross-national survey evidence in an effort to identify the roots of electoral support for these political parties in a variety of European societies.

## Notes

1. See also K. Deegan-Krause and T. Haughton. 2009. 'Toward a more useful conceptualization of populism: Types and degrees of populist appeals in the case of Slovakia.' *Politics and Policy* 37 (4): 821–841.
2. Cees van der Eijk, Wouter van der Brug, Martin Kroh, and Mark Franklin. 2005. 'Rethinking the dependent variable in voting behavior: The measurement and analysis of electoral utilities.' *Electoral Studies* 25 (3): 424–447.
3. For further discussion of this understanding, see Chapter 3 and also Jan-Werner Muller. 2016. *What is Populism?* Pennsylvania: University of Pennsylvania Press; Ernesto Laclau. 2005. *On Populist Reason.* London:

Verso; Benjamin Moffitt. 2016. *The Global Rise of Populism: Performance, Political Style and Representation*. Palo Alto, CA: Stanford University Press; Toril Aalberg, Frank Esser, Carsten Reinemann, Jesper Stromback, and Claes H. de Vreese. Eds. 2017. *Populist Political Communication in Europe*. London: Routledge; Paris Aslanidis. 2015. 'Is populism an ideology? A refutation and a new perspective.' *Political Studies* 64 (1): 88–104; Elena Block and Ralph Negrine. 2017. 'The populist communication style: Toward a critical framework.' *International Journal of Communication* 11: 178–197.

4. For the literature using the concept of the 'radical right,' see, for example, Herbert Kitschelt, with Anthony J. McGann. 1997. *The Radical Right in Western Europe*. Ann Arbor, MI: University of Michigan Press; Pippa Norris. 2005. *Radical Right: Voters and Parties in the Electoral Market*. New York: Cambridge University Press.
5. For the term 'populist radical right,' see Cas Mudde. 2007. *Populist Radical Right Parties in Europe*. New York: Cambridge University Press; H.G. Betz. 1994. *Radical Right-Wing Populism in Western Europe*. New York: St Martin's Press; Laurenz Ennser. 2012. 'The homogeneity of West European party families: The radical right in comparative perspective.' *Party Politics* 18 (2): 151–171.
6. For scholars using the term 'extreme right,' see Pierro Ignazi. 2003. *Extreme Right Parties in Western Europe*. Oxford: Oxford University Press; Elizabeth Carter. 2005. *The Extreme Right in Western Europe: Success or Failure?* Manchester: Manchester University Press.
7. Carlos de la Torre and Cynthia J. Arnson. Eds. 2013. *Latin American Populism in the Twenty-First Century*. Baltimore, MD: Johns Hopkins University Press; Yannis Stavrakakis, Alexandros Kioupkioli, and Gioros Katsambekis. 2016. 'Contemporary left-wing populism in Latin America: Leadership, horizontalism, and post-democracy in Chavez's Venezuela.' *Latin American Politics and Society* 58 (3): 51–76.
8. Noam Lupu. 2010. 'Who Votes for Chavismo? Class voting in Hugo Chavez's Venezuela.' *Latin American Research Review* 45 (1): 7–32.
9. Carlos de la Torre. Ed. 2015. *The Promise and Perils of Populism: Global Perspectives*. Lexington, KT: University of Kentucky Press; Karen Remmer. 2012. 'The rise of leftist-populist governance in Latin America: The roots of electoral change.' *Comparative Political Studies* 45: 947–972; A.E. van Niekerk. 1974. *Populism and Political Development in Latin America*. Rotterdam: Universitaire Pers Rotterdam; Erdem S. Aytac and Ziva Onis. 2014. 'Varieties of populism in a changing global context: The divergent paths of Erdogan and Kirchnerismo.' *Comparative Politics* 47 (1): 41–49.
10. Matthijs Rooduijn and Tjitske Akkerman. 2017. 'Flank attacks: Populism and left–right radicalism in Western Europe.' *Party Politics* 23 (3): 193–204.
11. Michael Kazin. 1998. *The Populist Persuasion: An American History*. Ithaca, NY: Cornell University Press.
12. Michele Lamont, Bo Yun Park, and Elena Ayala-Hurtado. 2017. 'Trump's electoral speeches and his appeal to the American white working class.' *British Journal of Sociology* 68: 153–180.

13. On the meaning of 'New York values,' see www.washingtonpost.com/blogs/post-partisan/wp/2016/04/19/ted-cruz-and-the-revenge-of-new-york-values/.
14. Ian Budge, Hans Keman, Michael McDonald, and Paul Pennings. 2012. *Organizing Democratic Choice: Party Representation over Time*. Oxford: Oxford University Press; T.J. Royed. 1996. 'Testing the mandate model in Britain and the United States: Evidence from the Reagan and Thatcher eras.' *British Journal of Political Science* 26 (1): 48–80.
15. For similar approaches, see Anthony Heath, Geoffrey Evans, and Jean Martin. 1994. 'The measurement of core beliefs and values: The development of balanced socialist/laissez faire and libertarian/authoritarian scales.' *British Journal of Political Science* 24 (1): 115–132; Simon Bornschier. 2010. *Cleavage Politics and the Populist Right: The New Cultural Conflict in Western Europe*. Philadelphia: Temple University Press.
16. See Alan Ware. 1996. *Political Parties and Party Systems*. Oxford: Oxford University Press; Peter Mair and Cas Mudde. 1998.'The party family and its study.' *Annual Review of Political Science* 1: 211–229.
17. www.socialistinternational.org/.
18. www.enfgroup-ep.eu/.
19. www.efddgroup.eu/about-us/our-president.
20. www.efddgroup.eu/about-us/our-charter.
21. Toril Aalberg, Frank Esser, Carsten Reinemann, Jesper Stromback, and Claes H. de Vreese. Eds. 2017. *Populist Political Communication in Europe*. London: Routledge; Jan Jagers and Stephan Walgrave. 2007. 'Populism as political communication style: An empirical study of political parties' discourse in Belgium.' *European Journal of Political Research* 46 (3): 319–345.
22. G. Mazzoleni, J. Stewart, and B. Horsfield. Eds. 2003. *The Media and Neo-populism: A Contemporary Comparative Analysis*. Westport, CT: Praeger.
23. Martin Conboy. 2006. *Tabloid Britain: Constructing a Community through Language*. London: Routledge.
24. Sean Carey and Jonathan Burton. 2004. 'Research note: The influence of the press in shaping public opinion towards the European Union in Britain.' *Political Studies* 52 (3): 623–640.
25. Juha Herkman. 2017. 'The life cycle model and press coverage of Nordic populist parties.' *Journalism Studies* 18 (4): 430–448.
26. H.G. Boomgaarden and R. Vliegenthart. 2007. 'Explaining the rise of anti-immigrant parties: The role of news media content.' *Electoral Studies* 26 (2): 404–417; Tjitske Akkerman. 2011. 'Friend or foe? Right-wing populism and the popular press in Britain and the Netherlands.' *Journalism* 12 (8): 931–945.
27. See, however, Matthijs Rooduijn. 2014. 'The mesmerising message: The diffusion of populism in public debates in Western European media.' *Political Studies* 62 (4): 726–744.
28. Toril Aalberg, Frank Esser, Carsten Reinemann, Jesper Stromback, and Claes H. de Vreese. 2017. *Populist Political Communication in Europe*. New York: Routledge; Alessandro Nai and Juergen Maier. 2018. 'Perceived

personality and campaign style of Hillary Clinton and Donald Trump.' *Personality and Individual Differences* 121: 80–83.

29. Bart Bonikowski and Noam Gidron. 2016. 'The populist style in American politics.' *Social Forces* 94 (4): 1593–1621.
30. Michele Lamont, Bo Yun Park, and Elena Ayala-Hurtado. 2017. 'Trump's electoral speeches and his appeal to the American white working class.' *British Journal of Sociology* 68: 153–180.
31. Ramona Kreis. 2017. 'The "Tweet Politics" of President Trump.' *Journal of Language and Politics* 16 (4): 607–618.
32. Delia Dumitrescu. 2017. 'Up, close and personal: The new Front National visual strategy under Marine Le Pen.' *French Politics* 15 (1): 1–26.
33. Kirk Hawkins. 2009. 'Is Chavez populist? Measuring populist discourse in comparative perspective.' *Comparative Political Studies* 42 (8): 1040–1067.
34. See, however, http://observatory.populismus.gr/.
35. See the Comparative Candidate Survey. www.comparativecandidates.org/.
36. See Members and Activists of Political Parties (MAPP). www.projectmapp.eu/.
37. Pippa Norris. 1995. 'May's law of curvilinear disparity revisited: Leaders, officers, members and voters in British political parties.' *Party Politics* 1 (1): 29–47; Pippa Norris and Joni Lovenduski. 2004. 'Why parties fail to learn: Electoral defeat, selective perception and British party politics.' *Party Politics* 10 (1): 85–104.
38. Andrea Volkens, Pola Lehmann, Theres Matthieß, Nicolas Merz, Sven Regel, and Bernhard Weßels. 2017. *The Manifesto Data Collection. Manifesto Project (MRG/CMP/MARPOR)*. Version 2017a. Berlin: Wissenschaftszentrum Berlin für Sozialforschung (WZB). https://manifesto-project.wzb.eu/. For some uses of the dataset, see, for example, Ian Budge and Dennis J. Farlie. 1983. *Explaining and Predicting Elections: Issue Effects and Party Strategies in Twenty-Three Democracies*. London: Allen & Unwin; Ian Budge, David Robertson, and Derek Hearl. Eds. 1987. *Ideology, Strategy and Party Change: Spatial Analysis of Postwar Election Programmes in 19 Democracies*. Cambridge: Cambridge University Press; Ian Budge, Hans-Dieter Klingemann, Andrew Volkens, Judith Bara, and Eric Tanenbaum. 2001. *Mapping Policy Preferences*. Oxford: Oxford University Press.
39. Michael Laver and Ian Budge. Eds. 1992. *Party Policy and Government Coalitions*. Houndmills, Basingstoke: Macmillan.
40. For the utility of the left–right schema, see Dieter Fuchs and Hans-Dieter Klingemann. 1989. 'The left–right schema.' In M.K. Jennings and Jan W. van Deth. Eds. *Continuities in Political Action*. Berlin: Walter de Gruyter, pp. 203–234. Several expert surveys classifying parties on the left–right ideological spectrum have been conducted, including by Francis Castles and Peter Mair. 1984. 'Left-right political scales: Some "expert" judgements.' *European Journal of Political Research* 12 (1): 73–88; John Huber and Ronald Inglehart. 1995. 'Expert interpretations of party space and party locations in 42 societies.' *Party Politics* 1: 73–111; Michael Laver. Ed. 2001. *Estimating the Policy Positions of Political Actors*. London: Routledge. For

critical discussions, see Ian Budge. 2000. 'Expert judgments of party policy positions: Uses and limitations in political research.' *European Journal of Political Research* 37 (1): 103–113; Peter Mair. 2001. 'Searching for the position of political actors: A review of approaches and a critical evaluation of expert surveys.' In M. Laver. Ed. *Estimating the Policy Positions of Political Actors.* London: Routledge.

41. Herbert Kitschelt and S. Hellemans. 1990. 'The left–right semantics and the new politics cleavage.' *Comparative Political Studies* 23 (2): 210–238; Michael McDonald and S. Mendes. 2001. 'The Policy Space of Party Manifestos.' In Michael Laver. Ed. *Estimating the Policy Position of Political Actors.* London: Routledge, pp. 90–114; Kostas Gemenis. 2013. 'What to do (and not to do) with the comparative manifestos project data.' *Political Studies* 61: 23–43; Elias Dinas and Kostas Gemenis. 2010. 'Measuring parties' ideological positions with manifesto data: A critical evaluation of the competing methods.' *Party Politics* 16 (4): 427–450.
42. Seymour Martin Lipset and Stein Rokkan. 1967. *Party Systems and Voter Alignments.* New York: Free Press.
43. Pippa Norris. 2005. *Radical Right: Voters and Parties in the Electoral Market.* New York: Cambridge University Press, Chapter 2; Marco R. Steenbergen and Gary Marks. 2007. 'Evaluating expert judgments.' *European Journal of Political Research* 46: 347–366; Peter Mair and Francis Castles. 1997. 'Reflections: Revisiting expert judgments.' *European Journal of Political Research* 31 (1–2): 150–157; John Huber and Ronald Inglehart. 1995. 'Expert interpretations of party space and party locations in 42 societies.' *Party Politics* 1: 73–111; Ian Budge, Hans-Dieter Klingemann, Andrew Volkens, Judith Bara, and Eric Tanenbaum. 2001. *Mapping Policy Preferences: Estimates for Parties, Electors and Governments, 1945–1998.* Oxford: Oxford University Press.
44. Ryan Bakker, Erica Edwards, Liesbet Hooghe, Seth Jolly, Gary Marks, Jonathan Polk, Jan Rovny, Marco Steenbergen, and Milada Vachudova. 2015. '2014 Chapel Hill Expert Survey.' Version 2015.1. Chapel Hill, NC: University of North Carolina, Chapel Hill. Available via chesdata.eu.
45. Mary Meyer and Jane Booker. 2001. *Eliciting and Analyzing Expert Judgment: A Practical Guide.* Society for Industrial and Applied Mathematics; Andreas Schedler. 2012. 'Judgment and measurement in political science.' *Perspectives on Politics* 10 (1): 21–36; Ferran Martinez i Coma and Richard W. Frank. 2014. 'Expert judgments.' In Pippa Norris, Richard W. Frank, and Ferran Martinez I. Coma. Eds. *Advancing Electoral Integrity.* New York: Oxford University Press, Chapter 4; Alexander Cooley and Jack Snyder. Eds. 2015. *Ranking the World.* New York: Cambridge University Press.
46. The CHES and the ESS datasets overlapped in coverage for 28 European countries but four countries contained in the pooled ESS were not classified in CHES (Ukraine, Russia, Iceland, and Israel). In these cases, other standard reference sources were used to classify populist parties, including Tim Immerzeel, Marcel Lubbers, and Hilde Coffé. 2011. *Expert Judgment Survey of European Political Parties.* Utrecht: Utrecht University; Marcel

Lubbers. 2000 [principal investigator]. *Expert Judgment Survey of Western-European Political Parties 2000* [machine readable data set]. Nijmegen, the Netherlands: NWO, Department of Sociology, University of Nijmegen; Tim Immerzeel, Marcel Lubbers, and Hilde Coffé. 2016. 'Competing with the radical right: Distances between the European radical right and other parties on typical radical right issues.' *Party Politics* 22 (6): 823–834.

47. Marco R. Steenbergen and Gary Marks. 2007. 'Evaluating expert judgments.' *European Journal of Political Research* 46: 347–366; Ryan Bakker *et al.* 2012. 'Measuring party positions in Europe: The Chapel Hill expert survey trend file, 1999–2010.' *Party Politics* 21 (1): 43–152.
48. It should be noted that the next wave of the CHES survey will include an item on populism and unfortunately the Comparative Manifesto Project also lacks suitable measures on this dimension.
49. Geoffrey Evans and Pippa Norris. Eds. *Critical Elections*. London: Sage.
50. Daniel Stockemer and Mauro Barisione. 2017. 'The "new" discourse of the Front National under Marine Le Pen: A slight change with a big impact.' *European Journal of Communication* 32 (2): 100–115.
51. Cronbach's Alpha. 75 ***.
52. Tim Immerzeel, Marcel Lubbers, and Hilde Coffé. 2011. *Expert Judgment Survey of European Political Parties*. Utrecht: Utrecht University.
53. The results of the CHES and the Immerzeel, Lubbers and Coffé estimates for the ideological position of parties were compared and the simple correlations were strong (R = .85***) for the cultural scale and also for the L-R economic scales (R = .88***).
54. Comparisons were drawn with populist radical right parties listed in Cas Mudde. 2007. *Populist Radical Right Parties in Europe*. New York: Cambridge University Press.
55. It should be noted that Nigel Farage has stood down as the official party leader of UKIP but he remains the most well-known spokesperson.
56. P. Aslanidis and C. Rovira Kaltwasser. 2016. 'Dealing with populists in government: The SYRIZA-ANEL coalition in Greece.' *Democratization* 23 (6): 1077–1091.
57. Iasonas Lamprianou and Antonis Ellinas. 2017. 'Institutional grievances and right-wing extremism: Voting for Golden Dawn in Greece.' *South European Society And Politics* 22 (1): 43–60.
58. www.ataka.bg/.
59. Venelin Ganev. 2017. 'Neoliberalism is fascism and should be criminalized: Bulgarian populism as left-wing radicalism.' *Slavic Review* 76: S9.
60. Luke March. 2012. *Radical Left Parties in Europe*. London: Routledge; Luis Orriols and Guillermo Coirdero. 2016. 'The breakdown of the Spanish two-party system: The upsurge of Podemos and Ciudadanos in the 2015 general election.' *South European Society and Politics* 21 (4): 469–492; Simon Otjes and Tom Louwerse. 2015. 'Populists in parliament: Comparing left-wing and right-wing populism in the Netherlands.' *Political Studies* 63 (1): 60–79; Davide Vittori. 2017. 'Podemos and the Five-star Movement: Populist, nationalist or what?' *Contemporary Italian Politics* 9 (2): 142–161.

61. Gilles Ivaldi, Maria Elisabetta Lanzone, and Dwayne Woods. 'Varieties of populism across a left–right spectrum: The case of the Front National, the Northern League, Podemos and Five Star Movement.' *Swiss Political Science Review* 23 (4): 354–376.
62. Paris Aslanidis and Cristóbal Rovira Kaltwasser. 2016. 'Dealing with populists in government: The SYRIZA-ANEL coalition in Greece.' *Democratization* 23 (6): 1077–1091; Cas Mudde. 2017. *SYRIZA: The Failure of the Populist Promise*. London: Palgrave Macmillan.
63. Simon Bornschier. 2010.*Cleavage Politics and the Populist Right: The New Cultural Conflict in Western Europe*. Philadelphia: Temple University Press.
64. D. Skenderovic. 2009. *The Radical Right in Switzerland: Continuity and Change, 1945–2000*. New York/Oxford: Berghahn Books.
65. Simon Bornschier. 2010.*Cleavage Politics and the Populist Right: The New Cultural Conflict in Western Europe*. Philadelphia: Temple University Press.
66. It should be noted that the SVP lost its second seat in 2008, when the BDP split from the SVP, but they regained it again after the 2015 elections.
67. Daniel Bochsler, Marlene Gerber, and David Zumbach. 2016. 'The 2015 national elections in Switzerland: Renewed polarization and shift to the right.' *Regional and Federal Studies* 26 (1): 95–106.
68. www.svp.ch/partei/positionen/themen/asylpolitik/.
69. Simon Bornschier. 2015. 'The new cultural conflict, polarization, and representation in the Swiss party system, 1975–2011.' *Swiss Political Science Review* 21(4): 680–701.
70. A. Ladner. 2001. 'Swiss political parties: Between persistence and change.' *West European Politics* 24 (2): 123–144; Daniele Albertazzi and Sean Mueller. 2013. 'Populism and liberal democracy: Populists in government in Austria, Italy, Poland and Switzerland.' *Government and Opposition* 48(3): 343–371.
71. Oscar Mazzoleni and Damir Skenderovic. 2007. 'The Rise and Impact of the Swiss People's Party: Challenging the Rules of Governance in Switzerland.' In Pascal Delwit and Philippe Poirier, *Extrême-droite et pouvoir en Europe*. Bruxelles: Editions de l'Université de Bruxelles.
72. The ILO estimates that the rate of unemployment in Switzerland was 5.2 percent in 2017.
73. Jacques Thomassen. 2012. 'The blind corner of representation.' *Representation* 48 (1): 13–27; Zoe Lefkofridi, Markus Wagner, and Johanna E. Willmann. 2014. 'Left-authoritarians and policy representation in Western Europe: Electoral choice across ideological dimensions.' *West European Politics* 37 (1): 65–90.
74. Alina Polyakova. 2015. 'The backward East? Explaining differences in support for radical right parties in Western and Eastern Europe.' *Journal of Comparative Politics* 8 (1): 49–74; Andrea Pirro. 2017. *The Populist Radical Right in Central and Eastern Europe: Ideology, Impact, and Electoral Performance*. London: Routledge.
75. Luke March. 2012. *Radical Left Parties in Europe*. London: Routledge.
76. Michael L. Conniff. Ed. 1982. *Latin American Populism in Comparative Perspective*. Albuquerque, NM: University of New Mexico Press; K. Burgess

and Stephen Levitsky. 2003. 'Explaining populist party adaptation in Latin America: Environmental and organizational determinants of party change in Argentina, Mexico, Peru, and Venezuela.' *Comparative Political Studies* 36 (8): 881–911; Sebastian Edwards. 2010. *Left Behind: Latin America and the False Promise of Populism.* Chicago: University of Chicago Press; Carlos de la Torre. Ed. 2015. *The Promise and Perils of Populism: Global Perspectives.* Kentucky: University Press of Kentucky; Cas Mudde and Cristóbal Rovira Kaltwasser. 2012. 'Exclusionary vs. inclusionary populism in Europe and Latin America.' *Government and Opposition* 48 (2): 147–174.

77. Michael L. Conniff. Ed. 1982. *Latin American Populism in Comparative Perspective.* Albuquerque, NM: University of New Mexico Press; K. Burgess and Stephen Levitsky. 2003. 'Explaining populist party adaptation in Latin America: Environmental and organizational determinants of party change in Argentina, Mexico, Peru, and Venezuela.' *Comparative Political Studies* 36 (8): 881–911; Carlos de la Torre. Ed. 2015. *The Promise and Perils of Populism: Global Perspectives.* Kentucky: University Press of Kentucky.
78. K. Weyland. 2003. 'Economic voting reconsidered: Crisis and charisma in the election of Hugo Chavez.' *Comparative Political Studies* 36 (7): 822–848; Richard Nadeau, Eric Belanger, and Thomas Didier. 2013. 'The Chavez vote and the national economy in Venezuela.' *Electoral Studies* 32 (3): 482–488.
79. www.vanderbilt.edu/lapop/.
80. Kirk Hawkins. 2010. *Venezuela's Chavismo and Populism in Comparative Perspective.* Cambridge: Cambridge University Press.
81. For some of the contemporary debate about this interpretation, see Matthew C. MacWilliams. 2016. 'Who decides when the party doesn't? Authoritarian voters and the rise of Donald Trump.' *PS: Political Science and Politics* 49 (4): 716–721; Amanda Taub. March 1, 2016. 'The rise of American authoritarianism.' *Vox.* www.vox.com/2016/3/1/11127424/trump-authoritarianism; Wendy Rahn and Eric Oliver. March 9, 2016. 'Trump's voters aren't authoritarians, new research says. So what are they?' *The Washington Post/Monkey Cage.* 'www.washingtonpost.com/news/monkey-cage/wp/2016/03/09/trumps-voters-arent-authoritarians-new-research-says-so-what-are-they/.
82. Martin Wolff. 2017. *Fire and Fury: Inside the Trump White House.* New York: Henry Holt & Co.
83. Michael Kazin. 1998. *The Populist Persuasion: An American History.* Ithaca, NY: Cornell University Press; John B. Judis. 2016. *The Populist Explosion: How the Great Recession Transformed American and European Politics.* New York: Columbia Global Reports.
84. Bart Bonikowski and Noam Gidron. 2016. 'The populist style in American politics: Presidential campaign discourse, 1952–1996.' *Social Forces* 94 (4): 1593–1621.
85. Bart Bonikowski and Noam Gidron. 2016. 'The populist style in American politics.' *Social Forces* 94 (4): 1593–1621.

86. Carlos de la Torre. Ed. 2015. *The Promise and Perils of Populism: Global Perspectives*. Kentucky: University Press of Kentucky; Cas Mudde. August 26, 2015. 'The Trump phenomenon and the European populist radical right.' *Monkey Cage/Washington Post*. www.washingtonpost.com/blogs/monkey-cage/wp/2015/08/26/the-trump-phenomenon-and-the-european-populist-radical-right/.
87. Sebastian Edwards. 2010. *Left Behind: Latin America and the False Promise of Populism*. Chicago: University of Chicago Press; Carlos de la Torre and Cynthia J. Arnson. Eds. 2013. *Latin American Populism in the Twenty-First Century*. Baltimore, MD: Johns Hopkins University Press; Karen Remmer. 2012. 'The rise of leftist-populist governance in Latin America: The roots of electoral change.' *Comparative Political Studies* 45: 947–972; Kurt Weyland. 2001. 'Clarifying a contested concept: Populism in the study of Latin American politics.' *Comparative Politics* 34 (1): 1–22; Kirk Hawkins. 2010. *Venezuela's Chavismo and Populism in Comparative Perspective*. Cambridge: Cambridge University Press.
88. Benjamin Moffat. 2015. 'Contemporary populism and "the people" in the Asia-Pacific region.' In Carlos de la Torre. Ed. *The Promise and Perils of Populism: Global Perspectives*. Kentucky: University Press of Kentucky.
89. Nicole Curato. 2017. 'Flirting with Authoritarian fantasies? Rodrigo Duterte and the new terms of Philippine Populis.' *Journal of Contemporary Asia* 47 (1): 142–153.
90. Danielle Resnick. 2015. 'Varieties of African populism in comparative perspective.' In Carlos de la Torre. Ed. *The Promise and Perils of Populism: Global Perspectives*. Kentucky: University Press of Kentucky; Nic Cheeseman and Miles Larmer. 2015. 'Ethno-populism in Africa: Opposition mobilization in diverse and unequal societies.' *Democratization* 22 (1): 22–50.
91. Kirk A. Hawkins. 2009. 'Is Chávez Populist? Measuring populist discourse in comparative perspective.' *Comparative Political Studies* 42 (8): 1040–1067.
92. Jan Jagers and Stafaan Walgrave. 2007. 'Populism as political communication style: An empirical study of political parties' discourse in Belgium.' *European Journal of Political Research* 46 (3): 319–345.

# 8

# Who Votes for Authoritarian-Populist Parties?

The surge of support for Authoritarian-Populist parties in a series of 2017 elections renewed concern about this phenomenon and its potential for destabilizing long-established patterns of party competition. In June 2017, the National Front's Marine Le Pen challenged Emmanuel Macron in the second round of the French presidential elections, after defeating the socialist party on the center-left and the republicans on the center-right in the first round contest. A few months later, in September, the xenophobic and racist Alternative for Germany challenged Angela Merkel's generous refugee policies, entering the Bundestag with 94 seats – the first time a far-right party had done so since 1948. This was followed a month later by the Austrian Freedom Party (FPÖ) coming second in parliamentary elections, winning one in four votes. In still other countries, including Austria, Switzerland, New Zealand, Norway, Finland, the Czech Republic, Italy, and Poland, Authoritarian-Populist parties have won legislative and ministerial office.[1] The performance of Authoritarian-Populist parties ebbs and flows over time but even where these parties have had only limited electoral success, their hardline anti-immigrant rhetoric, racist and religious intolerance, and nationalist policies can infect the policy agenda for governing parties on the center-right, such as the People's Party in Austria, the Republican Party in the US, and the Eurosceptic Conservative Party in the UK. All major parties have been affected by the voting success of far-right parties but they have been most damaging for Social Democratic and Labour parties.

It is important to understand the reasons why people vote for Authoritarian-Populist parties. Authoritarian-populist forces were decisive for the outcome of the Brexit referendum on the UK's membership in the European Union in June 2016, igniting anti-immigrant and nativist sentiments and generating a deep financial, political, and constitutional crisis within the United Kingdom. In the United States, Donald Trump has overthrown numerous conventions in American politics. His aggressive rejection of 'political correctness,' his belligerent style, and his willingness to engage in cultural wars against liberal targets seems to be particularly appealing to older, religious, white men in rural communities, especially social conservatives and xenophobes. These groups find themselves left behind by growing support for same-sex marriage, gender equality for women in politics, and immigration rights for 'Dreamers.' Rhetorical slogans to 'Build the wall,' 'Make America Great Again,' and 'Clean the Swamp' appeal deeply and symbolically to people who reject new values and establishment politics – a group that Trump mobilized to vote in the 2016 election, although it is a shrinking sector of the American electorate. Authoritarian-Populist and Progressive-Populist parties have advanced in many other post-industrial societies, disrupting long-established patterns of party competition and governing coalitions.

To understand the factors underlying electoral support for these parties, this chapter first discusses various approaches to analyzing the evidence. We then describe the research design used to analyze electoral behavior in this study, treating the individual-level indices of voting for populist and authoritarian parties developed in the previous chapter as the dependent variables. We again use data from the European Social Survey, pooling the surveys from 2002 to 2014, covering over 30 countries. When considering elections, citizens face two choices: (1) whether to cast a ballot, and (2) what party to support. Both decisions are equally important for estimating any compositional effects – and both are related in practice – although most attention has traditionally focused on analyzing who supports radical right or populist parties. This approach is inadequate, since voter turnout is not a random process and any analysis restricted to voters alone (rather than all citizens) provides an incomplete picture.[2] Young and old differ in their propensity to vote, and in their value preferences and party choices. We therefore use regression models to examine both stages of the voting process. We first examine *who participates*, demonstrating both generational and life-cycle effects. We then analyze the social and attitudinal characteristics of voters who support authoritarian parties – that is, parties that favor nationalism in foreign affairs, tough law and order, restrictions on the integration of immigrants and asylum seekers, opposing liberal lifestyles like homosexuality, and valuing order, tradition, and stability. We next analyze support for populist parties – those using anti-establishment and anti-corruption rhetoric. The direct role of political values and generational effects are examined in detail – along with the impact of period and life-cycle effects, education, social class, and urbanization – as we expect these factors to play a key role in driving long-term processes of cultural change and changes in voting behavior. Our models control for many other socio-economic factors that are often considered important in explaining patterns of turnout and party choices.

We arrive at several major findings.

With *turnout*, we find consistent and remarkably strong generational differences in the European electorate: members of the oldest (Interwar) generation are almost *twice* as likely to report casting a ballot as are members of the youngest (Millennial) generation – a finding that is observed across diverse societies. Some of the disparity reflects life-cycle effects – as people settle down to raise families – but most of it reflects enduring generational differences. This pattern was expected and is an important part of the backlash thesis, which argues that the impact of the growing cultural gap between young and old is conditioned by rates of voting participation.

Secondly, in explaining electoral support for authoritarian parties, we find that the Interwar generation is most likely to vote for parties that are more authoritarian, while the Millennials are least likely to support them. This pattern is also consistent and significant across 19 out of 26 European countries. The generation gap is not simply attributable to period or life-cycle effects. It weakens when we control for the background characteristics on which young and old differ, such as religiosity and education. It reverses itself when we introduce attitudinal controls. In the final model, among all the factors, voting for authoritarian parties is predicted most strongly (according to the standardized betas) by cultural attitudes: self-identified left–right ideology, authoritarian values, and political attitudes. In short, the political differences between old and young can be traced to deep-rooted differences in their values and attitudes.

Finally, in analyzing voting support for parties using populist rhetoric, the patterns differ; here Millennials are more likely to vote for these parties than older generations, not less. This generation gap remains significant after controlling for period, life-cycle, compositional, and attitudinal effects. It is observed in 17 of the 26 nations under comparison. Populist support is also stronger among the working class, the less educated, men, white Europeans, the economically insecure, and those expressing political mistrust.

The results suggest that Authoritarian-Populist parties and presidential candidates combining anti-elite language with authoritarian values and policies, exemplified by Donald Trump, tend to mobilize an older, more rural base. By contrast, progressive populists like Bernie Sanders, combining anti-elite rhetoric with socially liberal values, attract younger urban supporters. What matters here are mainly the values and ideological positions that are espoused – rather than the style of discourse used to communicate these values. These findings lay the foundations for subsequent chapters that examine the institutional context shaping how votes cast for Authoritarian-Populist parties are translated into seats, ministerial office, and how they influence the policy agenda.

## EXPLAINING VOTER SUPPORT FOR AUTHORITARIAN-POPULIST PARTIES

What evidence can help explain electoral support for authoritarian populists? Scholars have adopted several different approaches, each with certain pros and cons.

### Macro-level Evidence of Social Conditions and Electoral Rules

Cross-national comparisons often analyze the share of the vote won by the radical right or populist political parties by examining the impact of inflow by immigrants, refugees, and asylum seekers; the proportion of 'foreign citizens'; the distribution of racial minorities; the levels of unemployment and poverty; and so on.[3]

Comparative studies usually analyze the factors shaping the success of populist parties within relatively similar nations in given regions such as Western Europe, post-communist Europe, or Latin America, although a growing literature is expanding our understanding of this phenomenon around the world.[4] To reduce the risks of potentially confounding factors, scholars compare party performance and voting behavior across societies with common historical traditions, legacies of authoritarian regimes and democratic traditions, and similar levels of economic and human development. Hence, support for radical right parties has often been thought to reflect a grassroots reaction by European publics against growing ethnic heterogeneity and multiculturalism in society, using evidence such as rates of migration flows or levels of minority populations.[5] But, contrary to popular assumptions, previous research suggests that the share of the vote won by radical right parties at the national level cannot be explained satisfactorily by indicators of growing ethnic diversity in society, including both 'objective' measures, such as the rate of immigration and asylum seekers entering each nation, and 'subjective' measures, such as the strength of nativist attitudes among the publics of given countries.[6] Similarly, studies of economic performance across nine European countries have found that aggregate economic indices gauging objective economic hardships, such as levels of unemployment or poverty, do not predict populist attitudes, although citizen's *subjective* perceptions of economic conditions are significant.[7] Researchers have also explored the impact of the 2007/2008 financial crisis and economic recession by comparing national-level indicators on levels of populist voting across European states, reporting mixed results.[8]

## Within Country Comparisons

For more fine-grained analysis, political geographers have compared party support among electoral units within a single country, such as authoritarian-populist voting results in given provinces, states, regions, constituencies, wards, precincts, or counties. In America, for example, popular commentary focused on county-level results in the 2016 presidential elections and highlighted the way that Trump gained votes disproportionately in white, semi-rural small towns in the Rust Belt, characterized by low levels of education, depopulation, economic decline, and the loss of secure employment due to shuttered factories and mines.[9]

Similarly, in the UK Brexit referendum, as we will see in Chapter 11, the Leave vote was concentrated in the Midlands and North of England, areas characterized by low levels of college education and employment skills, and with many manual workers and retired citizens. By contrast, the Remain voters tended to live in constituencies that are more prosperous, containing many young people, university graduates, and ethnic minorities.[10] Major regional variations were evident, with Leave voting being weaker in Scotland (38%) and Northern Ireland (44%), than the 51.9 percent found across the entire UK.[11]

In Germany, as well, the Alternative for Germany (AfD) attracts the most support in former East Germany, where the party performed particularly well in the September 2017 parliamentary elections.[12] Studies suggest that many AfD supporters have attained an economically stable middle-class existence with relatively prosperous incomes and secure jobs, but they have also experienced profound political and cultural disruptions over the past three decades that have engendered a sense of disillusion and marginality.[13] AfD support is concentrated disproportionately among conservatives lamenting the negative consequences of immigration, especially when linked with access to welfare benefits and services. But the demographic profile of aggregate districts does not consistently support the conventional wisdom about the role of economic and social grievances, since other research states that radical right parties performed more strongly in European areas with high proportions of college-educated populations, not low, as well as in rural communities with few foreign residents and immigrants.[14]

Macro-level or aggregate-level studies may differ in their findings for many reasons, including the use of different model specifications, country coverage, time-periods, and measurement of the dependent variable.[15] The underlying reasons why any observed correlations exist, moreover, and which factors are generally most important for voting support for Authoritarian-Populist parties remains uncertain, partly because general theories are often poorly operationalized, and complex interactive causal pathways may be at work. For example, US maps of the census characteristics of county voting results demonstrate that small-town America in the Rust Belt and coal country swung toward Trump, who performed particularly well in counties with low levels of education, older white populations, while Clinton did better in urban areas with younger and more ethnically diverse populations.[16] But it remains unclear from the county-level evidence whether this pattern was due to the appeal of Trump's economic promises to restore blue-collar manufacturing jobs in middle America (as often assumed) or because his cultural message on wedge issues resonated particularly well in the Rust Belt states. We need to avoid the classic ecological fallacy in drawing inferences about individual motivations from observations of aggregate groupings to which the individuals belong.[17]

Moreover, previous literature analyzing voting for radical right populist parties across European countries and regions presents mixed and inconclusive results, partly because citizens are responding to complex structures of party choices in each election, where viable Authoritarian-Populist parties and candidates may or may not be listed on the ballot. Researchers also face challenges in establishing reliable evidence where party fortunes fluctuate sharply over successive contests; for example, where minor parties make sudden gains at the local level but fail to reach the minimal vote threshold for parliamentary representation in national elections, or if parties change issue positions and populist appeals strategically in response to evolving patterns of competition from their rivals.

Populist parties can also shift policy positions rapidly where they divide into factions and form new parliamentary alliances, such as the Finns Party leadership split in June 2017. Thus, Marine Le Pen dropped some of the most flagrant anti-immigrant, homophobic, and anti-Semitic diatribes of her father's National Front.[18] The rules of the game also matter for the credibility and electoral success of minor parties, and for tactical or strategic voting, such as the legal voting thresholds for gaining seats under Majoritarian and Proportional electoral systems.

## Micro-level Analysis of Citizens

Individual-level observational evidence derived from representative surveys of the electorate provides more fine-grained analysis of the attitudes and motivations underlying voting behavior, but this approach also faces several challenges.

When analyzing voting choices for smaller and fringe parties, one issue arises from the relatively small number of voters in the standard survey samples used in national election studies. This is a common problem when analyzing the standard categorical question used for monitoring voting choices: '*Which party/candidate will you/did you vote for?*' This limitation can be overcome, however, by using alternative measures to gauge the strength of voting preferences, such as 'thermometer' scales monitoring the propensity for electors to support each of the political parties or candidates listed on the ballot. For example, the European Election Study asks respondents to rate the probability that they would *ever* vote for each of the parties standing in the election in each country, measured using standardized 10-point scales.[19] But these types of questions are not often included in national election studies and social attitude surveys. Responses to hypothetical items ('would you ever') tend to be less reliable than reported voting choices ('how did you vote'), with the risk of generating 'manufactured' answers for parties that respondents have not seriously considered supporting. Moreover, reported party preferences may also diverge widely from the actual votes cast, especially for smaller parties, partly due to strategic or tactical voting considerations.

The dynamics of individual changes in voting choices are ideally measured from longitudinal studies of electoral behavior using multiwave election surveys (of different respondents over time, such as pre-post election studies), or, even better, panel surveys (repeated observations of the same respondents over time). Panel studies are usually conducted within specific countries, however, which limits their comparative value to test whether generalizations established in one case can be observed over many national contexts and over time.

Familiar challenges of disentangling endogeneity arise when analysis is limited to observed correlations linking attitudes and voting choices derived from cross-sectional surveys taken at one point in time, raising questions about how to interpret the direction of causality. For example, in the polls taken by the Pew Research Center during the Obama years, Republicans consistently reported being more pessimistic than Democrats about the future of the US economy and more negative in their assessment of current economic conditions.[20] This might be taken to support the theory that retrospective and prospective evaluations of the national economy shape candidate and party choices at the ballot box. But in subsequent surveys, conducted after the November 2016 election, Pew found that many Clinton and Trump voters had reversed positions in these evaluations, with Republicans becoming sharply more bullish on the current and future performance of the US economy after Trump was elected, although the underlying indicators, such as the unemployment rate, remained largely unchanged.[21] This suggests that partisanship functions as a prism that can color citizen's judgments about the state of the US economy.

Similarly, complex interaction effects have been observed in the relationship linking political discontent and populist support; for example, in the Netherlands, multiwave panel survey studies suggest that those disenchanted with established political elites were more likely to vote for populist parties, but that when Authoritarian-Populist parties subsequently blamed established political and economic elites for problems, this deepened feelings of discontent among their followers.[22] American studies have also found that partisan and media cues shape public beliefs about electoral integrity; their supporters are far more likely to believe that these specific malpractices have occurred when party leaders and candidates claim 'rigged' or 'fraudulent' elections, such as Republicans allegations about voting by undocumented immigrants, and Democratic complaints about Russian meddling in the US election.[23] The 'winners–losers' gap has also been found to be important; when populist parties are included in coalition governments, their supporters express more satisfaction with democracy than in countries where these parties are excluded from power.[24]

## DATA AND METHODS

The burgeoning literature on support for Authoritarian-Populist parties and candidates has no shortage of rival theories, but systematic analysis of comparative macro- and micro-level empirical evidence supporting these arguments remains inconclusive.[25] The research design most appropriate for analyzing micro-level attitudes and behavior from individual citizens also requires careful modeling of the decision-process. As we have seen, in elections citizens face two choices: firstly whether to cast a ballot or not, and, secondly, which candidate or party to support in the ballot. Both decisions are equally important. And the two are related – since parties seek to mobilize *and* to persuade. In practice, however, these steps are usually treated separately in the literature, with most attention being given to analyzing the profile of voters supporting radical right or populist parties. But who participates at the ballot box is far from random. Previous research has established that generations differ sharply in both their propensity to vote and in their values and party choices. Where turnout is particularly low – as in the US where around 40 percent of the eligible electorate generally stay home on polling day – examining only the preferences of voters discards information about large swathes of the public.[26] A two-step process determines the outcome of any election, involving (a) deciding whether to vote or not, and then (b) deciding which party to support. Both shape the share of votes and seats won by Authoritarian-Populist political parties. Hence, parties seek to mobilize their base and deter opposition supporters, as well as to persuade the undecided and to convert leaners.

The theoretical argument outlined in earlier chapters generates several claims about both voting turnout and party choices that can be tested using cross-national survey evidence from the pooled European Election Study. This chapter focuses on analyzing the social and demographic characteristics of the European electorate, especially the effects of generation, education, and urbanization. Our models include the year of the survey (to monitor period-effects), standard social controls, such as occupational class, sex, employment/unemployment, ethnicity, and religiosity. We also examine the role of authoritarian values and populist attitudes. Subsequent chapters examine the institutional context for how votes are translated into seats – and thus political representation.

This chapter again uses the European Social Survey (ESS) waves 1–7 (2002–2014).[27] This pooled dataset contains 331,877 respondents across all waves, providing a large sample of the European public in 32 countries. This enables us to analyze electoral behavior in diverse contexts since societies vary in their historical and contemporary experience of liberal democracy and in their levels of economic growth and experience of the financial crisis. The comparison includes Scandinavian and Mediterranean states, as well as contrasts between long-standing democracies in Western Europe and post-communist nations. We can also compare elections held under Majoritarian, Mixed, and Proportional electoral systems, parliamentary and presidential executives, and federal and unitary states. The ESS survey also allows comparison of trends over time in European attitudes toward specific issues, for example in surveys conducted before and after the financial crisis of 2007–2013 and the refugee crisis in 2008. Cases were weighted by post-stratification weights, including design weights.

## The Dependent Variable: Measuring Voting Participation and Party Support

Electoral participation is measured by whether respondents reported voting in a country's most recent national election, modeled as a simple binary (1=Yes/0=No) variable. Surveys usually over-report rates of voting participation when compared with the official record of electoral turnout, but there is no reason to believe that this will generate systematic problems for the analysis.[28]

Voting choices are more complex to measure. Many studies conventionally use a simple binary variable coded as to whether respondents voted for radical right or populist parties (1) or whether they voted for any other party (0). This process can be unreliable, as it is heavily conditioned by the prior classification of political party families. However, it can be relatively straightforward when analyzing support for mainstream Christian democratic or socialist parties, but there is considerable latitude for misclassifying populist parties. And newer parties are often ideologically unstable, dependent upon the preferences of particular factions or leaders, and they have not established a clear programmatic platform over successive elections or a record in office. In pragmatic terms, the use of categorical typologies for minor parties also limits the number of respondents available for analysis, even in large-scale samples, and also generates heavily skewed samples.

The standard approach also assumes that the goal is to understand a distinct *type* of authoritarian or libertarian populist party family, which is unified and cohesive in its programmatic appeals, rather than seeing populism as a communication style that can be adapted by politicians across the spectrum. For example, did the Republican Party suddenly become populist overnight when Trump became their standard-bearer at the national convention? We think not. It makes more sense to assume that some strands of the GOP used populist discourse well before Trump, notably many Tea Party candidates and Sarah Palin, while other wings of the Republican Party, represented by leaders such as Mitt Romney, Ted Cruz, and John McCain, endorsed different governing styles and philosophies. Previous research suggests that well before Trump, when predicting whether voters preferred Hillary Clinton over Barack Obama in the 2008 Democratic primary, authoritarian values mattered more than income, ideology, gender, age, and education.[29] Studies have also found that authoritarians have steadily moved from the Democratic to the Republican Party in a sorting process since the early 1990s.[30] In general, the use of continuous scales captures finer distinctions, rather than throwing away information by classifying diverse parties as one family, viewing UKIP, the True Finns and PVV as all alike. For all these reasons, in this chapter we treat the extent to which parties use populist rhetoric and endorse authoritarian values as a matter of degree not as categorical types. For the dependent variables, party choices, monitored in the ESS survey, are scaled and measured using the continuous 100-point indices estimating the salience of populist rhetoric and party positions toward authoritarian–libertarian values and left–right values for each party in each election. The populism–pluralism, authoritarian–libertarian and left–right indices are derived from the CHES expert estimates at party level, as discussed in the previous chapter.

## Authoritarian Values

The cultural backlash theory suggests that if citizens are choosing whether to vote and which parties to support based on their values, we will find a high level of congruence between authoritarian and socially conservative attitudes, and voting for parties that endorse these values in their policy platforms.

In seeking to disentangle the evidence, however, it is important to minimize the risks of endogeneity, especially with measures of authoritarian values. Direct measures, such as hostile attitudes toward immigrants and multiculturalism, probably influence support for parties that emphasize these issues. But it can also work the other way around, with people who endorse these parties (perhaps because of disillusionment with the mainstream parties) adopting their hardline attitudes toward immigrants.

To avoid these problems, previous studies that have measured authoritarian values have used a battery of items concerning child-rearing practices, including whether it is more important to have a child who is respectful or independent; obedient or self-reliant; well-behaved or considerate; and well-mannered or curious. In the American National Election Survey, for example, respondents selecting the first option in each of these questions were classified as strongly authoritarian.[31] Along similar lines, in successive waves since 1981, the World Values Survey has asked about the importance of many similar qualities for children, including obedience, independence, religious faith, and good manners.[32] As discussed earlier, to measure authoritarian values from the pooled European Social Survey 1–7, we selected five items derived from a battery originally developed by Schwartz as suitable for cross-national comparisons of personal values.[33] These items measure adherence to authoritarian values as indicated by the core concepts of: conformity (the importance of behaving properly and following traditions); security (the importance of living in secure surroundings and having a strong government to protect against threats); and deference (the importance of following rules and doing what one's told). These items refer to individual predispositions and personal preferences, not attitudes toward public policy issues, such as anti-immigration laws, that are more open to the risks of endogeneity. The scale was constructed by combining the five items and compares favorably with equivalent measures.[34]

We demonstrated in Chapter 4 how support for the authoritarian and libertarian value scales varied sharply by generation, as our theory predicts. Thus, the Interwar generation showed most authoritarian values while support steadily declines among the Millennials. The reverse pattern is evident for the libertarian values scale. As a result, the trend lines cross at a tipping point, reflecting rising levels of libertarian values among the younger cohorts. The patterns also reflect the distinct formative experiences of having grown up in different regions of Europe, with the balance of support between authoritarian and libertarian values differing among the post-war generation in Nordic and Northern Europe. The balance of support switches later, for those born in the mid-1970s, in Mediterranean Europe, and in post-communist Europe. We expect both the decision whether to vote, and the decision whether to vote for Authoritarian-Populist parties, to be influenced by generational cohort, educational characteristics, and urbanization – established earlier in the book as long-term drivers of cultural change – as well as by direct support for authoritarian values and socially conservative attitudes. Period-effects are monitored by the year of the survey and life-cycle effects are monitored, as in Chapter 4, by whether one has children living at home, and whether one is married, separated, or divorced.

## Populist Anti-establishment Protest and Political Trust

There are several ways to measure populist attitudes among the electorate.[35] Populism is often assumed to have been fueled by growing public alienation and anger toward the establishment and the core political institutions of representative democracy, especially by weakening loyalties toward mainstream political parties, mistrust of politicians, and disaffection with parliaments.[36] This assumption is widespread in the literature. For example, Latin America studies suggest that weakly legitimate political institutions can encourage populist left support; in particular, where the public is deeply cynical about political parties and leaders, voters are thought to be attracted to candidates portraying themselves as radical 'outsiders,' crusading against the established political order.[37] Numerous accounts suggest that political dissatisfaction and alienation motivate support for authoritarian populism, with resentment directed against both the out-groups, such as immigrants, who are blamed for taking welfare benefits, limiting job opportunities, and thereby reducing life chances for the white working-class population, and the establishment elites, who are blamed for failure to respond to these grievances.[38]

Similarly, in the US, the dominant media narrative of the 2016 US presidential election focused on 'angry' voters frustrated with the performance of their government, the economy, and the direction of the country. Thus Trump's bombastic promises to bring back mines and mills was thought to be particularly potent for exploiting grievances in communities where factory and plant closures triggered population decline, leading to a shrinking tax base, abandoned homes and empty housing lots, and a plague of pills and booze.[39] It is true that, during the campaign, according to Gallup polls, most Americans expressed distrust in government and said that the country was 'on the wrong track.' But this account encounters several problems in seeking to explain the support for Trump. For one thing, according to Gallup trends, levels of dissatisfaction and distrust with political institutions in 2016 were no lower than in several earlier years.[40] Moreover, the lack of trust that existed had no clear electoral implication. After all, President Obama had been comfortably reelected in 2012, when a similar percentage of Americans were saying that they trusted the government in Washington DC 'always' or 'most' of the time.[41] Much of the media claims about supposed voter 'anger' are not supported by solid evidence.

To test whether political disaffection in the mass electorate actually mobilized European voters to support parties and leaders expressing populist rhetoric, we compare several indicators of citizen's trust toward representative institutions linking citizens and the state. Public cynicism toward government is not unidimensional and five distinct levels of support for the political system can be distinguished, ranging from the most diffuse to the most specific.[42] These included feelings toward the nation-state, adherence to regime ideals and democratic principles, confidence in the performance of the regime, trust in the core political institutions, and approval of political actors. Supporters of populism are expected to be particularly likely to reject the legitimacy of mainstream parties, elected assemblies, and incumbent politicians. For these reasons, items were selected from the European Social Survey to develop a standardized scale based on mistrust of political parties, politicians, and national parliaments.

Even where a strong correlation is found between attitudes and voting choices, however, it is difficult to establish the direction of causality from cross-sectional social surveys alone, since complex reciprocal relationships can be at work. Thus, people dissatisfied with liberal elites in Washington DC, Paris, and London, and those with ethnocentric and hostile racist attitudes toward ethnic minorities, multiculturalism, and immigration may decide on this basis to cast their ballot for Authoritarian-Populist leaders and parties. But citizens may also rationalize their voting choice, expressing support for the policy issues most closely associated with a candidate or party although actually motivated by other reasons, such as seeing the world through strong partisan lenses. In the US, for example, Trump may have attracted votes for diverse reasons unrelated to his vague policy promises about restoring jobs, cutting taxes, or building a wall against Mexico. Thus, Trump support may come from die-hard Republicans out of a sense of party loyalty, from residents in the Rust Belt Mid-West and coal country discontented with the failure of the Democrats to stem community decline, from citizens disapproving of the Obama presidency and America's economic recovery, from Hillary Clinton haters concerned about emails, or from those attracted by Trump's flamboyant personality, pugilistic style, and belligerent campaign rhetoric. Similarly, deep cynicism about corrupt politicians and unresponsive bureaucratic elites may have led Latin American and European citizens to support populist outsiders crusading against established political order.[43] Reciprocal effects may underlie any observed correlations – in this regard, political discontent is best regarded as both a cause and a consequence of the rise of populist parties.[44]

## Controls

Our analysis examines the impact of the cultural values scrutinized earlier – including authoritarian values prioritizing security, conformity and loyalty, socially liberal or conservative attitudes, and the respondent's self-placement on the left–right ideological scale. We also control for several other factors emphasized in the literature on voting behavior.

Classic theories based on the Michigan model of voting behavior, suggest that voting turnout and party support are often driven by affective feelings of social identity in the mass electorate, including class cleavages. The role of socio-economic inequality is widely regarded as important in accounts emphasizing that the economically left-behind are the base for authoritarian-populist support.[45] But systematic individual-level survey evidence for this thesis remains mixed, and the role of social class on attitudes and values means that the impact may be indirect.[46] Occupational class is monitored using the five-fold Goldthorpe class schema.[47] The impact of several other economic indicators is also scrutinized, including long-term unemployment and subjective feelings of economic insecurity, as well as dissatisfaction with the performance of the national economy. The models also control for sex, religiosity, ethnicity, and urbanization. Many previous studies have found a significant gender gap, finding stronger support for radical right parties among men.[48] We expect religiosity to strengthen support for Authoritarian-Populist parties, which emphasize traditional morality, illustrated by the strong support of Evangelicals for Donald Trump. By contrast, members of ethnic minorities, and residents of ethnically diverse urban areas, are expected to reject authoritarian-populist appeals. The selected variables and the coding used in this chapter are listed in Appendix B. All models were checked and found by tolerance tests to be free of problems of multicollinearity.

## EXPLAINING VOTING PARTICIPATION

Table 8.1 shows logistic regression models of who votes in European national elections. Once all the factors were entered into the model, the results demonstrate that authoritarian values are significantly associated with *greater* voting turnout, not less, although the relationship is weak; thus around three-quarters (74%) of those scoring high on the authoritarian values scale reported voting in national elections, compared with two thirds (68%) of those scoring low. By contrast, authoritarian

TABLE 8.1. *Predicting who votes, Europe*

| | | B | S.E. | Sig. |
|---|---|---|---|---|
| Generation | Interwar (1900–1945) (Ref) | 0.00 | | |
| | Boomers (1946–1964) | − 0.44 | 0.02 | *** |
| | Gen X (1965–1979) | − 1.07 | 0.02 | *** |
| | Millennials (1980–1996) | − 1.98 | 0.02 | *** |
| Year (period) | 2002 (Ref) | 0.00 | | |
| | 2004 | − 0.40 | 0.03 | *** |
| | 2006 | − 0.19 | 0.02 | *** |
| | 2008 | − 0.08 | 0.02 | *** |
| | 2010 | − 0.11 | 0.02 | *** |
| | 2012 | 0.04 | 0.02 | * |
| Life cycle | Children | 0.26 | 0.01 | *** |
| | Married | 0.38 | 0.03 | *** |
| | Separated or divorced | − 0.02 | 0.04 | N/s |
| Class | Manager | 0.42 | 0.02 | *** |
| | Routine non-manual | 0.30 | 0.02 | *** |
| | Petty bourgeoisie | 0.27 | 0.02 | *** |
| | Skilled manual | 0.06 | 0.02 | * |
| | Manual (Ref) | 0.00 | | |
| Background | Education | 0.28 | 0.01 | *** |
| | Sex (male) | 0.08 | 0.01 | *** |
| | Urbanization (1–5 scale Most rural to most urban) | − 0.04 | 0.00 | *** |
| | How religious are you on 10-pt scale | 0.03 | 0.00 | *** |
| | Member of an ethnic minority | − 0.83 | 0.02 | *** |
| Economic | Income insecurity | − 0.12 | 0.01 | *** |
| | Ever been unemployed for 12 months or more | 0.01 | 0.01 | N/s |
| | Dissatisfaction with present state of national economy | 0.03 | 0.00 | *** |
| Values | Authoritarian values (Schwartz scale) | 0.01 | 0.00 | *** |
| | Political mistrust (in parliament, parties and politicians) | − 0.01 | 0.00 | *** |
| | Placement on left–right scale | 0.02 | 0.00 | *** |
| | Constant | 1.50 | 0.05 | *** |
| | Nagelkerke $R^2$ | 0.20 | | |
| | % Correctly predicted | 78.2 | | |
| | N | 155,443 | | |

*Note:* Logistic regression where reported voting participation (0/1) is the dependent variable. Sig *** .001, ** .01, * .05, N/s Not significant.

*Source:* European Social Survey, Cumulative File Rounds 1–7.

orientations were *not* significant predictors of engaging in direct participation, such as boycotts, demonstrations, and petitioning. This suggests that social conformity, deference toward authorities, and authoritarian orientations in general tend to encourage voting, which is a conventional norm in democratic societies. But elite-challenging types of activities such as street protests seem to be regarded by authoritarians as inappropriate forms of rowdy and disruptive behavior.

By contrast, populist mistrust of representative institutions was negatively related to turnout; not surprisingly, alienated citizens who generally don't trust politicians, parties, and parliaments are more likely to stay home (exit) rather than casting a ballot. To mobilize support, therefore, Authoritarian-Populist parties have an incentive to press the classic wedge issues that are likely to excite social conservatives, but their anti-establishment rhetoric may discourage voting participation.

The results confirm that the generation gap in turnout is substantial, as expected. Thus, if we compare mean turnout among generations across all European countries, almost twice as many of the oldest (Interwar) cohort reported casting a ballot as did the Millennials (82 percent to 43 percent respectively). As Figure 8.1 illustrates, this pattern is consistently observed across all European regions and in every country from Austria to Ukraine, whether long-established democracies such as Sweden and France or post-communist states such as Lithuania and the Czech Republic. In some cases, such as Switzerland and France, a steady drop in turnout can be seen across successive birth cohorts but in others, such as Turkey, Norway, and Sweden, there is a steady erosion over cohorts until the Millennials, when a precipitate fall in participation occurs.

Are these differences due to the formative socialization experiences of different birth cohorts? Young and old differ in many other forms of political activism, suggesting that value change may be altering orientations toward the role of citizens and the repertoires of action connecting citizens to the state.[49] In the ESS surveys, for example, while almost none of the Interwar generation (3%) reported engaging in a lawful demonstration within the previous 12 months, three times as many Millennials (9%) reported doing so. Previous research suggests that some of the observable age-related contrasts are attributable to life-cycle effects; for example, younger people tend to be more residentially mobile when college students and seeking employment away from home, making it more difficult for them to get listed on the electoral register or to vote, before settling down to raise a family and developing roots in a community.[50] Period-effects may also be at work; for example, if the European

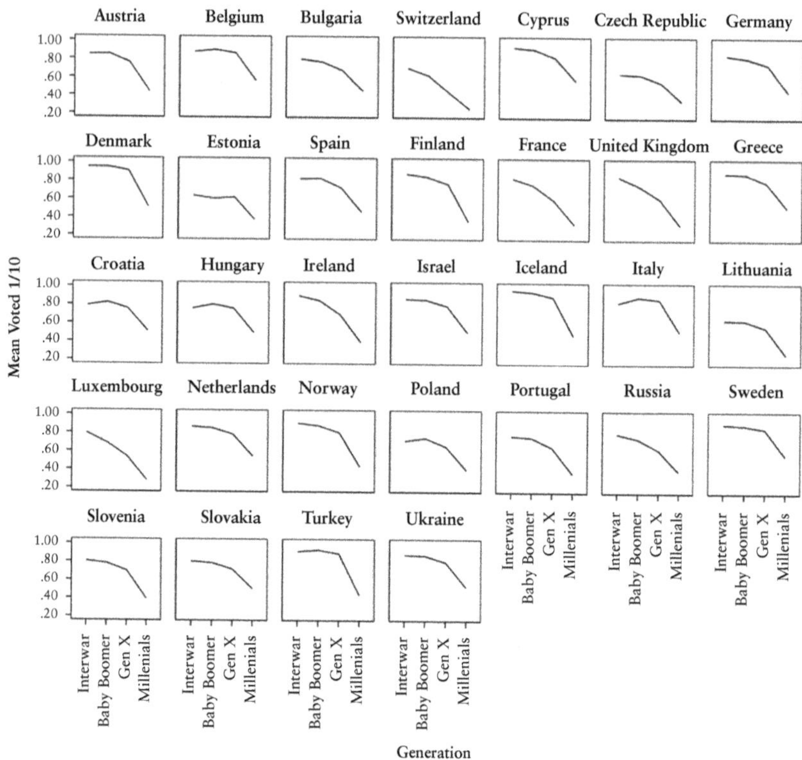


FIGURE 8.1. *Turnout by generation*
*Note:* Reported voting by generation.
*Source:* European Social Survey, Cumulative File Rounds 1–7.

financial crisis and subsequent austerity policies discouraged traditional center-left social democratic and labour supporters from going to the polls. Table 8.2 indicates that the generational effects in voting turnout are significant and large, without consistent period-effects linked with the year of the survey. Life-cycle effects are also observed; those who are married and with children (although not those divorced or separated) are significantly more likely to vote, although the effects of one's birth cohort are stronger.

The impact of education on voting participation was also significant. As has been observed for more than half a century, ever since the classic *Civic Culture* study, the cognitive skills, knowledge, and sense of efficacy associated with education consistently predict multiple forms of civic engagement, including registering and casting a ballot.[51] Thus, among

TABLE 8.2. *Predicting voting support for parties that are more authoritarian*

| | | Model 1 | | | | Model 2 | | | | Model 3 | | | | Model 4 | | | | Model 5 | | | |
|---|---|---|---|---|---|---|---|---|---|---|---|---|---|---|---|---|---|---|---|---|---|
| | | B | SE | Beta | Sig. | B | SE | Beta | Sig. | B | SE | Beta | Sig. | B | SE | Beta | Sig. | B | SE | Beta | Sig. |
| Generation | Interwar (1990–1945) (Ref) | 0.00 | | | | 0.00 | | | | 0.00 | | | | 0.00 | | | | 0.00 | | | |
| | Boomers (1946–1964) | −1.97 | 0.16 | −0.05 | *** | −2.08 | 0.16 | −0.05 | | −2.76 | 0.16 | −0.07 | *** | −0.92 | 0.17 | −0.02 | *** | 0.03 | 0.15 | 0.00 | N/s |
| | Gen X (1965–1979) | −1.69 | 0.17 | −0.04 | *** | −1.81 | 0.17 | −0.04 | | −2.77 | 0.19 | −0.06 | *** | 0.24 | 0.19 | 0.01 | N/s | 0.58 | 0.18 | 0.01 | *** |
| | Millennials (1980–1996) | −2.77 | 0.20 | −0.05 | *** | −3.09 | 0.20 | −0.05 | | −2.96 | 0.21 | −0.05 | *** | −0.14 | 0.21 | 0.00 | N/s | 0.46 | 0.20 | 0.01 | * |
| Year (Period) | 2002 (Ref) | | | | | 0.00 | | | ... | 0.00 | | | | 0.00 | | | | 0.00 | | | |
| | 2004 | | | | | −1.82 | 0.21 | −0.03 | | −4.58 | 0.37 | −0.08 | *** | −3.92 | 0.38 | −0.07 | *** | −2.47 | 0.35 | −0.04 | *** |
| | 2006 | | | | | −0.92 | 0.21 | −0.02 | | −0.97 | 0.21 | −0.02 | *** | −0.02 | 0.24 | 0.00 | N/s | 0.98 | 0.22 | 0.02 | *** |
| | 2008 | | | | | 0.67 | 0.19 | 0.01 | | −0.73 | 0.19 | −0.01 | *** | −0.47 | 0.22 | −0.01 | * | −0.13 | 0.20 | 0.00 | N/s |
| | 2010 | | | | | 0.95 | 0.20 | 0.02 | | 0.92 | 0.20 | 0.02 | *** | 1.61 | 0.22 | 0.03 | *** | 1.24 | 0.21 | 0.02 | *** |
| | 2012 | | | | | 0.61 | 0.20 | 0.01 | | 0.67 | 0.20 | 0.01 | *** | 1.25 | 0.20 | 0.02 | *** | 1.58 | 0.18 | 0.03 | *** |
| Life-cycle | Children | | | | | | | | | 1.88 | 0.13 | 0.05 | *** | 1.17 | 0.13 | 0.03 | *** | 0.75 | 0.12 | 0.02 | *** |
| | Married | | | | | | | | | 3.93 | 0.40 | 0.06 | *** | 3.44 | 0.39 | 0.05 | *** | 2.12 | 0.36 | 0.03 | *** |
| | Separated or divorced | | | | | | | | | 1.11 | 0.54 | 0.01 | * | 1.16 | 0.53 | 0.01 | * | 0.39 | 0.49 | 0.00 | N/s |

*(continued)*

TABLE 8.2. *(continued)*

| | | Model 1 | | | | Model 2 | | | | Model 3 | | | | Model 4 | | | | Model 5 | | | |
|---|---|---|---|---|---|---|---|---|---|---|---|---|---|---|---|---|---|---|---|---|---|
| | | B | SE | Beta | Sig. | B | SE | Beta | Sig. | B | SE | Beta | Sig. | B | SE | Beta | Sig. | B | SE | Beta | Sig. |
| Class | Manager | | | | | | | | | | | | | −1.78 | 0.24 | −0.03 | *** | −1.55 | 0.22 | −0.03 | *** |
| | Routine non-manual | | | | | | | | | | | | | −1.33 | 0.19 | −0.03 | *** | −1.12 | 0.18 | −0.02 | *** |
| | Petty bourgeoise | | | | | | | | | | | | | 1.04 | 0.19 | 0.02 | *** | −0.32 | 0.18 | −0.01 | N/s |
| | Skilled manual | | | | | | | | | | | | | −1.05 | 0.27 | −0.01 | *** | −0.66 | 0.25 | −0.01 | *** |
| | Manual (Ref) | | | | | | | | | | | | | 0.00 | | | | 0.00 | | | |
| Background | Education | | | | | | | | | | | | | −0.93 | 0.05 | −0.06 | *** | −0.61 | 0.05 | −0.04 | *** |
| | Sex (male) | | | | | | | | | | | | | 2.13 | 0.12 | 0.05 | *** | 1.57 | 0.11 | 0.04 | *** |
| | Urbanization (1–5 scale Most rural to most urban) | | | | | | | | | | | | | −0.86 | 0.05 | −0.05 | *** | −0.85 | 0.04 | −0.05 | *** |
| | How religious are you on 10-pt scale | | | | | | | | | | | | | 0.97 | 0.02 | 0.15 | *** | 0.44 | 0.02 | 0.07 | *** |
| | Member of an ethnic minority | | | | | | | | | | | | | −3.47 | 0.32 | −0.03 | *** | −2.13 | 0.30 | −0.02 | *** |
| Economic | Subjective financial insecurity | | | | | | | | | | | | | 1.14 | 0.08 | 0.05 | *** | 1.01 | 0.07 | 0.04 | *** |
| | Ever been unemployed for 12 months or more | | | | | | | | | | | | | −1.81 | 0.14 | −0.04 | *** | −0.90 | 0.13 | −0.02 | *** |
| | Dissatisfied with present state of national economy | | | | | | | | | | | | | 0.23 | 0.03 | −0.03 | *** | 0.27 | 0.03 | −0.03 | *** |
| Values | Authoritarian values (Schwartz scale) | | | | | | | | | | | | | | | | | 0.15 | 0.00 | 0.11 | *** |
| | Political mistrust (in parliament, parties, and politicians] | | | | | | | | | | | | | | | | | 0.05 | 0.00 | 0.05 | *** |
| | Placement on left-right scale | | | | | | | | | | | | | | | | | 3.02 | 0.02 | 0.35 | *** |
| | (Constant) | 51.98 | 0.12 | | *** | 52.36 | 0.18 | | *** | 52.06 | 0.18 | | *** | 50.10 | 0.37 | | *** | 21.88 | 0.51 | | *** |
| | Adjusted R2 | 0.00 | | | | 0.004 | | | | 0.007 | | | | 0.05 | | | | 0.19 | | | |

*Notes:* OLS regression models predicting whether respondents voted for a party scored by experts on the authoritarian values standardized scale (for the items and construction, see Table 7.1). Sig *** .001, ** .01, * .05, N/s Not significant. Ref = the excluded category.

*Source:* The European Social Survey Cumulative File Rounds 1–7 N, 119,7331 in 21 European countries.

those with low levels of formal education, around 71 percent of Europeans reported voting, compared with 81 percent among the group with high educational qualifications. Even larger educational disparities are found with more demanding forms of participation, such as contacting officials, working for parties, signing petitions, and consumer boycotts.

The remaining demographic and socio-economic predictors were largely consistent with past research; thus, on average, voting turnout was marginally higher among the rural and semi-rural European communities (areas with aging populations and long-established residents) compared with major cities (which are more often home to younger people, students, immigrants, and transient professional and service-sector employees). Turnout was generally much stronger among middle-class professionals and managers than among blue-collar workers; work by Sidney Verba and his colleagues has established the impact of socio-economic status to be one of the classic predictors of voter turnout, partly because occupational class is strongly associated with formal educational qualifications, and thus with stronger cognitive skills and civic knowledge, as well as feelings of political efficacy.[52] Turnout was also greater as expected among men than women, white Europeans rather than ethnic minorities (who may not be eligible citizens), and the more religious (who are also disproportionately older). Economic factors were not consistently or strongly associated with voting turnout. Although subjective financial insecurity is a significant predictor of lower turnout, having experienced unemployment was not important, and those less satisfied with the state of the national economy were *more* likely to vote.

Overall, the model explained about one-fifth of the variation in the propensity to vote. Meta-analysis of the extensive research literature suggests that other factors reported in other studies may also play an important role, such as micro-level political interest, media attention, and the strength of partisan identification, as well as macro-level variations in electoral contexts, such as the type of Majoritarian or Proportional Representation electoral system, the closeness of the race, and the frequency of contests.[53]

Our analysis largely confirms the typical social profile of voters, but it indicates that the Interwar and Baby Boom generations are far, far more likely to participate in elections than the Millennials – to a considerably greater extent than previous research has indicated. This leads to substantial disparities by birth cohort and the over-representation of the 'grey vote' in parties and elections. In addition, citizens with authoritarian values are more likely to vote, while those mistrusting political institutions are less likely to do so.

The evidence presented in previous chapters, combined with the findings in this one, points to three key conclusions:

(1) Millennials and Generation X hold far more socially liberal views on cultural issues than their parents and grandparents;
(2) the process of demographic turnover is gradually expanding the proportion of the population drawn from these younger birth cohorts, so that Millennials and Generation X have become the new majority in the electorate in Western societies; nevertheless,
(3) due to large differences in voter turnout, the values of the older birth cohorts are systematically over-represented in conventional party politics and elections.

This representation gap can have major consequences, generating tension between long-term processes of cultural change and processes of political representation. Before considering these issues, however, what predicts voting for authoritarian and populist parties?

## WHO SUPPORTS PARTIES THAT ARE MORE AUTHORITARIAN?

To summarize the key findings concerning who voted for parties that are more authoritarian in the most recent national election, Table 8.2 presents the results of series of OLS regression models. The dependent variable is the authoritarianism party scale, based on expert ratings of the degree to which political parties endorsed authoritarian policies. Model 1 includes the generational cohorts. Model 2 adds the year for period-effects. Model 3 adds life-cycle indices of children and marital status. Model 4 adds a range of demographic and social controls, including the Goldthorpe class schema, sex, education, the strength of religiosity, the degree of residential urbanization, belonging to an ethnic minority, experience of long-term unemployment, economic dissatisfaction, and subjective financial insecurity. Finally, Model 5 adds the key indicators of cultural values, including the authoritarian value scales, mistrust in national political institutions, and self-placement on the left–right ideological scale.

The models highlight several main findings.

First, the results in Model 1 confirm that older and younger birth cohorts differ significantly in voting for authoritarian parties. The Interwar cohort is far more likely to support authoritarian parties than younger cohorts, with least support found among Millennials. This provides further confirmation of the cultural backlash thesis, which emphasizes intergenerational differences as drivers of value change. The next two models show that these generational effects persist after we add the year of the survey (period-effects) and indicators of life-cycle effects (marriage and children). The year of the survey does not display a linear trend, but there is some indication of a rise in support in 2010, after the economic crisis. The indicators of marriage and the family are also related to voting for parties that are more authoritarian – although it cannot be determined whether this means that people become more favorable toward these values as they age or whether those with greater emphasis on social conformity and respect for traditions are more likely to marry and have children.

Model 4 reduces the statistical significance of generation once controlling for class: there is a steady increase in voting for authoritarian parties among blue-collar workers, as we observed in Chapter 4 in the class profile of those endorsing authoritarian values. After almost 60 years, the Lipset working-class authoritarianism thesis stands the test of time, although it remains unclear whether this is due to the association between occupational class and education or between class and material security. The consistent gender gap, documented in many previous studies, is further confirmed here, with men more likely to vote for authoritarian parties than women.[54]

Education also proves significant and negative, with authoritarian parties winning more support from the less educated sectors of the population. This effect could be attributed either to the role of formal education in determining subsequent social status and occupation, or to the values and knowledge acquired from formal schooling or to the fact that the more educated tend to come from relatively prosperous families and experienced greater levels of existential security during their formative years.

Urbanization was negative – indicating that voting for authoritarian parties is strongest in rural and non-metropolitan areas of Europe, in semi-rural villages and small towns, rather than in inner-city urban areas. The strength of religiosity, closely linked with a wide range of traditional values, is also positively associated with voting for authoritarian parties – and indeed is one of the strongest social predictors of authoritarian voting, just as it was a strong predictor of authoritarian values. Not surprisingly, members of ethnic minorities are less inclined to vote for these parties, given the close links between authoritarianism, anti-immigrant policies, and xenophobia.

Subjective income insecurity, measured by the difficulty of living on household savings, and dissatisfaction with the state of the national economy, are both significant predictors of support for authoritarian parties. At the same time, having experience of long-term unemployment is *negatively* correlated with support, which is inconsistent with one of the central assumptions of economic grievance theories.

In short, voting for authoritarian parties is strongest among the older generation, men, the less educated, white European populations, in semi-rural areas, and among the most religious. The effects of sex, education, religiosity, class, ethnicity, and urbanization remain stable across successive models, confirming the demographic profile found in earlier studies – although the reasons for these relationships remain open to alternative interpretations.[55]

In addition to all these controls, Model 5 enters the cultural values and attitudinal scales that we expected to predict voting support for authoritarian parties. Authoritarian values, political mistrust (toward politicians and parties), and right-wing position on the left–right ideological scale, were all significantly linked with voting for authoritarian parties. Most importantly, once these cultural measures were included in this model, the effects of being part of the Generation X or Millennial generations reversed, suggesting that the voting differences between the older and younger cohorts is due to their differing values. The final model 5, combining a wide range of social controls and cultural attitudes, provides a comprehensive account of voting support for authoritarian parties in Europe.

To look at the results descriptively, Figure 8.2 shows the links between voting for parties that are more authoritarian and the strength of authoritarian values, using the Schwartz scale. The results confirm the strong association, with countries such as Turkey, Slovakia, Hungary, and Greece high on both scales. These are also the societies that the next chapter demonstrates have some of the most electorally successful Authoritarian-Populist parties. By contrast, Sweden, France, and Germany have some of the lowest support for authoritarian values and authoritarian parties. The correlation between these factors was strong and significant ($R^2 = 0.442$ ***). Figure 8.3 illustrates the relationships broken down by country, showing the link between values and votes is clear in most countries under comparison, exemplified by the pattern observed in Germany, the Netherlands, and Switzerland.

Are the observed generational differences consistent across all countries? Table 8.3 presents the simple correlations between generation and voting support for authoritarian parties in 26 European states. It is

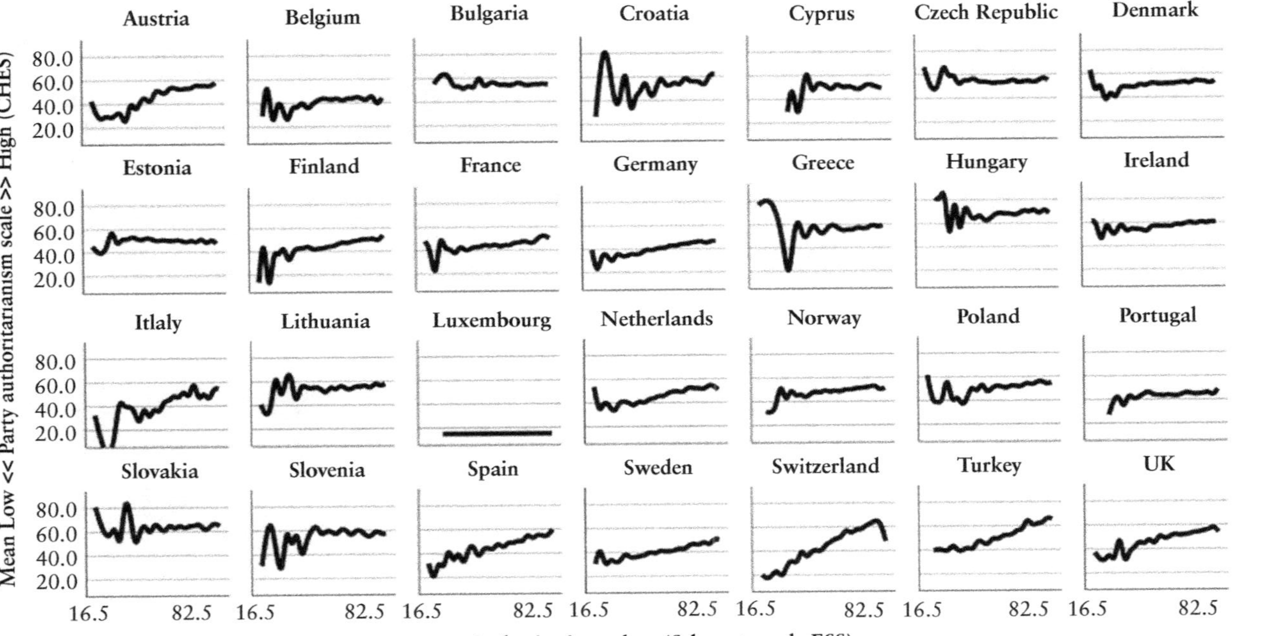


FIGURE 8.2. *Authoritarian values and voting for parties with policy positions that are more authoritarian, by country*
*Notes:* Political parties are classified according to their score on the authoritarian scale in CHES data. Authoritarian values in the electorate are measured by the Schwartz items in the ESS concerning the importance of security, social conformity, and deference, described in Table 4.3.
*Source:* European Social Survey, Cumulative File Rounds 1–7.

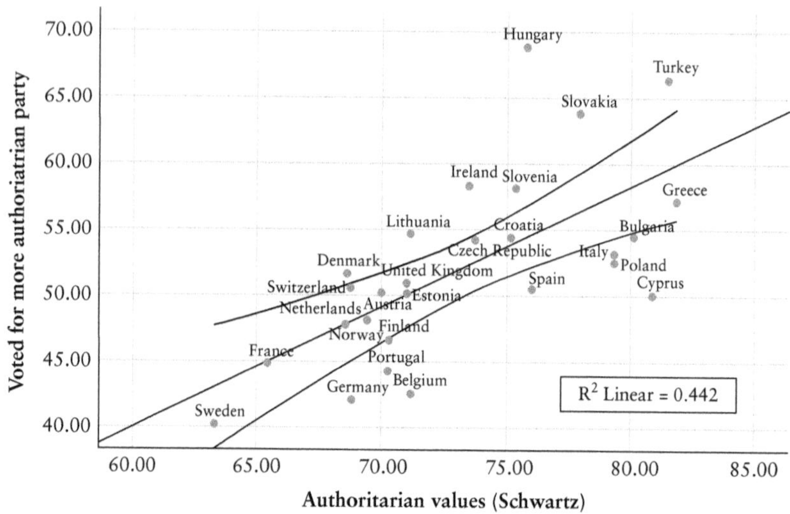


FIGURE 8.3. *Authoritarian values and support for parties that are more authoritarian*

*Notes:* Political parties are classified according to their score on the authoritarian scale in CHES data. Authoritarian values in the electorate are measured by the Schwartz items in the ESS concerning the importance of security, social conformity, and deference, described in Table 4.3.

*Source:* European Social Survey, Cumulative File Rounds 1–7.

striking that in nearly all countries, where significant differences can be observed, the older generations, that is the Interwar and Baby Boomer birth cohorts, were more likely to vote for authoritarian parties than younger generations. The only exceptions were Cyprus and Hungary, where parties endorsing authoritarian policies received more support from the younger cohorts.

## WHO SUPPORTS POPULIST PARTIES?

To explore further, Table 8.4 tests the effects of the same set of factors on voting for parties that were populist (those rated highly by experts as using anti-elitist and anti-establishment rhetoric).

The demographic and social controls for populism differ in several important regards from the results observed for authoritarian voting. In particular, across the series of models *it is the younger cohorts who are consistently drawn toward parties that are more populist.* The simple correlations in Table 8.3 show that this is a consistent pattern across

TABLE 8.3. *Generational cohorts and voting, by country*

| | Voted for parties that are more authoritarian | | Voted for parties that are more populist | | |
|---|---|---|---|---|---|
| | **R.** | **Sig.** | **R.** | **Sig.** | **N.** |
| Austria | −0.096 | ** | 0.201 | ** | 4,719 |
| Belgium | −0.019 | N/s | 0.091 | ** | 7,714 |
| Bulgaria | −0.025 | N/s | 0.118 | ** | 3,763 |
| Croatia | −0.108 | ** | −0.057 | ** | 1,300 |
| Cyprus | 0.052 | ** | −0.058 | ** | 2,527 |
| Czech Republic | −0.109 | ** | −0.008 | N/s | 5,908 |
| Denmark | −0.086 | ** | 0.041 | ** | 6,869 |
| Finland | −0.059 | ** | 0.102 | ** | 8,377 |
| France | −0.075 | ** | 0.072 | ** | 5,163 |
| Germany | −0.092 | ** | 0.102 | ** | 13,244 |
| Greece | −0.058 | ** | 0.166 | ** | 4,528 |
| Hungary | 0.194 | ** | 0.112 | ** | 4,279 |
| Ireland | −0.164 | ** | 0.146 | ** | 9,081 |
| Italy | −0.244 | ** | 0.218 | ** | 9,300 |
| Lithuania | −0.066 | ** | −0.002 | N/s | 2,426 |
| Netherlands | −0.088 | ** | 0.079 | ** | 9,456 |
| Norway | −0.008 | N/s | −0.022 | * | 7,635 |
| Poland | −0.042 | ** | −0.081 | ** | 5,294 |
| Portugal | −0.083 | ** | 0.130 | ** | 3,423 |
| Slovakia | −0.113 | ** | 0.125 | ** | 4,433 |
| Slovenia | −0.021 | N/s | 0.057 | ** | 3,342 |
| Spain | −0.109 | ** | 0.149 | ** | 7,367 |
| Sweden | −0.027 | * | 0.084 | ** | 8,405 |
| Switzerland | −0.087 | ** | −0.037 | * | 4,573 |
| Turkey | 0.012 | N/s | 0.031 | N/s | 4,272 |
| UK | −0.159 | ** | 0.109 | ** | 5,472 |

*Note:* The simple Pearson correlations (R) and significance (P) between generational cohort and voting for a party that was more authoritarian and a party that was more populist. A negative correlation implies that parties received more votes from the Interwar cohort. A positive correlation implies that parties received more votes from the Millennial cohort. Sig *** .001, ** .01, * .05, N/s Not significant.

*Source:* European Social Survey, Cumulative File Rounds 1–7.

TABLE 8.4. *Predicting voting support for parties that are more populist*

| | | Model 1 | | | | Model 2 | | | | Model 3 | | | | Model 4 | | | | Model 5 | | | |
|---|---|---|---|---|---|---|---|---|---|---|---|---|---|---|---|---|---|---|---|---|---|
| | | B | SE | Beta | Sig. | B | SE | Beta | Sig. | B | SE | Beta | Sig. | B | SE | Beta | Sig. | B | SE | Beta | Sig. |
| Generation | Interwar (1900–1945) (Ref) | 0.00 | | | | | | | | | | | | | | | | | | | |
| | Boomers (1946–1964) | 1.53 | 0.14 | 0.04 | *** | 1.41 | 0.14 | 0.04 | *** | 0.72 | 0.14 | 0.02 | *** | 1.23 | 0.14 | 0.03 | *** | 1.46 | 0.14 | 0.04 | |
| | Gen X (1965–1979) | 2.03 | 0.15 | 0.05 | *** | 1.87 | 0.15 | 0.05 | *** | 0.72 | 0.17 | 0.02 | *** | 1.78 | 0.17 | 0.05 | *** | 2.14 | 0.17 | 0.05 | *** |
| | Millennials (1980–1996) | 3.91 | 0.18 | 0.08 | | 3.53 | 0.18 | 0.07 | | 3.23 | 0.18 | 0.06 | *** | 3.82 | 0.18 | 0.08 | *** | 4.29 | 0.18 | 0.08 | *** |
| Year (Period) | 2002 (Ref) | | | | | 0.00 | | | | 0.00 | | | | 0.00 | | | | 0.00 | | | |
| | 2004 | | | | | −3.32 | 0.18 | −0.07 | *** | −1.95 | 0.32 | −0.04 | *** | −0.32 | 0.32 | −0.01 | N/s | 0.06 | 0.32 | 0.00 | N/s |
| | 2006 | | | | | −2.74 | 0.18 | −0.06 | *** | −2.82 | 0.18 | −0.06 | *** | −0.01 | 0.20 | 0.00 | N/s | −0.01 | 0.20 | 0.00 | N/s |
| | 2008 | | | | | −0.60 | 0.17 | −0.01 | *** | −0.67 | 0.17 | −002 | *** | −0.30 | 0.19 | −0.01 | N/s | −0.11 | 0.19 | 0.00 | N/s |
| | 2010 | | | | | −1.00 | 0.17 | −0.02 | *** | −1.03 | 0.17 | −0.02 | *** | −0.29 | 0.19 | −0.01 | N/s | −0.41 | 0.19 | −0.01 | * |
| | 2012 | | | | | −0.98 | 0.18 | −0.02 | *** | −0.92 | 0.18 | −002 | *** | 0.49 | 0.17 | 0.01 | | 0.48 | 0.17 | 0.01 | *** |
| Life-cycle | Children | | | | | | | | | 1.84 | 0.12 | 0.05 | *** | 1.13 | 0.11 | 0.03 | *** | 1.04 | 0.11 | 0.03 | *** |
| | Married | | | | | | | | | −1.90 | 0.35 | −0.03 | *** | −1.78 | 0.34 | −0.03 | *** | −2.12 | 0.33 | −0.04 | |
| | Separated or divorced | | | | | | | | | −1.75 | 0.47 | −0.01 | *** | −2.53 | 0.45 | −0.02 | *** | −2.71 | 0.45 | −0.02 | *** |
| Class | Manager | | | | | | | | | | | | | −1.47 | 0.20 | −0.03 | *** | −1.17 | 0.20 | −0.02 | *** |
| | Routine non-manual | | | | | | | | | | | | | −2.03 | 0.16 | −0.05 | *** | −1.95 | 0.16 | −0.05 | |
| | Petty bourgeoise | | | | | | | | | | | | | −1.36 | 0.17 | −0.03 | *** | −1.22 | 0.16 | −0.02 | |
| | Skilled manual | | | | | | | | | | | | | −0.55 | 0.23 | −0.01 | * | −0.62 | 0.23 | −0.01 | *** |
| | Manual (Ref) | | | | | | | | | | | | | 0.00 | | | | 0.00 | | | |
| Background | Education | | | | | | | | | | | | | −0.52 | 0.04 | −0.04 | *** | −0.34 | 0.04 | −0.03 | *** |
| | Sex (male) | | | | | | | | | | | | | 1.17 | 0.10 | 0.03 | *** | 1.23 | 0.10 | 0.04 | *** |
| | Urbanization (1–5 scale Most rural to most urban) | | | | | | | | | | | | | 0.65 | 0.04 | 0.05 | *** | 0.65 | 0.04 | 0.05 | |

| | | | | | | | | | | | | | | | | | | | | | |
|---|---|---|---|---|---|---|---|---|---|---|---|---|---|---|---|---|---|---|---|---|---|
| | How religious are you on 10-pt scale | | | | | | | | | | | | | 0.17 | 0.02 | 0.03 | *** | 0.13 | 0.02 | 0.02 | |
| | Member of an ethnic minority | | | | | | | | | | | | | −1.82 | 0.28 | −0.02 | *** | −1.96 | 0.28 | −0.02 | *** |
| Economic | Subjective financial insecurity | | | | | | | | | | | | | 2.60 | 0.07 | 0.12 | *** | 2.22 | 0.07 | 0.11 | *** |
| | Ever been unemployed for 12 months or more | | | | | | | | | | | | | 0.32 | 0.12 | 0.01 | *** | 0.38 | 0.12 | 0.01 | |
| | Dissatisfied with present state of national economy | | | | | | | | | | | | | 1.40 | 0.02 | −0.20 | *** | 0.89 | 0.03 | −0.13 | *** |
| Values | Authoritarian values (Schwartz scale) | | | | | | | | | | | | | | | | | 0.10 | 0.00 | 0.08 | *** |
| | Political mistrust (in parliament, parties, and politicians) | | | | | | | | | | | | | | | | | 0.11 | 0.00 | 0.13 | *** |
| | Placement on left-right scale | | | | | | | | | | | | | | | | | −0.16 | 0.02 | −0.02 | *** |
| | (Constant) | 34.56 | 0.11 | | *** | 36.02 | 0.16 | | *** | 35.86 | 0.16 | | *** | 35.55 | 0.32 | | *** | 20.62 | 0.47 | | *** |
| | Adjusted R2 | 0.00 | | | | 0.009 | | | | 0.011 | | | | 0.096 | | | | 114 | | | |

*Notes:* OLS regression models predicting whether respondents voted for a party scored by experts on the authoritarian values standardized scale (for the items and construction, see Table 7.1). Sig *** .001, ** .01, * .05, N/s Not significant. Ref = the excluded category.

*Source:* The European Social Survey, Cumulative File Rounds 1–7. N, 119,7331 in 21 European countries.

European countries; there are significant associations between birth cohort and voting for populist parties in 18 of the 26 countries under comparison: younger cohorts favor these parties more than older ones. As we have argued, populist anti-establishment rhetoric – criticizing the corruption of the political classes, mainstream parties, and elected assemblies, denigrating public-sector bureaucrats, judges and fake news media, claiming that more decisions need to be made by the 'real' people – is a handy stick that can be used by political outsiders from across the political spectrum. Thus, when populism is blended with progressive appeals, it can mobilize support among the young – if they can be persuaded to vote. By contrast, anti-establishment language about restoring power to the 'real' people linked with authoritarian positions promising tough law and order, restricted border flows, and the restoration of national sovereignty, appeals more strongly to older citizens who are easier to mobilize to vote.

Other factors from the analysis in Model 2 indicate that no consistent period-effect emerges; instead, there are trendless fluctuations over the years. The life-cycle effects in Model 3 are also inconsistent. Model 4 adds the battery of social controls, suggesting that voting for populist parties is stronger among blue-collar workers, the less educated, men, urban populations, and the religious. Parties using populist anti-elite discourse are also likely to appeal to financially insecure households without reservoirs of savings for rainy days, the unemployed, and those dissatisfied with the performance of the national economy. In this regard, the economic thesis finds support – although economic satisfaction may also be exogenous if cued by prior partisanship and candidate preferences. Finally with all these controls, the generational patterns remain consistent, and voting for populist parties is strongest among those holding authoritarian values, expressing political mistrust, and those placing themselves on the left of the left–right ideological spectrum.

The analysis in Table 8.4 leads us to conclude that a combination of several standard demographic and social controls with cultural values provides the most useful explanation for European voting behavior and party choices. But there are important tensions and contrasts in the observed patterns, with voting for authoritarian parties being concentrated disproportionately among the older generations, and among men, religious people, whites, rural communities, and the less educated, blue-collar workers, and less financially secure – all social sectors generally left behind by cultural value change. Voting for parties using populist rhetoric shares several similar characteristics, such as by class, education,

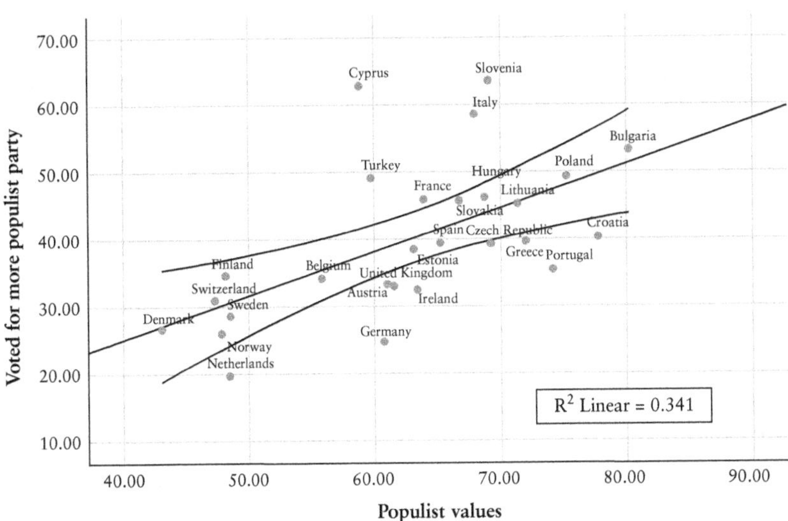


FIGURE 8.4. *Populist values and support for parties that are more populist*
*Notes:* Political parties are classified according to their score on the populism scale in CHES data. Populist values in the electorate are measured by the items in the ESS concerning trust in parliaments, parties, and politicians.
*Source:* European Social Survey, Cumulative File Rounds 1–7.

and sex, but there is one big exception: support for populist parties is strongest among the younger birth cohorts, not the older ones. Figure 8.4 illustrates the scatterplot associations between populist values and votes at national levels, confirming the significant linkages, although the overall correlation is weaker than that observed to be connecting authoritarian values and votes (R2 = .341**). The weaker correlation can be attributed in large part to the three outliers, notably Cyprus, Slovenia, and Italy, which have more populist voters than might be expected by the cultural values in these societies.

## CONCLUSIONS AND DISCUSSION

The evidence examined here points to several main findings.

First, it confirms that a substantial *generation gap in voting participation and party choices exists.* Younger cohorts are far less likely to vote – a widely observed and consistent pattern across European countries. As we demonstrated in earlier chapters, young people therefore differ sharply from their parents and grandparents in their socially liberal, libertarian, and post-materialist attitudes. Through population turnover, Millennials and Generation X are now a bare majority of citizens in the electorate. Because they are much less likely to vote, however, their preferences are systematically under-represented among the voting public. By contrast, the Interwar and Baby Boom generations are a steadily shrinking sector of the general population – but they are substantially more likely to vote, so their partisan preferences have a stronger impact on electoral outcomes.

If young and old shared broadly similar ideological values and party choices, then the lower rate of voting by younger citizens, while undesirable for civic engagement, would not matter. But voting for authoritarian parties in Europe is significantly stronger among the older generation, as well as among men, the less educated, the religious, and white populations living in rural areas. After applying socio-demographic controls, voting for parties endorsing authoritarian policy positions was also strengthened by mistrust of political institutions, authoritarian values, and right-wing ideological self-placement. Voting support for parties with populist anti-establishment appeals differs in several respects, however, particularly since it tends to be greater among younger than older cohorts.

The consistent patterns we have observed across diverse European societies take us further toward understanding this phenomenon but the exact reasons underlying some of these relationships remain open to interpretation. According to the economic grievance thesis, social class and educational correlations with voting support for authoritarian and populist parties reflect the level of economic security experienced because of socio-economic status, job security, salaries, and career opportunities. It does not imply the presence of intergenerational differences. The cultural backlash thesis suggests that the educational effects are linked with the acquisition of knowledge and cognitive skills, and the level of security experienced during one's formative years – which produces substantial intergenerational differences in cultural attitudes, levels of social tolerance, and adherence to socially liberal values.

The cultural backlash argument has significant implications. The generational gap in Western societies is likely to heighten the salience of the cultural cleavage in future politics, regardless of possible improvements in the underlying economic conditions or any slowdown in globalization. The orthogonal pull of cultural politics generates tensions and divisions within mainstream parties, allowing new opportunities for populist leaders to mobilize electoral support. Nevertheless, it often is difficult for Authoritarian-Populist parties to build an organizational base that persists beyond particular leaders. Party institutionalization is challenging for minor parties but essential to enable them to sustain themselves in legislative office and government coalitions. The net result is that Western societies may face increasingly unpredictable electoral outcomes, growing challenges to the legitimacy of liberal democracy and the liberal consensus about the values of engagement in the world and tolerance of diversity at home.

The evidence considered in this chapter raises several issues that will be examined in subsequent chapters. The pooled ESS from 2002 to 2014 provides sufficient cases to examine support for smaller parties, and European reactions to the period shock of the 2007–2013 financial crisis, but it does not permit the analysis of long-term dynamic patterns. Further chapters therefore scrutinize time-series data from selected cases, including time series from national election surveys, to examine long-term trends in cultural attitudes and populist voting support in cases of Brexit in the UK and the election of Trump in the US. This can help to establish more conclusive evidence of the linkages hypothesized to exist between *changes* in cultural values and *changes* in authoritarian-populist party support. Moreover, to understand more fully the varied electoral fortunes of political parties in different countries, the roles of supply-side party competition and electoral systems also need to be addressed. The next chapter analyzes how votes are translated into seats, and the institutional context that shapes electoral outcomes.

## Notes

1. Daniele Albertazzi and Sean Mueller. 2013. 'Populism and liberal democracy: Populists in government in Austria, Italy, Poland and Switzerland.' *Government and Opposition* 48(3): 343–371.
2. This is similar to the reasoning used in the approach used by Luigi Guiso, Helios Herrera, Massimo Morelli, and Tommaso Sonne. 2017. 'Demand and supply of populism.' www.heliosherrera.com/populism.pdf.
3. For a discussion, see Thomas F. Pettigrew. 1998. 'Reactions toward the new minorities of Western Europe.' *Annual Review of Sociology* 24: 77–103; Rachel Gibson. 2002. *The Growth of Anti-Immigrant Parties in Western Europe.* Lewiston, NY: The Edwin Mellen Press; Herbert Kitschelt, with Anthony J. McGann. 1995. *The Radical Right in Western Europe: A Comparative Analysis.* Ann Arbor, MI: University of Michigan Press; Matt Golder. 2003. 'Explaining variations in the success of extreme right parties in Western Europe.' *Comparative Political Studies* 36(4): 432–466; Christopher J. Anderson. 1996. 'Economics, politics, and foreigners: Populist party support in Denmark and Norway.' *Electoral Studies* 15 (4):

497–511; Kai Arzheimer. 2009. 'Contextual factors and the extreme right vote in Western Europe, 1980–2002.' *American Journal of Political Science* 53 (2): 259–275; T.E. Givens. 2005. *Voting Radical Right in Western Europe*. New York: Cambridge University Press.

4. On Latin America, see, for example, Michael L. Conniff. Ed. 1982. *Latin American Populism in Comparative Perspective*. Albuquerque, NM: University of New Mexico Press; Sebastian Edwards. 2010. *Left Behind: Latin America and the False Promise of Populism*. Chicago: University of Chicago Press; David Doyle. 2011. 'The legitimacy of political institutions: Explaining contemporary populism in Latin America.' *Comparative Political Studies* 44: 1447–1473. On Central and Eastern Europe, see Andrea Pirro. 2017. *The Populist Radical Right in Central and Eastern Europe: Ideology, Impact, and Electoral Performance*. London: Routledge. On Western Europe, see Cas Mudde. 2007. *Populist Radical Right Parties in Europe*. New York: Cambridge University Press; Ruth Wodak, Majid KhosraviNik, and Brigitte Mral. Eds. 2013. *Right-Wing Populism in Europe*. London: Bloomsbury Academic; Tjitske Akkerman, Sarah L. de Lange, and Matthijs Rooduijn. Eds. 2016. *Radical Right-Wing Populist Parties in Western Europe: Into the Mainstream?* New York: Routledge.
5. See Thomas F. Pettigrew. 1998. 'Reactions toward the new minorities of Western Europe.' *Annual Review of Sociology* 24: 77–103; Rachel Gibson. 2002. *The Growth of Anti-Immigrant Parties in Western Europe*. Lewiston, NY: The Edwin Mellen Press.
6. P. Knigge. 1998. 'The ecological correlates of right-wing extremism in Western Europe.' *European Journal of Political Research* 34: 249–279.
7. Eva Anduiza and Guillem Rico. 2016. 'Economic correlates of populist attitudes: An analysis of nine European countries.' www.ceu.edu/sites/default/files/attachment/event/14668/economic-correlates-populist-attitudes-eva anduiza.pdf.
8. Hans-Peter Kriesi and Takis S. Pappas. Eds. 2015. *European Populism in the Shadow of the Great Recession*. Colchester: ECPR Press.
9. Dante J. Scala and Kenneth M. Johnson. 2017. 'Political polarization along the rural–urban continuum? The geography of the presidential vote, 2000–2016.' *The Annals of the Academy of Political and Social Science* 672: 162; Loren Collingwood. 2016. 'The county-by-county data on Trump voters shows why he won.' *The Washington Post/Monkey Cage*. November 19, 2016. www.washingtonpost.com/news/monkey-cage/wp/2016/11/19/the-country-by-county-data-on-trump-voters-shows-why-he-won/.
10. Matthew J. Goodwin and Oliver Heath. 2016. 'The 2016 referendum, Brexit and the left behind? An aggregate-level analysis of the result.' *Political Quarterly* 87 (3):323–332.
11. Harold D. Clark, Matthew Goodwin, and Paul Whiteley. 2017. *Brexit: Why Britain Voted to Leave the European Union*. Cambridge: Cambridge University Press.
12. http://wahl.tagesschau.de/wahlen/2017-09-24-BT-DE/index.shtml.

13. Martin Eiermann. September 28, 2017. 'The geography of German populism: Reflections on the 2017 Bundestag election.' Tony Blair Institute for Global Change. https://institute.global/insight/renewing-centre/geography-german-populism-reflections-2017-bundestag-election.
14. Daniel Stockemer. 2017. 'The success of radical right-wing parties in Western European regions: New challenging findings.' *Journal of Contemporary European Studies* 25 (1): 41–56.
15. Cas Mudde. 2007. *Populist Radical Right Parties in Europe*. New York: Cambridge University Press, Chapter 9.
16. www.brookings.edu/blog/the-avenue/2017/03/23/a-substantial-majority-of-americans-live-outside-trump-counties-census-shows/.
17. Gary King, O. Rosen and M. Tanner. Eds. 2004. *Ecological Inference: New Methodological Strategies*. Cambridge: Cambridge University Press; Paul Brewer and Sunil Venaik. 2014. 'The ecological fallacy in national culture research.' *Organizational Studies* 35 (7): 1063–1086.
18. Daniel Stockemer and Mauro Barisione. 2017. 'The "new" discourse of the Front National under Marine Le Pen: A slight change with a big impact.' *European Journal of Communication* 32 (2): 100–115.
19. The European Election Study asks respondents: '*We have a number of political parties in (OUR COUNTRY) each of which would like to get your vote. How probable is it that you will ever vote for the following parties? Please answer on a scale where "0" means "not at all probable" and "10" means "very probable"*.' http://europeanelectionstudies.net/wp-content/uploads/2014/05/Master-Questionnaire.pdf.
20. www.pewresearch.org.
21. www.pewresearch.org/fact-tank/2017/04/03/americans-give-economy-highest-marks-since-financial-crisis/.
22. Matthijs Rooduijn, Wouter van der Brug, and Sarah de Lange. 2016. 'Expressing or fueling discontent? The relationship between populist voting and political discontent.' *Electoral Studies* 43: 32–40.
23. Emily Beaulieu. 2014. 'From voter ID to party ID: How political parties affect perceptions of election fraud in the US.' *Electoral Studies* 35: 24–32. See also Jeffrey Karp, Alessandro Nai, and Pippa Norris. 2018. 'Dial "F" for Fraud: Explaining Citizens Suspicions about Elections.' *Electoral Studies* 53: 11–19; Pippa Norris, Holly Ann Garnett, and Max Grömping. 2016. 'Roswell, grassy knolls and voter fraud: Explaining erroneous perceptions of electoral malpractices.' Paper presented at the 2016 APSA Annual Convention, San Francisco, CA.
24. Pippa Norris. 2005. *Radical Right: Voters and Parties in the Electoral Market*. New York: Cambridge University Press. pp. 158–165.
25. Pippa Norris. 2005. *Radical Right: Voters and Parties in the Electoral Market*. New York: Cambridge University Press; Agnes Akkerman, Cas Mudde, and Andrej Zaslove. 2014. 'How populist are the people? Measuring populist attitudes in voters.' Comparative Political Studies 47: 1324–1353; Mark Elchardus and Bram Spruyt. 2016. 'Populism, persistent republicanism and declinism: An empirical analysis of populism as a thin ideology.' *Government and Opposition* 51: 111–133.

26. Estimates suggest that around 60.1 percent of the eligible electorate voted in the 2016 US presidential election. www.nonprofitvote.org/america-goes-to-the-polls-2016/.
27. For details, see www.europeansocialsurvey.org/.
28. P. Selb and S. Munzert. 2013 'Voter overrepresentation, vote misreporting, and turnout bias in postelection surveys.' *Electoral Studies* 32: 186–196.
29. Mark Hetherington and Jonathan D. Weiler. 2009. *Authoritarianism and Polarization in American Politics*. New York: Cambridge University Press.
30. Mark Hetherington and Jonathan D. Weiler. 2009. *Authoritarianism and Polarization in American Politics*. New York: Cambridge University Press.
31. Matthew C. MacWilliams. 2016. 'Who decides when the party doesn't? Authoritarian voters and the rise of Donald Trump.' *PS: Political Science and Politics* 49 (4): 716–721; Matthew C. MacWilliams. 2017. 'Intolerant and afraid Authoritarians rise to Trump's call.' In Mari Fitzduff. Ed. *Why Irrational Politics Appeals: Understanding the Allure of Trump*. Santa Barbara, CA: Praeger.
32. See www.worldvaluessurvey.org.
33. Shalom Schwartz. 1992. 'Universals in the content and structure of values: Theoretical advances and empirical tests in 20 countries.' *Advances in Experimental Social Psychology* 25: 1–65.
34. The Cronbach Alpha for the five-item scale is 0.720. By contrast, the reliability of the similar Heath–Evans libertarian–authoritarian value 6-item scale is .53, see Anthony Heath, Geoffrey Evans, and Jean Martin. 1994. 'The measurement of core beliefs and values: The development of balanced socialist/laissez faire and libertarian/authoritarian scales.' *British Journal of Political Science* 24 (1): 115–132. The equivalent Tilley scale had a Cronbach Alpha of 0.51. See James R. Tilley. 2005. 'Research note: Libertarian–authoritarian value change in Britain, 1974–2001.' *Political Studies* 53: 422–453.
35. Agnes Akkerman, Cas Mudde, and Andrej Zaslove. 2014. 'How populist are the people? Measuring populist attitudes in voters.' *Comparative Political Studies* 47(9): 8–30.
36. Hans-Georg Betz. 1994. *Radical Rightwing Populism in Western Europe*. New York: St Martin's Press, pp. 37–38.
37. D. Doyle. 2011. 'The legitimacy of political institutions: Explaining contemporary populism in Latin America.' *Comparative Political Studies* 44: 1447–1473.
38. Elizabeth Ivarsflaten. 2008. 'What unites the populist right in Western Europe? Re-examining grievance mobilization models in seven successful cases.' *Comparative Political Studies* 41 (1): 3–23.
39. See, for example, www.politico.com/magazine/story/2017/11/08/donald-trump-johnstown-pennsylvania-supporters-215800.
40. www.gallup.com/poll/1597/confidence-institutions.aspx.
41. www.people-press.org/2017/05/03/public-trust-in-government-1958-2017/.
42. Pippa Norris. Ed. 1999. *Critical Citizens: Global Support for Democratic Governance*. Oxford: Oxford University Press.

43. David Doyle. 2011. 'The legitimacy of political institutions: Explaining contemporary populism in Latin America.' *Comparative Political Studies.* 44 (11): 1447–1473; Stijn Van Kessel. 2015. *Populist Parties in Europe: Agents of Discontent?* London: Palgrave Macmillan.
44. Matthijs Rooduijn, Wouter van der Brug, and Sarah de Lange. 2016. 'Expressing or fueling discontent? The relationship between populist voting and political discontent.' *Electoral Studies* 43: 32–40.
45. Justin Gest. 2016. *The New Minority: White Working Class Politics, Immigration and Inequality.* New York: Oxford University Press; Matthew J. Goodwin and Oliver Heath. 2016. 'The 2016 Referendum, Brexit and the left behind? An aggregate-level analysis of the result.' *Political Quarterly* 87 (3): 323–332; Harold Clarke, Matthew J. Goodwin, and Paul Whiteley. 2017. *Brexit! Why Britain Voted to Leave the European Union.* Cambridge: Cambridge University Press.
46. T. Smits, S. de Regt, and D. Mortelmans. 2012. 'The relevance of class in shaping authoritarian attitudes: A cross-national perspective.' *Research in Social Stratification and Mobility* 30: 280–295; Jens Rydgren. Ed. 2012. *Class Politics and the Radical Right.* New York: Routledge.
47. Geoffrey Evans. 1992. 'Testing the validity of the Goldthorpe class schema.' *European Sociological Review* 8 (3): 211–232.
48. Niels Spierings and Andrej Zaslove. 2017. 'Gender, populist attitudes, and voting: Explaining the gender gap in voting for populist radical right and populist radical left parties.' *West European Politics* 40 (4): 821–847; Rob Ford and Matthew Goodwin. 2010. 'Angry white men: Individual and contextual predictors of support for the British National Party.' *Political Studies* 58: 1–25.
49. Pippa Norris. 2003. *Democratic Phoenix.* New York: Cambridge University Press.
50. Achim Goerres. 2009. *The Political Representation of Older People in Europe.* London: Palgrave Macmillan; Gema Garcia Albacete. 2014. *Young People's Political Participation in Western Europe Continuity or Generational Change?* London: Palgrave Macmillan; Russell J. Dalton. 2015. *The Good Citizen: How a Younger Generation Is Reshaping American Politics.* 2nd revised edn. Washington DC: CQ Press.
51. Gabriel Almond and Sidney Verba. 1963. *The Civic Culture.* Princeton, NJ: Princeton University Press.
52. Sidney Verba, Norman Nie, and Jae-on Kim. 1978. *Participation and Political Equality.* New York: Cambridge University Press.
53. Kaat Smets and Carolien van Ham. 2013. 'The embarrassment of riches? A meta-analysis of individual-level research on voter turnout.' *Electoral Studies* 32 (2): 344–359.
54. Terri E. Givens. 2004. 'The radical right gender gap.' *Comparative Political Studies* 37 (1): 30–54.
55. Pippa Norris. 2005. *Radical Right: Voters and Parties in the Electoral Market.* New York: Cambridge University Press.

# 9

# Party Fortunes and Electoral Rules

In 2016, after the Brexit decision in June and then Trump's victory in November, widespread fears arose about an unstoppable authoritarian-populist surge at the polls, a domino effect disrupting European elections. The forces of Islamophobia, racism, and anti-immigration buffeted governments. During 2017, contests in Austria, the Netherlands, France, the UK, and Germany provided mixed signals. But it was not just Trump – politicians claimed to speak for the people but demonizing minorities, attacking human rights, and fueling distrust have risen to power as presidents or prime ministers in several countries around the world. This includes Recep Tayyip Erdoğan in Turkey, Nicolás Maduro in Venezuela, Lech and Jaroslaw Kacynski in Poland, Viktor Orbán in Hungary, Milos Zeman in the Czech Republic, Rafael Correa in Ecuador, and Rodrigo Duterte in the Philippines.[1] In the Netherlands and Germany, a cordon sanitaire has shut out Authoritarian-Populist parties from coalition governments, but elsewhere ministers from these parties have held office, including in Slovenia, Switzerland, and Austria. European parties from this family have gained 10 percent of more of the vote in recent contests – including the Norwegian Progress Party, the Danish People's Party, the Finnish Party – True Finns, and the Dutch Party for Freedom. Books warn darkly of the dangers of populism for '*How Democracies Die*,' how Trump is '*The Despot's Apprentice*,' and '*Why Our Freedom Is In Danger*.'[2]

Yet a more cautious story can also be told. Elsewhere on the continent, populists have often struggled to gain any parliamentary seats or else they prove to be poorly institutionalized 'flash' parties, such as UKIP, which surge temporarily and then collapse. Active resistance campaigns have mobilized against these forces suggesting that an authoritarian-populist surge can be contained.[3] Protest is exemplified by the first Women's March on the day of Trump's inauguration, estimated to have mobilized over 4.2 million people, the largest single day demonstration ever held in America.[4] The energies triggered by this protest continued to be evident a year later when around 2.5 million marched.[5]

What explains the varied electoral fortunes of Authoritarian-Populist parties across similar European societies? Has there been a resurgence of support for them? And how does the electoral system translate votes into seats – and thus government office?

To address these questions, Part I examines the evidence from national parliamentary elections from 1946 to 2015 in 27 European societies. The results indicate that, since the 1980s, Authoritarian-Populist parties have expanded their share of votes and seats substantially in national and European Parliament elections, but their success varies considerably cross-nationally and over time.[6] Many commentators have speculated about the recent resurgence of a populist wave in Europe or even regarded developments as a 'populist zeitgeist' in which this movement has become mainstream.[7] But electoral statistics show a mixed record for the success of Authoritarian-Populist parties and leaders. While they have made parliamentary gains and entered government office in some countries, such as Austria and Switzerland, they have fallen back and lost votes in others, such as the UK – suggesting a more cautious interpretation. Part II focuses on case-studies to illustrate how rules influence the fortunes of Authoritarian-Populist parties in elections from six selected European countries with varying electoral systems – Austria and the Netherlands using Proportional Representation electoral systems, France and the UK being Majoritarian-Plurality systems, and Germany and Hungary having two different type of Mixed systems. Part III shows how the electoral system and institutional rules governing party competition help to explain the varied performance of these parties even among relatively similar European societies. This analysis confirms the importance of institutional barriers, with seat gains being greater under Proportional systems but usually more limited under Majoritarian systems. Part IV discusses trends in parties' shifting policy agenda, demonstrating the rising importance of the cultural libertarian–authoritarian cleavage and the declining salience of the left–right economic cleavage. The conclusion considers how votes translate into seats and thus shape the electoral fortunes and power of Authoritarian-Populist parties and leaders.

## I THE ELECTORAL PERFORMANCE OF AUTHORITARIAN-POPULIST PARTIES

In this analysis, parties are classified using the typology developed in Chapter 7. Evidence is derived from the 1900 to 2016 ParlGov dataset, which compiles official statistics. We find that across 27 European societies, in the decades following the end of World War II Authoritarian-Populist parties were almost always confined to the political fringe. The historical memories of Bolshevism and Fascism were seared into the public's memories. Some of the parties under comparison have long historical roots; for example, the Freedom Party has been on the political stage in Austria since 1956, although it was an agrarian center-right party for many years and it was only after Jorg Haider became leader in 1986 that its program changed and its electoral fortunes surged when it become Authoritarian-Populist on an anti-immigration platform. National Front parties were established in the UK in 1967 and in 1972 in France, and the British National Party sprang up a decade later in 1982. It was only in the 1980s, however, that Authoritarian-Populist parties made substantial gains in their share of the vote and seats in Europe, moving from fringe to minor party status, with some parliamentary seats. This jump was followed by slower gains in subsequent decades.[8] As Figure 9.1 shows, the mean share of the vote for Authoritarian-Populist parties in the lower (or single) house in national parliamentary elections rose from 5.9 percent in the 1970s to 11.7 percent in the most recent decade. During the same period, their average share of seats reflected similar gains. Several parties which have grown rapidly in recent years are relative newcomers: for example, the Dutch Freedom Party (PVV) was created by Geert Wilders in 2006, while the Alternative for Germany was founded by Alexander Gauland and partners in 2013. In post-communist Europe, as well, several new Authoritarian-Populist parties like Law and Justice in Poland (founded in 2001) and Hungary's Jobbik (founded in 2003) quickly made rapid headway following the opening of party competition in Central and Eastern Europe. Authoritarian-Populist parties have also often performed particularly well in second-order elections, at both sub-national and supra-national levels. The 2014 European Parliament

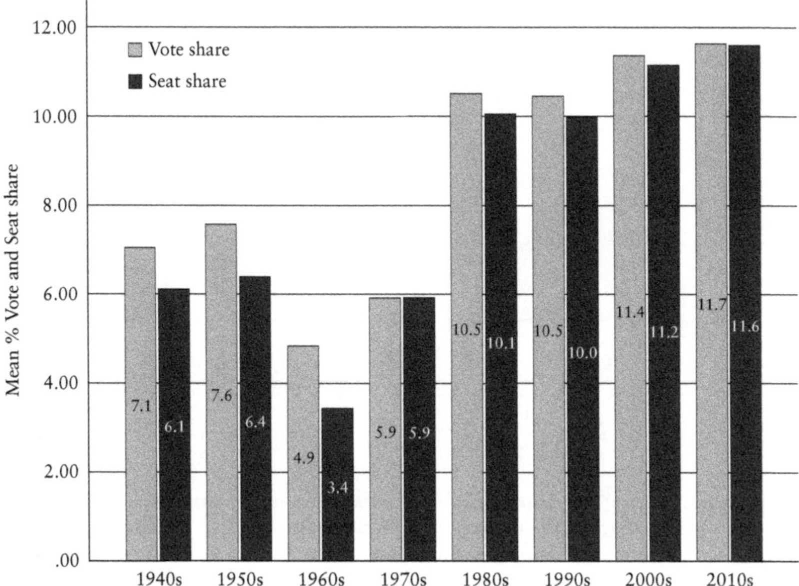


FIGURE 9.1. *Mean vote and seat for Authoritarian-Populist parties in Europe, 1946–2015*

*Note:* The mean share of the national vote won by Authoritarian-Populist parties in the lower (or single) house in national parliamentary elections in 27 European societies which contain at least one such party from 1946 to 2015. The classification of types of parties is based on the CHES dataset. See Table 7.1 for the indices used for classification and Table 7.2 for the list of parties.

*Source:* Calculated from Holger Döring and Philip Manow. 2017. *Parliaments and governments database* (ParlGov) 'Elections' dataset. www.parlgov.org/.

elections registered a surge of support for Euroscepticism, challenging the legitimacy of the EU from within. This included strong performances by the Austrian Freedom Party (FPO), the French Front National (FN), UKIP, the Danish People's Party, the Hungarian Jobbik, the True Finns, and the Greek Golden Dawn (XA).[9]

Figure 9.2 shows the share of the vote won by Authoritarian-Populist parties from 1990 to 2016 in national legislative elections for the lower house across more than two dozen Western democracies. The average vote for Authoritarian-Populist parties during this quarter century varies substantially even among relatively similar post-industrial neighboring European states with shared cultural legacies, and broadly similar Majoritarian or Proportional electoral systems. This is illustrated by the contrasts that can be observed between Norway (16%) and Sweden (6%),

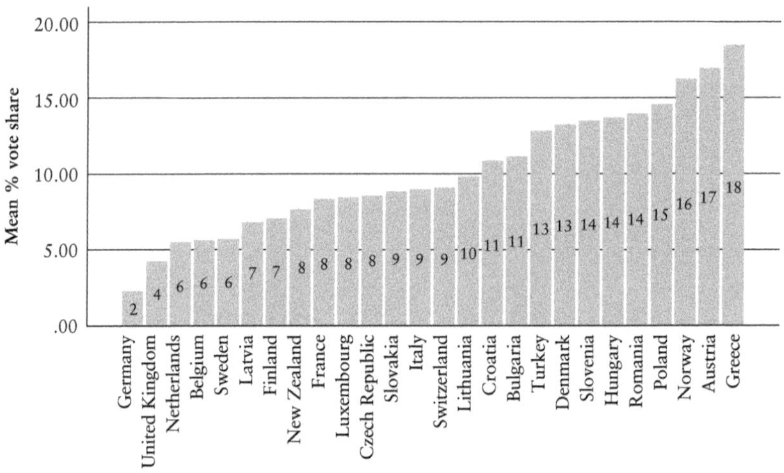


FIGURE 9.2. *Voting for Authoritarian-Populist parties by country, 1990–2016*
*Notes:* The mean share of the national vote won by Authoritarian-Populist parties in the lower (or single) house in national parliamentary elections in 27 European societies which contain at least one such party. The classification of types of parties is based on the CHES dataset. See Table 7.1 for the indices used for classification and Table 7.2 for the list of parties.
*Source:* Calculated from Holger Döring and Philip Manow. 2016. *Parliaments and governments database* (ParlGov) 'Elections' dataset. www.parlgov.org/.

Austria (17%) and Germany (2%), or Greece (18%) and Italy (9%). Overall, there appears to be little in common between the countries where these parties have made the most headway, with over 15 percent of the vote on average during this period – Greece, Austria, Norway, and Poland. And the countries where these parties fare most poorly also appear to have little in common – Germany, the UK, the Netherlands, and Belgium.

## II COMPARING EUROPEAN PARTY FORTUNES AND ELECTORAL RULES

An explanation for these differences may lie in the rules of the game and the electoral systems. If European societies are responding to demand-side structural changes in modern societies, like those in education and the labor force, and cultural shifts like the rising tide of social liberalism or processes of secularization, then we might expect to see a similar pattern in voting across Europe. Instead, as we can see from the election results, the fortunes of Authoritarian-Populist parties vary substantially, especially in translating votes into seats and ministerial office. One explanation for these contrasts lies in the role of electoral systems and patterns of party competition. The rules of the game are widely recognized as important for determining ballot access for minor parties, how votes are translated into seats – and then party competition determines how seats are translated into ministerial office through coalition politics.

To understand these institutional contrasts more fully, we selected six case studies illustrating the performance of some of the most successful Authoritarian-Populist parties in Western and Eastern Europe, examining several relatively similar prosperous post-industrial societies that operate contests under different electoral systems and structures of party competition. We compared the performance of these parties in the electoral systems used for the lower house of the national parliament. The performance of the Freedom Party in Austria and the PVV in the Netherlands were selected as these countries use Proportional Representation systems (with different district magnitudes and vote thresholds). The fortunes of the Alternative for Germany and both Fidesz and Jobbik in Hungary were compared, since both countries use Mixed Member electoral systems, where citizens cast two ballots in the same contest (one for a single member for your district and one for party lists), but with different rules. Finally, the results for the National Front in France and UKIP in Britain were compared as these countries use Majoritarian-Plurality systems.

## The Freedom Party and Austrian Elections

For parliamentary elections to the Nationalrat, Austria uses an open list Proportional Representation system in nine multimember districts to elect the 183 members of the National Council. Parties must win a minimum of 4 percent of the vote to win any seats. Seats are allocated via the d'Hondt method at the federal level. There is also a modest hurdle to ballot access; parties need the signatures of three MPs or must collect 2,600 signatures of eligible voters to be listed on the nation-wide ballot. This type of system is expected to be favorable for the parliamentary representation of minor parties, since Proportional Representation lowers the barriers for entry compared with Majoritarian systems.

At the presidential level, however, Austria uses a ballot system requiring an absolute majority of votes, similar to that used in France. The President is elected every six years. If a candidate wins an absolute majority of votes in the first round, they are elected. If not, then the top two candidates go head to head in the second round. The role of the Austrian president as Head of State is largely symbolic but the constitution grants powers of appointment for several senior members of the government. The winner-take-all system poses far greater challenges for minor parties given the vote threshold, and is designed to favor moderate center-right or center-left parties able to mobilize support among the majority of Austrians.

In these contests, the Freedom Party of Austria (Freiheitliche Partei Österreichs, FPÖ) hoped to do well given the campaign opinion polls. As we have seen, Austria was at the forefront of the wave of immigrants, refugees, and asylum seekers coming through the Balkan land route. By 2015, around one-fifth of the population was foreign born. The FPÖ was founded in 1956 as a center-right conservative party but it shifted toward the authoritarian-populist category when Jorg Haider became its leader in 1986. Haider was notorious for alleged Nazi sympathies and his plans to halt immigration, a particularly sensitive issue given Austria's past history. The party gained support from the early 1990s onwards and by the 1999 election it had become the second largest party in Austria with 26.9 percent of the vote and 55 seats in the Nationalrat. The entry of the FPÖ into government in 1999, with six FPÖ ministers in the coalition government with the conservative Österreichische Volkspartei (ÖVP, Austrian People's Party), triggered an international outcry and diplomatic sanctions were mounted against Austria by the European Union and the US. In February 2000, Haider was forced to resign as party leader and the FPÖ subsequently lost ground in national elections in November 2002, although they remain in a coalition government with the ÖVP, as well as holding pockets of electoral strength in local and regional politics. Under Strache's leadership, in opposition the party again rebuilt popular support, winning one fifth of the vote in the 2013 legislative elections. In the 2010 Federal presidential election, the FPÖ candidate, Barbara Rosenkranz, was knocked out in the first round, with only 15.2 percent of the vote.

The outcome of the presidential elections on 24 April 2016 was therefore all the more remarkable when the candidate of the Freedom Party of Austria (FPÖ), Norbert Hofer, took the lead in the first round with 35 percent of the vote, easily beating both the mainstream Social Democratic and the Austrian People's Party candidates. This generated a jolt to the party system and sparked international concern. Hofer had campaigned on an 'Austria First' platform emphasizing authoritarian and populist

TABLE 9.1. *Rules for parliamentary elections for the lower house in the selected case studies*

| | Majoritarian-Plurality | | Mixed Member | | Proportional Representation | |
|---|---|---|---|---|---|---|
| | UK | France | Germany | Hungary | Austria | Netherlands |
| | House of Commons | National Assembly | Federal | National Assembly | National Council | Second Chamber |
| Electoral system | Single Member Plurality | Second Ballot Majoritarian | Mixed Member Proportional | Mixed Member Parallel | Proportional Party List | Proportional Party List |
| Date of last parliamentary election | 8 June 2017 | 18 June 2017 | 24 Sept 2017 | 6 April 2014 | 15 Oct 2017 | 15 March 2017 |
| Registered electors | 46,800,000 | 47,293,103 | 61,500,000 | 8,029,829 | 5,120,881 | 10,563,456 |
| Turnout (%) | 69% | 38% | 75% | 60% | 79% | 82% |
| Legal Vote Threshold | None | 50% | 5% | 5% | 4% | None |
| Total number of seats | 650 | 577 | 598 | 199 | 183 | 150 |
| Total number of SMP seats | 650 | 577 | 299 | 106 | 0 | 0 |
| Total number of party list seats | 0 | 0 | 299 | 93 | 183 | 150 |
| Populist Authoritarian | UKIP | FN | AfD | Jobbik | FPO | PVV |
| Leader | Nuttall | Le Pen | Petry/Meuten | Vona | Strache | Wilders |
| Rank of party in % of vote | 5th | 3rd | 3rd | 3rd | 3rd | 2nd |
| Number of seats won | 0 (−1) | 8 (+6) | 94 (+94) | 23 | 51 (+11) | 20 (+5) |
| % Vote | 1.8 | 8.7 | 12.6 | 20.5% | 26.0 | 13.1 |
| % Seats | 0 | 1.4 | 15.7 | 11.6% | 27.8 | 13.3 |
| In government | No | No | Tbd | No | Yes (6 /16 ministers) | No |

*Source:* Compiled from IFES Election Guide. www.electionguide.org/.

values, including restrictions on immigration, tight border controls, anti-Islam, anti-establishment, welfare chauvinism, and Eurosceptic policies. If elected, he promised a referendum on Austria's membership of the EU, similar to Brexit. He was eventually defeated in the 22 May runoff by the Independent Green candidate, Alexander Van der Bellen, but the margin of victory was wafer-thin (0.3 percent of the vote). Van der Bellen consolidated his lead in the rerun contest on 4 December 2016, following a technical irregularity disqualifying the earlier election. Election-day surveys in the final round suggest that the Freedom Party mobilized their greatest support among men, blue-collar workers, those living in rural areas, and those lacking a high school diploma or more.[10] By contrast, Van der Bellen performed best among the college educated, those under 30, and in urban areas such as Vienna, and his support was driven in large part by voters seeking to stop Hofer more than by positive approval of der Bellen. The outcome sidelined both the center-left Social Democratic and the center-right People's Party, challenging the established party system that had dominated Austrian governments since the end of World War II.[11]

In the legislative elections held on October 15, 2017, the FPÖ again went into the contest with high expectations as they had been leading in the opinion polls from June 2015 until June 2017. Since then, their support has steadily declined in the opinion polls. By contrast, under a new young leader, Sebastian Kurz, the Österreichische Volkspartei (ÖVP) surged into a decisive lead, which it maintained until the election. Sixteen parties qualified for ballot access for the 2017 parliamentary elections and eight succeeded in winning seats. The ÖVP was elected as the largest party, winning 62 out of 183 seats, with Kurz becoming the youngest head of government in Europe. But the FPÖ performed strongly, with its best parliamentary result since 1999, winning 51 seats (gaining 11) with one-quarter of the vote, coming third behind the Social Democratic Party (SPÖ). The FPÖ leader, Heinz-Christian Strache entered in a right-wing coalition government as the junior partner, with the ÖVP led by Chancellor Kurz. Six ministers from the Freedom Party were appointed, forming one–third of the cabinet. The government held the presidency of the Council of the EU in 2018. On this occasion, after the rise of Authoritarian-Populist parties in many countries, the EU did not impose any sanctions against Austria. The Freedom Party illustrates the strength of authoritarian populism and their success in gaining access to government office with just 26 percent of the vote under a Proportional Representation electoral system.

## The Dutch Party for Freedom (PVV)

The Netherlands has a highly fragmented party system and coalition governments due to the Proportional Representation electoral system, and all 150 members are elected in a single nation-wide constituency. This generates an extremely low vote threshold, requiring only 0.66 percent of the vote for a party to enter parliament, which is highly favorable for small parties. Slightly less than 100,000 votes is sufficient to win one seat in the House of Representatives. The Netherlands has a reputation as an extremely liberal and tolerant multicultural society, a prosperous welfare state, and long-standing power-sharing democracy. Nevertheless, it has always had more conservative regions, especially in rural farming areas. Out of a population of around 16 million, more than 3 million are non-Dutch, including about 1.7 million from developing societies. Many of these are from Turkey, Morocco, Surinam, and the former Dutch West Indies colonies – and these and more recent waves of refugees are heavily concentrated in urban areas, making up four out of ten residents in Rotterdam, Amsterdam, the Hague, and Utrecht.[12] This background, and debate about whether Dutch society was effectively integrating Muslim populations, made conditions ripe for authoritarian-populist challengers.

There have been several minor populist parties on the right and left in the Netherlands but they never achieved electoral success during the post-war decades.[13] The agrarian Farmer's Party (BP) came closest to French Poujadism, opposing European integration and development aid. The BP support peaked in the 1960s, winning seven seats in 1967. In 1971, it lost much of that vote, and never regained it, losing its last remaining seat in 1981. The main Dutch radical right parties in the 1980s were the *Nederlanden Volksunie* (Netherland People's Union), which was succeeded by the *Centrum Partij* (Center Party – CP), and the splinter *Centrum Partij '86* (Center Party '86). The *Centrumdemocraten* (Center Democrats – CD) was formed in 1986, gaining marginal support throughout the 1990s (peaking with 2.5 percent of the vote in 1994). In November 2001, Pim Fortuyn was elected to parliament by a new party, Livable Netherlands. His comments, such as calling for an end to Muslim immigration, stirred controversy, however, and he was subsequently ejected from the party. On February 11, 2002, Fortuyn founded his own party, the anti-immigrant Pim Fortuyn List (LPF). In May 2002, just before the Dutch general election, his assassination by an animal rights activist led to a sudden surge of support for his party. Founded just three months earlier, in their first contest, the LPF entered parliament as the second largest party, joining a coalition government led by the Christian Democrats. Their initial success caused shockwaves in the Dutch political system; lacking experienced party leaders or clearly developed policies, and with scandal and divisions destabilizing the coalition, the government proved short-lived. In the subsequent general election in January 2003, the LPF vote plummeted from 17 percent to 5.7 percent, causing a loss of two-thirds of their elected members. The following year, in the 2004 elections to the European Parliament, the party achieved a marginal share of the vote and no members were elected.[14] The May 2002 election exemplified a 'deviating' election, providing a radical jolt to Dutch politics from a flash party that ultimately proved short-lived.

The most successful successor to the LPF is the Dutch Freedom Party (PVV), founded by Geert Wilders in 2006. PVV won nine seats in the 2006 parliamentary elections, surging to 24 to become the third largest party in 2010, before falling back to 15 in 2012. The 2012 parliamentary elections produced a coalition government led by Prime Minister Mark Rutte's People's Party for Freedom and Democracy (VVD), a conservative liberal party, in partnership with the Labour Party (PvdA). The Netherlands went to the polls on March 15, 2017 in parliamentary elections.

These contests posed a major test for Wilder's PVV, campaigning on a populist, nationalist, and anti-immigrant platform. A flamboyant, controversial and divisive figure, Wilders' campaign emphasized the need to protect Western liberal values against Islam, to take the Netherlands out of the EU, to close all mosques, and to ban the Koran, in the name of preserving traditional Dutch values.[15] He called Islam 'a backward culture,' a view which he expounded at length in his book called Against the Islamisation of Our Culture. He also said: 'This is a full society.' Like all populists, his rhetoric denigrated elites and called on the people. As he said in December 2017 at the Prague meeting of several Authoritarian-Populist parties, it is important to 'respect the wisdom of the people. Respect the wisdom of our ancestors. Our national values, our traditions, our identity, they make us who we are, and we will never give up!' Moreover, he argued that he would fight supra-nationalism and migration: 'At the moment Brussels wants to flood us with Third World immigrants. Predominantly from Islamic countries. It wants to distribute these immigrants across all EU member states. The result will be a disaster. It will weaken the Jewish-Christian and humanistic identity of our nations.'[16] His argument claimed that the traditional cultural values of many Muslim migrants failed to respect the tolerance of Dutch society, for example in attitudes toward religion, gender equality, and tolerance of homosexuality. The rhetoric appealed to his voters, who displayed nationalist, populist, and authoritarian attitudes.[17] The PVV had led in the opinion polls from September 2015 until late-February 2017. The final stage of the campaign generated a swing, however, with Mark Rutte's VVD regaining its lead. Media reports attributed this shift in part to Wilder's refusal to take part in two RTL televised debates, and to Rutte's strong stance in tit-for-tat criticism of Turkish President Erdoğan.

On election day in 2017, Wilder's PVV took second place, with 20 seats and a modest (+3%) gain in their share of the vote. The final result on 15 March 2017 saw Mark Rutte's VVD win first place with 21.3 percent of the vote (−5.3%) and 33 seats (down 8). By contrast, Gert Wilder's PVV came second with 13.1 percent of the vote (+3.0%) and 20 seats (up 5). The PVV had still made gains in parliament although it demonstrated a poorer performance than in previous European Parliamentary elections. The Christian Democrats (CDA) and the liberal D66 party were close behind with 19 seats each. Labour was badly squeezed by the fragmentation of the left. The negotiator tasked with exploring government coalition negotiations after the election immediately set about forming a coalition to achieve an overall parliamentary majority of at least 76 seats, led by the VVD in partnership with the centre-right CDA and liberal D66. There were considerable delays in trying to form a cross-party governing coalition, with talks persisting for many months. The new Rutte-led governing coalition was eventually installed in October 2017, made up of the People's Party for Freedom and Democracy (VVD), the leftist-liberal Democrats 66, the Christian Democrats (CDA), and the small Christian Union Party. The PVV won 20 seats in the March elections but they were excluded from the new coalition government as all the other parties ruled out any cooperation with them. The Dutch parliamentary elections can be seen as disappointing for the Freedom Party, which failed to become the largest parliamentary party, as had been expected in early opinion polls. But the outcome still saw PVV gains. Moreover, the populist surge arguably influenced Prime Minister Mark Rutte. who adopted a milder version of Geert Wilder's rhetoric and policies toward stricter restrictions on migrants, with a strong speech in January 2017 warning immigrants to 'be normal or be gone.' The new government is expected to implement measures to control immigration, boost defense spending, and cut taxes. Resurgent populist parties can influence mainstream party policies and rhetoric, even when they fail to gain an outright victory. Despite the small share of votes won by the PVV – just 13.1 percent – it was sufficient to make them the second largest party because the Proportional Representation electoral system allowed the vote to be divided by a large number of parties. Unlike the Austrian outcome, Wilders and the PVV were excluded from government office by an agreement to exclude them among other parties in the Rutte-led coalition.

## The National Front in the 2017 French Presidential and Legislative Elections

The French electoral system in the Fifth Republic, introduced by de Gaulle in 1958, was designed to curb extreme party system fragmentation and government instability. Under the Majoritarian Second Ballot electoral systems, many contenders can compete in the first ballot but if no one secures an absolute majority of the vote, a run-off election is held between the top two contenders – guaranteeing that the winner will represent a majority. The run-off system provides incentives for center-left and center-right party coalitions to unite behind two major party candidates. Under this system, coalitions led by the socialist and the republican center-right parties rotated in office and have won the presidency in every contest since 1958.

By contrast, 2017 shattered the dominance of the mainstream socialist and center-right parties. The unpopularity of President Francois Holland's government dragged down the socialist candidate, Benoit Hamon, who attracted just 6.4 percent of the vote in the first round, the worst result for the socialists since 1969. On the center-right, the republican candidate, Francois Fillon, damaged by accusations of corruption, came in third with 20 percent of the vote. Emmanuel Macron led the field, winning 24 percent of the vote in the first round, and triumphing with a decisive 65 percent of the vote in the second round runoff. A youthful newcomer who had held ministerial office under Holland, and who founded his own party (En Marche!) in April 2016, Macron had never held elected office. Pro-EU, he appealed to moderates and to tactical voters.

Jean-Marie Le Pen, founder of the party, was convicted of hate speech and described the Holocaust as a 'detail of history.' His daughter sought to project a more moderate image, rejecting the anti-Semitism of her father, although she continues to stand on an extreme nationalist platform against the European Union, immigration, and globalization. The National Front performed particularly well in the 1986 elections to the National Assembly, gaining 35 seats with 10 percent of the vote, in large part because in 1985 President Mitterrand had changed the electoral system to Proportional Representation, before the Second Ballot Majoritarian system was restored for the next elections. Her father's greatest success in mobilizing FN support came in the 2002 presidential elections, when he came second with 16.8 percent of the vote on the first ballot, rising to 17.8 percent in the second round run-off.

Brexit and Trump's victory reenergized the party: the deputy leader of the French National Front, Florian Philippot, crowed that 'their world is crumbling, ours is being built.' In the 2017 French presidential elections, under Marine Le Pen's leadership the National Front won a larger proportion of the presidential vote than ever before, pulling in 34 percent in the final runoff – almost twice the share of the vote that her father had won in the presidential contest 15 years earlier.[18] But she was still unable to prevent a remarkable victory for the pro-EU centrist Emmanuel Macron, who won a decisive two-thirds of the vote in the final round.[19]

The French National Assembly elections the following month confirmed the popularity of Macron's party, which won 43 percent of the vote in the second round, and 308 out of 577 seats in the National Assembly, gaining a comfortable parliamentary majority. By contrast, although Marine Le Pen was returned for her district, the National Front won only 8.8 percent of the national vote and just eight seats in the National Assembly, falling well below their target of 15 seats and losing votes between the first and second rounds, in part due to difficulties in mobilizing FN supporters to turn out.[20] The established French party system, dominated by the center-left and center-right and which had governed throughout the Fifth Republic, was upended – partly by the National Front, but even more by Emmanuel Macron, a centrist pro-EU outsider, political neophyte, and charismatic leader of a party that had only been founded a year earlier.

The second round of the French presidential elections in May 2017 saw the National Front (FN) score their highest share of the vote (33.9%) in any presidential, legislative, or European contest.[21] Marine Le Pen got almost twice as large a share of the votes in the second round of the 2017 presidential election as her father had in 2002. Unlike the age-profile of authoritarian-populist voters in the US and UK, exit polls reported that the FN received its highest support in the presidential and legislative elections from middle-aged voters, not the elderly. The party also performed best among rural voters with a low level of education and among blue-collar workers.[22] The series of presidential elections provide an opportunity to examine dynamic changes in the social and ideological basis of National Front support and the party's electoral fortunes over successive contests. Marine Le Pen sought to soften her father's hardline anti-immigrant and anti-EU appeal. But she was defeated in the 2017 presidential elections by the centrist-populist newcomer, Emmanuel Macron. The National Front performed poorly in National Assembly elections a month later and failed to mobilize their base.[23]

The French presidential and legislative elections in 2017 provides further evidence of the state of authoritarian populism in Europe – and how the electoral system is critical for translating popular support for these parties into seats in parliament and government office. In the April 2017 presidential elections, Le Pen won one–third of the vote in the second ballot, beating mainstream center-right and center-left opponents, a remarkable success for any Authoritarian-Populist leader. Nevertheless, they lost the election to a newcomer leading a new party. The electorate clearly rejected the old established parties – but was not willing to back an authoritarian populist. The consequences of the election were critical for the EU; Brexit in June 2016 was a major shock to the European Union, and it was widely predicted that a victory for Le Pen would have led to French exit – and the collapse of the EU.

## UKIP in the 2015 and 2017 UK General Elections

The electoral fortunes of the UK Independence Party (UKIP) in recent British general elections provides another illustration of the decisive impact of vote threshold hurdles in preventing support for minor parties from translating into seats. The case of Brexit is discussed in detail in Chapter 11, but first we will summarize some key aspects of the Plurality electoral system and why it proved critical for UKIP. The Single Member Plurality electoral system (known also as first-past-the-post) is used for elections to the House of Commons. There are 650 constituencies, voters cast a ballot for one candidate in their constituency, and the candidate winning the largest share (a simple plurality) wins the seat. During the post-war era, the electoral system usually produced a stable two-party system in which the Labour and Conservative parties rotated in office, winning an absolute majority of the seats in parliament, even with much less than a majority of the total votes. This enabled them to form one-party governments. Minor parties are penalized by the system: unless they come in first in a given constituency, they win no seats – even if they win votes in the country as a whole.

Since the 1970s, several Authoritarian-Populist parties have contested local and parliamentary elections, including the National Front and the British National Party. They registered sporadic gains in a few local council elections, especially in urban cities with immigrants, but their representation in the House of Commons was negligible. The UK Independence Party was established in 1993, but it remained on the fringe of British politics until the party adopted a broader party platform, including anti-immigration, making significant breakthroughs in the 2013 local elections and the 2014 European Parliament elections. In 1999, the Labour government, as part of a broader package of constitutional reforms, changed the electoral system used for the European Parliament from the Single Member Plurality system to Regional Party List Proportional Representation. This allowed UKIP to make substantial gains in the subsequent 2004 European elections held under these rules, since 16 percent of the national vote translated into a delegation of 15 percent of UK Members returned to the European Parliament. This gave UKIP's leader, Nigel Farage, a public platform and media visibility on their core anti-Brussels message. As Figure 11.2 shows, this strong performance was again repeated in the 2009 European Parliamentary elections – but not at the 2005 and 2010 general elections, which continued to be held under the first-past-the-post system. Their best performance, in terms of their share of the vote, came in the 2014 European elections, where UKIP broke through with more than a quarter of the vote and one-third of the seats. This surge in the vote, the gain of two Eurosceptic Conservative MPs who switched parties to join them, and the popularity of UKIP in the opinion polls during a mid-term period of government unpopularity, was critical in influencing Prime Minister David Cameron's promise to hold a referendum on Britain's membership in the European Union, if the Conservatives were returned to government in the next general election.

In the 2015 British general election, UKIP rose from 3.1 percent of the vote in 2010 to 12.6 percent of the nation-wide vote, a record share for them in any House of Commons contest, but because of the electoral system they won only one seat. The sudden surge in popularity proved short-term, however, for reasons discussed in Chapter 11. As a result, in the 2017 general election they fell back to 1.8 percent of the national vote with no parliamentary representatives. This does not mean that populism is dead in Britain, because – in order to steal their voters – the Conservative government under Theresa May has adopted their key policies. But it does mean that the viability of UKIP as a party is in doubt.

## The AFD and the 2017 German Bundestag Elections

The contrasts between the fortunes of Authoritarian-Populist parties under Proportional Representation and Majoritarian electoral system are further illustrated by contests in Germany and Hungary under Mixed Member electoral systems, although these differ in some important regards.[24] Germany's system is Mixed Member Proportional – meaning that the allocation of seats in the Bundestag is determined according to the proportion of votes won on the Proportional Representation Party List side of the ballot. Compensatory allocations are used to achieve proportional results. By contrast, Hungary's system uses Mixed Member, without compensatory allocations. This apparently small detail in design means that in practice Hungary's system is much closer to a pure Majoritarian system.

In Germany, 598 members are returned to the Bundestag, with half (299) elected through Regional Party List Proportional Representation elections in each state and half elected in a second vote on the ballot through Single Member Plurality districts. The system is highly proportional for parties that meet the 4 percent minimum vote threshold according to the share of ballots cast in the the second party list votes.

Article 21 of the German Constitution specifies that political parties that seek to impair German democratic principles shall be declared unconstitutional. Thus, in 1952 the Court outlawed the Sozialistsche Reichspartei (SRP), a successor to the Nazi party. Nevertheless, several attempts to disband the far-right Nationalist Party of Germany (NPD) failed in the Court as recently as January 2017. The Court has also outlawed many xenophobic skinhead groups, ultra-nationalist organizations, and neo-Nazi movements that were actively engaged in violent acts of intimidation and hate crimes against asylum seekers, Turkish migrants, foreigners, and Jews.

In 2013, reflecting developments across the continent, Alternative for Gemany (AfD) was founded, originally with a platform calling to end the Euro. In reaction to the upsurge in migrants arriving in mid-to late 2015, and in opposition to Merkel's open door refugee policy, the party shifted its focus to an anti-immigrant and nationalist platform. In regional contests, the AfD managed to gain entry to 11 state parliaments. A leadership change in April 2017 brought Alexander Gauland and Alice Weidel to the party's helm. The outcome of the September 2017 Bundestag elections sent a shockwave through Germany. For the first time since the Nazi era, an Authoritarian-Populist party – the Alternative for Gemany

(AfD) – won enough votes to enter the German federal parliament. In the 2017 elections, the AfD not only surpassed the 5 percent minimum needed to gain seats in the Bundestag, but won almost 13 percent of the vote, obtaining 94 of the seats in the lower house of parliament. Only three of the AfD seats were won in single member districts, while 91 seats were allocated through Party List Proportional Representation. Germany had been governed since 2013 by a coalition of the two largest parties, the Christian Democrats and Social Democrats, with Angela Merkel as Chancellor. Both major parties suffered significant losses in the 2017 elections, with the Christian Democrats winning 34.7 percent of the seats in the Bundestag and the Social Democrats winning 21.6 percent, their worst result since 1949.

Merkel managed to form a governing coalition. As in the Netherlands, negotiations over forming the governing coalition were prolonged, partly because none of the other parties was willing to enter a coalition that included the Alternative for Germany. This excludes the AfD from government, but their entry into parliament greatly complicated attempts to form a stable coalition under Angela Merkel's leadership.

### Hungary

The case of Hungary enables us to examine the working of a Mixed Member Parallel electoral system, combining Single Member Plurality and Party List Proportional Representation seats. This appears similar to the German system in many regards but which nevertheless has produced very different outcomes because there are no compensatory seats allocated for smaller parties. The results of votes cast for the Single Member Plurality seats and the Party List seats are each counted and allocated separately.[25]

Both Viktor Orbán's Hungarian Civic Union (Fidesz) and the Movement for a Better Hungary (Jobbik) are nationalist, economically left-wing, and socially conservative Authoritarian-Populist parties. Jobbik is more extreme in its ideology, however, being stringently anti-Roma and anti-Semitic in its discourse and pro-Russian in its foreign policy, describing itself in its manifesto as 'a value-centered, conservative, patriotic Christian party.'[26] The April 2010 parliamentary election was a major turning point in Hungarian history marking the start of the erosion of democratic rights.[27] Fidesz – the Hungarian Civic Alliance – became the dominant party, winning 54 percent of votes but 68 percent of the seats a highly disproportional result. The Fidesz government had won a super-majority (263 out of 386 parliamentary seats), empowering Orbán to amend the Fundamental Law (constitution) without challenge from the opposition parties. The MSZP (or HSP, Hungarian Socialist Party) was badly defeated with just 13 percent of the vote. The Movement for a Better Hungary or Jobbik Party also entered parliament for the first time with 5.7 percent of the vote. Fidesz's two-thirds super-majority in parliament empowered the government to push through a new constitution that strengthened the executive and destroyed many checks and balances in the previous political system, including weakening the independence of the Electoral Commission and the powers of the Constitutional Court.[28] The government also changed the electoral law toward a more Majoritarian system, abolishing the compensation list which benefitted smaller parties, while sharply reducing the number of seats in the National Assembly to 199. For the 2014 National Assembly elections, 106 members were elected from Single Member Plurality districts and 93 were elected under Party Lists, with a 5 percent threshold. But the system was designed to benefit Fidesz.

The subsequent April 2014 parliamentary, European, and local elections left Fidesz predominant with a comfortable two-thirds overall majority in parliament, and the left parties were further fragmented and weakened. In 2014, Fidesz won just 44 percent of the vote, less than in 2010, but under the new electoral rules they still swept up 69 percent of the seats. The district boundaries were heavily gerrymandered, with smaller sized electorates for the pro-government constituencies, and the results were highly disproportional: Fidesz-KDNP won one seat per 31,833 votes, whereas Unity needed 66,309, Jobbik 84,879, and LMP 94,424 votes.[29]

Led by János Volner, Jobbik surged to win one-fifth of the popular vote (20.5%), becoming the third largest party in the National Assembly, although without any ministerial offices. It is notable that all the 23 Jobbik MPs were elected from the Party List Proportional Representation system, and the party failed to win Plurality seats. Under a purely Single Member Plurality electoral system, it seems doubtful whether Jobbik would have been elected to parliament. The performance of Jobbik in both types of ballots again emphasizes the importance of the legal rules in translating popular support at the ballot box into parliamentary seats – and ultimately ministerial office.

Overall the integrity of the 2014 election was ranked poorly in new electoral laws, the process of drawing district boundaries, media coverage, and campaign finance, so that Hungary ranks 75th worldwide out of 161 countries in the Perceptions of Electoral Integrity Index.[30] Electoral officials at all levels are appointed by the majority of MPs, and the top officials are nominated by the president, so that in practice the ruling party dominates the administrative and appeal process.[31]

Overall in recent years, under the Fidesz government, Hungarian politics have seen a sharp deterioration in the quality of the country's political rights and freedoms, including laws, policies, and practices that have curtailed the ability of refugees to seek asylum in the country, deteriorating freedoms in the mass media, and large-scale government corruption.[32] The lack of electoral integrity has consolidated Fidesz' control. Developments in this country, along with those in Poland and the Czech Republic, have ushered in a return to more authoritarian rule in the region, despite membership in the EU and considerable economic gains experienced during the last decade. Growing support for other Authoritarian-Populist parties in the region include Poland's Law and Justice Party, Bulgaria's Political Party Attack (Ataka), and the Slovak National Party (SNS).[33] In September 2018 the European Parliament voted to punish Hungary over alleged breaches of the EU's core values.

## III MAKING SENSE OF CONTRASTING PARTY FORTUNES

In several European contests held in recent years, Authoritarian-Populist parties have increased their share of the vote. In the aftermath of the successive shockwaves of the Austrian presidential election, the Brexit referendum, and the US victory of President Trump, the stable foundations of the left–right cleavage in electoral competition, which Rokkan and Lipset claimed had 'frozen' party systems in Western democracies during the post-war decade, seemed to be collapsing.[34]

The outcomes of these contests appeared to be particularly damaging for moderate political parties in Europe, especially for the center-left Social Democrats. Some scholars argued that the traditional center-left was experiencing a 'death-spiral,' with global markets and austerity policies restricting welfare programs for those suffering from inequality, job losses, and stagnant wages, with community and class solidarity being splintered by growing social diversity.[35] Prospects for a revival of the center-left parties looked bleak. In France, in 2012, François Hollande won the Presidency for the center-left Socialist Party. Just five years later, in the first round of the 2017 elections, the Socialist candidate, Benoît Hamon, won just 6.2 percent of the vote, putting him in fifth place. The French legislative contests a month later saw no recovery from this drubbing; the socialists won just 30 out of 577 seats (5.2%). In Germany, Chancellor Angela Merkel had seemed, before the 2017 election, to be taking up the mantle as leader of the free world. But after the AfD performed so well, prolonged struggles to form a governing coalition raised questions about her future in politics. Prospects for moderate social democratic parties seemed equally poor elsewhere in Europe. Similarly, after the Democrats' stunning loss in the US 2016 presidential elections, Republicans controlled not just the White House, but also the Senate and House of Representatives, 32 State legislatures, and 33 Governorships, in a sea of red across the map. By contrast, the Democrats controlled just 14 state legislatures and 16 Governorships, including only five states where they controlled both.[36]

Yet the varied fortunes of Authoritarian-Populist parties across European elections, notably their failure to break through into governments in France and even the Netherlands, led other commentators to conclude that instead of a fatal virus sweeping across the continent, the initial enthusiasm to emulate Brexit elsewhere on the Continent may have been limited by the English Channel.[37]

But the electoral success or failure of parties cannot be read straightforwardly by their mixed performance in winning elected office. The electoral system and institutional context, in particular, helps to explain these divergent outcomes and how the demand-side of votes in the electorate interacts with both the supply-side of party competition and the regulation of electoral markets. For example, as is evident from the 2017 UK general election and the 2017 French presidential and National Assembly contests, under Majoritarian-Plurality electoral systems, UKIP and the National Front face major hurdles in translating potential gains in voting into electoral office. This emphasizes the importance of the institutional context and provides grounds for more cautious interpretations about long-term shifts in the stability of European party systems in parliament and governments.

## The Legal Framework for Elections

Institutional rules matter for converting votes into seats and the design of electoral systems vary substantially. These contrasts are exemplified by the role of Proportional Representation with an exceptionally low threshold for parliamentary elections in the Netherlands, the Mixed Member Proportional system used for the Bundestag elections in Germany, and the Majoritarian Second Ballot electoral system employed in the French and Austrian presidential elections. Thus, Hofer was defeated with

46.2 percent of the vote in the Austrian presidential runoff. By contrast, the proportionality of the electoral system used in the Netherlands allowed Geert Wilder's PVV to gain second place with only 13.1 percent of the national vote. Similarly, in the 2016 US elections, the disparities between Hillary Clinton winning the popular vote by a margin of 2.9 million votes, but Donald Trump winning in the Electoral College, underlines the critical role of constitutional and legal arrangements.

Electoral laws and regulations structure opportunities for party competition within each country. Thus, Jackman and Volpert conclude: 'Electoral disproportionality (through the mechanism of thresholds) increasingly dampens support for the extreme right as the number of parliamentary parties expands. At the same time, multi-partyism increasingly fosters parties of the extreme right with rising electoral proportionality.'[38] Proportional Representation systems play an important role in the electoral fortunes of the radical right. Ignazi summarizes this view: 'As with every new/minor party, extreme right parties need low institutional/electoral thresholds to enter the political arena. The thresholds are low when the electoral system is proportional, the requirements to participate (financial deposits, signatures, etc.) are minimal, and when the first electoral contest is run as a "second-order" election.'[39] Proportional Representation systems with low thresholds facilitate party fragmentation and extremism, which, in turn, is associated with hung parliaments, unstable and ineffective governments, and, in extreme cases, even state failure. An extensive literature providing systematic comparisons of the relationship between electoral systems and party systems has developed since the seminal work of Douglas Rae.[40] Much of this has focused upon the evidence surrounding Duverger's first 'law': (1) 'The plurality single-ballot rule tends to party dualism.' The second claim is that (2) 'The double-ballot system and proportional representation tend to multipartyism.'[41] While originally stated as a universal law, Duverger subsequently suggested that these claims were only probabilistic generalizations.[42] The conditions under which this relationship holds, and its status as a law, have attracted considerable debate in the literature marked by continued reformulations of the original statement and many efforts to define precisely what is to 'count' as a party in order to verify these claims.[43]

Much of the literature, notably Lijphart's classic study, supports Duverger's generalization that Plurality electoral systems tend toward party dualism, while Proportional Representation is associated with multipartyism.[44] Previous research compared the results of the national election for the lower house of parliament in 170 contests worldwide from

1995 to 2000.[45] It found that the mean number of parliamentary parties (based on the simplest definition of parties as holding at least one seat) was around 5.22 under Majoritarian systems, 8.85 under Mixed systems, and 9.52 under Proportional Representation. In other words, nations using Proportional Representation had almost twice as many parliamentary parties as countries using Majoritarian electoral systems.[46]

The literature has also established evidence supporting the thesis that extremist parties flourish best under Proportional Representation.[47] For example, Katz compared the ideological position of parties in established democracies, using expert scales, under different electoral systems. He concluded: 'Clearly, Proportional Representation is associated with more small parties and with more extreme and ideological parties, while single-member plurality and other barriers to the representation of small parties are associated with fewer parties and a tendency towards an abbreviated political spectrum.'[48]

But the evidence deserves to be reexamined because the validity of this claim continues to be debated.[49] Moreover, the contrast is not simply between the main types of Majoritarian versus Mixed versus Proportional electoral systems, since important variations exist in more detailed rules. For example, among nations using Proportional Representation, the Netherland's single nation-wide constituency with a very low legal vote threshold (0.75%) allows the election of far more minor parties than Poland, with a 7 percent legal vote threshold and 52 small electoral districts. We also need to examine the impact of the mean district magnitude and the level of proportionality. Evidence presented in earlier work confirmed that electoral laws have an important impact on the electoral fortunes of the minor parties on the radical right.[50] This impact was generated primarily through their mechanical effects in translating votes into seats (especially the role of legal thresholds in Proportional Representation systems), more than their psychological effects in deterring voting for minor parties. In this study, we can update the analysis and evidence for these observations to see if they still hold.

Moreover, 'before-and-after' case studies, monitoring the impact of electoral reform over successive elections within particular countries, lend credence to the conventional assumption that these rules matter for Authoritarian-Populist party fortunes. In France, for example, the Front National won no seats in the 1981 parliamentary elections (held under the Second Ballot Majoritarian electoral rules), but suddenly gained 35 deputies (6.3%) under the Proportional Representation system tried in the 1986 parliamentary election, and then plummeted to only one deputy in 1988, despite an unchanged share of the vote, after Proportional Representation was repealed.[51] The impact of changes through electoral reform can also be demonstrated by the success of New Zealand First under the Mixed Member Proportional system first adopted in 1993, when New Zealand's two party system suddenly became a multimember system.[52]

Despite this body of evidence, the claim that Proportional Representation necessarily depresses popular support for extremist parties, continues to be questioned. Kitschelt, for example, analyzed voting for the radical right in Western Europe during the 1980s and found that this did not vary significantly and consistently under Majoritarian, Combined, or Proportional electoral systems. On this basis, he dismisses the role of institutional rules: 'While electoral laws have a non-negligible impact on party formation and the fragmentation of party systems taken by themselves, they explain very little about the actual dynamics of competition.'[53] Another study by Carter compared the electoral formulae used in 16 West European countries and estimated the mean share of the vote won by extreme right-wing parties from 1979 to 2002 under each major types of system. The study suggested that, contrary to popular assumptions, Proportional Representation systems do not promote party extremism: 'The share of the vote won by the West European parties of the extreme right in the period 1979–2002 appears unrelated to the type of electoral system in operation in the various countries.'[54]

The idea that the type of electoral system should affect support for minor parties is based on the notion of strategic voting. In highly disproportional systems, in Duverger's words: 'The electors soon realize that their votes are wasted if they continue to give them to the third party, whereas their natural tendency is to transfer their vote to the less evil of its two adversaries.'[55] The basic simple idea of '*strategic*' voting (also known as *'tactical,' 'insincere,'* or *'pragmatic'* voting) is that these considerations come into play among voters whose favorite party has a poor chance of winning in their constituency, but who have a preference between the parties perceived to be in first and second place.[56] The necessary but not sufficient conditions for casting a tactical vote are threefold: voters need to have a clear *rank order* of preferences among parties; voters need to have certain *expectations* based on the available information about how well each party is likely to do in their constituency; and, lastly, voters need to *rationally calculate* that the benefit of casting a ballot for their second preference party outweighs the costs of not supporting their favorite party. The 'wasted vote' thesis assumes that higher thresholds commonly found in Majoritarian elections deter rational citizens from casting a ballot for minor parties on the radical right, if they believe that their chosen party stands little chance of entering parliament or government office. Such rational supporters of the minor parties, the wasted vote thesis assumes, should either stay home, thereby reducing levels of turnout, or they should switch support to another party on strategic or tactical grounds. Citizens are expected to cast a 'strategic' vote for their second preference choice, in the belief that casting a ballot for smaller radical right parties under these rules will generate no direct policy benefits. This thesis assumes that people are instrumentally rational, that is, they care about whom they vote for only insofar as this affects the outcome in seats, thereby maximizing their utility in terms of policy outcomes. They are not concerned to express their symbolic support for a party, nor do they wish to swell the national vote share for their favorite party, nor attempt to exercise indirect influence over the policy platforms of other parties.

To look at the comparative evidence, Figure 9.3 compares the vote share and seat share of Authoritarian-Populist parties in parliamentary elections for the lower house of parliament held under the major types of electoral system from 1990 to 2015 in 27 European societies. Compared with systems of Proportional Representation, Majoritarian elections characterized by high electoral thresholds are expected to create disproportional results with greater mechanical and psychological hurdles for minor parties, and hence to prevent many Authoritarian-Populist parties from gaining parliamentary seats.

To classify the electoral laws during these years, we use data from the Varieties of Democracy project.[57] Electoral systems in the European countries under comparison are classified into three major families, each including a number of sub-categories: *majoritarian* formula (including first-past-the-post, second ballot, the block vote, single non-transferable vote, and alternative voting systems); *mixed* systems (incorporating both majoritarian and proportional formula); and *proportional formula* (including party lists as well as the single transferable vote systems).[58]

The results of the comparison in Figure 9.3 confirm the importance of the electoral system. Authoritarian-Populist parties won on average 6.8 percent of the vote but only 0.2 percent of seats under Majoritarian-Plurality systems. These systems penalize any small party with geographically dispersed support. Under Proportional Representation systems, however, Authoritarian-Populist parties won on average 11.9 percent of the vote but 12.3 percent of the seats. Countries with the Mixed electoral systems fell between these poles. There are many factors that might

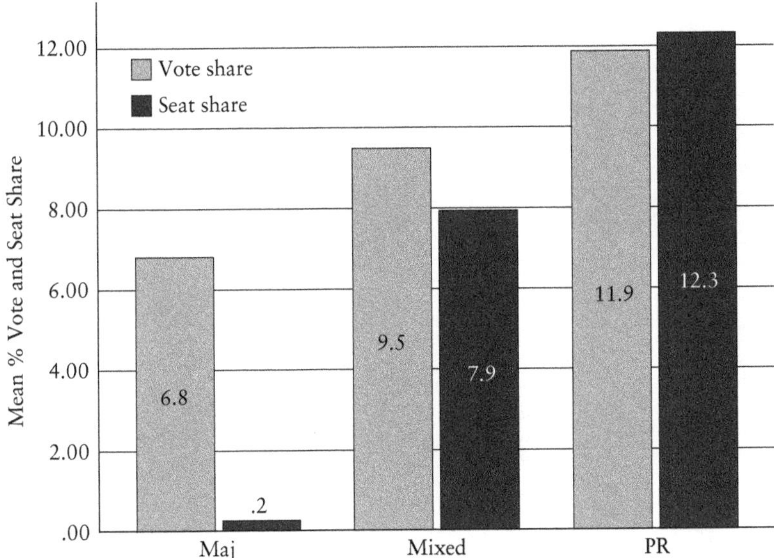


FIGURE 9.3. *Vote and seat share for Authoritarian-Populist parties by type of electoral system, 1990–2015*

*Notes:* The mean share of the vote won by all types of populist parties in national parliamentary elections in 27 societies from 1990 to 2015. The classification of types of parties is based on the CHES dataset. See Table 3A for the classification of Authoritarian-Populist parties. The classification of electoral systems for the lower house (or single chamber) of the national legislature is from V-Dem.

*Source:* Calculated from Holger Döring and Philip Manow. 2016. *Parliaments and governments database* (ParlGov) 'Elections' dataset. www.parlgov.org/.

influence European elections – from levels of turnout and party competition to the issues agenda and campaign media – so we cannot be sure that it is the rules that generated these observed patterns. Nevertheless further scrutiny showed that under the Mixed Member systems used in Germany and Hungary, in exactly the same contest and campaign, Authoritarian-Populist parties gained almost all their seats from the party list side of the ballot, with few winners from the plurality side. This supports the conclusion that the type of electoral system is an important factor in either generating substantial numbers of seats for minor parties, or systematically discriminating against smaller parties in favor of whichever party gets the largest share of the vote.[59]

For a closer look at the proportionality of the results for all populist parties (both libertarian and authoritarian), Figure 9.4 shows where parties fall in elections for the lower house of parliament from 2000 to 2015

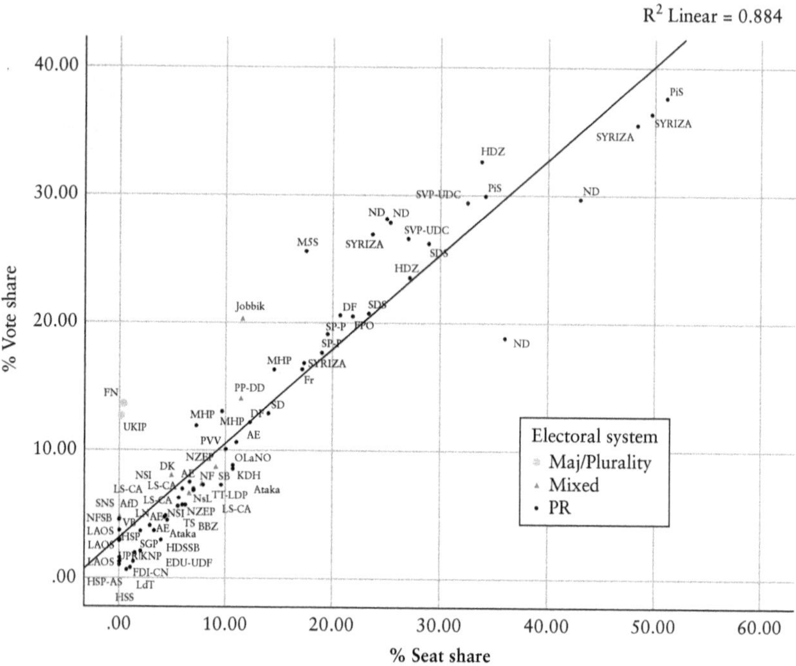


FIGURE 9.4. *The proportionality of votes–seats for Authoritarian-Populist parties, 2010*

*Notes:* The mean share of the vote and seats won by all types of populist parties in national parliamentary elections in 27 societies from 2000 to 2015. The classification of types of parties is based on the CHES dataset. See Table 3A for the classification of Authoritarian-Populist parties. The classification of electoral systems for the lower house (or single chamber) of the national legislature is from V-Dem.

*Source:* Calculated from Holger Döring and Philip Manow. 2016. *Parliaments and governments database* (ParlGov) 'Elections' dataset. www.parlgov.org/.

with the mean vote share depicted on the vertical axis and the seat share on the horizontal axis. The scatterplot shows that the National Front (FN) and UKIP, fighting in Majoritarian and Plurality systems, have some of the lowest vote–seat ratios. Several parties contesting elections under Mixed Member electoral systems, such as Jobbik and the Italian Five Star Movement are also penalized through the Single Member Plurality component. Under Proportional Representation, however, parties such as the Polish Law and Justice Party (PiS), Syriza and the Swiss People's Party perform strongly with much more favorable vote–seat ratios.

The Electoral College in the United States is a special case where the constitutional rules were designed to insure that even a close lead in the popular vote still generates a decisive outcome in Electoral College votes for the winning candidate, reinforcing the legitimacy of the winner. In the 2016 election, however, the Electoral College votes translated a 2.9 million vote lead for Hillary Clinton into a decisive electoral victory for Donald Trump, in large part because what matters for the Electoral College is not simply how many popular votes a candidate wins but also where these are distributed across the country. In this regard, the US uses a Plurality Single Member District system for voting and then doubles down in presidential contests through the Electoral College. The distribution of Electoral College votes is also weighted disproportionately toward more sparsely populated states, under-representing urbanized states.

Many other legal and constitutional arrangements governing all stages of the electoral cycle matter – including regulations concerning partisan gerrymandering and the allocation of seats through redistricting; the nomination process used to select candidates; the independence of the Electoral Management Body and the courts in any processes of appeal; the rules governing campaign funding and spending; regulations of campaign media, party broadcasts, and leadership debates; regulations of ballot access and gender or ethnic minority quotas; laws against electoral corruption, voter intimidation, and vote buying; and laws determining the allocation of Electoral College votes by the state. All of these arrangements influence the free and fair quality of contests and thus whether they meet international standards of electoral integrity.[60] Even long-established democracies such as the United States and Britain can have major flaws in electoral administration, restricting party competition.

Beyond the legal framework, party organizations also matter for the effective organizing of modern election campaigns. Thus, in the 2015 UK general election, the UK Independence Party had difficulties in organizing grassroots campaigns and raising sufficient funds capable of translating popular support for Euroscepticism into seats.[61] Fringe and minor parties generally lack the resources and experience essential for mounting effective election campaigns, lacking a strong grassroots membership base and often access to public funding subsidies available to parties in parliament. Weakly institutionalized minor parties are also particularly vulnerable to the sudden loss of charismatic leaders who may be difficult to replace, such as Jorg Haider standing down in the Freedom Party of Austria in 1986, as well as being at risk of internal factional splits and mergers.[62] The net result of these institutional contexts is that although we have seen that many Authoritarian-Populist parties compete for votes and seats, far fewer have held ministerial office in coalition governments, while still fewer have formed majority governments.

This suggests that comprehensive explanations cannot focus exclusively on demand-side factors (mass support in the electorate), without also taking into consideration supply-side factors, notably the institutional rules of the game. The results of recent elections indicate that Authoritarian-Populist parties and candidates face many organizational challenges in gaining office and translating popular support into seats, even though their level of voting has risen.

## Party Competition and the Issue Agenda

Patterns of party competition can also be critical for electoral success. Like a political game of chess, this includes how mainstream parties and leaders react to rising support for populist rivals. Chapter 7 suggested that party competition is multidimensional, so parties can place themselves strategically on the populist–pluralist dimension, the left–right economic dimension, and the authoritarian–libertarian dimension. When confronted by Authoritarian-Populist parties, mainstream center-right parties can either move further toward the policies of their rivals, or they can try to isolate Authoritarian-Populist politicians from any governing coalition. For example, Prime Minister Rutte attempted to deter support for Wilders' PVV in the Netherlands elections by adopting a hardline stance on immigration and tougher language toward Turkey. If mainstream parties adopt authoritarian-populist language and policies, this shifts the policy agenda, with potential consequences for government programs even if the populist parties fail to gain seats.

Evidence of the changing issue agenda underlying the traditional post-war left–right cleavage in party competition, and the growing importance of the cultural cleavage, was discussed in Chapter 7. Today economic inequality remains a major issue, and the classic bread-and-butter issues have not disappeared from the political agenda. But their relative prominence declined to such an extent that by the late 1980s, as Figure 9.6 shows, non-economic issues had become more prominent than economic issues in Western political party platforms. The growing salience of socially liberal values in society has stimulated the emergence of a new cultural cleavage in party competition that has undermined the post-war party systems. Today, many of the most heated conflicts are based on issues such as immigration and refugees, minority rights, the

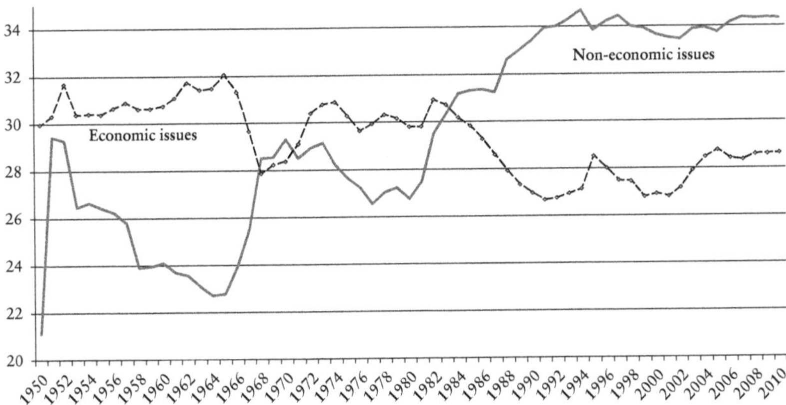


FIGURE 9.5. *Rising salience of non-economic issues in the party manifestos of 13 Western Democracies, 1950–2010*
*Notes:* Scores on the vertical axis are calculated by counting the number of economic issues, and non-economic issues mentioned in each party's electoral manifesto for the most recent election, weighted by each party's share of the vote in that election, giving equal weight to each country.
*Source:* Party Manifestos data from Austria, Belgium, Canada, Denmark, France, Germany, Ireland, Italy, Netherlands, Norway, Sweden, Switzerland, and United States, in Zakharov (2013).[63]

threat of terrorism, abortion rights, same-sex marriage, and more fluid gender identities, while support for progressive change on these issues increasingly comes from well-educated younger post-materialists, largely of middle-class origin.

Figure 9.5 illustrates how the issues emphasized in political party platforms evolved from 1950 to 2010 in 13 Western democracies (Austria, Belgium, Canada, Denmark, France, Germany, Ireland, Italy, the Netherlands, Norway, Sweden, Switzerland, and the United States). This figure shows the declining emphasis on economic issues, which dominated party programs until around 1968, when cultural issues raised by student protest briefly dominated the agenda. Economic issues once again dominated party competition and the policy agenda from 1970 to the early 1980s, when non-economic issues began to rise sharply. For the last two decades, non-economic issues have consistently dominated party competition and rival manifesto platforms by a wide margin.

For a more detailed comparison, Figure 9.6 breaks down the relative salience of economic and cultural issues in party manifestos from 1920 to 2016 in 21 Western democracies. The cultural issues have risen in

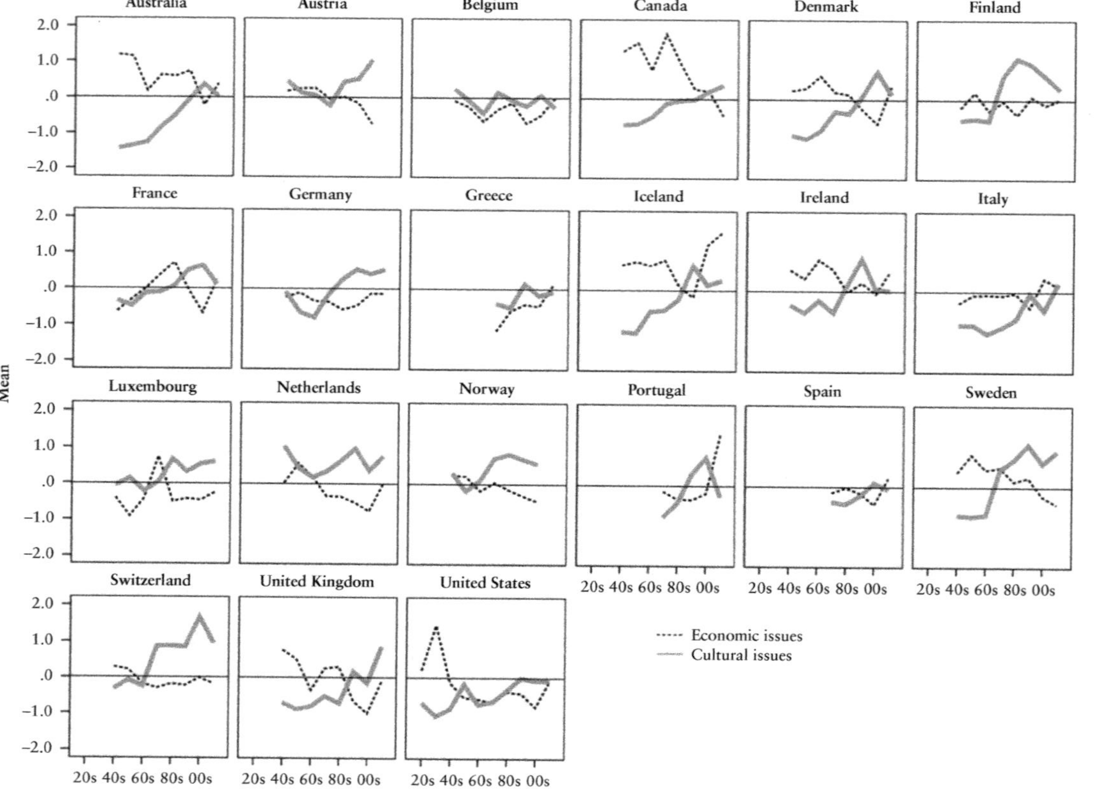


FIGURE 9.6. *Salience of economic and cultural issues, 1920–2016*

*Note:* The relative salience of economic and cultural issues from party manifestos 1920–2016. Importance is gauged by a standardized scale (Z-score) measuring the amount of coverage of issues in manifestos, irrespective of direction. 'Economic issues' includes free market economies, incentives, market regulation, protectionism, economic goals, demand management, economic growth, controlled economy, economic orthodoxy, and Marxist analysis. 'Cultural issues' include environmentalism, culture, social justice, national way of life, traditional morality, and multiculturalism.

*Source:* Comparative Manifestos Project, 2017.

importance in most of the societies under comparison – and have crossed over to become the most salient issues in many of the more prosperous societies such as Switzerland, Sweden, Austria, and Germany. The main exceptions are Portugal and Spain, where the economy has become a more important issue in recent years, partly because of the financial crash and debt crisis in the Eurozone.

## IV CONCLUSIONS

This chapter has demonstrated that the strength or weakness of Authoritarian-Populist parties cannot be read straightforwardly by scrutinizing where they have gained office – or failed to do so. Several findings deserve to be highlighted.

Firstly, the case-studies and comparative data show that the rules of the game matter a lot for how popular support at the ballot box translates into parliamentary seats – and how this feeds into the process of negotiating governing coalitions and allocating Ministerial portfolios. To give an example, in the 2015 UK General election UKIP won 12.6 percent of the nation-wide vote – but under the plurality system won only one seat in the House of Commons. By contrast, in the 2017 German Federal elections, the Alternative for Germany won exactly the same share of the nation-wide vote (12.6%) – and, under a Mixed Member Proportional system, catapulted into third position, winning 94 seats in the Bundestag. This outcome made it difficult for Angela Merkel to assemble a new government and led to uncertainty about the stability of German party politics.

In addition, Proportional Representation systems with low vote thresholds and high district magnitudes, as in the Netherlands, usually offers more opportunities for smaller parties. Majoritarian and Plurality systems usually favor larger parties, with a systematic winners bonus for the party with the largest share of the vote. These patterns hold unless there are special conditions, such as Trump's hostile take-over of the Republican Party in the primaries and then the role of the Electoral College in awarding the presidential candidate with the lower share of the vote the keys to the White House.

To examine how supply-side factors like the party campaigns, leaders, and institutional rules interact with demand-side factors in the electorate, we need to delve in greater depth into specific cases. To explore these issues, the next chapters turn to two events having immense consequences: the 2016 US elections that brought Donald Trump to the Presidency and the Brexit referendum.

## Notes

1. Daniele Albertazzi and Duncan McDonnell. 2015. *Populists in Power*. London: Routledge.
2. Steven Levitsky and Daniel Ziblatt. 2018. *How Democracies Die*. New York: Crown; Brian Klass. 2018. *The Despot's Apprentice: Donald Trump's Attack on Democracy*. New York: Hot Books; Yasha Mounk. 2018. *The People versus Democracy: How our Democracy is in Danger (and How to Save it)*. Cambridge, MA: Harvard University Press.
3. Kenneth Roth. 2018. 'The pushback against the populist challenge.' *Human Rights Watch*. www.hrw.org/world-report/2018/pushback-against-the-populist-challenge
4. Erica Chenoweth and Jeremy Pressman. February 7, 2017. This is what we learned by counting the women's marches.' *Washington Post/Monkey Cage*. www.washingtonpost.com/news/monkey-cage/wp/2017/02/07/this-is-what-we-learned-by-counting-the-womens-marches/.
5. German Lopez. January 23, 2018. 'A year after the first Women's March, millions are still actively protesting Trump.' *Vox*. www.vox.com/policy-and-politics/2018/1/23/16922884/womens-march-attendance.
6. Holger Döring and Philip Manow. 2016. *Parliaments and governments database (ParlGov)* 'Elections' dataset: www.parlgov.org/.
7. Cas Muddle. 2004. 'The populist zeitgeist.' *Government and Opposition* 39 (4): 541–563.
8. www.parlgov.org/.
9. Daphne Halikiopoulou and Sophia Vasilopoulou. 2014. 'Support for the far right in the 2014 European Parliament elections: A comparative perspective.' *Political Quarterly* 85 (3): 285–288; Nathalie Brack. 2015. 'The roles of Eurosceptic members of the European Parliament and their implications for the EU.' *International Political Science Review* 36 (3): 337–350; Cas Mudde. 2014. 'The far right and the European elections.' *Current History* March: 98–103. See also *European Parliament Results of the 2014 European elections*. www.europarl.europa.eu/elections2014-results/en/election-results-2014.html.
10. SORA Institute for Social Research and Consulting. *Election Day Survey*. December 4, 2016. www.sora.at/en/topics/electoral-behavior/election-analyses/bp-revote16.html.
11. Mario Gavenda and Resul Umit. 2016. 'The 2016 Austrian presidential election: A tale of three divides.' *Regional and Federal Studies* 26 (3): 419–432.
12. www.ucl.ac.uk/dutchstudies/an/SP_LINKS_UCL_POPUP/SPs_english/multicultureel_gev_ENG/pages/allochtonen.html.
13. Stijn Van Kessel. 2011. 'Explaining the electoral performance of populist parties: The Netherlands as a case study.' *Perspectives on European Politics and Society* 12 (1): 68–88.
14. Joop van Holsteyn and Josje M. den Ridder. 2003. 'In the eye of the beholder: The perception of the List Pim Fortuyn and the Parliamentary Elections of May 2002.' *Acta Politica* 38 (1): 69–88; Joop van Holsteyn.

2003. 'A new kid on the block: Pim Fortuyn and the Dutch Parliamentary Election of May 2002.' In Colin Rallings *et al.* Eds. 2003. *British Elections and Parties Review*. London: Frank Cass, pp. 29–46; Joop van Holsteyn and G.A. Irwin. 2003. 'Never a dull moment: Pim Fortuyn and the Dutch Parliamentary Election of 2002.' *West European Politics* 26 (2): 41–66.

15. Koen Vossen. 2016. *The Power of Populism: Geert Wilders and the Party for Freedom in the Netherlands*. New York: Routledge; Koen Vossen. 2011. 'Classifying Wilders: The ideological development of Geert Wilders and his Party for Freedom.' *Politics* 31 (3): 179–189.
16. www.pvv.nl/36-fj-related/geert-wilders/9674-speech-geert-wilders-in-praag-16-12-2017-menf-congres.html.
17. Matthijs Rooduijn. 2014. 'Vox populismus: A populist radical right attitude among the public?' *Nations and Nationalism* 20 (1): 80–92.
18. Pippa Norris. May 1, 2017. 'So is the wave of populist nationalism finished? Hardly.' *Washington Post/Monkey Cage*.
19. IPSOS. *2017 Election Presidentielle*. www.ipsos.fr/presidentielle2017/.
20. www.ipsos.fr/decrypter-societe/2017-06-11-1er-tour-legislatives-2017-sociologie-electorats-et-profil-abstentionnistes.
21. Nonna Mayer. 2013. 'From Jean-Marie to Marine Le Pen: Electoral change on the far right.' *Parliamentary Affairs* 66: 160–178; IPSOS. *2017 Election Presidentielle*. www.ipsos.fr/presidentielle2017/.
22. IFOP-Fiducial. April 2017. *Radioscopie de l'électorat du National Front*. Paris: IFOP-Fiducial for Le Journal du Dimanche and Sud Radio; www.ipsos.fr/decrypter-societe/2017-06-11-1er-tour-legislatives-2017-sociologie-electorats-et-profil-abstentionnistes.
23. www.ipsos.fr/decrypter-societe/2017-06-11-1er-tour-legislatives-2017-sociologie-electorats-et-profil-abstentionnistes.
24. Matthew Shugart and Martin Wattenberg Eds. 2003. *Mixed Member Electoral Systems*. Oxford University Press.
25. Alina Polyakova. 2015. 'The backward East? Explaining differences in support for radical right parties in Western and Eastern Europe.' *Journal of Comparative Politics* 8 (1): 49–74; Andrea Pirro. 2017. *The Populist Radical Right in Central and Eastern Europe: Ideology, Impact, and Electoral Performance*. London: Routledge.
26. A. Kovács. 2013. 'The post-communist extreme right. The Jobbik Party in Hungary.' In R. Wodak, M. KhosraviNik, and B. Mral. Eds. *Right-Wing Populism in Europe: Politics and Discourse*. London: Bloomsbury, pp. 223–234. For details, see www.jobbik.com/policies.
27. Attila Agh. 2016. 'The decline of democracy in East-Central Europe Hungary as the worst-case scenario.' *Problems of Post-Communism* 63 (5–6): 277–287.
28. Andrea Pirro. 2015. *The Populist Radical Right in Central and Eastern Europe: Ideology, Impact, and Electoral Performance*. London: Routledge; Attila Agh. 2016. 'The decline of democracy in East-Central Europe: Hungary as the worst-case scenario.' *Problems of Post-Communism* 63 (5–6): 277–287.

29. Cas Mudde. 2014. 'The 2014 Hungarian parliamentary elections or how to craft a constitutional majority.' *The Washington Post/Monkey Cage*. www.washingtonpost.com/news/monkey-cage/wp/2014/04/14/the-2014-hungarian-parliamentary-elections-or-how-to-craft-a-constitutional-majority/.
30. Pippa Norris, Thomas Wynter, Max Gromping, and Sarah M. Cameron. 2017. *The Year in Elections, 2017 Mid Year Report*. University of Sydney: Electoral Integrity Project.
31. OSCE. 2014. *Hungary-Parliamentary Elections, April 6, 2014*. Budapest: OSCE. www.osce.org/odihr/elections/117205.
32. https://freedomhouse.org/report/freedom-world/2016/hungary.
33. Attila Agh. 2016. 'The decline of democracy in East-Central Europe: Hungary as the worst-case scenario.' *Problems of Communism* 63 (5): 277–287; Andrea Pirro. 2017. *The Populist Radical Right in Central and Eastern Europe: Ideology, Impact, and Electoral Performance*. London: Routledge.
34. Seymour Martin Lipset and Stein Rokkan. 1967. *Party Systems and Voter Alignments*. New York: Free Press.
35. Sheri Berman. 2016. 'The specter haunting Europe: The lost left.' *Journal of Democracy* 27 (4): 69–76.
36. www.ncsl.org/research/about-state-legislatures/partisan-composition.aspx.
37. Larry Bartels. June 2017. 'The wave of right-wing populist sentiment is a myth.' www.washingtonpost.com/news/monkey-cage/wp/2017/06/21/the-wave-of-right-wing-populist-sentiment-is-a-myth/; Kim Sengupta. April 24, 2017. 'French election results shows that populist wave is not sweeping Europe.' *The Independent*. www.independent.co.uk/news/world/europe/marine-le-pen-france-election-macron-right-wing-populist-vote-not-sweeping-europe-a7700131.html.
38. Robert W. Jackman and Karin Volpert. 1996. 'Conditions favouring parties of the extreme right in Western Europe.' *British Journal of Political Science* 264: 501–522.
39. Piero Ignazi. 2003. *Extreme Right Parties in Western Europe*. Oxford: Oxford University Press, p. 205. See also Robert W. Jackman and Karin Volpert. 1996. 'Conditions favouring parties of the extreme right in Western Europe.' *British Journal of Political Science* 264: 501–522.
40. Douglas W. Rae 1967. *The Political Consequences of Electoral Laws*. 1971 revised edn. New Haven, CT: Yale University Press.
41. Maurice Duverger. 1954. *Political Parties: Their Organization and Activity in the Modern State*. New York: Wiley.
42. Maurice Duverger. 1986. 'Duverger's Law: Forty years later.' In Bernard Grofman and Arend Lijphart. Eds. *Electoral Laws and Their Political Consequences*. New York: Agathon Press.
43. Douglas W. Rae. 1967. *The Political Consequences of Electoral Laws*. 1971 revised edn. New Haven, CT: Yale University Press; William H. Riker. 1976. 'The number of political parties: A reexamination of Duverger's law.' *Comparative Politics* 9: 93–106; William H. Riker. 1982. 'The two-party system and Duverger's Law: An essay on the history of political science.' *American Political Science Review* 76: 753–766; William H. Riker. 1986.

'Duverger's Law revisited.' In Bernard Grofman and Arend Lijphart. Eds. *Electoral Laws and Their Political Consequences*. New York: Agathon Press; Arend Lijphart. 1994. *Electoral Systems and Party Systems: A Study of Twenty-Seven Democracies, 1945–1990*. Oxford: Oxford University Press; Rein Taagepera. 1999. 'The number of parties as a function of heterogeneity and electoral system.' *Comparative Political Studies* 32 (5): 531–548; Patrick Dunleavy and Françoise Boucek. 2003. 'Constructing the number of parties.' *Party Politics* 9 (3): 291–315.

44. Arendt Lijphart. 1994. *Electoral Systems and Party Systems: A Study of Twenty-Seven Democracies, 1945–1990*. Oxford: Oxford University Press. See also Richard S. Katz. 1997. *Democracy and Elections*. New York/Oxford: Oxford University Press.
45. Pippa Norris. 2004. *Electoral Engineering*. New York: Cambridge University Press, Chapter 4.
46. Similar patterns were found when the analysis was confined to the 37 nations classified worldwide by the Freedom House Gastil index as 'older' or 'newer' democracies. In these countries, the mean number of parliamentary parties was 7.4 in Majoritarian systems and 10.2 in Proportional Representation systems. The mean effective number of relevant parties was 3.0 in Majoritarian systems and 5.5 in Proportional Representation systems.
47. Arend Lijphart. 2001. 'The pros and cons – but mainly pros – of consensus democracy.' *Acta Politica* 35: 363–398; R.B. Andeweg. 2001. 'Lijphart v. Lijphart: The cons of consensus democracy in homogeneous societies.' *Acta Politica* 36: 117–128.
48. Richard S. Katz. 1997. *Democracy and Elections*. New York/Oxford: Oxford University Press, p. 154. See also David M. Farrell. 2001. *Electoral Systems: A Comparative Introduction*. London: Palgrave, pp. 199–200.
49. Matt Golder. 2003. 'Electoral institutions, unemployment and extreme right parties: A correction.' *British Journal of Political Science* 33 (3): 525–534; Elisabeth Carter. 2002. 'Proportional representation and the fortunes of right-wing extremist parties.' *West European Politics* 25 (3): 125–146; Matt Golder. 2003. 'Explaining variation in the electoral success of extreme right parties in Western Europe.' *Comparative Political Studies* 36 (4): 432–466; Elisabeth Carter. 2004. 'Does Proportional Representation promote political extremism? Evidence from the West European parties of the extreme right.' *Representation* 40 (2): 82–100.
50. Pippa Norris. 2005. *Radical Right: Voters and Parties in the Electoral Market*. New York: Cambridge University Press, Chapter 5.
51. Paul Hainsworth. 2004. 'The extreme right in France: The rise and rise of Jean-Marie Le Pen's Front National.' *Representation* 40 (2): 101–114.
52. Jack Vowles, Peter Aimer, Susan Banducci, and Jeffrey Karp. 1998. *Voters' Victory? New Zealand's First Election under Proportional Representation*. Auckland: Auckland University Press; Jack Vowles. 1995. 'The politics of electoral reform in New Zealand.' *International Political Science Review* 16 (1): 95–116; D. Denemark and Shaun Bowler. 2002. 'Minor parties and

protest votes in Australia and New Zealand: Locating populist politics.' *Electoral Studies* 21 (1): 47–67.

53. Herbert Kitschelt, with Anthony J. McGann. 1995. *The Radical Right in Western Europe: A Comparative Analysis*. Ann Arbor, MI: University of Michigan, Table 2.4, p. 60.
54. Elisabeth Carter. 2002. 'Proportional representation and the fortunes of right-wing extremist parties.' *West European Politics* 25 (3): 125–146; Elisabeth Carter. 2004. 'Does Proportional Representation promote political extremism? Evidence from the West European parties of the extreme right.' *Representation* 40(2): 82–100; Elisabeth Carter. 2005. *The Extreme Right in Western Europe: Success or Failure?* Manchester: Manchester University Press. It should be noted that both Kitschelt and Carter limited their comparison to examining the evidence for the effect of the major type of electoral systems on the radical right share of *voting*, rather than seats.
55. Maurice Duverger. 1954. *Political Parties: Their Organization and Activity in the Modern State*. New York: Wiley, p. 226.
56. For a detailed discussion, see Gary W. Cox. 1997. *Making Votes Count*. New York/Cambridge: Cambridge University Press.
57. Varieties of Democracy V7.1. Michael Coppedge, John Gerring, Steffan I. Lindberg, Svend-Erik Skaaning, Jan Teorell, David Altman, Michael Bernhard, M. Steven Fish, Adam Glynn, Allen Hicken, Carl Henrik Knutsen, Joshua Krusell, Anna Lührmann, Kyle L. Marquardt, Kelly McMann, Valeriya Mechkova, Moa Olin, Pamela Paxton, Daniel Pemstein, Josefine Pernes, Constanza Sanhueza Petrarca, Johannes von Römer, Laura Saxer, Brigitte Seim, Rachel Sigman, Jeffrey Staton, Natalia Stepanova, and Steven Wilson. 2017. *V-Dem [Country-Year/Country-Date] Dataset v7.1* Varieties of Democracy (V-Dem) Project.
58. It can be argued that a further distinction needs to be drawn between majority and plurality elections, given the higher effective electoral threshold used in the former. Nevertheless, the classification used in this study is more parsimonious, the ballot structure used for Plurality and Majoritarian elections is similar (casting a vote for a single candidate), and it reflects the standard typology used in the literature.
59. Pippa Norris. 2004. *Electoral Engineering*. New York: Cambridge University Press.
60. Pippa Norris. 2015. *Why Elections Fail*. New York: Cambridge University Press.
61. David Cutts, Matthew Goodwin, and Caitlin Milazzo. 2017. 'Defeat of the People's Army? The 2015 British general election and the UK Independence Party (UKIP).' *Electoral Studies* 48 (3): 70–83.
62. Scott Mainwaring and Timothy R. Scully. Eds. 1995. *Building Democratic Institutions: Party Systems in Latin America*. Stanford, CA: Stanford University Press.
63. Alexei Zakharov. 2013. 'Changes in European voting patterns: Is the new left–right dimension becoming more important, and why.' Working Paper. Higher School of Economics, Moscow, Russia. https://lcsr.hse.ru/en/zakharov.

# 10

# Trump's America

The outcome of the 2016 American presidential election can be attributed to many situation-specific factors, such as the Obama legacy, the 2016 primaries, campaign strategies and finance, news coverage, and the performance of the economy.[1] The result was determined by the Electoral College, which awarded Trump the White House, although Hillary Clinton won almost three million more votes. Suspicions swirl about FBI-chief Comey's intervention during the campaign and Russian hacking of emails and trolling on social media.[2] Nation-specific events clearly played a role, as in any election. But Trump's victory was rooted in cultural changes that began decades earlier. It began with the intergenerational shift from materialist to post-materialist values that led to growing support for socially liberal attitudes, among younger and educated Americans in the 1960s and 1970s. Reflecting the changing values of their electorates, the two major parties gradually shifted to become more homogeneous internally in their cultural positions and more polarized between parties. Over successive decades, as Southern segregationists deserted the party, Democrats became steadily more consistently socially liberal. And, starting with Nixon's strategy of appealing to Southern conservatives, the Republicans gradually became increasingly socially conservative. From the mid-1990s onwards, these developments led to a growing generational gap in the American electorate. Birth cohorts sorted their support for the major parties, with younger cohorts becoming a core part of the post-materialist and socially liberal Democratic coalition under Bill Clinton, while the older generation moved toward the socially conservative GOP. The defeat of the Republican mainstream nominees in the 2016 primaries, and Trump's eventual victory, was a culmination of these long-term developments, with his campaign energizing older and non-college educated white men who felt that their most-cherished values and their way of life were being eroded by socially liberal cultural currents.

To explain the context of these developments, we will briefly discuss the historical roots of populism in America and present longitudinal evidence of partisan sorting in Congress and the electorate that laid the foundations for the 2016 elections. The outcome depended upon a contingent alignment of candidates, issues, and events. Nevertheless, Trump's victory was built on an authoritarian-populist faction of the Republican Party that had been growing for many years. His strategy to reach the White House exploited divisive and controversial cultural wedge issues about race, gender, religion, and nation that have divided American party politics for decades. We then will examine the cultural trends in post-materialist values and socially liberal attitudes in America and trace the relationship between these values and patterns of voting behavior since the early seventies. Building on this foundation, we will examine how economic and cultural factors shaped whether people voted for Clinton or Trump in the 2016 presidential election. The concluding part of this chapter reflects on these findings' implications for party polarization and cultural cleavages in American politics.

## THE ROOTS OF AMERICAN POPULISM

America has a long tradition of populist leaders and movements emerging to lambast the establishment and demand power for the people, but no one before Trump had achieved a hostile take-over of one of the major parties and gained the Presidency.[3] The most successful of the early movements, the People's Party, emerged from the populist movement in 1892 as a left-wing coalition of cotton and wheat farmers and the labor movement, railing against capitalism, banks, and gold.[4] This party was short-lived, however, merging with the Democratic Party in 1896. Some regard this movement as progressive, but others see it as a nostalgic reaction against industrial America. The populism rhetorical style was manifest in demagogic spokesmen like Father Charles Coughlin in the 1930s, who attracted a massive radio listenership through his strident left-wing anti-Semitic appeals.[5] Radical populism also characterized outspoken leaders like Huey Long, elected Governor and then Senator for Louisiana on a Share the Wealth program, calling for radical economic redistribution in the wake of the Great Depression. The style was also exemplified by Governor George Wallace in the 1960s, elected in Alabama on a Southern segregationist platform.[6]

The phenomenon did not originate when Donald Trump descended the golden escalator at Trump Tower on June 15, 2016 to announce his presidential bid, with racist comments disparaging Mexican immigrants as drug dealers, criminals, and rapists ('And some, I assume, are good people').[7] He inherited the populist mantle pioneered by Ross Perot's third-party challenge in 1992, when Perot presented himself as a modern-day common-sense Mr. Deeds promising to restore a healthy America by cleaning up 'the system' on behalf of 'the people.'[8] Presidential candidates – for both major parties – have used populist language, as in the campaign speeches of Jimmy Carter and Ronald Reagan.[9] Patrick Buchanan's 1992 run for the GOP nomination was cut from the same cloth; as he said at the 1992 GOP convention: 'The agenda Clinton & Clinton would impose on America – abortion on demand, a litmus test for the Supreme Court, homosexual rights, discrimination against religious schools, and women in combat units – that's change, all right. But it is not the kind of change America needs. It is not the kind of change America wants. And it is not the kind of change we can abide in a nation we still call God's country.'[10] Trump's roots can also be traced back to Sarah Palin's critique of the 'Washington establishment' as McCain's running mate in 2008, and to the Tea Party organization launched the following year – a predominately white, male, movement of disgruntled anti-government social conservatives stoking racial resentment and welfare chauvinism, with a strong authoritarian streak.[11] And subsequent candidates, such as Roy Moore's controversial Alabama primary bid for the Senate, suggest that Trump will not be the last American politician drawn from this tradition. Authoritarian populism has now spread well beyond President Trump to infect the bloodstream of the body politic, including the Congressional Republican Party leadership, media outlets like Breitbart News and Fox TV, and extremist white supremacist groups.

During the contemporary era, many previous Republican and Democratic presidential contenders have used populist rhetoric.[12] Signs of growing polarization between liberal and conservative members have been observed in Congressional parties for decades. In the mid-1950s, the Democratic Party started to shift its position on civil rights, a critical issue dividing Northern liberal representatives from Southern segregationists. In the 1960s, during the era of President Johnson, Congressional Democrats from Northern states moved in a more socially liberal direction on issues such as the War on Poverty, Civil Rights, and the Equal Rights Amendment. When the liberal wing of the Democratic Party pushed through the 1964 Civil Rights Act, it began shifting their core base toward African-Americans, Hispanics, and other ethnic minorities. Segregationist white Southerners, who previously provided a solid bloc of support for the Democrats, increasingly shifted to the Republicans.[13] During these years, the Republican Party remained fairly moderate and mainstream – with the notable exception of the 1964 Goldwater presidential campaign, in which the Republicans suffered a crushing defeat. From the mid-1970s onwards, however, the Congressional Republican Party gradually shifted toward more consistent social conservatism on key issues, including abortion, affirmative action, and LGBTQ rights, accompanied by a growing role for the GOP evangelical base. Under President Reagan, however, the GOP remained a broad coalition combining three factions: traditional 'country club' Republicans, small-government, tax cut fiscal conservatives, and the Christian Right. The timing of these ideological shifts in the leadership of each of the major parties over successive decades can be characterized as a staggered realignment. The Congressional Democratic and Republican Parties, once big-tent catch-all coalitions, sorted into two distinct camps divided along increasingly sharply drawn ideological lines.[14]

The story of party polarization in Congress is illustrated by the longitudinal trends shown by roll call voting records, monitoring the median liberal or conservative ideology of each of the major parties' members in Congress.[15] Figure 10.1 illustrates party positions using standardized scores on which a lower line means a more liberal party, while a higher line indicates a more conservative party. The evidence shows the Congressional Democratic Party becoming increasingly liberal since the mid-twentieth century; shifting 16 points from a score of –22 around 1948, when Truman submitted a civil rights plan to Congress and ended racial segregation in the armed forces, down to –38 during the Trump era. The Congressional Republican Party reacted somewhat later, moving under successive administrations from the mid-1970s onwards in a steadily more conservative direction; the party scored +.25 under Nixon, but +.49 in the 115th Congress today, a 24-point shift.

Many factors help to explain this staggered realignment and growing party polarization in Congress.[16] We suggest that one major driver was the transformation in the priority given to cultural issues in the party platforms of the major US parties. As the American electorate became increasingly polarized over divisive cultural issues, the party manifestos reflected these cleavages. The evolving policy agenda is illustrated in Figure 10.2, drawing on data from the Comparative Manifesto Project.[17] 'Economic issues' are defined here as the *proportion* of coverage in party

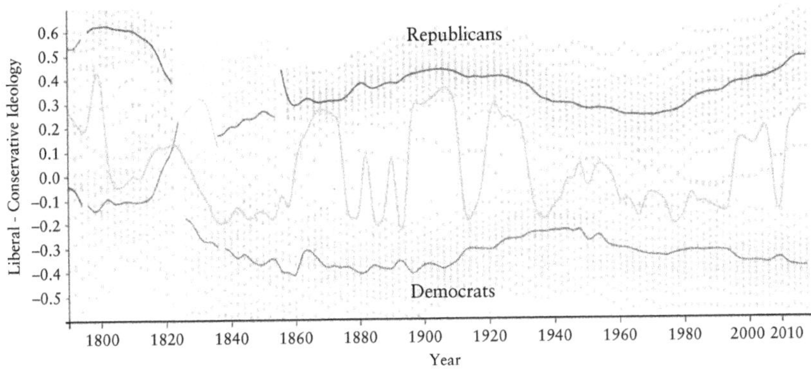


FIGURE 10.1. *Party polarization in Congress*
*Note:* This chart shows the ideologies of major parties in Congress according to DW-Nominate. The top line is the Republicans and the bottom line is the Democrats. Each line represents the median (mid-point) ideology of members of a single party. A lower line means a more liberal party, while a higher line means a more conservative party. The original dataset was developed by Keith T. Poole and Howard Rosenthal.
*Source:* DW-Nominate. https://voteview.com/parties/all.

programs devoted to issues such as free market economies, incentives, market regulation, protectionism, economic goals, and economic growth. By contrast, 'cultural issues' are issues such as environmentalism, culture, social justice, traditional morality, and multiculturalism. The salience of issues is monitored through the total *amount* of attention issues are given in manifesto programs for each party, regardless of their direction.

The results in Figure 10.2 show that bread-and-butter economic policies were the primary focus in the programs of both major parties during the Interwar decades, especially after the Stock Market crash led to the massive unemployment and the economic dislocation of the Great Depression and its aftermath. The two major parties reflected the classic left–right economic cleavages, with Roosevelt quickly abandoning austerity and orthodox fiscal and budgetary policies in favor of New Deal programs reflecting Keynesian ideas of economic management, emphasizing government regulation of the marketplace, and the expansion of spending on federally funded emergency relief and public works programs designed to put Americans back to work, reduce widespread poverty and hunger, and win World War II. The post-war decades saw the growing salience of important cultural issues, notably the Civil Rights movement, desegregation, and the Civil Rights Act of 1957 prohibiting discrimination by federal and state governments based on race, color, sex, and national origin – and

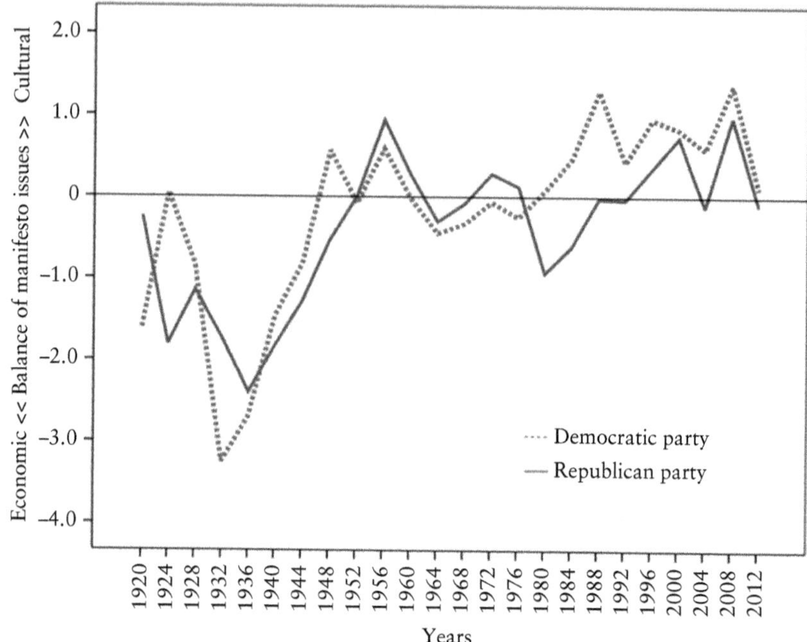


FIGURE 10.2. *The rising salience of cultural issues on the Democrat and Republican Party platforms*

*Note:* The relative salience of economic and cultural issues from party manifestos for the major US parties from 1920 to 2016. Relative importance is calculated using standardized scales (Z-score) measuring the amount of coverage of issues in manifestos, irrespective of direction. 'Economic issues' includes free market economies, incentives, market regulation, protectionism, economic goals, demand management, economic growth, controlled economy, economic orthodoxy, and Marxist analysis. 'Cultural issues' include environmentalism, culture, social justice, national way of life, traditional morality, and multiculturalism. The balance of issue salience is estimated as the mean economic score minus the mean cultural score.

*Source:* Comparative Manifestos Project, 2017.

the backlash among Southern segregationists who fled to the Republican Party. But these decades also saw a rough balance of concern about the relative importance of material economic policies and those reflecting cultural issues in both major party platforms. This pattern persisted until the mid-1970s and early 1980s, when the Democratic platform started to shift toward giving far greater emphasis on cultural rather than economic issues. As Figure 10.2 shows, with a staggered realignment, starting around the mid-1990s, the Republican platform followed suit. As a result, during the last two decades the policy platforms of both major parties have come to offer increasingly divergent positions on a wide range of social issues, such as reproductive rights and affirmative action, race relations and criminal justice, same sex marriage and transsexual rights, environmental protection and climate change, sexual harassment, the role of religion, and immigration. On economic issues, such as healthcare or taxation, there is room for bargaining between the leaders of both parties. On cultural issues, however, politics is more often depicted as a battleground between good and evil where compromise and negotiation are signs of moral weakness. Combative debates demonize opponents, compromise becomes difficult, and language is infused with a sense of moral self-righteousness on both sides.

Indications of the right-ward drift in the House Republican Party in recent years include the 2004 'Gingrich revolution,' where the GOP won control of both the House and the Senate on a socially conservative and small government platform. The revolution was fueled by populist language, campaigns focused on wedge issues, and a new generation of freshmen elected on a radical agenda to balance the budget, cut taxes, and reform government. These short-term gains were tempered, however, by Gingrich's willingness to work with President Clinton after the Democratic victory in 2006. These events were followed by the unexpected choice of Sarah Palin as the Republican Party nominee for Vice President and John McCain's running mate in the 2008 elections. Her populist outsider-status, folksy style, anti-elitist rhetoric, and socially conservative views appealed to the grassroots base of the party. Similar forces led the following year to the emergence of the Tea Party organization as an anti-government, low-tax Republican movement discontented with Washington DC, the election of President Barack Obama, and the moderate position of the Congressional GOP leadership.[18] Well before Trump, in the 2008 Democratic primary, authoritarian values mattered more than income, ideology, gender, age, and education in predicting whether voters preferred Hillary Clinton over Barack Obama.[19] Since the mid-1990s, in a process of political sorting, socially conservative voters steadily drifted from the Democratic to the Republican Party, catalyzing a new generation gap in the voting base of both the major parties.

Despite these historical roots in American politics and society, it is almost impossible for third parties to gain office in the US due to institutional barriers, including the first-past-the-post (Single Member Plurality) electoral system for legislative office, gerrymandered House districts favoring the incumbent, the Electoral College used for the White House, as well as Republican and Democrat restrictions on state laws governing ballot access.[20] The Majoritarian electoral system of Single Member Plurality Districts and the Electoral College used in the United States places almost insuperable institutional barriers on the success of independent candidates and minor parties, especially if their support is geographically dispersed.[21] Yet in 2016, populist forces broke through in the primaries and nomination process for the presidential election, despite these obstacles, stimulating major revolts *within* each of the two major parties – with Donald Trump, backed by older, less-educated rural Americans, capturing the Republican nomination and then the White House, while Bernie Sanders, endorsed by younger, better-educated supporters, mounted a strong challenge for the Democratic nomination and policy platform.

We argue that a tipping point has been reached in the gradual erosion of the socially conservative hegemony of traditional values in America. This has triggered a negative authoritarian counter-reaction among the moral conservatives threatened by these cultural shifts – a backlash that has been especially powerful in mobilizing older generations of white men in rural communities. Although a shrinking sector of the population, they remain a bare majority of those who actually vote, due to age-related differences in turnout.[22] Numerous fringe movements outside the mainstream have long sought to exploit the politics of racial resentment, hate-speech, and anti-Muslim sentiments.[23] But in the past, the leadership of both major parties was unwilling to condone extreme forms of racism, nativism, or Islamophobia – out of respect for the core principles of American democracy. Party polarization frayed the consensus about these conventions in the heated battles, since Bush versus Gore in 2000, over US state laws governing processes of electoral registration and balloting.[24] But the liberal consensus about America's leadership role in the world, and the benefits of global free trade, international cooperation, and liberal democracy largely held among leaders of both major parties.

Trump's victory was the culmination of these long-term developments – but the President has been further deepening divisions between the major parties, and within the Congressional GOP, on the classic wedge issues of race/ethnicity, immigration, and gender. Trump's defeat of his rivals to become the Republican nominee, his belligerent campaign against Hillary Clinton, and the shock of his unexpected victory in the 2016 Electoral College, posed a major challenge to the liberal consensus, and energized the cultural backlash in the American electorate. Trump galvanized support through authoritarian-populist appeals, especially by articulating a dog-whistle version of racist and xenophobic rhetoric, and by appeals to strongman executive rule, disregarding conventional constitutional checks and balances. Though his racist appeal was more subtle than that of the 1960s Southern segregationists, it is unmistakable.[25] He first became a prominent political figure as a leader of the birther movement questioning whether Barack Obama was born in the US. Trump pledged to build a wall along the Mexican border to stop the influx of Mexican 'criminals and rapists.' In seeking to implement a ban against entry from several Muslim-majority countries, President Trump has repeatedly implied that all Muslim immigrants are potential terrorists, while failing to condemn outright extremist groups like the neo-Nazis engaged in the violent Charlottesville, VA protests, and re-tweeting extremist Britain First Islamophobic hate videos. After entering the White House, when Trump's speeches constantly attack 'fake news' media, when he claims falsely that he won the 2016 election by a landslide of popular votes, when he charges that the American system is 'rigged' and elections are 'fraudulent,' when he assaults the intelligence services as 'Hillary-sympathizers' and judges as 'biased,' when he cries 'lock her up' against 'Crooked Hillary,' when he stokes racist hatred, Islamophobia, misogyny, and white supremacism, he is damaging public confidence in the principles and institutions of American democracy. His campaign rhetoric appeals directly to social conservatives concerned with their declining position. He addressed this group's concern by raising their moral status, describing 'hard-working' Americans as victims of globalization, voicing concern about elites, drawing strong moral boundaries toward undocumented immigrants, refugees, and Muslims, and stressing the traditional role of men as protectors of wives, mothers, and daughters.[26]

In practice, the Trump administration has joined Republicans in Congress to scrap many government regulations that protect families and the environment and undermined the Affordable Care Act (Obamacare). Tax reform, the major legislative achievement of Trump's first year in office, has closely followed the traditional agenda of the GOP leadership, donors, and organized interests, enriching corporations by reducing taxes on profits, capital gains, and dividends, and benefitting big ticket donors, like the Koch brothers, while also weakening healthcare and exacerbating government debt. These policies worsen economic inequality, already at the highest levels in America since the nineteenth century.[27]

We argue that the apparent paradox of ordinary, hard-working blue-collar Americans voting against their own narrow economic self-interests by supporting Trump and conservative Republican politicians who lean heavily toward the wealthy and powerful corporate interests is motivated by a powerful emotional response. It is not just that Evangelical Christian leaders and Republican politicians are duping voters by directing their anger away from the 'real' sources of grievance.[28] Millions of older white Americans living in declining communities feel, with some justification, that they have become 'strangers in their own land.'[29] They see themselves as victims of immigration and affirmative action policies. Men with traditional views of masculinity feel undermined and ridiculed by feminists.[30] Extreme alt-right groups and leaders claim that 'white identity' and Western civilization is under attack by multicultural forces.[31] They feel betrayed by 'line-cutters' – black people, immigrants, women, and gays – whom they see as jumping ahead in the queue for social mobility. They see themselves as patronized by arrogant and self-righteous coastal liberals who tell them whom to feel sorry for and then dismiss them as bigots or deplorables when they don't. Trump's supporters are attracted by appeals to turn back the clock to earlier eras – exemplified by the President's campaign to bring back the greeting 'Merry Christmas!' that had been taken for granted during earlier decades, but had become a non-denominational 'Happy Holidays!' during an era of rapid cultural change. The nostalgic appeal of a mythical Norman Rockwell America calls for a return to taking pride in America's dominant world role, respect for military service, churchgoing, marriage and children, and a world in which the male breadwinner could give his family a more comfortable lifestyle than their parents, through hard work. Unlike other politicians, Donald Trump provides emotional support when he expresses racist, ethnocentric, homophobic, and xenophobic views that transgress politically correct language, and outrage liberals.[32] The backlash theory argues that Trump was able to be so successful in exploiting cultural divisions because a gradual process of cultural change had reached a tipping point by 2016 (see Figure 2.1). This amplified a conservative counter-attack against the long-term spread of post-material values and socially liberal attitudes in American society that brought growing polarization along ideological lines, and increased the salience of cultural issues.

Trump voters and Clinton voters live in two different worlds. Figure 10.3 illustrates their perceptions of who is discriminated against in contemporary American society. It shows the mean score of Trump voters' perceptions of which groups are victims of discrimination, minus the mean scores of Clinton voters. Scores to the left of the zero point indicate that Clinton voters are more likely than Trump voters to see a given

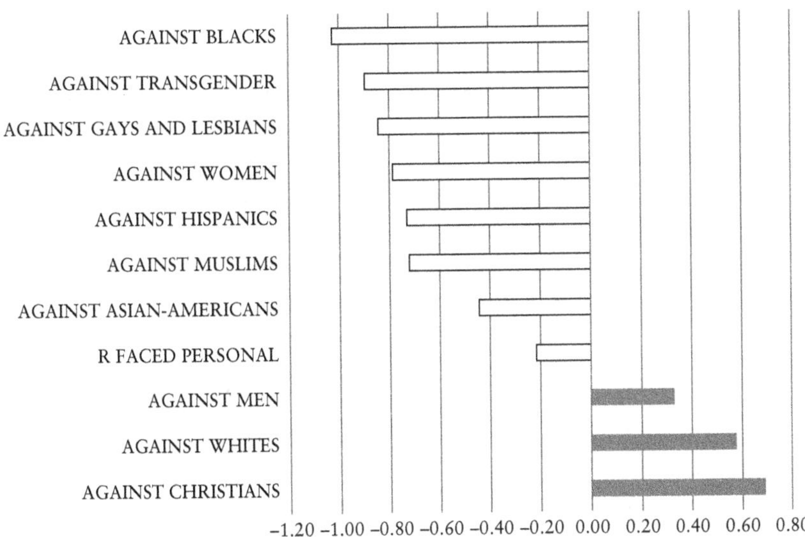


FIGURE 10.3. *Perceptions of the degree of group discrimination by Trump and Clinton voters, US 2016*
*Notes:* Estimates are calculated as the mean scores for Trump voters minus the mean scores for Clinton voters.
*Source:* 2016 American National Election Study.

group as being discriminated against. Scores to the right of the zero point indicate that Trump voters are more likely to see that group as being discriminated against. As Figure 10.3 indicates, Clinton voters are relatively likely to see blacks, transgender people, gays, and women as victims of discrimination – while Trump voters are likelier to see Christians, whites, and men as victims of discrimination.

The unprecedented economic and physical security that Western societies experienced in the decades after World War II and the dramatic expansion of higher education led to an intergenerational shift toward post-materialist values, bringing greater emphasis on individual choice, tolerance of multicultural diversity, freedom of expression, open borders, democratization, environmental protection, gender equality, and acceptance of the rights of gays, handicapped people, and religious minorities. From the start, these cultural changes provoked a reaction among the older and less secure strata threatened by the erosion of respect for familiar values, declining deference toward traditional authority, and declining religious faith, producing a 'Silent Counter-revolution.'[33]

Moreover, as Figure 10.2 demonstrates, from the 1970s onwards, the cultural political agenda introduced by post-materialists gradually came to overshadow the classic left–right economic cleavage, drawing attention away from the class politics of redistribution and welfare. Post-materialists are concentrated among the more secure, mobile, and better-educated strata, and they are relatively open to social change and intolerant of those who are not. Consequently, though recruited from the strata of society that traditionally supported right-wing parties, they have gravitated toward parties that endorse cultural change – weakening social class voting. Authoritarian-Populist parties have been present for decades in the parliaments of some European countries, and these forces remained an extremist fringe in the US and UK, where it was almost impossible for them to gain seats because both countries have first-past-the-post electoral systems with high vote thresholds.[34] But in 2016, populist movements broke through in the US, stimulating major upheavals within each of the two major parties – with Trump, backed by older, less-secure voters, capturing the Republican presidential nomination and Sanders, backed by younger, better-educated voters, mounting a strong challenge for the Democratic nomination. This breakthrough reflected the growing salience of cultural issues.

## AMERICAN TRENDS IN POST-MATERIALISM AND SOCIAL LIBERALISM

Does our theory fit the American evidence? Let's start by examining the impact of post-materialist values since the early 1970s. There is no reason why post-materialists would necessarily support Democratic candidates and materialists would support Republicans – unless the parties shifted from the traditional left–right dimension to the cultural dimension. The extent to which they did so has fluctuated over time, as Figure 10.4 demonstrates. This figure shows how strongly the US presidential vote was correlated with materialist/post-materialist values from 1972 to 2016, using three different databases that are not directly comparable but provide a rough idea of how strongly US presidential elections were influenced by cultural issues over the past five decades. From 1972 through 1992, the National Election Surveys (ANES) included the four-item materialist/post-materialist values battery and as the graph indicates, the strength of the correlation between values and reported presidential vote varied considerably from one presidential election to the next.

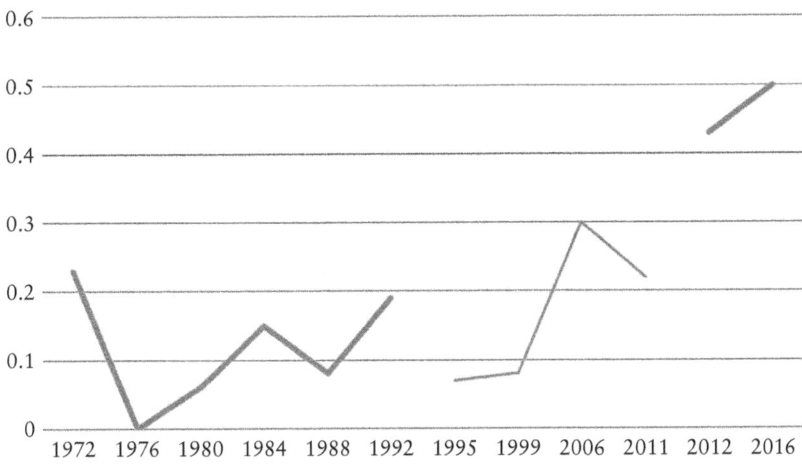


FIGURE 10.4. *Vote and materialist/post-materialist values, 1972–2016*
*Note:* Correlations between US presidential vote (or party preference) and materialist/post-materialist values. — (1976–1992) ANES surveys, using the 4-item index; — (1995–2011) WVS surveys, using the 12-item index asking about party vote (instead of Presidential vote); — (2012–2016) WVS surveys, using the 12-item index.
*Sources:* American National Election Study (ANES) 1972–92; WVS 1995.

The 1972 presidential election mobilized student protesters behind George McGovern in a counter-cultural movement that demanded an end to the Vietnamese war, against Richard Nixon who stood for order, economic growth, and other materialist goals. Post-materialists backing socially liberal cultural values were still a relatively small share of the electorate and Nixon won handily, but the cultural cleavage had a significant impact, producing a .23 correlation between values and the vote.

The 1976 presidential election pitted Jimmy Carter, an outsider to Washington DC politics and a born-again Christian from Plains, Georgia, against Gerald Ford, a mainstream Republican who campaigned on traditional issues. In Carter's victory, the correlation between post-materialist values and the presidential vote fell to zero. In the 1980 contest between Carter and Reagan, the correlation was only slightly higher. It rose to .15 in the 1984 contest between Reagan and Mondale, declined to .08 in the 1988 contest between Bush and Dukakis, and then rose to .19 in the 1992 Clinton–Bush election.

After 1992, the ANES no longer included the materialist/post-materialist battery so we turn to data from the World Values Surveys (WVS) to trace the impact of values, using the 12-item materialist/post-materialist values battery. Being designed for world-wide comparisons, the WVS monitors

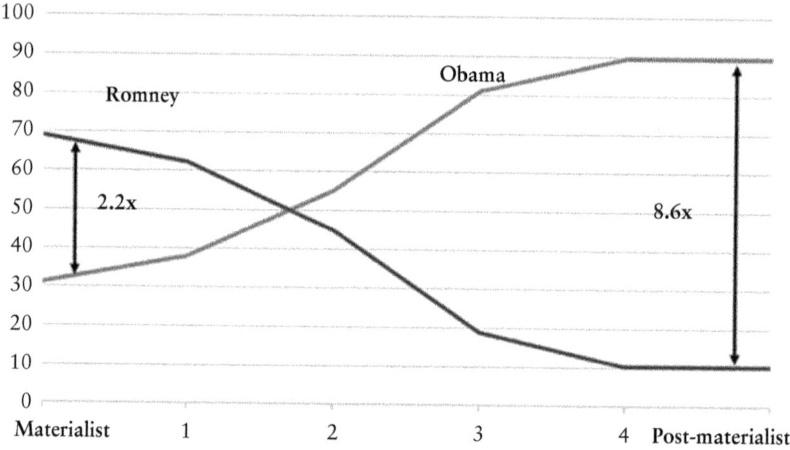


FIGURE 10.5. *The 2012 US presidential vote by materialist/post-materialist values*
*Source:* World Values Survey, US 2012.

which political party the respondent supports, rather than one's vote for specific candidates. As we have suggested, materialist/post-materialist values are not necessarily linked with support for a given party unless that party promotes a materialist or post-materialist agenda, and in the 1990s we find relatively weak correlations between values and party preference. But after 2000, we find relatively strong correlations, as both parties prioritized cultural over economic issues.

The most dramatic such phenomenon occurred in 2008 and 2012, when the Democratic Party nominated an African-American, Barack Obama, as their presidential candidate. This was a sharp symbolic break with the politics of race in previous American elections. The most recent US World Values Survey asked which candidate the respondent voted for in both the 2012 and the 2016 presidential elections, and measured materialist/post-materialist values (using the 12-item battery). The correlations between values and vote are dramatically stronger than previously. The correlation between values and the reported presidential vote in 2012 was .43, and the correlation between values and presidential vote in 2016 was .50. In contrast with its modest role in some previous elections, in recent presidential contests, materialist/post-materialist values became a substantial factor – dwarfing the standard demographic predictors linked with social class, and causing generation gaps to become much stronger predictors.

Figure 10.5 depicts the relationship between values and vote in the 2012 presidential election as we move from the pure materialist type (which

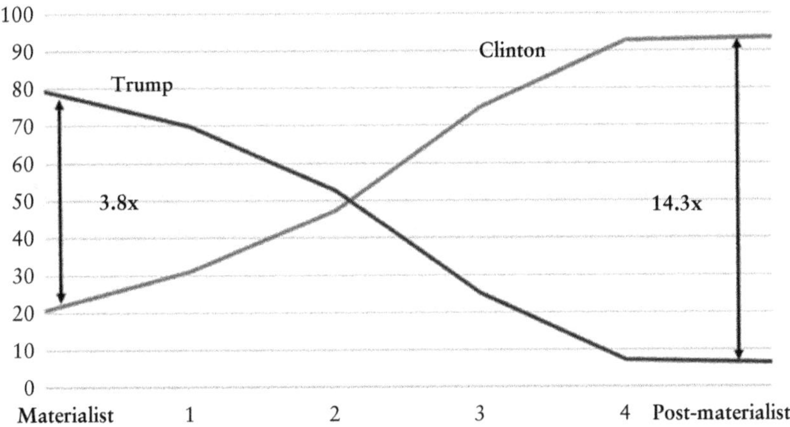


FIGURE 10.6. *The 2016 US presidential vote by materialist/post-materialist values*
*Source:* World Values Survey, US 2017.

gave low priority to the post-materialist goals) to the pure post-materialists (which gave high priority to all five of the post-materialist goals). Pure materialists were 2.2 times as likely to have voted for Romney as for Obama – while at the opposite end of the spectrum, pure post-materialists were 8.6 times as likely to have voted for Obama as for Romney.

This was a strikingly strong relationship, but it became even stronger in 2016 when Trump, an openly racist, sexist, and xenophobic candidate, was running against Hillary Clinton, a relatively liberal and cosmopolitan candidate who was also the first woman to win a major party's presidential nomination. Figure 10.6 shows the relationship between values and vote in the 2016 presidential election. As it indicates, pure materialists were 3.8 times as likely to have voted for Trump as for Clinton – while pure post-materialists were 14.3 times as likely to have voted for Clinton as for Trump.

The fact that materialist/post-materialist values had a strong impact on the 2016 presidential vote suggests that we will also find a strong relationship with age – and we do. Among Americans over 65 years of age, fully 54 percent expressed favorable attitudes toward Trump – while among those less than 30 years old, only 20 percent did so: older Americans are 2.7 times as likely to support Trump as are younger Americans. This large generational gap in support for the two main parties has not always been present. As Figure 10.7 indicates, time series data from the American

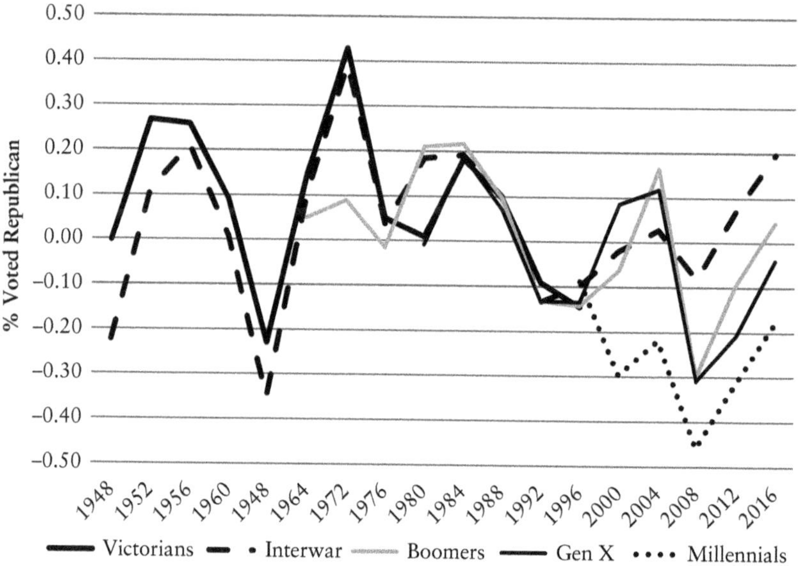


FIGURE 10.7. *Generational shifts in voting, US presidential elections 1948–2016*
*Note:* Proportion voting Republican by generational birth cohort classified as Victorians (Pre-1900), Interwar (1900–1945), Baby Boomers (1946–1964), Generation X (1964–1979), and Millennials (1980).
*Source:* American National Election Study Time Series Cumulative Data File 1948–2012; American National Election Study 2016 Time Series Study.

National Election Study show relatively small differences between the voting preferences of different birth cohorts until about 2000, when generationally linked differences in basic values became a major influence on how people voted, making age one of the strongest demographic predictor of electoral behavior.

A sexist, racist, xenophobic, authoritarian, anti-environmentalist figure, Trump is the antithesis of everything that post-materialists value. Accordingly, he was precisely the type of candidate that the silent revolution thesis predicts would polarize the vote between materialists and post-materialists – and he did so to a striking extent.[35]

As Chapter 2 pointed out, the post-war intergenerational value shift eventually launched a positive feedback loop. For the world into which one is born seems normal and legitimate. And in high-income societies, for the past several decades each successive birth cohort has been born into a world in which tolerance of gender equality and gays and racial minorities was becoming more widespread and ethnic diversity was increasing. For the youngest birth cohort, the election of an African-American President simply continued a familiar trend. For the oldest cohort, it was an event that had been inconceivable in the world in which they had been born. Consequently, the gap between contemporary reality and the world one had known since birth was much greater for the oldest cohort than for the youngest one – so older people felt much more threatened by contemporary levels of social tolerance and ethnic diversity than younger ones. Accordingly, intergenerational population replacement continued to bring greater acceptance of the new cultural norms. This also applies to geographic differences. For people born in New York or Los Angeles in 1960, ethnic and cultural diversity were familiar and relatively acceptable. For those born in the same year in rural Montana or West Virginia, they were not. Accordingly, younger people born in metropolitan regions were disproportionately likely to support Sanders or Clinton, while older people from ethnically homogeneous rural counties tended to vote for Trump.

As we found when tracing the evolution of party platforms, the conflict over social and moral values has become a major factor in party polarization, shifting it away from the economic-based left–right axis toward the cultural-based axis. As Table 10.1 indicates, materialist/post-materialist values by themselves explained fully 25 percent of the variance in the Clinton or Trump vote (see Model 1). As noted earlier, age and education are strongly correlated with support for Trump versus Clinton (or for Le Pen versus Macron in France, or for Leave versus Remain in the UK) but age and education overlap strongly with materialist/post-materialist values. Consequently, when we add them to the regression equation, they increase the explained variance only slightly (raising it from 25 percent to 27 percent – see Model 2). Adding household income to the equation explains no additional variance whatsoever (Model 3). The standard social class-linked demographic indicators have little explanatory power – they are dominated by cultural factors.

As one would expect, most Obama voters in 2012 supported Clinton in 2016: their party loyalties, demographic characteristics, and ideological preferences (and the fact that Obama campaigned for Clinton) all push them in that direction. Accordingly, when we use the respondent's

TABLE 10.1. *Predicting the Trump vote, US 2016*

| | Model 1 | Model 2 | Model 3 | Model 4 | Model 5 | Model 6 |
|---|---|---|---|---|---|---|
| Materialist/post-materialist values | −.50 | −.47 | −.47 | – | −.19 | −.17 |
| Age (4-categories) | – | .10 | .10 | – | – | .03 |
| Education (4-category) | – | −.06 | −.08 | – | – | −.09 |
| Household Income | – | – | .05 | – | – | .01 |
| 2012 Republican presidential vote | – | – | – | .77 | .69 | .69 |
| Adjusted $R^2$ | .25 | .27 | .27 | .59 | .63 | .64 |

*Note:* Logistic regression models where the dependent variable is the 2016 presidential vote for Trump (1) or Clinton (0). The coefficients are standardized betas and their significance. N. 1182.
*Source:* World Values Survey, US 2017.

reported vote in 2012 as a predictor of how he or she voted in 2016, this variable alone explains 59 percent of the variance (Model 4).

When we add the respondent's materialist/post-materialist values to the equation, it explains only 4 points of additional variance, which is not surprising: whether the respondent had materialist or post-materialist values in 2012 is already captured in the reported vote in 2012 (along with all other influences on that vote). Nevertheless, the respondent's values as measured in the 2017 survey do make a significant contribution to explaining how the 2016 presidential vote *deviated* from that person's vote in 2012 (Model 5). Post-materialists were even more likely to have voted for Clinton than for Obama. But adding age, education, and income to the model only explains an additional 1 percent of the variance in how people voted in 2016 (Model 6).

## THE ROLE OF ECONOMIC AND CULTURAL GRIEVANCES IN THE 2016 ELECTION

Are these patterns limited to materialist/post-materialist values – or are they also consistently found for other measures of social attitudes? And do the cultural effects persist as significant when a more comprehensive range of demographic and socio-economic factors are taken into account, including economic grievance explanations?

Previous chapters have focused largely on European evidence but the 2016 presidential election presents a classic case study allowing us to see whether similar patterns can be observed in the US. Many commentators have found it difficult to understand the rise of Donald Trump. His rhetoric is a mixture of xenophobic fear mongering, deep-seated misogyny, paranoid conspiracy theories, and isolationist 'America First' foreign policies. His populism is rooted in claims that he is an outsider to DC politics, a self-made billionaire leading an insurgency movement on behalf of ordinary Americans. Despite being located on opposite sides of the ideological spectrum, Trump's rhetoric taps some of the same populist anti-elite anger articulated by Bernie Sanders when attacking big corporations, big donors, and big banks.

Numerous studies have sought to explain the outcome of the 2016 US presidential election, but they have not resolved the debate about the role of economic and cultural grievances in Trump's victory and Clinton's defeat. Chapters 5 and 6 reviewed some of the theories and the comparative evidence for value change – but the American case provides a particularly good test of these arguments.

## Economic Grievances

Perhaps the most widely held view – the *economic grievance* perspective – emphasizes the consequences for electoral behavior arising from profound changes transforming the workforce and society in post-industrial economies. There is overwhelming evidence of powerful trends toward greater income and wealth inequality in the West, based on the rise of the knowledge economy, technological automation, and the collapse of the manufacturing industry, global flows of labor, goods, peoples, and capital (especially the inflow of migrants and refugees), the erosion of organized labor, shrinking welfare safety-nets, and neo-liberal austerity policies.[36] According to this view, rising economic insecurity and social deprivation among the left-behinds has fueled popular resentment of the political classes. This situation is believed to have made the less secure strata of society susceptible to the anti-establishment, nativist, and xenophobic scare-mongering exploited of authoritarian-populist movements, parties, and leaders, blaming 'Them' for stripping prosperity, job opportunities, and public services from 'Us.' In this view, Trump's base is attracted by his Make America Great Again promises to restore blue-collar jobs lost in factories, mills, and mines, to attack the opioid crisis devastating local communities, to rebuild America's crumbling infrastructure of roads and bridges, to scrap or renegotiate free trade deals like NAFTA and TPP, to reduce the costs of healthcare insurance, and to implement massive tax cuts for the less well-off.

The contemporary version of the economic grievance argument links globalization directly with rising mass support for populism, which is understood to reflect divisions between the winners and losers from labor markets.[37] In this argument, economic vulnerability is conducive to in-group solidarity, rigid conformity to group norms, and rejection of outsiders. Threatened people tend to seek strong, authoritarian leaders to protect them from dangerous outsiders who are seen as threatening jobs and benefits.[38] Anxiety arising from contemporary events – migrants and refugees flooding into Texas and New Mexico, random acts of domestic terrorism in Paris, Brussels, and Berlin, and austerity measures – are blamed for exacerbating economic grievances linked with growing income inequality, the loss of secure manufacturing jobs, and stagnant wages.

These developments are often assumed to have played an important role in the election of Donald Trump. Several economists have argued that globalization, in particular the effects of the import of cheap Chinese goods in electronics and textiles, has had a devastating effect upon employment in American factories and mills, and that communities most affected by the loss of economic opportunities swung decisively toward populist leaders such as Trump.[39] Social individualization and fragmentation have eroded the grassroots membership of traditional collective organizations, social networks, and mass movements that once mobilized workers' cooperatives and trade unions.[40] Collective movements and organized labor, which in the past mobilized the expression of working-class grievances, have found their negotiating powers undermined by open labor markets and multinational corporations. Movements like Black Lives Matter have mobilized strongly around issues of social justice, including the appropriate use of police violence – but this has divided poorer communities around issues of race. The Democratic Party has found its traditional electoral base depleted by the shrinking numbers of industrial workers in the Rust Belt states, forcing them to widen their electoral appeals as catch-all parties to attract public-sector professionals and liberal coastal communities focused on issues such as environmental protection.[41] Socially disadvantaged groups are most prone to blame ethnic minorities and migrant populations for deteriorating conditions, loss of manufacturing jobs, and inadequate welfare services. Populists often advocate trade barriers and tariffs to protect workers from foreign competition, and they attack governments for failing to provide the growing prosperity and sense of shared community that characterized post-war societies (hence Trump's slogan of 'Make America Great Again'). The failure of the Clinton and Obama administrations to restore a sense of security and prosperity to the unemployed and depopulated rural communities in heartland America, this account suggests, has led many of their traditional supporters to flee to Trump, who promises to restore America's past golden age.[42] In short, the economic grievance thesis explains the loyalty of Trump's base as a product of stagnant or declining real incomes for the average family, loss of secure blue-collar jobs in the manufacturing heartland, and lack of opportunities for social mobility, combined with the feeling that, despite rising levels of national income, successive Democratic administrations have failed to respond effectively to these concerns.[43]

Much of the evidence used to buttress the economic grievance thesis is derived from county-level comparisons. For example, Trump made above average vote gains in non-metropolitan communities heavily dependent on manufacturing industries particularly vulnerable to competition from Chinese trade imports, such as electronics and textiles.[44] This suggests that economic shocks arising from global trade are important for voting behavior. Non-metropolitan counties have seen their populations shrink during the last decade, in contrast to major urban areas. Employment in places like the Appalachian coal country is heavily vulnerable to commodity prices and technological changes affecting the costs of extraction of energy products.[45] Analysis of the census characteristics of county voting results demonstrate that small-town America in the Rust Belt and coal country swung toward Trump, who performed particularly well in counties with less-educated older white populations, while Clinton did better in urban areas with younger and more ethnically diverse populations.[46]

Despite these observations, which have colored much of the popular commentary, county-level analysis is unable to determine the underlying reasons for the vote swings. They could have been driven by Trump's campaign pledge to restore automobile plants in Detroit, coal mines in Kentucky, and factories in Indiana in local communities that have lost well-paid blue-collar jobs to cheaper labor in Mexico and technological automation (as the economic grievance argument assumes). Or these counties could have swung to Trump because of the resonance of his cultural message on wedge social issues of race, gender, religion, and nation, which appeal most to the less educated and working-class sectors of America – notably his anti-immigrant rhetoric and his aggressive stance against 'foreigners,' in stark contrast to the traditional messages of diversity and respect for multiculturalism that characterized Hillary Clinton's Democratic campaign. As Chapter 5 argued, the culture of rural communities in heartland America differs from that of coastal cities in numerous ways – including the strength of religiosity, the lack of ethnic diversity, and the presence of elderly populations with low levels of education that were left behind as more geographically mobile younger, college-educated professionals left for opportunities in the service, financial, and technology sectors in metropolitan areas.[47] The classic ecological fallacy arises using county-level voting results when inferences about the nature of individual voters are deduced from observations of the aggregate characteristics of the place where they live.[48]

If the economic grievance thesis is correct, it predicts that electoral support for Trump should be concentrated among economically marginalized sectors who are the main losers from global labor markets and technological advances. Thus, in terms of objective economic indicators, votes for Trump (and the vote switch from Obama in 2012 to Trump in 2016) should be strongest amongst unskilled manual workers, especially those working in manufacturing industries most depressed by imports, such as textiles and electronics, the unemployed, those lacking college degrees, low-income households, and those dependent on welfare benefits as their main source of income. In addition, support for Trump should also be linked with subjective feelings of economic insecurity, both egotropic, such as those worried about their own and their family's financial savings, those feeling worse off, and those believing that social mobility to achieve a more comfortable lifestyle than their parents is harder today than earlier. Support for Clinton and Trump should also be associated with socio-tropic economic attitudes, such as positive or negative judgments about the past and future performance of the national economy. Among these indices, the objective measures are likely to be the more reliable predictors. Even where measured before election day, subjective judgments of the performance of the economy are vulnerable to questions about the direction of the causal arrow. For example, those already supporting Trump (for whatever reason) could have subsequently become more critical of Obama's management of the economy.[49]

## Cultural Grievances

The main alternative account to the economic grievance school is provided by the cultural backlash thesis which has been supported primarily from European evidence so far in this book. If the American case also fits this explanation, Trump's base support should be explained not as a purely economic phenomenon but in large part as a reaction against cultural change. This argument builds on the 'silent revolution' theory of value change, which tends to move post-industrial societies in a more progressive direction, as opportunities for college education were made open to growing segments of the population and as younger cohorts gradually replaced their parents and grandparents in the population. But the silent revolution thesis also emphasizes that, from the start, these developments triggered a powerful reaction in America, especially among authoritarians and social conservatives who are angered by the erosion of familiar norms and who actively resent the rising tide of post-materialist and progressive values – eventually providing a pool of potential supporters for Trump.[50] Members of once culturally predominant groups in America, notably older white working-class men, may react angrily against the loss of their former privileges and status, blaming liberal elites and out-groups for these developments. In this view, Trump's base will continue to be faithful irrespective of liberal outrage over his words and deeds, and indeed because of these transgressions (such as the infamous video of him describing his sexual harassment of women), so long as he delivers symbolically through rhetorical channels of expression, such as his pugilistic attacks on opponents and critics via Twitter, media interviews, and rallies. He also delivers to his base symbolically through executive actions, signed in the Oval Office with much flourish, on key issues fulfilling campaign pledges, such as attempts to tighten border security against perceived threats of Muslim terrorists, to implement more aggressive ICE deportation of illegal immigrants, and to roll back environmental protection such as by withdrawing from the Paris climate accord, eliminating protection of public lands in the American West, and lifting restrictions on building the oil pipeline from Canada.

This perspective emphasizes that Trump's support can be explained largely as a social psychological phenomenon, reflecting a nostalgic reaction among social conservatives and older sectors of the electorate seeking a bulwark against long-term processes of value change, the 'silent revolution' that transformed American culture during the second half of the twentieth century. Hence Trump's slogan 'Make America Great Again' – and his rejection of 'political correctness' – appeals sentimentally to a mythical 'golden past,' especially for older white men in small-town America, when society was less diverse, US leadership was unrivalled among Western powers during the Cold War era, threats of terrorism pre-9/11 were in distant lands but not at home, and conventional sex roles for women and men reflected familiar power relationships in the family and workforce.

The backlash approach predicts that cultural grievances and therefore voting support for Trump will be especially strong among those holding authoritarian values and morally conservative attitudes, both of which tend to be concentrated among the older generation and the less-educated groups. The appeal to authoritarian values like nativism, racism, and strongman rule is clear. Trump declared his candidacy promising to wall off Mexico and deport millions of illegal aliens: 'When Mexico sends its people, they're not sending their best ... they're bringing drugs, they're bringing crime, they're rapists, and some I assume are good people but I speak to border guards and they tell us what we're getting.' On the campaign trail, Trump called for 'a total and complete shutdown of Muslims entering the United States,' declaring on CNN that 'Islam hates us,' although on coming to office the initial botched executive order banning travel from seven Muslim-majority countries was quickly overturned by the courts. He has repeatedly attacked African-American leaders and athletes on Twitter. Abroad, he has demonstrated a striking affinity with many of the world's autocrats, from Saudi Arabia's Crown Prince Mohammed bin Salman who carried out mass arrests without due process to cement his control ('I have great confidence in King Salman and the Crown Prince of Saudi Arabia, they know exactly what they are doing'), Turkey's Erdogan ('very high marks') to Rodrigo Duterte of the Philippines (a 'great relationship') – and the administration's numerous dark links with President Putin remain under active investigation.

As Chapter 8 demonstrated, voting support for parties endorsing authoritarian values in a wide range of European societies is strongly predicted by one's birth cohort, college education, and sex. If the cultural backlash thesis also holds in America, then this argument predicts that the strongest support for Trump in the 2016 election will also be observed among the older generation, men, those lacking college education, and among those holding authoritarian values and socially conservative attitudes toward the family and sexuality, religion and multiculturalism, cosmopolitanism and tolerance of foreigners.

The analytical distinction between economic grievances accounts and cultural backlash theories becomes somewhat artificial, however, if interactive processes link these factors. For example, structural changes in the workforce and social trends in globalized markets may heighten economic grievances, and this, in turn, may stimulate a negative backlash among social traditionalists and authoritarians blaming cultural changes for the loss of jobs, like the growing role of women in the workforce. And, as we have pointed out, even if the proximate cause of voting for an authoritarian populist is cultural backlash, long-term trends could explain why the overall level of authoritarian-populist voting is much stronger now than it was 30 years ago. It is not an either/or question.

## Evidence

To consider the evidence for these arguments, we will examine the social, cultural, and economic factors predicting the 2016 presidential vote, using survey data from the American National Election Study (ANES). The study contains several items that are designed to tap the cultural attitudes that we hypothesize are conducive to Trump support. As shown in Table 10.2, these selected items were tested using factor analysis and four dimensions emerged. The first concerns *moral conservatism*, measured by opposition to change, rejection of moral relativism, disapproval of newer lifestyles, and the importance of family values. The second clustered the four classic items about the desirability of childhood traits, such as good manners, being well-behaved, respect, and obedience, which have long been used to measure *authoritarian* predispositions. The third concerned agreement with a series of three statements reflecting the *anti-establishment component of populism*, such as agreement that most politicians do not care about the people and most politicians only care about the interests of the rich. Finally, three items tap the *populism* claim that the will of the majority should always prevail, approval of strong leaders even if they bend the rules, and the belief that minorities should adapt to American customs. These clusters of items were summed and transformed into four standardized cultural scales. It should be noted that these items were measured in the pre-election survey, so they were not contaminated by the outcome. The selected items also did not refer to candidate characteristics or policy issues, such as support for same sex marriage, for homosexual rights, or immigration, which would be vulnerable to endogeneity, but rather to more general value orientations and perceptions. The models also excluded direct measures of liberal or conservative self-identification, and partisan identification. These factors were strongly correlated with the Trump vote, but it would have been difficult to interpret the causal direction of this correlation.

The models also selected a wide range of economic items from the ANES, listed in Table 10.3, including objective indices such as unemployment and reported level of household income, as well as subjective

TABLE 10.2. *Cultural scales, US 2016*

| | Moral conservatism | Authoritarian values | Populism1 Anti-politician | Populism2 Vox pop |
|---|---|---|---|---|
| Agree: More emphasis on traditional family values | 0.76 | | | 0.44 |
| Agree: Newer lifestyles are breaking down society | 0.76 | | | 0.44 |
| Disagree: The world is always changing & we should adjust our view of moral behavior to that change | 0.73 | | | |
| Disagree: Be more tolerant of other moral standards | 0.71 | | | |
| Child trait more important: curiosity or *good manners* | | 0.83 | | |
| Child trait more important: considerate or *well-behaved* | | 0.80 | | |
| Child trait more important: independence or *respect* | | 0.75 | | |
| Child trait more important: *obedience* or self-reliance | | 0.57 | | |
| Most politicians do not care about the people | | | 0.85 | |
| Politicians are the main problem in the US | | | 0.78 | |
| Most politicians only care about interests of rich and powerful | | | 0.77 | |
| Strong leader is good for US even if bends rules to get things done | | | | 0.72 |
| The will of the majority should always prevail | | | | 0.70 |
| Minorities should adapt to customs/traditions of US | | | | 0.60 |
| % Variance | 23.2 | 19.7 | 11.8 | 7.7 |

*Note:* Principal Component Factor analysis with Varimax rotation.
*Source:* 2016 American National Election Study.

TABLE 10.3. *Predicting the Trump presidential vote, US 2016*

| | | Model A | | | Model B | | | Model C | | | Model D | | |
|---|---|---|---|---|---|---|---|---|---|---|---|---|---|
| | | B | S.E. | Sig. | B | S.E. | Sig. | B | S.E. | Sig. | B | S.E. | Sig. |
| Generation | Interwar (1900–1945) (Ref) | 0.00 | | | 0.00 | | | 0.00 | | | 0.00 | | |
| | Baby boomer (1946–64) | –0.36 | 0.13 | *** | –0.29 | 0.14 | * | 0.03 | 0.18 | N/s | 0.04 | 0.21 | N/s |
| | Generation X (1965–79) | –0.53 | 0.14 | *** | –0.41 | 0.17 | * | 0.50 | 0.21 | * | 0.51 | 0.25 | * |
| | Millennial (1980–96) | –0.79 | 0.14 | *** | –0.65 | 0.17 | *** | 0.57 | 0.21 | ** | 0.61 | 0.26 | ** |
| Social | Race (Black) (Ref) | | | | 0.00 | | | 0.00 | | | 0.00 | | |
| | Race (white) | | | | 2.31 | 0.19 | *** | 3.06 | 0.23 | *** | 2.93 | 0.27 | *** |
| | Race (Hispanic) | | | | 0.86 | 0.25 | *** | 1.25 | 0.29 | *** | 1.16 | 0.35 | *** |
| | Sex (male) | | | | 0.29 | 0.09 | *** | 0.41 | 0.12 | *** | 0.56 | 0.15 | *** |
| | Education (4 cat High School to Masters) | | | | –0.36 | 0.04 | **** | –0.05 | 0.15 | N/s | –0.05 | 0.08 | N/s |
| | Have children under 18 living at home | | | | 0.23 | 0.12 | * | 0.12 | 0.00 | N/s | 0.06 | 0.18 | N/s |
| | Married | | | | 0.34 | 0.10 | *** | 0.17 | 0.01 | N/s | 0.23 | 0.16 | N/s |
| Culture | Childhood traits authoritarian values scale | | | | | | | 0.01 | 0.01 | *** | 0.01 | 0.00 | * |

(*continued*)

TABLE 10.3 (*continued*)

| | | Model A | | | Model B | | | Model C | | | Model D | | |
|---|---|---|---|---|---|---|---|---|---|---|---|---|---|
| | | B | S.E. | Sig. | B | S.E. | Sig. | B | S.E. | Sig. | B | S.E. | Sig. |
| | Populism 1 Anti-politician scale | | | | | | | 0.00 | 0.01 | N/s | –0.01 | 0.00 | N/s |
| | Populism 2 Vox pop/ majority rule scale | | | | | | | 0.04 | 0.01 | *** | 0.04 | 0.01 | *** |
| | Moral conservatism (against moral change) | | | | | | | 0.06 | 0.01 | *** | 0.05 | 0.00 | *** |
| | Religion important | | | | | | | 0.73 | 0.14 | *** | 0.77 | 0.16 | *** |
| Economy | Working class | | | | | | | | | | 0.19 | 0.20 | N/s |
| | Household income scale (Low to High) | | | | | | | | | | 0.02 | 0.01 | N/s |
| | Unemployed (0/1) | | | | | | | | | | 0.03 | 0.33 | N/s |
| | Larger income gap today | | | | | | | | | | –0.21 | 0.08 | ** |
| | Economy worse in last year | | | | | | | | | | 0.60 | 0.09 | *** |
| | Current economy very bad | | | | | | | | | | 0.62 | 0.09 | *** |
| | Economy worse in next year | | | | | | | | | | –0.16 | 0.08 | * |

| | | | | | | | | | | | | |
|---|---|---|---|---|---|---|---|---|---|---|---|---|
| More unemployment in last year | | | | | | | | | | 0.67 | 0.09 | *** |
| Worry about household financial situation | | | | | | | | | | −0.28 | 0.07 | *** |
| Economic mobility harder compared to 20 yrs ago | | | | | | | | | | 0.00 | 0.05 | N/s |
| Feel worse off than one year ago | | | | | | | | | | 0.20 | 0.09 | * |
| Constant | 0.36 | | | −1.15 | | | −2.67 | | | −10.1 | 0.92 | *** |
| Nagelkerke $R^2$ | 0.02 | | | 0.21 | | | 0.58 | | | 0.72 | | |

*Note:* Logistic regression analysis with the presidential vote for Trump (1) or Clinton (0) as the dependent variable.
*Source:* 2016 ANES.

evaluations of the past and future performance of the US economy, household financial insecurity, and feelings about opportunities for economic mobility and income gaps in America. Most of the economic performance items were selected from the pre-election survey to avoid the results being colored by the outcome.

Table 10.3 presents the results of a series of binary logistic regression models predicting vote for Trump (1) or Clinton (0) in the 2016 presidential election.

As in earlier chapters, the first model enters the birth cohorts that we have found to be important in Europe. The results confirm the social profile of Trump voters is consistent with that found in European support for Authoritarian-Populist parties. A large generation gap in the American election was evident, with Millennials being least likely to vote for Trump.

The second model enters the other social and demographic factors, confirming their importance. Votes for Trump came disproportionately from whites. The usual gender gap was evident, with Trump getting more support from men, those with lower education, and those who were married and with children living at home. All these social characteristics were consistent with the social profile observed in earlier chapters in predicting support for Authoritarian-Populist parties in Europe.

After introducing all of these social and demographic controls, the third model entered the cultural scales. The results show that Trump votes were associated with authoritarian orientations, as predicted, and with the vox pop component of populism, moral conservatism, and the strength of religiosity. By contrast, however, the anti-establishment scale of populism was not significant; one reason is that these attitudes were so broadly shared in the American electorate that Clinton voters did not differ from Trump supporters in their distaste for politicians. As we have argued, the anti-establishment claims of populism reflects a malleable form of discourse that can be adapted by politicians of all ideological stripes, especially those seeking to depict themselves as outsiders and challengers to the major parties. The underlying values linked with the particular variety of populism advocated is far more important than the anti-establishment claims. As Figure 10.8 shows, there is a strong and consistent link between morally conservative attitudes, reflecting beliefs that newer lifestyles are breaking down society and a rejection of other moral standards, and favorable feelings toward both the major candidates, as measured by the thermometer ratings. Once cultural values were entered into the model, the generation gap reversed, indicating that the birth cohort differences reflect distinctive values.

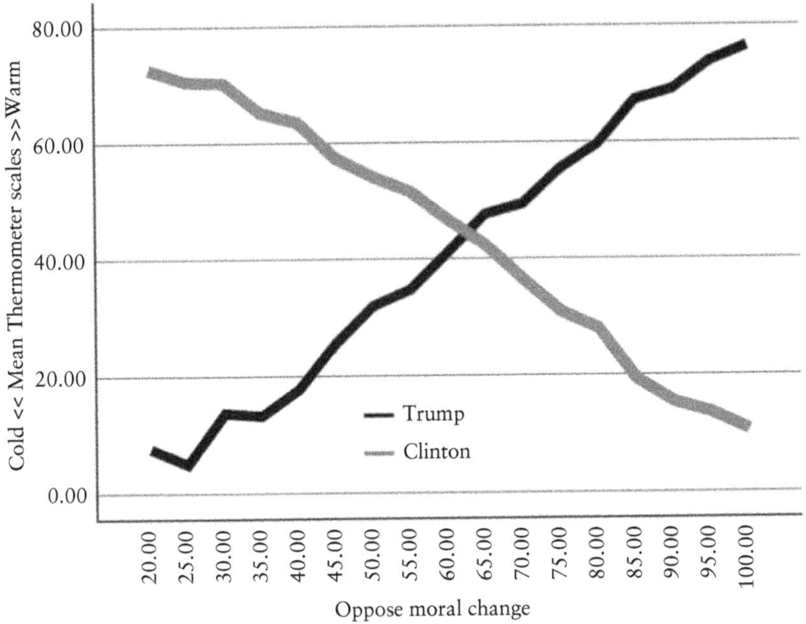


FIGURE 10.8. *Moral conservatism predicts support for Trump and Clinton*
*Note:* Moral conservatism is measured by a standardized 100 point summing agreement/disagreement about four statements: 'There should be more emphasis on traditional family values' (agree); 'Newer lifestyles are breaking down society' (agree); 'The world is always changing & we should adjust our view of moral behavior to that change' (disagree); and 'We should be more tolerant of other moral standards' (disagree). See Table 10.2 for details. Support for the two major candidates are measured by 100-point thermometer scores.
*Source:* 2016 American National Election Study.

The final model in Table 10.3 incorporates the full range of items, including the economic indices. What this shows is that several, though not all of them, were significantly related to votes for Trump. This included retrospective evaluations about economic performance; those who thought it was poor were more likely to support Trump. But these can be problematic since such judgments can be colored by candidate preferences. Those who reported feeling worse off than one year ago were more likely to vote for Trump, but this effect was sharply conditioned by race; whites who felt worse off were more likely to vote for Trump than Clinton, but among the non-white population this group overwhelmingly supported Clinton. By contrast, the indicators of subjective class reported household income and unemployment were not significant. Once these items were entered, three of the cultural factors remained significant, namely support for majority rule populism, attitudes of moral conservatism, and religiosity. Those who wanted greater emphasis on traditional family values, who feared modern lifestyles, and who believed in absolute moral standards supported Trump, all indicators of the underlying cultural grievances held by those endorsing Authoritarian-Populist candidates and parties.

## CONCLUSIONS AND IMPLICATIONS

There are many reasons why electoral behavior in Europe and the United States might be expected to differ: religion is much more important in American society than in secular Europe. Surveys report contrasting cultural attitudes on a range of issues, such as toward the role of government, willingness to use military force, and attitudes toward race. Nevertheless, the phenomenon of authoritarian populism seems strikingly similar on both sides of the Atlantic, as indicated by the dynamics of the Leave decision in the Brexit referendum in June 2016 and the Trump victory in November 2016. These events generated an enormous amount of speculation about the reasons for these political earthquakes. Both the economic and cultural grievance theories have attracted supporters – but few have examined a comprehensive range of evidence for both arguments, and few have examined these issues in both Europe and America.

The economic grievance thesis suggests that rising economic insecurity and social deprivation among the left-behinds has fueled populist resentment against Washington DC. This is believed to have made the less affluent susceptible to the anti-establishment, nativist, and xenophobic scare mongering exploited of authoritarian-populist movements, parties, and leaders like Trump. The main alternative account is the cultural backlash thesis which suggests that Trump's base is largely a reaction against cultural change. In particular the rise of social liberalism is thought to have triggered a powerful reaction among authoritarians and social conservatives angered by the erosion of familiar norms and politically correct elites telling them what to think – providing a pool of potential supporters for Trump.

Several conclusions can be drawn from the evidence presented in this chapter.

First, the results of analyzing voting behavior in the 2016 election confirmed the existence of a large generation gap in the American electorate, with Millennials least likely to vote for Trump. Other social and demographic factors were as expected, with votes for Trump coming disproportionately from whites, men, and those with lower education. Even with these controls, Trump votes were significantly associated with authoritarian orientations, as predicted, and with the vox pop/popular rule component of populism, moral conservatism, and the strength of religiosity. Those who thought that the economy had performed badly and those who felt worse off were also more likely to support Trump.

Overall, we find support for both the economic grievances theory and the cultural backlash theory. They seem to reinforce each other – but cultural backlash clearly played the dominant role in people's decision to vote for Trump or Clinton. Table 10.3 indicates that education, race, and sex explain 21 percent of the variance in the vote for Clinton versus Trump. But when we add the cultural values and religiosity to the model, we explain an additional 37 percent of the variance. And when we take economic factors into account, we explain an additional 14 percent of the variance. Therefore, cultural indicators play the dominant role, but several economic factors are also important for comprehensive explanations.

The time series evidence examined in the American case gives a clearer idea of the conditions under which cultural backlash is likely to play a major role. There is no reason why the polarization between materialist and post-materialist values would shape political choice unless the respective candidates take distinctive positions on the issues linked with these values.

The 2016 presidential election presented an exceptionally clear-cut choice. An openly sexist, racist, and xenophobic candidate was running against a socially liberal woman. As a result, materialist/post-materialist values alone explained fully 25 percent of the variance in the vote. The fact that materialist/post-materialist values had such a strong impact suggests that we will also find a strong relationship with age – and we do. Among the Interwar generation, the majority expressed favorable attitudes toward Trump – while among the Millennials, only a fifth did so. We get a similar result when analyzing the impact of other indicators of socially liberal versus authoritarian values. Moreover, as we have seen, since about 1980, cultural values have become far more liberal among the younger generations, while real income and job security have declined for a large share of the American population, which helps to explain why the authoritarian populist vote was much stronger in 2016 than in earlier elections.

The following chapter examines to what extent we find similar dynamics at work in the British decision to leave the European Union.

## Notes


1. Larry Sabato, Kyle Kondik, and Geoffrey Skelley. Eds. *Trumped: The 2016 Elections that Broke all the Rules*. New York: Rowman & Littlefield; James W. Ceaser, Andrew E. Busch, and John J. Pitney. 2017. *Defying the Odds: The 2016 Elections and American Politics*. New York: Rowman & Littlefield.
2. Office of the Director of National Intelligence. January 6, 2017. *Assessing Russian Activities and Intentions in Recent US Elections*. Unclassified version. www.scribd.com/document/335885580/Unclassified-version-of-intelligence-report-on-Russian-hacking-during-the-2016-election.
3. Norman Pollack. 1962. *The Populist Response to Industrial America*. Cambridge, MA: Harvard University Press; Ronald P. Formisano. 2008. *For the People: American Populist Movements from the Revolution to the 1850s*. Chapel Hill: The University of North Carolina Press; Chip Berlet and Matthew N. Lyons. 2010. *Right-Wing Populism in America: Too Close for Comfort*. NY: Guilford Press.
4. Michael Kazin. 1998. *The Populist Persuasion: An American History*. Ithaca, NY: Cornell University Press; Walter Nugent. 2013.*The Tolerant Populists: Kansas Populism and Nativism*. 2nd edn. Chicago: University of Chicago Press.
5. Donald Warren. 1996. *Radio Priest: Charles Coughlin The Father of Hate Radio*. New York: The Free Press.
6. Michael Kazin. 1995. *The Populist Persuasion*. Ithaca, NY: Cornell University Press.
7. www.washingtonpost.com/news/post-politics/wp/2015/06/16/full-text-donald-trump-announces-a-presidential-bid/.
8. Linda Schulte-Sasse. 1993. 'Meet Ross Perot: The lasting legacy of Capraesque populism.' *Cultural Critique* 25: 91–119.
9. Bart Bonikowski and Noam Gidron. 2016. 'The populist style in American politics: Presidential campaign discourse, 1952–1996.' *Social Forces* 94 (4): 1593–1621.
10. Patrick J. Buchanan. 1992. Republican National Convention Speech. Houston, TX. August 17, 1992. https://web.archive.org/web/20061012133633/www.buchanan.org/pa-92-0817-rnc.html.
11. Kevin Arceneaux and Stephen P. Nicholson, 2012. 'Who wants to have a Tea Party? The who, what, and why of the Tea Party Movement.' *PS: Political Science and Politics* 45 (4): 700–710.
12. Bart Bonikowski and Noam Gidron. 2016. 'The populist style in American politics: Presidential campaign discourse, 1952–1996.' *Social Forces* 94 (4): 1593–1621.
13. Earl Black and Merle Black. 2003. *The Rise of Southern Republicans*. Cambridge, MA: Harvard University Press.
14. Alan Abramowitz. 2012. *The Polarized Public*. New York: Pearson; James E. Campbell. 2016. *Polarized: Making Sense of a Divided America*. Princeton, NJ: Princeton University Press; Morris Fiorina. 2017. *Unstable Majorities: Polarization, Party Sorting, and Political Stalemate*. Stanford, CA: Hoover Institute Publications.

15. https://voteview.com/parties/all.
16. James E. Campbell. 2016. *Polarized: Making Sense of a Divided America.* Princeton, NJ: Princeton University Press.
17. The Comparative Manifesto Project. https://manifesto-project.wzb.eu/. Dataset Release 2017a (August 18, 2017). For more details, see Ian Budge, Hans-Dieter Klingemann, Andrew Volkens, Judith Bara, and Eric Tanenbaum. 2001. *Mapping Policy Preferences.* Oxford: Oxford University Press.
18. Kevin Arceneaux and Stephen P. Nicholson. 2012. 'Who wants to have a Tea Party? The who, what, and why of the Tea Party Movement.' *PS: Political Science and Politics* 45 (4): 700–710.
19. Mark Hetherington and Jonathan D. Weiler. 2009. *Authoritarianism and Polarization in American Politics.* New York: Cambridge University Press; J. Eric Oliver and Wendy M. Rahn. 2016. 'Rise of the Trumpenvolk: Populism in the 2016 election.' *Annals of the American Academy of Political and Social Science* 667 (1): 189–206; A.M. Cizmar *et al.* 2014. 'Authoritarianism and American political behavior from 1952 to 2008.' *Political Research Quarterly* 67 (1): 71–83.
20. Steven J. Rosenstone, Roy L. Behr, and Edward H. Lazarus. 1996. *Third Parties in America.* 2nd edn. Princeton, NJ: Princeton University Press.
21. Pippa Norris. 2005. *Radical Right: Voters and Parties in the Electoral Market.* New York: Cambridge University Press; Elisabeth Carter. 2004. 'Does PR promote political extremism? Evidence from the West European parties of the extreme right.' *Representation* 40(2): 82–100; Elisabeth Carter. 2005. *The Extreme Right in Western Europe: Success or Failure?* Manchester: Manchester University Press.
22. Russell J. Dalton. 2015. *The Good Citizen: How a Younger Generation is Reshaping American Politics.* 2nd revised edn. Washington DC: CQ Press.
23. Jean Hardisty. 1999. *Mobilizing Resentment: Conservative Resurgence from John Birch to the Promise Keepers.* Boston, MA: Beacon Press.
24. Richard Hasen. 2012. *The Voting Wars: From Florida 2000 to the Next Election Meltdown.* New Haven, CT: Yale University Press.
25. I. Haney-Lopez. 2015. *Dog Whistle Politics: How Coded Racial Appeals Have Reinvented Racism and Wrecked the Middle Class.* New York: Oxford University Press; Lawrence D. Bobo. 2017. 'Racism in Trump's America: Reflections on culture, sociology, and the 2016 US presidential election.' *British Journal of Sociology* 68: 85–104.
26. Michele Lamont, Bo Yun Park, and Elena Ayala-Hurtado. 2017. 'Trump's electoral speeches and his appeal to the American white working class.' *British Journal of Sociology* 68: 153–180.
27. The Joint Committee on Taxation. November 24, 2017. *Distributional effects of the 'Tax Cuts and Jobs Act.'* Washington DC: US Congress. www.jct.gov/publications.html?func=startdown&id=5044; Benjamin I. Page and Martin Gilens. 2017. *Democracy in America? What Has Gone Wrong and What We Can Do About It.* Chicago: University of Chicago Press.
28. Thomas Frank. 2005. *What's the Matter with Kansas?: How Conservatives Won the Heart of America.* New York: Holt.

29. Arlie Russell Hochschild. 2016. *Strangers in Their Own Land: Anger and Mourning on the American Right*. New York: The New Press; Katherine J. Cramer. 2016. *The Politics of Resentment: Rural Consciousness in Wisconsin and the Rise of Scott Walker*. Chicago: University of Chicago Press; Justin Gest. 2016. *The New Minority: White Working Class Politics, Immigration and Inequality*. New York: Oxford University Press.
30. For extreme version of this thesis by the alt-right, see www.manosphere .com/.
31. www.splcenter.org/fighting-hate/extremist-files/ideology/alt-right.
32. M. Abrajano and Z.L. Hajnal. 2015. *White Backlash: Immigration, Race, and American Politics*. Princeton, NJ: Princeton University Press.
33. Piero Ignaz. 1992. 'The silent counter-revolution.' *European Journal of Political Research* 22 (1): 3–34; Piero Ignazi. 2003. *Extreme Right Parties in Western Europe*. Oxford: Oxford University Press.
34. Pippa Norris. 2005. *Radical Right: Voters and Parties in the Electoral Market*. New York: Cambridge University Press.
35. When data become available from the most recent wave of the World Values Surveys, we expect that they will also show strong value-based polarization in the vote for Authoritarian-Populist parties such as the National Front and the Alternative for Germany.
36. See, for example, Thomas Piketty. 2014. *Capital*. Cambridge, MA: Belknap Press; Jacob Hacker. 2006. *The Great Risk Shift: The New Economic Insecurity and the Decline of the American Dream*. New York: Oxford University Press.
37. Simon Bornschier. 2010. *Cleavage Politics and the Populist Right: The New Cultural Conflict in Western Europe*. Philadelphia: Temple University Press.
38. See Ronald F. Inglehart. 2016. 'Modernization, existential security and cultural change: Reshaping human motivations and society.' In M. Gelfand, C.Y. Chiu, and Y.-Y. Hong. Eds. *Advances in Culture and Psychology*. New York: Oxford University Press.
39. David Autor, David Dorn, Gordon Hanson, and Kaveh Majlesi. 2017. 'A note on the effect of rising trade exposure on the 2016 presidential election.' MIT Working Paper. https://economics.mit.edu/files/12418; Luigi Guiso, Helios Herrera, Massimo Morelli, and Tommaso Sonne. 2017. 'Demand and Supply of Populism.' www.heliosherrera.com/populism.pdf; Caroline Freund and Dario Sidhu. 2017. Manufacturing and the 2016 election: An analysis of US presidential election data.' Peterson Institute for International Economics Working Paper No. 17-7. SSRN: https://ssrn.com/abstract=2983872.
40. Michael Keating and David McCrone. Eds. 2015. *The Crisis of Social Democracy*. Edinburgh: University of Edinburgh Press.
41. Russell J. Dalton and Martin Wattenberg. 2002. *Parties without Partisans: Political Change in Advanced Industrial Democracies*. Oxford: Oxford University Press.
42. Hans-Georg Betz. 1994. *Radical Rightwing Populism in Western Europe*. New York: St Martin's Press.

43. Michael Hirsh. February 28, 2016. 'Why Trump and Sanders were inevitable.' *Politico Magazine* www.politico.com/magazine/story/2016/02/why-donald-trump-and-bernie-sanders-were-inevitable-213685.
44. Italo Colantone and Piero Stanig. 2016. 'Global competition and Brexit.' *Science Research Network*. http://ssrn.com/abstract=2870313.
45. www.ers.usda.gov/webdocs/publications/80894/eib-162.pdf.
46. Dante J. Scala and Kenneth M. Johnson. 2017. 'Political polarization along the rural–urban continuum? The geography of the presidential vote, 2000–2016.' *The Annals of the Academy of Political and Social Science* 672: 162–169. www.brookings.edu/blog/the-avenue/2017/03/23/a-substantial-majority-of-americans-live-outside-trump-counties-census-shows/.
47. US Department of Agriculture. 2016. *Rural America at a Glance*; Shannon Monnat. 2016. 'Deaths of despair and support for Trump in the 2016 presidential election.' Department of Agricultural Economics, Sociology and Education Research Brief 12/04/16. Pennsylvania State University. http://aese.psu.edu/directory/smm67/Election16.pdf.
48. Gary King, O. Rosen, and M. Tanner. Eds. 2004. *Ecological Inference: New Methodological Strategies*. Cambridge: Cambridge University Press; Paul Brewer and Sunil Venaik. 2014. 'The ecological fallacy in national culture research.' *Organizational Studies* 35 (7): 1063–1086.
49. Geoffrey Evans and Mark Pickup. 2010. 'Reversing the causal arrow: The political conditioning of economic perceptions in the 2000–2004 US presidential election cycle.' *Journal of Politics* 72 (4): 1236.
50. Ronald Inglehart. 1990. *Cultural Shift in Advanced Industrial Society*. Princeton, NJ: Princeton University Press; Ronald Inglehart. 1997. *Modernization and Postmodernization: Cultural, Economic and Political Change in 43 Societies*. Princeton, NJ: Princeton University Press.

# 11

# Brexit

The outcome of the Brexit referenda on 23 June 2016 generated international concern about the effects of populist forces, and stunned disbelief from Berlin to Paris that Britain had voted to withdraw from the European Union after more than four decades of membership.[1] Brexit has been widely seen as a watershed signaling an end to the era of faith in the benefits of globalization, open labor markets, and European integration. The development was welcomed by Le Pen and Trump ('so smart in getting out'), foreshadowing the outcome of the 2016 US elections in the fall. The results of the non-binding referendum were extremely tight: 48.1 percent (16.1m) voted Remain while 51.9 percent (17.4m) voted Leave, with 72 percent of registered electors casting a ballot.[2] Given the immense repercussions, the government could have treated the outcome as indicative but open to negotiation and further public consultations in another contest, as happened earlier following similar referenda in Denmark and Ireland.[3] Other countries often require a 'qualified' or super-majority to pass major constitutional referenda.[4] The majority of MPs backed Remain ('Britain Stronger in Europe') – as did the leaders of the major parties (David Cameron, Nick Clegg, Jeremy Corbyn, and Nichola Sturgeon), distinguished experts as diverse as the Governor of the Bank of England, the General Secretary of the Trade Union Congress, the head of the IMF, the Russell Group of top universities, the head of NATO, economists, scientists, scholars and businesspersons, and a panoply of world leaders such as Barack Obama, Angela Merkel, Nicolas Sarkozy, Justin Trudeau, and Shinzo Abe.[5] A petition to parliament with over 4 million signatories asked for a do-over. Instead, a few weeks later, on 13 July, after Theresa May succeeded David Cameron as Prime Minister and first entered Downing Street, she treated the outcome as definitive. Brexit means Brexit. The people had spoken. 'The campaign was fought, the vote was held, turnout was high, and the public gave their verdict. There must be no attempts to remain inside the EU, no attempts to rejoin it through the back door, and no second referendum. The country voted to leave the European Union, and it is the duty of the Government and of Parliament to make sure we do just that.'[6] She sounded a populist tone by declaring on the doorstep of No. 10 that she intended to make Britain a country 'that works for everyone,' in the interests of those 'just about managing' rather than 'the privileged few.'

But what does the outcome of the Brexit referendum – in context with plummeting support for the UK Independence Party just a year later in the June 8, 2017 general election, indicate about the state of populism in the UK? This is another case, like the Netherlands and Sweden, where populist clothes have been stolen by center-right parties. Under David Cameron and Theresa May's leadership, the Conservative government's policies toward Europe and immigration have been profoundly influenced by strategic attempts to placate their own Eurosceptic wing, and to prevent a substantial electoral breakthrough by the United Kingdom Independence Party (UKIP). Even though UKIP stock has fallen, populism seems alive and well in the UK in mainstream parties, the tabloid press, and in public opinion. For example, polls differ slightly, but at the time of writing there appears to be little buyer's regret among the British public suggesting that the Leave decision should be reversed.[7]

Multiple 'supply-side' and 'demand-side' factors led to the outcome of Brexit and support for UKIP – including competition for power among party leaders, the institutional rules of the game, and public opinion.[8] After considering these issues, this chapter examines survey evidence testing alternative 'demand-side' explanations, focusing on the heated debate about the role of economics and culture in explaining the electorate's decisions over Brexit and their support for UKIP.[9] This gives us another perspective on the dynamics of Trump's victory in the 2016 US election, discussed in the preceding chapter. Some argue that the Leave–Remain divide, the Brexit outcome, and UKIP's initial rise were driven mainly by economic factors, emphasizing the role of the economically 'left-behinds' who had not experienced the instrumental benefits of EU membership in jobs or wages – observing that Remain votes were strongest among educated professionals, financial managers, and stockbrokers in prosperous metropolitan London. By contrast, the Leave vote was exceptionally strong in the struggling areas of the North of England, the Midlands, and

Wales that were historically dependent on mills and mines, as well as in places with poor households, few college graduates, and unemployment.[10]

Others emphasize cultural factors such as the long-term British suspicion about the European Union project, public disgust with the political class at Westminster,[11] anxiety about the effects of the refugee crisis and migration from other EU countries, and opposition to the government's austerity cuts on NHS funding, schools, and public services.[12] These theories can also be regarded as complementary rather than rivals, for example if economic deprivation catalyzed resentment about immigrants and the rejection of open borders.

To examine these issues, Part I sets out the electoral context and historical background in the run up to Brexit – and its implications for party competition in the UK. Part II outlines the arguments based on economic and cultural theories about the British electorate. Part III describes the evidence from the British Election Study panel surveys, which allows us to examine the factors dividing supporters in the Leave and Remain camps in the 2016 Brexit referendum, as well as those predicting support for UKIP from 2015 to 2017. Part IV examines the evidence including the impact of demographic control factors like age and sex, indicators of economic grievances, and the cultural profile of voters in their authoritarian and populist values, as well as their attitudes toward the European Union, immigration, and left–right ideology. The conclusion considers developments since Brexit and their implications for the future of populism in the UK. The main advocate of Brexit, UKIP, succeeded in attaining this goal, but then failed to achieve a decisive breakthrough as a parliamentary party. Yet populist authoritarianism remains alive and well in post-Brexit Britain.

## I BACKGROUND AND CONTEXT

Brexit was born in a speech on January 23, 2013, when the Prime Minister, David Cameron, promised that if the Conservatives won the next general election they would hold an in–out referendum on the UK's membership of the European Union, letting the British people 'have their say.'[13] This commitment was subsequently included in the 2015 Conservative Party election manifesto. After being returned to No. 10 Downing Street, Cameron introduced the European Union Referendum Act 2015 to parliament. This was passed a year later and received the royal assent in December 2015, triggering the Brexit referendum on June

23, 2016. Britain woke the morning after to discover, shocked, that it had voted to Leave. Cameron immediately resigned as Prime Minister.

The Prime Minister's decision to hold a referendum was not driven by personal convictions, since he campaigned to Remain. It seems to have been influenced by strategic calculations.[14]

One was an attempt to stem rising support for the Eurosceptic populist UKIP. In 1999 the electoral system that was used to elect UK members to the European Parliament switched from first-past-the-post to Regional Party List Proportional Representation. This lower vote threshold allowed the UK Independence Party (UKIP) to enjoy its first real breakthrough by winning 7 percent of the vote and three seats in the European Parliament on a strongly Eurosceptic platform (see Figure 11.1). The party doubled its share of the vote in the 2004 European Parliamentary elections and maintained this position in 2009, before surging in 2014 to win more than a quarter of the vote and one-third of MEPs. This provided a platform and the oxygen of publicity, as well as more party members, so that they were taken more seriously by the news media and rival parties. Previous fringe parties on the extreme right, including the National Front and British National Party, had focused mainly on the xenophobic politics of race and immigration. By emphasizing hostility toward the European Union as their core issue, and pushing for a hardline exit, UKIP presented a more acceptable and moderate profile, even if dog-whistle xenophobia and anti-immigration attitudes were a large part of their electoral appeal.[15]

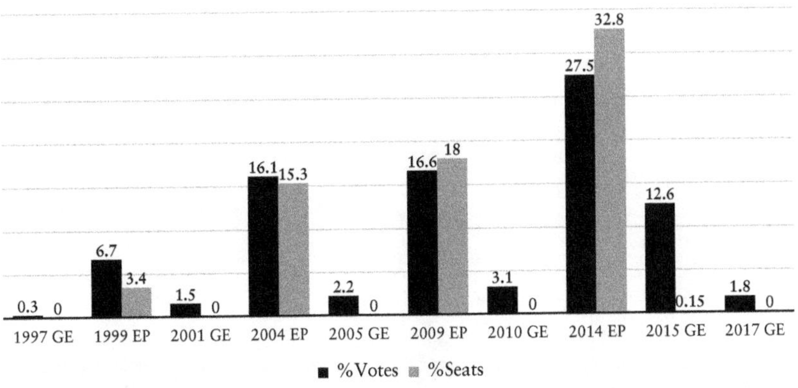


FIGURE 11.1. *UKIP's share of votes and seats in UK European and general elections, 1997–2017*

At Westminster, however, under first-past-the-post (Single Member Plurality) elections and higher vote thresholds, UKIP faced similar hurdles to those confronting other minor parties with spatially dispersed support, like the Green Party and the ultra-nationalist British National Party. In a series of general elections from 1997 to 2010, UKIP modestly increased its share of the vote but failed to gain a single seat. In the 2010 general elections, for example, UKIP won only 3.1 percent of the vote and lost many candidate deposits. Following this contest, however, under the leadership of Nigel Farage, the party saw its poll ratings rise, in part by winning parliamentary by-elections in August and November 2014 where two rebellious Eurosceptic Conservative MPs resigned (including the aptly named Mr. Reckless) and switched to UKIP. As shown in Figure 11.2, UKIP's rise in the opinion polls mirrored the Conservative-led government period of mid-term blues. This was exacerbated from 2010 to 2013 by lackluster economic growth, roughly 8 percent unemployment, and austerity cuts in public spending for schools, healthcare, and housing in an effort to reduce the debt.[16] Moreover, the pro-European Liberal Democrats lost support

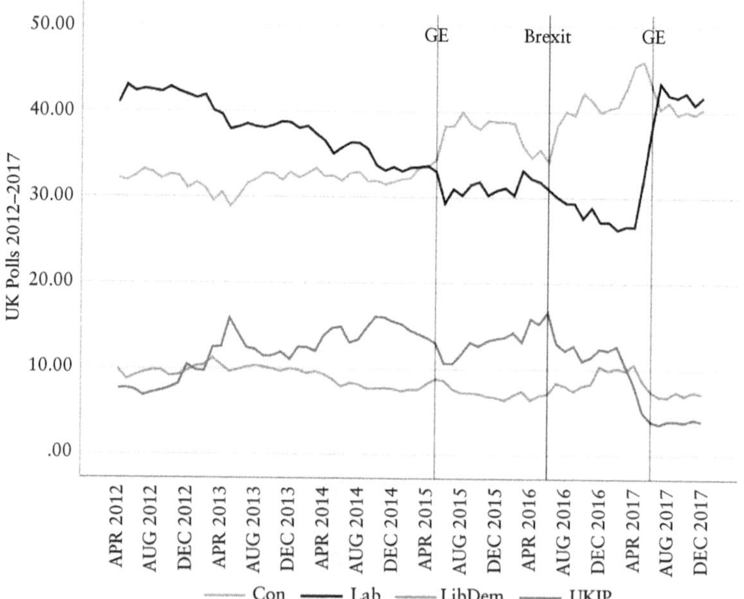


FIGURE 11.2. *Party voting intentions in UK polls, 2012–2017*
*Notes:* These estimate voting intentions for the four largest nation-wide parties based on the monthly average in 649 published national polls by major pollsters (MORI, ICM, YouGov, Populus, Communicate Research, NOP, Opinium, Survation, ORB, Ashcroft).
*Source:* Calculated from data from http://ukpollingreport.co.uk/voting-intention-2.

in the opinion polls, alienating its center-left supporters both through the party's participation as junior partners in the Con-Lib/Dem coalition government and through participating in the austerity programs. The 2015 general election saw a disastrous performance for the Lib-Dems, with their parliamentary party drastically reduced, falling from 57 to just 8 MPs.[17] By contrast, UKIP quadrupled its share of the vote in this contest, surging to 12.6 percent or almost 4 million ballots, representing a record performance for the party in a general election, although only retaining one of its by-election seats (Clacton).[18] Based on the closeness of major parties in the final polls, the 2015 campaign generated much speculation about a possible hung parliament, or even a Labour victory under Ed Miliband. Instead, to everyone's surprise, David Cameron was returned for a second term of Conservative government with a narrow overall parliamentary majority (330). By holding a decisive referendum on Britain's EU membership – and winning it – Cameron gambled that in future contests the Conservatives could strengthen their lead and see off the UKIP challenge.

Moreover, over successive decades the Conservative Party had become increasingly divided over Britain's membership in the European Union. Under Edward Heath's leadership in the early 1970s, the Tories had been the most pro-EU of the two major parties, but party positions gradually switched on this issue among parliamentarians and their supporters.[19] Mrs. Thatcher regarded deeper European integration and the Single European Act as imposing heavy regulatory burdens and limits on the sovereignty of its member states. During the Thatcher era of the 1980s, Euroscepticism became more common among Tory backbenchers. The chorus of criticism of Europe became far louder after the Maastricht Treaty of 1992, with the move toward adopting a single currency sparking major backbench rebellions within the Major government.[20] The May 6, 2010 UK general Election saw the return of a minority government with the Conservatives winning the largest number of seats and votes but falling 20 seats short of an overall parliamentary majority. Talks produced a Conservative–Liberal Democrat governing coalition, led by Prime Minister David Cameron, with the leader of the Liberal Democrats, Nick Clegg, serving as his Deputy. This coalition caused new tensions, however, as Cameron sought to placate his Eurosceptic backbench rebels while satisfying his pro-EU Liberal Democrat partners. Cameron calculated that holding a referendum on Britain's membership could help silence the Eurosceptic wing within his own party, settling internal battles in a decisive fashion. He blundered by banking on the widespread expectation that the pro-EU forces would win.[21] But European problems multiplied, not least by the Eurozone crisis in countries like Spain and Greece, and by the refugee crisis. The 'Vote Leave' campaign emphasized the potential saving to the taxpayer from EU withdrawal which could, supposedly, channel more funds into the NHS, regaining sovereignty over British borders, control of immigration, and the ability of the UK to trade freely with the rest of the world.[22] The Remain side, 'Britain Stronger in Europe,' focused on the economic risks of withdrawal for jobs, prices, trade, businesses, and investments. Campaign coverage in the news media was dominated by the issue of the economy, immigration, and the conduct of the referendum.[23] Newspaper endorsements were divided evenly between Ins and Outs, although in terms of mass circulation, 80 percent of published articles favored Leave. As illustrated in Figure 11.3, combining all major published national opinion polls, the long campaign from January to June 2016 saw a tight contest without Leave or Remain moving consistently ahead and considerable fluctuations over time. Polls also differed; Remain was projected to have a modest lead in the telephone polls and the betting markets during the May campaign, but online polls showed greater uncertainty.[24]

On June 23, 2016, the Brexit referendum upended UK politics. The margin of victory was modest, with 51.9 percent of the electorate voting

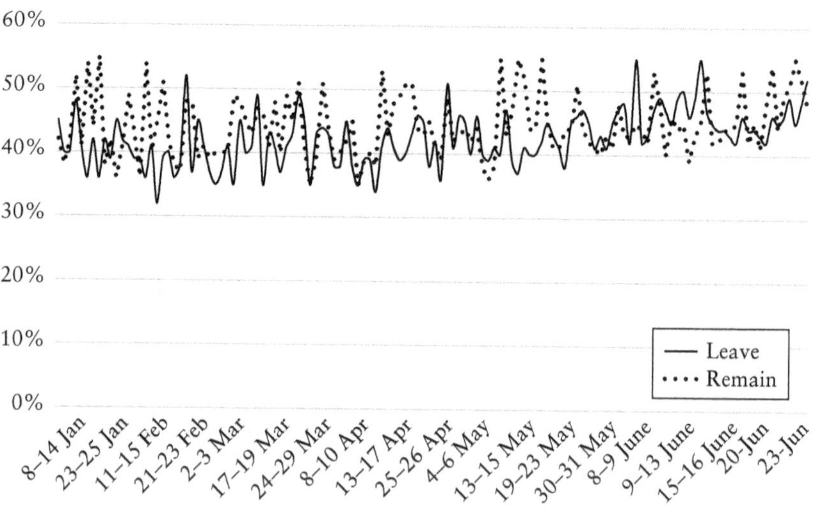


FIGURE 11.3. *The dynamics of the Leave–Remain voting intentions, January–June 2016*

*Note:* All national British opinion polls published on Brexit from January–June 23, 2016.

to leave the European Union. Although strictly consultative, the outcome was treated by parliament as decisive and binding, rather than as catalyzing the sort of re-run referendum held in Ireland in 2008–2009 over approval of the Lisbon Treaty.[25] Cameron immediately resigned after the result was declared, to be replaced a few weeks later by Theresa May, who promised to lead the withdrawal negotiations on the grounds that 'Brexit means Brexit.'

The results demonstrated deep divisions between the Leave areas of the UK – economically disadvantaged communities with many older, less educated, white voters, in the Midlands, the North East, Yorkshire and Humber, and Eastern England – versus the Remain territories of Scotland, metropolitan London, and Northern Ireland.[26] Some scholars concluded that the mainstream parties, especially the Labour Party under Tony Blair, Gordon Brown, and Jeremy Corbyn, offered policies that failed to appeal to their base; British political elites shared similar values endorsing social liberalism, multiculturalism, and EU membership, but working-class voters and older social conservatives held values that reflected a more authoritarian, xenophobic, and nativist response to immigration and EU membership.[27] But others challenge this claim, citing evidence that it was the 'squeezed middle' or intermediary class who reported financial decline and who voted Leave, not the working class.[28]

## The June 8, 2017 UK General Elections

Brexit was followed by a surge in support for the Conservative Party under Theresa May's leadership (see Figure 11.2). Leaving the European Union was adopted as official Conservative Party policy as the new Prime Minister pledged to negotiate Britain's exit from the EU, with the Home Office implementing stricter control of immigration numbers. The Conservative manifesto promised to cut net migration below 100,000 a year. When the party decided to negotiate a European divorce, UKIP lost ownership of its signature issue, and their support plummeted; thus, UKIP lost 140 councilors in the May 4, 2017 local elections as their voters switched in droves to the Tories. Moreover, the Labour Party continued to be divided over Europe and they became locked in an internal battle over Jeremy Corbyn's leadership, as he tried to move the party in a more radically left-wing direction, with support from the grassroots membership but on-again, off-again rebellions from his backbenchers.[29]

Seeking to capitalize on the Conservative's comfortable 20-point lead in the opinion polls, in spring 2017 Theresa May decided to go for a snap general election on June 8, 2017.[30] The Prime Minister hoped to secure a comfortable overall parliamentary majority, and some even hoped for a landslide, which would thereby strengthen the government's hand in the lengthy two-year negotiations with the EU. But May's campaign skills came into question. During the campaign, Theresa May repeatedly pledged to provide 'strong and stable' leadership, and to be tough with the EU in the Brexit negotiations.[31] Since her speech to the Conservative Party conference in 2015, as Home Secretary she had advocated stricter limits on asylum seekers and immigration, but polls reported that this was not the most important issue in the campaign. For the Labour Party, after being dismissed by many pundits, Jeremy Corbyn mounted what was seen as a surprisingly effective policy-oriented campaign, arguing for more generous government spending on the public sector, especially healthcare.[32] On the EU, he shilly-shallied and vaguely endorsed a 'soft' Brexit in negotiations with Europe, remaining strategically ambiguous.[33] The 'Remain' camp was quiescent and defeated, with talk of a second referendum being seen as a betrayal, and parliamentary dissent portrayed as acting like 'tyrants to the people.' Tony Blair reappeared to fly the tattered pro-EU flag, like Marley's ghost of Christmas past, still shackled by the chains of Iraq. The Liberal Democrats remained pro-Brussels in a rear-guard action but they failed to regain their popularity, dogged by the long shadow of the Cameron–Clegg coalition. UKIP battled on under the leadership of Paul Nuttall, with candidates in around half of all constituencies, but they had lost their key issue of EU withdrawal and received little coverage in the news media, their membership fell to around 39,000, and they organized a poor grassroots campaign.[34]

The June 2017 general election registered a disastrous performance by the UK Independence Party; on election night, UKIP lost their only seat, and their share of the vote plummeted to just 1.8 percent, from 12.6 percent in the 2015 general election. The Conservatives gained votes in 'Leave' constituencies, such as Clacton, Doncaster Central, and Don Valley, and where the UKIP vote plummeted most sharply.[35] Election day polls suggest that only around one fifth of UKIP 2015 voters remained faithful, while the majority (57%) switched to the Conservatives, with around one fifth returning to Labour.[36] Many Leave voters in the referendum appear to have switched back to the Conservatives in the general election, generating the collapse in UKIP support.[37] Nevertheless, the risky bet Theresa May placed on securing a comfortable parliamentary majority failed to pay off; instead, the Conservatives lost seats and while they remained the largest party with 317 MPs, they lost their majority, resulting in a hung parliament. Labour treated defeat like victory, given their unexpected surge in the polls under Corbyn, confounding his critics.[38] The aftermath saw much chatter about the resignation of the Prime Minister but she clung on. In late June 2017, a deal was struck with the hardline Democratic Unionist Party (DUP), who promised their support for key parliamentary votes, allowing May to form a minority Conservative government, which started negotiations for a messy divorce from the EU.

## II THEORIES OF ECONOMIC OR CULTURAL GRIEVANCES

Like the US 2016 elections, the key debate in the UK case concerns whether the Leave camp in Brexit in June 2016, and voting for UKIP in the 2015 and 2017 general elections, were motivated primarily by economic grievances among the least well off, because jobs and wages had been stagnant in the most economically depressed areas of Britain, or whether cultural values played a bigger role, including mistrust of Westminster, attitudes toward Europe, and immigration.

The economic thesis dominated the early popular commentary, based on scrutinizing the geography of the Leave vote. The outcome of Brexit was widely regarded in media coverage as a consequence of the 'left behind,' or 'economic-have-nots,' delivering a protest against Westminster. Rational choice theories of political economy argue that voters calculated the instrumental benefits and costs arising from EU membership or withdrawal. On the one hand, the middle-class professionals, managers, and executives in the service sector, typically university educated, affluent, and mobile, seem to have benefitted from EU membership through the lower costs of imported goods, and the broader access to trade and investment opportunities, while taking advantage of opportunities for international travel and broader educational and professional possibilities within a borderless Europe.[39] By contrast, however, those with low-paid, low-skill jobs, without college degrees, found themselves competing with migrant workers from Poland, Bulgaria, and the Czech Republic, while competing with companies employing cheaper labor in China and India. Economic globalization has been blamed for a trade 'shock' hitting the profitability of manufacturing, jobs, and the domestic costs of labor.[40] These developments have been linked with the growing proportion of low-wage, unskilled immigrant workers, drawn from within and outside the EU, and outsourcing as companies moved jobs abroad. The cumulative impact of these economic shifts was held to be responsible for working-class support for UKIP in the 2015 UK general election and the unexpected Brexit Leave outcome.[41]

But studies by other scholars find that some of these claims were not supported by individual-level survey evidence. The impact of social class on the voting preferences of the British electorate, including for or against Brexit, which had been the predominant cleavage in the post-war period, gradually dwindled over successive elections to become insignificant in recent years. The most comprehensive recent analysis of class politics in Britain, by Evans and Tilley, found that the class cleavage had diminished or even reversed itself by the time of the 2015 general election: in this contest, some middle-class professional groups were more likely to vote for Labour than the working class.[42] This study attributed these developments to 'top' down changes in the supply-side of party competition, including the growth of the college-educated middle classes in the social composition of parliament and the development of catch-all party appeals weakening class-based campaigns. These factors might have contributed to the erosion of the class cleavage in British elections, but it seems implausible to attribute this development wholly to supply-side factors, like Labour Party campaign strategies, as we have observed that this phenomenon is not sui generis but applies to many established democracies.

With greatly weakened class and economic appeal to the less well-off, feelings of identity and cultural grievances may come to the fore, with the Leave vote being driven by a populist protest directed 'upwards' against the establishment such as party leaders, journalists, economists, scientists, Eurocrats, bankers, and world leaders telling 'us' what to think, and by authoritarian antipathy toward perceived threats from 'Them' (whether Polish shopkeepers, Syrian refugees, or second-generation Bangladeshi). As Chapter 6 showed, even after including multiple controls, negative attitudes toward immigration were significant predictors of authoritarian and populist values in the pooled European Social Survey. This linkage was confirmed in many West European and Scandinavian societies that had attracted a high proportion of immigrants, refugees, and asylum seekers – although not in many Eastern and Central European nations, which had seen a net loss. Many other studies have reported that immigration attitudes are strongly linked with voting for radical right parties.[43]

The British case is also suitable to examine this phenomenon within the context of a plural multicultural Western democracy. Major cities in England and Wales have long attracted waves of migrants, often from Commonwealth countries in South East Asia and the Caribbean, as well as from states like Uganda and Nigeria in sub-Saharan Africa. The OECD estimates that today, around one in seven British residents is foreign-born – not including the second-generation of British-born citizens with parents who immigrated from such countries as India, Pakistan, Bangladesh, and the Caribbean from the 1950s onwards.[44] Britain has long been an attractive destination for migrants, as a prosperous English-speaking society with cultural ties to Commonwealth countries, an open labor market, a university system aggressively recruiting international students, and a comprehensive welfare state. Today cities such as London, Manchester, Birmingham, Leicester, Leeds, and Coventry have become diverse multiethnic and multicultural societies. Based on official statistics, the Institute for Race Relations estimates that in terms of ethnicity, in 2014 around 87 percent of the total UK resident population are White British. This proportion drops to 80 percent in England and Wales and only 45 percent in cosmopolitan London.[45]

It would be a mistake to see the complex issue of immigration in Britain purely through the lens of the politics of racism or Islamophobia. The UK has one of the highest levels of inward migration within the EU, attracting almost nine million migrants as of 2017, more than any other EU state except Germany (see Figure 6.2).[46] Many migrants are high-skilled professionals, such as doctors in the NHS, financial managers in the city, and entrepreneurs in the retail sector. The right for European citizens to live and work anywhere within the European Union, and the removal of restrictions on open access to labor markets for citizens from Central and Eastern European accession states, attracted many high-educated migrants. It is estimated that by the time of Brexit, around one million Poles lived and worked in Britain, while around 400,000 French expats lived in London alone, a number equal to France's sixth largest city.[47] Others are unskilled and less-educated workers, often second-generation from the African-Caribbean, Indian, Bangladeshi, and Pakistani communities. Only a minority comes from the influx of more recent refugees and asylum seekers fleeing developing countries with weak states, conflict, and poverty. Compared with other West European countries such as Germany, Britain has one of the least generous policies for supporting asylum seekers with financial aid, housing, and benefits.[48]

## III EVIDENCE AND DATA

Many factors on the 'demand-side' of the equation may have contributed toward the Brexit Leave vote – as well as support for UKIP. If the economic grievance thesis is correct, then voting for Leave and UKIP in the electorate should be stronger among low-income households, unskilled manual workers, the unemployed, those with subjective feelings of economic insecurity, as well as those with left-wing economic attitudes and values. On the other hand, as Chapter 8 demonstrated, populist attitudes political distrusting, and authoritarian values, were strong predictors of support for Authoritarian-Populist parties across Europe. If the cultural grievance thesis is also correct for the British case, then voting for UKIP and for Leave should be predicted by authoritarian and populist values. The literature suggests that many other cultural values may also matter, including attitudes toward immigration, and toward European integration.

The British Election Study multiwave panel data provide rich opportunities to test these relationships in more depth, throughout the period from 2014 to 2017. If similar patterns are observed over time, this increases confidence in the reliability of the results. The UK case study also allows us to explore the dynamics of support for authoritarian populism in terms of both issues (Brexit) and parties (UKIP) by comparing voting behavior and public opinion over time, including the May 7, 2015 British general election, the June 23, 2016 non-binding referendum on Britain's membership of the EU (Brexit), and the June 8, 2017 British general election. For evidence at individual level, we draw on the British Election Study panel survey, a large study of 31,196 people conducted by YouGov over 13 waves from February 2014, from the first wave in advance of the May 2015 general election until the final wave immediately after the June 2017 general election.[49] For constituency-level analysis over successive elections, we can also use the British General Election Constituency Results 2010–2017, which also include the estimated Brexit vote by seat.[50]

In the British Election Study panel survey, three scale measures of values are particularly useful for analysis in this study, measuring libertarian/authoritarian, left–right economic values, and populist attitudes.

The first concerns the *libertarian/authoritarian* cleavage, which we have already demonstrated is a strong influence on voting behavior in many European societies. The British Election Study (BES) libertarian-authoritarian scale is calculated from responses to the following statements in the panel survey: '(1) Young people today don't have enough respect for traditional British values; (2) People who break the law should be given stiffer sentences; (3) For some crimes, the death penalty is the most appropriate sentence; (4) Schools should teach children to obey authority; (5) The law should always be obeyed, even if a particular law is wrong; (6) Censorship of films and magazines is necessary to uphold moral standards.' The battery taps similar values to those in the Schwartz values scales used in earlier chapters. The scale is also strongly correlated with the classic childrearing right-wing authoritarian value scale monitoring obedience and social conformity.[51] The BES scale is summed across all six items. Those classified as most 'authoritarian' are amongst the one-fifth with the highest scores (i.e. scoring eight or more on the 10-point scale), while those classified as 'libertarian' are among the one-fifth with the lowest scores (i.e. 2 or less). Similar batteries have been used in successive surveys since 1992 in the British Social Attitudes and the British Election Study.[52] The BES scale also taps broad social values without any reference to policy issues debated during the Brexit and general election campaigns, avoiding problems of circularity and endogeneity. In a 'funnel of causality' model, values can be understood as further from the voting decision than attitudes toward immigration, European integration, party identification, or support for party leaders. If this value cleavage has become more important in the UK, as the cultural backlash thesis argues, this should be a strong predictor of both UKIP and Leave support.

For comparison, we can also measure left–right economic attitudes, reflecting the classic cleavage over state socialism versus free markets. If the economic grievance thesis is correct, then this should also predict UKIP and Brexit voting, with the 'left-behind' sectors supporting redistribution of wealth and income. These values are monitored using similar procedures to the libertarian–authoritarian scale in the BES based on 5-point agreement or disagreement responses to the following Likert-style items: '(1) Government should redistribute income from the better off to those who are less well off; (2) Big business benefits owners at the expense of workers; (3) Ordinary working people do not get their fair share of the nation's wealth; (4) There is one law for the rich and one for the poor; (5) Management will always try to get the better of employees if it gets the chance.' The left–right scale is constructed by summing the five items and standardizing the scale. Again, these items are designed to monitor broad values and do not tap the core campaign issues debated during Brexit. These batteries of questions were included in successive BES and BSA surveys and have been widely tested in the research literature.[53] If economic considerations continue to shape patterns of party competition and voting behavior, then this cleavage should be a strong predictor of both party choices in recent general elections as well as the Brexit Leave/Remain vote.

In previous chapters using the ESS survey data, we needed to reply on indirect measures of the core concept of *populism*, such as feelings of mistrust of political parties, politicians, and parliaments. This has limitations, since these measures only capture the anti-establishment dimension, but not the 'power to the people' aspect of this concept. New survey instruments are emerging to examine the latter dimension, not just dissatisfaction with the political establishment but also whether the public endorses the principle of popular sovereignty.[54] Analyzing evidence from nine European countries with these items suggests that populist attitudes do serve to shape support for populist parties and also moderate the impact of policy issues.[55] To explore this issue we will analyze a specially designed battery of items in the BES panel which is closer to the notion of populism outlined in Chapter 3. Some of these questions were first used in a pioneering study developed by Akkerman, Mudde, and Zaslove which was tested in a small Dutch survey designed to establish public attitudes toward populism.[56] Accordingly we constructed a Populist standardized scale as a summary (Z-score) measured in BES (Waves 7 and 10) from the following five Likert-style agree/disagree items: '(1) The politicians in the UK Parliament need to follow the will of the people; (2) The people, and not politicians, should make our most important policy decisions; (3) I would rather be represented by a citizen than by a specialized politician; (4) Elected officials talk too much and take too little action; (5) What people call 'compromise' in politics is really just selling out on one's principles.' In factor analysis and reliability tests, these items generate consistent scales in a single dimension.[57] Similar procedures were followed to classify the most and least populist categories.

Table 11.1 presents the results of logistic regression models where the dependent variable is the vote to Leave (1) or Remain (0) in the European Union in Wave 9 (24 June–4 July 2016), from the post-Brexit wave of the BES survey. Descriptive statistics are used to compare the typical profile of the Brexit Leave vote with patterns of voting for UKIP in 2015, 2016, and 2017. For comparisons with previous chapters, the models in Table 11.1 control for several factors expected to prove important in predicting support for UKIP as a party, as well as Leave as an issue, with items matched to the closed wave of the panel prior to Brexit, including the effects of birth cohort, social background (using having children and marital status as proxies for life-cycle effects), as well as gender, education, and ethnicity (White British nor not). Economic indicators include occupational class (a five-fold schema based on the occupational status of the head of household), feelings of economic inequality (subjective

TABLE 11.1. *Predicting Leave Vote in Brexit*

| | | Model 1 | | | Model 2 | | | Model 3 | | | Model 4 | | |
|---|---|---|---|---|---|---|---|---|---|---|---|---|---|
| | | B | S.E. | Sig. | B | S.E. | Sig. | B | S.E. | Sig. | B | S.E. | Sig. |
| Generation | Interwar (1900–1945) (Ref) | 0.00 | | | 0.00 | | | 0.00 | | | 0.00 | | |
| | Boomers (1946–1964) | −0.18 | 0.15 | N/s | −0.27 | 0.15 | N/s | −0.16 | 0.16 | N/s | 0.12 | 0.29 | N/s |
| | Gen X (1965–1979) | −0.43 | 0.20 | ** | −0.58 | 0.20 | *** | −0.38 | 0.23 | N/s | −0.01 | 0.39 | N/s |
| | Millennials (1980–1996) | −0.88 | 0.25 | *** | −1.00 | 0.25 | *** | −0.87 | 0.28 | *** | −0.78 | 0.48 | N/s |
| Background | Married | 0.27 | 0.16 | N/s | 0.34 | 0.16 | * | 0.22 | 0.18 | N/s | 0.03 | 0.31 | N/s |
| | Children | 0.04 | 0.15 | N/s | 0.00 | 0.15 | N/s | −0.06 | 0.17 | N/s | 0.13 | 0.28 | N/s |
| | Education | −0.53 | 0.04 | *** | −0.47 | 0.05 | *** | −0.24 | 0.05 | *** | −0.14 | 0.08 | N/s |
| | Sex (Male) | 0.00 | 0.10 | N/s | 0.02 | 0.10 | N/s | −0.01 | 0.12 | N/s | −0.28 | 0.19 | N/s |
| | White British | 0.30 | 0.19 | N/s | 0.35 | 0.19 | N/s | 0.42 | 0.22 | * | −0.44 | 0.36 | N/s |
| Class | Professional and managerial | | | | −0.30 | 0.17 | N/s | −0.03 | 0.19 | N/s | 0.09 | 0.32 | N/s |
| | Skilled clerical | | | | −0.07 | 0.19 | N/s | 0.09 | 0.21 | N/s | 0.08 | 0.35 | N/s |
| | Foremen and technicians | | | | 0.17 | 0.19 | N/s | 0.14 | 0.21 | N/s | 0.54 | 0.36 | N/s |
| | Skilled manual | | | | 0.00 | 0.24 | N/s | 0.14 | 0.26 | N/s | −0.14 | 0.44 | N/s |
| | Unskilled manual (Ref) | | | | 0.00 | | | 0.00 | | | 0.00 | | |

(*continued*)

TABLE 11.1 (*continued*)

| | | Model 1 | | | Model 2 | | | Model 3 | | | Model 4 | | |
|---|---|---|---|---|---|---|---|---|---|---|---|---|---|
| | | B | S.E. | Sig. | B | S.E. | Sig. | B | S.E. | Sig. | B | S.E. | Sig. |
| Economic | Unemployed | | | | 0.21 | 0.46 | N/s | 0.81 | 0.53 | N/s | 0.76 | 0.87 | N/s |
| | Subjective economic insecurity | | | | 0.06 | 0.03 | * | 0.03 | 0.03 | N/s | 0.10 | 0.05 | * |
| Culture | Libertarian-authoritarian BES scale | | | | | | | 0.41 | 0.03 | *** | 0.11 | 0.06 | * |
| | Populism scale | | | | | | | 0.47 | 0.06 | *** | 0.37 | 0.13 | *** |
| Values | Left–right economic scale | | | | | | | | | | −0.03 | 0.06 | N/s |
| | Allow more or fewer immigrants | | | | | | | | | | 0.00 | 0.00 | N/s |
| | European Integration scale | | | | | | | | | | 0.74 | 0.05 | *** |
| | Like/dislike: UKIP | | | | | | | | | | 0.44 | 0.04 | *** |
| | Constant | 1.39 | 0.31 | *** | 1.02 | 0.36 | *** | −2.36 | 0.47 | *** | −6.15 | 0.85 | *** |
| | Nagelkerke R2 | 0.17 | | | 0.19 | | | 0.38 | | | 82.40 | | |
| | % Correct | 65.4 | | | 66.5 | | | 74.3 | | | 91.6 | | |

*Note:* Logistic regression analysis where the dependence variable is vote Leave in Brexit. See Appendix B for all variables.
*Source:* British Election Study Internet Panel Waves 8–9. www.britishelectionstudy.com/data-objects/panel-study-data/.

economic security from the perceived risks of low savings and unemployment), and experience of unemployment.[58] The left–right economic values scale is also included. Gross household income was also compared descriptively but dropped from the multivariate model to avoid problems of multicollinearity. Cultural scales include those for the core values of authoritarianism and populism, at the heart of this book, as well as attitudes toward immigration, European integration, and like/dislike of UKIP.

## IV ANALYZING THE RESULTS

### Generation Gaps

The results of the first model in Table 11.1 confirms that there was a major generational cleavage dividing the Leave–Remain camps. In keeping with many other studies, we find that Millennials were far less likely to vote Leave than the Interwar generation.[59] And according to the British Election Study, the generation gap has widened over successive elections in the UK (as in the US). Thus, in general elections held from 1970 to 2010, the Conservatives consistently held a modest advantage among the older generations when compared with the support they attracted among younger cohorts. But the gap among birth cohorts has expanded in recent contests. Thus, younger people were significantly less likely to cast a Brexit ballot but when they did so, according to the BES, around 38 percent of the youngest (Millennial) cohort voted to Leave the EU in contrast to almost two–thirds of the Interwar cohort (65%) (see Figure 11.4). Moreover, strikingly similar generation gaps were found in the proportion of the electorate voting for UKIP in the 2015 and 2017 British general elections (and saying that they would vote for UKIP in 2016) (see Figure 11.5). There is not much difference between the Interwar and Boomer birth cohorts, but voting for UKIP drops a lot among the Generation X and Millennials. In the 2015 general election, while 8.4 percent of the Interwar generation reported voting UKIP, only 2 percent of the Millennials did so.

As well as birth cohorts, Model 1 in Table 11.1 also includes a range of social background factors; none is significant except for education. This finding has been widely noted in previous studies of Brexit as well as in classic studies of authoritarianism.[60] College education is consistently one of the strongest predictors of socially liberal and socially conservative values – and of support for Authoritarian-Populist parties and

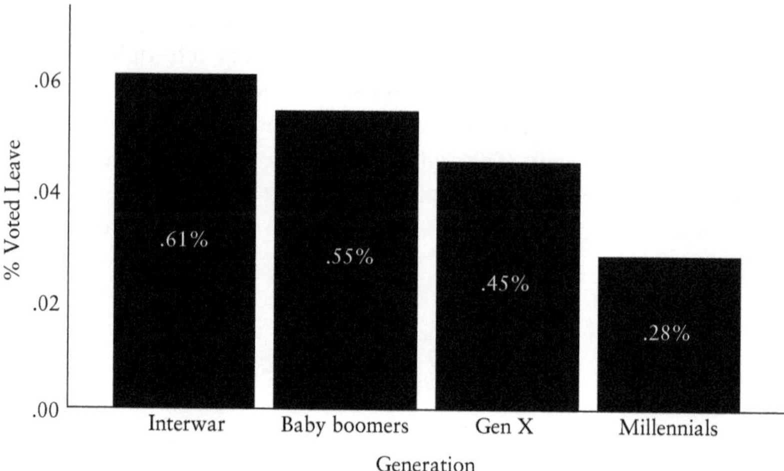


FIGURE 11.4. *Vote Leave by birth cohort*
*Note:* 'In the referendum on Britain's membership of the European Union, how did you vote?'
*Source:* British Election Study Internet Panel Waves 1–13. Wave 9 post-Brexit (24 June to 6 July 2016). www.britishelectionstudy.com/data-objects/panel-study-data/.

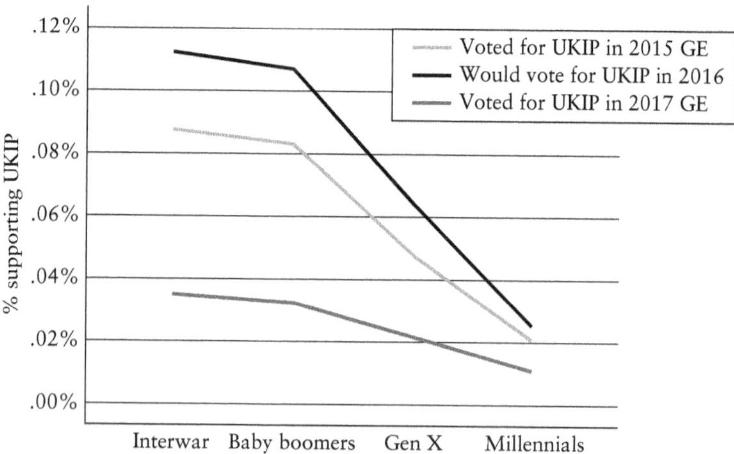


FIGURE 11.5. *Generation gaps in UKIP voting, 2015–2017*
*Source:* British Election Study Internet Panel Waves 1–13. www.britishelectionstudy.com/data-objects/panel-study-data/.

leaders. The linkage between education and libertarian views seems to arise from socialization effects.[61] College graduates were likely to vote Remain because tolerance toward diversity is fostered by the values, knowledge, and cognitive skills acquired through formal schooling.[62] More awareness and information about other peoples and places tends to generate greater trust.[63] But, surprisingly, ethnicity (being White British) did not predict whether someone voted to Remain or Leave. Support for the European Union and attitudes toward immigration are so much more complicated than a simple racial or ethnic divide might suggest.

## Economic Grievances and the Have-Nots

To test the economic grievance thesis, Model 2 adds several economic indicators – including occupational class – which remains statistically insignificant across all models in predicting the Leave vote. There is a significant difference between the middle and working-class categories in the Leave vote (as illustrated in Figure 11.8) – but support for Leave was not greatest among the unskilled manual working-class households with the lowest levels of pay in Table 11.1, occupational status, and job security. Social class was not significant when one controls for education and birth cohort. The least well-off are often assumed to be the most Eurosceptic, based on the characteristics of the constituencies that voted to Leave. But, as with the US vote for Trump, the have-not's (or have-least's) did not predict the Brexit vote – as other survey-based studies have also observed.[64] And, despite extensive discussion about the importance of economic deprivation due to the decline of British factories in global markets, individual-level unemployment was also not a significant predictor of how someone voted in Brexit. The only economic indicator in model 2 that was associated with Leave voting tapped subjective feelings of economic insecurity. In other words, those who *felt* more vulnerable to the risks of unemployment or inadequate income were more likely to vote Leave – although the coefficients were not consistently significant across all models. Moreover, the left–right economic value scale is insignificant in the models – a further indication that these attitudes were not important in explaining the Brexit vote.

## Cultural Values

What are the effects of cultural values? To test these, Model 3 adds the Authoritarian–Libertarian BES scale and the populism scale. In keeping

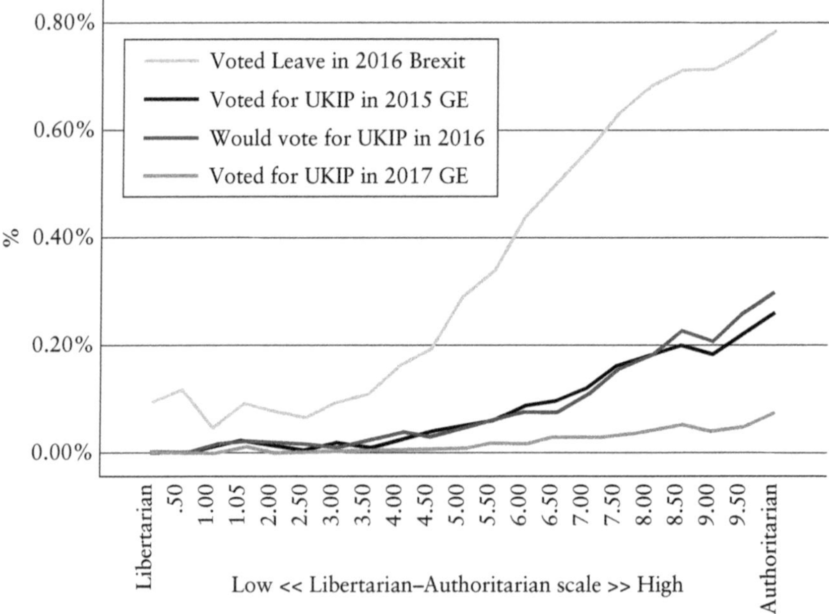


FIGURE 11.6. *Vote Leave and UKIP by authoritarian–libertarian values*
*Notes:* The libertarian–authoritarian standardized 10-point scale is constructed by summing the following items: '(1) Young people today don't have enough respect for traditional British values; (2) People who break the law should be given stiffer sentences; (3) For some crimes, the death penalty is the most appropriate sentence; (4) Schools should teach children to obey authority; (5) The law should always be obeyed, even if a particular law is wrong; (6) Censorship of films and magazines is necessary to uphold moral standards.'
*Source:* British Election Study Internet Panel Waves 1-13. Wave 9 post-Brexit (24 June to 6 July 2016). www.britishelectionstudy.com/data-objects/panel-study-data/.

with findings presented in previous chapters, both of these proved strong and significantly associated with Leave voting in Brexit. As Figure 11.6 illustrates, 60 percent or more of those who were most authoritarian (scoring above 8 on the 10 point scale) voted to Leave. By contrast, among those who were most libertarian (scoring below 2 points on the scale) only 10 percent voted to Leave – a massive gap. Moreover, this was not simply confined to Brexit; instead, similar linear patterns can be observed (at lower levels) for reported UKIP voting in the 2015 and 2017 general elections, and intentions to vote for UKIP in 2016. When UKIP surged in the 2015 general election, almost none of the support came from the most libertarian voters – but UKIP picked up the support

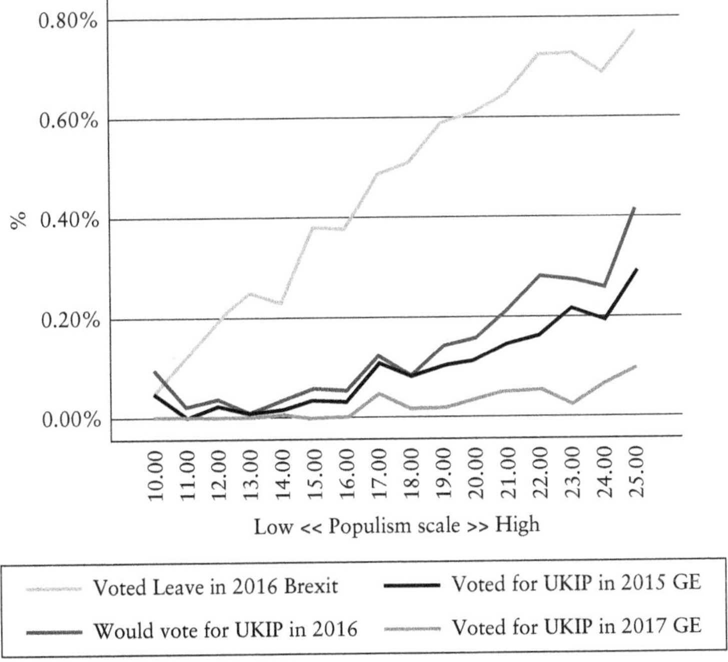


FIGURE 11.7. *Vote Leave and UKIP by populist values*
*Notes:* The *Populist* standardized scale is a summary (Z-score) measured in BES W7 from the following 5 Likert-style agree/disagree items: '(1) The politicians in the UK Parliament need to follow the will of the people; (2) The people, and not politicians, should make our most important policy decisions; (3) I would rather be represented by a citizen than by a specialized politician; (4) Elected officials talk too much and take too little action; (5) What people call "compromise" in politics is really just selling out on one's principles.'
*Source:* British Election Study Internet Panel Waves 1–13. www.britishelectionstudy.com/data-objects/panel-study-data/.

of over one-fifth of the most authoritarian voters. It is worth emphasizing that authoritarian–libertarian values were measured one year before the general election, and policy debates during the campaign did not focus on any of the items in the authoritarianism scale, so this finding does not seem to be attributable to endogeneity. This increases our confidence that these core values drive subsequent voting choices, and reduce the risk that pre-existing party preferences and voting choices shape core authoritarian values.

The measure of populism used in the BES scale is designed to tap orientations toward the role of elected representatives versus the will of the people – the heart of the populism concept. We were unable to monitor

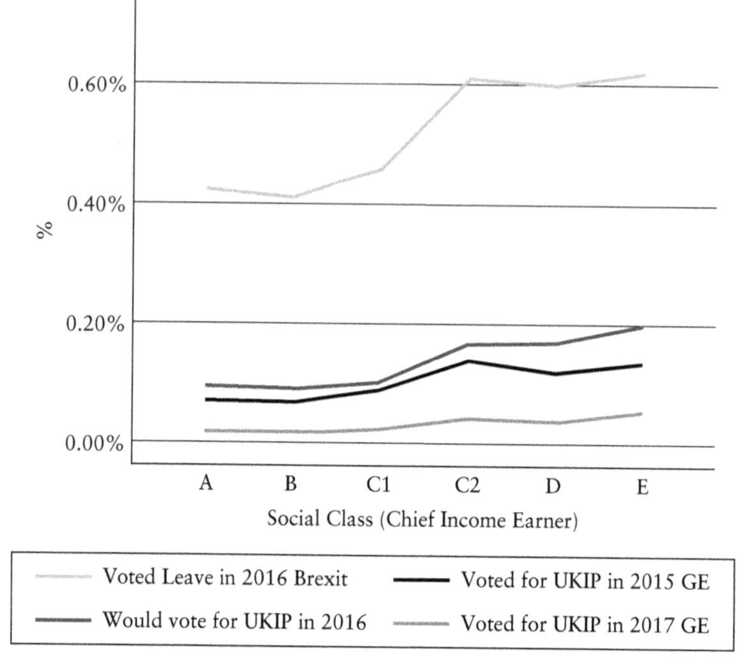


FIGURE 11.8. *Vote Leave and UKIP by social class*
*Note:* Social Class. A Professionals and higher managerial, B Lower managerial, C1 Skilled non-manual, C2 Foremen and supervisors, D Skilled manual, D Unskilled manual.
*Source:* British Election Study Internet Panel Waves 1–13. www.britishelectionstudy.com/data-objects/panel-study-data/.

this dimension in earlier chapters, due to lack of relevant data in the ESS. But the results of the BES scale presented in model 3 in Table 11.1 confirms that populism is indeed statistically significant as a predictor of voting Leave and supporting UKIP, as hypothesized. Figure 11.7 illustrates the remarkable strength of the relationship. Among those scoring lowest in populism (12 or below) around 15 percent voted Leave. In stark contrast, among those scoring highest in populism (23 or above on the 25 point scale) around 70 percent voted Leave. A similar profile is found for those supporting UKIP in the 2015 and 2017 general elections – and expressing voting intentions for UKIP in 2016. This party campaigned almost solely on the issue of withdrawing Britain from the European Union. But beyond this issue, supporters were strongly attracted by the deeper populist appeal that a vote for UKIP and for Brexit reflected a way to restore popular sovereignty to the people – or at least that it delivered a well-aimed kick at 'Them' – the elected representatives at Westminster and European officials in Brussels and Strasbourg.

Finally, Model 4 adds the left–right economic value scale, and whether respondents favored more or fewer immigrants. After controlling for the other characteristics of voters, neither of these was statistically significant. Further examination suggests that without any controls, attitudes toward immigration were indeed directly correlated with the vote to Leave, as expected. But the effect of attitudes toward immigration on Leave voting disappeared once authoritarian and populist values were added to the model. As Chapter 6 demonstrated, attitudes toward immigration are consistently linked with authoritarian populism. In this regard, we concur with a study based on the British Social Attitudes that concluded: 'The [Brexit] result reflected the concerns of older, more "authoritarian" or social conservative voters who were particularly worried about immigration.'[65] The BSA time-series surveys since 2002 suggest that in fact British society as a whole has become slightly more tolerant over time in their views toward the effects of immigration. Growing acceptance of multiculturalism in British society seems to have triggered an authoritarian backlash among the minority of racist and xenophobic sectors of society who endorse these values as a form of collective security to protect 'Us' from 'Them.'

Two other cultural items were very strongly linked to Leave voting in Model 4, namely being for or against further European Integration and whether respondents liked or disliked UKIP. These linkages are highly predictable, indeed almost tautological. They do not help much, in themselves, to enrich our understanding of why people favored or opposed European Union membership or why they support UKIP. In the final model, the addition of these items wiped out the effects of nearly all other factors but the Authoritarian–Libertarian and populism scales and feelings of economic insecurity. It is especially noteworthy that neither the authoritarian nor the populism scales make any explicit references to Europe – yet they are powerful predictors of voting to Leave and supporting UKIP.

How do these patterns relate to Britain's electoral cleavages? No one party has a monopoly on appealing to authoritarian populism. Figure 11.9 compares the position of voters for all the main British parties (excluding Northern Ireland) in terms of where they stood in endorsing authoritarian and populist values, and whether they voted Leave or Remain. As the scatterplot shows, authoritarian and populist values formed a cleavage dividing Leave from Remain supporters in all parties. The Leave

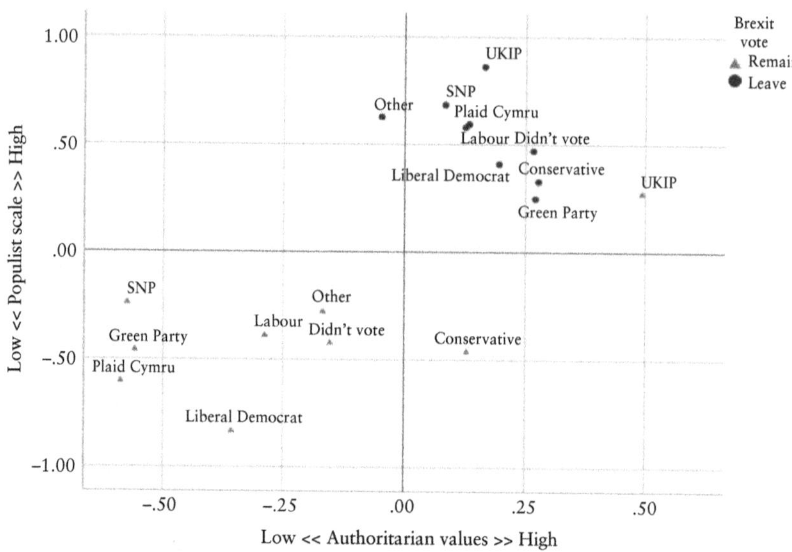


FIGURE 11.9. *Populist and authoritarian values of voters in the UK 2017 general election*

*Note:* The *Populist* standardized scale is a summary (Z-score) measured in BES W10 post-Brexit from the following 5 Likert-style agree/disagree items: '(1) The politicians in the UK Parliament need to follow the will of the people; (2) The people, and not politicians, should make our most important policy decisions; (3) I would rather be represented by a citizen than by a specialized politician; (4) Elected officials talk too much and take too little action; (5) What people call "compromise" in politics is really just selling out on one's principles.' The *Authoritarian* values standardized scale is a summary (Z-score) measured in BES W10 post-Brexit from the following items: 'Please tell me which one you think is more important for a child to have: (1) independence/respect for elders; (2) obedience/self-reliance; (3) consideration/well-behaved; (4) curiosity/good-manners.' The Brexit Leave/Remain vote was measured post-Brexit (W9). The recalled party vote was measured post-2017 UK general election vote (W13).

*Source:* British Election Study Internet Panel Waves 1–13. www.britishelectionstudy.com/data-objects/panel-study-data/.

voters from each party are located in the top-right quadrant, expressing the highest support for authoritarian populism. Of these, UKIP voters are the most populist – but they are located near the Leave supporters from the other parties. By contrast, the Remain supporters from all the parties except UKIP are clustered in the bottom-left quadrant, with the Conservative Remainers more authoritarian, and the Liberal Democrats the least populist. The distribution confirms the importance of the cultural cleavage around these values and the way that this divided supporters *within* each party into Leave and Remain camps.

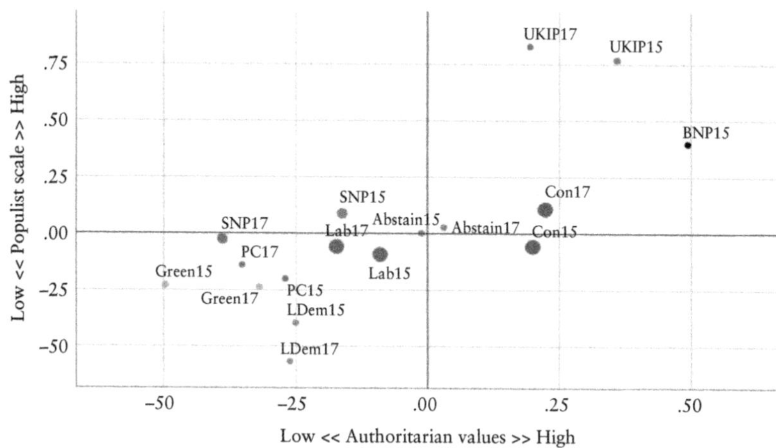


FIGURE 11.10. *Populist and authoritarian values of voters in the UK 2015 and 2017 general election*

*Note:* The *Populist* standardized scale is a summary (Z-score) measured in BES W10 post-Brexit from the following 5 Likert-style agree/disagree items: '(1) The politicians in the UK Parliament need to follow the will of the people; (2) The people, and not politicians, should make our most important policy decisions; (3) I would rather be represented by a citizen than by a specialized politician; 4) Elected officials talk too much and take too little action; (5) What people call "compromise" in politics is really just selling out on one's principles.' The *Authoritarian* values standardized scale is a summary (Z-score) measured in BES W10 post-Brexit from the following items: 'Please tell me which one you think is more important for a child to have: (1) independence/respect for elders; (2) obedience/self-reliance; (3) consideration/well-behaved; (4) curiosity/good-manners.' The Brexit Leave/Remain vote was measured post-Brexit (W9). The recalled party vote was measured post-2017 UK general election vote (W13).

*Source:* British Election Study Internet Panel Waves 1–13. www.britishelectionstudy.com/data-objects/panel-study-data/.

And how do the median positions of party supporters vary *across* these cultural scales and are these positions reasonably stable or do we find major changes over successive elections? Figure 11.10 shows the median position of party voters on these issues scales in the 2015 and 2017 general elections. It is evident that voters for UKIP are consistently the most authoritarian populist in their values – in the top-right quadrant located at some distance from all the other parties except the ultra-fringe British National Party in the 2015 election, which was even more extreme in its racist, anti-immigrant, and xenophobic appeal. The Conservative Party voters are the closest to UKIP voters – but located nearer the center of the political spectrum. Moreover, compared with 2015, Conservative Party voters become slightly more populist and authoritarian in 2017, tacking closer to UKIP under Theresa May's hardline policies toward Europe and immigration. The supporters of the other main British parties cluster in the bottom-right quadrant with less populist and more libertarian values – where they compete with each other for votes. Labour voters are relatively centrist, located near the median voter, while Green voters are most libertarian in their values, and the Liberal Democrat supporters are least populist and most favorable to pluralist democracy. The next chapter builds on these findings to consider the consequences of authoritarian populism for party competition – and the policy agenda.

## V CONCLUSIONS

Brexit shocked Britain's image of itself – and sent reverberations around Europe and the world. Until recently, a broad consensus about the liberal international order abroad and the importance of liberal democratic governance at home was widely shared on both sides of the aisle at Westminster. This consensus also reflected the views of many European heads of state, central bankers, top corporate executives, Silicon Valley leaders, media commentators, academic experts, and the global elites who gathered at Davos. The accord reflected a cosmopolitan vision, convinced of the benefits of access to global markets, open borders, and international cooperation. In Europe, this was seen as a 'permissive consensus' in which Brussels Eurocrats pursued a common vision of deepening and enlarging the European Union, without giving a voice to the European public on the matter – even though this goal was increasingly rejected by many of their own citizens.[66]

At home, as well, the political leadership in all major UK parties differed on many economic and social policies but seemed to share wide agreement about the values of pluralism, tolerance, and respect for diversity, the protection of minority rights, and the rejection of racism, xenophobia, and Islamophobia. In practice, there were always important social tensions and challenges to the tradition of live-and-let-live tolerance – exemplified by regular expressions of xenophobia, Islamophobia, sexism, and racism in the tabloid press. But the worst extremist politics of hate, exemplified by the National Front and the British National Party, were largely confined to the far fringe and quarantined from mainstream British electoral politics. The elite consensus was buttressed by deeply entrenched political norms endorsing the importance of parliamentary democracy, devolved assemblies in the UK regions, a long tradition of free speech supported by a pluralistic and lively free press and an active civil society, rule of law through an independent judiciary, professionalism in the public sector, and strong and stable majoritarian governments counterbalanced by the protection of minority rights. In Almond and Verba's *Civic Culture*, the predominant norms and values in Britain were seen as a model for other democracies. The rise of UKIP, and the Brexit decision and its deeply divisive consequences in its aftermath have shaken faith in the traditional tolerance of British society, raised challenges to the liberal consensus concerning the principles of democratic governance, and even threatened the stability and unity of the United Kingdom.

The story behind Britain's momentous decision to withdraw from the European Union after more than 40 years of membership, and the historical legacy of UKIP in this process, rests ultimately on 'supply-side' factors in Westminster politics – including the critical role of contingent historical events and key decisions made by leading politicians. David Cameron chose for strategic reasons, not personal convictions, to hold a referendum on EU membership – hoping to secure his authority over his recalcitrant backbenchers and to see off UKIP.[67] Yet rather than proving a major threat to the electoral fortunes of the Conservative Party, like many related fringe parties, UKIP has remained a marginal force in British politics. It lost its raison d'etre once the Conservative Party pledged to Leave but also, like many fringe parties, it was unable to overcome the many logistical, financial, and organizational obstacles facing small parties contesting seats in Majoritarian electoral systems. The leaders of Leave – Boris Johnson and Michael Gove – were motivated recklessly by their own leadership aspirations to take over from Cameron more than any deep rooted Euroscepticism or even belief that they would actually win.[68] The result of the consultative Brexit referendum was extremely close and, like similar contests in Ireland and Denmark, could have been rerun, or the rules could have required a qualified majority to win. But instead, Leave's wafer-thin victory was treated by Theresa May as decisive, in part to secure ministerial backing for her own position as party leader. After she entered No. 10, parliament triggered Article 50 of the Lisbon Treaty and endorsed negotiations leading to Britain's eventual divorce from the EU, which is due to occur by midnight March 29, 2019. Yet during negotiations the government appears to have no clear plan of what it wants to secure from these talks – and no realistic chance of securing its goals of restricting the right of Europeans to live and work in Britain while simultaneously maintaining tariff-free access to European markets.[69] May also miscalculated by calling the snap general election in June 2017, losing her parliamentary majority, eroding her authority as party leader, and weakening her negotiating hand in Europe by becoming dependent on the DUP.[70] Like Trump's unexpected edge in the Electoral College in the 2016 election, there are multiple 'what-ifs' in the series of steps leading toward Brexit that could have led to a very different outcome.

Nevertheless, on the 'demand-side' of the equation, the evidence we have scrutinized suggests more predictable and consistent patterns about the main drivers of public opinion and voting behavior in the Brexit referendum, once the referendum had been called, and in patterns of electoral support for UKIP in the 2015 and 2017 general elections.

Three key findings deserve emphasizing from this case study.

The cultural backlash theory argues that a new cleavage emerged in both party competition and in the electorate in many Western societies. In Goodhart's depiction of this situation, Britain has become split between the 'Anywheres,' the degree-educated geographically mobile professionals who embrace new people and experiences, and define themselves by their achievements. In contrast, the 'Somewheres' have an identity rooted in their hometown and find rapid change unsettling, particularly that brought on by the flow of migrants, the growth of multiethnic cities, and more fluid gender identities.[71] We believe that the heart of this cultural division concerns authoritarian values, endorsed by socially conservative groups that feel most threatened by the rapid pace of cultural change and the loss of respect for traditional ways of life. This triggers an authoritarian reflex – emphasizing the importance of maintaining collective security by enforcing conformity with traditional mores, a united front against outsiders, and loyalty to strong leaders. This orientation is reinforced by anti-establishment populist rhetoric kicking 'Them' and reasserting the legitimate voice of 'Us' through claiming 'power to the people.' The cultural backlash thesis suggests that authoritarian and populist values among the older generation and less educated sectors have generated a new cultural cleavage that can be mobilized by populist leaders such as Nigel Farage, and opportunities to express public preferences, such as the Brexit referendum. The empirical evidence in this chapter confirms that both authoritarian and populist values are strongly linked with voting behavior in the United Kingdom, as hypothesized. These patterns persist in predicting not only Leave support in the EU referendum, but also the votes cast for UKIP in the 2015 and 2017 general elections. The results of the analysis remain significant and strong in size, even with multiple controls for the social background of British voters and their economic characteristics.

This chapter also examined the economic grievance thesis, which holds that those who are less well-off – the economic losers from globalization – will be more likely to embrace Brexit and UKIP. Although a widely popular argument in media commentary, and supported by studies in political economy based on the areas where the Leave vote was strongest, this chapter (like other individual-level analyses) found little support for this thesis.[72] In the analytical models, *support for Brexit was not significantly stronger among unskilled manual workers, among the unemployed, and among those with left-wing economic values.*

*Striking generation gaps are evident in voting for Brexit and in recent general elections in the UK.* This confirms the patterns already observed in Europe and the US, and raises important questions about the changing nature of electoral cleavages and party competition in these countries. If these patterns persist and if younger generations can be mobilized to vote, this is likely to be important. We consider the implications in the next chapter, including the potential for transforming the policy agenda, for the future of party competition, and for long-term electoral change in Britain and elsewhere.

What explains the large and growing generational gaps in Brexit and UKIP? On the one hand, it could be that younger people feel that they face more limited economic opportunities than their parents and grandparents. Howker and Malik argue that, in stark contrast to the older generations, millions of young Britons today face the most uncertain future since the early 1930s, without good pensions, secure jobs, and affordable housing.[73] Moreover, Millennials face the costs of attending university and growing levels of student debt,[74] lack of secure well-paid jobs,[75] stagnant wages, and relatively high levels of youth unemployment (with rates more than double the national average).[76] In this sense, age may have become the new social class. If young people feel less well off than their parents and grandparents, they may be attracted by the radical socialist message of the Labour leader, Jeremy Corbyn. But systematic evidence for this claim is mixed. For example, a study using the British Social Attitudes data from 1985 to 2012 reported that young people who came of age under Thatcher were more right-wing in their economic attitudes than previous generations, not more left-wing.[77]

An alternative argument, which is more persuasive, is that the Millennials and Generation X in Britain dislike the Leave camp and UKIP's appeals to English nationalism and white nativism, racial and ethnic intolerance, and social conservatism. They were more strongly attracted to other parties with a cosmopolitan outlook on Britain's place in the EU and socially liberal policies on cultural and moral issues, such as Labour's manifesto pledges to support LGBTQ equality, women's rights, anti-racism, protecting animal welfare, lowering the voting age to 16, supporting international development, and building sustainable environments.[78] But as Figure 11.10 demonstrates, Labour supporters are far from alone in endorsing these values, since voters for the Green Party, the Liberal Democrats, Plaid Cymru, and the Scottish National Party were also all clustered in the quadrant endorsing pluralism over populism and libertarian over authoritarian values. There is widespread evidence from the British Attitudes Survey that British society continues to move in a socially liberal direction, with younger and college-educated people being far more tolerant than older and less-educated groups on same-sex marriage, abortion, euthanasia, pornography, and pre-marital sex.[79] Millennials are also far more likely to have voted Remain – especially university students, because Britain's membership in the European Union presents opportunities to work, live, and study in Paris, Berlin, or Rome. A post-Brexit study of young people in Britain, involving focus groups and a large-scale survey, concluded that many are concerned about the negative impact of Brexit on multiethnic communities – and they expressed concern about rising intolerance, discrimination, racism, and the decline of Britain's multicultural image.[80] They were also resentful that the decision to leave the EU was made by the older generation, and concerned that Brexit would limit their opportunities to live and work in Europe. Meanwhile the Interwar generation was drawn toward Leave, and UKIP, because they tend to endorse a broader range of socially conservative and authoritarian values associated with nationalism, Euroscepticism, and immigration. We have already demonstrated how strongly the generation gap in Europe and America is associated with cultural cleavages around these issues. As the old left–right divisions of social class identities have faded in Britain, an emerging cultural war deeply divides voters and parties around values of national sovereignty versus cooperation among EU member states, respect for traditional families and marriage versus support for gender equality and feminism, tolerance of diverse lifestyles and gender fluid identities, the importance of protecting manufacturing jobs versus environmental protection and climate change, and restrictions on immigration and closed borders versus openness toward refugees, migrants, and foreigners. These are the issues that divide contemporary societies. The next chapter considers their consequences.

## Notes

1. www.bbc.co.uk/news/uk-politics-eu-referendum-36616018.
2. www.electoralcommission.org.uk/find-information-by-subject/elections-and-referendums/past-elections-and-referendums/eu-referendum/electorate-and-count-information.
3. On June 2, 1992, Denmark held a referendum which failed to endorse the decision to join the Maastricht Treaty. After renegotiating some clauses, a second Danish referendum was held on May 18, 1993, which passed. Similarly, Ireland held a referendum to approve the Treaty of Lisbon on June 12, 2018. After this was rejected by the public, a second referendum was held on October 2, 2009, when it passed.
4. Stephan Michel and Ignacio N. Cofone. 2017. 'Majority rules in constitutional referendums.' *Kyklos* 70 (3): 402–424.
5. www.strongerin.co.uk/experts#y5OkcYwCaYQ8qpEl.97.
6. www.conservativehome.com/parliament/2016/06/theresa-mays-launch-statement-full-text.html.
7. https://yougov.co.uk/news/2017/10/27/there-has-been-shift-against-brexit-public-still-t/.
8. For a discussion about a range of alternative explanatory theories, see Harold Clarke, Matthew J. Goodwin, and Paul Whiteley. 2017. *Brexit! Why Britain Voted to Leave the European Union*. Cambridge: Cambridge University Press.
9. John Curtice. 2015. 'A question of culture or economics? Public attitudes to the European Union in Britain.' *Political Quarterly* 87 (2): 209–218.
10. Matthew J. Goodwin and Oliver Heath. 2016. 'The 2016 Referendum, Brexit and the left behind? An aggregate-level analysis of the result.' *Political Quarterly* 87 (3): 323–332; Italo Colantone and Piero Stanig. 2016. 'Global competition and Brexit.' Science Research Network. http://ssrn.com/abstract=2870313; Sasha Becker, Thiemo Fetzer, and Dennis Novy. 2017. 'Who voted for Brexit? A comprehensive district-level analysis.' Munich: CESifo Working Papers 6438-2017. Paper presented at the 65th Panel Meeting of Economic Policy. http://cep.lse.ac.uk/pubs/download/dp1480.pdf; Lorenza Antonucci, Laszlo Horvath, Yordan Kutiyski, and Andre Krouwel. 2017. 'The malaise of the squeezed middle: Challenging the narrative of the "left behind" Brexiter.' *Competition and Change* 21 (3): 211–229.
11. Nick Clarke, Will Jennings, Jonathan Moss, and Gerry Stoker. 2017. 'Changing spaces of political encounter and the rise of anti-politics: Evidence from Mass Observation's General Election diaries.' *Political Geography* 56: 13–33.
12. Geoffrey Evans and Anand Menon. 2017. *Brexit and British Politics*. Oxford: Polity.
13. www.bbc.co.uk/news/uk-politics-21148282.
14. There are several accounts of the politics of the Brexit decision and the referendum campaign. See, for example, Andrew Glencross. 2016. *Why the UK Voted for Brexit: David Cameron's Great Mistake*. London: Palgrave

Macmillan; Owen Bennett. 2016. *The Brexit Club: The Inside Story of the Leave Campaign's Shock Victory.* London: Backbite Books; Tim Ross and Tom McTague. 2017. *Betting the House: The Inside Story of the 2017 Election.* London: Biteback Publishers; Kenneth A. Armstrong. 2017. *Brexit: Leaving the EU – Why, How and When?* Cambridge: Cambridge University Press; Tim Shipman. 2016. *All Out War: The Full Story of Brexit.* London: William Collins.

15. Rob Ford and Matthew J. Goodwin. 2014. *Revolt on the Right. Explaining Support for the Radical Right in Britain.* London: Routledge; Matthew J. Goodwin and Caitlin Milazzo. 2015. *UKIP: Inside the Campaign to Redraw British Politics.* Oxford: Oxford University Press; Harold Clarke, Matthew J. Goodwin, and Paul Whiteley. 2017. *Brexit! Why Britain Voted to Leave the European Union.* Cambridge: Cambridge University Press; Robert Ford, Matthew J. Goodwin, and David Cutts. 2012. 'Strategic Eurosceptics and polite xenophobes: Support for the United Kingdom Independence Party (UKIP) in the 2009 European Parliament elections.' *European Journal of Political Research* 51 (2): 204–234.
16. Andrew Gamble. 2015. 'The Economy.' *Parliamentary Affairs* 68: 154–167.
17. For details about the campaign and results, see Philip Cowley and Dennis Kavanagh. 2016. *The British General Election of 2015.* London: Palgrave Macmillan.
18. David Cutts, Matthew Goodwin, and Caitlin Milazzo. 2017. 'Defeat of the People's Army? The 2015 British general election and the UK Independence Party (UKIP).' *Electoral Studies* 48 (3): 70–83.
19. Tim Bale. 2016. *The Conservative Party: From Thatcher to Cameron.* Cambridge: Polity Press; Geoffrey Evans. 1999. 'Europe: A new electoral cleavage?' In Geoffrey Evans and Pippa Norris. Eds. *Critical Elections.* London: Sage.
20. Timothy Heppell. 2002. 'The ideological composition of the parliamentary Conservative Party 1992–1997.' *British Journal of Politics and International Relations* 4 (2): 299–324; Philip Lynch. 2015. 'Conservative modernisation and European integration: From silence to salience and schism.' *British Politics* 10 (2): 185–203; Timothy Heppell, Andrew Crines, and David Jeffery. 2017. 'The UK Referendum in European Union Membership: The voting of Conservative parliamentarians.' *Journal of Common Market Studies* 55 (4): 762–778.
21. Tim Ross and Tom McTague. 2017. *Betting the House: The Inside Story of the 2017 Election.* London: Biteback Publishers.
22. www.voteleavetakecontrol.org/why_vote_leave.html.
23. www.referendumanalysis.eu/eu-referendum-analysis-2016/section-3-news/the-narrow-agenda-how-the-news-media-covered-the-referendum/.
24. www.ft.com/content/6a63c2ca-2d80-11e6-bf8d-26294ad519fc.
25. Oier Vincenzo Uleri and Michael Gallagher. Eds. 1996. *The Referendum Experience in Europe.* London: Macmillan.
26. Richard Harris and Martin Charlton. 2016. 'Voting out of the European Union: Exploring the geography of Leave.' *Environment and Planning*

48 (11): 2116–2128; Elise Uberoi. 2016. *European Union Referendum 2016*. London: House of Commons Briefing Paper CBP-7639.
27. Rob Ford and Matthew J. Goodwin. 2014. *Revolt on the Right: Explaining Public Support for the Radical Right in Britain*. Abingdon: Routledge; Matthew J. Goodwin and Oliver Heath. 2016. 'The 2016 Referendum, Brexit and the left behind? An aggregate-level analysis of the result.' *Political Quarterly* 87 (3): 323–332; Agnieszka Golec de Zavala, Rita Guerra, and Claudia Simao. 2017. 'The relationship between the Brexit Vote and individual predictors of prejudice: Collective narcissism, right-wing authoritarianism, social dominance orientation.' *Frontiers In Psychology* 8. doi: 10.3389/fpsyg.2017.02023.
28. Lorenza Antonucci, Laszlo Horvath, Yordan Kutiyski, and Andre Krouwel. 2017. 'The malaise of the squeezed middle: Challenging the narrative of the "left behind" Brexiter.' *Competition and Change* 21 (3): 211–229.
29. Peter Dorey and Andrew Denham. 2016. 'The longest suicide vote in history: The Labour Party leadership election of 2015.' *British Politics* 11 (3): 259–282.
30. Tim Ross and Tom McTague. 2017. *Betting the House: The Inside Story of the 2017 Election*. London: Biteback Publishers; Nicholas Allen and John Bartle. Eds. 2018. *None Past the Post: Britain at the Polls 2017*. Manchester: Manchester University Press.
31. www.conservatives.com/manifesto.
32. Peter Dorey. 2017. 'Jeremy Corbyn confounds his critics: Explaining the Labour party's remarkable resurgence in the 2017 election.' *British Politics* 12 (3): 308–334; https://labour.org.uk/manifesto/.
33. Tim Shipman. 2017. *Fall Out: A Year of Political Mayhem*. New York: Harper Collins.
34. http://blog.lboro.ac.uk/crcc/general-election/conservatives-media-strategy-collapsed-election-campaign/.
35. Pippa Norris. June 2017. *British Parliamentary Constituency Database 2010–2017*, V1.2. www.pippanorris.com/data/; Einar Thorsen, Daniel Jackson, and Darren Lilleker. Eds. *UK Election Analysis 2017*. Center for the Study of Journalism, Culture & Community, Bournmouth University. http://ElectionAnalysis.UK.
36. Lord Ashcroft. 'UK General Election Day poll.' June 6–9, 2017. N. 14,384.
37. John Curtice. 2017. *Has Brexit Reshaped British Politics? What the UK Thinks*. https://whatukthinks.org/eu/wp-content/uploads/2017/12/EU-Briefing-Paper-12-Brexit-and-the-election_V2.pdf.
38. Peter Dorey. 2017. 'Jeremy Corbyn confounds his critics: Explaining the Labour party's remarkable resurgence in the 2017 election.' *British Politics* 12 (3): 308–334.
39. David Goodhart. 2017. *The Road to Somewhere: The Populist Revolt and the Future of Politics*. London: Hurst & Company.
40. Dani Rodrik. 2017. 'Populism and the economics of globalization.' https://drodrik.scholar.harvard.edu/files/dani–rodrik/files/populism_and_the_economics_of_globalization.pdf.

41. Italo Colantone and Piero Stanig. 2017. 'The trade origins of economic nationalism: Import competition and voting behavior in Western Europe.' Carefen Working Papers 2017–49. http://ssrn.com/abstract=2904105; Sasha Becker, Thiemo Fetzer, and Dennis Novy. 2017. 'Who voted for Brexit? A comprehensive district-level analysis.' Munich: CESifo Working Paper 6438-2017. Paper presented at the 65th Panel Meeting of Economic Policy. http://cep.lse.ac.uk/pubs/download/dp1480.pdf; Matthew J. Goodwin and Oliver Heath. 2016. 'The 2016 referendum, Brexit and the left behind? An aggregate-level analysis of the result.' *Political Quarterly* 87 (3): 323–332; Luigi Guiso, Helios Herrera, Massimo Morelli, and Tommaso Sonne. November 8, 2017. 'Populism: Demand and supply.' www.heliosherrera.com/populism.pdf.
42. Geoffrey Evans and James Tilley. 2017. *The New Politics of Class*. Oxford: Oxford University Press. See also Lorenza Antonucci, Laszlo Horvath, Yordan Kutiyski, and Andre Krouwel. 2017. 'The malaise of the squeezed middle: Challenging the narrative of the "left behind" Brexiter.' *Competition and Change* 21 (3): 211–229.
43. Hans-Georg Betz. 1994. *Radical Rightwing Populism in Western Europe*. New York: St Martin's Press. Chapter 3; Roger Karapin. 2002. 'Far right parties and the construction of immigration issues in Germany.' In Martin Schain, Aristide Zolberg, and Patrick Hossay. Eds. *Shadows Over Europe: The Development and Impact of the Extreme Right in Western Europe*. Houndsmill: Palgrave Macmillan; Cas Mudde. 1999. 'The single-issue party thesis: Extreme right parties and the immigration issue.' *West European Politics* 22 (3): 182–197; Rachel Gibson. 2002. *The Growth of Anti-Immigrant Parties in Western Europe*. Lewiston, NY: The Edwin Mellen Press; Elizabeth Ivarsflaten. 2008. 'What unites right-wing populists in Western Europe? Re-examining grievance mobilization models in seven successful cases.' *Comparative Political Studies* 41 (1): 3–23; Tjitske Akkerman. 2012. 'Comparing radical right parties in government: Immigration and integration policies in nine countries (1996–2010),' *West European Politics* 35 (3): 511–529.
44. OECD. 2017. *International Migration Outlook, 2017 – Statistical Annex*. Version 2. Last updated June 8, 2017. www.oecd-ilibrary.org/social-issues-migration-health/international-migration-outlook-2017_migr_outlook-2017-en.
45. www.irr.org.uk/research/statistics/ethnicity-and-religion/.
46. United Nations Population Division, Department of Economic and Social Affairs. 2017. *International Migrant Stock, 2015*. New York: United Nations. www.un.org/en/development/desa/population/migration/data/estimates2/estimates15.shtml.
47. www.independent.co.uk/news/world/europe/french-say-au-revoir-to-france-over-two-million-french-people-now-live-abroad-and-most-are-crossing-9788348.html.
48. www.theguardian.com/uk-news/2017/mar/01/britain-one-of-worst-places-western-europe-asylum-seekers.
49. Ed Fieldhouse, Jane Green, Geoffrey Evans, Herman Schmitt, Cees van der Eijk, J. Mellon, and Christopher Prosser. 2017. British Election Study

Internet Panel Waves 1–13. www.britishelectionstudy.com/data-objects/panel-study-data/.

50. Pippa Norris. June 2017. British Parliamentary Constituency Database 2010–2017, V1.2. www.pippanorris.com/data/. Data draw upon Chris Hanretty's estimated Brexit vote by seat from https://secondreading.uk/brexit/brexit-votes-by-constituency/; and also http://researchbriefings.parliament.uk/ResearchBriefing/Summary/CBP-7979.
51. The correlation between the BES authoritarian–liberalism scale and the four-item classic right-wing authoritarian child-rearing values scale in the same BES panel wave is strong and significant (R = .440***).
52. Anthony Heath, Geoffrey Evans, and Jean Martin. 1994. 'The measurement of core beliefs and values: The development of balanced socialist/laissez faire and libertarian/authoritarian scales.' *British Journal of Political Science* 24 (1): 115–132; Geoffrey Evans, Anthony Heath, and Mansur Lalljee. 1996. 'Measuring left–right and Libertarian–Authoritarian Values in the British Electorate.' *The British Journal of Sociology* 47 (1): 93–112.
53. Geoffrey Evans, Anthony Heath, and Mansur Lalljee. 1996. 'Measuring left–right and Libertarian–Authoritarian Values in the British Electorate.' *The British Journal of Sociology* 47 (1): 93–112.
54. A. Akkerman, Cas Mudde, and A. Zaslove. 2014. How populist are the people? Measuring populist attitudes in voters. Comparative Political Studies 47(9): 1324–1353; M. Rooduijn. 2014. 'Vox populismus: A populist radical right attitude among the public?' Nations and Nationalism 20 (1): 80–92.
55. Steven M. Van Hauwaert and Stijn Van Kessel. 2018. 'Beyond protest and discontent: A cross-national analysis of the effect of populist attitudes and issue positions on populist party support.' *European Journal of Political Research* 57 (1): 68–92.
56. Agnes Akkerman, Cas Mudde, and Andrej Zaslove. 2014. 'How populist are the people? Measuring populist attitudes in voters.' *Comparative Political Studies* 47(9): 8–30.
57. Cronbach Alpha =.68.
58. Economic insecurity was measured by combining responses to the following questions: '*During the next 12 months, how likely or unlikely is it that ... 1) There will be times when you don't have enough money to cover your day to day living costs; 2) You will be out of a job and looking for work.*'
59. Harold Clarke, Matthew J. Goodwin, and Paul Whiteley. 2017. *Brexit! Why Britain Voted to Leave the European Union*. Cambridge: Cambridge University Press, Figure 7.3.
60. Matthew J. Goodwin, Paul Whiteley, and Harold Clarke. 2017. 'Why Britain voted for Brexit: An Individual-level analysis of the 2016 referendum vote.' *Parliamentary Affairs* 70 (3): 439–464; Harold D. Clarke, Matthew J. Goodwin, and Paul Whiteley. 2017. *Brexit! Why Britain Voted to Leave the European Union*. Cambridge: Cambridge University Press.
61. Rune Stubager. 2008. 'Educational effects on authoritarian–libertarian values: A question of socialization.' *British Journal of Sociology* 59 (2): 327–350;

Paula Surridge. 'Education and liberalism: Pursuing the link.' *Oxford Review of Education* 42 (2): 146–164.

62. Anders Todal Jenssen and Heidi Engesbak. 1994. 'The many faces of education: Why are people with lower education more hostile toward immigrants than people with higher education?' *Scandinavian Journal of Educational Research* 38: 33–50; Paul W. Vogt. 1997. *Tolerance and Education: Learning to Live with Diversity and Difference.* Thousand Oaks, CA: Sage Publications; Becky L. Choma and Yaniv Hanoch. 2017. 'Cognitive ability and authoritarianism: Understanding support for Trump and Clinton.' *Personality and Individual Differences* 106: 287–291.
63. Russell Hardin. 2002 *Trust and Trustworthiness.* NY: Russell Sage Foundation.
64. Geoffrey Evans and Anand Menon. 2017. *Brexit and British Politics.* Oxford: Polity; Harold Clarke, Matthew J. Goodwin, and Paul Whiteley. 2017. *Brexit! Why Britain Voted to Leave the European Union.* Cambridge: Cambridge University Press, Table 7.2.
65. British Social Attitudes 34. 'Immigration: How attitudes in the UK compare with Europe.' www.bsa.natcen.ac.uk/media/39148/bsa34_immigration_final.pdf.
66. Achim Hurrelmann. 2007. 'European Democracy, the "Permissive Consensus" and the Collapse of the EU Constitution.' *European Law Journal* 13 (3): 343–359.
67. Andrew Glencross. 2016. *Why the UK voted for Brexit: David Cameron's Great Mistake.* London: Palgrave Macmillan.
68. Owen Bennett. 2016. *The Brexit Club: The Inside Story of the Leave campaign's Shock Victory.* London: Backbite books; Tim Shipman. 2017. *Fall Out: A Year of Political Mayhem.* New York: Harper Collins.
69. Kenneth A. Armstrong. 2017. *Brexit: Leaving the EU – Why, how and when?* Cambridge: Cambridge University Press.
70. Tim Ross and Tom McTague. 2017. *Betting the House: The Inside Story of the 2017 Election.* London: Biteback Publishers.
71. David Goodhart. 2017. *The Road to Somewhere.* London: Hurst & Co.
72. See also Lorenza Antonucci, Laszlo Horvath, Yordan Kutiyski, and Andre Krouwel. 2017. 'The malaise of the squeezed middle: Challenging the narrative of the "left behind" Brexiter.' *Competition and Change* 21 (3): 211–229.
73. Ed Howker and Shiv Malik. 2010. *Jilted Generation: How Britain has Bankrupted Its Youth.* London: Icon Books.
74. www.ft.com/content/55f4a6f6-3eab-11e6-9f2c-36b487ebd80a?mhq5j=e1.
75. www.understandingsociety.ac.uk/research/publications/524045.
76. http://researchbriefings.parliament.uk/ResearchBriefing/Summary/SN05871#fullreport.
77. Maria Teresa Grasso, Stephen Farrall, Emily Gray, and Colin Hay. 2017. 'Thatcher's children, Blair's babies, political socialization and trickle-down value change: An age, period and cohort analysis.' *British Journal of Political Science.* doi:10.1017/S0007123416000375.
78. https://labour.org.uk/manifesto/.

79. Kirby Swales and Eleanor Attar Taylor. 2017. 'Moral issues: Sex, gender identity and euthanasia.' *British Social Attitudes* 34. London: City University. www.bsa.natcen.ac.uk/media/39147/bsa34_moral_issues_final .pdf.
80. Sam Mejias and Shakuntala Banaji. October 2017. *UK Youth Perspectives and Priorities for Brexit Negotiations*. Report for the All Party Parliamentary Group on a Better Brexit for Young People conducted by the London School of Economics and Political Science. www.lse.ac.uk/ media-and-communications/assets/documents/research/A-Better-Brexit-for-Young-People.pdf.

# PART IV

# CONCLUSIONS

# 12

# Eroding the Civic Culture

Now let us examine the consequences of authoritarian populism and the question of whether democratic cultures are sufficiently robust to resist its dangers. Many observers have reacted with intense alarm to the threat that authoritarian-populist forces pose to the post-war liberal consensus and traditional norms of liberal democracy. These concerns have existed since the rise of radical right parties in Europe during the 1980s but they sharply accelerated following Brexit and the election of President Trump.[1] Until recently, it was widely assumed that Western societies would be governed by moderate political parties, committed to liberal democracy, open economies, and multilateral cooperation. The core values respecting free and fair elections, rule of law, human rights, and civil liberties seemed sacrosanct. Despite some major challenges and notable setbacks, as the twenty-first century opened, elections and democratic values appeared to be spreading to every corner of the world. The rise of authoritarian-populist forces challenges these sanguine assumptions, arousing intense debate.[2]

This chapter examines the potential impact of rising authoritarian populism at three distinct levels. Part I looks at the trends in democratic regimes. Part II turns to patterns of party competition and the policy agenda on issues such as immigration and Europe. Finally, Part III analyzes public confidence in democracy and support for the civic culture.

## I DEMOCRATIC REGIMES

Several watchdog agencies concur in detecting worrying signs of a global democratic retreat: in Huntington's classic formulation, the world is experiencing another reverse wave of democratization.[3] Hence, in its

2018 report, Freedom House warns that democracies around the world are battered and weaker, with more losses than gains in 2017, and populism is highlighted as one of the factors contributing to this development: 'Democracy is in crisis. The values it embodies – particularly the right to choose leaders in free and fair elections, freedom of the press, and the rule of law – are under assault and in retreat globally.'[4] Freedom House blames populist leaders for fueling anti-immigrant sentiment and undermining fundamental civil and political liberties, assuming that 'the fish rots from the head.' The Economist Intelligence Unit reports that their Democracy Index for 2017 registered a worldwide fall; compared with the previous year, 89 countries experienced a decline in their score, more than three times as many as the 27 countries showing an improvement (the 51 other countries were unchanged).[5] The report highlights that Western Europe recorded a regression in the Democracy Index during the last decade, including falling participation in elections and parties, declining institutional trust, weakening media freedoms, and the erosion of civil liberties like free speech.

Human Rights Watch notes the dangerous rise of populism and global attacks on human rights values: 'Claims of unfettered majoritarianism, and the attacks on the checks and balances that constrain governmental power, are perhaps the greatest danger today to the future of democracy in the West.'[6]

Scholars of comparative politics have also sounded the alarm about 'how democracies die' through the corrosion of the unwritten rules that make formal institutions work, mutual toleration, and confidence in representative institutions. Demagogic populists have been blamed for weakening democratic institutions by rejecting the democratic rules of the game, denying the legitimacy of political opponents, tolerating violence, and curtailing civil liberties.[7] Leaders such as Alberto Fujimori, Hugo Chavez, Evo Morales, Victor Orbán, Recep Tayyip Erdoğan, and Nicolás Maduro have destroyed basic human rights and liberal freedoms.[8] Venezuela, in particular, has seen a crackdown on dissent, brutality, and political persecution of opponents, with pro-democracy protests repressed by security forces.[9] In Eastern Europe, human rights abuses are most evident in the hybrid regimes that partially liberalized in the late-1980s but subsequently slipped back into authoritarian rule, despite growing economies and EU membership.

Yet is there evidence of a deeper problem in the mass culture beyond specific leadership elites? And is populism to blame for these setbacks? Some see democracy as more resilient and the crisis as exaggerated – and in part this depends on the time period being examined. International IDEA's Global State of Democracy indicators, derived from the Varieties of Democracy project, suggest that the years from 1975 to 2015 were a period of growth and more recent years have seen trendless fluctuations rather than decline.[10]

Since the mid-1970s, the long-term trend has been toward the spread of liberal democracy around the world, for reasons closely linked with modernization. But it has not been a simple, linear trend. The past two centuries have seen major advances, followed by severe setbacks.[11] The net result has been increasing numbers of liberal democratic regimes. Freedom House estimates that by the end of 2017, 88 countries qualified as 'free' or fully democratic, while 58 were 'partly free' or hybrid regimes, and 49 are 'Not free' or autocratic. Modernization led to the spread of democracy for several reasons:

(1) Urbanization and industrialization bring formerly scattered and illiterate peasants into factories where they can communicate with each other and organize politically.
(2) Economic development makes survival more secure, eventually bringing an intergenerational value shift in which people come to give freedom of expression high priority, making them more likely to *want* democracy.
(3) Rising educational levels make people more articulate, better informed, and more skilled at organizing – making them more effective at *getting* democracy.
(4) As industrial societies mature, jobs shift from industry into the knowledge sector. People no longer follow routines dictated from above, but increasingly have jobs that require them to think for themselves. This tends to spill over from their work into the political realm.

These aspects of modernization help explain why the number of democracies has grown so dramatically since the nineteenth century.

Democracy has another big advantage: it provides a non-violent way to replace a country's leaders. All power corrupts, and an unlimited time in power corrupts limitlessly. Democratic institutions do not guarantee that the people will elect wise and benevolent rulers, but honest elections provide a non-violent way to remove unwise and malevolent ones from office. Autocratic succession struggles can be bloody and costly. Democracy has spread for strong reasons.

During early industrialization, authoritarian states can attain high rates of economic growth, but knowledge economies flourish best in relatively open societies. In the long run, democracy seems to be the best way discovered so far to govern developed countries. History is not predetermined. But the long-term trend favors democracy.

As Figure 12.1 shows, using the Liberal Democracy index from the Varieties of Democracy (V-Dem) project, the long-term trend toward democracy has always moved in surges and declines. At the start of the twentieth century only a handful of democracies existed, and even they were not full democracies by today's standards (lacking universal suffrage). The number of democracies increased sharply after World War I, with another surge following World War II, and a third surge at the end of the Cold War. As Huntington noted, each wave was eventually followed by a decline, notably the spread of Bolshevism and Fascism during the 1930s.[12] But each decline was eventually followed by a new surge.

In the decades after World War II, unprecedentedly high levels of economic and physical security brought a pervasive intergenerational value shift. A large share of the post-war generation no longer gave top priority to economic and physical safety and conformity to group norms, but to freedom of choice for the individual. They favored gender equality; tolerance of gays, foreigners, and other out-groups; freedom of expression and more say in decision-making. This led to stronger environmental

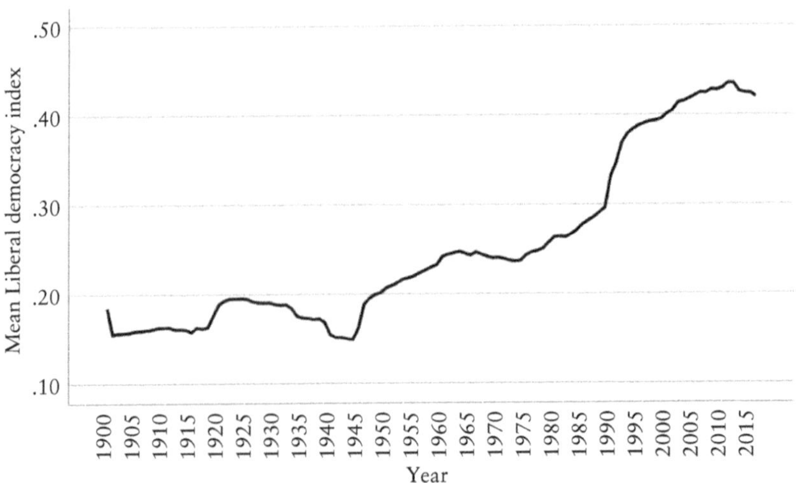


FIGURE 12.1. *Trends in liberal democracy worldwide, V-Dem, 1900–2016*
*Note:* Annual estimates of liberal democracy by the Varieties of Democracy project measured as a 100-point standardized scale.
*Source:* Varieties of Democracy Project (V-Dem). Version 7.1.

protection policies, anti-war movements, higher levels of gender equality in government, business, and public life, and the spread of democracy.

It is not a linear trend, however, because the extent to which people feel secure or uncertain has a major impact on the balance between authoritarianism and democracy. We are currently facing challenges similar to the reverse waves experienced during the 1930s and again in the 1970s. Today strongman leaders such as Donald Trump, Nicolás Maduro, and Viktor Orban threaten liberal checks and balances. They probably do not represent the long-term trend, but history is probabilistic, not deterministic: democracy could be eroded.

The V-Dem data suggest a slight downturn in recent years. For comparison, we can also look at the global trends in levels of democratization estimated from Freedom House data 1972–2017. Figure 12.2 confirms the rising waves of democratization during the third wave era since the 1970s – and suggests that there has been a more significant and steady global reversal since 2005.

Numerous factors can contribute toward the downturn, and authoritarian populism cannot be blamed for the entire global pattern. What we can claim is that significant setbacks have occurred under Authoritarian-Populist leaders in hybrid states.

In Hungary, as discussed in Chapter 9, Victor Orbán was able to form a one-party government in 2010 when the Fidesz Party won just

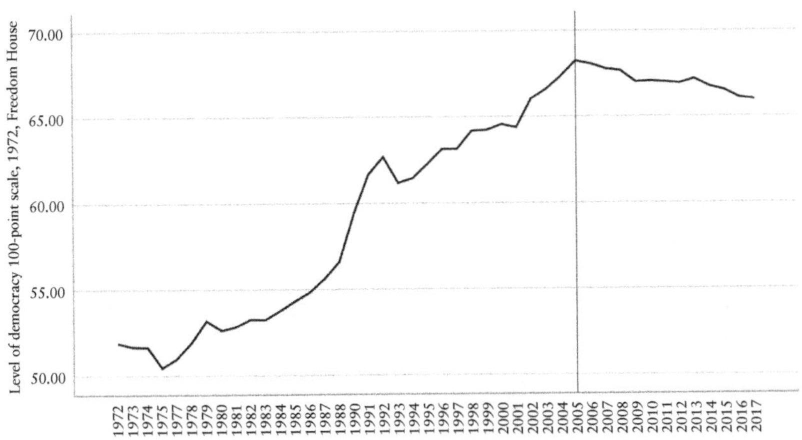


FIGURE 12.2. *Trends in democratization worldwide, FH 1972–2017*
*Note:* Freedom House's annual estimates of civil liberties and political rights, worldwide, 1972–2017. These are converted into a 0–100 point scale, where high is more democratic.
*Source:* Calculated from Freedom House Freedom in the World. www.freedomhouse.org.

52 percent of the vote but swept up two-thirds of the seats in parliament. The opposition Hungarian Socialist Party (MSZP) was left in disarray. With a super-majority in the legislature, the government was able to push through a new electoral system and a series of constitutional reforms which dismantled checks and balances on executive powers, limited the power of the constitutional court, and undermined the multiparty composition of the Electoral Commission.[13] Formal democratic institutions had been in place in Hungary, though undermined by clientalism and other informal practices. As a result of the new Mixed electoral system, in the 2014 elections Fidesz was able to retain two-thirds (67%) of all parliamentary seats, despite the fact that the party's share of the vote dropped from 52 percent to 44 percent. The Orbán government incorporated many economic and social policies into the constitution, so that these become entrenched, even if Fidesz lost power.

In Poland, since Lech and Jarosław Kaczyński's Law and Justice Party came to power in December 2015, the government has undermined democracy and fought a rear-guard culture war against socially liberal norms on everything from gay rights to women's equality. In late 2015, the Law and Justice (PiS) party passed legislation that politicized public media, neutered the constitutional court, handed the security services sweeping powers of surveillance, restricted the right of public protest, and proposed regulations on NGOs.[14] The European Commission has been critical of the country's deteriorating human rights record arguing that the new laws breach European values by threatening the rule of law and judicial independence. As a result, the EU has debated suspending Polish voting rights in the EU.

In the Czech Republic, Milos Zeman was elected in 2013 in the first direct presidential vote held in the Czech Republic and he was reelected in January 2018. In his campaign, he cast himself as a populist savior working for the common man using the slogan 'You are not alone anymore.'[15] Running on an anti-immigrant and Eurosceptic platform, Zeman was one of the first European leaders to advocate sealing national borders against refugees and for the Czech Republic to refuse EU quotas. He favors stronger ties with Russia and his transgressive and blunt language echoes that of Trump. His campaign was supported by the prime minister, the billionaire Andrej Babis, who was appointed by the president.

In Turkey, after a botched coup attempt in July 2016, President Recep Tayyip Erdoğan imposed emergency rule and arrested nearly 40,000 civilians, imprisoned hundreds of army officers, opposition party officials, journalists and academics, shuttered hundreds of media outlets and non-governmental organizations (NGOs), and fired more than a hundred thousand civil servants.[16] He has also renewed the offensive against the Kurdish minority in Turkey and in neighboring Syria. A flawed constitutional referendum centralized the power of the presidency, allowed arbitrary prosecutions of human rights activists, and replaced elected mayors with government appointees. As a result, in 2018 Freedom House downgraded their rating of the country from Partly to Not Free.[17]

When populist authoritarian leaders say something that violates norms of human rights, you had better believe them. In the Philippines, in June 2016 Rodrigo Duterte campaigned for the presidency promising execution without trial of alleged drug carriers: 'Forget the laws on human rights. If I make it to the presidential palace, I will do just want I did as mayor. You drug pushers, hold-up men, and do-nothings, you better go out, because I'd kill you. I'll dump all of you into Manila Bay and fatten the fishes there.'[18] Since then, Amnesty International reports that thousands have been murdered by police, killed without trial, in his controversial anti-drug campaign.

In Venezuela, Hugo Chavez promised wealth redistribution, land reform, and using state oil revenues to subsidize living standards, but the country experienced drastic economic decline.[19] Under his successor, President Nicolás Maduro, faced with a falling petro-dollar and a humanitarian crisis, the country slid into outright authoritarian rule in 2017, when the Supreme Court suspended the powers of the National Assembly, triggering widespread protests, mass detentions, and a rising death toll. The general secretary of the Organization of American States condemned Maduro as a repressive dictator guilty of human rights violations that involved killings and hundreds of political prisoners, leading Venezuela to quit the organization.[20]

There are many other cases where Authoritarian-Populist leaders have centralized power in the presidency, weakened opposition movements, and undermined human rights. Latin America has a long legacy of Presidents who have followed populist strategies from Argentina's Peron and Peru's Alberto Fujimori to Argentina's Cristina Fernández, Ecuador's Rafael Correa, and Venezuela's Hugo Chavez and Nicolás Maduro.[21]

Moreover, a club of authoritarian leaders has been strengthening linkages. It is notable that Trump has been particularly friendly toward the leaders of authoritarian states, notably Russia, Saudi Arabia, North Korea, China, and the Philippines, while often more distant toward long-established democratic allies such as Canada, Mexico, the UK, Germany, France, and the other members of NATO. Thus, early in his administration he berated Germany's 'massive' trade imbalance with the US but congratulated the Philippine President Duterte, saying that he was doing 'an unbelievable job' in fighting his country's illegal drug trade, although it has led to thousands of extra-judicial deaths.[22] This tilt has shaped foreign policy priorities in the new administration as well. Under Trump, the US State Department has cut back further on the promotion of human rights and democracy. As one important indicator, when speaking about the State Department budget for fiscal year 2018, the Secretary of State, Rex Tillerson, was silent about human rights and democracy: 'This budget request reflects the president's 'America First' agenda that prioritizes the well-being of Americans, bolsters US national security, secures our borders, and advances US economic interests.' The budget slashed spending for the sector on 'governing justly and democratically' from $2.3 billion in 2016 to $1.6 billion in 2018. Without funding, the US Agency for International Development was forced to cut back on programs on rule of law and human rights, good governance, political competition, and civil society.[23]

But is populism to blame for the deterioration of democracy and authoritarian rule in these countries – or would it have happened anyway? Are populist leaders, political elites, and weak institutions the problem, as Levitsky and Zimblatt assume, or does it reflect an authoritarian culture in mass society? Cas Mudde cautions that, at least in Western democracies, fears about the impact of populism are largely overblown and he argues that the rise of the populist radical right has had far less serious political consequences than many pessimistic prophecies had long predicted.[24] Mudde noted that the average share of the vote for radical right populists in Western European Parliamentary elections has grown but it remains limited. Our estimates, based on the comparison of a broad range of 56 parties in 27 European societies, suggests that the mean share of the vote for Authoritarian-Populist parties doubled from around 5 percent during their nadir in the 1960s to around 12 percent during the last decade, the highest level they have ever achieved since the end of World War II (see Figure 1.1). Nevertheless, as we observed in Chapter 9, even in Proportional Representation electoral systems, fringe and minor parties often face formidable challenges in surmounting vote thresholds and then translating popular votes into parliamentary seats and ministerial offices – as well as influencing the parliamentary policy agenda across a wide range of issues.

Populists also face a particular conundrum – the more they enter the corridors of power, the more difficult it is for them to hold onto their credentials as outsiders.[25] Chapter 8 demonstrated that populists typically attract disproportionate support among disillusioned citizens distrusting parliament, parties, and politicians. Populists therefore may have a problem in campaigning as radical outsiders fighting mainstream elites once they join the parliamentary backbenches, enter governing coalitions, or even hold executive office. For example, popular support for the Austrian Freedom Party fell dramatically once they entered the ÖVP-led government, from 26.9 percent in the 1999 legislative elections to 10 percent in 2002. Governing may take a toll on populist support so that they can only maintain their support in opposition.[26]

Arguably, when populist outsiders from sectors such as the military or corporate world are suddenly thrust into high level government office, without the usual lengthy apprenticeship that comes with professional politicians who have climbed the greasy ladder, the lack of experience in how public-sector agencies and legislatures work can prove a major obstacle to filling posts, passing laws, managing complex bureaucracies, and implementing radical policy change. Every politician can blunder, no matter how skilled and knowledgeable, but reports about the Trump White House suggest that many of the administration's actions, like the early Executive Orders designed to ban visitors from Muslim majority countries, backfired due to inadequate experience about how the federal government works.[27]

## II CONTAGION ON THE RIGHT IN POLICY AGENDAS?

What about the impact of Authoritarian-Populist parties on patterns of party competition and the policy agenda? Here Mudde also argues that the main effects in Western Europe have been largely limited to the signature issue of immigration, and even on this topic Authoritarian-Populist parties should be regarded as catalysts more than initiators, since they are neither necessary nor sufficient for the introduction of stricter immigration policies. Since then, post-Brexit, the impact of these parties on EU politics must also be acknowledged, including why Poland and Hungary have rejected compliance with EU quotas on refugees and asylum seekers.

Several scholars suggest that radical right populists heighten public concern about race relations, immigration policy, welfare reform, and law and order, thereby pulling moderate parties toward the extreme right.[28] Many examples can be given. Thus, Bornschier argues that where Authoritarian-Populist parties have succeeded in expanding their share of the popular vote, as in France and Switzerland, this has generated a new cultural cleavage in party politics, heightening the salience of issues such as immigration and the European Union. Where mainstream parties have been successful in preventing serious threats from such parties, by absorbing these issues, this has weakened support for minor parties.[29]

Schain also suggests that in France, the center-right parties, the RPR, and UDF, adopted the *National Front* anti-immigrant rhetoric after 1986, in an attempt to preempt Jean-Marie Le Pen's support.[30] Along similar lines, Pettigrew argues that Austria implemented more restrictive policies toward refugees after Jorg Haider's FPÖ entered coalition government with the center-right ÖVP.[31] In the October 2017 parliamentary elections, the ÖVP adopted far more hardline language against immigrants and asylum seekers, legitimizing tough xenophobic policies as mainstream, rising to first place in the polls under the leadership of Sebastian Kurz. During the spring 2017 campaign for parliamentary elections in the Netherlands, the Dutch Prime Minister from the center-right People's Party for Freedom (VVD), Mark Rutte, adopted a tough line toward immigrants who failed to integrate, telling them to 'act normal or go away,' when faced with fierce political competition from Geert Wilders' Party for Freedom (PVV).[32]

Finally, it can be argued that despite UKIP winning only one seat in the May 2015 general election, Cameron's pledge to hold the Brexit referendum the following year would not have happened without UKIP's popularity in the opinion polls. After Cameron's resignation, also Theresa May adopted a hardline stance toward UK negotiations on Brexit in the leadership contest for the Conservative Party, both to reassure Eurosceptic backbenchers within her own party and also to attract UKIP voters. This strategy apparently worked in the 2017 local and general elections, causing UKIP to hemorrhage local councilors and votes, as former supporters switched (back) to the Tories.[33]

Can all these events be attributed to the rise of Authoritarian-Populist parties? It is conceivable these policy developments might have occurred anyway, regardless of populist party competition, as European governments respond directly to public concern. Government needed to revise their policies following Angela Merkel's decision to open Germany's borders, in September 2015, triggering a flood of Syrian, Turkish, and Afghan refugees and asylum seekers. In recent years, many EU countries have tightened immigration policies even where populist parties remain weak.[34] Nevertheless, it seems likely that these parties contributed toward this process, by challenging the liberal consensus among mainstream parties, altering the boundaries of public debate, heightening the salience and polarization of the immigration issue on the legislative agenda, and legitimating policies founded on racism and intolerance that had previously been quarantined by the elite liberal consensus.[35] For example, content analysis of party manifestos in Norway and Denmark since the early 1970s suggests that the policy platforms of the moderate conservative parties moved rightwards in response to the electoral challenge of authoritarian-populist rivals on their extreme flank.[36]

Electoral gains by minor Authoritarian-Populist parties remain limited but their popular support has been expanding.[37] As we have seen, their average share of the vote for the lower house in national parliamentary elections in Europe has more than doubled since the 1960s, from around 4.9 percent to 11.7%, while their share of seats has more than tripled, from 3.4 percent to 11.6 percent.[38]

Given these developments, how do other parties respond strategically? If mainstream parties win a majority of parliamentary seats, then they can form a one-party government excluding all rivals. If there is a minority government, however, falling short of an overall parliamentary majority, as is common under Proportional Representation elections, then strategically the largest party can seek to form a coalition with other parties but exclude populists from negotiations, isolating them, for example as was done when the 2017 Rutte government in the Netherlands excluded the PVV. But where the populist party wins a substantial number of seats, this process can generate lengthy negotiations and a prolonged period of uncertainty, as in Germany following the entry of AfD into the Bundestag. Or the largest party can invite populists to join a coalition government. For example, in late 2017, Norwegian elections returned prime minister Erna Solberg in a Conservative-led coalition government in partnership with the Norwegian Progress Party and two other right-wing partners. Contests in Austria produced the OVP–FPO coalition led by Sebastian Kurz, while New Zealand saw a Labour coalition government led by Jacinda Ardern in partnership with the Greens and New Zealand First.[39] Elsewhere Authoritarian-Populist parties have entered government coalitions in many countries, including the Italian Northern League, the Slovak National Party, and the Swiss People's Party.[40]

Even in countries with few authoritarian populists in parliament, however, these parties can still exert 'blackmail' pressure on governments, public discourse, and the policy agenda.[41] They need not gain many votes or seats to exert substantial influence, as illustrated by UKIP's role in catalyzing British exit (Brexit) from the European Union. Though the UK Independence Party won only one constituency in the 2015 general election, its populist rhetoric fueled rabid anti-European and anti-immigration sentiment in Britain, pressuring the Conservatives to call the Brexit referendum.[42] The consequences of the vote for withdrawal have been profound, instigating Britain's messy divorce from the European Union, the resignation of Prime Minister David Cameron, divisions in the Labour Party, prospects for the disintegration of the United Kingdom, uncertainty in financial markets, and outbreaks of hate speech attacking immigrants.[43] Brexit encouraged other populist parties to call for similar referenda over EU membership in France, the Netherlands, Austria, Germany, Denmark, Italy, and elsewhere, although none has yet followed.[44] In Britain's June 2017 snap general election, UKIP's vote share plummeted dramatically; it lost its raison d'etre once the Conservative Party embraced Brexit wholeheartedly and Theresa May's rhetoric pledged to preserve 'our values, our country and our way of life' through providing 'strong and stable' leadership. The Conservatives made some headway with the Leave constituency. But once Brexit was regarded as inevitable, many 2015 UKIP supporters appear to have switched back to Labour, who also gained seats with Remain votes.[45] This does not mean that authoritarian populism is dead in Britain; on the contrary, its anti-European policies and nationalist rhetoric have been absorbed into the Conservative mainstream.

## III DAMAGING THE CIVIC CULTURE?

But the impact on party competition does not address the debate about the potential consequences of the rise of authoritarian populism on the civic culture.

By deepening public disenchantment with the workings of political institutions, such as elections, the news media, and the courts, populism can have destabilizing effects upon the body politic. Public confidence in democracy seems vulnerable to being undermined by demagogues impugning the impartiality of the courts, alleging widespread electoral fraud, and attacking the role of the free press, as well as potentially heightening social intolerance, xenophobia, and Islamophobia. Public skepticism about democracy may tip into cynicism.[46]

It is too early to determine the full consequence of the Trump presidency on American civic culture. His heated rhetoric and belligerent no-holds-barred style has been widely blamed for deepening party polarization, political tolerance, and mistrust in the American electorate.[47] At the same time, alarm bells about the state of the civic culture in American politics were ringing loudly before Obama left the White House. There was growing party polarization in Congress (see Figure 10.2), deepening racial resentment, and religious intolerance of Muslims, and widespread loss of public trust in American political institutions, especially Congress. In the United States, public trust in government is near an historic low.[48]

On the positive side, moreover, populism can function as a useful correction to liberal democracy.[49] By calling attention to genuine problems, populist movements can spur grassroots pressures for much-needed democratic reforms, such as reenergizing American initiatives designed to strengthen electoral integrity, restore voting rights, clean up campaign funding, and eradicate gerrymandering.[50] Through expanding party competition and electoral choices on the ballot, populism may serve as a useful corrective to reengage disenchanted citizens and strengthen turnout.[51] Instead of sweeping problems under the carpet, populism may force political representatives to listen more carefully to genuine public concerns about the rapid pace of social change, the economic disruptions caused by globalization, and the negative consequences of migration.[52] In states where corruption is endemic and political elites are lining their pockets, populist reforms to 'clean the stables' can serve as a useful corrective. In practice, sudden electoral gains by populist parties and leaders, while attracting headline news, have often proved volatile and fleeting.[53] Liberal democracy is a form of government universally valued by citizens all over the world, and it may remain resilient in the West.[54]

One way to understand these issues is to examine the roots of how ordinary people feel about their system of government. If there were evidence of long-term erosion of support for the political system, across many Western democracies, then this would suggest that the election of particular Authoritarian-Populist parties and leaders is more a symptom than the fundamental cause. To understand these issues, we can turn to Juan Linz and Alfred Stepan's concept of regime consolidation, meaning that democracy has become 'the only game in town.'[55] This is claimed to depend on three characteristics.

(1) Culturally, the overwhelming majority of people believe that democracy is the best form of government, so that any further reforms reflect these values and principles.
(2) Constitutionally, all the major actors and organs of the state reflect democratic norms and practices.
(3) Behaviorally, no significant groups actively seek to overthrow the regime or secede from the state.

What does evidence suggests about the contemporary state of the first of these conditions and the health of the civic culture in Western democracies?

In tackling this issue, three considerations are important. First, we need trend data over an extended period of time, to help determine the effects of changes in party competition. For such evidence, we turn to the World Values Survey/European Values Survey, containing several suitable indicators in five successive waves stretching over more than 20 years. Fieldwork for the most recent wave was conducted in the US in May 2017, a few months after Trump's inauguration.

In addition, we can break down the American data by party support, to see whether there is a broad consensus about the rules of the game across both parties, suggesting a stable system, or whether party polarization is evident. In particular, we can see whether trends show that there were partisan differences in attitudes toward democracy well before the 2016 election, or whether a change occurred with the campaign and election of Donald Trump.

Finally, it is important to distinguish between levels of public support. Ever since Almond and Verba's seminal *The Civic Culture* (1963), social-psychological theories have suggested that stable regimes depend on congruence between political values and institutional practices.[56] In David Easton's conceptualization of levels of system support, dissatisfaction with the performance of specific leaders and political institutions can be regarded relatively sanguinely as part of the normal give-and-take of politics.[57] If the acid of disaffection has spread upwards to corrode the more diffuse level of support for democratic ideals and core regime principles, however, then this is seen as far more problematic for system stability. We therefore need to scrutinize the public's endorsement of democratic principles like press freedom and equal rights, satisfaction with how democracy is perceived to perform in each country, and confidence in core representative institutions connecting citizens and the state, notably trust in parliament and political parties.

## Public Support for Democratic Principles

First, let us look at the American evidence in attitudes toward democracy. The World Values Survey contains a battery of items that have been widely used since the mid-1990s to establish how people feel about government.[58] Churchill once remarked that democracy is the worst form of government, except for all the others that have been tried from time to time. Accordingly, respondents are asked to express approval or disapproval using four-point scales to the following statements: 'I'm going to describe various types of political systems and ask what you think about each as a way of governing this country. For each one, would you say it is a very good, fairly good, fairly bad, or very bad way of governing this country? Having a democratic political system. Having experts, not government, make decisions according to what they think is best for the country. Having a strong leader who doesn't have to bother with elections. Having the army rule.' These range from approval of democracy through support for progressively more repressive regimes. The items have been carried now over five waves spanning more than two decades and the results are broken down by party voters to see whether there was any 'Trump effect.'

The results in Figure 12.3 show an overwhelming consensus among both Democrats and Republicans in endorsing democracy as a 'very good' or 'fairly good' way of governing America. Thus, eight out of ten American voters support the principle of democracy during these years. Nevertheless,

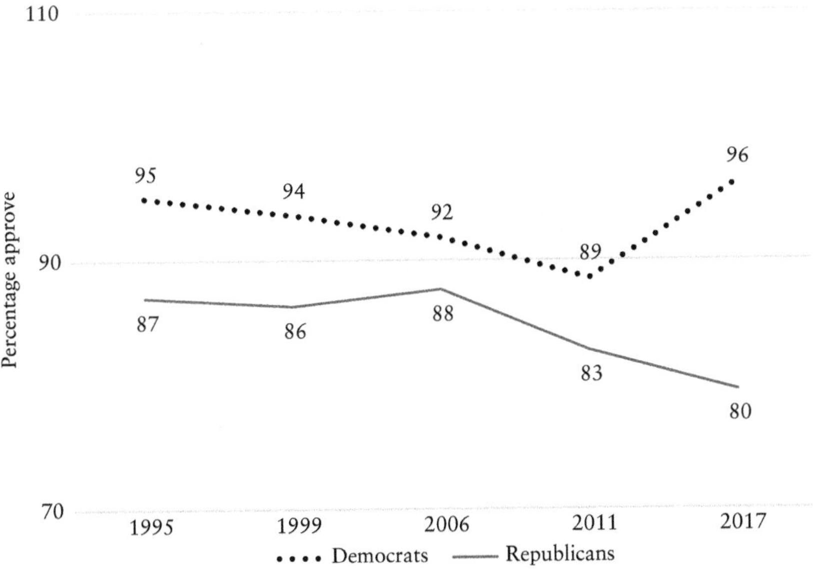


FIGURE 12.3. *Approval of democratic governance, US 1995–2017*
*Note:* Q: 'I'm going to describe various types of political systems and ask what you think about each as a way of governing this country. For each one, would you say it is a very good, fairly good, fairly bad or very bad way of governing this country? Having a democratic political system.' The proportion of Democratic and Republican voters expressing approval.
*Source:* World Values Survey, US 2005–2017.

it is also apparent that Republicans are consistently slightly less positive than Democrats – and this is not simply a 'winners–losers' partisan effect, since this period includes successive presidents from both parties in the White House. Moreover, partisan polarization over the value of democracy widened substantially in the most recent wave; by May 2017, 96 percent of Democrats endorsed democracy – compared with only 80 percent of Republicans. The partisan gap widened sharply from 6 percentage points in 2011 to 16 points in 2017. The contrasts were even greater among those with the strongest approval; two-thirds of Democrats (64%) thought that democracy was a 'very good' way of governing America – compared with less than a majority of Republicans (44%).

What was the approval of the alternative forms of governance? In terms of meritocracy – the idea of having policy experts take decisions saw growing approval in America – but on this item, it is the Democrats who endorse the idea most strongly. By spring 2017, more than half of the Democrats (55%) thought this was a good way of governing, with fewer Republicans expressing approval (47%) (see Figure 12.4). But

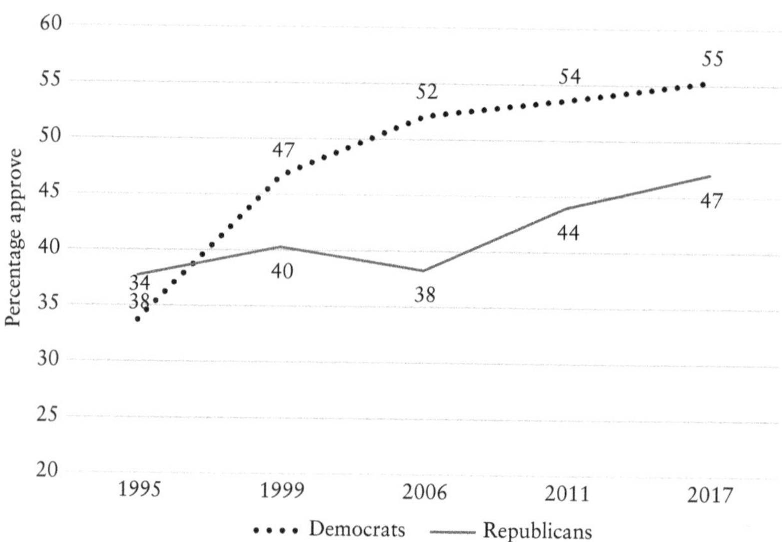


FIGURE 12.4. *Approval of governance by experts, US 1995–2017*
*Note:* Q: 'I'm going to describe various types of political systems and ask what you think about each as a way of governing this country. For each one, would you say it is a very good, fairly good, fairly bad or very bad way of governing this country? Having experts, not government, make decisions according to what they think is best for the country.' The proportion of Democratic and Republican voters expressing approval.
*Source:* World Values Survey, US 2005–2017.

party polarization was clearest on approval of a strong leader *without elections*; from 1995 to 2011, Democrats approved of this idea more than Republicans. From 2011 to 2017, however, partisans switched positions; by the latest wave, almost one-third of Republicans (31%) approved of strongman rule without elections, compared with only one fifth (21%) or Democrats (see Figure 12.5). This is one of the clearest indicators that Trump's appeal to his supporters reflected his 'strongman' image – and perhaps his supporters were also persuaded by Republican claims of fraud and Trump's attacks on the integrity of elections ('I won the popular vote if you deduct the millions of people who voted illegally'). Moreover, responses on this item were not isolated; when asked about the most extreme form of authoritarian rule, having the army rule, most Americans expressed clear disapproval. But amongst those who approved, in 2017 fully one fifth of Republican voters endorsed this idea, with this proportion jumping from 12 to 20 percent from 2011 to 2017 (see Figure 12.6). This provides strong indications concerning the appeal of authoritarian governance among Trump voters – a finding that we have already

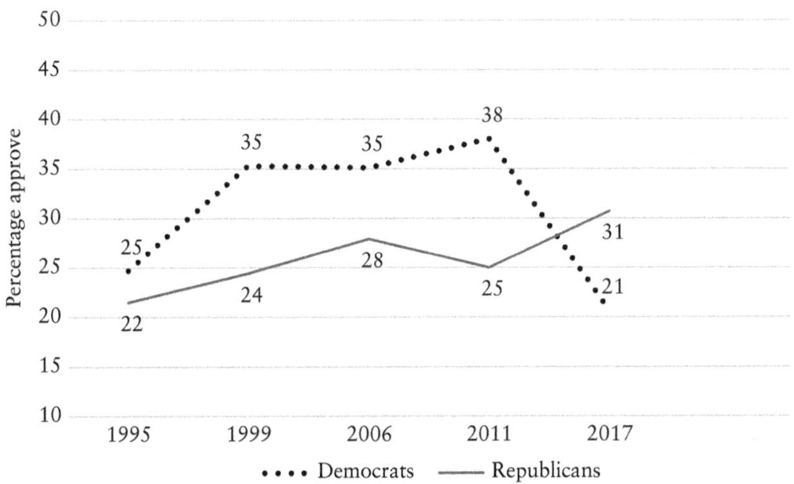


FIGURE 12.5. *Approval of governance by strongman rule without elections, US 1995–2017*

*Note:* Q: 'I'm going to describe various types of political systems and ask what you think about each as a way of governing this country. For each one, would you say it is a very good, fairly good, fairly bad or very bad way of governing this country? Having a strong leader who doesn't have to bother with elections.' The proportion of Democratic and Republican voters expressing approval.

*Source:* World Values Survey, US 2005–2017.

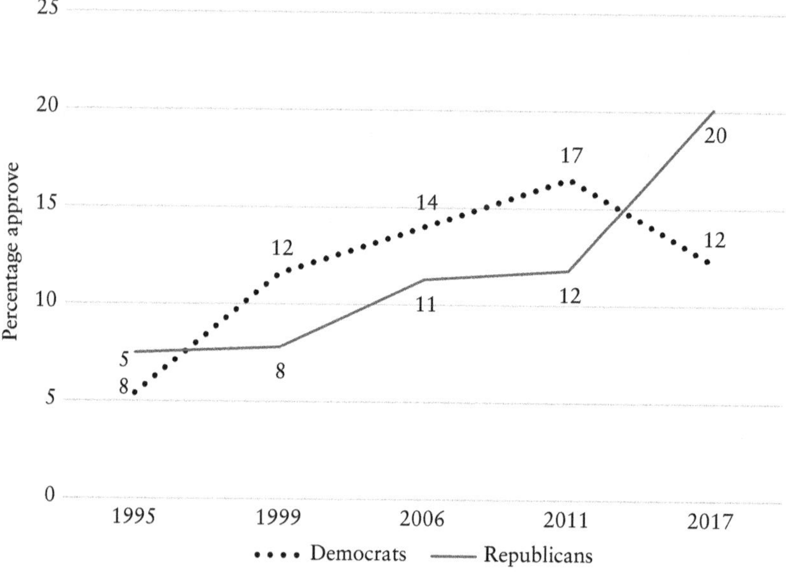


FIGURE 12.6. *Approval of army rule, US 1995–2017*
*Note:* Q: 'I'm going to describe various types of political systems and ask what you think about each as a way of governing this country. For each one, would you say it is a very good, fairly good, fairly bad or very bad way of governing this country? Having the army rule.' The proportion of Democratic and Republican voters expressing approval.
*Source:* World Values Survey, US 1995–2017.

documented in terms of support for authoritarian personal values. This reflects a general orientation among Republican voters that tends to be intolerant of unconventional life-styles, favors tough collective security over personal freedom, and is deferential toward strongman leaders.

## Public Satisfaction with Democratic Performance

But is America exceptional or are similar patterns found in Europe? One standard explanation for the rise in support for Populist parties is that it reflects growing discontent with liberal democracy – although this could be either a cause or a consequence – or both.[59] For clarification, let us examine satisfaction with how democracy works across a wide range of European societies. The Eurobarometer provides the longest regular time-series, having monitored how well people believe that democracy works in their own country since the early 1970s. The standard annual Eurobarometer question asks: '*On the whole, are you very satisfied, fairly satisfied, not very satisfied or not at all satisfied with the way democracy works in (OUR COUNTRY)?*' The country coverage expanded as

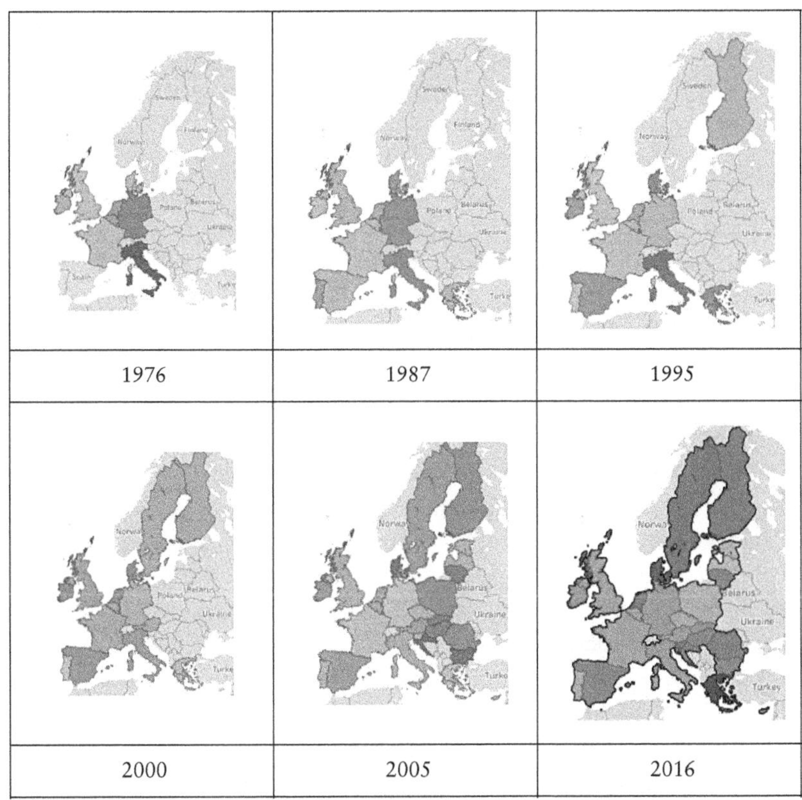


FIGURE 12.7. *Citizen dissatisfaction with the performance of democracy in their own country, EU 1976–2016*
*Note:* Q 'On the whole, are you very satisfied, fairly satisfied, not very satisfied or not at all satisfied with the way democracy works in (OUR COUNTRY)?' Proportion responding 'Not very' and 'Not at all' satisfied. Darker grey indicates more dissatisfaction.
*Source:* Eurobarometer surveys 1976–2016.

EU membership increased during these three decades. The item has been widely used in research, although its interpretation remains a matter of debate.[60] Some argue that it taps approval of 'democracy' as a value or ideal, but we agree with Linde and Ekman that the phrasing of the question (emphasizing how democracy is *performing)* tends to tap public evaluations of the actual workings of democratic regimes.[61] The most extensive recent study of how Europeans see democracy also concluded that responses to this item largely reflect how well people believe that institutions such as elections work in practice.[62]

As shown by Figure 12.7, based on Eurobarometer survey data from 1976 to 2016, satisfaction with how well democracy works persistently differs between Northern and Southern Europe. Democratic satisfaction was consistently low in Italy throughout these decades and satisfaction fell across the Mediterranean countries. By contrast, high satisfaction persists in the Nordic countries.

This North–South pattern has been consistently observed elsewhere using multiple indicators of public opinion and it seems to reflect enduring contrasts.[63] For example, more than a half century ago *The Civic Culture* identified the Italian case as exemplifying an *alienated* political culture: 'The picture of Italian political culture that has emerged from our data is one of relatively unrelieved political alienation and distrust.'[64] Persistent divergent responses across similar European regions can probably be explained, at least in part, by enduring historical cultures, by the democratic quality of their political institution, as well as by the relative capacity of national governments to manage economic growth and deliver inclusive public goods and services. As Lijphart argues, these two factors are linked; parliamentary democracies with Proportional Representation elections and stable multiparty coalition governments, typical of the Nordic region, avoid the adversarial winner-take-all divisive politics and social inequality more characteristic of majoritarian systems as well as generating a broader consensus about welfare policies addressing inequality, exclusion, and social justice.[65]

At the same time, it is apparent that contemporary levels of democratic satisfaction in European societies are only weakly linked with the electoral strength of Authoritarian-Populist parties. Thus the strong populist tradition in Italy – reflected in the electoral success of Berlosconi's Forza Italia, the Northern League, and the Five Star Movement – could potentially be attributed to the persistent lack of public confidence in Italian democracy. A similar narrative could be constructed for the success of Golden Dawn and Syriza in Greece or Podemos in Spain (but with no equivalent in neighboring Portugal). At the same time, however, although Nordic cultures have high levels of democratic satisfaction, the True Finns, the Sweden Democrats, and the Norwegian Progress parties have been very successful in elections; thus, in the September 2017 parliamentary elections the Sweden Democrats returned to power under their leader Siv Jensen as part of the right-wing Solberg-led governing coalition.[66] Earlier chapters demonstrated that at the individual level, even with multiple controls, political mistrust (of parliament, parties and politicians) was a strong and significant predictor of voting for parties endorsing populist anti-establishment values (see Table 8.4). At the societal level, however, it is not clear that the success of populist parties is directly related to levels of democratic satisfaction. One reason for the lack of consistent linkages could be that populism is a two-edged sword.[67] On the one hand, populists can provide an outlet of expression for critical citizens dissatisfied with established political parties, expanding choices on the ballot, and issues on the policy agenda, and thereby providing a corrective for liberal democracy. At the same time, populism may also be a threat to liberal democracy: leadership rhetoric alleging 'corrupt politicians,' 'fake news,' and 'out-of-touch parties' can erode institutional confidence among their supporters, as is illustrated by the way that American beliefs about alleged voter fraud are strongly cued by partisanship.[68]

Younger respondents tend to be particularly critical of the performance of democracy. If this reflects an enduring birth cohort effect, rather than a life-cycle effect, it suggests that several Western democracies are in potential danger of 'deconsolidation.'[69] Foa and Mounk used cohort analysis to compare public attitudes, values, and behavioral indicators derived from the World Values Survey in several affluent post-industrial societies. The authors concluded that significant generation gaps could be observed: compared with their parents and grandparents, the Millennial generation (born after 1980) are significantly *less* supportive of democratic values and institutions, and are more disengaged with both civic and protest forms of political activism. These symptoms are interpreted by the authors as signs of a broader malaise among the younger generation. The argument attracted considerable attention in the mass media.[70] If true, this should indeed be a genuine cause for concern.

But is there convincing evidence to support these claims? In Chapter 8 we demonstrated in multivariate models that younger generations were *less* likely to support authoritarian parties – but they were *more* likely to support populist parties. This phenomenon was observed in 23 out of 26 European societies under comparison. At the individual level, there is evidence that compared with older cohorts, younger generations are more likely to favor Libertarian-Populist parties such as Podemos. But there are reasons to doubt the most pessimistic interpretation of the generational trends.[71] Culturally, when systematic survey data are examined across more than two-dozen Western democracies and over an extended time-period, Foa and Mounk's claims of deconsolidation do not find consistent support.

Figure 12.8 displays approval of the principles of democratic governance by birth cohort using the pooled 5th and 6th waves of the World Value Survey (WVS) across two-dozen post-industrial societies.

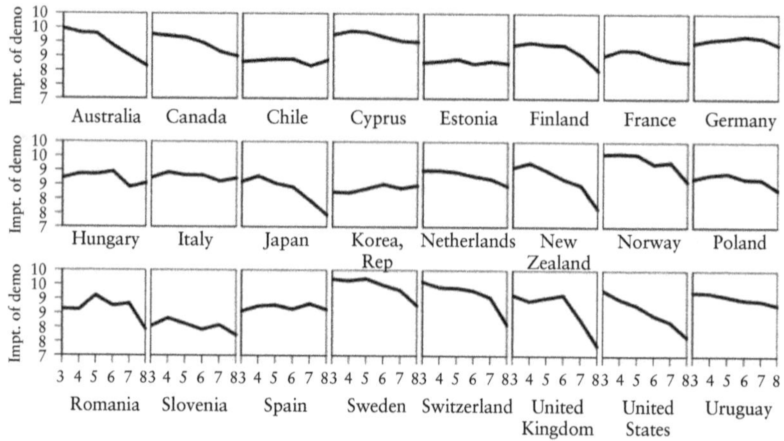


FIGURE 12.8. *Importance of democracy by birth cohort across post-industrial democracies*

*Note:* Q 'How important is it for you to live in a country that is governed democratically? On this scale where 1 means it is "not at all important" and 10 means "absolutely important" what position would you choose?' Mean importance by birth cohort. 3 "Born 1930s" 4 "Born 1940s" 5 "Born 1950s" 6 "Born 1960s" 7 "Born 1970s" 8 "Born 1980s." N. 43,432. Correlation indicates a significant decline by birth cohort in 18 societies (Australia, Canada, Cyprus, Finland, France, Hungary, Japan, Netherlands, NZ, Norway, Poland, Romania, Slovenia, Sweden, Switzerland, UK, US, and Uruguay).

*Source:* World Values Survey 2005–2014, 5th and 6th waves.

The countries are all classified by Freedom House as democratic states, and they share similar characteristics as high-income societies.[72] The correlation between birth cohort and responses are also tested. As Figure 12.8 illustrates, far from a uniform 'European' pattern, the countries under comparison show widely varying trends by birth cohort. Thus, the Anglo-American democracies (including Australia, the US, Canada, the UK, and New Zealand) do indeed display a statistically significant decline in support for democracy by birth cohort. More modest generation gaps can also be observed in several other countries, including Slovenia, Uruguay, Japan, and the Republic of Korea. But in half of the post-industrial democracies under comparison no significant difference by birth cohort can be observed, including Spain, Norway, the Netherlands, Chile, Germany, Hungary, and France. Striking contrasts in the overall levels of democratic approval are also clearly evident among societies, particularly the low approval recorded in America, displaying a profile more like Slovenia than Sweden.[73] The contrasts observed across similar post-industrial democracies are usually greater than the contrasts by cohort within each society.

## Public Trust in Representative Institutions and Elections

What about the impact of populism on trust on core democratic institutions? There has long been concern about an erosion of trust in political parties, parliaments and governments in Western societies.[74] This is also where populism might be expected to have the strongest impact. For example, repeated rhetorical claims of 'fake news' by President Trump and White House spokespersons have sought to construct an alternative reality portraying facts as fungible and journalists as the partisan tool of an arrogant elite.[75] This phrase has spread to many dictators when rejecting critical news reports, including Venezuela's Nicolás Maduro, Syrian president Bashar al-Assad, Myanmar government officials dismissing news about genocide, and by Russia's Foreign Ministry and the Chinese Communist Party's *People's Daily*.[76] The fake news narrative from Trump, combined with social media users actually being targeted by Russian misinformation campaigns, is widely believed to have eroded public trust in the news media.[77] For example, Gallup polls report that most Americans say that it is harder to be well informed and to determine which information is accurate today, with social media 'bubbles' reinforcing partisan polarization among like-minded networks.[78]

To examine the trends, we turn to the Eurobarometer surveys which have monitored institutional trust in political parties, national parliaments and national governments in EU member states from 2001 to 2017. These institutions are some of the core pillars of representative democracies which are commonly attacked by populist leaders. Figure 12.9 shows the trends and suggests that in fact, rather than a steady slide in institutional confidence, we observe patterns closely associated with the onset of the economic recession in 2007. The overall pattern across the EU displays largely flat lines for trust in political parties from 2001 to 2017, not a steady erosion. The trends for trust in national governments and national parliaments show a dip in 2007, followed by recovery as the economy improved, and then another slight erosion starting in 2013. The European survey does not support the more extreme 'crisis of legitimacy' theories.

## Social Tolerance and Trust

Finally, what are the broader effects on society – including tolerance and trust. Authoritarian values, especially when promoted by extremist groups, are widely believed to pose serious dangers for the values of social tolerance and trust, by vilifying or attacking foreigners, immigrants, Muslims, women, and sexual minorities. Racial discrimination and ethnic intolerance remain

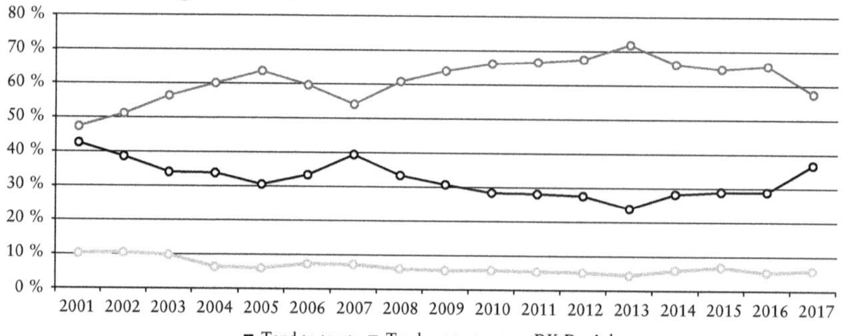


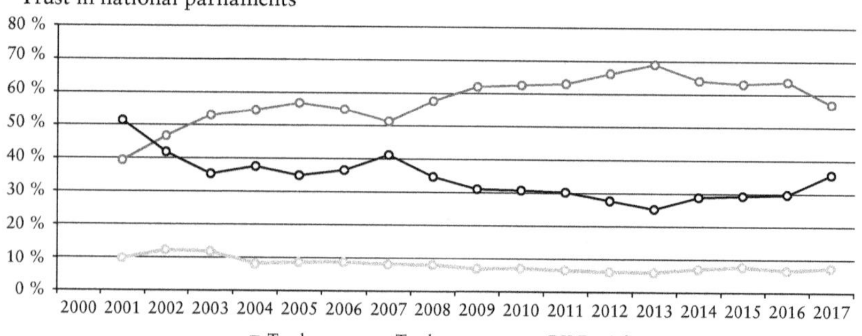


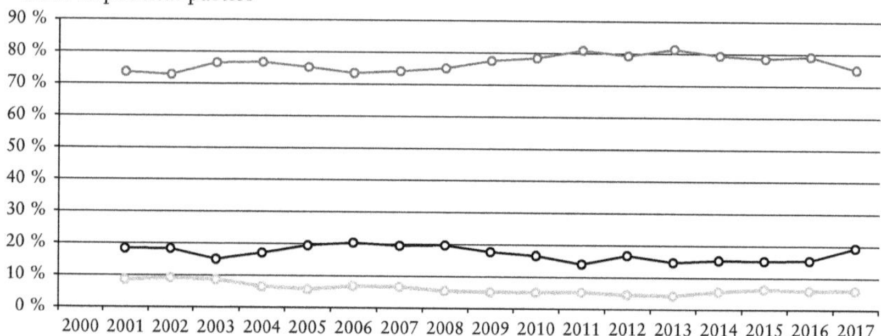


FIGURE 12.9. *Institutional trust, EU 2001–2017*
*Notes:* Q 'I would like to ask you a question about how much trust you have in certain institutions. For each of the following institutions, please tell me if you tend to trust it or tend not to trust it. The national government. The national Parliament. Political Parties. The Press.'
*Source:* Eurobarometer, EU member states.

a major social problem in Western societies, with Islamophobia and Anti-Semitism in Europe, and white nationalist hate groups in America.[79] The messages and actions of extreme-right activists have been widely condemned by the vast majority of people in democratic societies, as demonstrated by the marginalization in American society of white supremacists, neo-Nazis, racist skinheads, and Klansmen.[80] Nevertheless, events such as President Trump's equivocation of the protests 'on many sides' in Charlottesville, his use of racist language denigrating Mexicans, Muslims, and African-Americans throughout his campaign, Trump's supporting the 'birther' conspiracy, and a series of signals through tweets attacking black sportsmen and celebrities, seem to function as dog-whistle politics encouraging David Duke and extremist groups such as White Supremacist, neo-Nazi, neo-Confederate, alt-right, Patriot, and Klan. The Southern Poverty Law Center has tracked rising numbers of hate groups during recent decades, especially anti-Muslim groups.[81] The Anti-Defamation League, tracking extremism and terrorism in the United States, reports that most of the ideologically motivated extremist-related killings in the US were conducted by perpetrators affiliated with White Supremacists, Anti-Government, and Anti-Abortion groups, but some smaller groups of extremist radicals condoning violence can also be found among the radical left, exemplified by the 1999 anti-globalization and anti-capitalist property damage by anarchists protesting the WTO meeting in Seattle, lethal acts of police shooting by black nationalists, and violent protests by the Atifa (anti-fascist) movement.[82] Authoritarian orientations typically underlie acts of political violence, assaults, riots, and hate crimes.

There are many measures of social tolerance but perhaps the key issue in Europe concerns the influx of immigrants from outside the EU. If the focus on this signature issue by Authoritarian-Populist parties has gradually altered public opinion, then we might expect to see growing European hostility toward immigrants. On the other hand, if public opinion responds more to the refugee crisis triggered by the flood of migrants overland and by sea, and by Angela Merkel's open borders decision in September 2015, then any fluctuations in attitudes could be expected to prove more temporary.

The Eurobarometer has monitored European attitudes toward immigrants in recent years and Figure 12.10 illustrates the trends. The graphs show a fairly stable pattern over successive surveys from 2014 to 2017. Where there is some movement, however, then the proportion who are 'very' or 'fairly' negative toward immigrants from outside the EU peaks in 2015, around the height of the flood of migrants – before returning to the more tolerant direction two years later. The proportion of Europeans who are very negative falls from one-quarter to one-fifth during this period. Similarly, when asked about immigrants from other EU member states, the largest

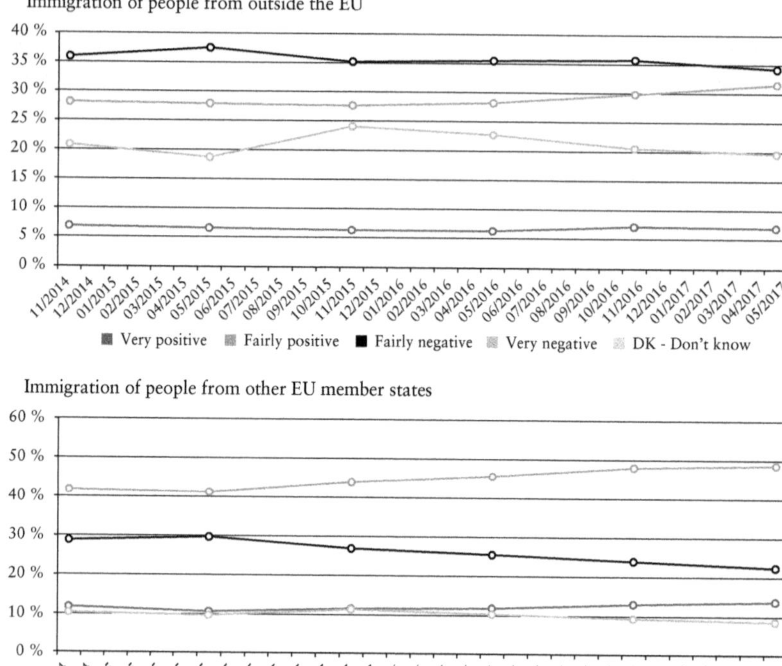


FIGURE 12.10. *European tolerance of immigration*
*Note:* Q 'Please tell me whether each of the following statements evokes a positive or negative feeling for you. Immigration of people from outside the EU. Immigration of people from other EU member states'.
*Source:* Eurobarometer.

category in public opinion is fairly positive and this proportion grows from May 2015 to May 2017 (from 41 to 49%) while the proportion who are fairly negative falls by similar amounts. There is also a slight fall in the proportion who are 'very negative.' It seems that far from rising social intolerance, attitudes toward immigration reflect the actual crisis, widely reported in the news media, more than a steadily growing hostility toward immigration and social intolerance stirred up by authoritarian-populist rhetoric.

## III CONCLUSIONS

In conclusion, there is widespread concern about the impact of populist forces on the health of democracy, with agencies like Human Rights Watch and Freedom House reporting a significant erosion in liberal democracy and the rise of authoritarianism around the world. But how widespread are these problems and how far is the rise of Authoritarian-Populist leaders and parties to blame for these developments? The evidence examined in this chapter points to several conclusions.

First, there are debates about how to interpret worldwide trends in democratization. Both Freedom House and the Economist Intelligence Unit report a global erosion of democracy during the last decade, shrinking the number of democratic states. The EUI estimate that during 2017 more than three times as many countries recorded a worse score than an improvement.[83] They also conclude that US democracy faces growing risk from polarization. Similarly, Freedom House highlights more countries suffering democratic setbacks than gains in 2017, the twelfth consecutive year this has occurred. These developments are also attributed to the rise of populist leaders who appeal to anti-immigrant sentiments and fail to respect civil and political liberties.[84] On the other hand, International IDEA's analysis suggests that democratic institutions remain resilient.[85] We examined the long-term trends from the turn of the twentieth century and concluded that successive waves can be observed, as Huntington argued.[86] Levels of liberal democracy estimated by the Varieties of Democracy project suggests a modest downturn worldwide that started in 2013–2016. The Freedom House estimates of civil liberties and political rights provide stronger evidence of a reverse wave for 2005–2017. This global backsliding should not necessarily be blamed wholly on the rise of authoritarian populism, however, since multiple factors can shape regime transitions, including economic conditions, the onset of military conflicts and civil wars, the effects of the Arab uprisings, and so on. Nevertheless, several leading cases such as Turkey, Venezuela, and Hungary indicate that the rise of particular Authoritarian-Populist leaders has damaged checks and balances on executive powers and led to a deterioration of human rights in some countries.

We also discussed the argument that the growing popularity of authoritarian populism in the electorate leads to a 'contagion of the right' – where center-right parties move rightwards on issues such as control of immigration and Euroscepticism, without necessarily taking up the more extreme xenophobia or nativism. It could be argued that this is a positive development for democracy, making elites pay attention to issues of genuine public concerns. From this perspective, the liberal consensus on the benefit of European Membership and open borders have stifled debate for Eurosceptics and limited choices at the ballot box. On the other hand, by heightening party polarization over the complex and sensitive issue of immigration, authoritarian-populist rhetoric can stir up racial resentment and social intolerance. Again, there are several cases supporting the 'contagion of the right' thesis, such as in France, Switzerland, the Netherlands, France, and Britain. The Brexit case study in the previous chapter and the 2015 and 2017 UK general elections provided a detailed illustration of how this process works – and how this strategy can quickly and effectively under-cut voting support for smaller parties. After Brexit in 2016, once Theresa May's Conservative government declared that it was going to negotiate Britain's exit from the EU, UKIP voters switched back to the Conservatives in the general election the following year.

Finally, the chapter examined whether the rise of authoritarian populism should be understood as a cause – or a consequence – of an erosion of the civic culture. When populists attack the legitimacy of the core channels linking citizens and the state – mainstream political parties, parliaments, and the media – it can erode support for democracy – and the evidence suggests that there are genuine reasons for concern about this phenomenon. But European trends in recent years also suggest that talk of a 'crisis of legitimacy' is probably unduly alarmist.

What is to be done? The concluding chapter recapitulates our core theory, summarizes this book's main findings, and considers the strategic options to fight back.

## Notes

1. See, for example, Brian Klass. 2017. *The Despot's Apprentice: Donald Trump's Attack on Democracy.* New York: Hot Books; Cass R. Sunstein. Ed. 2018.*Can It Happen Here? Authoritarianism in America.* New York: Dey Street Books; David Frumm. 2018. *Trumpocracy: The Corruption of the American Republic.* New York: Harper.
2. Cas Mudde and C.R. Kaltwasser. Eds. 2012. *Populism in Europe and the Americas: Threat or corrective for democracy?* New York: Cambridge University Press; Patrick Hossay and Aristide Zolberg. 2002. 'Democracy in peril?' In Martin Schain, Aristide Zolberg, and Patrick Hossay. Eds. *Shadows Over Europe: The Development and Impact of the Extreme Right in Western Europe.* Houndsmill: Palgrave Macmillan, Chapter 13.
3. Joshua Kurlantzick. 2014. *Democracy in Retreat: The Revolt of the Middle Class and the Worldwide Decline of Representative Government.* New Haven, CT: Yale University Press; Larry Diamond and Marc F. Plattner. Eds. 2015. *Democracy in Decline?* Baltimore: Johns Hopkins University Press. The classic work classifying distinct periods of democratization is Samuel Huntington. 1993. *The Third Wave.* Oklahoma: University of Oklahoma Press.
4. Freedom House. 2018. *Freedom in the World, 2018.* https://freedomhouse.org/report/freedom-world/freedom-world-2018.

5. The Economist Intelligence Unit. *Democracy Index 2017: Free Speech Under Attack*. London: The Economist.
6. Kenneth Roth. November 6, 2016. *The Dangerous Rise of Populism*. Human Rights Watch. www.hrw.org/world-report/2017/country-chapters/dangerous-rise-of-populism.
7. Steven Levitsky and Daniel Ziblatt. 2018. *How Democracies Die*. New York: Crown; Yasha Mounk. 2018. *The People vs. Democracy: Why Democracy Is in Danger & How to Save It*. Cambridge, MA: Harvard University Press.
8. Allan R. Brewer-Carías. 2010. *Dismantling Democracy in Venezuela: The Chávez Authoritarian Experiment*. Cambridge: Cambridge University Press.
9. Human Rights Watch. November 29, 2017. *Crackdown on dissent*. www.hrw.org/report/2017/11/29/crackdown-dissent/brutality-torture-and-political-persecution-venezuela.
10. International IDEA. 2017.*The Global State of Democracy: Exploring Democracy's Resilience*. Stockholm: International IDEA. www.idea.int/publications/catalogue/global-state-democracy-exploring-democracys-resilience.
11. Samuel Huntington. 1993. *The Third Wave of Democratization*. Oklahoma: University of Oklahoma Press.
12. Samuel Huntington. 1993. *The Third Wave of Democratization*. Oklahoma: University of Oklahoma Press.
13. Andrea Pirro. 2015. *The Populist Radical Right in Central and Eastern Europe: Ideology, Impact, and Electoral Performance*. London: Routledge; Attila Agh. 2016. 'The decline of democracy in East-Central Europe: Hungary as the worst-case scenario.' *Problems of Post-Communism* 63 (5–6): 277–228.
14. Freedom House. 2018. *Freedom in the World, 2018*. https://freedomhouse.org/report/freedom-world/freedom-world-2018.
15. www.nytimes.com/2018/01/27/world/europe/czech-election-milos-zeman.html.
16. Freedom House. 2018. *Freedom in the World, 2018*. https://freedomhouse.org/report/freedom-world/freedom-world-2018; Berk Esen and Sebnem Gumuscu. 2016. 'Rising competitive authoritarianism in Turkey.' *Third World Quarterly* 37 (9): 1581–1606.
17. Freedom House. 2018. *Freedom in the World, 2018*. https://freedomhouse.org/report/freedom-world/freedom-world-2018.
18. www.bbc.co.uk/news/world-asia-36251094.
19. R.D. Sylvia and C.P. Danopoulos. 2003. 'The Chavez phenomenon: Political change in Venezuela.' *Third World Quarterly* 24 (1): 63–76; Leonardo Vera. 2015. 'Venezuela 1999–2014: Macro-policy, oil governance and economic performance.' *Comparative Economic Studies* 57 (3): 539–568.
20. www.oas.org/en/media_center/press_release.asp?sCodigo=E-042/17.
21. Michael L. Conniff. Ed. 1982. *Latin American Populism in Comparative Perspective*. Albuquerque, NM: University of New Mexico Press.
22. Julio C. Teehankee. 2016. 'Weak state, strong presidents: Situating the Duterte presidency in Philippine political time.' *Journal of Developing Societies* 32 (3): 293–321; Nicole Curato. 2017. 'Flirting with authoritarian

fantasies? Rodrigo Duterte and the new terms of Philippine populism.' *Journal of Contemporary Asia* 47 (1): 142–153.

23. Pippa Norris. September 7, 2017. 'Trump's Global democracy retreat.' *New York Times*. www.nytimes.com/2017/09/07/opinion/trump-democracy-state-department.html.
24. Cas Mudde. 2013. 'Three decades of populist radical right parties in Western Europe: So what?' *European Journal of Political Research* 52: 1–19; Cas Mudde. 2014. 'Fighting the system? Populist radical right parties and party system change.' *Party Politics* 20 (2): 217–226.
25. Paul Taggart. *Populism*. Buckingham: Open University Press; Cristóbal Rovira Kaltwassera and Paul Taggart. 2016. 'Dealing with populists in government: A framework for analysis.' *Democratization* 23 (2): 201–220; Paul Taggart and Cristóbal Rovira Kaltwasser. 2016. 'Dealing with populists in government: Some comparative conclusions.' *Democratization* 23 (2): 345–365.
26. Tjitske Akkerman and Sarah L. De Lange. 2012. 'Radical right parties in office: Incumbency records and the electoral cost of governing.' *Government and Opposition* 47 (4): 574–596.
27. Michael Wolff. 2018. *Fire and Fury*. New York: Henry Holt.
28. Tim Bale. 2003. 'Cinderella and her ugly sisters: The mainstream and extreme right in Europe's bipolarizing party systems.' *West European Politics* 26 (3): 67–90; Tjitske Akkerman. 2012. 'Comparing radical right parties in government: Immigration and integration policies in nine countries (1996–2010).' *West European Politics* 35 (3): 511–529; Tjitske Akkerman. 2015. 'Immigration policy and electoral competition in Western Europe: A fine grained analysis of party positions over the past two decades.' *Party Politics* 21 (1): 54–67.
29. Simon Bornschier. 2010. *Cleavage Politics and the Populist Right: The New Cultural Conflict in Western Europe*. Philadelphia: Temple University Press.
30. Martin Schain. 1987. 'The National Front in France and the construction of political legitimacy.' *West European Politics* 10 (2): 229–252.
31. Thomas F. Pettigrew. 1998. 'Reactions toward the new minorities of Western Europe.' *Annual Review of Sociology* 24: 77–103.
32. www.washingtonpost.com/news/worldviews/wp/2017/01/23/dutch-pm-tells-immigrants-act-normal-or-go-away/.
33. http://ukpollingreport.co.uk/blog/archives/9879.
34. Christof Roos. 2013. *The EU and Immigration Policies: Cracks in the Walls of Fortress Europe?* New York: Palgrave Macmillan.
35. Ruud Koopmans and Paul Statham. Eds. 2000. *Challenging Immigration and Ethnic Relations Politics: Comparative European Perspectives*. Oxford: Oxford University Press. See also the comparison of Germany and Italy on this issue in Ted Perlmutter. 2002. 'The politics of restriction.' In Martin Schain, Aristide Zolberg, and Patrick Hossay. Eds. *Shadows Over Europe: The Development and Impact of the Extreme Right in Western Europe*. Houndsmill: Palgrave Macmillan.
36. Robert Harmel and Lars Svasand. 1997. 'The influence of new parties on old parties' platforms: The cases of the progress parties and conservative

parties of Denmark and Norway.' *Party Politics* 3 (3): 315–340; W.M. Downs. 2001. 'Pariahs in their midst: Belgian and Norwegian parties react to extremist threats.' *West European Politics* 24 (3): 23–42.

37. Cas Mudde. 2013. 'Three decades of populist radical right parties in Western Europe: So what?' *European Journal of Political Research* 52: 1–19; Cas Mudde. 2014. 'Fighting the system? Populist radical right parties and party system change.' *Party Politics* 20 (2): 217–226; Cas Mudde and Cristóbal Rovira Kaltwasser. Eds. 2012. *Populism in Europe and the Americas: Threat or Corrective for Democracy?* Cambridge: Cambridge University Press.
38. Calculated from Holger Döring and Philip Manow. 2017. *Parliaments and Governments Database* (ParlGov) 'Elections' dataset: www.parlgov.org/. See Chapter 8, Figure 9.1.
39. Cristóbal Rovira Kaltwasser and Paul Taggart. 2015. 'Dealing with populists in government: A framework for analysis.' *Democratization* 23 (2): 201–220.
40. Sarah L. De Lange 2012 'New alliances: Why mainstream parties govern with radical right-wing populist parties.' *Political Studies* 60: 899–918; Daniele Albertazzi and Sean Mueller. 2013. 'Populism and liberal democracy: Populists in government in Austria, Italy, Poland and Switzerland.' *Government and Opposition* 48(3): 343–371; Daniele Albertazzi and Duncan McDonnell. 2014. *Populists in Power*. London: Routledge.
41. Michael Minkenberg. 2001. 'The radical right in public office: Agenda-setting and policy effects.' *West European Politics* 24: 1–21; Tjitske Akkerman and Matthijs Rooduijn. 2014. 'Pariahs or partners? Inclusion and exclusion of radical right parties and the effects on their policy positions.' *Political Studies* 62: 1–18.
42. Harold Clarke, Matthew J. Goodwin, and Paul Whiteley. 2017. *Brexit! Why Britain Voted to Leave the European Union*. Cambridge: Cambridge University Press.
43. Matthew J. Goodwin and Robert Ford. 2017. 'Britain after Brexit: A nation divided.' *Journal of Democracy* 28 (1): 17–30.
44. European Council on Foreign Relations. 2016. *The World According to Europe's Insurgent Parties*. London: European Council on Foreign Relations. www.ecfr.eu.
45. See Philip Lynch. 2017. 'The Conservatives and Brexit' and also Ron Johnston and Charles Pattie. 2017. 'UKIP's former supporters were crucial for the outcome.' Both in Einar Thorsen, Daniel Jackson, and Darren Lilleker. Eds. *UK Election Analysis 2017*. Center for the Study of Journalism, Culture & Community, Bournmouth University. http://ElectionAnalysis.UK.
46. Klaus Armingeon and Kai Guthmann. 2014. 'Democracy in crisis? The declining support for national democracy in European countries, 2007–2011.' *European Journal of Political Research* 53 (3): 423–442.
47. See, for example, The Pew Center. October 2017. *Political Typology Reveals Deep Fissures on the Right and Left*. www.people-press.org/2017/10/24/political-typology-reveals-deep-fissures-on-the-right-and-left/.

48. www.people-press.org/2017/05/03/public-trust-in-government-remains-near-historic-lows-as-partisan-attitudes-shift/.
49. Cas Mudde and Cristóbal Rovira Kaltwasser. Eds. 2012. *Populism in Europe and the Americas: Threat or Corrective for Democracy?* New York: Cambridge University Press.
50. Pippa Norris. 2017. *Why American Elections Are Flawed (and How to Fix Them)*. Ithaca, NY: Cornell University Press.
51. Tim Immerzeel and Mark Pickup. 2015. 'Populist radical right parties mobilizing "the people"? The role of populist radical right success in voter turnout.' *Electoral Studies* 40: 347–360.
52. Göran Adamson. 2016. *Populist Parties and the Failure of the Political Elites: The Rise of the Austrian Freedom Party (FPÖ)*. Germany: Peter Lang; Koen Abts and Stefan Rummens. 2007. 'Populism versus democracy.' *Political Studies* 55 (2): 405–424.
53. R. Heinisch. 2003. 'Success in opposition – failure in government: Explaining the performance of right-wing populist parties in public office.' *West European Politics* 26 (3): 91–130.
54. International IDEA. 2017.*The Global State of Democracy: Exploring Democracy's Resilience*. Stockholm: International IDEA. www.idea.int/publications/catalogue/global-state-democracy-exploring-democracys-resilience; Pippa Norris. 2017. 'Is Western democracy backsliding? Diagnosing the risks.' *Journal of Democracy* 28 (2).
55. Juan Linz and Alfred Stephan. Eds. 1978. *The Breakdown of Democratic Regimes: An Introduction*. Baltimore, MD: The Johns Hopkins University Press; Juan J. Linz and Alfred Stephan. 1996. *Problems of Democratic Transition and Consolidation*. Baltimore, MD: The Johns Hopkins University Press, p. 5.
56. Gabriel Almond and Sidney Verba. 1963. *The Civic Culture*. Princeton, NJ: Princeton University Press.
57. Pippa Norris. Ed. 1999. *Critical Citizens: Global Support for Democratic Governance*. Oxford: Oxford University Press; Pippa Norris. 2011. *Democratic Deficits*. Cambridge: Cambridge University Press.
58. See also the Pew Global Attitudes survey. www.pewresearch.org/fact-tank/2017/10/30/global-views-political-systems/.
59. Matthijs Rooduijn, Wouter Van Der Brug, and Sarah L. de Lange. 2016. 'Expressing or fueling discontent? The relationship between populist voting and political discontent.' *Electoral Studies* 43: 32–40.
60. For some of the many previous studies using this measure, see Christopher J. Anderson and Christine A. Guillory. 1997. 'Political institutions and satisfaction with Democracy.' *American Political Science Review* 91 (1): 66–81; Marta Lagos. 2003. 'Support for and satisfaction with democracy.' *International Journal of Public Opinion Research* 15 (4): 471–487; André Blais and François Gélineau. 2007. 'Winning, losing and satisfaction with democracy.' *Political Studies* 55: 425–441; Kees Aarts and Jacques Thomassen. 2008. 'Satisfaction with democracy: Do institutions matter?' *Electoral Studies* 27 (1): 5–18; Alexander F. Wagner, Friedrich Schneider, and Martin Halla. 2009. 'The

quality of institutions and satisfaction with democracy in Western Europe: A panel analysis.' *European Journal of Political Economy* 25 (1): 30–41.

61. Jonas Linde and Joakim Ekman. 2003. 'Satisfaction with democracy: A note on a frequently used indicator in comparative politics.' *European Journal of Political Research* 42 (3): 391–408; Damarys Canache, Jeffrey J. Mondak, and Mitch A. Seligson. 2001. 'Meaning and measurement in cross-national research on satisfaction with democracy.' *Public Opinion Quarterly* 65 (4): 506–528.
62. Monica Ferrin and Hanspeter Kriesi. Eds. 2016. *How Europeans View and Evaluate Democracy.* Oxford: Oxford University Press.
63. Carolien van Ham, Jacques Thomassen, Kees Aarts, and Rudy Andeweg. Eds. 2017. *Myth and Reality of the Legitimacy Crisis: Explaining Trends and Cross-National Differences in Established Democracies.* Oxford: Oxford University Press.
64. Gabriel A. Almond and Sidney Verba. 1963. *The Civic Culture.* Princeton, NJ: Princeton University Press, p. 308; Paolo Segatti. 2006. 'Italy, forty years of political disaffection: A longitudinal exploration.' In Mariano Torcal and José R. Montero. Eds. *Political Disaffection in Contemporary Democracies: Social Capital, Institutions, and Politics.* London: Routledge.
65. Arend Lijphart. 1999. *Patterns of Democracy.* New Haven, CT: Yale University Press.
66. www.ft.com/content/abbd83f6-97a5-11e7-b83c-9588e51488a0.
67. Cas Mudde and Cristóbal Rovira Kaltwasser. Eds. 2012. *Populism in Europe and the Americas: Threat or Corrective for Democracy?* New York: Cambridge University Press.
68. John Kane. 2017. 'Why can't we agree on Id? Partisanship, perceptions of fraud, and public support for voter identification laws.' *Public Opinion Quarterly* 81 (4): 943–955; Emily Beaulieu. 2014. 'From voter ID to party ID: How political parties affect perceptions of election fraud in the US.' *Electoral Studies* 35: 24–32; Jake Sherman. 'Poll: 1-in-4 voters believe Trump's vote-fraud claims.' *Politico.* www.politico.com/story/2017/02/poll-donald-trump-voter-fraud-234458.
69. Roberto Stephen Foa and Yasha Mounk. 2016. 'The dangers of deconsolidation: The democratic disconnect.' *Journal of Democracy* 27: 5–17; Roberto Stephen Foa and Yasha Mounk. 2017. 'The signs of deconsolidation.' *Journal of Democracy* 28 (1): 5–15.
70. Amanda Taub. November 29, 2016. 'How stable are democracies? "Warning signs are flashing red".' *New York Times.*
71. For critiques, see Ronald Inglehart. 2016. 'The danger of deconsolidation: How much should we worry?' *Journal of Democracy* 27: 18–23; Erik Voeten. December 5, 2016. 'That viral graph about millennials' declining support for democracy? It's very misleading.' *The Washington Post/Monkey Cage*; Erik Voeten. December 14, 2016. 'It's actually older people who have become more cynical about US democracy.' *The Washington Post/Monkey Cage.*
72. Measured by the World Development Indicators and defined as societies with per capita GDP (in purchasing power parity) above $16,000.

73. The Pew Research Center. February 7–12, 2017. www.people-press.org.
74. Susan J. Pharr and Robert D. Putnam. Eds. 2000. *Disaffected Democracies: What's Troubling the Trilateral Countries?* Princeton, NJ: Princeton University Press; Mattei Dogan. Ed. 2005. *Political Mistrust and the Discrediting of Politicians.* The Netherlands: Brill; Gerry Stoker. 2006. *Why Politics Matters: Making Democracy Work.* London: Palgrave/Macmillan; Mariano Torcal and José R. Montero. Eds. 2006. *Political Disaffection in Contemporary Democracies: Social Capital, Institutions, and Politics.* London: Routledge; Colin Hay. 2007. *Why We Hate Politics.* Cambridge: Polity Press; Russell J. Dalton. 2004. *Democratic Challenges, Democratic Choices: The Erosion of Political Support in Advanced Industrial Democracies.* New York: Oxford University Press.
75. Shorenstein Center. May 2017. *Combatting Fake News: An Agenda for Research and Action.* https://shorensteincenter.org/combating-fake-news-agenda-for-research/.
76. www.nytimes.com/2017/12/12/world/europe/trump-fake-news-dictators.html.
77. M. Mitchell Waldrop. 2017. 'News feature: The genuine problem of fake news.' *Proceedings of the National Academy of Arts and Sciences* 114 (48): 12631–12634.
78. Knight Foundation. 2017. *American Views: Trust, Media and Democracy.* Gallup/Knight Foundation Survey. https://kf-site-production.s3.amazonaws.com/publications/pdfs/000/000/242/original/KnightFoundation_AmericansViews_Client_Report_010917_Final_Updated.pdf.
79. See the Southern Policy Law group, www.splcenter.org/hate-map.
80. See the Southern Policy Law group's *Intelligence Report*, which monitors activities by these groups in America. www.splcenter.org/fighting-hate/extremist-files/groups.
81. Mark Potok. 2017. *The Year in Hate and Extremism.* Montgomery, AL: Southern Poverty Law Center. www.splcenter.org/fighting-hate/intelligence-report/2017/year-hate-and-extremism.
82. Anti-Defamation League. 2017. *Murder and Extremism in the United States in 2016.* ADL Report. www.adl.org/sites/default/files/documents/MurderAndExtremismInUS2016.pdf.
83. *The Economist. Democracy Index 2017: Free Speech Under Attack.* London: The Economist Intelligence Unit.
84. Freedom House. 2018. *Freedom in the World, 2018.* https://freedomhouse.org/report/freedom-world/freedom-world-2018.
85. International IDEA. 2017. *The Global State of Democracy: Exploring Democracy's Resilience.* Stockholm: International IDEA. www.idea.int/publications/catalogue/global-state-democracy-exploring-democracys-resilience.
86. Samuel Huntington. 1993. *The Third Wave of Democratization.* Oklahoma: University of Oklahoma Press.

# 13

# The Authoritarian-Populist Challenge

The surge of support for Authoritarian-Populist parties in contemporary elections has mobilized a resistance concerned about its potential consequences for liberal democracy. It is not just Trump: Authoritarian-Populist parties have won legislative and presidential contests in many places, and advanced into ministerial office in Austria, Switzerland, New Zealand, Norway, Finland, the Czech Republic, Italy, and Poland.[1] Elsewhere, European parties within this family group have often seen upswings in support even if they have not won office. Since the 1980s, the vote for Authoritarian-Populist parties in Europe has risen to the highest level recorded since World War II. In the first round of the June 2017 French presidential elections, the anti-immigrant and Eurosceptic National Front's Marine Le Pen defeated both the Socialist Party on the center-left and the Republicans on the center-right. A few months later, in September, the xenophobic, and racist Alternative for Germany won 94 seats, the first time such a party had gained entry into the Bundestag since 1948. A month later, the Austrian Freedom Party (FPÖ) came second in national elections, becoming junior partners in the OVP government. The populist tide did not always advance. Thus, UKIP rose in 2015 only to fall back into disarray after Brexit. Authoritarian Populism support ebbs and flows. Yet even where parties have had limited electoral success in winning office, their ideas can still influence the policy agenda for the center-right such as the Austrian People's Party and the UK Conservatives. And Trump's election has emboldened authoritarian leaders around the world.

How can we account for this development?

This chapter recapitulates our core theory, summarizes how far it is supported by the evidence, and considers the broader lessons for the resistance seeking to counter authoritarian populism.

## I THE THEORETICAL ARGUMENT

We will start by summarizing our theoretical argument.

Populist rhetoric holds that legitimate power rests with the ordinary people not the mainstream parties, the news media, and elected representatives. But in practice, this façade allows authoritarian leaders to step into the power vacuum, claiming legitimacy as the voice of the real people. Populist rejection of established elites can be linked with libertarian attitudes and progressive policies, but, more often, the discourse is coupled with authoritarian values emphasizing security, conformity, and loyalty toward tribal leaders at the expense of individual freedom. This mix corrodes faith in pluralism, openness, and the safeguards of individual liberty such as freedom of speech, the rule of law, an independent judiciary, and checks on the abuse of executive power. It fails to recognize the importance of protecting minority rights, the virtues of deliberation and consensus-building, and the importance of transparency, accountability, and the clear separation between personal and political interests. The state is seen as an instrument at the service of the leader. Authoritarian populists attach little importance to the rules-based international world order and the role of multilateral cooperation to strengthen human development. Regimes based on authoritarian cultures maintain control by restricting individual rights, silencing the free press, limiting opposition, and strengthening the army and police.

Authoritarian cultures are based on two premises:

First, authoritarians draw a sharp distinction between 'Us' and 'Them.' The in-group is an imagined community based on the belief that it has shared values and attitudes and a common social identity that can be based on nationality, race, religion, language, socio-economic status, partisanship, location, sex, or gender. Whatever the basis of group membership, it is sharply divided from other tribes.

Second, group security is seen to be under threat. The authoritarian culture depicts a dog-eat-dog world where it is vital to be on guard. In this view, suckers and losers trust in fair-dealing, the loyalty of allies, and objective truth. Outsiders and politicians cannot be trusted; they are out to swindle you and lies are everywhere. In a zero-sum game, their gain is our loss. Authoritarians know that in this world, the only protection is strength.

Given these assumptions, the authoritarian culture is a rational response to perceived tribal threats. If life is insecure, the community needs to close ranks behind strong leaders, with in-group solidarity, rejection of outsiders, and conformity to group norms. This orientation is linked with xenophobic nationalism, racism, misogyny, homophobia, conventionalism, loyalty to the group, and obedience to its leaders. Although often described as 'right-wing,' in fact authoritarian intolerance cuts across the conventional economic-based left–right dimension. Although racism, nationalism and ethnocentrism tend to be dismissed by liberals and educated elites as irrational and deplorable feelings, if one perceives the world as a dangerous place, if elected representatives are failing to defend us, the authoritarian reflex seems to be a rational response to protecting the tribe, even at the expense of individual freedom.

The notion that the authoritarianism is fed by perceptions of threat has always been central to the concept. But what fears trigger the authoritarian reflex? There is surprisingly little consensus.[2] It could be stimulated by material and physical insecurities, such as poverty, crime, or war. But it could also be linked with cultural anxieties, such as the perceived threat to the once-predominant groups from growing ethnic diversity, rapid value change, and the loss of status, privilege, and power. Or a mix of material and cultural factors could be at work. The book has analyzed a large body of empirical evidence to understand the impact of different types of threats on authoritarian and populist values and, in turn, how these values lead to support for Authoritarian-Populist parties.

Our theoretical argument is based on the following building blocks, illustrated in Figure 13.1.

### 1) Social Structural Change in Post-Industrial Societies

Our account starts with long-term transformations in the social structure of post-industrial societies arising from processes of economic growth, demographic turnover, the expansion of access to higher education, more egalitarian roles of women and men, and the growing ethnic diversity of large cities combined with processes of urbanization. These processes interact to reinforce the direction of change, with younger generations leaving rural communities to study and then to live and work in ethnically diverse urban and suburban conurbations. The net effect has been to depopulate rural and older industrialized communities, leaving behind disproportionately white, older, less educated, and working-class communities.

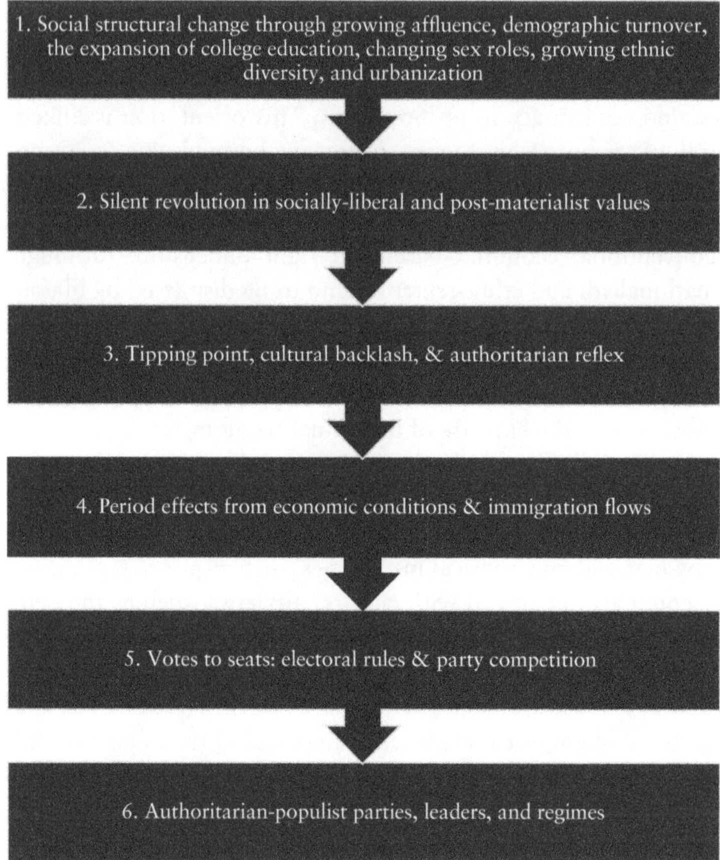


FIGURE 13.1. *The sequence of steps in the cultural backlash theory*

## 2) The Silent Revolution in Cultural Values

The book emphasizes the consequences of the silent revolution's intergenerational value shift, with cultures gradually evolving from socially conservative to socially liberal and post-material values. As Chapter 4 shows, a large body of evidence illustrates this development. In economically and physically secure high-income societies – although not most of the developing world – traditional moral beliefs about sex, marriage, and the family have eroded in recent decades, with growing public acceptance of lesbian and gay relations and more fluid identities based on gender and sexuality.[3] Younger people have been at the forefront in growing recognition of gay rights.[4] Increasingly secure societies have become increasingly secular – with the fading of religious identities, everyday practices like prayer and attending religious services, and feelings about the central importance of religion in people's lives.[5] Secularization has undercut the authority of church authorities, moral beliefs, and faith-based teachings concerning the importance of the conventional two-parent family, the strict division of sex roles, and policies restricting contraception, abortion, and divorce. These value shifts have been associated with major changes in social lifestyles and the public policy agenda in many Western societies, exemplified by laws establishing LGBTQ rights and same-sex marriage, preventing sexual harassment in the workplace and domestic violence at home, and implementing gender quotas for elected office.[6]

Complex shifts have also been observed in feelings of identity with the nation, policies protecting native-born populations against immigrants, and racial prejudice. A sense of belonging to the nation-state has traditionally been expressed through deep-rooted feelings of pride and patriotism, willingness to fight for one's country, and support for closed borders as security against foreign threats. Acceptance of these norms has been challenged in contemporary societies by globalization, international communication technologies, migrant population flows accelerating the spread of multicultural lifestyles and multiethnic communities, and the growth of transnational networks around the world.[7] Successive waves of immigration have transformed once-homogeneous European populations through an influx of foreign laborers, family reunifications, refugees, and asylum seekers.[8]

A substantial body of evidence demonstrates the trajectory of cultural evolution.[9] Today the balance of public opinion has moved in a more socially liberal direction on these issues, with fewer located in the middle. This is not merely an American phenomenon; the direction of value change is clear and consistent across multiple cultural issues and across many developed societies. Thus, the British Social Attitudes survey has tracked the expansion of steadily more socially liberal attitudes since the early 1980s on a range of personal and political issues, such as attitudes toward sex before marriage, same-sex relationships, abortion, and pornography, and the impact of immigration on the country – although with growing Euroscepticism.[10] These issues divide young and old, the college educated and the school leavers, the urban metropolis and rural communities, affluent professionals and the working-class. And parties and partisans. In America, for example, well before Trump entered the White House, Pew Center surveys over the last quarter century show widening party polarization dividing Democrats and Republicans in the electorate on social and lifestyle issues concerning abortion, race and immigration, homosexuality, the use of military force, gun control, and the role of government.[11] The moderate middle has disintegrated; in 1994, along the liberal vs. conservative spectrum on these values, most Americans were at the center. At the elite level, 'big tent' parties in America used to include a mixture of diverse viewpoints: in the Democratic Party under Truman, a coalition of New York liberal elites, Chicago meat-packers, and Alabama traditionalists, and similarly in the GOP under Reagan, Texas oil executives, Iowa farmers, and Christian Right fundamentalists. Under Nixon, the Republican Party of Lincoln favored civil rights and reproductive rights. Well before the election of Trump, however, members of Congress had become sorted into cohesive and deeply opposing camps without the capacity to compromise on many issues.[12]

The silent revolution gave rise to long-term generational shifts in which younger birth cohorts and the more-educated became consistently less nationalistic and socially conservative than the older and less educated groups.[13] For example, data from the World Values Survey found that cosmopolitan orientations, such as a sense of belonging 'to the world as a whole,' were strongest among the young.[14] Similar findings are reported in survey-based cross-sectional studies of national identities, national pride, and support for the agencies of multilateral governance in Britain, Australia, and Sweden.[15] Analysis of Islamophobia in the US and in Europe finds that negative views of Muslims are far more common among older people, and among the less educated and lower socio-economic sectors.[16] If these age-differences reflect generational differences rather than life-cycle effects (as the evidence indicates), then a gradual transformation of worldviews will tend to emerge over successive decades, as older generations with anti-immigrant and anti-Muslim prejudices are replaced by younger birth cohorts holding more cosmopolitan and tolerant attitudes.[17] In post-industrial societies, younger, more-educated people have generally shown relatively trusting attitudes toward outsiders (people of other nationalities or religions), positive views of multicultural diversity, disavowal of racial prejudice, and support for minority rights.[18] These attitudes may interact with urbanization; studies suggest that ethnic prejudice provides cognitive shortcuts that can be reduced by intergroup contact and familiarity.[19] Millennials are more likely than their parents and grandparents to live in ethnically diverse cities and conurbations, than in rural areas and small towns inhabited predominately by older, ethnically homogeneous residents.

Generational change has also transformed conventional forms of political mobilization and political activism. Millennials are engaged in politics – but they generally vote at far lower rates than the Interwar generation. Almost two decades ago, the rise of 'critical citizens' was documented, showing that many people endorsed democratic ideals but they were deeply disenchanted with the performance of representative institutions.[20] These patterns have persisted – providing opportunities for populists to turn rightful skepticism about liberal democracy into a deeper cynicism about 'the establishment.'

### 3) Tipping Points and the Authoritarian Reflex

We theorize that the silent revolution eventually produced a major cultural backlash. The first stage of the silent revolution, during the post-war decades, transformed the cultures of post-industrial societies. It eroded support for socially conservative and materialist values, bringing a gradual rise of socially liberal and post-materialist values that give top priority to individual free choice and self-expression. This long-term evolution has shifted the balance of public opinion in high-income countries. The moral beliefs, values, and social norms that used to be mainstream in affluent nations during the mid-twentieth century are endorsed today by shrinking segments of the population.

The post-war era saw a broad consensus emerge about the values of democratic decision-making and the goals of building prosperity, expanding the welfare safety net and opportunities for the less well-off, and developing international cooperation and peace. The central debates in the policy agenda, dividing the electorate and mainstream political parties on both left and right, centered on the role of markets versus states in redistributive and regulatory policies designed to achieve these common goals. The rise of post-material values brought increased tensions that deeply divide social liberals and social conservatives over identity politics, religiosity versus secularism, sexuality and gender, the role of family and marriage, support for LGBTQ rights, environmental protection, and nationalism versus cosmopolitanism. The new cultural cleavages are reflected in the heated debate over these issues, on which it is relatively difficult to compromise.

Moreover, the rising numbers of those holding socially liberal values have triggered a counter-reaction as cultural change eventually reached a tipping point. The proportion of social conservatives has gradually shrunken to become a new cultural minority. Traditional values remain most widespread among the older generation, less-educated white men, and people living in rural communities – all declining sectors of the population. This has produced a feeling among social conservatives that they have become strangers in their own country, holding views that are no longer respected by educated elites – or tolerated by society as a whole.

Culture wars between socially liberal and socially conservative values have become highly polarized. Social conservatism per se does not generate tensions. The crucial point is whether socially conservative values are combined with authoritarian predispositions emphasizing: (1) the importance of *conformity* with social conventions and established traditions; (2) the need for *security* to protect against risks threatening the group; and (3) the value of *loyalty* and *deference* to group leaders.[21] This orientation is not necessarily 'right-wing' – intolerance of 'out-groups' exists on the left as well. But it is most compatible with socially conservative attitudes, because authoritarian values are closely linked with emphasis on social order, tradition, and stability. Thus, the rise of socially liberal and post-materialist values threatens authoritarians and those losing status and respect from the silent revolution.

Groups can react to long-term cultural changes in society in several ways. The 'spiral of silence' thesis advanced by Noelle-Neuman argues that people are unlikely to express dissent if they feel that their views are out of step with the majority – they want to avoid social isolation or sanctions.[22] Another option is adaptation, as groups gradually come to accept societal shifts during their lifetimes, like growing acceptance of homosexuality or the decline of religious values and churchgoing practices in Europe.[23] A third way to cope with dissonance is to retreat into social bubbles of like-minded people, facilitated by social media and the partisan press, helping to avoid the risks of social conflict.[24]

But another alternative is that as the formerly predominant majority becomes a steadily shrinking share of the population, a tipping point triggers an authoritarian reflex, mobilizing socially conservative groups who feel that their core values are no longer widely respected. They react against condescending cosmopolitan elites dominating the popular media, the professional political classes, and the literary, legal, academic, and scientific establishment. And they feel displaced by growing social diversity linked with the influx of out-groups with different nationalities, languages, lifestyles, traditions, and religions. Older members of the major ethnic group feel out of step with cultural changes, moving the more educated younger generation toward more socially liberal values. The authoritarian reflex seeks to defend the tribe against outside threats, seeking collective support from a community of like-minded social conservatives, endorsing leaders defending tribal values.

## 4) Economic Conditions and Immigration

Recent decades have seen a growing influx of people with different religions, languages, and customs into Western societies – reinforcing the tendency for people to feel that their basic values are threatened by rapid cultural change. Media coverage of terrorist attacks (often by people of a different ethnic group) further strengthens the authoritarian reflex.

Period effects are also evident in cultural reactions to given events; for example Euro-barometer surveys show that the public's identification with Europe has fluctuated over time, rising and falling in response to such developments as the Maastricht Treaty and the launch of the euro, and responding to economic downturns and the 2008 refugee crisis.[25] Economic and political integration has not necessarily strengthened feelings of European identity and community, even in long-standing member states.[26] The revival of Euroscepticism reflected in the Brexit decision to leave the European Union, and popular demands for secession in Scotland and Catalonia, indicate that nationalism remains a potent force in contemporary politics.

Confidence in government also fluctuates across countries and over time, reflecting factors such as the performance of European governments and major economic events like the 2008 financial crisis. There are ups and downs but the long-term trend across many Western societies since the 1960s and 1970s has been to weaken public trust and confidence in representative institutions – parliaments, elections, news media, and political parties – undermining partisan loyalties, eroding voting turnout, and encouraging a shift toward direct involvement through mass demonstrations, referenda, and net activism.[27]

## 5) Values to Votes and Seats

Support for authoritarian and populist values are only translated into votes and seats for political parties through the rules of the game, especially the electoral system, and patterns of party competition. In this regard, the electoral fortunes of authoritarian parties differ across societies and across contests within each country, depending upon the electoral system and the thresholds which parties have to surmount. It is easier for minor parties to break through into the legislature, and to become part of governing coalitions, in elections using Party List Proportional Representation with large district magnitudes and low vote threshold requirements.

## 6) Authoritarian Cultures, Leaders, and Regimes

When Authoritarian-Populist leaders and parties rise to power, it poses risks for liberal democracy institutions, and for the political culture that supports democracy. Authoritarian leaders delegitimize the checks and balances on the power of the executive. They claim that elections are rigged, politicians are corrupt, and interest groups are hijacking democracy. Strongman leaders claim to empower ordinary people as a smokescreen behind which they demand loyal obedience and are intolerant of dissent ('I demand absolute loyalty to my leadership ... anything else is betrayal').[28] And they heighten divisions by seeking to impose socially conservative policies even if these are rejected by the majority of society. The populist claim to empower ordinary people is hollow since contemporary societies lack mechanisms allowing the regular expression of public preferences on important issues. Blunt instruments for mass decision-making exist, such as opinion polls and referenda, but in the absence of genuine opportunities for the expression of public voice, populist leaders step into the void by claiming that they alone reflect the voice of the ordinary people, fighting to protect the group against corrupt interests, a rigged system, and the deep state. Power is exercised by leaders and their acolytes claiming to act on behalf of 'Us' versus 'Them.' Leadership communication is usually top-down – mass rallies, TV studio interviews, Twitter feeds – not interactive opportunities for grassroots participation. And authoritarian leaders seek to strengthen their powers and suppress dissent.

Authoritarian populists dismantle tolerance of the opposition and constraints on leaders, but they do so in the name of restoring power to the '*real* people.' This was encapsulated in Trump's inauguration speech: 'For too long, a small group in our nation's Capital has reaped the rewards of government while the people have borne the cost. Washington flourished – but the people did not share in its wealth. Politicians prospered – but the jobs left, and the factories closed. The establishment protected itself, but not the citizens of our country. Their victories have not been your victories; their triumphs have not been your triumphs; and while they celebrated in our nation's Capital, there was little to celebrate for struggling families all across our land. That all changes – starting right here, and right now, because this moment is your moment: it belongs to you.'[29]

This rhetoric is a false façade, however, which can empower illiberal forces, especially when authoritarian leaders suppress opposition in the name of the authentic concerns of 'ordinary' people. Long-established democratic institutions in Western democracies are resilient but not immune to these challenges. In hybrid regimes, however, such as Turkey, Hungary, Venezuela, and the Philippines, this culture corrodes liberal democratic institutions and facilitates the slide into full-blown authoritarian regimes with strong leaders who are intolerant of opposition. This may prove a passing phase that changes with the downfall of particular strongmen. But where the authoritarian culture takes root and people lose faith in democracy, where extreme polarization becomes deeply embedded in party politics, and where executive powers become institutionalized through constitutional changes, then authoritarianism becomes the only game in town. Authoritarian regimes reflect the institutionalization of these forms of power over successive leaders.

## II EVIDENCE AND KEY FINDINGS

The cultural backlash theory argues that a new cleavage has emerged in both party competition and in the electorate in many Western societies. Rapid cultural change, immigration, and economic conditions have triggered an authoritarian reflex among those that feel most threatened by these changes – emphasizing the importance of maintaining collective security by enforcing conformity with traditional mores, a united front against outsiders, and loyalty to strong leaders. This orientation is reinforced by anti-establishment populist rhetoric attacking 'Them' and reasserting the legitimate voice of 'Us' through claiming 'power to the people.'

### What Drives Support for Authoritarian and Populist Values?

Many parts of this theory are supported by evidence from multiple sources of data. But the story continues to unfold and the outcome is unknown. After laying out the conceptual framework and theory, Chapter 4 examined a large body of survey data demonstrating long-term trends in social value change across diverse societies. The results confirmed several important findings.

First, updating previous research, the evidence demonstrated that the silent revolution continues to transform Western societies on a wide range of social issues, including those involving sexuality and gender, religion and faith, race and ethnicity, and national versus cosmopolitan identities.

Far from a conservative revival, or slow-down in progressive change, the survey data demonstrate that the long-term trajectory of cultural evolution has continued to move Western societies in a more socially liberal direction over successive decades.

Moreover, these underlying value shifts are unlikely to reverse in the near future because they are driven by long-term and enduring changes in social structures common across Western societies. The evidence confirms that the 'silent revolution' during the second half of the twentieth century was closely associated with processes of intergenerational value change, as the Interwar and Baby Boomer generations are gradually replaced by Generation X and Millennials. This demographic process is reinforced by the expansion of university education in knowledge societies, generating more acceptance of multicultural diversity, by growing gender equality as women have entered the paid workforce and public sphere, and by urbanization as younger professionals have deserted rural areas to live in metropolitan cities. The tectonic plates of culture have shifted.

The silent revolution has catalyzed a major cultural backlash. Socially conservative and authoritarian values are strongest among the Interwar Generation (born 1900–1945) and Baby Boomers (born 1946–1964), a steadily shrinking sector of the general population due to demographic turnover. Social conservatives tend to respond to these trends with growing feelings of resentment at the erosion of respect for their core beliefs – catalyzing the authoritarian reflex. This generates resentment directed both upwards toward elites who are no longer seen to share these values, and downwards toward out-groups of lower status, opening the way for populist authoritarian parties.

Many accounts see authoritarian populism as a consequence of economic globalization, viewing rising support for these parties as largely the product of stagnant and declining real incomes, growing inequality, and loss of faith that mainstream parties have the capacity or the will to respond to these concerns. Chapter 5 scrutinized the available European evidence concerning these claims. The results demonstrated that support for authoritarian values and populist attitudes were indeed concentrated among the 'losers' from processes of economic globalization, the manual workers, and low-income families, on many indicators. In particular, authoritarian and populist values are consistently stronger among less prosperous people, who are most likely to feel a sense of economic insecurity. The key exceptions – and they are important – that this pattern was not found among those who have experienced long-term unemployment and dependency on state benefits.

Similar relationships can be observed when we examine support for post-materialism. The longitudinal analysis of support for values in six West European countries from 1970 to 2008 demonstrates the existence of distinct birth cohort effects, with the youngest birth cohort being consistently the most post-materialist, while the oldest cohort is consistently the most materialist. But it is also clear that period-effects exist, with all birth cohorts shifting toward materialist values when there are economic downturns, and moving back toward post-materialist values with economic recovery.

The macro-level evidence also provided strong confirmation that populist attitudes were strongly linked with economic conditions within given regions of European countries. People are most mistrustful of mainstream political parties, parliaments, and politicians in poorer regions that have suffered from declining populations – providing a natural constituency for populist appeals. The effects of social deprivation were less consistent and weaker as predictors of authoritarian values. But it remains unclear whether these findings reflect economic or cultural grievances among the 'left behinds.' These places have suffered economically, but they are also disproportionately rural areas with older white residents, where younger people have left for educational and employment opportunities in metropolitan cities.

To what extent have other major changes also contributed to this backlash – particularly the influx of people with diverse nationalities, religions, languages, customs, and ethnic backgrounds into Western societies? These developments could lead more socially conservative people to feel that their basic values are threatened by rapid cultural change – reinforced by growing ethnic diversity and the specter of Islamic terrorism. Chapter 6 examined a range of evidence. It confirms extensive previous research linking anti-immigration attitudes with authoritarian values. Authoritarianism is about protecting 'Us' from 'Them' – those who transgress community norms. Immigrants who differ from the native population in the color of their skin or their religion, lifestyle, or language tend to be perceived as dangerous – especially by those with little direct personal contact with ethnic minorities. Moreover, cultural threats associated with immigration are found to be more closely linked with authoritarian and populist values than instrumental concerns about protecting economic interests.

Cultural grievances are particularly strong among the older generation of white social conservatives, the people most likely to feel disoriented by the rapid transformation of their societies. The evidence suggests that rapidly growing racial and ethnic diversity, not immigration per se, is most closely associated with authoritarian values. Finally, even after controlling for attitudes toward immigrants and economic conditions, generation remains the most important predictor of authoritarian values. Long-term intergenerational population replacement is transforming the predominant values of European societies, and it is accelerated by immigration. But the reaction to rapidly growing ethnic diversity by social conservatives who feel threatened by these developments leads to support for Authoritarian-Populist parties.

## From Values to Votes

How values are translated into votes, however, is complex. The anti-immigrant backlash provides opportunities for Authoritarian-Populist parties to gain support by advocating hardline nationalist policies. They can exploit issues such as immigration, particularly where mainstream politicians share a liberal consensus that deters them from following suit. But if mainstream parties react by adopting more restrictive immigration policies and nationalistic language, stealing their rival's clothes while simultaneously ostracizing Authoritarian-Populist parties, the latter may find themselves squeezed out.[30]

To analyze these issues we need to identify and classify parties on a consistent basis. Chapter 7 described how party positions are measured in this study and mapped on a multidimensional issue space. We used the Chapel Hill Expert Survey (CHES) to create indices of left–right, authoritarian–libertarianism, and populism–pluralism. This enabled us to identify the positions of 270 political parties on the left–right and authoritarian–libertarian dimensions, and to what extent they adopt Populist discourse. The results suggest that populism is not confined to a specific party type, as much of the literature assumes, but is a pervasive rhetorical style. Politicians of many political persuasions can adopt populist language – especially challengers and outsiders – because this is an effective way to tap public disenchantment with the performance of mainstream parties and other representative institutions.

The classification developed in this chapter replaced the conventional language that labels populist parties as 'radical right,' 'extreme right, and 'populist right,' as conceptually flawed. Instead, we identified the party positions of a wide range of European parties on three dimensions. The measures capture contemporary patterns of party competition in European societies, distinguishing the classic left–right economic cleavage, the authoritarian–libertarian cultural cleavage and the populist–pluralist dimension that overlays both. On this basis, we identified a sub-category of European parties that combines both authoritarianism and populism – the combination we regard as most dangerous for undermining liberal democracy. Our final list of parties is similar to classifications used in previous research – but the key difference is that the position of all parties can be analyzed using continuous standardized scales for each dimension – avoiding potential boundary errors and problems of sample size associated with dichotomous classifications.

This lays the foundation for analyzing voting support for relatively authoritarian and relatively populist parties in Chapter 8. The analysis confirms the existence of a substantial generation gap in voting participation and in party choices. Younger cohorts are far less likely to vote – a pattern found consistently across European countries and the US. Earlier chapters demonstrated that young people differ sharply from their parents and grandparents in their socially liberal, libertarian, and post-materialist attitudes. Through population turnover, Millennials and Generation X have now become a bare majority of those eligible to vote. But because they are much less likely to vote, their preferences are systematically under-represented. By contrast, the Interwar and Baby Boom generations are a steadily shrinking sector of the general population – but they are substantially more likely to vote, so their partisan preferences have a stronger impact on electoral outcomes. If young and old had similar ideological values and party choices, then the lower rate of voting by Millennials would not matter. But in fact voting for authoritarian parties in high-income societies is significantly stronger among the older generation. The generational gap in Western societies is likely to heighten the salience of the cultural cleavage in future politics, regardless of possible improvements in economic conditions or any slowdown in globalization. The orthogonal pull of cultural politics generates divisions within mainstream parties, allowing new opportunities for populist leaders to mobilize electoral support.

But party fortunes are determined not only by popular support in the electorate but also by how votes are translated into seats by the electoral system. Chapter 9 examined these issues. Case studies illustrated how rules influence the fortunes of Authoritarian-Populist parties in elections in Austria and the Netherlands using Proportional Representation electoral systems, France and the UK using Majoritarian-Plurality systems, and Germany and Hungary with Mixed systems. The results demonstrated that the strength or weakness of Authoritarian-Populist parties among the electorate cannot be read straightforwardly by knowing where they have gained office – or failed to do so. The rules of the game determine how popular support at the ballot box translates into parliamentary seats – and how this shapes the process of negotiating governing coalitions and allocating Ministerial portfolios. In general, Proportional Representation systems with low vote thresholds and high district magnitudes, as in the Netherlands, offer opportunities that are more favorable for smaller parties. Majoritarian and Plurality systems usually favor larger parties, with a systematic winner's bonus for the party with the largest share of the vote. These patterns hold unless there are special conditions, such as the role of the Electoral College in awarding the Presidency.

Chapter 10 analyzed the reasons for Trump's victory in the 2016 US presidential election. We argue that it was built on an authoritarian-populist faction of the Republican Party that had been growing for many years. His strategy to reach the White House exploited cultural wedge issues about race, religion, and nation that have divided American party politics for decades. Several conclusions can be drawn from the evidence presented in this chapter.

Analyzing voting behavior confirmed the existence of a large generation gap in the American electorate, with the youngest birth cohort being least likely to vote for Trump. Other social factors performed as expected: as many other studies have reported, votes for Trump came disproportionately from whites, men, and those without college education, and from those who were married and with children living at home. All these social characteristics were consistent with the social profile observed in support for Authoritarian-Populist parties in Europe.

Secondly, even with these controls, Trump votes were associated with authoritarian orientations, and with the popular rule component of populism, moral conservatism, and the strength of religiosity. The anti-establishment scale of populism did not play a significant role: these attitudes were so broadly shared in the American electorate that Clinton voters did not differ from Trump supporters in their distaste for politicians. Once cultural values were entered into the model, the generation gap reversed, indicating that the birth cohort differences reflect distinctive values.

Thirdly, when economic measures were included in the analysis, several, though not all of them, were significantly related to votes for Trump. Those who thought the economy was doing poorly and those who felt worse off were more likely to support Trump.

We found support for both the economic grievances theory and the cultural backlash theory. They seem to reinforce each other – but the cultural factors clearly played the dominant role in people's decision to vote for Trump or Clinton.

Chapter 11 examined Britain's closely contested decision to leave the European Union. The results point to three key findings.

The cultural backlash thesis suggests that authoritarian and populist values among the older generation and less educated sectors have generated a new cultural cleavage that can be mobilized by populist leaders, such as Nigel Farage, and by opportunities to express public preferences, such as the Brexit referendum. The empirical evidence in this chapter confirms that both authoritarian and populist values were strongly linked with voting behavior in the United Kingdom, as hypothesized. These values predict not only Leave support in the EU referendum, but also the votes cast for UKIP in the 2015 and 2017 general elections. The results of the analysis remain significant and strong in size, even with multiple controls for the social background of British voters and their economic characteristics.

This chapter also examined individual-level evidence for the economic grievance thesis, which holds that those who are less well-off – the economic losers from globalization – would be more likely to embrace Brexit and UKIP. Although a common claim, and supported by the areas where the Leave vote was strongest, this chapter found little support for this thesis.[31] In particular, support for Brexit was not significantly stronger among unskilled manual workers, among the unemployed, and among those with left-wing economic values.

Finally, there are striking generation gaps in who voted for Brexit and for UKIP in recent British general elections. This confirms the patterns already observed in Europe and America and raises important questions about the changing nature of electoral cleavages and party competition in these countries. If these patterns persist, and if younger generations can be mobilized to vote, it can have important consequences. The Millennials and Generation X in Britain generally disliked the Leave camp and UKIP's appeals to English nationalism and white nativism, racial and ethnic intolerance, and social conservatism. They were more strongly attracted to other parties with a cosmopolitan outlook on Britain's place in the EU and socially liberal policies on cultural and moral issues. As the old left–right divisions of social class identities have faded in Britain, an emerging cultural war deeply divides voters and parties.

Chapter 12 examined to what extent the rise in support for Authoritarian-Populist parties has affected democratic regimes, the issues agenda, and support for civic cultures.

Debate continues about worldwide trends in democratization. Both Freedom House and the Economist Intelligence Unit report a global erosion of democracy during the last decade, but International IDEA's analysis suggests that democratic institutions are more resilient.[32] We examined long-term trends since the start of the twentieth century and concluded that successive waves can be observed, as Huntington claimed. The data from the Varieties of Democracy project suggest a relatively modest democratic downturn worldwide has occurred but similar estimates by Freedom House provide stronger evidence of a reverse wave in liberal democracy in the last few years. Many factors can contribute to backsliding toward autocracy but several leading cases – Turkey, Venezuela, and Hungary – indicate that the rise of particular populist authoritarian leaders has led to more repression and worsening human rights.

We also considered the claim that rising support for Authoritarian-Populist parties leads to a 'contagion of the right' – where center-right parties move toward their policy positions on issues such as control of immigration and Euroscepticism. Evidence from many persuasive cases supports the 'contagion of the right' thesis, including those of France, Switzerland, Germany, the Netherlands, and Britain. Many factors could have led governments to adopt more restrictive immigration policies – including changes in the actual number of refugees and asylum seekers. But it seems likely that electoral pressures contributed to these policy changes. Whether this is viewed as a positive or negative aspect of democracy depends on one's values.

When a large segment of the population comes to feel they no longer are living in the country in which they grew up, society is in danger of cultural backlash. Earlier investigators have calculated precise tipping points for other phenomena, arguing, for example, that white flight will occur when the percentage of blacks in a neighborhood reaches a specific level. It would be difficult to do this with cultural backlash because it involves several different factors, including (1) the ratio of those holding socially liberal values to those holding socially conservative values, but also (2) the contemporary level of economic and physical security, (3) the rate of immigration by culturally distinct people, and (4) the level of ethnic diversity prevailing during the host population's formative years. Calculating the level and relative weight of each variable involved in this process would be a very difficult task, but it seems clear that no society – not even Norway or Sweden – has an unlimited capacity to absorb immigration, especially in a context of rapid cultural change, without experiencing some degree of cultural backlash, particularly among the older and less secure segments of the population. The disorientation and anxiety that these people experience is genuine, and dismissing their feelings as irrational bigotry does not solve the problem. In the long run, doing so can lead to levels of cultural backlash that endanger civility and democracy itself.

## III WHAT IS TO BE DONE?

We need to understand the roots of populist sentiments. They have the potential to be a force for good in the world when grassroots reform movements help reduce corruption, strengthen responsive governance, expand the issue agenda that are debated and the electoral choices on the ballot, and reengage participation among groups alienated by mainstream party politics.[33] Libertarian populists like Pablo Iglesias' Podemos have been experimenting with alternative forms of participation in internal party decision-making processes.[34] Several other populist parties associated with the European Parliament's Alliance for Direct Democracy in Europe advocate expanding opportunities for direct democracy, like the use of citizen initiatives and referenda.[35]

But authoritarian populism can also prove dangerous. When populist rhetoric is coupled with authoritarian values, emphasizing the importance of group conformity, security, and loyalty, this combination can generate a combustible mix that challenges the legitimate authority of institutions checking executive power, opening the door for rule by strongman leaders, social intolerance, and illiberal governance.[36] By undermining the legitimacy of the conventional power structures in democracies, and providing no effective channels for 'the people' to speak, populist language provides rich opportunities for demagogues to claim sweeping powers – ostensibly on behalf of the people.[37] Populist agitators like Trump and his supporters are most effective in disrupting the old equilibrium, spreading paranoid conspiracy theories (the 'Birther' movement, 'Pizzagate'), and polarizing politics around divisive wedge issues like race and immigration. When actually in office, they are less effective in implementing political reforms, forging legislative compromises, and rebuilding trust in democratic governance.[38] Actors of various political persuasions who adopt populist discourse share a common language about what they are *against*, depicting themselves as radical insurgents fighting the establishment on behalf of the people.

What are the broader lessons for citizens, activists and policymakers seeking to address the root causes of this phenomenon? The political response depends, in large part, upon interpretations about the nature of the phenomenon.

## Mobilizing Civil Resistance and Electoral Opposition

The standard political reaction in democratic societies is for opponents to organize public protests, dispute executive actions and challenge laws through the courts, lobby representatives and express outrage through social media, and mobilize through elections. The challenge of authoritarian-populism may be purely temporary if the main problem arises from contingent factors, such as the way that Cameron recklessly decided to bet Britain's future on the Brexit referendum. Strategic miscalculations, leadership blunders, personal scandals, and mistakes by leaders and party elites are all part of the story. In multiparty democracies that meet international standards of electoral integrity, opponents get another chance to go to the polls and an opportunity to 'throw them out.' In this context, through regular electoral processes, opposition parties eventually have an opportunity to reverse government leaders and decisions.

On the other hand, even if energized Democrats mobilized a blue wave election reversing party control of both ends of Pennsylvania Avenue, it might not have the capacity to heal deep cultural fractures in American society or fix the dysfunctionality and bitter party polarization pervading Washington DC. And many structural flaws limit party competition and reinforce incumbent advantages, including in the US through gerrymandering of House district boundaries, the distorting role of money in politics, the way that the Electoral College systematically over-represents sparsely populated rural states, and state laws suppressing voting rights and electoral turnout.[39] The balance of voices in society is also critical – the younger generation is the most socially liberal but also the least likely to turnout; and voting participation among African-Americans and Hispanics is usually lower than among Whites. By contrast, the older white generation, who are most likely to vote, are the strongest base for authoritarian-populism. Mobilizing the younger generation and ethnic minorities is critical for closing the representation gap in democratic politics.

A substantial resistance has been mobilized on the streets to protest the Trump administration's policies, especially on issues of gender, race and sexuality, immigration and religion, the dismantling of environmental and consumer protections, the violation of democratic norms, and creeping authoritarianism. Activism around the Women's March, the Black Lives Matter movement, DACA protests, and the '#MeToo' movements are indicative of civil society resistance. Protests have mobilized enormous crowds; for example, the January 2018 women's march on the anniversary of Trump's inauguration drew an estimated 2.67 million people onto the streets across America.[40] What matters for reversing effective action, however, is whether these energies can be transferred from the streets and Twitter feeds to the ballot box and elected office.

## Reducing Economic Inequality

Western societies have increasingly become winner-take-all economies dominated by a small minority, while the overwhelming majority have precarious jobs. If left to market forces, this tendency will prevail. But government can be a countervailing force that reallocates resources for the benefit of society as a whole. In recent decades, neo-liberal policies of deregulation and austerity cuts in social welfare have mainly had the opposite effect, fueling growing insecurity.

A wide range of economic policies and social reforms could help address the problem. Examples include apprenticeship programs and vocational training for retraining miners and factory workers, addressing social deprivation and the opioid drug crisis in Ohio, providing tax breaks attracting companies to invest in rural communities in former East Germany, language programs integrating immigrants living in public housing on the outskirts of Paris, Budapest, and Oslo, tighter security to reduce the risks of terrorist incidents in Brussels and London, and offering better health services, good schools, and transportation services in deprived areas. High-income countries can use taxation policies and public spending to expand employment, educational opportunities, and public services addressing material inequalities.

In response to party polarization on the right, Social Democratic parties are most likely to shift leftwards, as illustrated by Bernie Sanders' platform in the 2016 Democratic primaries and the British Labour Party's manifesto under the leadership of Jeremy Corbyn. In the face of the rapidly increasing concentration of wealth and political power in the hands of the top one percent that has occurred in the last four decades, government intervention is probably the only feasible way to offset rising economic inequality. During the New Deal era in the US, government-sponsored programs built highways and post offices, protected the environment and contributed to education and cultural life. Today, people are as imaginative and as capable of designing effective programs that require humans as they were then – but they are not yet effectively organized. Western societies are currently regressing toward the authoritarian politics that is linked historically with economic insecurity. But – unlike the rise of Fascism during the Great Depression – this does not result from objective scarcity. Western societies possess abundant and growing resources, but they are increasingly misallocated from the standpoint of maximizing human well-being. Insecurity today results from growing inequality – which is ultimately a political question. Government intervention could reallocate a significant part of these resources to create meaningful jobs in healthcare, education, building infrastructure, environmental protection, research and development, care of the elderly, and the arts and humanities – with the goal of improving the quality of life for society as a whole, rather than maximizing corporate profits.

## Responding to Cultural Anxieties

But insofar as the authoritarian reaction is motivated by a cultural backlash against growing ethnic diversity in multicultural Western societies, however, it requires another set of policy responses responding to issues such as Islamophobia, Euroscepticism, xenophobia, racial resentment, and fears from terrorist incidents.

These are complex issues and the most obvious political response concerns immigration policies. European Union rules guarantee freedom of movement for EU citizens across national borders. But a number of governments have refused to follow these rules, in part due to electoral threats from authoritarian-populist rivals.[41] For example, in reaction to the Wilders' PVV, the Netherlands has toughened its immigration policies in recent years, making family reunification more difficult, criminalizing illegal residence, and moving to stricter curbs on dual nationality. Influenced by the Swiss People's Party, Switzerland tightened its immigration law, prioritizing Swiss job seekers over EU citizens. Canada has adopted a merit-based points program, with generous targets for new permanent residents and admissions criteria that emphasize education, work experience, and fluency in English or French, but disregard race and country of origin.[42] Admission policies and programs assisting newcomers with housing, jobs, and training need to be carefully calibrated to avoid cultural backlash and accusations of 'queue jumping.' No society has an unlimited capacity to absorb immigration, particularly during periods of economic stagnation, not even the Netherlands or the Nordic countries.[43] Governments face a difficult balancing act. They need to respond to anti-immigrant concerns in the electorate but also meet international human rights obligations to accept genuine refugees and asylum seekers fleeing persecution in war-torn societies.

In an early study of the rise of the radical right, Lipset sought to explain the extremism and intolerance associated with social movements popular in mid-twentieth century America, such as the John Birch Society, the Ku Klux Klan, and McCarthyism.[44] He noted that if the root cause of these forces was class based, then economic and social policies could be potentially effective in addressing these problems, such as measures reducing white rural poverty, improving schools and clinics, and investing in public works programs. But if the politics of unreason – racial violence, hatred, and intolerance – was rooted in a perceived loss of status by white rural populations, who felt threatened by the civil rights movement and growing racial equality, then it was more difficult to identify policy solutions that were compatible with American values. This observation remains true today. The inflection point in cultural change is likely to generate more heated polarization in society and politics about the issues that divide us, threatening the social tolerance and mutual trust that allow democratic societies to thrive. It calls above all for leaders who can help to bridge divisions – not exacerbate them.

Liberal democracies continue to prove resilient to the abuse of power by strongman leaders – especially through push back by the courts, the news media, and civil society.[45] Nevertheless, fundamental freedoms are under increasing threat particularly in hybrid regimes that transitioned from dictatorship but have never developed strong institutional safeguards to protect human rights from repressive leaders.[46] It remains to be seen how resilient liberal democracy will be in Western societies, or whether it will be damaged irreparably by authoritarian populist forces. The problem is not just Trump, nor is the problem just America. It reflects pervasive economic and cultural changes, for which there are no easy answers.

## Notes

1. Daniele Albertazzi and Sean Mueller. 2013. 'Populism and liberal democracy: Populists in government in Austria, Italy, Poland and Switzerland.' *Government and Opposition* 48(3): 343–371.
2. John Duckitt. 2013. 'Introduction to the special section on authoritarianism in societal context: The role of threat.' *International Journal of Psychology* 48 (1): 1–5.
3. See, for example, Ronald Inglehart and Pippa Norris. 2003. *Rising Tide: Gender Equality and Cultural Change around the World*. New York: Cambridge University Press; Benjamin Page and Robert Shapiro. 1992. *The Rational Public: Fifty Years of Trends in Americans' Policy Preferences*. Chicago: University of Chicago Press.
4. See, for example, Phillip M. Ayoub and Jeremiah Garretson. 2017. 'Getting the message out: Media context and global changes in attitudes toward homosexuality.' *Comparative Political Studies* 50 (8): 1055–1085; Nicholas Alozie, Kathy Thomas, and Patience Akpan-Obong. 2017. 'Global liberalization on homosexuality: Explaining the African gap.' *Social Science Journal* 54 (2): 120–131.
5. Pippa Norris and Ronald Inglehart. 2011. *Sacred and Secular*. 2nd edn. New York: Cambridge University Press.
6. Aengus Carroll. October 2016. *State-Sponsored Homophobia: A World Survey of Sexual Orientation Laws*. International Lesbian Gay, Bisexual, Trans and Intersex Association. ilga.org/downloads/02_ILGA_State_Sponsored_Homophobia_2016_ENG_WEB_150516.pdf; www.pewforum.org/2017/08/08/gay-marriage-around-the-world-2013/.
7. Pippa Norris and Ronald Inglehart. 2009. *Cosmopolitan Communications*. New York: Cambridge University Press.
8. Jocelyne Cesari. 2004. *When Islam and Democracy Meet: Muslims in Europe and in the United States*. New York: Palgrave Macmillan.
9. Ronald Inglehart. 1990. *Cultural Shift in Advanced Industrial Society*. Princeton, NJ: Princeton University Press; Ronald Inglehart. 1997. *Modernization and Postmodernization: Cultural, Economic and Political Change in 43 Societies*. Princeton, NJ: Princeton University Press; Ronald Inglehart and Christian Welzel. 2005. *Modernization, Cultural Change and Democracy: The Human Development Sequence*. New York: Cambridge University Press; Christian Welzel. 2013. *Freedom Rising: Human Empowerment and the Quest for Emancipation*. New York: Cambridge University Press; Ronald Inglehart. 2018. *Cultural Evolution: People's Motivations Are Changing, and Transforming the World*. New York: Cambridge University Press.
10. British Social Attitudes. www.bsa.natcen.ac.uk/latest-report/british-social-attitudes-34/moral-issues.aspx; see also James Tilley. 2005. 'Research note: Libertarian–authoritarian value change in Britain, 1974–2001.' *Political Studies* 53: 422–453.
11. The Pew Research Center. October 5, 2017. *The Partisan Divide on Political Values Grows Even Wider*. Washington DC: Pew Research

Center. www.people-press.org/2017/10/05/1-partisan-divides-over-political-values-widen/.

12. Thomas E. Mann and Norman J. Ornstein. 2012. *Its Even Worse than It Looks*. New York: Basic Books; James E. Campbell. 2016. *Polarized: Making Sense of a Divided America*. Princeton, NJ: Princeton University Press; E.J. Dionne, Norman J. Ornstein, and Thomas E. Mann. 2017. *One Nation Under Trump*. New York: St Martin's Press.
13. Pippa Norris. 2008. 'Confidence in the United Nations: Cosmopolitan and nationalistic attitudes.' In Yilmaz Esmer and Thorleif Pettersson. Eds. *The Global System, Democracy and Values*. Uppsala: Uppsala University Press; Jai Kwan Jung. 2008. 'Growing supranational identities in a globalizing world? A multilevel analysis of the World Values Surveys.' *European Journal of Political Research* 47: 578–609.
14. S. Schueth and J. O'Laughlin. 2008. 'Belonging to the world: Cosmopolitanism in geographic contexts.' *Geoforum* 39 (2): 926–941; Jai Kwan Jung. 2008. 'Growing supranational identities in a globalizing world? A multilevel analysis of the World Values Surveys.' *European Journal of Political Research* 47: 578–609.
15. On Australia, see Ian Woodward, Zlato Skrbis, and Clive Bean. 2008. 'Attitudes towards globalization and cosmopolitanism: Cultural diversity, personal consumption and the national economy.' *British Journal of Sociology* 59 (2): 207–226. On Sweden, see A. Ofsson and S. Ohman. 2007. 'Cosmopolitans and locals: An empirical investigation of transnationalism.' *Current Sociology* 55(6): 877–895. On Britain, see James Tilley and Anthony Heath. 2007. 'The decline of British national pride.' *British Journal of Sociology* 58: 661–678.
16. Charles R. Chandler and Yung-Mei Tsai. 2001. 'Social factors influencing immigration attitudes: An analysis of data from the general social survey.' *The Social Science Journal* 38 (2): 177–188; Serdar Kaya. 2015. 'Islamophobia in Western Europe: A comparative, multilevel study.' *Journal of Muslim Minority Affairs* 35 (3): 450–465.
17. James Tilley and Anthony Heath. 2007. 'The decline of British national pride.' *British Journal of Sociology* 58: 661–678.
18. Marc Helbling. Ed. 2012. *Islamophobia in the West: Measuring and Explaining Individual Attitudes*. New York: Routledge; L. Bobo. 2001 'Racial attitudes and relations at the close of the twentieth century.' In N.J. Smelser, W.J. Wilson, and F. Mitchell. Eds. *America Becoming: Racial Trends and Their Consequences*. Washington DC: National Academy Press; M. Coenders and P. Scheepers. 2008. 'Changes in resistance to the social integration of foreigners in Germany 1980–2000: Individual and contextual determinants.' *Journal of Ethnic and Migration Studies* 34 (1): 1–26; Rob Ford. 2008. 'Is racial prejudice declining in Britain?' *The British Journal of Sociology* 59 (4): 609–636.
19. G.W. Allport. 1954. *The Nature of Prejudice*, Reading, MA: Addison-Wesley; T.F. Pettigrew and L.R. Tropp. 2008. 'How Does Intergroup Contact Reduce Prejudice? Meta-Analytic Tests of Three Mediators.' *European Journal of Social Psychology* 38 (6): 922–934.

20. Pippa Norris. Ed. 1999. *Critical Citizens: Global Support for Democratic Government*. Oxford: Oxford University Press.
21. For the social psychological debate about the concept of authoritarian dispositions, and measurement, see Theodore W. Adorno, Else Fraenkel-Brunswick, David J. Levinson, and R. Nevitt Sanford. 1950. *The Authoritarian Personality*. New York: Harper & Row; Bob Altemeyer. 1998. 'The other "authoritarian personality".' In M.P. Zanna. Ed. *Advances in Experimental Social Psychology*. New York: Academic Press, pp. 47–91; Bob Altemeyer. 1996. *The Authoritarian Specter.* Cambridge, MA: Harvard University Press; Stanley Feldman. 2003. 'Values, ideology, and the structure of political attitudes.' In Donald Sears, Leonie Huddy, and R. Jervis. Eds. *Oxford Handbook of Political Psychology*. New York: Oxford University Press; Karen Stenner. 2005. *The Authoritarian Dynamic.* New York: Cambridge University Press; Marc J. Hetherington and Jonathan D. Weiler. 2009. *Authoritarianism and Polarization in American Politics*. New York: Cambridge University Press; Stefano Passini. 2017. 'Different ways of being authoritarian: The distinct effects of authoritarian dimensions on values and prejudice.' *Political Psychology* 38 (1): 73–86; Karen Stenner. 2005. *The Authoritarian Dynamic.* New York: Cambridge University Press; Marc J. Hetherington and Jonathan Weiler. 2009. *Authoritarianism and Polarization in American Politics*. New York: Cambridge University Press.
22. Elizabeth Noelle Neuman. 1984. *The Spiral of Silence: Public Opinion – Our Social Skin.* Chicago: University of Chicago Press; J.C. Glynn, F.A. Hayes, and J. Shanahan. 1997. 'Perceived support for one's opinions and willingness to speak out: A meta-analysis of survey studies on the "spiral of silence".' *Public Opinion Quarterly* 61 (3): 452–463.
23. Pippa Norris and Ronald Inglehart. 2011. *Sacred and Secular*. New York: Cambridge University Press.
24. Jack Shafer and Tucker Doherty. May/June 2017. 'The media bubble is worse than you think.' *Politico*. www.politico.com/magazine/story/2017/04/25/media-bubble-real-journalism-jobs-east-coast-215048.
25. S. Ciftci. 2005. 'Treaties, collective responses and the determinants of aggregate support for European integration.' *European Union Politics* 6 (4): 469–492; Richard C. Eichenberg and Russell J. Dalton. 2007. 'Post-Maastricht blues: The transformation of citizen support for European integration, 1973–2004.' *Acta Politica* 42 (2–3): 128–152.
26. Sophie Duchesne and André-Paul Frognier. 1995. 'Is there a European identity?' In Oskar Niedermayer and Richard Sinnott. Eds. *Public Opinion and Internationalized Governance*. Oxford: Oxford University Press; Angelika Scheuer. 1999. 'A political community?' In Hermann Schmitt and Jacques Thomassen. Eds. *Political Representation and Legitimacy in the European Union*. Oxford: Oxford University Press; T. Risse. 2001. 'A European identity? Europeanization and the evolution of nation-state identities.' In M.G. Cowles, J. Caporaso, and T. Risse. Eds. *Transforming Europe*. Ithaca, NY: Cornell University Press. See also B. Nelson, D. Roberts, and W. Veit. Eds. *The Idea of Europe: Problems of*

National and Transnational Identity. Oxford: Berg; Lauren M. McLaren. 2005. *Identity, Interests and Attitudes to European Integration.* London: Palgrave Macmillan.

27. Pippa Norris. 2002. *Democratic Phoenix: Reinventing Political Activism.* New York: Cambridge University Press; Pippa Norris. 2011. *Democratic Deficit.* Cambridge: Cambridge University Press; Carolien van Ham, Jacques Thomassen, Kees Aarts, and Rudy Andeweg. Eds. 2017. *Myth and Reality of the Legitimacy Crisis: Explaining Trends and Cross-National Differences in Established Democracies.* Oxford: Oxford University Press.
28. Hugo Chavez. Campaign speech, Caracas, January 24, 2010. www.smh.com.au//breaking-news-world/i-am-the-people-chavez-tells-followers-ahead-of-polls-20100124-mryf.html.
29. Donald Trump. January 20, 2017. *The Inaugural Address.* www.whitehouse.gov/briefings-statements/the-inaugural-address/.
30. Rooduijn Matthijs, S.L. De Lange, and Wouter van der Brug. 2014. 'A populist Zeitgeist? Programmatic contagion by populist parties in Western Europe.' *Party Politics* 20 (4): 563–575; Joost van Spanje and Nan Dirk de Graaf. 2018. 'How established parties reduce other parties' electoral support: The strategy of parroting the pariah.' *West European Politics* 41 (1): 1–27.
31. See also Lorenza Antonucci, Laszlo Horvath, Yordan Kutiyski, and André Krouwel. 2017. 'The malaise of the squeezed middle: Challenging the narrative of the "left behind" Brexiter.' *Competition and Change* 21 (3): 211–229.
32. International IDEA. 2017.*The Global State of Democracy: Exploring Democracy's Resilience.* Stockholm: International IDEA. www.idea.int/publications/catalogue/global-state-democracy-exploring-democracys-resilience.
33. Margaret Canovan. 1999. 'Trust the people! Populism and the two faces of democracy.' *Political Studies* 47: 2–16.
34. Simon Tormey. 2015. *The End of Representative Democracy.* Oxford: Polity.
35. Sherman J. Clark. 1998. 'A populist critique of direct democracy.' *Harvard Law Review* 112 (2): 434–482.
36. Cas Mudde. 2007. *Populist Radical Right Parties in Europe.* New York: Cambridge University Press.
37. Yves Mény and Yves Surel. Eds. 2002. *Democracies and the Populist Challenge.* Basingstoke: Palgrave, pp. 25–44.
38. Cristóbal Rovira Kaltwasser and Paul Taggart. 2015. 'Dealing with populists in government: A framework for analysis.' *Democratization* 23 (2): 201–220.
39. Pippa Norris. 2016. *Why Elections Fail.* New York: Cambridge University Press.
40. Jeremy Pressman and Erica Chenoweth. *Crowd Counting Consortium.* www.crowdcounting.org. https://docs.google.com/spreadsheets/d/1vl1MlIZP2i87TFvSVDUY1zkRgmSfe-_-Ae_I3pr-cQA/edit#gid=272855497.

41. Matthijs Rooduijn, Sarah L. de Lange, and Wouter van der Brug. 2014. 'A populist Zeitgeist? Programmatic contagion by populist parties in Western Europe.' *Party Politics* 20 (4): 563–575; Joost van Spanje and Nan Dirk de Graaf. 2018. 'How established parties reduce other parties' electoral support: The strategy of parroting the pariah.' *West European Politics* 41 (1): 1–27.
42. Richard Alba and Nancy Foner. 2017. *Strangers No More: Immigration and the Challenges of Integration in North America and Western Europe.* Princeton, NJ: Princeton University Press.
43. Sarah Spencer. Ed. 2003. *The Politics of Migration.* Oxford: Blackwell; Grete Brochmann and Tomas Hammar. Eds. 1999. *Mechanisms of Immigration Control: A Comparative Analysis of European Regulation Policies.* New York: Berg; Andrew Geddes and Peter Scholten. 2016. *The Politics of Migration and Immigration in Europe.* London: Sage.
44. Seymour Martin Lipset. 1955. 'The sources of the radical right.' In Daniel Bell. Ed. *The New American Right.* New York: Criterion Books; Seymour Martin Lipset and Earl Raab. 1978. *The Politics of Unreason: Rightwing extremism in America 1790–1977.* 2nd edn. Chicago: University of Chicago Press.
45. International IDEA. 2017. *The Global State of Democracy: Exploring Democracy's Resilience.* Stockholm: International IDEA. www.idea.int/publications/catalogue/global-state-democracy-exploring-democracys-resilience.
46. Steven Levitsky and Daniel Ziblatt. 2018. *How Democracies Die.* New York: Crown; Yasha Mounk. 2018. *The People vs. Democracy: Why Democracy Is in Danger & How to Save It*, Cambridge, MA: Harvard University Press; The Economist Intelligence Unit. *Democracy Index 2017: Free Speech Under Attack.* London: The Economist; Freedom House. 2018. *Freedom in the World, 2018.* Washington DC: Freedom House. https://freedomhouse.org/.

# TECHNICAL APPENDICES

# Cultural Backlash: Technical Appendix A: Classification of Parties

| Country-party | Authoritarian or Libertarian party | | Populist or Pluralist party | | Economic Left-right party | | Vote/Seats in national elections (2014) | | | EP vote | CHES party_id |
|---|---|---|---|---|---|---|---|---|---|---|---|
| | Score | Type | Score | Type | Score | Type | % Votes | % Seats | Type | % | |
| Aus_BZO | 77 | Lib | 59 | Populist | 71 | Right | 3.5 | 0.0 | Extra-Parl | 1 | 1307 |
| Aus_FPO | 87 | Auth | 67 | Populist | 53 | Right | 20.5 | 21.9 | Major | 20 | 1303 |
| Aus_Grune | 18 | Lib | 66 | Populist | 28 | Left | 12.4 | 13.1 | Minor | 15 | 1304 |
| Aus_OVP | 71 | Lib | 20 | Pluralist | 62 | Right | 24.0 | 25.7 | Major | 27 | 1302 |
| Aus_SPO | 41 | Lib | 25 | Pluralist | 22 | Left | 26.8 | 28.4 | Major | 24 | 1301 |
| Aus_TS | 74 | Lib | 79 | Populist | 86 | Right | 5.7 | 6.0 | Minor | | 1310 |
| Bel_CD&V | 57 | Lib | 26 | Pluralist | 56 | Right | 11.6 | 12.0 | Minor | 13 | 109 |
| Bel_cdH | 48 | Lib | 26 | Pluralist | 49 | Left | 5.0 | 6.0 | Minor | 4 | 108 |
| Bel_ECOLO | 15 | Lib | 47 | Pluralist | 20 | Left | 3.3 | 4.0 | Minor | 4 | 104 |
| Bel_FDF | 42 | Lib | 45 | Pluralist | 59 | Right | 1.8 | 1.3 | Fringe | 1 | 111 |
| Bel_Groen | 15 | Lib | 47 | Pluralist | 23 | Left | 5.3 | 4.0 | Minor | 7 | 105 |
| Bel_MR | 46 | Lib | 24 | Pluralist | 77 | Right | 9.6 | 13.3 | Minor | 10 | 106 |
| Bel_N_VA | 72 | Lib | 53 | Populist | 85 | Right | 20.3 | 22.0 | Major | 17 | 110 |
| Bel_PP | 80 | Auth | 60 | Populist | 72 | Right | 1.5 | 0.7 | Fringe | 2 | 120 |
| Bel_PS | 26 | Lib | 25 | Pluralist | 21 | Left | 11.7 | 15.3 | Major | 11 | 102 |
| Bel_PVDA | 23 | Lib | 73 | Populist | 3 | Left | 3.7 | 1.3 | Fringe | 4 | 119 |
| Bel_SPA | 25 | Lib | 29 | Pluralist | 25 | Left | 8.8 | 8.7 | Minor | 8 | 103 |
| Bel_VB | 86 | Auth | 75 | Populist | 54 | Right | 3.7 | 2.0 | Fringe | 4 | 112 |
| Bel_VLD | 46 | Lib | 24 | Pluralist | 79 | Right | 9.8 | 9.3 | Minor | 13 | 107 |

| | | | | | | | | | | | |
|---|---|---|---|---|---|---|---|---|---|---|---|
| Bul_ABV | 59 | Lib | 61 | Populist | 35 | Left | 4.2 | 4.6 | Minor | 4 | 2016 |
| Bul_Ataka | 96 | Auth | 83 | Populist | 14 | Left | 4.5 | 4.6 | Minor | 3 | 2007 |
| Bul_BBT | 81 | Auth | 81 | Populist | 37 | Left | 5.7 | 6.3 | Minor | 5 | 2015 |
| Bul_BSP | 59 | Lib | 45 | Pluralist | 34 | Left | 14.6 | 15.4 | Major | 19 | 2003 |
| Bul_DBG | 41 | Lib | 63 | Populist | 69 | Right | 2.7 | 2.9 | Fringe | 2 | 2013 |
| Bul_DPS | 54 | Lib | 37 | Pluralist | 45 | Left | 14.8 | 15.8 | Major | 17 | 2004 |
| Bul_DSB | 47 | Lib | 63 | Populist | 82 | Right | 3.5 | 3.8 | Minor | 3 | 2008 |
| Bul_GERB | 57 | Lib | 58 | Populist | 69 | Right | 32.7 | 35.0 | Major | 30 | 2010 |
| Bul_NFSB | 86 | Auth | 76 | Populist | 36 | Left | 4.2 | 4.6 | Minor | 3 | 2014 |
| Bul_SDS | 45 | Lib | 62 | Populist | 78 | Right | 1.5 | 1.7 | Fringe | 1 | 2002 |
| Bul_VMRO-BND | 90 | Auth | 79 | Populist | 32 | Left | 3.1 | 3.3 | Fringe | 5 | 2005 |
| Cro_HDSSB | 86 | Auth | 61 | Populist | 46 | Left | 3.0 | 4.0 | Minor | 2 | 3107 |
| Cro_HDZ | 80 | Auth | 39 | Pluralist | 62 | Right | 21.9 | 27.2 | Major | 28 | 3101 |
| Cro_HL_SR | 31 | Lib | 80 | Populist | 23 | Left | 4.2 | 4.0 | Minor | 3 | 3112 |
| Cro_HNS | 26 | Lib | 80 | Populist | 69 | Left | 4.2 | 8.6 | Minor | 8 | 3105 |
| Cro_HSLS | 44 | Lib | 35 | Pluralist | 77 | Right | 3.0 | 0.0 | Extra-Parl | 1 | 3104 |
| Cro_HSP | 92 | Auth | 65 | Populist | 49 | Left | 3.0 | 0.0 | Extra-Parl | 2 | 3109 |
| Cro_HSP-AS | 90 | Auth | 75 | Populist | 53 | Right | 0.6 | 0.7 | Fringe | 7 | 3113 |
| Cro_HSS | 86 | Auth | 43 | Pluralist | 44 | Left | 0.6 | 0.7 | Fringe | 7 | 3103 |
| Cro_IDS | 26 | Lib | 36 | Pluralist | 56 | Right | 1.5 | 2.0 | Fringe | 8 | 3106 |
| Cro_ORaH | 14 | Lib | 59 | Populist | 35 | Left | 2.0 | 0.0 | Extra-Parl | 9 | 3114 |
| Cro_SDP | 31 | Lib | 41 | Pluralist | 50 | Right | 31.3 | 40.4 | Major | 15 | 3102 |
| Cyp_AKEL | 33 | Lib | 71 | Populist | 26 | Left | 32.7 | 33.9 | Major | 27 | 4003 |

(*continued*)

(*continued*)

| Country-party | Authoritarian or Libertarian party | | Populist or Pluralist party | | Economic Left-right party | | Vote/Seats in national elections (2014) | | | EP vote | CHES party_id |
|---|---|---|---|---|---|---|---|---|---|---|---|
| | Score | Type | Score | Type | Score | Type | % Votes | % Seats | Type | % | |
| Cyp_DIKO | 67 | Lib | 56 | Populist | 65 | Right | 15.8 | 16.1 | Major | 11 | 4004 |
| Cyp_Disy | 60 | Lib | 56 | Populist | 83 | Right | 34.3 | 35.7 | Major | 38 | 4001 |
| Cyp_EDEK | 58 | Lib | 71 | Populist | 48 | Left | 8.9 | 8.9 | Minor | 8 | 4005 |
| Cyp_EVROKO | 74 | Lib | 61 | Populist | 74 | Right | 3.9 | 3.6 | Minor | 0 | 4002 |
| Cyp_KOP | 52 | Lib | 77 | Populist | 48 | Left | 2.2 | 1.8 | Fringe | 0 | 4006 |
| Cze_ANO | 52 | Lib | 83 | Populist | 62 | Right | 18.7 | 23.5 | Major | 16 | 2111 |
| Cze_CSSD | 47 | Lib | 34 | Pluralist | 32 | Left | 20.5 | 25.0 | Major | 14 | 2101 |
| Cze_KDEU_CSL | 75 | Lib | 41 | Pluralist | 51 | Right | 6.8 | 7.0 | Minor | 10 | 2104 |
| Cze_KSCM | 64 | Lib | 57 | Populist | 12 | Left | 14.9 | 16.5 | Major | 11 | 2103 |
| Cze_ODS | 67 | Lib | 27 | Pluralist | 82 | Right | 7.7 | 8.0 | Minor | 8 | 2102 |
| Cze_SVOBODNI | 62 | Lib | 66 | Populist | 97 | Right | 2.5 | 0.0 | Extra-Parl | 5 | 2113 |
| Cze_SZ | 18 | Lib | 66 | Populist | 43 | Left | 3.2 | 0.0 | Extra-Parl | 4 | 2107 |
| Cze_TOP | 53 | Lib | 36 | Pluralist | 79 | Right | 12.0 | 10.5 | Minor | 12 | 2109 |
| Cze_USVIT | 84 | Auth | 92 | Populist | 47 | Left | 6.9 | 7.0 | Minor | 3 | 2112 |
| Del_EL | 17 | Lib | 47 | Pluralist | 7 | Left | 6.6 | 6.7 | Minor | | 213 |
| Den_DF | 83 | Auth | 48 | Pluralist | 44 | Left | 12.2 | 12.3 | Minor | 27 | 215 |
| Den_FolkB | 28 | Lib | 52 | Populist | 23 | Left | 8.1 | 0.5 | | 8 | 217 |

| | | | | | | | | | | | |
|---|---|---|---|---|---|---|---|---|---|---|---|
| Den_KF | 70 | Lib | 24 | Pluralist | 71 | Right | 4.9 | 4.5 | Minor | 9 | 203 |
| Den_LA | 42 | Lib | 27 | Pluralist | 92 | Right | 4.9 | 5.0 | Minor | 3 | 218 |
| Den_RV | 25 | Lib | 17 | Pluralist | 58 | Right | 9.4 | 9.5 | Minor | 7 | 202 |
| Den_SD | 48 | Lib | 26 | Pluralist | 38 | Left | 24.5 | 24.6 | Major | 19 | 201 |
| Den_SF | 28 | Lib | 27 | Pluralist | 21 | Left | 9.1 | 8.9 | Minor | 11 | 206 |
| Den_V | 67 | Lib | 25 | Pluralist | 73 | Right | 26.4 | 26.3 | Major | 17 | 211 |
| Est_EER | 44 | Lib | 78 | Populist | 54 | Right | 3.8 | 0.0 | Extra-Parl | | 2207 |
| Est_EK | 48 | Lib | 41 | Pluralist | 36 | Left | 23.3 | 25.7 | Major | 22 | 2202 |
| Est_ER | 48 | Lib | 31 | Pluralist | 84 | Right | 28.6 | 32.7 | Major | 24 | 2203 |
| Est_EVE | 55 | Lib | 80 | Populist | 70 | Right | 8.7 | 7.9 | Minor | | 2208 |
| Est_IRL | 68 | Lib | 36 | Pluralist | 84 | Right | 20.5 | 22.8 | Major | 14 | 2201 |
| Est_SDE | 36 | Lib | 47 | Pluralist | 43 | Left | 17.1 | 18.8 | Major | 14 | 2204 |
| Fin_KD | 77 | Lib | 32 | Pluralist | 54 | Right | 4.0 | 3.0 | Fringe | 5 | 1409 |
| Fin_KESK | 70 | Lib | 36 | Pluralist | 58 | Right | 15.8 | 17.5 | Major | 20 | 1403 |
| Fin_KOK | 55 | Lib | 20 | Pluralist | 77 | Right | 20.4 | 22.0 | Major | 23 | 1402 |
| Fin_PS | 90 | Auth | 81 | Populist | 40 | Left | 19.1 | 19.5 | Major | 13 | 1405 |
| Fin_RKP_SFP | 34 | Lib | 24 | Pluralist | 71 | Right | 4.3 | 4.5 | Minor | 7 | 1406 |
| Fin_SDP | 42 | Lib | 29 | Pluralist | 39 | Left | 19.1 | 21.0 | Major | 12 | 1401 |
| Fin_VAS | 27 | Lib | 51 | Populist | 19 | Left | 8.1 | 7.0 | Minor | 9 | 1404 |
| Fin_VIHR | 15 | Lib | 46 | Pluralist | 48 | Left | 7.3 | 5.0 | Minor | 9 | 1408 |
| Fra_AC | 63 | Lib | 33 | Pluralist | 65 | Right | 0.6 | 0.3 | Extra-Parl | 1 | 623 |
| Fra_EELV | 17 | Lib | 58 | Populist | 23 | Left | 5.5 | 2.9 | Fringe | 9 | 605 |
| Fra_Ens | 42 | Lib | 73 | Populist | 22 | Left | | | | | 625 |
| Fra_FN | 88 | Auth | 89 | Populist | 47 | Left | 13.6 | 0.3 | Extra-Parl | 25 | 610 |

*(continued)*

(*continued*)

| Country-party | Authoritarian or Libertarian party | | Populist or Pluralist party | | Economic Left-right party | | Vote/Seats in national elections (2014) | | | EP vote | CHES party_id |
|---|---|---|---|---|---|---|---|---|---|---|---|
| | Score | Type | Score | Type | Score | Type | % Votes | % Seats | Type | % | |
| Fra_MODEM | 60 | Lib | 52 | Populist | 67 | Right | 1.8 | 0.3 | Extra-Parl | 6 | 613 |
| Fra_MPF | 91 | Auth | 66 | Populist | 67 | Right | 0.2 | 0.0 | Extra-Parl | 0 | 612 |
| Fra_NC | 64 | Lib | 32 | Pluralist | 69 | Right | 2.2 | 2.1 | Fringe | 1 | 621 |
| Fra_PCF | 39 | Lib | 55 | Populist | 8 | Left | 4.8 | 1.2 | Fringe | 2 | 601 |
| Fra_PG | 27 | Lib | 83 | Populist | 8 | Left | 0.7 | 0.2 | Extra-Parl | 2 | 624 |
| Fra_PRG | 41 | Lib | 37 | Pluralist | 35 | Left | 1.7 | 2.1 | Fringe | 1 | 603 |
| Fra_PRV | 60 | Lib | 38 | Pluralist | 62 | Right | 1.2 | 1.0 | Fringe | 1 | 622 |
| Fra_PS | 40 | Lib | 35 | Pluralist | 39 | Left | 29.4 | 48.5 | Major | 13 | 602 |
| Fra_UMP | 76 | Lib | 33 | Pluralist | 74 | Right | 27.1 | 33.6 | Major | 21 | 609 |
| Ger_AfD | 88 | Auth | 59 | Populist | 80 | Right | 4.7 | 0.0 | Extra-Parl | 7 | 310 |
| Ger_CDU | 62 | Lib | 19 | Pluralist | 59 | Right | 34.1 | 40.4 | Major | 30 | 301 |
| Ger_CSU | 79 | Lib | 22 | Pluralist | 64 | Right | 7.4 | 8.9 | Minor | 5 | 308 |
| Ger_DT | 18 | Lib | 74 | Populist | 21 | Left | 0.3 | 0.0 | Extra-Parl | 1 | 312 |
| Ger_FDP | 40 | Lib | 22 | Pluralist | 77 | Right | 4.8 | 0.0 | Extra-Parl | 3 | 303 |
| Ger_Grunen | 22 | Lib | 33 | Pluralist | 33 | Left | 8.4 | 10.0 | Minor | 11 | 304 |
| Ger_Linke | 39 | Lib | 44 | Pluralist | 11 | Left | 8.6 | 10.1 | Minor | 7 | 306 |
| Ger_NPD | 92 | Auth | 62 | Populist | 44 | Left | 1.3 | 0.0 | Extra-Parl | 1 | 309 |
| Ger_Piraten | 21 | Lib | 67 | Populist | 30 | Left | 2.2 | 0.0 | Extra-Parl | 1 | 311 |
| Ger_SPD | 41 | Lib | 22 | Pluralist | 36 | Left | 25.7 | 30.6 | Major | 27 | 302 |

| | | | | | | | | | | | |
|---|---|---|---|---|---|---|---|---|---|---|---|
| Gre_ANEL | 94 | Auth | 85 | Populist | 44 | Left | 7.5 | 6.7 | Minor | 4 | 412 |
| Gre_DIMAR | 27 | Lib | 60 | Populist | 32 | Left | 6.3 | 5.7 | Minor | 1 | 414 |
| Gre_KKE | 48 | Lib | 94 | Populist | 4 | Left | 4.5 | 4.0 | Minor | 6 | 405 |
| Gre_LAOS | 93 | Auth | 76 | Populist | 51 | Right | 1.6 | 0.0 | Extra-Parl | 3 | 410 |
| Gre_ND | 82 | Auth | 35 | Pluralist | 63 | Right | 29.7 | 43.0 | Major | 23 | 402 |
| Gre_PASOK | 48 | Lib | 39 | Pluralist | 49 | Left | 12.3 | 11.0 | Minor | 8 | 401 |
| Gre_Pot | 30 | Lib | 69 | Populist | 53 | Right | 4.1 | 2.6 | Fringe | 7 | 413 |
| Gre_Syriza | 25 | Lib | 84 | Populist | 14 | Left | 26.9 | 23.7 | Major | 27 | 403 |
| Gre_XA | 100 | Auth | 91 | Populist | 18 | Left | 6.9 | 6.0 | Minor | 9 | 415 |
| Hun_DK | 29 | Lib | 63 | Populist | 59 | Right | 2.8 | 2.0 | Fringe | 10 | 2311 |
| Hun_E14 | 25 | Lib | 69 | Populist | 59 | Right | 2.1 | 1.5 | Fringe | 4 | 2310 |
| Hun_Fidesz | 87 | Auth | 39 | Pluralist | 45 | Left | 39.5 | 58.8 | Major | 47 | 2302 |
| Hun_Jobbik | 95 | Auth | 87 | Populist | 31 | Left | 20.2 | 11.6 | Minor | 15 | 2308 |
| Hun_LMP | 28 | Lib | 82 | Populist | 35 | Left | 5.3 | 2.5 | Fringe | 5 | 2309 |
| Hun_MSZP | 43 | Lib | 47 | Pluralist | 44 | Left | 20.6 | 14.6 | Major | 11 | 2301 |
| Ire_FF | 71 | Lib | 30 | Pluralist | 58 | Right | 17.5 | 11.5 | Minor | 22 | 701 |
| Ire_FG | 67 | Lib | 27 | Pluralist | 66 | Right | 36.1 | 46.1 | Major | 22 | 702 |
| Ire_GP | 30 | Lib | 52 | Populist | 36 | Left | 1.9 | 0.0 | Extra-Parl | 5 | 705 |
| Ire_PBPA | 26 | Lib | 66 | Populist | 9 | Left | 1.0 | 1.2 | Fringe | 1 | 709 |
| Ire_SF | 48 | Lib | 60 | Populist | 23 | Left | 9.9 | 8.5 | Minor | 20 | 707 |
| Ire_SP | 29 | Lib | 65 | Populist | 11 | Left | 1.2 | 1.2 | Fringe | 2 | 708 |
| It_CD | 57 | Lib | 50 | Populist | 56 | Right | 0.5 | 1.0 | Fringe | 0 | 843 |
| It_Fdl | 91 | Auth | 62 | Populist | 49 | Left | 2.0 | 1.5 | Fringe | 4 | 844 |
| It_Fl | 76 | Lib | 37 | Pluralist | 84 | Right | 21.6 | 15.7 | Major | 17 | 815 |

*(continued)*

(*continued*)

| Country-party | Authoritarian or Libertarian party | | Populist or Pluralist party | | Economic Left-right party | | Vote/Seats in national elections (2014) | | | EP vote | CHES party_id |
|---|---|---|---|---|---|---|---|---|---|---|---|
| | Score | Type | Score | Type | Score | Type | % Votes | % Seats | Type | % | |
| It_LN | 86 | Auth | 78 | Populist | 64 | Right | 4.1 | 2.9 | Fringe | 6 | 811 |
| It_MSS | 39 | Lib | 100 | Populist | 40 | Left | 25.6 | 17.5 | Major | 21 | 845 |
| It_NCD | 74 | Lib | 37 | Pluralist | 72 | Right | 4.4 | 4.4 | Minor | 3 | 848 |
| It_PD | 37 | Lib | 58 | Populist | 47 | Left | 25.4 | 47.3 | Major | 41 | 837 |
| It_RC | 19 | Lib | 92 | Populist | 5 | Left | 2.3 | 0.0 | Extra-Parl | 1 | 803 |
| It_SC | 55 | Lib | 41 | Pluralist | 82 | Right | 8.3 | 6.0 | Minor | 1 | 846 |
| It_Sel | 20 | Lib | 71 | Populist | 11 | Left | 3.2 | 6.0 | Minor | 1 | 838 |
| It_SVP | 60 | Lib | 49 | Pluralist | 49 | Left | 0.4 | 0.8 | Fringe | 1 | 827 |
| It_UDC | 70 | Lib | 34 | Pluralist | 53 | Right | 1.8 | 1.3 | Fringe | 2 | 814 |
| It_VdA | 47 | Lib | 46 | Pluralist | 38 | Left | 0.0 | 1.0 | Fringe | | 847 |
| Lat_LKS | 56 | Lib | 80 | Populist | 29 | Left | 1.6 | 0.0 | Extra-Parl | 6 | 2402 |
| Lat_LRA | 69 | Lib | 76 | Populist | 56 | Right | 6.7 | 8.0 | Minor | 3 | 2414 |
| Lat_NA | 80 | Auth | 61 | Populist | 60 | Right | 16.6 | 17.0 | Major | 14 | 2406 |
| Lat_NSL | 64 | Lib | 87 | Populist | 51 | Right | 6.9 | 7.0 | Minor | | 2413 |
| Lat_SDPS | 50 | Lib | 58 | Populist | 40 | Left | 23.0 | 24.0 | Major | 13 | 2410 |
| Lat_V | 52 | Lib | 52 | Populist | 67 | Right | 21.9 | 23.0 | Major | 46 | 2412 |
| Lat_ZZS | 68 | Lib | 47 | Pluralist | 63 | Right | 19.5 | 21.0 | Major | 8 | 2405 |
| Lith_DK | 80 | Auth | 91 | Populist | 37 | Left | 8.0 | 5.0 | Minor | | 2520 |
| Lith_DP | 55 | Lib | 42 | Pluralist | 48 | Left | 19.8 | 20.6 | Major | 13 | 2516 |

| | | | | | | | | | | | |
|---|---|---|---|---|---|---|---|---|---|---|---|
| Lith_LLRA | 70 | Lib | 54 | Populist | 40 | Left | 5.8 | 5.7 | Minor | 8 | 2511 |
| Lith_LRLS | 35 | Lib | 41 | Pluralist | 86 | Right | 8.6 | 7.1 | Minor | 17 | 2518 |
| Lith_LSDP | 46 | Lib | 34 | Pluralist | 32 | Left | 18.4 | 26.2 | Major | 17 | 2501 |
| Lith_LVZS | 65 | Lib | 56 | Populist | 37 | Left | 3.9 | 0.7 | Fringe | 7 | 2507 |
| Lith_TS_LKD | 69 | Lib | 44 | Pluralist | 53 | Right | 15.1 | 23.4 | Major | 17 | 2506 |
| Lith_TT | 78 | Lib | 71 | Populist | 39 | Left | 7.3 | 7.8 | Minor | 14 | 2515 |
| Luc_CSV | 68 | Lib | 26 | Pluralist | 55 | Right | 33.7 | 38.3 | Major | 38 | 3801 |
| Lux_ARD | 87 | Auth | 87 | Populist | 62 | Right | 6.6 | 5.0 | Minor | 8 | 3805 |
| Lux_DL | 17 | Lib | 87 | Populist | 4 | Left | 4.9 | 3.3 | Fringe | 6 | 3806 |
| Lux_DP | 41 | Lib | 51 | Populist | 74 | Right | 18.3 | 21.7 | Major | 15 | 3803 |
| Lux_Greng | 28 | Lib | 69 | Populist | 51 | Right | 10.1 | 10.0 | Minor | 15 | 3802 |
| Lux_LSAP | 36 | Lib | 56 | Populist | 49 | Left | 20.3 | 21.7 | Major | 12 | 3804 |
| Mal_PL | 51 | Lib | 32 | Pluralist | 55 | Right | 54.8 | 56.5 | Major | 53 | 3701 |
| Mal_PN | 59 | Lib | 63 | Populist | 67 | Right | 43.3 | 43.5 | Major | 40 | 3702 |
| NEOS | 32 | Lib | 68 | Populist | 77 | Right | 5.0 | 4.9 | Major | 8 | 1306 |
| Net_50+ | 51 | Lib | 42 | Pluralist | 47 | Left | 1.9 | 1.3 | Fringe | 4 | 1020 |
| Net_CDA | 69 | Lib | 14 | Pluralist | 67 | Right | 8.5 | 8.7 | Minor | 15 | 1001 |
| Net_CU | 65 | Lib | 18 | Pluralist | 45 | Left | 3.1 | 3.3 | Fringe | 4 | 1016 |
| Net_D66 | 21 | Lib | 16 | Pluralist | 64 | Right | 8.0 | 8.0 | Minor | 16 | 1004 |
| Net_GL | 17 | Lib | 18 | Pluralist | 32 | Left | 2.3 | 2.7 | Fringe | 7 | 1005 |
| Net_PvcD | 29 | Lib | 37 | Pluralist | 23 | Left | 1.9 | 1.3 | Fringe | 4 | 1018 |
| Net_PvdA | 40 | Lib | 14 | Pluralist | 41 | Left | 24.8 | 25.3 | Major | 9 | 1002 |
| Net_PVV | 82 | Auth | 74 | Populist | 51 | Right | 10.1 | 10.0 | Minor | 13 | 1017 |
| Net_SGP | 89 | Auth | 11 | 0 | 63 | Right | 2.1 | 2.0 | Fringe | 4 | 1006 |

(*continued*)

(*continued*)

| Country-party | Authoritarian or Libertarian party | | Populist or Pluralist party | | Economic Left-right party | | Vote/Seats in national elections (2014) | | | EP vote | CHES party_id |
|---|---|---|---|---|---|---|---|---|---|---|---|
| | Score | Type | Score | Type | Score | Type | % Votes | % Seats | Type | % | |
| Net_SP | 46 | Lib | 51 | Populist | 13 | Left | 9.7 | 10.0 | Minor | 10 | 1014 |
| Net_VVD | 59 | Lib | 16 | Pluralist | 83 | Right | 26.6 | 27.3 | Major | 12 | 1003 |
| Nor_AP | 48 | Lib | 12 | Pluralist | 43 | Left | 30.8 | 32.5 | Major | | 3501 |
| Nor_FrP | 81 | Auth | 39 | Pluralist | 67 | Right | 16.3 | 17.1 | Major | | 3502 |
| Nor_H | 60 | Lib | 12 | Pluralist | 69 | Right | 26.8 | 28.4 | Major | | 3503 |
| Nor_KrF | 63 | Lib | 20 | Pluralist | 53 | Right | 5.6 | 5.9 | Minor | | 3506 |
| Nor_MDG | 26 | Lib | 37 | Pluralist | 38 | Left | 2.8 | 1.7 | Fringe | | 3508 |
| Nor_Sp | 63 | Lib | 26 | Pluralist | 43 | Left | 5.5 | 5.9 | Minor | | 3505 |
| Nor_SV | 32 | Lib | 36 | Pluralist | 33 | Left | 4.1 | 4.1 | Minor | | 3504 |
| Nor_V | 39 | Lib | 20 | Pluralist | 62 | Right | 5.2 | 5.3 | Minor | | 3507 |
| Pol_KNP | 85 | Auth | 91 | Populist | 100 | Right | 1.1 | 0.0 | Extra-Parl | 7 | 2614 |
| Pol_PiS | 83 | Auth | 83 | Populist | 33 | Left | 29.9 | 34.1 | Major | 32 | 2605 |
| Pol_PO | 47 | Lib | 30 | Pluralist | 62 | Right | 39.2 | 45.0 | Major | 32 | 2603 |
| Pol_PR | 71 | Lib | 70 | Populist | 71 | Right | 0.2 | 0.0 | Extra-Parl | 3 | 2615 |
| Pol_PSL | 71 | Lib | 31 | Pluralist | 37 | Left | 8.4 | 6.1 | Minor | 7 | 2606 |
| Pol_RP | 17 | Lib | 56 | Populist | 48 | Left | 10.0 | 8.7 | Minor | 4 | 2613 |
| Pol_SLD | 35 | Lib | 36 | Pluralist | 32 | Left | 8.2 | 5.9 | Minor | 8 | 2601 |
| Pol_SP | 87 | Auth | 84 | Populist | 35 | Left | 1.9 | 1.9 | Fringe | 4 | 2616 |
| Por_BE | 15 | Lib | 79 | Populist | 10 | Left | 5.4 | 3.5 | Minor | 5 | 1208 |

| | | | | | | | | | | | |
|---|---|---|---|---|---|---|---|---|---|---|---|
| Por_CDU | 35 | Lib | 78 | Populist | 7 | Left | 8.2 | 7.0 | Minor | 14 | 1201 |
| Por_MPT | 64 | Lib | 80 | Populist | 49 | Left | 0.4 | 0.0 | Extra-Parl | 8 | 1209 |
| Por_PP | 75 | Lib | 26 | Pluralist | 68 | Right | 12.2 | 10.4 | Minor | 4 | 1202 |
| Por_PS | 42 | Lib | 38 | Pluralist | 39 | Left | 29.2 | 32.2 | Major | 34 | 1205 |
| Por_PSD | 61 | Lib | 27 | Pluralist | 75 | Right | 40.3 | 47.0 | Major | 26 | 1206 |
| Rom_PC | 72 | Lib | 34 | Pluralist | 48 | Left | 2.8 | 3.2 | Fringe | 5 | 2702 |
| Rom_PDL | 54 | Lib | 56 | Populist | 74 | Right | 15.3 | 12.6 | Minor | 12 | 2704 |
| Rom_PMP | 55 | Lib | 60 | Populist | 75 | Right | 5.0 | 5.5 | Minor | 6 | 2711 |
| Rom_PNL | 53 | Lib | 50 | Populist | 70 | Right | 21.5 | 24.3 | Major | 15 | 2705 |
| Rom_PP-DD | 82 | Auth | 79 | Populist | 33 | Left | 14.0 | 11.4 | Minor | 4 | 2710 |
| Rom_PSD | 70 | Lib | 36 | Pluralist | 41 | Left | 32.2 | 36.4 | Major | 28 | 2701 |
| Rom_UDMR | 46 | Lib | 43 | Pluralist | 63 | Right | 5.1 | 4.4 | Minor | 6 | 2706 |
| Rom_UNPR | 75 | Lib | 34 | Pluralist | 38 | Left | 2.1 | 2.4 | Fringe | 5 | 2709 |
| Sel_ZL | 14 | Lib | 79 | Populist | 14 | Left | 6.0 | 6.7 | Minor | 6 | 2912 |
| Sle_DeSUS | 50 | Lib | 55 | Populist | 42 | Left | 10.2 | 11.1 | Minor | 8 | 2906 |
| Sle_NSI | 82 | Auth | 69 | Populist | 82 | Right | 5.6 | 5.6 | Minor | 8 | 2905 |
| Sle_PS | 35 | Lib | 57 | Populist | 50 | Left | 3.0 | 0.0 | Extra-Parl | 7 | 2914 |
| Sle_SD | 34 | Lib | 59 | Populist | 36 | Left | 6.0 | 6.7 | Minor | 8 | 2903 |
| Sle_SDS | 82 | Auth | 69 | Populist | 81 | Right | 20.7 | 23.3 | Major | 25 | 2902 |
| Sle_SLS | 71 | Lib | 61 | Populist | 64 | Right | 4.0 | 0.0 | Extra-Parl | 8 | 2904 |
| Sle_SMC | 43 | Lib | 68 | Populist | 57 | Right | 34.5 | 40.0 | Major | | 2911 |
| Sle_ZaAB | 36 | Lib | 57 | Populist | 54 | Right | 4.4 | 4.4 | Minor | | 2913 |
| Slo_KDH | 84 | Auth | 49 | Pluralist | 55 | Right | 8.8 | 10.7 | Minor | 13 | 2805 |
| Slo_MH | 51 | Lib | 50 | Populist | 62 | Right | 6.9 | 8.7 | Minor | 6 | 2813 |

*(continued)*

(*continued*)

| Country-party | Authoritarian or Libertarian party | | Populist or Pluralist party | | Economic Left-right party | | Vote/Seats in national elections (2014) | | | EP vote | CHES party_id |
|---|---|---|---|---|---|---|---|---|---|---|---|
| | Score | Type | Score | Type | Score | Type | % Votes | % Seats | Type | % | |
| Slo_Nova | 70 | Lib | 69 | Populist | 76 | Right | 0.7 | 1.3 | Fringe | 7 | 2815 |
| Slo_OLaNO | 75 | Lib | 87 | Populist | 64 | Right | 8.6 | 10.7 | Minor | 8 | 2814 |
| Slo_SaS | 40 | Lib | 66 | Populist | 92 | Right | 5.9 | 7.3 | Minor | 7 | 2812 |
| Slo_SDKU_DS | 52 | Lib | 50 | Populist | 77 | Right | 6.1 | 7.3 | Minor | 8 | 2802 |
| Slo_Siet | 68 | Lib | 69 | Populist | 73 | Right | 5.6 | 1.3 | Fringe | | 2816 |
| Slo_Smer_SD | 70 | Lib | 38 | Pluralist | 24 | Left | 44.4 | 55.3 | Major | 24 | 2803 |
| Slo_SMK_MKP | 61 | Lib | 47 | Pluralist | 54 | Right | 4.3 | 0.0 | Extra-Parl | 7 | 2804 |
| Slo_SNS | 96 | Auth | 60 | Populist | 49 | Left | 4.6 | 0.0 | Extra-Parl | 4 | 2809 |
| Spa_Amaiur | 40 | Lib | 57 | Populist | 17 | Left | 1.2 | 1.7 | Fringe | | 524 |
| Spa_BNG | 37 | Lib | 57 | Populist | 19 | Left | 0.8 | 0.6 | Fringe | 0 | 513 |
| Spa_CC | 60 | Lib | 31 | Pluralist | 61 | Right | 0.6 | 0.6 | Fringe | 0 | 517 |
| Spa_CiU | 70 | Lib | 27 | Pluralist | 69 | Right | 4.2 | 4.6 | Minor | 4 | 505 |
| Spa_Cs | 49 | Lib | 74 | Populist | 59 | Right | 13.6 | 9.1 | Minor | 3 | 526 |
| Spa_EA | 58 | Lib | 30 | Pluralist | 43 | Left | 0.2 | 0.3 | Extra-Parl | 2 | 507 |
| Spa_EAJ_PNV | 62 | Lib | 27 | Pluralist | 60 | Right | 1.4 | 1.4 | Fringe | 2 | 506 |
| SPA_ERC | 43 | Lib | 45 | Pluralist | 31 | Left | 1.1 | 0.9 | Fringe | 4 | 511 |
| SPA_ICV | 27 | Lib | 64 | Populist | 15 | Left | 1.3 | 0.6 | Fringe | 2 | 518 |
| SPA_IU | 24 | Lib | 67 | Populist | 11 | Left | 5.0 | 2.3 | Fringe | 7 | 504 |
| Spa_Pod | 25 | Lib | 101 | Populist | 10 | Left | 21.0 | 19.7 | Major | 8 | 525 |

| | | | | | | | | | | | |
|---|---|---|---|---|---|---|---|---|---|---|---|
| Spa_PP | 80 | Auth | 25 | Pluralist | 79 | Right | 41.9 | 53.1 | Major | 26 | 502 |
| Spa_PSOE | 36 | Lib | 47 | Pluralist | 29 | Left | 28.8 | 31.4 | Major | 23 | 501 |
| Spa_UpyD | 44 | Lib | 75 | Populist | 50 | Right | 4.8 | 1.4 | Fringe | 7 | 523 |
| Swe_C | 36 | Lib | 20 | Pluralist | 74 | Right | 6.1 | 6.3 | Minor | 7 | 1603 |
| Swe_FI | 12 | Lib | 50 | Populist | 14 | Left | 3.1 | 0.0 | Extra-Parl | 6 | 1612 |
| Swe_FP | 35 | Lib | 19 | Pluralist | 71 | Right | 5.4 | 5.4 | Minor | 10 | 1604 |
| Swe_KD | 57 | Lib | 20 | Pluralist | 68 | Right | 4.6 | 4.6 | Minor | 6 | 1606 |
| Swe_M | 44 | Lib | 18 | Pluralist | 74 | Right | 23.3 | 24.1 | Major | 14 | 1605 |
| Swe_MP | 15 | Lib | 29 | Pluralist | 35 | Left | 6.9 | 7.2 | Minor | 15 | 1607 |
| Swe_Pirat | 23 | Lib | 59 | Populist | 57 | Right | 0.4 | 0.0 | Extra-Parl | 2 | 1611 |
| Swe_SAP | 34 | Lib | 20 | Pluralist | 32 | Left | 31.0 | 32.4 | Major | 24 | 1602 |
| Swe_SD | 92 | Auth | 60 | Populist | 48 | Left | 12.9 | 14.0 | Minor | 10 | 1610 |
| Swe_V | 17 | Lib | 38 | Pluralist | 7 | Left | 5.7 | 6.0 | Minor | 6 | 1601 |
| Swi_BDP | 66 | Lib | 22 | Pluralist | 66 | Right | 4.1 | 3.5 | Fringe | | 3612 |
| Swi_CSP_PCS | 53 | Lib | 20 | Pluralist | 41 | Left | 0.2 | 0.0 | Extra-Parl | | 3611 |
| Swi_CVP_PVC | 66 | Lib | 20 | Pluralist | 53 | Right | 11.6 | 13.5 | Minor | | 3604 |
| Swi_EDU | 86 | Auth | 36 | Pluralist | 55 | Right | 1.2 | 0.0 | Extra-Parl | | 3608 |
| Swi_EVP_PEV | 68 | Lib | 26 | Pluralist | 45 | Left | 1.9 | 1.0 | Fringe | | 3607 |
| SWI_FDP_PLR | 54 | Lib | 20 | Pluralist | 79 | Right | 16.4 | 16.5 | Major | | 3603 |
| Swi_GLP_PVL | 31 | Lib | 25 | Pluralist | 67 | Right | 4.6 | 3.5 | Minor | | 3606 |
| Swi_GPS_PES | 17 | Lib | 25 | Pluralist | 24 | Left | 7.1 | 5.5 | Minor | | 3605 |
| Swi_LdT | 80 | Auth | 43 | Pluralist | 48 | Left | 1.0 | 1.0 | Fringe | | 3610 |
| Swi_SP_PS | 21 | Lib | 27 | Pluralist | 19 | Left | 18.8 | 21.5 | Major | | 3602 |
| Swi_SVP_UDC | 89 | Auth | 49 | Pluralist | 76 | Right | 29.4 | 32.5 | Major | | 3601 |

(*continued*)

(*continued*)

| Country-party | Authoritarian or Libertarian party | | Populist or Pluralist party | | Economic Left-right party | | Vote/Seats in national elections (2014) | | | EP vote | CHES party_id |
|---|---|---|---|---|---|---|---|---|---|---|---|
| | Score | Type | Score | Type | Score | Type | % Votes | % Seats | Type | % | |
| Tur_AKP | 79 | Lib | 43 | Pluralist | 66 | Right | 49.5 | 57.6 | Major | | 3401 |
| Tur_CHP | 38 | Lib | 66 | Populist | 36 | Left | 25.3 | 24.4 | Major | | 3402 |
| Tur_HDP | 21 | Lib | 68 | Populist | 28 | Left | 10.8 | 10.7 | Minor | | 3407 |
| Tur_MHP | 83 | Auth | 62 | Populist | 52 | Right | 13.0 | 12.9 | Minor | | 3403 |
| Uere_Lab | 44 | Lib | 29 | Pluralist | 44 | Left | 19.5 | 22.4 | Major | 5 | 703 |
| UK_Cons | 71 | Lib | 27 | Pluralist | 79 | Right | 36.1 | 47.2 | Major | 24 | 1101 |
| UK_Green | 18 | Lib | 65 | Populist | 19 | Left | 1.0 | 0.2 | Extra-Parl | 8 | 1107 |
| UK_IP | 92 | Auth | 82 | Populist | 86 | Right | 3.1 | 0.0 | Extra-Parl | 28 | 1108 |
| UK_Lab | 43 | Lib | 39 | Pluralist | 40 | Left | 29.0 | 39.7 | Major | 25 | 1102 |
| UK_LD | 33 | Lib | 34 | Pluralist | 51 | Right | 23.0 | 8.8 | Minor | 7 | 1104 |
| UK_PC | 35 | Lib | 50 | Populist | 36 | Left | 0.6 | 0.5 | Fringe | 1 | 1106 |
| UK_SNP | 43 | Lib | 57 | Populist | 34 | Left | 1.7 | 0.9 | Fringe | 3 | 1105 |
| Total | 54 | Lib | 50 | Populist | 49 | Left | 11.3 | 11.7 | Minor | 11 | 1779 |

# Technical Appendix B: The Variables and Coding Used in the Multivariate Analysis

*European Social Survey 1-7 Classifying the European Electorate*

| ESS variable | Question topic | Study coding |
|---|---|---|
| **PARTY VOTE** | | |
| Party Vote | Party voted for in the last general election in each country scored by the CHES estimated party position scales on authoritarian values and the salience of populist rhetoric | 0-100 |
| **SOCIAL CHARACTERISTICS** | | |
| Edulvla | Highest level of education, ES – ISCED | Categories from low (1) to high (5) |
| Income | Household total net income | Low (1) to high (12) |
| Age | Age of respondent | In years |
| Malesex | Sex | Male (1) Female (0) |
| Ethnic | Belong to minority ethnic group in country | Ethnic minority (1), not (0) |
| Unemp3m | Ever been unemployed for more than 3 months | Yes (1), No (0) |
| Unemp12m | Ever been unemployed for more than 12 months | Yes (1), No (0) |

(*continued*)

(*continued*)

| ESS variable | Question topic | Study coding |
|---|---|---|
| **SOCIAL CHARACTERISTICS** | | |
| Hincsrca | Social benefits are the main source of household income | Unemployment/ redundancy benefits or Any other social benefits or grants (1)/ Else (eg wages)=0. |
| Hincfel | Subjective economic insecurity: Reported difficulties about living on household's income | 4-pt scale from 'Living comfortably on present income' (1) to 'Very difficult on present income' (4) |
| rlgdgr | Strength of religiosity | Low (0) to High (10) |
| Class | ISCOCO Occupation recoded into the Goldthorpe class schema | Manager/prof (1), Lower managerial (2), Petty bourgeoisie (3), Skilled worker (4), Unskilled worker (5) |
| Urbanization | Urbanization scale | Big city (5), Suburb (4), Town (3), Village (2), Rural (1) |
| Generational cohort | Recoded from year of birth | Interwar (Born before 1945)<br>Baby Boomers (Born 1946–1964)<br>Generation X (1946–1964)<br>Millennials (Born 1980–1996) |
| **CULTURAL ATTITUDES** | | |
| **Anti-Immigration scale** | Sum: Imbgeco, imueclt, imwbcnt (Standardized scale) | Scale 0–100 |
| imbgeco | Immigration bad or good for the country's economy | Scale 0–10 |
| imueclt | Country's cultural life undermined or enriched by immigrants | Scale 0–10 |
| imwbcnt | Immigrants make country worse or better place to live | Scale 0–10 |
| **Trust in global governance** | Sum: Trstun, trstep (Standardized scale) | Scale 0–100 |

| ESS variable | Question topic | Study coding |
|---|---|---|
| **CULTURAL ATTITUDES** | | |
| trstun | Trust in the United Nations | Scale 0–10 |
| trstep | Trust in the European Parliament | Scale 0–10 |
| **Trust in national political institutions** | Sum: Trstplt, trstplc, trstprt, trstprl, trstlgl (Standardized scale) | Scale 0–100 |
| trstplt | Trust in politicians | Scale 0–10 |
| trstplc | Trust in police | Scale 0–10 |
| trstprt | Trust in political parties | Scale 0–10 |
| trstprl | Trust in country's parliament | Scale 0–10 |
| trstlgl | Trust in the legal system | Scale 0–10 |
| **Satisfaction scale** | Sum: stlife, stfgov, stfdem, stfedu, stfhlth (Standardized scale) | Scale 0–100 |
| stlife | How satisfied with life as a whole | Scale 0–10 |
| stfgov | How satisfied with the national government | Scale 0–10 |
| stfdem | How satisfied with the way democracy works in country | Scale 0–10 |
| stfedu | How satisfied with the state of education in country | Scale 0–10 |
| stfhlth | How satisfied with state of health services in country | Scale 0–10 |
| **Social trust** | Sum: ppltrst, pplfair, pplhlp (Standardized scale) | Scale 0–100 |
| ppltrst | Most people can be trusted/can't be too careful | Scale 0–10 |
| pplfair | Most people try to take advantage of you/try to be fair | Scale 0–10 |
| pphlp | Most people are looking out for themselves/try to be helpful | Scale 0–10 |
| **Authoritarian values** | Sum: impsafe, ipfruler, ipbhprp, ipstrgv, imptrad (Standardized Schwartz scale) | Scale 0–100 |
| impsafe | Important to live in secure and safe surroundings | Scale 1–6 |
| ipfrule | Important to do what is told and follow rules | Scale 1–6 |
| ipbhprp | Important to behave properly | Scale 1–6 |

*(continued)*

(*continued*)

| ESS variable | Question topic | Study coding |
|---|---|---|
| **CULTURAL ATTITUDES** | | |
| ipstrgv | Important that government is strong and ensures safety | Scale 1–6 |
| imptrad | Important to follow traditions and customs | Scale 1–6 |
| **Populist values** | | |
| trstplt | Trust in politicians | Scale 0–10 |
| trstplc | Trust in police | Scale 0–10 |
| trstprt | Trust in political parties | Scale 0–10 |
| trstprl | Trust in country's parliament | Scale 0–10 |
| trstlgl | Trust in the legal system | Scale 0–10 |
| **Populist values** | Trust in politicians, parties, and parliament (sum) | Scale 0–100 |
| **Libertarian values** | Sum: impdiff, impadvnt, ipcrtiv, impfree, ipudrst (Standardized scale) | Scale 0–100 |
| impdiff | Important to do different things in life | Scale 1–6 |
| impadvnt | Important to have an exciting life | Scale 1–6 |
| ipcrtiv | Important to be creative | Scale 1–6 |
| impfree | Important to be free | Scale 1–6 |
| ipudrst | Important to listen to people different from her/him | Scale 1–6 |
| **Right-wing self-placement scale** | Self-placement on the left–right ideological scale | Left (0) to right (10) |
| **Anti-Immigration scale** | Imbgeco, imueclt, imwbcnt | Scale 0–100 |
| imbgeco | Immigration bad or good for country's economy | Scale 0–10 |
| imueclt | Country's cultural life undermined or enriched by immigrants | Scale 0–10 |
| imwbcnt | Immigrants make country worse or better place to live | Scale 0–10 |

*Notes:* Items were selected to be consistent across all rounds of the survey, unless otherwise noted. Scales were summed from each of the relevant items and standardized to 100-points for ease of comparison.

*Source:* European Social Survey, Cumulative File Rounds 1–7. www.europeansocialsurvey.org/.

| Authoritarian position scale | | 100-points from the following items |
|---|---|---|
| Galtan | Party positions toward democratic freedoms and rights; libertarian parties favor expanding personal freedoms; authoritarian parties value order, tradition, and stability. | Scale 1–10 |
| Nationalism | Pro-nationalism | Scale 1–10 |
| Civlib_laworder | Favors tough measures to fight crime rather than the protection of civil liberties | Scale 1–10 |
| Multiculturalism | Against multiculturalism and the integration of immigrants and asylum seekers | Scale 1–10 |
| Sociallifestyle | Opposes liberal social lifestyles (e.g. homosexuality) | Scale 1–10 |
| Immigrate_policy | Favors restrictive policy on immigration | Scale 1–10 |
| Ethnic_minorities | Opposes rights for ethnic minorities | Scale 1–10 |
| **Populist position scale** | | **100-points from the following items** |
| Anti-corrupt salience | Salience of anti-corruption | Scale 1–10 |
| Anti-elite_salience | Salience of anti-elite and anti-establishment rhetoric | Scale 1–10 |
| **Left–right position scale** | | **100-points from the following items** |
| Deregulation | Favors market regulation or deregulation | Scale 1–10 |
| Econ_interven | Favors or opposed to state intervention on the economy | Scale 1–10 |
| Redistribution | Favors or opposed to redistribution of wealth from the rich to the poor | Scale 1–10 |
| Spendvtax | Favor or opposes cutting taxes and public services | Scale 1–10 |

*Notes:* CHES 2014 expert survey of political party positions in 31 countries, including all EU member states plus Norway, Switzerland, and Turkey, December 2014–February 2015. The scales were constructed by factor analysis with rotated varimax and Kaiser normalization (see Table 7.1).

*Source:* Ryan Bakker, Erica Edwards, Liesbet Hooghe, Seth Jolly, Gary Marks, Jonathan Polk, Jan Rovny, Marco Steenbergen, and Milada Vachudova. 2015. '2014 Chapel Hill Expert Survey.' Version 2015.1. Available on chesdata.eu. Chapel Hill, NC: University of North Carolina, Chapel Hill (Subsequently referenced as the 2014 Chapel Hill Expert Survey or just abbreviated as CHES 2014).

# Bibliography

Aalberg, Toril, Frank Esser, Carsten Reinemann, Jesper Stromback, and Claes H. de Vreese. Eds. 2017. *Populist Political Communication in Europe*. London: Routledge.

Abedi, Amir. 2002. 'Challenges to established parties: The effects of party system features on the electoral fortunes of anti-political-establishment parties.' *European Journal of Political Research*, 41(4): 551–583.

Abou-Chadi, Tarik. 2016. 'Niche party success and mainstream party policy shifts: How green and radical right parties differ in their impact.' *British Journal of Political Science*, 46(2): 417–436.

Abrajano, Marisa and Zoltan L. Hajnal. 2015. *White Backlash: Immigration, Race, and American Politics*. New Jersey: Princeton University Press.

Abts, Koen and Stefan Rummens. 2007. 'Populism versus democracy.' *Political Studies*, 55(2): 405–424.

Adamson, Göran. 2016. *Populist Parties and the Failure of the Political Elites: The Rise of the Austrian Freedom Party (FPÖ)*. Germany: Peter Lang.

Adorno, Theodore W., Else Fraenkel-Brunswick, David J. Levinson, and R. Nevitt Sanford. 1950. *The Authoritarian Personality*. New York: Harper & Row.

Agh, Attila. 2016. 'The decline of democracy in East-Central Europe: Hungary as the worst-case scenario.' *Problems of Post-Communism*, 63(5–6): 277–228.

Akkerman, Tjitske. 2012. 'Comparing radical right parties in government: Immigration and integration policies in nine countries (1996–2010).' *West European Politics*, 35(3): 511–529.

2015. 'Immigration policy and electoral competition in Western Europe: A fine grained analysis of party positions over the past two decades.' *Party Politics*, 21(1): 54–67.

Akkerman, Tjitske and Sarah L. de Lange. 2012. 'Radical right parties in office: Incumbency records and the electoral cost of governing.' *Government and Opposition*, 47(4): 574–596.

Akkerman, Agnes, Cas Mudde, and Andrej Zaslove. 2014. 'How populist are the people? Measuring populist attitudes in voters.' *Comparative Political Studies*, 47(9): 8–30.

Akkerman, Tjitske and Matthijs Rooduijn. 2015. 'Pariahs or partners? Inclusion and exclusion of radical right parties and the effects on their policy positions.' *Political Studies*, 62: 1–18.

Akkerman, Tjitske, Sarah L. de Lange, and Matthijs Rooduijn. Eds. 2016. *Radical Right-Wing Populist Parties in Western Europe: Into the Mainstream?*. New York: Routledge.

Albertazzi, Daniele. 2008. 'Switzerland: Yet another populist paradise.' In Daniele Albertazzi and Duncan McDonnell. Eds. *Twenty-First Century Populism*. New York: Palgrave Macmillan, pp. 100–118.

Albertazzi, Daniele and Duncan McDonnell. 2005. 'The Lega Nord in the second Berlusconi government: In a league of its own.' *West European Politics*, 28(5): 952–972.

2010. 'The Lega Nord back in government.' *West European Politics*, 33(6): 1318–1340.

2015. *Populists in Power*. London: Routledge.

Eds. 2008. *Twenty-First Century Populism: The Specter of Western European Democracy*. Basingstoke, UK: Palgrave Macmillan.

Albertazzi, Daniele and Sean Mueller. 2013. 'Populism and liberal democracy: Populists in government in Austria, Italy, Poland and Switzerland.' *Government and Opposition*, 48(3): 343–371.

Albertson, Bethany and Shana Kushner Gadarian. 2015. *Anxious Politics: Democratic Citizenship in a Threatening World*. New York: Cambridge University Press.

Aldrich, John H. 1995. *Why Parties? The Origin and Transformation of Party Politics in America*. Chicago: University of Chicago Press.

Alford, Robert R. 1967. 'Class voting in the Anglo-American political systems.' In Seymour M. Lipset and Stein Rokkan. Eds. *Party Systems and Voter Alignments: Cross National Perspectives*. New York: The Free Press.

Allcott, Hunt and Matthew Gentzkow. 2017. 'Social media and fake news in the 2016 election.' *Journal of Economic Perspectives*, 31(2): 211–236.

Allen, Chris. 2014. 'Britain First: The "frontline resistance" to the Islamification of Britain.' *The Political Quarterly*, 85(3): 354–361.

Allen, Trevor J. 2017. 'All in the party family? Comparing far right voters in Western and post-communist Europe.' *Party Politics*, 23(3): 274–285.

Allport, Gordon W. 1954. *The Nature of Prejudice*. London: Addison-Wesley.

Almond, Gabriel A. and Sidney Verba. 1963. *The Civic Culture: Political Attitudes and Democracy in Five Nations*. Princeton, NJ: Princeton University Press.

Alonso, Sonia and Sara Claro Da Fonseca. 2012. 'Immigration, left and right.' *Party Politics*, 18(6): 865–884.

Alonso, Sonia and Cristóbal Rovira Kaltwasser. 2016. 'Spain: No country for the populist radical right?' *South European Society and Politics*, 20(1): 21–45.

Altemeyer, Bob. 1981. *Right-Wing Authoritarianism*. Winnipeg: University of Manitoba Press.

1988. *Enemies of Freedom: Understanding Right-Wing Authoritarianism*. San Francisco: Jossey-Bass Publishers.

1996. *The Authoritarian Specter*. Cambridge, MA: Harvard University Press.
1998. 'The other authoritarian personality.' *Advances in Experimental Social Psychology*, 30: 47–92.
Ames, Barry. 1995. 'Electoral strategy under open-list proportional representation.' *American Journal of Political Science*, 39(2): 406–433.
Anderson, Christopher J. 1995. *Blaming the Government: Citizens and the Economy in Five European Democracies*. New York: M.E. Sharpe.
1996. 'Economics, politics, and foreigners: Populist party support in Denmark and Norway.' *Electoral Studies*, 15(4): 497–511.
Anderson, Christopher J. and Christine A. Guillory. 1997. 'Political institutions and satisfaction with democracy.' *American Political Science Review*, 91(1): 66–81.
Antonucci, Lorenza, Laszlo Horvath, Yordan Kutiyski, and Andre Krouwel. 2017. 'The malaise of the squeezed middle: Challenging the narrative of the "left behind" Brexiter.' *Competition and Change*, 21(3): 211–229.
Armingeon, Klaus and Kai Guthmann. 2014. 'Democracy in crisis? The declining support for national democracy in European countries, 2007–2011.' *European Journal of Political Research*, 53(3): 423–442.
Arnold, Edwards J. Ed. 2000. *The Development of the Radical Right in France: From Boulanger to Le Pen*. Basingstoke: Macmillan Press.
Art, David. 2007. 'Reacting to the radical right: Lessons from Germany and Austria.' *Party Politics*, 13(3): 331–349.
2011. *Inside the Radical Right: The Development of Anti-Immigrant Parties in Europe*. Cambridge: Cambridge University Press.
Arter, David. 2010. 'The breakthrough of another West European populist radical right party? The case of the True Finns.' *Government and Opposition*, 45(4): 484–504.
Arzheimer, Kai. 2009. 'Contextual factors and the extreme right vote in Western Europe, 1980–2002.' *American Journal of Political Science*, 53(2): 259–275.
2012. 'Electoral sociology: Who votes for the extreme right and why – and when?' In Uwe Backes and Patrick Moreau. Eds. *The Extreme Right in Europe: Current Trends and Perspectives*. Göttingen: Vandenhoeck & Ruprecht, pp. 35–50.
Arzheimer, Kai and Elisabeth Carter. 2006. 'Political opportunity structures and rightwing extremist party success.' *European Journal of Political Research*, 45(3) 419–444.
2009. 'Christian religiosity and voting for West European radical right parties.' *West European Politics*, 32(5): 985–1011.
Aslanidis, Paris and Cristóbal Rovira Kaltwasser. 2016. 'Dealing with populists in government: The SYRIZA-ANEL coalition in Greece.' *Democratization*, 23(6): 1077–1091.
Atkin, Nicholas and Frank Tallett. 2003. *The Right in France: From Revolution to Le Pen*. London: I.B. Tauris.
Autor, David, David Dorn, Gordon Hanson, and Kaveh Majlesi. 2017. 'A note on the effect of rising trade exposure on the 2016 Presidential Election.' MIT Working Paper https://economics.mit.edu/files/12418.
Aylott, Nick. 1995. 'Back to the future: The 1994 Swedish election.' *Party Politics*, 1(3): 419–429.

Backes, Uwe and Patrick Moreau. Eds. 2012. *The Extreme Right in Europe: Current Trends and Perspectives*. Göttingen: Vandenhoeck and Ruprecht.

Bakker, Bert N., Matthijs Rooduijn, and Gijs Schumacher. 2016. 'The psychological roots of populist voting: Evidence from the United States, the Netherlands and Germany.' *European Journal of Political Research*, 55(2): 302–320.

Bale, Tim. 2003. 'Cinderella and her ugly sisters: The mainstream and extreme right in Europe's bipolarizing party systems.' *West European Politics*, 26(3): 67–90.

2008. 'Turning round the telescope: Centre-right parties and immigration and integration policy in Europe.' *Journal of European Public Policy*, 15(3): 315–330.

Bale, Tim, Christofer Green-Pedersen, and André A. Krouwel. 2010. 'If you can't beat them, join them? Explaining social democratic responses to the challenge from the populist radical right in Western Europe.' *Political Studies*, 58(3): 410–426.

Barker, David C. and James D. Tinnick. 2006. 'Competing visions of parental roles and ideological constraint.' *American Political Science Review*, 100(2): 249–263.

Barnes, Samuel and Max Kaase. 1979. *Political Action: Mass Participation in Five Western Democracies*. Beverley Hills, CA: Sage.

Barnes, Samuel and Janos Simon. Eds. 1998. *The Post-Communist Citizen*. Budapest, Hungary: Erasmus Foundation.

Barr, Robert R. 2009. 'Populists, outsiders and anti-establishment politics.' *Party Politics*, 15(1): 29–48.

Bartolini, Stephano and Peter Mair. 1990. *Identity, Competition, and Electoral Availability: The Stabilization of European Electorates*, 1885–1985. Cambridge: Cambridge University Press.

Bayle, Marc. 1995. *Le Front national: ça n'arrive pas qu'aux autres*. Toulon: Plein Sud.

Beaulieu, Emily. 2014. 'From voter ID to party ID: How political parties affect perceptions of election fraud in the US.' *Electoral Studies*, 35: 24–32.

Becker, Sasha, Thiemo Fetzer, and Dennis Novy. 2017. *'Who voted for Brexit? A comprehensive district-level analysis.'* Munich: CESifo Working Papers 6438–2017.

Bélanger Eric and Kees Aarts. 2006. 'Explaining the rise of the LPF: Issues, discontent, and the 2002 Dutch election.' *Acta Politica*, 41(1): 4–20.

Bell, Daniel. Ed. 2001 [1995/1963]. *The Radical Right*. New York: Transaction Books.

Bell, David S. and Byron Criddle. 2002. 'Presidentialism restored: The French elections of April–May and June 2002.' *Parliamentary Affairs*, 55(4): 643–663.

Ben-Moshe, D. 2001. 'One Nation and the Australian far right.' *Patterns of Prejudice*, 35(3): 24–40.

Bennett, David. *The Party of Fear: The American Far Right from Nativism to the Militia*.

Benoit, Ken. 2001. 'District magnitude, electoral formula, and the number of parties.' *European Journal of Political Research*, 39(2): 203–224.

2002. 'The endogeneity problem in electoral studies: A critical re-examination of Duverger's mechanical effect.' *Electoral Studies*, 21(1): 35–46.

Berbuir, Nicole, Marcel Lewandowsky, and Jasmin Siri. 2015. 'The AfD and its sympathisers: Finally a right-wing populist movement in Germany?' *German Politics*, 24(2): 154–178.

Berelson, Bernard, Paul F. Lazarsfeld, and William N. McPhee, 1954. *Voting*. Chicago: University of Chicago Press.

Berglund, Sten and Jan A. Dellenbrant. 1994. *The New Democracies in Eastern Europe: Party Systems and Political Cleavages*. Aldershot: Edward Elgar.

Berlet, Chip and Matthew N. Lyons. 2010. *Right-Wing Populism in America: Too Close for Comfort*. New York: Guilford Press.

Berman, Sheri. 2016. 'The specter haunting Europe: The lost left.' *Journal of Democracy*, 27(4): 69–76.

Bermanis, Shai, Daphna Canetti-Nisim, and Ami Pedahzur. 2004. 'Religious fundamentalism and the extreme right-wing camp in Israel.' *Patterns of Prejudice*, 38(2): 159–176.

Berning, Carl C. and Elmar Schlueter. 2016. 'The dynamics of radical right-wing populist party preferences and perceived group threat: A comparative panel analysis of three competing hypotheses in the Netherlands and Germany.' *Social Science Research*, 55: 83–93.

Best, Robin E. 2011. 'The declining electoral relevance of traditional cleavage groups.' *European Political Science Review*, 3(2): 279–300.

Betz, Hans-George. 1994. *Radicalism and Right-Wing Populism in Western Europe*. New York: St. Martin's Press.

Betz, Hans-George and Carol Johnson. 2004. 'Against the current – stemming the tide: The nostalgic ideology of the contemporary radical populist right.' *Journal of Political Ideologies*, 9(3): 311–327.

Betz, Hans-George and Stefan Immerfall. Eds. 1998. *The New Politics of the Right: Neo-Populist Parties and Movements in Established Democracies*. New York: St Martin's Press.

Beyme, Klaus von. Ed. 1988. *Right-wing Extremism in Western Europe*. London: Frank Cass.

Bielasiak, Jack. 2002. 'The institutionalization of electoral and party systems in post-Communist states.' *Comparative Politics*, 34(2): 189.

Billiet, Jack. 1995. 'Church involvement, ethnocentrism, and voting for a radical right-wing party: Diverging behavioral outcomes of equal attitudinal dispositions.' *Sociology of Religion*, 56(3): 303–326.

Billiet, Jack and Hans de Witte. 1995. 'Attitudinal dispositions to vote for a "new" extreme right-wing party: The case of "Vlaams Blok."' *European Journal of Political Research*, 27(4): 181–202.

Bitrin, Yves. 2003. *Vote Le Pen et psychologie des foules: 21 avril 2002, 'un coup de tonnerre dans un ciel bleu.'* Paris: Harmattan.

Bjørklund, Tor and Jørgen Goul Andersen. 2002. 'Anti-immigration parties in Denmark and Norway.' In Martin Schain, Aristide Zolberg, and Patrick Hossay. Eds. *Shadows Over Europe: The Development and Impact of the Extreme Right in Western Europe*. Houndsmill: Palgrave Macmillan.

Blee, Kathleen M. and Kimberly A. Creasap. 2010. 'Conservative and right-wing movements.' *Annual Review of Sociology*, 36: 269–286.

Bleich, Erik. 2003. *Race Politics in Britain and France: Ideas and Policymaking since the 1960s*. Cambridge: Cambridge University Press.

Block, Elena and Ralph Negrine. 2017. 'The populist communication style: Toward a critical framework.' *International Journal of Communication*, 11: 178–197.

Bohman, Andrea. 2011. 'Articulated antipathies: Political influence on anti-immigrant attitudes.' *International Journal of Comparative Sociology*, 52(6): 457–477.

Bohman, Andrea and Mikael Hjerm. 2016. 'In the wake of radical right electoral success: A cross-country comparative study of anti-immigration attitudes over time.' *Journal of Ethnic and Migration Studies*, 42(11): 1729–1747.

Bonikowski, Bart and Noam Gidron. 2016. 'The populist style in American politics: Presidential campaign discourse, 1952–1996.' *Social Forces*, 94(4): 1593–1621.

Boomgaarden, Hajo G. and Rens Vliegenthart. 2007. 'Explaining the rise of anti-immigrant parties: The role of news media content.' *Electoral Studies*, 26(2): 404–417.

Bornschier, Simon. 2010. *Cleavage Politics and the Populist Right: The New Cultural Conflict in Western Europe*. PA: Temple University Press.

2015. 'New cultural conflict, polarization, and representation in the Swiss Party System, 1975–2011.' *Swiss Political Science Review*, 21(4): 680–701.

Bos, Linda, Wouter van der Brug, and Claes de Vreese. 2010. 'Media coverage of right-wing populist leaders.' *Communications*, 35(2): 141–163.

Bovens, Mark and Anchrit Wille. 2010. 'The education gap in participation and its political consequences.' *Acta Politica*, 45(4): 393–422.

2017. *Diploma Democracy: The Rise of Political Meritocracy.* Oxford: Oxford University Press.

Bowler, Shaun and David J. Lanoue. 1992. 'Strategic and protest voting for 3rd parties: The case of the Canadian NDP.' *Western Political Quarterly*, 45(2): 485–499.

Braun, Aurel and Stephen Scheinberg. 1997. *The Extreme Right: Freedom and Security at Risk*. Boulder, CO: Westview Press.

Bresson, Gilles and Christian Lionet. 1994. *Le Pen: biographie*. Paris: Seuil.

Breuning M. and John T. Ishiyama. 1998. 'The rhetoric of nationalism: Rhetorical strategies of the Volksunie and Vlaams Blok in Belgium, 1991–1995.' *Political Communication*, 15(1): 5–26.

Broughton, David and Mark Donovan. Eds. 1999. *Changing Party Systems in Western Europe*. London: Pinter.

Brubaker, Rogers. 2017. 'Between nationalism and civilizationism: The European populist moment in comparative perspective.' *Ethnic and Racial Studies*, 40(8): 1191–1226.

Brug, Wouter Van der. 2003. 'How the LPF fueled discontent: Empirical tests of explanations of LPF support.' *Acta Politika*, 38(1): 89–106.

Brug, Wouter Van der and Meidert Fennema. 2003. 'Protest or mainstream? How the European anti-immigrant parties developed into two separate groups by 1999.' *European Journal of Political Research*, 42: 55–76.

Brug, Wouter Van der, Meidert Fennema, and Jean Tillie. 2000. 'Anti-immigrant parties in Europe: Ideological or protest vote?' *European Journal of Political Research*, 37(1): 77–102.

2005. 'Why some anti-immigrant parties fail and others succeed: A two-step model of aggregate electoral support.' *Comparative Political Studies*, 38(5): 537–573.

Bryk, Anthony S. and Stephen W. Raudenbush. 1992. *Hierarchical Linear Models*. Newbury Park, CA: Sage.

Budge, Ian. 2000. 'Expert judgments of party policy positions: Uses and limitations in political research.' *European Journal of Political Research*, 37(1): 103–113.

Budge, Ian and Dennis J. Farlie. 1983. *Explaining and Predicting Elections: Issue Effects and Party Strategies in Twenty-Three Democracies*. London: Allen & Unwin.

Budge, Ian, Hans-Dieter Klingemann, Andrew Volkens, Judith Bara, and Eric Tanenbaum. 2001. *Mapping Policy Preferences*. Oxford: Oxford University Press.

Budge, Ian, Ivor Crewe, and Dennis Farlie. Eds. 1976. *Party Identification and Beyond*. New York: John Wiley.

Budge, Ian and Michael J. Laver. Eds. 1992. *Party Policy and Government Coalitions*. Basingstoke: Macmillan.

Budge, Ian, David Robertson, and Derek Hearl. Eds. 1987. *Ideology, Strategy and Party Change: Spatial Analysis of Postwar Election Programmes in 19 Democracies*. Cambridge: Cambridge University Press.

Bukodi, Erzsébet, Marii Paskov, and Brian Nolan. 2017. 'Intergenerational class mobility in Europe: A new account and an old story.' INET Oxford Working Paper, 2017–03.

Burgess, Katrina and Stephen Levitsky. 2003. 'Explaining populist party adaptation in Latin America: Environmental and organizational determinants of party change in Argentina, Mexico, Peru, and Venezuela.' *Comparative Political Studies*, 36(8): 881–911.

Busher, Joel. 2013. 'Grassroots activism in the English Defence League: Discourse and public (dis)order.' In Max Taylor, P.M. Currie, and Donald Holbrook. Eds. *Extreme Right-Wing Political Violence and Terrorism*. London: Bloomsbury, pp. 65–84.

Bustikova, Lenka and Herbert Kitschelt. 2009. 'The radical right in post-communist Europe: Comparative perspectives on legacies and party competition.' *Communist and Post-Communist Studies*, 42(4): 459–483.

Caiani Manuela, Donatella Della Porta, and Claudius Wagemann. 2012. *Mobilizing on the Extreme Right: Germany, Italy, and the United States*. Oxford: Oxford University Press.

Caiani, Manuela and Donatella Della Porta. 2011. 'The elitist populism of the extreme right: A frame analysis of extreme right-wing discourses in Italy and Germany.' *Acta Politica*, 46(2): 180–202.

Caiani, Manuela and Linda Parenti. 2013. *European and American Extreme Right Groups and the Internet*. London: Routledge.

Cambadélis, Jean-Christophe and Eric Osmond. 1998. *La France blafarde: Une histoire politique de l'extrême droite*. Paris: Plon.

Campbell, Angus, Philip Converse, Warren Miller, and Donald Stokes. 1960. *The American Voter*. New York: Wiley.

1966. *Elections and the Political Order.* New York: Wiley.

Camus, Jean-Yves and Nicolas Lebourg. 2017. *Far-Right Politics in Europe.* Cambridge, MA: Belknap Press.

Canache, Damarys, Jeffrey J. Mondak, and Mitch A. Seligson. 2001. 'Meaning and measurement in cross-national research on satisfaction with democracy.' *Public Opinion Quarterly*, 65(4): 506–528.

Canovan, Margaret. 1981. *Populism.* New York: Harcourt, Brace, Jovanovich.

1999. 'Trust the people! Populism and the two faces of democracy.' *Political Studies*, 57 :2–16.

2002. 'Taking politics to the people: Populism as the ideology of democracy.' In Yves Mény and Yves Surel. Eds. *Democracies and the Populist Challenge.* Basingstoke: Palgrave, pp. 25–44.

2005. *The People.* Cambridge: Polity.

Carothers, Thomas. 2002. 'The end of the transition paradigm.' *Journal of Democracy*, 13(1): 5–21.

Carstairs, Andrew McLaren. 1980. *A Short History of Electoral Systems in Western Europe.* London: George Allen & Unwin.

Carter, Elisabeth. 2002. 'Proportional representation and the fortunes of right-wing extremist parties.' *West European Politics*, 25(3): 125–146.

2004. 'Does PR promote political extremism? Evidence from the West European parties of the extreme right.' *Representation*, 40(2): 82–100.

2005. *The Extreme Right in Western Europe: Success or Failure?* Manchester: Manchester University Press.

Castells, Manuel. 1997. *The Information Age: Economy, Society and Culture. Vol. 2, The Power of Identity.* London: Blackwell.

Castles, Francis G. and Peter Mair. 1984. 'Left–right political scales: Some "expert" judgments.' *European Journal of Political Research*, 12(1): 73–88.

Ceobanu, Alin M. and Xavier Escandell. 2010. 'Comparative analyses of public attitudes toward immigrants and immigration using multinational survey data: A review of theories and research.' *Annual Review of Sociology*, 36: 309–328.

Cesarani, David and Mary Fulbrook. Eds. 1996. *Citizenship, Nationality and Migration in Europe.* London: Routledge.

Chapin, Wesley D. 1992. 'Explaining the electoral success of the new right: The German case.' *West European Politics*, 20(2): 53–72.

Chebel d'Appollonia, Ariane. 1996. *L'extrême-droite en France: de Maurras à Le Pen.* Bruxelles: Editions complexe.

Cheles, Luciano, Ronnie Ferguson, and Michalina Vaughan. 1995. *The Far Right in Western and Eastern Europe.* New York: Longman.

Cizmar, A.M. *et al.* 2014. 'Authoritarianism and American political behavior from 1952 to 2008.' *Political Research Quarterly*, 67(1): 71–83.

Clark, Harold D., Matthew Goodwin, and Paul Whiteley. 2017. *Brexit: Why Britain Voted to Leave the European Union.* Cambridge: Cambridge University Press.

Clark, Terry Nichols and Seymour Martin Lipset. Eds. 2001. *The Breakdown of Class Politics.* Baltimore, MD: The Johns Hopkins University Press.

Clarke, Harold D, Alan Kornberg, Faron Ellis, and Jon Rapkin. 2000. 'Not for fame or fortune: A note on membership and activity in the Canadian Reform Party.' *Party Politics*, 6(1): 75–93.

Clarke, Harold, Matthew J. Goodwin, and Paul Whiteley. 2017. *Brexit! Why Britain Voted to Leave the European Union*. Cambridge: Cambridge University Press.

Clarke, Harold, Paul Whiteley, Walter Borges *et al.* 2016. 'Modelling the dynamics of support for a right-wing populist party: The case of UKIP.' *Journal of Elections, Public Opinion and Parties*, 26(2): 135–154.

Clarke, J. and J. Newman. 2017. '"People in this country have had enough of experts": Brexit and the paradoxes of populism.' *Critical Policy Studies*, 11: 101–106.

Cochrane, Christopher and Neil Nevitte. 2014. 'Scapegoating: Unemployment, far-right parties and anti-immigrant sentiment.' *Comparative European Politics*, 12(1): 1–32.

Coffé, Hilde. 2005. 'Do individual factors explain the different success of the two Belgian extreme right parties.' *Acta Politica*, 40(1): 74–93.

Cohen, Mollie J. and Amy Erica Smith. 2016. 'Do authoritarians vote for authoritarians? Evidence from Latin America.' *Research & Politics*, 3: 1–8.

Cohen, Patrick and Jean-Marc Salmon. 2003. *21 avril 2002: Contre-enquête sur le choc Le Pen*. Paris: Denoël.

Colantone, Italo and Piero Stanig. 2016. 'Global competition and Brexit.' *Science Research Network*. http://ssrn.com/abstract=2870313.

2017. 'The trade origins of economic nationalism: Import competition and voting behavior in Western Europe.' Carefen Working Papers 2017–49. http://ssrn.com/abstract=2904105.

Conniff, Michael L. Ed. 1982. *Latin American Populism in Comparative Perspective*. Albuquerque, NM: University of New Mexico Press.

Converse, Philip E. 1964. 'The nature of belief systems in mass publics.' In David Apter. Ed. *Ideology and Discontent*. New York: Free Press.

1969. 'Of time and partisan stability.' *Comparative Political Studies*, 2: 139–71.

1970. 'Attitudes vs. non-attitudes: The continuation of a dialogue.' In E.R. Tufte. Ed. *The Quantitative Analysis of Social Problems*. Reading, MA: Addison-Wesley.

Coppedge, Michael. 1997. 'District magnitude, economic performance, and party-system fragmentation in five Latin American countries.' *Comparative Political Studies*, 30(2): 156–185.

1998. 'The dynamic diversity of Latin American party systems.' *Party Politics*, 4(4): 547–568.

Cox, Gary W. 1987. 'Electoral equilibrium under alternative voting institutions.' *American Journal of Political Science*, 31: 82–108.

1987. *The Efficient Secret: The Cabinet and the Development of Political Parties in Victorian England*. Cambridge: Cambridge University Press.

1990. 'Centripetal and centrifugal incentives in electoral systems.' *American Journal of Political Science*, 34: 903–935.

1997. *Making Votes Count: Strategic Coordination in the World's Electoral Systems*. Cambridge: Cambridge University Press.

Cramer, Katherine J. 2016. *The Politics of Resentment: Rural Consciousness in Wisconsin and the Rise of Scott Walker.* Chicago: University of Chicago Press.

Crewe, Ivor and David Denver. Eds. 1985. *Electoral Change in Western Democracies: Patterns and Sources of Electoral Volatility*. New York: St. Martin's Press.

Crothers, Lane. 2003. *Rage on the Right: The American Militia Movement from Ruby Ridge to Homeland Security*. Lanham, MD: Rowman & Littlefield.

Curato, Nicole. 2017. 'Flirting with authoritarian fantasies? Rodrigo Duterte and the new terms of Philippine populism.' *Journal of Contemporary Asia*, 47(1): 142–153.

Curtice, John. 2016. 'A question of culture or economics? Public attitudes to the European Union in Britain.' *The Political Quarterly*, 87: 209–218.

Cutts, David, Matthew Goodwin, and Caitlin Milazzo. 2017. 'Defeat of the People's Army? The 2015 British general election and the UK Independence Party (UKIP).' *Electoral Studies*, 48(3): 70–83.

D'Amato, Gianni. 2003. 'Origins of right-wing extremism: A programmatic approach for social research in Switzerland.' *Schweizerische Zeitschrift fur Politikwissenschaft*, 9(2): 89–106.

Dalton, Russell J. 1999. 'Political support in advanced industrial democracies.' In Pippa Norris. Ed. *Critical Citizens: Global Support for Democratic Governance*. Oxford: Oxford University Press.

2000. 'Citizen attitudes and political behavior.' *Comparative Political Studies*, 33(6–7): 912–940.

2004. *Democratic Challenges: Democratic Choices*. Oxford: Oxford University Press.

2014. *Citizen Politics*. 6th edn. Irvine, CA: Sage Publications.

2015. *The Good Citizen: How a Younger Generation is Reshaping American Politics*. 2nd edn. Washington DC: CQ Press.

Dalton, Russell J. and Martin Wattenberg. Eds. 2002. *Parties without Partisans: Political Change in Advanced Industrial Democracies*. New York: Oxford University Press.

Dalton, Russell J., Scott C. Flanigan, and Paul Allen Beck. Eds. 1984. *Electoral Change in Advanced Industrial Democracies: Realignment or Dealignment?* Princeton, NJ: Princeton University Press.

Darmon, Michaël and Romain Rosso. 1998. *L'après Le Pen: enquête dans les coulisses du Front national*. Paris: Seuil.

Davidov, E., B. Meuleman, J. Billiet, and P. Schmidt. 2008. 'Values and support for immigration: A cross-country comparison.' *European Sociological Review*, 24(5): 583–599.

Davis, Peter. 2002. *The Extreme Right in France, 1789 to the Present: From De Maistre to Le Pen*. London: Routledge.

De Koster, Willem, Peter Achterberg, Jeroen Van der Waal *et al.* 2014. 'Progressiveness and the new right: The electoral relevance of culturally progressive values in the Netherlands.' *West European Politics*, 37(3): 584–604.

De Lange, Sarah L. 2007. 'A new winning formula? The programmatic appeal of the radical right.' *Party Politics*, 13: 411–35.

2012. 'New alliances: Why mainstream parties govern with radical right-wing populist parties.' *Political Studies*, 60: 899–918.

2012. Radical right-wing populist parties in offices: A cross-national comparison. In Uwe Backes and Patrick Moreau. Eds. *The Extreme Right in Europe: Current Trends and Perspectives*. Göttingen: Vandenhoeck & Ruprecht, pp. 171–194.

De Lange, Sarah L. and David Art. 2011. 'Fortuyn versus Wilders: An agency-based approach to radical right party building.' *West European Politics*, 34(6): 1229–1249.

de Regt, Smits T. and Dimitri Mortelmans. 2012. 'The relevance of class in shaping authoritarian attitudes: A cross-national perspective.' *Research in Social Stratification and Mobility*, 30: 280–295.

De Vries, Catherine E. and E.E. Edwards (2009), 'Taking Europe to its extremes: Extremist parties and public Euroscepticism.' *Party Politics*, 15(1): 5–28.

De Vries, Catherine E., Armen Hakhverdian, and Bram Lancee. 2013. 'The dynamics of voters' left/right identification: The role of economic and cultural attitudes.' *Political Science Research & Methods*, 1(2): 223–238.

De Winter, Leuvan and Johan Ackaert. 1998. 'Compulsory voting in Belgium: A reply to Hooghe and Pelleriaux.' *Electoral Studies*, 17(4): 425–428.

De Witte, Hans and Bert Klandermans. 2000. 'Political racism in Flanders and the Netherlands: Explaining differences in the electoral success of extreme right-wing parties.' *Journal of Ethnic and Migration Studies*, 26(4): 699–717.

DeAngelis, Richard A. 2003. 'A rising tide for Jean-Marie, Jorg, and Pauline? Xenophobic populism in comparative perspective.' *Australian Journal of Politics and History*, 49(1): 75–92.

DeClair, Edward G. 1999. *Politics on the Fringe: The People, Policies, and Organization of the French National Front*. Durham, NC: Duke University Press.

Denemark, David and Shaun Bowler. 2002. 'Minor parties and protest votes in Australia and New Zealand: Locating populist politics.' *Electoral Studies*, 21(1): 47–67.

Dennison, James and Matthew Goodwin. 2015. 'Immigration, issue ownership and the rise of UKIP.' *Parliamentary Affairs*, 68: 168–187.

Deutchman, Iva Ellen. 2000. 'Pauline Hanson and the rise and fall of the radical right in Australia.' *Patterns of Prejudice*, 34: 49–62.

Diamond, Larry and Juan J. Linz. 1989. 'Introduction: Politics, society, and democracy in Latin America.' In Larry Diamond, Juan J. Linz, and Seymour Martin Lipset. Eds. *Democracy in Developing Countries, vol. 4, Latin America*. Boulder, CO: Lynne Rienner.

DiTella, Torcuato. 1965. 'Populism and reform in Latin America.' In Claudio Véliz. Ed. *Obstacles to Change in Latin America*. Oxford: Oxford University Press, pp. 47–74.

Dix, Robert H. 1989. 'Cleavage structures and party systems in Latin America.' *Comparative Politics*, 22: 23–37.

Dominguez, Jorge I. and James A. McCann. 1996. *Democratizing Mexico: Public Opinion and Electoral Choices*. Baltimore, MD: Johns Hopkins University Press.

Dow, Jay K. 2001. 'A comparative spatial analysis of majoritarian and proportional elections.' *Electoral Studies*, 20: 109–125.

Down, Ian and Carole Wilson. 2013. 'A rising generation of Europeans? Life-cycle and cohort effects on support for "Europe".' *European Journal of Political Research*, 52(4): 431–456.

Downs, Anthony. 1957. *An Economic Theory of Democracy*. New York: Harper & Row.

Downs, William M. 2001. 'Pariahs in their midst: Belgian and Norwegian parties react to extremist threats.' *West European Politics*, 24(3): 23–42.

Doyle, David. 2011. 'The legitimacy of political institutions: Explaining contemporary populism in Latin America.' *Comparative Political Studies*, 44: 1447–1473.

Duckitt, John. 1989. 'Authoritarianism and group identification: A new view of an old construct.' *Political Psychology*, 10(1): 63–84.

2009. 'Authoritarianism and dogmatism.' In Mark Leary and Rick Hoyle. Eds. *Handbook of Individual Differences in Social Behavior.* New York: Guilford Press, pp. 298–317.

2013. 'Introduction to the special section on authoritarianism in societal context: The role of threat.' *International Journal of Psychology*, 48(1): 1–5.

Duckitt, John and Boris Bizumic. 2013. 'Multidimensionality of right-wing authoritarian attitudes: Authoritarianism–conservatism–traditionalism.' *Political Psychology*, 34(6): 841–862.

Duckitt, John and Chris G. Sibley. 2010. 'Personality, ideology, prejudice, and politics: A dual-process motivational model.' *Journal of Personality*, 78(6): 1861–1894.

Duckitt, John, Boris Bizumic, Stephen W. Krauss, and Edna Heled. 2010. 'A tripartite approach to right-wing authoritarianism: The authoritarianism–conservatism–traditionalism model.' *Political Psychology*, 31(5): 685–715.

Dunn, Kris. 2015. 'Preference for radical right-wing populist parties among exclusive-nationalists and authoritarians.' *Party Politics*, 21(3): 367–380.

Dunn, Kris and Shane P. Singh. 2011. 'The surprising non-impact of radical right-wing populist party representation on public tolerance of minorities.' *Journal of Elections, Public Opinion and Parties*, 21(3): 313–331.

Durand, Géraud. 1996. *Enquête au cur du Front national.* Paris: J. Grancher.

Duverger, Maurice. 1954. *Political Parties, Their Organization and Activity in the Modern State.* New York: Wiley.

1986. 'Duverger's Law: Forty years later.' In Bernard Grofman and Arend Lijphart. Eds. *Electoral Laws and Their Political Consequences*. New York: Agathon Press.

Eatwell, Roger. 1994. 'Why are fascism and racism reviving in Western Europe?' *The Political Quarterly*, 65(3): 313–325.

1997. 'Toward a new model of the rise of the extreme right.' *German Politics*, 6(3): 166–184.

1998. 'The dynamics of right-wing electoral breakthrough.' *Patterns of Prejudice*, 32(3): 3–31.

2000. 'The rebirth of the "extreme right" in Western Europe?' *Parliamentary Affairs*, 53(3): 407–425.

2002. 'The rebirth of right-wing charisma? The cases of Jean-Marie Le Pen and Vladimir Zhirinovsky.' *Totalitarian Movements and Political Religions*, 3(3): 1–24.

2003. 'Ten theories of the extreme right.' In Peter Merkl and Leonard Weinberg. Eds. *Right-Wing Extremism in the Twenty-first Century.* London: Frank Cass.

2004. 'Charisma and the revival of the European extreme right.' In Jens Rydgren. Ed. *Movements of Exclusion: Radical Right-Wing Populism.* New York: Nova Science Publishers, pp. 165–183.

2005. Charisma and the revival of the European extreme right. In Jens Rydgren. Ed. *Movements of Exclusion: Radical Right-Wing Populism in the Western World.* New York: Nova Publishers, pp. 101–120.

Eatwell, Roger and Cas Mudde. Eds. 2004. *Western Democracies and the New Extreme Right Challenge.* London: Routledge.

Edwards, Sebastian. 2010. *Left Behind: Latin America and the False Promise of Populism.* Chicago: University of Chicago Press.

Eger, Maureen A. and Sarah Valdez. 2015. 'Neo-nationalism in Western Europe.' *European Sociological Review*, 31(1): 115–130.

Eijk, Cees van der, Mark Franklin *et al.* 1996. *Choosing Europe? The European Electorate and National Politics in the Face of the Union.* Ann Arbor, MI: University of Michigan Press.

Eldersveld, Samuel James. 1982. *Political Parties in American Society.* New York: Basic Books.

Ellinas, Antonis A. 2007. 'Phased out: Far right parties in Western Europe.' *Comparative Politics*, 39(3): 353–371.

2009. 'Chaotic but popular? Extreme-right organisation and performance in the age of media communication.' *Journal of Contemporary European Studies*, 17(2): 209–221.

Enelow, James and Melvin Hinich. Eds. 1984. *The Spatial Theory of Voting.* New York: Cambridge University Press.

Engesser, Sven, Nicole Ernst, Frank Esser, and Florin Buechel. 2017. 'Populism and social media: How politicians spread a fragmented ideology.' *Information Communication and Society*, 20(8): 1109–1126.

Epstein, Leon. 1980. *Political Parties in Western Democracies.* New Brunswick, NJ: Transaction Books.

Esping-Anderson, Gosta. 1990. *The Three Worlds of Welfare Capitalism.* Princeton, NJ: Princeton University Press.

1999. *The Social Foundations of Post-industrial Economies.* Oxford: Oxford University Press.

Eulau, Heinz and Michael S. Lewis-Beck. Eds. 1985. *Economic Conditions and Electoral Outcomes: The United State and Western Europe.* New York: Agathon Press.

Evans, Geoffrey. 1999. *The Decline of Class Politics?* Oxford: Oxford University Press.

2000. 'The continued significance of class voting.' *Annual Review of Political Science*, 3: 401–417.

Evans, Geoffrey and James Tilley. 2017. *The New Politics of Class.* Oxford: Oxford University Press.

Evans, Geoffrey and Pippa Norris. Eds. 1999. *Critical Elections: British Parties and Voters in Long-term Perspective.* London: Sage.

Fallend, Franz. 2012. 'Populism in government: The case of Austria.' In Cas Mudde and Cristóbal Rovira Kaltwasser. Eds. *Populism in Europe and the Americas: Threat or Corrective for Democracy?* New York: Cambridge University Press, pp. 113–135.

Feldman, Stanley. 2003. 'Enforcing social conformity: A theory of authoritarianism.' *Political Psychology* 24(1): 41–74.

2013. 'Comments on authoritarianism in social context: The role of threat.' *International Journal of Psychology*, 48(1): 55–59.

Feldman, Stanley and Karen Stenner. 1997. 'Perceived threat and authoritarianism.' *Political Psychology*, 18(4): 741–770.

Fella, Stefano and Carlo Ruzza. 2013. 'Populism and the fall of the centre-right in Italy: The end of the Berlusconi model or a new beginning?' *Journal of Contemporary European Studies*, 21(1): 38–52.

Fennema, Meindert. 1997. 'Some conceptual issues and problems in the comparison of anti-immigrant parties in Western Europe.' *Party Politics*, 3: 473–492.

2000. 'Legal repression of extreme-right parties and racial discrimination.' In Ruud Koopmans and Paul Statham. Eds. *Challenging Immigration and Ethnic Relations Politics*. Oxford: Oxford University Press.

Ferber, Abby L. Ed. 2004. *Home-Grown Hate: Gender and Organized Racism*. New York: Routledge.

Fernández-Albertos, José. 2015. *The Voters of Podemos: From the Party of the Indignant to the Palada of the Excluded*. Madrid: La Catarata Books.

Ferrin, Monica and Hanspeter Kriesi. Eds. 2016. *How Europeans View and Evaluate Democracy*. Oxford: Oxford University Press.

Fieschi, Catherine. 2000. 'The far right in the context of the European Union.' *Parliamentary Affairs*, 53(3): 517–531.

2004. *Fascism, Populism and the Fifth Republic: In the Shadow of Democracy*. Manchester: Manchester University Press.

Fieschi, Catherine, James Shields, and Roger Woods. 1996. 'Extreme right-wing parties in Europe.' In John Gaffney. Ed. *Political Parties and the European Union*. London: Routledge.

Filc, Dani. 2015. 'Latin American inclusive and European exclusionary populism: Colonialism as an explanation.' *Journal of Political Ideologies*, 20(3): 263–283.

Flanagan, Scott C. and Aie-Rie Lee. 2003. 'The new politics, culture wars, and the authoritarian–libertarian value change in advanced industrial democracies.' *Comparative Political Studies*, 36(3): 235–270.

Ford, Rob and Matthew Goodwin. 2010. 'Angry white men: Individual and contextual predictors of support for the British National Party.' *Political Studies*, 58: 1–25.

Ford, Rob and Matthew J. Goodwin, 2014. *Revolt on the Right: Explaining Public Support for the Radical Right in Britain*. Abingdon: Routledge.

Franklin, Mark. 1985. *The Decline of Class Voting in Britain: Changes in the Basis of Electoral Choice, 1964–1983*. Oxford: Clarendon Press.

Franklin, Mark, Tom Mackie, Henry Valen *et al.* 1992. *Electoral Change: Responses to Evolving Social and Attitudinal Structures in Western Countries*. Cambridge: Cambridge University Press.

Freund, Caroline and Dario Sidhu. 2017. 'Manufacturing and the 2016 Election: An Analysis of US Presidential Election Data.' Peterson Institute for International Economics Working Paper No. 17–7. https://ssrn.com/abstract=2983872.

Frölich-Steffen, Susanne and Lars Rensmann. 2007. Conditions for failure and success of right-wing populist parties. In Pascal Delwit and Philippe Poirier. Eds. *Extreme droite et pouvoir en Europe*. Brussels: Université de Bruxelles, pp. 117–141.

Fromm, Erich. 1941. *Escape from Freedom*. New York: Holt, Rinehart & Winston.

Fukuyama, Francis. 1992. *The End of History and the Last Man*. London: Hamish Hamilton.

Funke, Manuel, Moritz Schularick, and Christoph Trebesch. 2016. 'Going to extremes: Politics after financial crises, 1870–2014.' *European Economic Review*, 88: 227–260.

Gallagher, Michael. 1992. 'Comparing proportional representation electoral systems: Quotas, thresholds, paradoxes, and majorities.' *British Journal of Political Science*, 22: 469–496.

Gallego, Ferran. 2002. *Por qué Le Pen*. Barcelona: Ediciones de Intervención Cultural.

Garcia-Albacete, Gema M. 2014. *Young People's Political Participation in Western Europe*. New York: Palgrave Macmillan.

Gavenda, Mario and Resul Umit. 2016. 'The 2016 Austrian Presidential Election: A tale of three divides.' *Regional and Federal Studies*, 26(3): 419–432.

Geiges, Lars, Stine Marg, and Franz Walter. 2015. *Pegida: Die schmutzige Seite der Zivilgesellschaft*. Bielefeld: Transcript Verlag.

Gest, Justin. 2016. *The New Minority: White Working Class Politics, Immigration and Inequality*. New York: Oxford University Press.

Gibson, Rachel. 1995. 'Anti-immigrant parties: The roots of their success.' *Current World Leaders*, 38(2): 119–130.

2002. *The Growth of Anti-Immigrant Parties in Western Europe*. Lewiston, NY: The Edwin Mellen Press.

Gibson, Rachel, Ian McAllister, and Tami Swenson. 2002. 'The politics of race and immigration in Australia: One nation voting in the 1998 election.' *Ethnic and Racial Studies*, 25(5): 823–844.

Gidengil, Elisabeth, André Blais, Richard Nadeau, and Neil Nevitte. 1999. 'Making sense of regional voting in the 1997 Canadian federal election: Liberal and Reform support outside Quebec.' *Canadian Journal of Political Science-Revue Canadienne De Science Politique*, 32(2): 247–272.

Gidengil, Elisabeth, André Blais, Neil Nevitte, and Richard Nadeau. 2001. 'The correlates and consequences of anti-partyism in the 1997 Canadian election.' *Party Politics*, 7(4): 491–513.

Gillespie, Richard. 2017. 'Spain: The forward march of Podemos halted?' *Mediterranean Politics*, 22(4): 537–544.

Givens, Terri E. 2004. 'The radical right gender gap.' *Comparative Political Studies*, 37(1): 30–54.

2005. *Voting Radical Right in Western Europe*. Cambridge: Cambridge University Press.

Goeres, Achim. 2009. *The Political Participation of Older People in Europe*. New York: Palgrave Macmillan.

Golder, Matthew. 2003. 'Explaining variation in the success of extreme right parties in Western Europe.' *Comparative Political Studies*, 36(4): 432–466.

2016. 'Far right parties in Europe.' *Annual Review of Political Science*, 19: 477–497.

Goldstein, Harvey. 1995. *Multilevel Statistical Models*. 3rd Edn. New York: Halstead Press.

Golsan, Richard J. Ed. 1995. *Fascism's Return: Scandal, Revision and Ideology since 1980*. Lincoln, NE: University of Nebraska Press.

Goodhart, David. 2017. *The Road to Somewhere: The Populist Revolt and the Future of Politics*. London: Hurst & Company.

Goodwin, Matthew J. 2006. 'The rise and faults of the internalist perspective in extreme right studies.' *Representation*, 42(4): 347–364.

2009. 'The radical right in contemporary Europe: Past, present and future.' *Political Studies Review*, 7(3): 322–329.

Goodwin, Matthew J. and Robert Ford. 2017. 'Britain after Brexit: A nation divided.' *Journal of Democracy*, 28(1): 17–30.

Goodwin, Matthew J. and Oliver Heath. 2016. 'The 2016 referendum, Brexit and the left behind? An aggregate-level analysis of the result.' *Political Quarterly*, 87(3): 323–332.

Goodwin, Matthew J. and Caitlin Milazzo. 2015. *UKIP: Inside the Campaign to Redraw British Politics*. Oxford: Oxford University Press.

Goodwin, Matthew J., Paul Whiteley, and Harold Clarke. 2017. 'Why Britain voted for Brexit: An individual-level analysis of the 2016 referendum vote.' *Parliamentary Affairs*, 70(3): 439–464.

Grasso, Maria Teresa, Stephen Farrall, Emily Gray, and Colin Hay. 2017. 'Thatcher's children, Blair's babies, political socialization and trickle-down value change: An age, period and cohort analysis.' *British Journal of Political Science*, 1–20.

Grendstad, Gunnar. 2003. 'Reconsidering Nordic party space.' *Scandinavian Political Studies*, 26(3): 193–217.

Greven, Thomas. 2016. *The Rise of Right-Wing Populism in Europe and the United States: A Comparative Perspective*. Berlin: Friedrich-Ebert-Stiftung.

Guilledoux, Frédéric-Joël. 2004. *Le Pen en Provence*. Paris: Fayard.

Guiso, Luigi, Helios Herrera, Massimo Morelli, and Tommaso Sonne. 8 November 2017. 'Populism: Demand and supply.' www.heliosherrera.com/populism.pdf.

Guiso, Luigi, Helios Herrera, Massimo Morelli, and Tommaso Sonne. Forthcoming. 'Global crisis and populism: The role of Eurozone Institutions.' *Economic Policy*.

Gunther, Richard and Larry Diamond. 2003. 'Species of political parties: A new typology.' *Party Politics*, 9(2): 167–199.

Hacker, Joseph and Paul Pierson. 2011. *Winner-Take-All Politics: How Washington Made the Rich Richer–and Turned Its Back on the Middle Class*. New York: Simon & Schuster.

Hainmueller, Jens and Daniel J. Hopkins. 2014. 'Public attitudes toward immigration.' *Annual Review of Political Science*, 17: 225–249.

Hainsworth, Paul. Ed. 1992. *The Extreme Right in Europe and the USA*. New York: St Martin's Press.

Ed. 2000. *The Politics of the Extreme Right: From the Margins to the Mainstream*. London: Pinter.

Hakhverdian, Armen and Christel Koop. 2007. 'Consensus democracy and support for populist parties in Western Europe.' *Acta Politica*, 42(4): 401–420.

Halikiopoulou, Daphne and Sophia Vasilopoulou. 2014. 'Support for the far right in the 2014 European Parliament Elections: A comparative perspective.' *Political Quarterly*, 85(3): 285–288.

Halikiopoulou, Daphne, K. Nanou, and Sophia Vasilopoulou. 2012. 'The paradox of nationalism: The common denominator of radical right and radical left Euroscepticism.' *European Journal of Political Research*, 51(4): 504–539.

Halikiopoulos, Daphne and T. Vlandas. 2017. 'Voting to leave: Economic insecurity and the Brexit vote.' In B. Leruth, N. Startin, and S. Usherwood. Eds. *The Routledge Handbook of Euroscepticism*. Abingdon: Routledge.

Halikiopoulou, Daphne and Tim Vlandas. 2015. 'The rise of the far right in debtor and creditor European Countries: The case of European Parliament Elections.' *Political Quarterly*, 85(2): 279–288.

Han, Kyung Joon. 2014. 'The impact of radical right-wing parties on the positions of mainstream parties regarding multiculturalism.' *West European Politics*, 38(3): 1–20.

2015. 'The impact of radical right-wing parties on the positions of mainstream parties regarding multiculturalism.' *West European Politics*, 38(3): 557–576.

Hardisty, Jean. 1999. *Mobilizing Resentment: Conservative Resurgence from John Birch to the Promise Keepers*. Boston, MA: Beacon Press.

Harmel, Robert and Kenneth Janda. 1994. 'An integrated theory of party goals and party change.' *Journal of Theoretical Politics*, 6: 259–287.

Harmel, Robert and Lars Svasand. 1997. 'The influence of new parties on old parties' platforms: The cases of the progress parties and conservative parties of Denmark and Norway.' *Party Politics*, 3(3): 315–340.

Harris, Richard and Martin Charlton. 2016. 'Voting out of the European Union: Exploring the geography of Leave.' *Environment and Planning*, 48(11): 2116–2128.

Hawkins, Kirk. 2010. *Venezuela's Chavismo and Populism in Comparative Perspective*. Cambridge: Cambridge University Press.

Hazan, Reuven Y. 1997. 'Three levels of election in Israel: The 1996 party, parliamentary and prime ministerial elections.' *Representation*, 34(3/4): 240–249.

Hazan, Reuvan Y. and Abraham Diskin. 2000. 'The 1999 Knesset and prime ministerial elections in Israel.' *Electoral Studies*, 19(4): 628–637.

Heath, Anthony, Geoffrey Evans, and Jean Martin. 1994. 'The measurement of core beliefs and values: The development of balanced socialist/laissez faire and libertarian/authoritarian scales.' *British Journal of Political Science*, 24(1): 115–132.

Heinisch, Reinhard. 2003. 'Success in opposition – failure in government: Explaining the performance of right-wing populist parties in public office.' *West European Politics*, 26(3): 91–130.

Heinisch, Reinhard and Oscar Mazzoleni. Eds. 2016. *Understanding Populist Party Organisation: The Radical Right in Western Europe*. London: Palgrave Macmillan.

Herkman, Juha. 2017. 'The life cycle model and press coverage of Nordic populist parties.' *Journalism Studies*, 18(4): 430–448.

Hernandez, Enrique and Hanspeter Kriesi. 2016. 'The electoral consequences of the financial and economic crisis in Europe.' *European Journal of Political Research*, 55(2): 203–224.

Hetherington, Mark and Elizabeth Suhay. 2011. 'Authoritarianism, threat, and Americans' support for the war on terror.' *American Journal of Political Science*, 55: 546–560.

Hetherington, Mark and Jonathan D. Weiler. 2009. *Authoritarianism and Polarization in American Politics*. Cambridge and New York: Cambridge University Press.

Hirsch-Hoefler, Sivan and Cass Mudde. 2013. 'Right-wing movements.' In David A. Snow, Donatella Della Porta, Bert Klandermans, and Doug McAdam. Eds. *The Wiley-Blackwell Encyclopedia of Social and Political Movements*. London: Blackwell, pp. 1–8.

Hirschman, Albert O. 1970. *Exit, Voice and Loyalty*. Cambridge, MA: Harvard University Press.

Hobolt, Sara B. 2016. 'The Brexit vote: A divided nation, a divided continent.' *Journal of European Public Policy*, 23(9): 1259–1277.

Hochschild, Arlie Russell. 2016. *Strangers in Their Own Land: Anger and Mourning on the American Right*. New York: The New Press.

Hoffman, Stanley. 1956. *Le Mouvement Poujade*. Paris: A. Colin.

Hofstedter, Richard. 1967. *The Paranoid Style in American Politics*. New York: Vintage Books.

Holmberg, Sören. 1994. 'Party identification compared across the Atlantic.' In M. Kent Jennings and Thomas Mann. Eds. *Elections at Home and Abroad*. Ann Arbor, MI: University of Michigan Press.

Holsteyn, Joop van. 2003. A new kid on the block: Pim Fortuyn and the Dutch Parliamentary Election of May 2002. In Colin Rallings *et al.* Eds. *British Elections and Parties Review*. London: Frank Cass, pp. 29–46.

Holsteyn, Joop van and Galen A. Irwin. 2003. 'Never a dull moment: Pim Fortuyn and the Dutch Parliamentary Election of 2002.' *West European Politics*, 26(2): 41–66.

Holsteyn, Joop van and Josje M. den Ridder. 2003. 'In the eye of the beholder: The perception of the List Pim Fortuyn and the Parliamentary Elections of May 2002.' *Acta Politica*, 38(1): 69–88.

Hooghe L., Gary Marks, and C.J. Wilson. 2002. 'Does left/right structure party positions on European integration?' *Comparative Political Studies*, 35(8): 965–989.

Hooghe, Marc and K. Pelleriaux. 1998. 'Compulsory voting in Belgium: An application of the Lijphart thesis.' *Electoral Studies*, 17(4): 419–424.

Huber, John and Ronald Inglehart. 1995. 'Expert interpretations of party space and party locations in 42 societies.' *Party Politics*, 1: 73–111.

Huntington, Samuel P. 1968. *Political Order in Changing Societies*. New Haven, CT: Yale University Press.

1993. *The Third Wave: Democratization in the late Twentieth Century Oklahoma*. Oklahoma: University of Oklahoma Press.

Husbands, Christopher T. 1988. 'The dynamic of racial exclusion and expulsion: Racist policy in Western Europe.' *European Journal of Political Research*, 16: 688–700.

1989. *Racist Political Movements in Western Europe*. London: Routledge.

1992. 'The other face of 1992: The extreme-right explosion in Western Europe.' *Parliamentary Affairs*, 45: 267–284.

Hutter, Swen. 2014. *Protesting Culture and Economics in Western Europe: New Cleavages in Left and Right Politics*. Minneapolis: University of Minnesota Press.

Hutter, Swen and Hanspeter Kriesi. 2013. 'Movements of the left, movements of the right reconsidered.' In Jacquelien van Stekelenburg, Conny Roggeband, and Bert Klandermans. Eds. *The Future of Social Movement Research*. Minneapolis: University of Minnesota Press, pp. 281–298.

Ignazi, Piero. 1992. 'The silent counter-revolution: Hypotheses on the emergence of extreme right-wing parties in Europe.' *European Journal of Political Research*, 22: 3–34.

1993. 'The changing profile of the Italian social movement.' In Peter H. Merkl and Leonard Weinberg. Eds. *Encounters with the Contemporary Radical Right*. Oxford: Westview Press, pp. 75–94.

2003. *Extreme Right Parties in Western Europe*. New York: Oxford University Press.

Immerzeel, Tim. 2015. *'Voting for a change: The democratic lure of populist radical right parties in voting behavior.'* PhD dissertation, Utrecht University, the Netherlands.

Immerzeel, Tim and Mark Pickup. 2015. 'Populist radical right parties mobilizing "the people"? The role of populist radical right success in voter turnout.' *Electoral Studies*, 40: 347–360.

Immerzeel, Tim, Marcel Lubbers, and Hilde Coffé. 2016. 'Competing with the radical right: Distances between the European radical right and other parties on typical radical right issues.' *Party Politics*, 22(6): 823–834.

Inglehart, Ronald. 1977. *The Silent Revolution: Changing Values and Political Styles among Western Publics*. Princeton, NJ: Princeton University Press.

1990. *Culture Shift in Advanced Industrial Society*. Princeton, NJ: Princeton University Press.

1997. *Modernization and Postmodernization: Cultural, Economic and Political Change in 43 Societies*. Princeton, NJ: Princeton University Press.

2018. *Cultural Evolution*. New York: Cambridge University Press.

Inglehart, Ronald, Mansoor Moaddel, and Mark Tessler. 2006. 'Xenophobia and in-group solidarity in Iraq: A natural experiment on the impact of insecurity.' *Perspectives on Politics*, 4(3): 495–505.

Inglehart, Ronald and Pippa Norris. 2003. *Rising Tide: Gender Equality and Cultural Change around the World*. Cambridge: Cambridge University Press.

2016. 'Trump, Brexit, and the rise of populism: Economic have-nots and cultural backlash.' HKS Working Paper No. RWP16-026, Harvard University.

2017. 'Trump and the Populist Authoritarian parties: The silent revolution in reverse.' *Perspectives on Politics*, 15(2): 443–454.

Inglehart, Ronald and Christian Welzel. 2005. *Modernization, Cultural Change and Democracy: The Human Development Sequence.* New York: Cambridge University Press.

International IDEA. 2004. *Handbook on Funding of Parties and Election Campaigns.* Stockholm: International IDEA.

Ivaldi, Gilles, Maria Elisabetta Lanzone, and Dwayne Woods. 'Varieties of populism across a left–right spectrum: The case of the Front National, the Northern League, Podemos and Five Star Movement.' *Swiss Political Science Review*, 23(4): 354–376.

Ivarsflaten, Elizabeth. 2005. 'Threatened by diversity: Why restrictive asylum and immigration policies appeal to Western Europeans.' *Journal of Elections, Public Opinion and Parties*, 15(1): 21–45.

2008. 'What unites right-wing populists in Western Europe? Re-examining grievance mobilization models in seven successful cases.' *Comparative Political Studies*, 41(1): 3–23.

Jäckle, Sebastian and Pascal D. König. 2017. 'The dark side of the German "welcome culture": Investigating the causes behind attacks on refugees in 2015.' *West European Politics*, 40(2): 223–251.

Jackman, Robert W. and Karin Volpert. 1996. 'Conditions favouring parties of the extreme right in Western Europe.' *British Journal of Political Science*, 26(4): 501–521.

Jackman, Simon. 1998. 'Pauline Hanson, the mainstream and political elites: The place of race in Australian political ideology.' *Australian Journal of Political Science*, 33(2): 167–186.

Jagers, Jan and Stephan Walgrave. 2007. 'Populism as political communication style: An empirical study of political parties' discourse in Belgium.' *European Journal of Political Research*, 46(3): 319–345.

Janda, Kenneth, Robert Harmel, Christine Edens, and Patricia Goff. 1995. 'Changes in party identity: Evidence from party manifestos.' *Party Politics*, 1: 171–196.

Jansen, Robert S. 2011. 'Populist mobilization: A new theoretical approach to populism.' *Sociological Theory*, 29(2): 75–96.

Jelen, Ted Gerard and Clyde Wilcox. Eds. 2002. *Religion and Politics in Comparative Perspective.* New York: Cambridge University Press.

Jenssen, Anders Todal. 1999. 'All that is solid melts into air: Party identification in Norway.' *Scandinavian Political Studies*, 22(1): 1–27.

Jesse, Eckhard. 2003. 'The performance of the PDS and the right-wing parties at the Bundestag election 2002.' *Zeitschrift fur Politik*, 50(1): 17–36.

Jesuit, David K., Piotr R. Paradowski, and Vincent A. Mahler. 2009. 'Electoral support for extreme right-wing parties: A sub-national analysis of Western European elections.' *Electoral Studies*, 28: 279–290.

John, Peter and Helen Margetts. 2009. 'The latent support for the extreme right in British politics.' *West European Politics*, 32(3): 496–513.

Jones, Robert P. 2016. *The End of White Christian America.* New York: Simon & Schuster.

Judis, John B. 2016. *The Populist Explosion: How the Great Recession Transformed American and European Politics.* New York: Columbia Global Reports.

Jungar, Ann-Cathrine and Anders Ravik Jupskas. 2014. 'Populist radical right parties in the Nordic Region: A new and distinct party family?' *Scandinavian Political Studies*, 37(3): 215–238.

Kang, Won-Taek. 2004. 'Protest voting and abstention under plurality rule elections: An alternative public choice approach.' *Journal of Theoretical Politics*, 16(1): 79–102.

Karapin, Roger. 1998. 'Radical-right and neo-fascist political parties in Western Europe.' *Comparative Politics*, 30(2): 213–34.

Karp, Jeffrey A., Susan A. Banducci, and Shaun Bowler. 2003. 'To know it is to love it? Satisfaction with democracy in the European Union.' *Comparative Political Studies*, 36(3): 271–292.

Katz, Richard S. 1997. *Democracy and Elections*. Oxford: Oxford University Press.

Katz, Richard S. and Peter Mair. 1992. 'The membership of political parties in European democracies, 1960–1990.' *European Journal of Political Research*, 22: 329–345.

1995. 'Changing models of party organization and party democracy: The emergence of the cartel party.' *Party Politics*, 1(1): 5–28.

1996. 'Cadre, catch-all or cartel? A rejoinder.' *Party Politics*, 2(4): 525–534.

Eds. 1992. *Party Organizations: A Data Handbook on Party Organizations in Western Democracies, 1960–1990*. London: Sage.

Katz, Richard S. and Peter Mair. Eds. 1994. *How Parties Organize: Change and Adaptation in Party Organizations in Western Democracies*. London: Sage.

Kazin, Michael. 1998. *The Populist Persuasion: An American History*. Ithaca, NY: Cornell University Press.

Keman, Hans. Ed. 2002. *Comparative Democratic Politics*. London: Sage.

Key, Vladimer O., Jr. 1949. *Southern Politics in State and Nation*. New York: Vintage.

1964. *Politics, Parties, and Pressure Groups*. 5th edn. New York: Crowell.

Kim, Heemin and Richard C. Fording. 2001. 'Does tactical voting matter? The political impact of tactical voting in recent British elections.' *Comparative Political Studies*, 34(3): 294–311.

Kinder, Donald R. and Allison Dale-Riddle. 2012. *The End of Race? Obama, 2008, and Racial Politics in America*. New Haven, CT: Yale University Press.

Kinder, Donald R. and David O. Sears. 1981. 'Prejudice and politics: Symbolic racism vs. racial threats to the good life.' *Journal of Personality and Social Psychology*, 40: 414–431.

Kinder, Donald R. and Lynn M. Sanders. 1996. *Divided by Color*. Chicago: University of Chicago Press.

Kirchheimer, Otto. 1966. 'The transformation of Western European party systems.' In Joseph La Palombara and Myron Weiner. Eds. *Political Parties and Political Development*. Princeton, NJ: Princeton University Press.

Kirscht, John P. and Ronald C. Dillehay. 1967. *Dimensions of Authoritarianism: A Review of Research and Theory*. Lexington: University of Kentucky Press.

Kitschelt, Herbert. 1988. 'Organization and strategy of Belgian and West European parties: A new dynamic of party politics in Western Europe?' *Comparative Politics*, 20: 127–154.

1989. *The Logics of Party Formation: Ecological Politics in Belgium and West Germany.* Ithaca, NY: Cornell University Press.

1992. 'The formation of party systems in East Central Europe.' *Politics and Society*, 20: 7–50.

1993. 'Class-structure and Social-Democratic party strategy.' *British Journal of Political Science*, 23(3): 299–337.

1994. *The Transformation of European Social Democracy.* Cambridge: Cambridge University Press.

1995. 'Formation of party cleavages in post-communist democracies – theoretical propositions.' *Party Politics*, 1(4): 447–472.

2000. 'Linkages between citizens and politicians in democratic polities.' *Comparative Political Studies*, 33(6–7): 845–879.

2007. 'Growth and persistence of the radical right in postindustrial democracies: Advances and challenges in comparative research.' *West European Politics*, 30(5): 1176–1206.

Kitschelt, Herbert, Zdenka Mansfeldova, Radoslaw Markowski, and Gabor Toka. 1999. *Post-Communist Party Systems.* Cambridge: Cambridge University Press.

Kitschelt, Herbert, with Anthony J. McGann. 1995. *The Radical Right in Western Europe: A Comparative Analysis.* Ann Arbor: University of Michigan.

Klingemann, Hans-Dieter. 1979. 'Measuring ideological conceptualizations.' In Samuel Barnes, Max Kaase *et al.* Eds. *Political Action.* Beverley Hills, CA: Sage Publications.

1995. 'Party positions and voter orientations.' In Hans-Dieter Klingemann and Dieter Fuchs. Eds. *Citizens and the State.* Oxford: Oxford University Press.

Klingemann, Hans-Dieter, Richard Hofferbert, and Ian Budge. 1994. *Parties, Policies and Democracy.* Boulder, Co: Westview.

Klingemann, Hans-Dieter and Dieter Fuchs. Eds. 1995. *Citizens and the State.* Oxford: Oxford University Press.

Klandermans, Bert and Nonna Mayer. Eds. 2006. *Extreme Right Activists in Europe: Through the Magnifying Glass.* London: Routledge.

Knapp, Andrew. 1987. 'Proportional but Bipolar: France's Electoral System in 1986.' *West European Politics*, 10(1): 89–114.

Knigge, Pia. 1998. 'The ecological correlates of right-wing extremism in Western Europe.' *European Journal of Political Research* 34: 249–279.

Koopmans, Ruud. 1996. 'Explaining the rise of racist and extreme right violence in Western Europe: Grievances or opportunities?' *European Journal of Political Research*, 30(2): 185–216.

1999. 'Political. Opportunity. Structure. Some splitting to balance the lumping.' *Sociological Forum*, 14(1): 93–105.

Koopmans, Ruud and Jasper Muis. 2009. 'The rise of right-wing populist Pim Fortuyn in the Netherlands: A discursive opportunity approach.' *European Journal of Political Research*, 48(5): 642–664.

Koopmans, Ruud and Susan Olzak. 2004. 'Discursive opportunities and the evolution of right-wing violence in Germany.' *American Journal of Sociology*, 110(1): 198–230.

Koopmans, Rudd, Paul Statham, Marco Giugni, and Florence Passy. 2005. *Contested Citizenship: Immigration and Cultural Diversity in Europe.* Minneapolis: University of Minnesota Press.

Koopmans, Ruud and Paul Statham. Eds. 2000. *Challenging Immigration and Ethnic Relations Politics: Comparative European Perspectives*. Oxford: Oxford University Press.

Kovács, András. 2013. 'The post-communist extreme right. The Jobbik Party in Hungary.' In Ruth Wodak, Majid KhosraviNik, and Brigitte Mral. Eds. *Right-Wing Populism in Europe: Politics and Discourse*. London: Bloomsbury, pp. 223–234.

Kriesi, Hanspeter. 2014. 'The populist challenge.' *West European Politics*, 37: 361–378.

Kriesi, Hanspeter, Edgar Grande, Romain Lachat, Martin Dolezal, Simon Bornschier, and Timotheos Frey. 2006. 'Globalization and the transformation of the national political space: Six European countries compared.' *European Journal of Political Research*, 45(6): 921–5.

Kriesi, Hanspeter, Edgar Grande, Romain Lachat *et al.* 2008. *West European Politics in the Age of Globalization*. Cambridge: Cambridge University Press.

Kriesi, Hanspeter, Edgar Grande, Martin Dolezal *et al.* 2012. *Political Conflict in Western Europe*. Cambridge: Cambridge University Press.

Kriesi, Hanspeter and Takis S. Pappas. Eds. 2015. *European Populism in the Shadow of the Great Recession*. Colchester: ECPR Press.

Laakso, Markku and Rein Taagepera. 1979. 'Effective number of parties: A measure with application to Western Europe.' *Comparative Political Studies*, 12: 3–27.

Laclau, Earnest. 2005. 'Populism: What's in a Name?' In Francisco Panizza. Ed. *Populism and the Mirror of Democracy*. London and New York: Verso.

Ladner, Andreas. 2001. 'Swiss political parties: Between persistence and change.' *West European Politics*, 24(2): 123–144.

Lamont, Michele, Bo Yun Park, and Elena Ayala-Hurtado. 2017. 'Trump's electoral speeches and his appeal to the American white working class.' *British Journal of Sociology*, 68: 153–180.

Landman, Todd. 2000. *Issues and Methods in Comparative Politics*. London: Routledge.

Lane, Jan-Erik, David McKay, and Kenneth Newton. Eds. 1997. *Political Data Handbook*. 2nd edn. Oxford: Oxford University Press.

Laver, Michael and Ian Budge. 1992. *Party Policy and Government Coalitions*. Houndmills: Macmillan.

Laver, Michael and William Ben Hunt. 1992. *Policy and Party Competition*. New York: Routledge.

Laver, Michael and Norman Schofield. 1990. Multiparty government. *The Politics of Coalition in Europe*. Oxford: Oxford University Press.

Laver, Michael and Kenneth A. Shepsle. 1996. *Making and Breaking Governments: Cabinets and Legislatures in Parliamentary Democracies*. Cambridge: Cambridge University Press.

Lavine, Howard *et al.* 2002. 'Explicating the black box through experimentation: Studies of authoritarianism and threat.' *Political Analysis*, 10(4): 343–361.

Lavine, Howard, Milton Lodge, and Kate Freitas. 2005. 'Threat, authoritarianism, and selective exposure to information.' *Political Psychology*, 26: 219–244.

Lawson, Kay. 1980. *Political Parties and Linkage: A Comparative Perspective.* New Haven, CT: Yale University Press.

Lazarsfeld, Paul F., Bernard Berelson, and Hazel Gaudet. 1948. *The People's Choice.* New York: Columbia University Press.

LeDuc, Lawrence. 1979. 'The dynamic properties of party identification: A four nation comparison.' *European Journal of Political Research*, 9: 257–268.

LeDuc, Lawrence, Richard G. Niemi, and Pippa Norris. Eds. 1996. *Comparing Democracies: Elections and Voting in Global Perspective.* Thousand Oaks, CA: Sage.

LeDuc, Lawrence, Richard Niemi, and Pippa Norris. Eds. 2002. *Comparing Democracies 2: New Challenges in the Study of Elections and Voting.* Thousand Oaks, CA: Sage.

Lefkofridi, Zoe, Markus Wagner, and Johanna E. Willmann. 2014. 'Left-authoritarians and policy representation in Western Europe: Electoral choice across ideological dimensions.' *West European Politics*, 37(1): 65–90.

LeVine, Robert A. and Donald T. Campbell. 1972. *Ethnocentrism: Theories of Conflict, Ethnic Attitudes and Group Behavior.* New York: Columbia University Press.

Levitsky, Stephen and Daniel Ziblatt. 2018. *How Democracies Die.* New York: Crown.

Lewis-Beck, Michael S. 1988. *Economics and Elections: The Major Western Democracies.* Ann Arbor, MI: University of Michigan Press.

Lewis-Beck, Michael S., and Glenn E. Mitchell. 1993. 'French electoral theory: The National Front test.' *Electoral Studies*, 12: 112–27.

Lewis-Beck, Michael S. and M. Stegmaier. 2000. 'Economic determinants of electoral outcomes.' *Annual Review of Political Science*, 3: 183–219.

Lewis, Paul G. 2000. *Political Parties in Post-Communist Eastern Europe.* London: Routledge.

2001. *Party Development and Democratic Change in Post-Communist Europe: The First Decade.* London: Frank Cass.

Lijphart, Arend. 1979. 'Religion vs. linguistic vs. class voting.' *American Political Science Review*, 65: 686.

1980. 'Language, religion, class, and party choice: Belgium, Canada, Switzerland and South Africa Compared.' In Richard Rose. Ed. *Electoral Participation: A Comparative Analysis.* Beverly Hills, CA: Sage.

1984. *Democracies: Patterns of Majoritarian and Consensus Government in Twenty-One Countries.* New Haven, CT: Yale University Press.

1994. *Electoral Systems and Party Systems: A Study of Twenty-Seven Democracies 1945–1990.* New York: Oxford University Press.

1999. *Patterns of Democracy: Government Forms and Performance in 36 Countries.* New Haven, CT: Yale University Press.

2001. 'The pros and cons – but mainly pros – of consensus democracy.' *Acta Politica*, 35: 363–398.

Linde, Jonas and Joakim Ekman. 2003. 'Satisfaction with democracy: A note on a frequently used indicator in comparative politics.' *European Journal of Political Research*, 42(3): 391–408.

Lipset, Seymour Martin. 1955. 'The sources of the radical right.' In Daniel Bell. Ed. *The New American Right.* New York: Criterion Books.

1959. 'Democracy and working-class authoritarianism.' *American Sociological Review*, 24: 482–501.

1960. *Political Man: The Social Basis of Politics*. New York: Doubleday.

Lipset, Seymour Martin and Earl Raab. 1978. *The Politics of Unreason: Rightwing Extremism in America 1790–1977*. 2nd edn. Chicago: University of Chicago Press.

Lipset, Seymour Martin and Stein Rokkan. 1967. *Party Systems and Voter Alignments*. New York: Free Press.

Lubbers, Marcel. 2000. [principal investigator] *Expert Judgment Survey of Western-European Political Parties 2000* [machine readable data set]. Nijmegen, the Netherlands: NWO, Department of Sociology, University of Nijmegen.

Lubbers, Marcel, Merove Gijsberts, and Peer Scheepers. 2002. 'Extreme right-wing voting in Western Europe.' *European Journal of Political Research*, 41(3): 345–378.

Lubbers, Marcel and Peer Scheepers. 2000. 'Individual and contextual characteristics of the German extreme right-wing vote in the 1990s: A test of complementary theories.' *European Journal of Political Research*, 38(1): 63–94.

2001. 'Explaining the trend in extreme right-wing voting: Germany 1989–1998.' *European Sociological Review*, 17(4): 431–449.

Lucassen, Geertje and Marcel Lubbers. 2012. 'Who fears what? Explaining far right-wing preference in Europe by distinguishing perceived cultural and economic ethnic threats.' *Comparative Political Studies*, 45: 547–574.

Luther, Kurt R. 2003. 'The self-destruction of a right-wing populist party? The Austrian parliamentary election of 2002.' *West European Politics*, 26(2): 136–152.

2011. 'Of goals and own goals: A case study of right-wing populist party strategy for and during incumbency.' *Party Politics*, 17(4): 453–470.

MacDonald, Stuart Elaine, Ola Listhaug, and George Rabinowitz. 1991. 'Issues and party support in multiparty systems.' *The American Political Science Review*, 85(4): 1107–1131.

Mackie, Thomas J. and Richard Rose. 1991. *The International Almanac of Electoral History*. Washington DC: Congressional Quarterly Press.

1991. *The International Almanac of Electoral History*, 3rd edn. Washington DC: Congressional Quarterly.

1997. *A Decade of Election Results: Updating the International Almanac*. Glasgow: Centre for the Study of Public Policy, University of Strathclyde.

MacWilliams, Matthew C. 2016. 'Who decides when the party doesn't? Authoritarian voters and the rise of Donald Trump.' *PS: Political Science & Politics*, 49(4): 716–721.

2017. 'Afraid and intolerant: Authoritarians rise to Trump's call.' In Mari Fitzduff. Ed. *Why Irrational Politics Appeals: Understanding the Allure of Trump*. Connecticut: Praeger Publishers.

Maguire, Maria. 1983. 'Is there still persistence? Electoral change in Western Europe, 1948–1979.' In Hans Daalder and Peter Mair. Eds. *Western European Party Systems: Continuity and Change*. Beverly Hills, CA: Sage Publications.

Mainwaring, Scott and Timothy R. Scully. 1995. 'Introduction: Party systems in Latin America.' In Scott Mainwaring and Timothy Scully. Eds. *Building*

*Democratic Institutions: Party Systems in Latin America*. Stanford, CA: Stanford University Press, 1–34.

Mainwaring, Scott and Timothy Scully. 1995. *Building Democratic Institutions: Party Systems in Latin America*. Stanford, CA: Stanford University Press.

Mair, Peter and Cas Mudde. 1998. 'The party family and its study.' *Annual Review of Political Science*, 1: 211–229.

Mair, Peter and Francis Castles. 1997. 'Reflections: Revisiting expert judgments.' *European Journal of Political Research*, 31(1–2): 150–157.

Mair, Peter. 1983. 'Adaptation and control: Towards an understanding of party and party system change.' In Hans Daalder and Peter Mair. Ed. *Western European Party Systems: Continuity and Change*. Beverly Hills, CA: Sage Publications.

1993. 'Myths of electoral change and the survival of traditional parties.' *European Journal of Political Research*, 24: 121–33.

1997. *Party System Change*. Oxford: Oxford University Press.

2000. 'The limited impact of Europe on national party systems.' *West European Politics*, 23(4): 27–51.

2001. 'In the aggregate: Mass electoral behaviour in Western Europe, 1950–2000.' In Hans Keman. Ed. *Comparative Democracy*. London: Sage.

2001. 'Party membership in twenty European democracies 1980–2000.' *Party Politics*, 7(1): 5–22.

Mammone, Andrea, Emmanuel Godin, and Brian Jenkins. Eds. 2013. *Varieties of Right-wing Extremism in Europe*. London: Routledge.

Manucci, Luca and Edward Weber. 2017. 'Why the big picture matters: Political and media populism in Western Europe since the 1970s. *Swiss Political Science Review*, 23(4): 313–334.

Manza, Jeff and Clem Brooks. 1999. *Social Cleavages and Political Change: Voter Alignments and US Party Coalitions*. New York: Oxford University Press.

March, James and Johan Olsen. 1989. *Rediscovering Institutions: The Organizational Basis of Politics*. New York: Free Press.

March, Luke. 2012. *Radical Left Parties in Europe*. London: Routledge.

Marcus, Jonathan. 1995. *The National Front and French Politics: The Resistible Rise of Jean-Marie Le Pen*. Washington Square, NY: New York University Press.

Maréchal, Yann and Nicolas Gauthier. 2001. *Le Pen*. Paris: Editions Objectif France.

Marsh, Alan. 1977. *Protest and Political Consciousness*. Beverly Hills, CA: Sage.

1990. *Political Action in Europe and the USA*. London: Macmillan.

Mason, William M., G.M. Wong, and Barbara Entwistle. 1983. 'Contextual analysis through the multilevel linear model.' *Sociological Methodology*, 3: 72–103.

Massicotte, Louis, André Blais, and Antoine Yoshinaka. 2004. *Establishing the Rules of the Game*. Toronto: University of Toronto Press.

Mayer, Lawrence C., Erol Kaymak, and Jeff W. Justice. 2000. 'Populism and the triumph of the politics of identity: The transformation of the Canadian party system.' *Nationalism and Ethnic Politics*, 6(1): 72–102.

Mayer, Nonna and Pascal Perrineau. 1992. 'Why do they vote for Le Pen?' *European Journal of Political Research*, 22(1): 123–141.

Mayer, Nonna. 2002. *Ces Français qui votent Le Pen*. Paris: Flammarion.

Mayhew, David R. 2002. *Electoral Realignments: A Critique of the American Genre*. New Haven, CT: Yale University Press.

Mazzoleni, Gianpietro. 2008. 'Populism and the media.' In Daniele Albertazzi and Duncan McDonnell. Eds. *Twenty-First Century Populism*. Basingstoke: Palgrave Macmillan, pp. 49–64.

McConahay, John B. and Joseph C. Hough. 1976. 'Symbolic racism.' *Journal of Social Issues*, 32: 23–45.

McDonald, Ronald H. and J. Mark Ruhl. 1989. *Party Politics and Elections in Latin America*. Boulder, CO: Westview.

McKenzie, Robert T. 1955. *British Political Parties*. New York: St. Martin's Press.

McLaren, Lauren M. 2002. 'Public support for the European Union: Cost/benefit analysis or perceived cultural threat?' *Journal of Politics*, 64(2): 551–566.

2003. 'Anti-immigrant prejudice in Europe: Contact, threat perception, and preferences for the exclusion of migrants.' *Social Forces*, 81(3): 909–936.

Meguid, Bonnie M. 2008. *Party Competition between Unequals: Strategies and Electoral Fortunes in Western Europe*. Cambridge: Cambridge University Press.

Meny, Yves and Yves Surel. Eds. 2002. *Democracies and the Populist Challenge*. Houndsmill: Palgrave/MacMillan.

Merkl, Peter and Leonard Weinberg. Eds. 2003. *Right-wing Extremism in the Twenty-First Century*. London: Frank Cass.

Merkl, Peter H. and Leonard Weinberg. Eds. 1993. *Encounters with the Contemporary Radical Right*. Boulder: Westview.

Eds. 1997. *The Revival of Right-Wing Extremism in the Nineties*. London: Frank Cass.

Merolla, Jennifer L. and Elizabeth J. Zechmeister. 2009. *Democracy at Risk: How Terrorist Threats Affect the Public*. Chicago: University of Chicago Press.

Merrill, III, Samuel and Bernard Grofman. 1999. *A Unified Theory of Voting: Directional and Proximity Spatial Models*. Cambridge: Cambridge University Press.

Merrill, III, Samuel and James Adam. 'Centifugal incentives in multi-candidate elections.' *Journal of Theoretical Politics*, 14(3): 275–300.

Miguet, Arnauld. 2002. 'The French elections of 2002: After the earthquake, the deluge.' *West European Politics*, 25(4): 207–220.

Miller, Arthur H. 2000. 'The development of party identification in post-soviet societies.' *American Journal of Political Science*, 44(4): 667–686.

Miller, Warren E. 1991. 'Party identification, realignment, and party voting: Back to the basics.' *American Political Science Review*, 85(2): 557–568.

Miller, Warren E. and J. Merrill Shanks. 1996. *The New American Voter*. Cambridge: Harvard University Press.

Miller, William L., Stephen White, and Paul Heywood. 1998. *Values and Political Change in Post-communist Europe*. New York: St. Martin's Press.

Minkenberg, Michael. 2000. 'The renewal of the radical right: Between modernity and anti-modernity.' *Government and Opposition*, 35(2): 170–188.

2001. 'The radical right in public office: Agenda-setting and policy effects.' *West European Politics*, 24: 1–21.

2002. 'The radical right in post-socialist Central and Eastern Europe: Comparative observations and interpretations.' *East European Politics and Societies*, 16(2): 335–362.

2003. 'The West European radical right as a collective actor: Modeling the impact of cultural and structural variables on party formation and movement mobilization.' *Comparative European Politics*, 1(2): 149–170.

2011. 'The radical right in Europe today: Trends and patterns in East and West.' In Nora Langenbacher and Britta Schellenberg. Eds. *Is Europe on the 'Right' Path?* Berlin: FriedrichEbert-Stiftung, pp. 37–55.

2017. *The Radical Right in Eastern Europe: Democracy under Siege?* New York: Palgrave Macmillan.

Ed. 2015. *Transforming the Transformation? The East European Radical Right in the Political Process*. New York: Routledge.

Mitra, Subrata. 1988. 'The National Front in France: A single-issue movement?' *West European Politics*, 11(2): 47–64.

Moffitt, Benjamin. 2016. *The Global Rise of Populism: Performance, Political Style and Representation*. Palo Alto, CA: Stanford University Press.

Morlino, Leonardo. 1998. *Democracy between Consolidation and Crisis: Parties, Groups, and Citizens in Southern Europe*. Oxford: Oxford University Press.

Moser, Robert G. 1999. 'Electoral systems and the number of parties in post-communist states.' *World Politics*, 51(3): 359.

2001. *Unexpected Outcomes: Electoral Systems, Political Parties and Representation in Russia*. Pittsburgh: University of Pittsburgh Press.

Mudde, Cas and Cristóbal Rovira Kaltwasser. Eds. 2012. *Populism in Europe and the Americas: Threat or Corrective for Democracy?* New York: Cambridge University Press.

2012. 'Exclusionary vs. Inclusionary Populism in Europe and Latin America.' *Government and Opposition*, 48(2): 147–174.

Mudde, Cas. 1996. 'The paradox of the anti-party party: Insights from the extreme right.' *Party Politics*, 2(2): 265–276.

1999. 'The single-issue party thesis: Extreme right parties and the immigration issue.' *West European Politics*, 22(3): 182–197.

2000. *The Ideology of the Extreme Right*. New York: St. Martin's Press.

2004. 'The populist zeitgeist.' *Government and Opposition*, 39(4): 541–563.

2007. *Populist Radical Right Parties in Europe*. New York: Cambridge University Press.

2010. 'The populist radical right: A pathological normalcy.' *West European Politics*, 33: 1167–1186.

2013. 'The 2012 Stein Rokkan Lecture: Three decades of populist radical right parties in Western Europe – so what?' *European Journal of Political Research*, 52(1): 1–19.

2014. 'Fighting the system? Populist radical right parties and party system change.' *Party Politics*, 20(2): 217–226.

2016. 'The study of populist radical right parties: Towards a fourth wave.' C-REX Working Paper Series No. 1, Centre for Research on Extremism, the Extreme Right, Hate Crime, and Political Violence. Oslo: University of Oslo.

2017. *Populism: A Very Short Introduction*. 2nd edn. New York: Oxford University Press.
2017. *SYRIZA: The Failure of the Populist Promise*. London: Palgrave Macmillan.
Ed. 2016. *The Populist Radical Right: A Reader*. London: Routledge.
Mughan, Anthony, Clive Bean, and Ian McAllister. 2003. 'Economic globalization, job insecurity and the populist reaction.' *Electoral Studies*, 22(4): 617–633.
Mughan, Anthony and David Lacy. 2002. 'Economic performance, job insecurity and electoral choice.' *British Journal of Political Science*, 32(3): 513–533.
Muis, Jasper. 2015. 'The rise and demise of the Dutch extreme right: Discursive opportunities and support for the Center Democrats in the 1990s.' *Mobilization: An International Quarterly*, 20(1): 41–60.
Muis, Jasper and Tim Immerzeel. 2017. 'Causes and consequences of the rise of the populist radical right parties and movements in Europe.' *Current Sociological Review*, 65(6): 909–930.
2018. 'Causes and consequences of the rise of populist radical right parties and movements in Europe.' *Current Sociology*, 65(6): 909–930.
Muis, Jasper, Tim Immerzeel, Robert Andersen. and Jocelyn A.J. Evans. 2003. 'Social-political context and authoritarian attitudes: Evidence from seven European countries.' In EREPS Annual Meeting, Ghent, December 5–7.
Muis, Jasper, Tim Immerzeel, and Chantal Mouffe. 2005. 'The "end of politics" and the challenge of right-wing populism.' In Francisco Panizza. Ed. *Populism and the Mirror of Democracy*. London: Verso, pp. 50–71.
Muis, Jasper, Tim Immerzeel, Joost van Spanje, and Wouter Van der Brug. 2009. 'Being intolerant of the intolerant: The exclusion of Western European anti-immigration parties and its consequences for party choice.' *Acta Politica*, 44(4): 353–384.
Muis, Jasper and Michel Scholte. 2013. 'How to find the "winning formula"? Conducting simulation experiments to grasp the tactical moves and fortunes of populist radical right parties.' *Acta Politica*, 48(1): 22–46.
Muis, Jasper, Tim Immerzeel, Maik Fielitz, and Laura L. Laloire. Eds. 2016. *Trouble on the Far Right: Contemporary Right-Wing Strategies and Practices in Europe*. Bielefeld: Transcript.
Muller-Rommel, Ferdinand and Geoffrey Pridham. Eds. 1991. *Small parties in Western Europe*. London: Sage.
Muller, Jan-Werner. 2016. *What is Populism?* PA: University of Pennsylvania Press.
Müller, Wolfgang C. 2000. 'The Austrian election of October 1999: A shift to the right.' *West European Politics*, 23(3): 191–200.
2000. 'Wahlen und die Dynamik des österreichischen Parteiensystems seit 1986.' In Fritz Plasser, Peter A. Ulram, and Franz Sommer. Eds. *Das österreichische Wahlverhalten*. Vienna: Signum, pp. 13–54.
2004. 'The parliamentary election in Austria, November 2002.' *Electoral Studies*, 23(2): 346–353.
Napier, Jaime L. and John T. Jost. 2008. 'The "antidemocratic personality" revisited: A cross-national investigation of working-class authoritarianism.' *Journal of Social Issues*, 64: 595–617.

Nelson, Michael. Ed. 2017. *The Elections of 2016*. Washington, DC: CQ Press.

Neto, Octavio Amorim and Gary Cox. 1997. 'Electoral institutions, cleavage structures and the number of parties.' *American Journal of Political Science*, 41(1): 149–174.

Newton, David E. 2016. *Same-Sex Marriage: A Reference Handbook*. 2nd edn. New York: ABC-CLIO.

Nie, Norman, Sidney Verba, and John Petricik. 1976. *The Changing American Voter*. Cambridge, MA: Harvard University Press.

Niekerk, A.E. van. 1974. *Populism and Political Development in Latin America*. Rotterdam: Universitaire Pers Rotterdam.

Nielsen, Hans J. 1999. 'The Danish election 1998.' *Scandinavian Political Studies*, 22(1): 67–81.

Nieuwbeerta, Paul. 1995. *The Democratic Class Struggle in Twenty Countries 1945–90*. Amsterdam: Amsterdam Thesis Publishers.

Nieuwbeerta, Paul and Nan Dirk De Graaf. 1999. 'Traditional class voting in 20 postwar societies.' In Geoffrey Evans. Ed. *The End of Class Politics?* Oxford: Oxford University Press.

Nohlen, Dieter. 1996. *Elections and Electoral Systems*. Delhi: Macmillan.

Norpoth, Helmut, Michael S. Lewis-Beck, and Jean-Dominique Lafay. Eds. 1991. *Economics and Politics: The Calculus of Support*. Ann Arbor, MI: University of Michigan Press.

Norris, Pippa. 2000. *A Virtuous Circle: Political Communication in Post-Industrial Democracies*. New York: Cambridge University Press.

2001. *Digital Divide: Civic Engagement, Information Poverty and the Internet Worldwide*. New York: Cambridge University Press.

2002. *Democratic Phoenix: Political Activism Worldwide*. New York: Cambridge University Press.

2004. *Electoral Engineering: Voting Rules and Political Behavior*. New York: Cambridge University Press.

2005. *Radical Right: Voters and Parties in the Electoral Market*. Cambridge: Cambridge University Press.

2005. *Radical Right: Voters and Parties in the Electoral Market*. New York: Cambridge University Press.

2011. *Democratic Deficit*. Cambridge: Cambridge University Press.

2015. *Why Elections Fail*. New York: Cambridge University Press.

2016. 'Its not just Trump: Authoritarian populism is rising across the West. Here's why.' *Monkey Cage/Washington Post*. 11 March 2016.

2017. 'Is Western democracy backsliding? Diagnosing the risks.' *Journal of Democracy*, 28(2).

2017. *Strengthening Electoral Integrity*. New York: Cambridge University Press.

Ed. 1999. *Critical Citizens: Global Support for Democratic Governance*. Oxford: Oxford University Press.

Norris, Pippa and Ronald Inglehart. 2003. *Rising Tide: Gender Equality and Cultural Change Worldwide*. New York: Cambridge University Press.

2004. *Sacred and Secular: Religion and Politics Worldwide*. New York: Cambridge University Press.

Norris, Pippa and Joni Lovenduski. 2004. 'Why parties fail to learn: Electoral defeat, selective perception and British party politics.' *Party Politics*, 10(1): 85–104.

North, Douglas, C. 1990. *Institutions, Institutional Change, and Economic Performance*. Cambridge: Cambridge University Press.

O'Malley, Eoin. 2008. 'Why is there no radical right party in Ireland?' *West European Politics*, 31(5): 960–977.

2017. 'A Populist Vote in the 2016 General Election in Ireland.' *PSAI Blog*. https://politicalreform.ie/2017/01/17/a-populist-vote-in-the-2016-general-election-in-ireland/.

O'Malley, Eoin. and J. FitzGibbon. 2015. 'Everywhere and nowhere: Populism and the puzzling non-reaction to Ireland's crises,' in Hans Kriesi and T.S. Pappas Eds. *European Populism in the Shadow of the Great Recession*. Colchester: ECPR Press, 287–302.

Oesch, Daniel. 2008. 'Explaining workers' support for right-wing populist parties in Western Europe: Evidence from Austria, Belgium, France, Norway, and Switzerland.' *International Political Science Review*, 29: 349–373.

Oesterreich, Detlef. 2005. 'Flight into security: A new approach and measure of the authoritarian personality.' *Political Psychology*, 26: 275–298.

Oliver, J. Eric and Wendy Rahn. 2016. 'Rise of the Trumpenvolk: Populism in the 2016 Election.' *Annals of the American Academy of Political and Social Science*, 667(1): 189–206.

Olzak, Susan. 1993. *The Dynamics of Ethnic Competition and Conflict*. Stanford, CA: Stanford University Press.

Oppenhuis, Eric. 1995. *Voting Behavior in Europe: A Comparative Analysis of Electoral Participation and Party Choice*. Amsterdam: Het Spinhuis.

Ordeshook, Peter C. and Olga Shvetsova. 1994. 'Ethnic heterogeneity, district magnitude and the number of parties.' *American Journal of Political Science*, 38: 100–123.

Orriols, Lluis and Guillermo Cordero. 2016. 'The breakdown of the Spanish two-party system: The upsurge of Podemos and Ciudadanos in the 2015 general election.' *South European Society and Politics*, 21(4): 469–492.

Otjes, Simon and Tom Louwerse. 2015. 'Populists in parliament: Comparing left-wing and right-wing populism in the Netherlands.' *Political Studies*, 63(1): 60–79.

Oyamot Clifton M., Jr, Eugene Borgida, and E.L. Fisher. 2006. 'Can values moderate the attitudes of right-wing authoritarians?' *Personality and Social Psychology Bulletin*, 32: 486–500.

Oyamot Clifton M., Jr, Emily L. Fisher, and Grace Deason. 2012. 'Attitudes toward immigrants: The interactive role of the authoritatian predisposition, social norms, and humanitarian values.' *Journal of Experimental Social Psychology*, 48: 97–105.

Pammett, Jon H. and Joan DeBardeleben. Eds. 1998. 'Voting and elections in post-communist states.' *Electoral Studies*, 17(2 Special Issue).

Panebianco, Angelo. 1988. *Political Parties: Organization and Power*. Cambridge: Cambridge University Press.

Pascal, Perrineau. 2017. *The Disruptive Vote: The Presidential and Legislative Elections of 2017*. Paris: Sciences Po Presses.

Passini, Stefano. 2017. 'Different ways of being authoritarian: The distinct effects of authoritarian dimensions on values and prejudice.' *Political Psychology*, 38(1): 73–86.

Patzelt, Werner J. and Joachim Klose. Eds. 2016. *PEGIDA. Warnsignale aus Dresden*. Dresden: Thelem Universitätsverlag.

Pauwels, Teun. 2010. 'Explaining the success of neo-liberal populist parties: The case of Lijst Dedecker in Belgium.' *Political Studies*, 58(5): 1009–1029.

2011. 'Measuring populism: A quantitative text analysis of party literature in Belgium.' *Journal of Elections, Public Opinion and Parties*, 21(1): 97–119.

Pauwels, Teun. 2011. 'Explaining the strange decline of the populist radical right Vlaams Belang in Belgium: The impact of permanent opposition.' *Acta Politica*, 46(1): 60–82.

2016. *Populism in Western Europe: Comparing Belgium, Germany and the Netherlands*. New York: Routledge.

Pedahzur, Ami. 2003. 'The potential role of pro-democratic civil society in responding to extreme right-wing challenges: The case of Brandenburg.' *Contemporary Politics*, 9(1): 63–74.

Pedahzur, Ami and Arie Perliger. 2004. 'An alternative approach for defining the boundaries of "party families": Examples from the Israeli extreme right-wing party scene.' *Australian Journal of Political Science*, 39(2): 285–305.

Pederson, Morgens N. 1979. 'The dynamics of European party systems: Changing patterns of electoral volatility.' *European Journal of Political Research*, 7: 1–26.

Pelinka, Anton. 2013. 'Right-wing populism: Concept and typology.' In Ruth Wodak, Majod KhosravNik, and Brigitte Mral. Eds. *Right-Wing Populism in Europe: Politics and Discourse*. London: Bloomsbury, pp. 3–22.

Peretz, Don and Gideon Doron. 1996. 'Israel's 1996 elections: A second political earthquake?' *Middle East Journal*, 50(4): 529–546.

Peretz, Don, Rebecca Kook, and Gideon Doron. 2003. 'Knesset election 2003: Why Likud regained its political domination and Labor continued to fade out.' *Middle East Journal*, 57(4): 588–603.

Perrineau, Pascal. 1997. *Le symptome Le Pen: radiographie des électeurs du Front national*. Paris: Fayard.

Pettigrew, Thomas F. 1998. 'Intergroup contact theory.' *Annual Review of Psychology*, 49: 65–85.

1998. 'Reactions toward the new minorities of Western Europe.' *Annual Review of Sociology*, 24: 77–103.

Pettigrew, Thomas F. and R.W. Meertens. 1995. 'Subtle and blatant prejudice in Western Europe.' *European Journal of Social Psychology*, 25: 57–77.

Pierson, Paul. 1998. 'Irresistible forces, immovable objects: Post-industrial welfare states confront permanent austerity.' *Journal of European Public Policy*, 5: 539–560.

Pirro, Andrea. 2015. *The Populist Radical Right in Central and Eastern Europe: Ideology, Impact, and Electoral Performance*. London: Routledge.

Plasser, F. and P.A. Ulram. 2003. 'Striking a responsive chord: Mass media and right-wing populism in Austria.' In Gianpietro Mazzoleni, Julianne Stewart, and Bruce Horsfield. Eds. *The Media and Neo-Populism: A Comparative Analysis*. Westport, CT: Praeger, pp. 21–43.
Pomper, Gerald. 1997. *The Election of 1996*. Chatham, NJ: Chatham House.
Powell, G. Bingham, Jr. 1982. *Contemporary Democracies: Participation, Stability, and Violence*. Cambridge, MA: Harvard University Press.
2000. *Elections as Instruments of Democracy*. New Haven, CT: Yale University Press.
Pratto, Felicia, James Sidanius, Lisa M. Stallworth, and Bertram F. Malle. 1994. 'Social dominance orientation: A personality variable predicting social and political attitudes.' *Journal of Personality and Social Psychology*, 67: 741–763.
Pridham, Geoffrey and Paul G. Lewis. Eds. 1996. *Stabilizing Fragile Democracies: Comparing Party Systems in Southern and Eastern Europe*. London: Routledge.
Przeworski, Adam and Henry Teune. 1970. *The Logic of Comparative Social Inquiry*. New York: Wiley–Interscience.
Przeworski, Adam and John Sprague. 1986. *Paper Stones: A History of Electoral Socialism*. Chicago: The University of Chicago Press.
Przeworski, Adam, Michael E. Alvarez, Jose Antonio Cheibub, and Fernando Limongi. 2000. *Democracy and Development: Political Institutions and Well-Being in the World, 1950–1990*. New York: Cambridge University Press.
Pytlas, Bartek. 2016. *Radical Right Parties in Central and Eastern Europe: Mainstream Party Competition and Electoral Fortune*. London: Routledge.
Quillian, Lincoln. 1995. 'Prejudice as a response to perceived group threat: Population composition and anti-immigrant and racial prejudice in Europe.' *American Sociological Review*, 60: 586–611.
Rabinowitz, George and Stuart Elaine Macdonald. 1989. 'A directional theory of issue voting.' *American Political Science Review*, 83: 93–121.
Rae, Douglas W. 1967. *The Political Consequences of Electoral Laws*. 2nd edn. New Haven, CT: Yale University Press.
Rahn, Wendy and Eric Oliver. 2016. 'Trump's voters aren't authoritarians, new research says: So what are they?' *The Washington Post/Monkey Cage*. March 9, 2016. https://www.washingtonpost.com/news/monkey-cage/wp/2016/03/09/trumps-voters-arent-authoritarians-new-research-says-so-what-are-they/.
Rallings, Colin and Michael Thrasher. 2000. 'Personality politics and protest voting: The first elections to the Greater London Authority.' *Parliamentary Affairs*, 53(4): 753–764.
Ramiro, Luis and Raul Gomez. 2017. 'Radical-left populism during the Great Recession: Podemos and its competition with the established radical left.' *Political Studies*, 65: 108–126.
Ravndal, Jacob A. 2016. 'Right-wing terrorism and violence in Western Europe: Introducing the RTV dataset.' *Perspectives on Terrorism* 10(3).
Reif, Karl-Heinz. 1997. 'European elections as member state second-order elections revisited.' *European Journal of Political Research*, 31(1–2): 115–124.

Reif, Karl-Heinz and Herman Schmitt. 1980. 'Second-order national elections: A conceptual-framework for the analysis of European election results.' *European Journal of Political Research*, 8(1): 3–44.

Renouvin, Bertrand. 1997. *Une tragédie bien française: le Front national contre la nation*. Paris: Ramsay.

Reuband, Karl-Heinz. 2015. 'Wer demonstriert in Dresden für Pegida? Ergebnisse empirischer Studien, methodische Grundlagen und offene Fragen.' *Mitteilungen des Instituts für Parteienrecht und Parteienforschung*, 21: 133–143.

Riedisperger, Max. 1992. 'Heil Haider! The revitalization of the Austrian Freedom Party since 1986.' *Politics and Society in Germany, Austria and Switzerland*, 4(3): 18–47.

Riker, William H. 1962. *The Theory of Political Coalitions*. New Haven, CT: Yale University Press.

1976. 'The number of political parties: A reexamination of Duverger's law.' *Comparative Politics*, 9: 93–106.

1982. 'The two-party system and Duverger's Law: An essay on the history of political science.' *American Political Science Review*, 76: 753–766.

1986. 'Duverger's Law Revisited.' In Bernard Grofman and Arend Lijphart. Eds. *Electoral Laws and Their Political Consequences*. New York: Agathon Press, Inc.

Rodrik, Dani. 2017. 'Populism and the economics of globalization.' CEPR DP11871.

Rokeach, Milton. 1960. *The Open and Closed Mind*. New York: Basic Books.

Rokkan, Stein. 1970. *Citizens, Elections, Parties: Approaches to the Comparative Study of the Processes of Development*. New York: McKay.

Rooduijn, Matthijs. 2014 'The mesmerising message: The diffusion of populism in public debates in Western European media.' *Political Studies*, 62(4): 726–744.

2014. 'The nucleus of populism: In search of the lowest common denominator.' *Government and Opposition*, 49(4): 572–598.

2014. 'Vox populismus: A populist radical right attitude among the public?' *Nations and Nationalism*, 20(1): 80–92.

2017. 'What unites the voter bases of populist parties? Comparing the electorates of 15 populist parties.' *European Political Science Review*, 1–18.

Rooduijn, Matthijs and Tjitske Akkerman. 2017. 'Flank attacks: Populism and left–right radicalism in Western Europe.' *Party Politics*, 23(3): 193–204.

Rooduijn, Matthijs, Brian Burgoon, and Erika J. van Elsas. 2017. 'Radical distinction: Support for radical left and radical right parties in Europe.' *European Union Politics*, 18(4): 536–559.

Rooduijn, Matthijs, Sarah L. de Lange, and Wouter Van Der Brug. 2014. 'A populist Zeitgeist? Programmatic contagion by populist parties in Western Europe.' *Party Politics*, 20(4): 563–575.

Rooduijn, Matthijs and Teun Pauwels. 2011. 'Measuring populism: Comparing two methods of content analysis.' *West European Politics*, 34(6): 1272–1283.

Rooduijn, Matthijs, Wouter Van Der Brug, and Sarah L. de Lange. 2016. 'Expressing or fueling discontent? The relationship between populist voting and political discontent.' *Electoral Studies*, 43: 32–40.

Rosanvallon, Pierre. 2008. *Counter-Democracy: Politics in an Age of Distrust.* New York: Cambridge University Press.

Rose, Richard. 2000. 'The end of consensus in Austria and Switzerland.' *Journal of Democracy*, 11(2): 26–40.

Rose, Richard and Neil Munro. 2002. *Elections without Order: Russia's Challenge to Vladimir Putin.* New York: Cambridge University Press.

Rose, Richard and Derek W. Urwin. 1969. 'Social cohesion, political parties and strains in regime.' *Comparative Political Studies*, 2: 7–67.

1970. 'Persistence and change in Western party systems since 1945.' *Political Studies*, 18: 287–319.

Rosenstone, Stephen, Roy L. Behr, and Edward H. Lazarus. 1996. *Third Parties in America.* Princeton, NJ: Princeton University Press.

Rovira Kaltwasser, Cristóbal. 2012. 'The ambivalence of populism: Threat and corrective for democracy.' *Democratization*, 19(2): 184–20.

Rovira Kaltwasser, Cristóbal and Paul Taggart. 2015. 'Dealing with populists in government: A framework for analysis.' *Democratization*, 23(2): 201–220.

Rovira Kaltwasser, Cristóbal, Paul A. Taggart, Paulina Ochoa Espejo, and Pierre Ostiguy. Eds. 2017. *The Oxford Handbook of Populism.* Oxford: Oxford University Press.

Rydgren, Jens. 2002. 'Radical right populism in Sweden: Still a failure, but for how long?' *Scandinavian Political Studies*, 25(1): 27–56.

2003. 'Meso-level reasons for racism and xenophobia: Some converging and diverging effects of radical right populism in France and Sweden.' *European Journal of Social Theory*, 6(1): 45–68.

2004. 'Explaining the emergence of radical right-wing populist parties: The case of Denmark.' *West European Politics*, 27(3): 474–502.

2004. *The Populist Challenge: Political Protest and Ethno-Nationalist Mobilization in France.* New York: Berghahn Books.

2005. 'Is extreme rightwing populism contagious? Explaining the emergence of a new party family.' *European Journal of Political Research*, 44(3): 413–437.

2007. 'The sociology of the radical right.' *Annual Review of Sociology*, 33: 241–262.

2011. 'A legacy of "uncivicness"? Social capital and radical right-wing populist voting in Eastern Europe.' *Acta Politica*, 46(2): 132–157.

2013. 'Introduction: Class politics and the radical right.' In Jens Rydgren. Ed. *Class Politics and the Radical Right.* London: Routledge, pp. 1–9.

Ed. 2005a. *Movements of Exclusion: Radical Right-Wing Populism in the Western World.* New York: Nova Publishers.

Ed. 2012. *Class Politics and the Radical Right*, London and New York: Routledge.

Sabato, Larry J., Kyle Kondik, and Geoffrey Skelley. 2017. *Trumped: The 2016 Election that Broke All the Rules.* New York: Rowman & Littlefield.

Sartori, Giovanni. 1966. 'European political parties: The case of polarized pluralism.' In Joseph LaPalombara and Myron Weiner. Eds. *Political Parties and Political Development.* Princeton, NJ: Princeton University Press.

1976. *Parties and Party Systems: A Framework for Analysis.* New York: Cambridge University Press.

1994. *Comparative Constitutional Engineering: An Inquiry into Structures, Incentives, and Outcomes.* New York: Columbia University Press.

Sawer, Marian. Ed. 2001. *Elections: Full, Free and Fair.* Sydney: The Federation Press.

Schain, Martin. 1987. 'The National Front in France and the construction of political legitimacy.' *West European Politics*, 10(2): 229–252.

Schain, Martin A. 2006. 'The extreme-right and immigration policy-making: Measuring direct and indirect effects.' *West European Politics*, 29(2): 270–289.

Schain, Martin, Aristide Zolberg, and Patrick Hossay. Eds. 2002. *Shadows Over Europe: The Development and Impact of the Extreme Right in Western Europe.* Houndsmill: Palgrave Macmillan.

Schattschneider, E.E. 1942. *Party Government.* New York: Farrar & Rinehart.

Schedler, Andreas. 1996. 'Antipolitical establishment parties.' *Party Politics*, 2: 291–312.

Scheepers, P., H. Schmeets, and A. Felling. 1997. 'Fortress Holland? Support for ethnocentric policies among the 1994-electorate of the Netherlands.' *Ethnic and Racial Studies*, 20(1): 145–159.

Schickler, Eric and Donald P. Green. 1997. 'The stability of party identification in Western democracies: Results from eight panel surveys.' *Comparative Political Studies*, 30(4): 450–483.

Schmitt-Beck, Rüdiger. 2016. 'The "Alternative für Deutschland in the electorate": Between single-issue and right-wing populist party.' *German Politics*, 26(1): 124–148.

Schmitt, Herman and Sören Holmberg. 1995. 'Political parties in decline?' In Hans-Dieter Klingemann and Dieter Fuchs. Eds. *Citizens and the State.* Oxford: Oxford University Press.

Schugart, Mathew Soberg and Martin P. Wattenberg. Eds. 2001. *Mixed-Member Electoral Systems: The Best of Both Worlds?* Oxford: Oxford University Press.

Schumacher, Gijs and Matthijs Rooduijn. 2013. 'Sympathy for the "devil"? Voting for populists in the 2006 and 2010 Dutch general elections.' *Electoral Studies*, 32(1): 124–133.

Schumann, Siegfried and Jurgen Falter. 1988. 'Affinity towards right-wing extremism in Western Europe.' *West European Politics*, 11(2): 96–110.

Schumpeter, Joseph A. 1952. *Capitalism, Socialism and Democracy.* 4th edn. London: George Allen & Unwin.

Schwartz, Shalom. 1992. 'Universals in the content and structure of values: Theoretical advances and empirical tests in 20 countries.' *Advances in Experimental Social Psychology*, 25: 1–65.

Selle, Per. 1991. 'Membership in party organizations and the problems of the decline of parties.' *Comparative Political Studies*, 23(4): 459–477.

Semyonov, Moshe, Rebeca Raijman, and Anastasia Gorodzeisky. 2006. 'The rise of anti-foreigner sentiment in European societies, 1988–2000.' *American Sociological Review*, 71(3): 426–449.

Sidanius, James and Felicia Pratto. 1999. *Social Dominance: An Intergroup Theory of Social Hierarchy and Oppression*. New York: Cambridge University Press.

Sides, John and Jack Citrin. 2007. 'European opinion about immigration: The role of identities, interests and information.' *British Journal of Political Science*, 37(3): 477–504.

Sides, John, Michael Tesler, and Lynn Vavreck. 2017. 'How Trump lost and won.' *Journal of Democracy*, 28(2): 34–44.

Simmons, Harvey Gerald. 1995. *The French National Front: The Extremist Challenge to Democracy*. Boulder, CO: Westview Press.

Smith, J. 2002. 'European right-wing: A turn to the right.' *World Today*, 58(6): 7–8.

Smith, Tom. 1982. 'General liberalism and social change in post World War II America: A summary of trends.' *Social Indicators Research*, 10(1): 1–28.

Sniderman, Paul M., Loek Hagendoorn, and Marcus Prior. 2004. 'Predisposing factors and situational triggers: Exclusionary reactions to immigrant minorities.' *American Political Science Review*, 98: 35–49.

Sniderman, Paul, Michael Bang Petersen, Rune Slothuus, and Rune Stubager. 2016. *Paradoxes of Liberal Democracy: Islam, Western Europe, and the Danish Cartoon Crisis*. Princeton, NJ: Princeton University Press.

Snijders, Tom A.B. and R.J. Bosker. 1999. *Multilevel Analysis: An Introduction to Basic and Advanced Multilevel Modelling*. London: Sage.

Spierings, Niels and Andrej Zaslove. 2017. 'Gender, populist attitudes, and voting: Explaining the gender gap in voting for populist radical right and populist radical left parties.' *West European Politics*, 40(4): 821–847.

Spies, Dennis, and Simon T. Franzmann. 2011. 'A two-dimensional approach to the political opportunity structure of extreme right parties in Western Europe.' *West European Politics*, 34: 1044–1069.

Sprague-Jones, Jessica. 2011. 'Extreme right-wing vote and support for multiculturalism in Europe.' *Ethnic and Racial Studies*, 34(4): 535–555.

Stanley, Ben. 2008. 'The thin ideology of populism,' *Journal of Political Ideologies*, 13(1): 95–110.

Stavrakakis, Yannis and Giorgos Katsambekis. 2014. 'Left-wing populism in the European periphery: The case of SYRIZA.' *Journal of Political Ideologies*, 19(2): 119–142.

Stavrakakis, Yannis, Alexandros Kioupkioli, and Gioros Katsambekis. 2016. 'Contemporary left-wing populism in Latin America: Leadership, horizontalism, and post-democracy in Chavez's Venezuela.' *Latin American Politics and Society*, 58(3): 51–76.

Stenner, Karen. 2005. *The Authoritarian Dynamic*. New York: Cambridge University Press.

2009. 'Three kinds of conservatism.' *Psychological Inquiry*, 20: 142–159.

Stephan, W.G. and Renfro, C.L. 2002. 'The role of threats in intergroup relations.' In U. Wagner, L.R. Tropp, G. Finchilescu, and C. Tredoux. Eds. *Improving Intergroup Relations: Building on the Legacy of Thomas F. Pettigrew*. Oxford: Blackwell, pp. 55–72.

Stewart, Julianne, Gianpietro Mazzoleni, and Bruce Horsfield. 2003. 'Conclusion: Power to the media managers.' In Gianpietro Mazzoleni, Julianne Stewart, and Bruce Horsfield. Eds. *The Media and Neo-Populism: A Comparative Analysis*. Westport, CT: Praeger, pp. 217–237.

Stockemer, Daniel. 2017. 'The success of radical right-wing parties in Western European regions: New challenging findings.' *Journal of Contemporary European Studies*, 25(1): 41–56.

2017. *The Front National in France: Continuity and Change under Jean-Marie Le Pen and Marine Le Pen*. Germany: Springer.

Stockemer, Daniel and Mauro Barisione. 2017. 'The "new" discourse of the Front National under Marine Le Pen: A slight change with a big impact.' *European Journal of Communication*, 32(2): 100–115.

Stöss, Richard. 1988. 'The problem of rightwing extremism in West Germany.' In Klaus von Beyme. Ed. *Right Extremism in Western Europe*. London: Frank Cass.

Strøm, Kaare. 1990. *Minority Government and Majority Rule*. New York: Cambridge University Press.

Stubager, Rune. 2013. 'The changing basis of party competition: Education, authoritarian–libertarian values and voting.' *Government and Opposition*, 48(3): 372–397.

Studlar, Donley T. 1979. 'Individual socioeconomic attributes and attitudes towards coloured immigrants.' *New Community*, 10: 228–52.

Svåsand, Lars. 1998. 'Scandinavian right-wing radicalism.' *The New Politics of the Right: Neo-Populist Parties and Movements in Established Democracies*. New York: St. Martin's Press, pp. 77–94.

Swami, Viren, David Barron, Laura Weis *et al.* 2018. 'To Brexit or not to Brexit: The roles of Islamophobia, conspiracist beliefs, and integrated threat in voting intentions for the United Kingdom European Union membership referendum.' *British Journal of Psychology*, 109(1): 156–179.

Swank, Duane and Betz Hans-Georg. 2003. 'Globalization, the welfare state and right-wing populism in Western Europe.' *Socio-Economic Review*, 1(2): 215–245.

Swyngedouw, Marc. 1992. 'National elections in Belgium: The breakthrough of the extreme right in Flanders.' *Regional Politics and Policy*, 2(3): 62–75.

2001. 'The subjective cognitive and affective map of extreme right voters: Using open-ended questions in exit polls.' *Electoral Studies*, 20(2): 217–241.

Swyngedouw, Marc and Giles Ivaldi. 2001. 'The extreme right utopia in Belgium and France: The ideology of the Flemish Vlaams Blok and the French Front National.' *West European Politics*, 24(3): 1–22.

Taagepera, Rein. 1998. 'Effective magnitude and effective threshold.' *Electoral Studies*, 17(4): 393–404.

1999. 'The number of parties as a function of heterogeneity and electoral system.' *Comparative Political Studies*, 32(5): 531–548.

2002. 'Nationwide threshold of representation.' *Electoral Studies*, 21(3): 383–401.

Taagepera, Rein and Bernard Grofman. 1985. 'Rethinking Duverger's Law: Predicting the effective number of parties in plurality and PR systems – parties minus issues equals one.' *European Journal of Political Research*, 13: 341–352.

Taagepera, Rein and Matthew Soberg Shugart. 1989. *Seats and Votes: The Effects and Determinants of Electoral Systems*. New Haven, CT: Yale University Press.

Taggart, Paul. 1995. 'New populist parties in Western Europe.' *West European Politics*, 18(1): 34–51.

1996. *The New Populism and New Politics: New Protest Parties in Sweden in Comparative Perspective*. London: Macmillan.

2000. *Populism*. Buckingham: Open University Press.

Taggart, Paul and Cristóbal Rovira Kaltwasser. 2016. 'Dealing with populists in government: Some comparative conclusions.' *Democratization*, 23(2): 345–365.

Taub, Amanda. 2016. 'The rise of American authoritarianism.' *Vox* www.vox.com/2016/3/1/11127424/trump-authoritarianism.

Tavits, Margit. 2006. 'Party system change testing a model of new party entry.' *Party Politics*, 12(1): 99–119.

Teehankee, Julio C. 2016. 'Weak state, strong presidents: Situating the Duterte Presidency in Philippine political time.' *Journal of Developing Societies*, 32(3): 293–321.

Tesler, Michael and David O. Sears. 2010. *Obama's Race: The 2008 Election and the Dream of a Post-Racial America*. Chicago: University of Chicago Press.

Thranhardt, Dietrich. 1995. 'The political uses of xenophobia in England, France and Germany.' *Party Politics*, 1: 323–345.

Thurlow, R. 1998. *Fascism in Britain: From Oswald Mosley's Blackshirts to the National Front*. London: I.B. Tauris.

Tilley, James R. 2005. 'Libertarian–authoritarian value change in Britain, 1974–2001.' *Political Studies*, 53: 422–453.

Torre, Carlos de la. Ed. 2014. *The Promise and Perils of Populism: Global Perspectives*. Kentucky: University Press of Kentucky.

Torre, Carlos de la and Cynthia J. Arnson. Eds. 2013. *Latin American Populism in the Twenty-First Century*. Baltimore, MD: Johns Hopkins University Press.

Tossutti, Livianna S. 2002. 'How transnational factors influence the success of ethnic, religious and regional parties in 21 states.' *Party Politics*, 8(1): 51–74.

Uberoi, Elise. 2016. *European Union Referendum 2016*. Briefing paper CBP-7639. London: House of Commons.

Van der Brug, Wouter and Meindert Fennema. 2003. 'Protest or mainstream? How the European anti-immigrant parties developed into two separate groups by 1991.' *European Journal of Political Research*, 42: 55–76.

2007. 'Causes of voting for the radical right.' *International Journal of Public Opinion Research*, 19(4): 474–487.

Van der Brug, Wouter, Miendert Fennema, and Jean Tillie. 2000. 'Anti-immigrant parties in Europe: Ideological or protest vote?' *European Journal of Political Research*, 37(1): 77–102.

2005. 'Why some anti-immigrant parties fail and others succeed.' *Comparative Political Studies*, 38(5): 537–573.

Van der Brug, Wouter and Anthony Mughan. 2007. 'Charisma, leader effects and support for right-wing populist parties.' *Party Politics*, 13(1): 29–51.

Van der Brug, Wouter and Joost van Spanje. 2009. 'Immigration, Europe and the "New sociocultural dimension".' *European Journal of Political Research*, 48(3): 309–334.

Van Ham, Carolien and Jacques Thomassen. Eds. 2017. *Myth and Reality of the Legitimacy Crisis: Explaining Trends and Cross-National Differences in Established Democracies*. Oxford: Oxford University Press.

Van Holsteyn, Joop J.M. and Galen A. Irwin. 2002. 'Never a dull moment: Pim Fortuyn and the Dutch parliamentary election of 2002.' *West European Politics*, 26(2): 41–66.

Van Kessel, Stijn. 2011. 'Explaining the electoral performance of populist parties: The Netherlands as a case study.' *Perspectives on European Politics and Society*, 12(1): 68–88.

2015. *Populist Parties in Europe: Agents of Discontent?* London: Palgrave Macmillan.

Van Spanje, Joost. 2010. 'Contagious parties: Anti-immigration parties and their impact on other parties' immigration stances in contemporary Western Europe.' *Party Politics*, 16(5): 563–586.

2011. 'The wrong and the right: A comparative analysis of "anti-immigration" and "far right" parties.' *Government and Opposition*, 46(3): 293–320.

2011. 'Keeping the rascals in: Anti-political-establishment parties and their cost of governing in established democracies.' *European Journal of Political Research*, 50(5): 609–635.

Van Spanje, Joost and Claes De Vreese. 2015. 'The good, the bad and the voter: The impact of hate speech prosecution of a politician on electoral support for his party.' *Party Politics*, 21(1): 115–130.

Van Spanje, Joost and Nan Dirk de Graaf. 2018. 'How established parties reduce other parties' electoral support: The strategy of parroting the pariah.' *West European Politics*, 41(1): 1–27.

Vance, J.D. 2016. *Hillbilly Elegy: A Memoir of Family and Culture in Crisis*. New York: Harper.

Vasilakis, Chrysovalantis. 2017. 'Massive migration and elections: Evidence from the refugee crisis in Greece.' *International Migration*.

Veugelers, John W.P. 1997. 'Social cleavage and the revival of far right parties: The case of France's National Front.' *Acta Sociologica*, 40(1): 31–49.

1999. 'A challenge for political sociology: The rise of far right parties in contemporary Western Europe.' *Current Sociology*, 47: 78–105.

2000. 'Right-wing extremism in contemporary France: A "silent counterrevolution"?' *Sociological Quarterly*, 41(1): 19–40.

Veugelers, John and Andre Magnan. 2005. 'Conditions of far right strength in contemporary Western Europe: An application of Kitschelt's theory.' *European Journal of Political Research*, 44(6): 837–860.

Vittori, Davide. 2017. 'Podemos and the Five Star Movement: Populist, nationalist or what?' *Contemporary Italian Politics*:1–20.

Vliegenthart, Rens, Hajo G. Boomgaarden, and Joost Van Spanje. 2012. 'Anti-immigrant party support and media visibility: A cross-party, over-time perspective.' *Journal of Elections, Public Opinion and Parties*, 22: 315–358.

Vossen, Koen. 2011. 'Classifying Wilders: The ideological development of Geert Wilders and his Party for Freedom.' *Politics*, 31(3): 179–189.

2016. *The Power of Populism: Geert Wilders and the Party for Freedom in the Netherlands*. New York: Routledge.

Vowles, Jack, Peter Aimer, Susan Banducci, and Jeffrey Karp. 1998. *Voters' Victory? New Zealand's First Election under Proportional Representation.* Auckland: Auckland University Press.

Wagner, Markus and Thomas M. Meyer. 2017. 'The Radical Right as niche parties? The ideological landscape of party systems in Western Europe, 1980–2014.' *Political Studies*, 65(1): 84–107.

Wagner, Ulrich and Andreas Zick. 1995. 'The relationship of formal education to ethnic prejudice: Its reliability, validity and explanation.' *European Journal of Social Psychology*, 25: 41–56.

Wald, Kenneth and Samuel Shye. 1995. 'Religious influence in electoral-behavior: The role of institutional and social forces in Israel.' *Journal of Politics*, 57(2): 495–507.

Walgrave, Steffan and Knut De Swert. 2004. 'The making of the (issues of the) Vlaams Blok.' *Political Communication*, 21(4): 479–500.

Walker, Martin. 1977. *The National Front.* London: Fontana/Collins.

Walter, Dean Burnham. 1970. *Critical elections and the Mainsprings of American Politics.* New York: Norton.

Wattenberg, Martin P. 1998. *The Decline of American Political Parties 1952–1996.* Cambridge, MA: Harvard University Press.

2002. *Where Have all the Voters Gone?* Cambridge, MA: Harvard University Press.

Webb, Paul. 2013. 'Who is willing to participate? Dissatisfied democrats, stealth democrats and populists in the United Kingdom.' *European Journal of Political Research*, 52(6): 747–772.

Webb, Paul, David Farrell, and Ian Holliday. Eds. *Political Parties in Advanced Industrial Democracies.* Oxford: Oxford University Press.

Werts, Han, Peer Scheepers, and Marcel Lubbers. 2013. 'Euro-scepticism and radical right-wing voting in Europe, 2002–2008: Social cleavages, socio-political attitudes and contextual characteristics determining voting for the radical right.' *European Union Politics*, 14(2): 183–205.

White, Stephen, Richard Rose, and Ian McAllister. 1996. *How Russia Votes.* New Jersey, Chatham House.

Whitefield, Stephen. 2002. 'Political cleavages and post-communist politics.' *Annual Review of Political Science*, 5: 181–200.

Widfeldt, Andre. 2000. 'Scandinavia: Mixed success for the populist right.' *Parliamentary Affairs*, 53(3): 468–500.

Wilkes, Rima, Neil Guppy, and Lily Farris. 2007. 'Right-wing parties and anti-foreigner sentiment in Europe.' *American Sociological Review*, 72(5): 831–840.

Williams, Joan C. 2017. *White Working Class.* Boston, MA: Harvard Business Review Press.

Williams, Michelle H. 2006. *The Impact of Radical Right-Wing Parties in West European Democracies.* New York: Palgrave Macmillan.

2010. 'Can leopards change their spots? Between xenophobia and trans-ethnic populism among West European far right parties.' *Nationalism and Ethnic Politics*, 16(1): 111–134.

Wilson, Frank L. Ed. 1998. *The European Center-Right at the End of the Twentieth Century.* New York: St. Martin's Press.

Wodak, Ruth. 2015. *The Politics of Fear: What Right-wing Populist Discourses Mean*. London: Sage.

Wodak, Ruth, Majid KhosraviNik, and Brigitte Mral. Eds. 2013. *Right-Wing Populism in Europe*. London: Bloomsbury Academic.

Wolintz, Steven B. 1979. 'The transformation of Western European party systems revisited.' *West European Politics*, 2: 7–8.

1988. *Parties and Party Systems in Liberal Democracies*. London: Routledge.

Zaslove Andrej. 2004. 'Closing the door? The ideology and impact of radical right populism on immigration policy in Austria and Italy.' *Journal of Political Ideologies*, 9(1): 99–118.

2008. 'Here to stay? Populism as a new party type.' *European Review*, 16(3): 319–336.

Zhirkov, Kirill. 2014. 'Nativist but not alienated: A comparative perspective on the radical right vote in Western Europe.' *Party Politics*, 20(2): 286–296.

Zielinski, Jakub. 2002. 'Translating social cleavages into party systems: The significance of new democracies.' *World Politics*, 54: 184–211.

Zukin, Cliff, Scott Keeter, Molly Andolina, Krista Jenkins, and Michael X. Delli Carpini. 2006. *A New Engagement? Political Participation, Civic Life and the Changing American Citizen*. Oxford: Oxford University Press.

# Index


Adorno, Theodore W., 70
Allport, G. W., 112
Almond, Gabriel A., 394, 422
Altemeyer, Bob, 70
Alternative for Germany (AfD), 9, 17, 51, 111, 186, 224, 231, 257, 261–262, 296, 299, 325
'America First', 8, 220, 349, 416
Asia, 246–247
Ataka (Bulgaria), 154, 239–240
Austria, 181, 186, 200, 203, 257, 295, 296, 298, 299, 299–302, 314–315, 321, 323, 325, 418
  Freedom party, 186, 200, 224, 240, 257, 296, 297, 299, 300–302, 417
  People's Party, 257
authoritarian left parties, 244–245
Authoritarian-Pluralist parties, 240–242, 342
authoritarian populism
  European states, 9–12, 234–240
  surge in support, 257
  reasons for support, 258–289
  religiosity, 271
  resentment, 48
  rise of, 9–12
authoritarian populist parties, 122, 234–240, 319, *see also* individual parties
  electoral system, 295–322
  effect on mainstream center-right parties, 322
  party competition, 322–325
  support for, 257–289
authoritarian right parties, 244
authoritarian values, 68–71
  class, 113
  democratic cultures resistance to, 409–417
  defining, 71
  economic insecurity, 156–164, 280
  gender, 114
  predicting, 108–117
  2008 Democratic primary, 267
authoritarianism
  defining, 6–8, 69
  loyalty, 74–76
  social conservatism
  security, 76–78

Babis, Andrej, 154
Baby Boomers, 36, 56, 89, 91, 97, 101, 117, 145, 146, 277, 454
Barr, Robert R., 67
Belgium, 202, 298, 323, *see also* Vlaams Belang
Berlusconi, Silvio, 75, 225
Betz, Hans-George, 182
Blocher, Christoph, 241
Black Lives Matter, 44, 95, 350, 463
Bonikowski, Bart, 226
Bornschier, Simon, 51, 417
Brexit, 5–6, 17, 23, 36, 52, 53, 56, 77, 89, 138, 189, 191, 202, 257, 261, 289, 294, 368–397, 419–420, 462
  class, 378
  competing theories, 377–379, 387–393

Brexit (*cont.*)
generation gaps, 396
ethnicity, 387
immigrants, 391
referendum results, 374–389
2017 General elections, 375–377
British Conservative Party, 55, 245, 257, 373–387, 392–393
British Election Study, 380, 389–390
British Labour Party, 225, 376, 377, 378, 393, 397
British Liberal Democrats, 372, 373, 393
British National Party, 372, 393
British Social Attitudes, 391, 447
Brunner, Toni, 211
Buchanan, Patrick, 333
Bulgaria, 9, 195, 239–240
Ataka, 154, 239–240
United Patriots, 240
Bulgarian National Movement, 244

Cameron, David, 370, 373, 375, 394
Canada, 323
Carter, Jimmy, 317, 344
Chapel Hill Expert Survey, 215, 229–234, 456
Charlottesville, VA, 47
Chavez, Hugo, 5, 75, 218, 244, 415
*Civic Culture* study, 274, 394, 422, 428
class
authoritarian values, 113
blue collar, 279
Brexit, 378
Clinton, Hillary, 191, 262, 340, 345, 352
voters, 360, 361
Comparative Manifesto Project, 227–229, 230
conformity
social conservatism, 71–73
contagion of the right, 417–420, 460
Converse, Philip, 98
Corbyn, Jeremy, 43, 225, 376, 377, 397
Coughlin, Father Charles, 332
counter-culture, 33
Cruz, Ted, 220
cultural backlash theory, 267, 362–363, 387–393, 446–451, 460–461
Brexit, 377–379, 395–396
Secularization, 447
cultural values, *see* cultural backlash theory

Cyprus, 195, 281, 287
Czech Republic, 9, 122, 154, 180, 257, 414

Dahlerup, Drude, 45
Dalton, Russell J., 96
Danish People's Party, 297
Democracy Index for 2017 (EIU), 410
democratization, 409–417
modernization, 411
Denmark, 93, 125, 185, 192, 203, 297, 323, 419
People's Party, 297
der Bellen, Alexander Van, 302
Die Linke (Germany), 240
Duckitt, John, 72
Duerte, Rodrigo, 75, 415
Dutch Freedom Party (PVV), 54, 180, 185, 296, 299, 418, 466
Duverger's First Law, 315, 317

economic grievances
Brexit, 377–379, 387
populism and authoritarianism, 140, 143–144, 156, 166
2016 election, 139, 262, 349–352, 362, 363
Economist Intelligence Unit, 410, 435, 460
education, 89, 279, 387
Electoral College, 321, 338
electoral participation, 275
electoral systems and voting outcomes, 53
elite education, 193
Erdoğan, Recep Tayyip, 6, 68, 414–415
Estonia, 122
ethnic diversity, 40–42, 45, 50, 182
EU enlargement, 183
immigration, 177–182, 192, 194–206
Eurobarometer surveys, 93, 183
Europe, 9–10, 96, 101, 122, 146, 221–245, 286, 287–289
political disaffection, 269–270
value survey, 426–431, 433–434
voting participation, 271–281
European Election Study, 140, 263, 265–266
European Social Survey, 108, 270
Europe of Freedom and Direct Democracy (EFD), 224
Europe of Nations and Freedom (EU Parliament), 186, 224

European Social Survey, 96, 103, 232
Evans, Geoffrey, 378

'fake news', 431
Farage, Nigel, 5, 309, 372
Farmer's Party (BP) (Netherlands), 303
Fidesz (Hungary – classical liberal), 185, 240, 299, 311–313, 466
financial crisis, 149
Finland, 257
Five Star Movement (Italy), 43, 124, 193, 224, 225, 240, 320
Foa, Roberto Stephen, 429
Fortuyn, Pim, 125, 303–304
Fox TV, 225
France, 93, 181, 263, 280, 295, 296, 306–308, 313–314, 316, 323, 418
  immigration, 186
Freedom House, 410, 411, 413, 435, 460
Freedom Party (FPO) (Austria), 186, 200, 224, 240, 257, 296, 297, 299, 300–302, 417
Freedom party (PVV) (Netherlands), 54, 180, 185, 296, 299, 418, 466
Fromm, Erich, 69, 70

Gallup Values and Beliefs polls, 98, 99–100
gender, 90
Generation X, 36, 90, 92, 97, 100, 101, 117, 278, 397, 457
generations
  Generation X, 36, 90, 92, 97, 100, 101, 117, 278, 397, 457
  Interwar, 36, 49, 55, 89, 91, 101, 105, 107, 108, 259, 273, 277, 278, 397, 448, 454
  Millennials, 34, 36, 39, 43, 49, 55, 56, 89, 90, 92, 97, 100, 101, 105, 107, 108, 117, 120, 122, 145, 149, 259, 277–278, 279, 360, 362, 363, 385, 396, 397, 448, 457
  post-Millennial, 40
Germany, 11, 12, 17, 93, 149, 153, 177, 181, 195, 203, 231, 261–262, 280, 295, 298, 310–311, 314, 323, 325
  Alternative for Germany (AfD), 9, 17, 51, 111, 186, 224, 231, 257, 261–262, 296, 299, 325
  Die Linke, 240
  immigration, 179
Gingrich revolution (2004), 337
Giuseppe 'Beppe' Grillo, 75
Gladwell, Malcolm, 45
globalization, 136, 137, 164, 166, 350
Golden Dawn (Greece), 150–151, 225, 239, 297
Goodhardt, David, 395
Granovetter, Mark, 45
Great Recession (2007–2009), 149
Greece, 9, 42, 150–151, 194–195, 280, 297, 298
  Golden Dawn, 150–151, 225, 239, 297
  Syriza (left), 240
Green parties, 44, 50, 51, 56, 94, 223, 302, 372, 393

Hacker, Joseph, 154
Haider, Jorg, 296, 300, 321
Hardin, Russell, 112
Hofer, Norbet, 5, 300, 314–315
homophobia, 70, 111
Howker, Ed, 396
Hungary, 9, 68, 154, 183–185, 202, 280, 281, 295, 296, 297, 310, 311–313, 413–414, 466
Huntington, Samuel, 409, 412, 435

IDEA's Global State of Democracy indicators, 411
Iglesias, Pablo, 151, 225
Ignazi, Pierro, 51, 315
immigrants, values of, 202
immigration, 40–42, 50, 111
  Europe, 177–182
  exclusion of those concerned from open debate, 190–191
  Fortune list, 176
  Muslim, 154, 241
  Switzerland, 241
inequality, 136
Inglehart, Ronald, 50
intergenerational change, 15, 32, 77, 88, 96, 101, 123, 143
  education, 38–39
  growing liberalism, 96, 454
  political consequences, 124
  tipping point, 103–106
  urbanization, 39–40
Interwar generation, 36, 49, 55, 89, 91, 101, 105, 107, 108, 259, 273, 277, 278, 397, 448, 454

Ireland, 323
Islamophobia, 47, 50, 70, 73, 111, 182, 190, 241, 354, 379, 394, 448
Italian Five Star Movement, 43, 124, 193, 224, 225, 240, 321
Italy, 93, 257, 287, 298, 323, 428, *see also* Five Star Movement, Northern League
Ivarsflaten, Elizabeth, 182

Jackman, Robert W., 315
Jobbik (Hungary), 154, 185, 296, 297, 299, 311–326

Kanter, Rosbeth Moss, 45
Katz, Richard S., 316
Kitschelt, Herbert, 317
Kurz, Sebastian, 302

Latin America, 244, 246, 269
Le Pen, Jean-Marie, 306
Le Pen, Marine, 5, 231, 257, 263, 306–308
Levitsky, Stephen, 416
'liberal', 230
liberalism, 78
libertarian pluralist parties, 242
libertarian right and left parties, 245
libertarian populists, 43, 78, 240
libertarianism, 73, 230
Lijphart, Arend, 315
Linde, Jonas, 427
Linz, Juan, 421
Lipset, Seymour Martin, 6, 113, 135, 228, 466
Lithuania, 120
Lithuanian Way of Courage (DK), 244
Long, Huey, 3, 246, 332
Luxemberg, 93, 180

McCarthy, Joe, 3
Macron, Emmanuel, 306
McGovern, George, 343
MacWilliams, 191
Maduro, Nichol, 68, 244, 413, 415
Make America Great Again (MAGA) slogan, 349, 351, 353
materialists
  voting US elections, 345–346, 363
May, Theresa, 5, 203, 309, 368, 375, 395, 420
Merkel, Angela, 12, 111, 231, 257, 310–311, 314, 325, 368
Merton, Robert, 79
Millennials, 34, 36, 39, 43, 49, 55, 56, 89, 90, 92, 97, 100, 101, 105, 107, 108, 117, 120, 122, 145, 149, 259, 277–278, 279, 362, 448, 457
  2016 US election, 360, 363
  Brexit, 385, 396, 397
misogyny, 70
Mixed Member Parallel representation, 310
Mixed Member Proportional, 319
Mudde, Cas, 24, 416, 417

National Election Surveys (ANES), 343, 344
National Front for the Salvation of Bulgaria, 244
National Front Party (France), 51, 182, 186, 224, 226, 231, 257, 263, 297, 306–308, 316
Netherlands, 54, 73, 181, 185, 264, 280, 295, 296, 298, 299, 303–306, 315, 316, 322, 323, 325, 418, 466
  Party for Freedom (Netherlands), 73, 180
New Zealand, 257, 317
Noelle-Neumann, Elisabeth, 46
Northern League, 186, 223, 224, 428
Norway, 153, 202, 203, 240, 257, 297, 298, 323, 419, 461
Norwegian Progress Party, 73, 153

Obama, Barack, 13, 347–348, 352, 368
Orbán, Viktor, 68, 154, 185, 413–414

Padermos (Spain), 74, 124, 151–152, 193, 225, 240, 461
Palin, Sarah, 333
Party for Freedom (Netherlands), 73
party loyalties, 53
periodic effects, 145–146, 148, 273–274
Peronism, 74, 244
Perot, Ross, 333
Pew Research Center, 98
Philippines, 415
Piketty, Thomas, 136
Poland, 9, 154, 180, 195, 203, 257, 296, 298, 414
Polish Law and Justice Party (PiS), 244

political parties
  authoritarian left parties, 244–245
  authoritarian-pluralist parties, 240–242, 342
  authoritarian populist parties, 122, 234–240, 319, *see also* individual parties
    electoral system, 295–322
    effect on mainstream center-right parties, 322
    party competition, 322–325
    support for, 257–289
  authoritarian right parties, 244
  categorization, 215–248
  electoral rules, 295–322
  Green parties, 44, 50, 51, 56, 94, 223, 302, 372, 393
  libertarian pluralist parties, 242
  libertarian right and left parties, 245
populism
  alternative conceptions, 24
  authoritarian culture here or above??, 444–445
  defining, 4–6, 66, 217
  exclusionary forms, 192
  inclusive, 193
  left-wing, 218–219
  legitimacy, 444
  rhetoric, 247
  targets of, 4
populist parties, 44
Portugal, 325
post-industrial societies, 35, 88
post-materialism, 92–98, 145–148
post-Millennial, 40
PPV (Party for Freedom – Netherlands), 186, 224, 304–306, 315, 322
press, 225–226
proportional representation, 310, 315–320, 325, 416, 418, 452, 458
Putnam, Robert, 112

radical right parties
  support, 261
Rae, Douglas, 315
Reagan, Ronald, 334
representative democracy, 74, 78
resistance, 463–464
Rokeach, Milton, 35, 69
Rokkan, Stein, 313
Russia, 23, 55, 120, 195, 203
Rust Belt states, 350, 351
Rutte, Mark VVD, 305–306, 322

Sanders, Bernie, 43, 67, 124, 135, 219, 260, 338, 342, 349
Scandinavia, 195, 203, 206, 234
Schelling, Thomas, 44
Schwartz, 102, 103, 268
Shain, Martin, 418
*Silent Revolution, The*, 32, 145
silent revolution theory, 87–91, 341
Slovak National Party, 244
Slovakia, 122, 195, 280
Slovenia, 9, 195, 287
social conservatives, 45, 48, 90, 123, 220, 450
  conformity, 71–73
  voting, 49
*Social Contract, The*, 217
Social Democratic parties, 464–465
social media, 55
Southern Poverty Law Center, 433
Spain, 42, 74, 151–152, 240, 325
  Padermos, 74, 124, 151–152, 193, 225, 240
Stiglitz, Joseph, 154
Strache, Heinz-Christian, 302
supply side (parties positions), 54
Sweden, 154–155, 202, 203, 206, 280, 297, 323, 325, 428, 461
Swiss People's Party (SVP), 241–242, 245
Switzerland, 180, 202, 203, 241–242, 257, 280, 295, 323, 325
Syriza (left – Greece), 240, 320

Tea Party, 333
terrorism and appeal to authoritarian values, 192
Thatcher, Margret, 373
tribalism, 8
True Finns, 297
Trump, Donald J., 3, 4, 8, 12–13, 52, 67, 75, 124, 135, 203, 258, 294–295, 325, 333, 345–361, 413, 452
  Administration, 463–464
  support for appeal to base, 260, 262, 270–284, 338
  categorizing, 219–221, 245–246
  Charlottesville, 433
  consequences, 420

Trump, Donald J. (*cont.*)
election, 56, 75, 89, 161, 192, 200, 349–355
electoral college, 75
Evangelical Christian, 340
immigration, 186–187, 200
nicknames, 75, 339
rhetoric, 76–77, 220, 339, 461
Russia investigation, 354
traditional agenda of the GOP leadership, 339
'Trump effect', 423
victory, 338–342
Turkey, 68, 180, 280, 414–415
2008 Democratic primary, Clinton v Obama authoritarian values, 267
2012 US election, 161
2016 US election, 12–13, 17, 261, 270, 315, 321, 331–332, 349–363, 385, 458–459
cultural revolution, 352–355
economic grievances, 139, 262
race, 18, 191–192

UK, 12, 38, 93, 135, 154–155, 203, 221, 257–258, 295, 297, 298, 308–309, 314, 321, 325, 368–397, 459–460, *see also* Brexit, UKIP
conservative, 55, 245, 257, 369, 373, 392–393
immigration, 181, 185, 202, 205, 206
populist parties, 296
press, 226
UKIP, 52, 137, 186, 206, 308–309, 321, 325, 369, 370, 375, 376, 378, 379–382, 388–393, 418, 419–420
Ukraine, 120, 203
urbanization, 279
US, 23, 47, 48, 155, 160–161, 219–221, 257–258, 261, 264, 265, 323, 415
causes populism, 269
Democratic party, 331, 350, 352
Electoral College, 321
immigration, 176–177, 181, 186–187, 191–192
liberal trends, 97–98
partisan cues, 264
party and perception of economic performance, 264
populist candidates, 245–246
populism, roots of, 332–342
public confidence, 24
race and 2016 election race, 18, 191–192
Republican Party, 221, 225, 257, 266–267, 331, 333–338
Trust in media, 431
Values survey, 422

Varieties of Democracy project, 318, 412, 460
Venezuela, 218, 244, 245, 410, 415
Verba, Sidney, 277, 422
Vlaams Belang (VB - Flemish) (Authoritarian-Populist), 186, 200, 224
Volpert, Karen, 315
Von Beyme, Klaus, 3

Wallace, George, 3, 442
Weidel, Alice, 111
Wilders, Geert, 185, 190, 304–306, 315, 322, 418, 466
World Values Surveys, 94, 95, 102, 429

xenophobia, 70, 76, 234, 340, 354

Zeman, Milos, 414

CPSIA information can be obtained
at www.ICGtesting.com
Printed in the USA
LVHW041736260319
611895LV00004B/344